THE AMERICAN REPUBLIC
for Christian Schools®

The Teacher's Edition

The teacher's edition of THE AMERICAN REPUBLIC *for Christian Schools* (Second Edition) has been designed to help you in your history teaching. Many tools have been provided to allow the teacher to break away from the sometimes stagnant lecture method and give more room for student participation, which is so essential to the junior high student. It is recommended that the teacher begin each lesson with review of past learning using student feedback so that the teacher can accurately determine whether learning is taking place. The sug-gested activities are designed as a part of the educational experience and are integral to the text. Materials lists and adequate directions should make these activities easy to incorporate.

Lessons and Scheduling

Although some of the second-edition student text will be familiar to the teacher who has used the first edition, we recommend that the teacher read each chapter prior to beginning lesson plans. This allows you to note changes and additions to the text as well as any newly available ancillary material. Then you can prepare accordingly.

Each chapter has three to six sections that divide the information into convenient reading assignments. You can combine sections into a single day's lesson or divide them into two or more days, as indicated in the Lesson Plan Chart at the beginning of each chapter. Your students' ability and your own interests will determine how you schedule lessons.

i

the AMERICAN

Rachel C. Larson, M.A.
Pamela B. Creason, M. Ed.
Michael D. Matthews, M. Ed.

How many chapters should I cover in the first semester?

Most teachers find it convenient to end a semester with a unit break. A natural break occurs after Unit 3, Chapter 18, but you will find it difficult to cover all the material in Unit 3 in your first semester. An alternate stopping point is after Chapter 17. This would allow you to begin second semester with Chapter 18 (Reconstruction), which is an appropriate beginning for the second half of the school year.

How many days do I spend on a chapter?

Once you have perused the teacher's edition and determined your end goal for the semester, look at your school calendar and take note of how many actual teaching days are available. Most chapters will require five to eight teaching days plus a day for review and a day for testing. You can take more or less time on each chapter as long as you balance out the days to meet your semester goal.

Just a Note

Even though this teacher's edition has been designed to assist the teacher in his teaching of *The American Republic*, it cannot replace teacher preparation. It is a supplement of teaching methods, information, and ideas. Likewise, this manual is not a complete and final authority; it contains only a sample and partial listing of suggested sources, methods, background information, and review techniques. It is the teacher's responsibility to select and develop those items that best meet the students' needs.

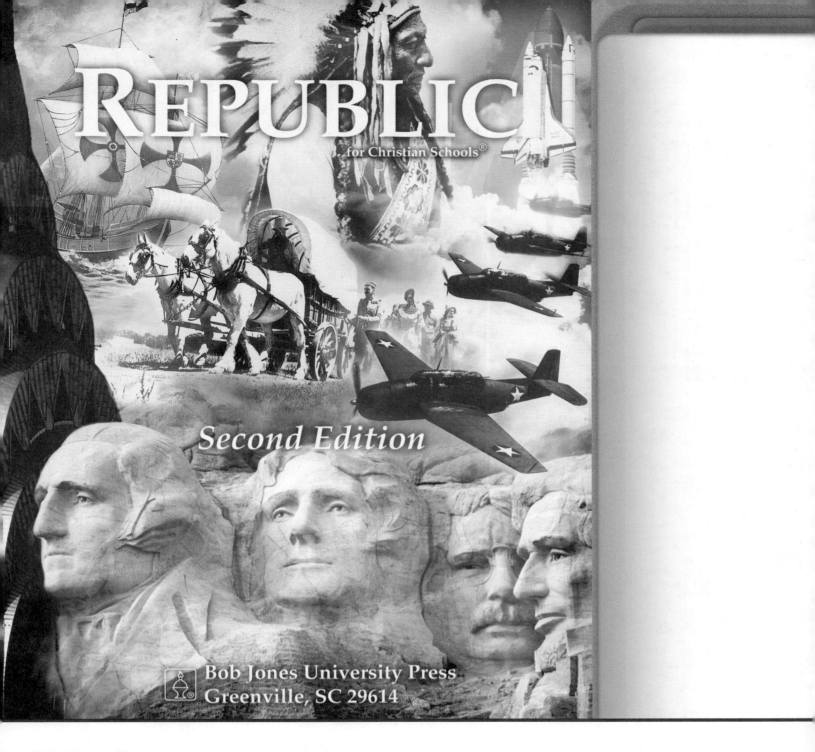

REPUBLIC
for Christian Schools®

Second Edition

Bob Jones University Press
Greenville, SC 29614

Side Margin Notes

Goals and Objectives

The first information in the side margin of a chapter is a box containing the student goals for the entire chapter. These general goals are what you want your students to achieve while studying the chapter. Read these carefully to get an overview of the chapter. One of the goals is in bold type, which denotes that goal as the most important of the chapter.

Chapter Motivation

The teacher should begin every chapter with the motivation idea. It will help tie the chapter to previous learning and show the students why the information contained in the chapter is important. Usually the motivator will involve some class discussion.

Chapter Materials List

The materials list includes all the materials needed for all the activities suggested in the chapter. You can see at a glance any items you may want to gather for your teaching.

Section Objectives

Each section has specific objectives. These are important facts and principles that your students should learn while studying that section. This is a suggested list. You may make changes to the objectives list as necessary.

Additional Information

Information provided in the side margins corresponds to information in the text. It is for the teacher's information and can be shared with the students as the teacher desires. It is designed to be interesting or to

To the Teacher

THE AMERICAN REPUBLIC for Christian Schools (Second Edition) is the eighth book in the Heritage Studies series. It is a comprehensive survey of United States history, intended to give the junior high student a solid foundation of knowledge about the heritage of this country.

The primary purpose of any Christian course of study is to produce students who are conformed to Christ's image. For the young student who is just discovering his own abilities and responsibilities in life, there may be no more valuable study than the lives of others in the light of Scripture. Throughout the history course are many examples of people who either followed God's standard or failed to do so. From these examples, the student will see the truth of God in action and develop values and principles for living.

General Objectives

The general course objectives can be broken into two categories.

Basic Comprehension Goals

There is basic historical information that all students should understand. By the end of the year, the students should be able to identify the following:

1. God's providence in the seven eras of U.S. history and the outline of major periods within each era.

2. Continuity and change in the six spheres of human activity—politics, economics, religion, society, science, and arts.

3. Continuity and change in foreign relations, including past wars, and the roots of modern foreign policy.

4. God's supervision of American church history as God's people have interacted with secular society.

5. The consequences of past decisions, good and bad, which testify that Bible principles are true and that God

NOTE:
The fact that materials produced by other publishers are referred to in this volume does not constitute an endorsement by Bob Jones University Press of the content or theological position of materials produced by such publishers. The position of Bob Jones University Press, and the University itself, is well known. Any references and ancillary materials are listed as an aid to the student or the teacher and in an attempt to maintain the accepted academic standards of the publishing industry.

THE AMERICAN REPUBLIC for Christian Schools® Teacher's Edition
Second Edition

Authors
Rachel C. Larson, M.A.
Pamela B. Creason, M.Ed.
Michael D. Matthews, M.Ed.

Contributing Authors
Terri L. Koontz
Thomas G. Luttmann
Jill M. Blackstock, M.Ed.

Consultants
John A. Matzko, Ph.D.
Professor, Department of History, Bob Jones University
Steven N. Skaggs
Supervisor, Secondary Authors
Daniel P. Olinger, Ph.D.
Strategic Planning Coordinator, Bob Jones University Press
Mark Sidwell, Ph.D.
Director, Fundamentalism File
David Fisher, M.A.
Instructor, Bob Jones Academy
Elizabeth Olsen, M.Ed.
Instructor, Bob Jones Junior High School

Compositor
Nancy C. Lohr

Designers
Ellyson Kalagayan
John W. Bjerk

Graphics
Timothy Banks
John W. Bjerk
H.P. Gravely, Jr.
Dyke Habegger
James H. Hargis
Ellyson Kalagayan
Asher Parris
Kathy Pflug
Wendy Searles
Linda Slattery

Editor
Manda Kalagayan

Photo Acquisition
Terry R. Latini

"I Have a Dream" speech reprinted by arrangement with The Heirs to the Estate of Martin Luther King, Jr., c/o Writers House, Inc. as agent for the proprietor.

Produced in cooperation with the Bob Jones University Departments of History and Social Studies of the College of Arts and Science, the School of Education, and Bob Jones Academy and Junior High School.

for Christian Schools is a registered trademark of Bob Jones University Press.

ISBN 1-57924-341-X

©2000 Bob Jones University Press
Greenville, South Carolina 29614
First Edition ©1988, 1993

Printed in the United States of America
All rights reserved

15   14   13   12   11   10   9   8   7   6   5   4   3   2

stimulate discussion but is not necessarily designed to be tested.

Chapter Review

An idea, activity, or game is suggested for class review.

Bottom Margin Notes

Lesson Plan Chart

As mentioned above, a lesson plan chart is featured at the beginning of every unit and chapter to aid the teacher in scheduling lessons. It is only a proposed plan and will still greatly depend on the teacher's style of teaching, the inclusion of class activities, and extracurricular activities that affect class participation. The chart includes the title of each chapter or section, the main activity in the chapter or section, the pages covered by each chapter or section, and the suggested time frame for teaching. The time frame includes a day for review and testing.

Materials List

At the beginning of each section is a list of materials for the suggested activities in that section. If you do not have access to certain materials, you might choose to skip those activities or design substitute activities.

Teaching Strategies

Suggested teaching strategies are given immediately after the materials list. Many of these varied activities are labeled with icons to help the teacher identify the type of teaching activity suggested without necessarily reading the entire description. If the activity does not have an icon, it is most likely a suggested discussion topic. The icons are as follows:

CONTENTS

oversees the course of U.S. history.

6. Every major event and date in each era, including the leading causes and effects of the events.

7. Every major individual of U.S. history, including his role in the past as well as lessons for today.

8. The fundamental traits of Americanism—the American dream, limited government, popular culture—and how they have changed over the nation's history.

Basic Skills Goals

In addition to understanding basic historical information, students should develop skills in using information that will help them for the rest of their lives. By the end of the year, they should be able to

1. Define and use basic terms from U.S. history that are essential in understanding and explaining God's providence.

2. Interpret historical maps that are found in atlases of U.S. history.

3. Evaluate historical narratives and original documents for accuracy and historic perspectives.

4. Interpret common tools of historians, such as time lines, graphs, and charts.

5. Discern God's providence in any era by showing the impact of physical geography and circumstances on the course of events in U.S. history.

6. Use the Bible to evaluate social, economic, and political systems or philosophies in any era.

7. Identify the variety of challenges that Christians faced in each era and draw lessons for today.

8. Explain the causes of historic crises, give the Bible's solution, and find parallels to current issues in America.

 Arts and Crafts

 Bible Study

 Bulletin Board

 Charts and Graphs

 Group Activity

 Home School Activity

 Listening Activity

 Map Activity

 Multiple Perspectives

 Music

 Outside Reading

 Photographs

 Reading Between the Lines

 Special Speaker

 Think About It

 Turning Points

 Video

 Writing

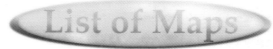

List of Maps

Section Review Answers

At the end of each section are the answers to the review questions and the thinking question.

Chapter Review Answers

At the end of the chapter are the answers to the chapter review questions and the discussion questions.

Teaching *The American Republic*

Many students are not excited about Heritage Studies. If you questioned them to find out why they think it is boring, you would probably discover that they resent having to memorize mountains of meaningless facts from monotonous reading assignments. For them Heritage Studies has no life; it is simply a pile of dry, dusty skeletons that are better left buried. Your job, then, is to show your students that this class is a living, meaningful, relevant subject in their everyday lives. How do you do this? Make it active. The activities, mental or physical, are attention-getters, interest-sustainers, and long-lasting memory makers that will make Heritage Studies exciting for your students.

Evaluation

There are many ways to evaluate the students' understanding of the material being taught. Whatever testing methods you use, be sure to adapt them to the specific needs and abilities of your class as well as to the material that you have emphasized in your teaching. Do not fall into the habit of giving the same type of questions on all your tests and quizzes throughout the year. By varying the type of questions that you use within each test, you will separate students who are having problems understanding a certain type of question from students who

Regions of American Geography

Forces on American Society

vii

The Student Text

Finishing a history text is essential to the students' understanding of God's hand working in history and each student's place in God's plan. Finishing a history text while making the material interesting is even more important because it gives students a love for the subject and makes application to their lives more enjoyable.

The student text has the following features.

Organization

The student text includes thirty chapters divided into seven units. Each chapter has an outlined structure with boldfaced headings. Important terms are also boldfaced.

Unit Divisions

Each of the seven units begins with a quick overview of the chapters, photos that illustrate important events, and a time line of events covered in the unit. A third page features an original document or speech transcript that highlights a central issue of the era included in the unit.

Interest Boxes

The textbook contains about fifty interest boxes that supplement the text, as well as information boxes for each president of the United States. All of these boxes are designed to spark student interest and to encourage deeper study into particular subjects.

Maps

Over forty maps, including a United States map and a world map at the back of the book, help to illustrate the events of American history. Refer to these maps often as you teach the related material. A list of all the maps is found on pages vi and vii.

Illustrations

The textbook contains hundreds of color and black-and-white photographs that are closely related to the content. In addition, the text contains several original drawings produced by the BJU Press art department.

are having problems learning the material. Tests should contain enough questions to avoid allowing one section to make or break a student's grade.

Long essay questions are probably not appropriate for this age level; however, short essays (three to five sentences) are a good way to help students learn to express their ideas effectively. Check with the seventh-grade Heritage Studies teacher to see if essays were assigned last year. Your expectations for your students' essays should be based on their experience. In any event, you may want to give a short expla-

nation of essay writing before the first test to show the students the difference between a well-developed answer and an incomplete answer, a rambling answer, or an answer with too much extraneous information. Essays should be fully developed and in sentence form. The students' essay-writing ability should improve as they gain experience throughout the year.

Note: Prepared tests are available for THE AMERICAN REPUBLIC for Christian Schools (Second Edition).

Feature Sections

The text contains eight two-page features. Four features discuss geographic regions of America, and the remaining four discuss forces that have changed American society. Each feature contains a map or original cartoon to add interest to the students' study.

The Constitution

Chapter 8 contains a complete annotated copy of the United States Constitution. The student book in no way intends to be a complete text for studying American government, but it provides an introduction and may also stimulate an appreciation for this amazing document.

Section Review Questions

Several questions follow each section. The numbered questions are designed as a reading check of general information from the section. Also included for each section is a thinking question that asks the students to go beyond what they have read and apply the information.

Chapter Reviews

Every chapter ends with a fully developed chapter review, including a list of terms. These pages provide students with an opportunity to review factual knowledge covered in the chapter. At the end of the review are two discussion questions that require students to apply information they have learned in the chapter.

History Skills

History Skills pages follow selected chapters. These pages are designed to help students become more skillful in using common tools of the historian.

Pronunciation Guide

The pronunciation key used in this text is designed to give readers a self-evident, acceptable pronunciation for a word as they read it from the page. For more nearly accurate pronunciations, consult a dictionary.

Syllables with primary stress appear in LARGE CAPITAL letters. Syllables with secondary stress and one-syllable words appear in SMALL CAPITAL letters; for example, Afghanistan appears as (af GAN uh STAN). Where two or more words appear together, hyphens separate the syllables within each word; for example, the Rub al Khali appears as (ROOB ahl KHAH-lee).

Most sounds are readily apparent. Here are the possible exceptions:

SYMBOL	EXAMPLE	SYMBOL	EXAMPLE
g	get = GET	th	thin = THIN
j	gentle = JEN tul	th	then = *THEN*
s	cent = SENT	zh	lesion = LEE zhun
a	cat = KAT	i-e	might = MITE
ah	cot = KAHT	eye	icy = EYE see
ar	car = KAR	oh	slow = SLOH
aw	all = AWL	ou	loud = LOUD
a-e	cape = KAPE	oy	toil = TOYL
ay	paint = PAYNT	u	some = SUM
e	jet = JET	uh	abet = uh BET
		oo	crew = CROO
		oo	push = POOSH

Home School Ideas

The flexibility inherent in the home schooling schedule allows parents and students to focus on specific topics. As much as possible, allow your child to pursue those interesting topics. Taking field trips to local historical sites, museums (art or history), and places of business helps to make history come alive. (Join other home schoolers in your area to receive group discounts and guided tours.) Inviting missionaries and older friends into your home to share firsthand experiences from other countries and to give accounts of life in the past adds a personal dimension to impersonal historical facts. Incorporating other academic disciplines, such as music and literature, with historical study broadens the scope of learning. (Remember that although the side pursuits are fun and interesting, the ultimate purpose for this course is for your child to understand the framework of United States history.)

The home schooling parent will be able to use any hands-on activities, listening activities, and creative writing opportunities given in this volume. For convenience, some activities have a home school icon.

Project Ideas

You may wish to include extended student projects in your plan for the school year. These projects give students an opportunity to use the information they are learning throughout the year. It also gives your students an opportunity to demonstrate their creative skills. Ideas include the following:

Introduction

This Page
The sermon quoted in the introduction is "God in History" by R. G. Lee and was preached in 1930 at the Winona Lake Bible Conference in Winona Lake, Indiana.

A Baptist minister asked a Midwestern audience in the 1930s, "Who, knowing the facts of our history, can doubt that the United States of America has been a thought in the mind of God from all eternity?" Indeed, Christians must realize that nothing in history is accidental; our sovereign God directs the affairs of men and nations to accomplish His will. As you begin your study of the history of the United States, keep in mind that God has likewise directed—and is still directing—America's history. The story of the United States is but one part of God's overall design for the ages. You will read about human failure and weakness, but remember that God superintends all things for His glory and purpose. "For of him, and through him, and to him, are all things: to whom be glory for ever. Amen." (Romans 11:36)

- Biographical reports, papers, or presentations on famous people from the era you are studying. These can range from two-page papers to oral reports to dramatic presentations about the chosen person. Give your students a check sheet detailing the requirements of the assignment so that they have every opportunity to be successful.

- State reports. Each student would research a state; write a two-page paper about its geography, resources, and culture; and present a five-minute talk to the class. This gives an excellent opportunity to overview the nation through student projects.

- Art projects. Students can make models of famous structures with a short report about their features. They can construct three-dimensional maps of the nation or a region, highlighting geographic features. They can make projects similar to early American crafts, such as samplers, pottery, or leather items.

Unit Four

The three chapters in this unit deal with the Civil War. You may want to end your first semester mid-unit and take up Reconstruction at the start of the new semester. This will give more time to cover the Civil War, a topic that usually interests students. Use these chapters to discuss the fact that often there are good people on both sides of a conflict. Discuss ways that the Civil War may have been circumvented.

Battle Scars

On the bulletin board, post pictures of Civil War battlefields and destroyed cities. Copies of Mathew Brady's photographs may be available in a teacher supply store. These can be posted on a map of the eastern half of the United States with string going from the picture to the battle location on the map. Other scars of war could be portrayed by images of the death of Lincoln, carpetbaggers in the South, and ruined fields and homes.

Materials

You will need the following special materials for your teaching of Unit Four.

- *Student Activities* manual for THE AMERICAN REPUBLIC for *Christian Schools* (Second Edition)
- An anthology of historical documents containing Thomas Dew's argument in favor of slavery
- *The Narrative of the Life of Frederick Douglass, an American Slave* by Frederick Douglass
- *Free Indeed: Heroes of Black Christian History* (BJUP)
- *American History in Verse* by Burton Stevenson (BJUP)
- Charles Ludwig's *Champion of Freedom* (1987)
- Harriet Beecher Stowe's *Uncle Tom's Cabin*
- A book of Mathew Brady photographs
- Special speaker: a Civil War historian

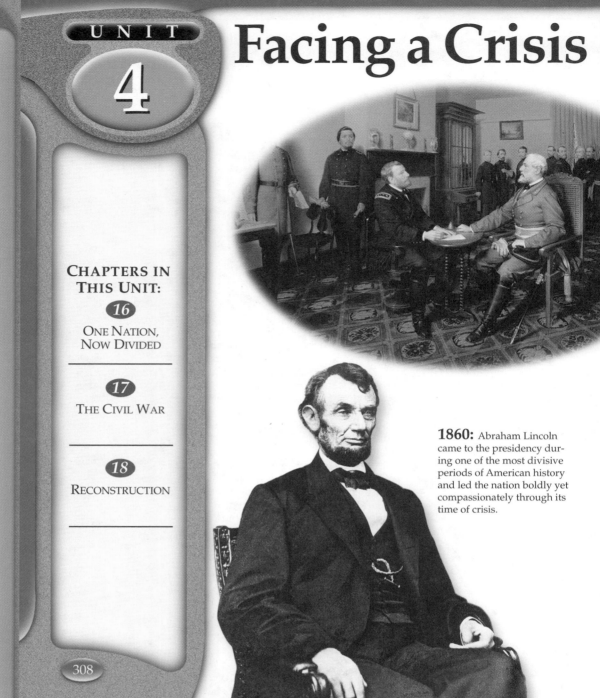

UNIT 4

Facing a Crisis

CHAPTERS IN THIS UNIT:

16
ONE NATION, NOW DIVIDED

17
THE CIVIL WAR

18
RECONSTRUCTION

308

1860: Abraham Lincoln came to the presidency during one of the most divisive periods of American history and led the nation boldly yet compassionately through its time of crisis.

Unit 4	Lesson Plan Chart		
Chapter Title	**Main Goal**	**Pages**	**Time Frame**
16. One Nation, Now Divided	To explain how consequences of past decisions, good and bad, testify that biblical principles are true and that God oversees the course of U.S. history	311-31	5-9 days
The South	To identify the social and geographic features of the South	332-33	½-1 day
17. The Civil War	To analyze the reasons for and effects of the Civil War	334-59	7-11 days
18. Reconstruction	To define greed and corruption as two prevalent problems when the government attempts to remedy social ills	360-81	6½-10 days
Free Speech in Action	To identify key people involved in civil rights efforts	382-83	½-1 day
Total Suggested Days			19½-32 days

- Video: *Red Runs the River* (BJUP)
- A Civil War documentary video
- A copy of the "Gettysburg Address"
- A copy of the Emancipation Proclamation
- A copy of *Roll of Thunder, Hear My Cry* (1976) by Mildred D. Taylor

1865: After four years of bloody civil war, Confederate general Robert E. Lee surrendered his troops to Ulysses S. Grant in the McLean House at Appomattox Courthouse, Virginia.

1850

1852 *Uncle Tom's Cabin* published

1854 Kansas-Nebraska Act; Founding of Republican Party

1855

1857 Dred Scott decision

1859 John Brown's raid on Harpers Ferry

1860 — 1860 South Carolina secedes

1861 ——— Firing on Fort Sumter

— **Civil War**

1863 Emancipation Proclamation

1865 — 1865 ——— Lee surrenders at Appomattox; Lincoln assassinated

1867 Reconstruction Act of 1867; Purchase of Alaska

1868 Impeachment of Andrew Johnson

1870 — 1870 Fifteenth Amendment

1875

1877 Last federal troops withdrawn from the South

1880

1861-65: There were over one million casualties in the Civil War, including Confederate private Edwin Francis Jemison, who died on July 1, 1863, at Malvern Hill.

Time Out

Ask the following questions about the time line.

- What event started the Civil War? *(firing on Fort Sumter)* In what year? *(1861)*

- What event ended the Civil War? *(Lee's surrender at Appomattox)* In what year? *(1865)*

- What event does not seem connected to the Civil War? *(the purchase of Alaska)*

- What year was the Emancipation Proclamation signed? *(1863)* How do you think the signing affected the war? *(became a rallying point for blacks in the North and South and for whites who were sympathetic to their cause)*

Stowe's Account of the Publication of *Uncle Tom's Cabin*

Harriet Beecher Stowe gave the story behind the writing of *Uncle Tom's Cabin,* the most influential book in American history. Read this excerpt and the questions below. Then write the first five words of the sentence in the text that answers each question.

With astonishment and distress Mrs. Stowe heard on all sides, from humane and Christian people, that the slavery of the blacks was a guaranteed constitutional right, and that all opposition to it endangered the national Union. With this conviction she saw that even earnest and tenderhearted Christians seemed to feel it a duty to close their eyes, ears, and hearts to the harrowing details of slavery, to put down all discussion of the subject, and even to assist slave owners to recover fugitives in Northern States. She said to herself, These people can not know what slavery is: they do not see what they are defending; and hence arose a purpose to write some sketches which would show to the world of slavery as she had herself seen it. . . .

In shaping her material, the author had but one purpose, to show the institution of slavery truly, just as it existed. She had visited Kentucky, had formed the acquaintance of people who were just, upright, and generous, and yet slave holders. She had heard their views and appreciated their situation. She felt that justice required that their difficulties should be recognized and their virtues acknowledged. It was her object to show that the evils of slavery were the inherent evils of a bad system, and not always the fault of those who had become involved in it and were its actual administrators. . . .

Uncle Tom's Cabin was published March 20, 1852. The despondency of the author as to the question whether anybody would read or attend to her appeal was soon dispelled. Ten thousand copies were sold in a few days, and over 300,000 within a year; and eight power presses, running day and night, were barely able to keep pace with the demand for it. It was read everywhere, apparently, and by everyone; and she soon began to hear echoes of sympathy all over the land. The indignation, the pity, the distress that had long weighed upon her soul, seemed to pass off from her and into the readers of the book.

In one respect, Mrs. Stowe's expectations were strikingly different from fact. She had painted slaveholders as amiable, generous, and just. She had shown examples among them of the noblest and most beautiful traits of character, had admitted fully their temptations, their perplexities, so that a friend of hers who had many relatives in the South wrote to her in exultation, "Your book is going to be the great pacificator: it will unite both North and South." Her expectation was that the professed Abolitionists would denounce it as altogether too mild in its dealings with slaveholders. To her astonishment, it was the extreme Abolitionists who received it, and the entire South who rose up against it.

1. According to Stowe, why did Northerners shut their eyes to slavery?
2. Stowe did not write her novel simply to entertain her readers. What did she want to "pass into them"?
3. Did Stowe write her novel to help the cause of extreme abolitionism?
4. Did Stowe expect the Southerners to ban her novel?

Uncle Tom's Cabin

1. because slavery was a guaranteed right and to oppose it endangered the Union

2. the indignation, pity, and distress that had weighed upon her heart

3. No, she expected them to denounce it.

4. No, she was astonished that they rose up against slavery.

What was the author's purpose in writing her book? *(to show the institution of slavery accurately)*

16

One Nation, Now Divided

Goals
Students should be able to
1. Define and use the basic terms from the chapter.
2. List the steps that led to the Civil War.
3. **Explain how the consequences of past decisions, good and bad, testify that biblical principles are true and that God oversees the course of U.S. history.**

 Ready to Fight
This photo shows a cannon emplacement at Fort Sumter, where the Civil War began. Ask students what they think the tracks in the floor are for. *(aiming the cannon)*

Chapter Motivation
A popular topic of discussion is the divisions in America today. Regional divisions are not as strong as they once were. Into what distinct groups are Americans still divided? *(Answers will vary but will probably include ethnic groups, religious groups, and political groups.)* Ask the students to name a moral issue that divides Americans today. *(Answers include abortion, legalized gambling, and assisted suicide.)* Make parallels between the debate over slavery and the debate over abortion. Note that people are divided into pro-life and pro-abortion camps, but both camps are further divided over how to resolve the problems. Could the issue of abortion ever lead to war?

Materials
SECTION 1
• Activity A from Chapter 16 of the *Student Activities* manual

SECTION 2
• Activities B and C from Chapter 16 of the *Student Activities* manual
• An anthology of historical documents containing Thomas Dew's argument in favor of slavery

In the 1850s, the United States experienced new growth and, except for a brief financial panic in 1857, prosperity. The population reached thirty-one million, a thirty-five percent increase in just ten years. Production of foodstuffs and manufactured goods reached new heights. The resources that God had given the United States, acres of unoccupied land, a network of navigable rivers, and huge amounts of timber, would allow the country to sustain progress. But this economic boom was only part of the picture of the United States at that time. Greater problems were about to rend the nation in two.

Differences Between the North and the South

There were several key issues that led to a division between the North and the South. Although the issues were not new, more people were beginning to see the issues as matters of right and wrong instead of as mere regional preferences. There was no longer much room for compromise between the two regions of the country.

Differing Economies and Lifestyles

There were major economic differences between the North and the South. The South

CHAPTER 16	Lesson Plan Chart		
Section Title	**Main Activity**	**Page**	**Time Frame**
1. Differences Between the North and the South	On Civil Wars	311-13	½-1 day
2. Slavery: America's Great Debate	Autobiography of a Freed Slave	314-18	1-2 days
3. Final Eruptions of the Slavery Issue	The Straw That Broke the Camel's Back	318-22	1-2 days
4. The Election of 1860 and Secession	Identify the Border States	322-24	½-1 day
5. Fort Sumter and War	Political Strategy—You Are There	325-29	1-2 days
Total Suggested Days (including 1 day for review and testing)		5-9 days	

SECTION 1

Objectives

Students should be able to
1. Describe the differing economies and lifestyles of the North and South.
2. Explain the differing political views of the North and South.

Recurring Issues

The divisive issues that led the country into war in the 1860s were not original to that time period. They had simmered below the surface for many years. One of the best examples of these controversies concerns the social contract. It said that the people of a country voluntarily submit to a ruler for the protection of their natural rights. If he exceeds the appropriate boundaries of his power, however, the people have the right to nullify his laws or even to remove him as the ruler. This issue was raised several times prior to the Civil War, even as far back as the American Revolution, for which the social contract was used as justification.

was agricultural. Towns and villages were few—cities, scarcer yet. Furthermore, nearly all of the South's cities, such as Charleston, Richmond, and Savannah, were relatively small, having populations under 40,000. Only New Orleans, with its population of 150,000, compared to northern cities in size and diversity. Instead of factories, the South had plantations and farms that raised cotton and other crops for sale. Much of the business of southern cities revolved around the trade of agricultural materials and crops.

In the South, the upper class, one percent of the population, was made up of planters owning large plantations and many slaves. This top one percent was the ruling class politically, socially, and economically. Other white farmers owned only a few slaves (generally fewer than ten). A much larger part of the southern white population, however, owned no slaves at all. (Owners of small farms and other Southerners without slaves made up three-quarters of the white population.) Yet the way of life of all Southerners was greatly influenced by the needs and desires of the slaveholders.

In contrast to the agricultural, slaveholding South, the North was industrialized and had few slaves. Its many cities were crowded and noisy. Some grew so quickly that it was hard for them to handle the growth. New York City's population soared to over 800,000. When Chicago became incorporated in 1837, it had only 4,170 people. In 1860 the census takers counted 112,000 Chicago residents.

One reason for the great population increase in the North was immigration. More

This photograph taken in South Carolina in 1862 shows a slave family that was fortunate enough to have several generations living on one plantation.

than 2.8 million immigrants had come to America, and seven out of eight settled in the North or West. Initially many were forced to live in filth and misery in the cities while laboring long hours for low wages. The working and living conditions of some northern workers were so poor that Southerners called them "wage slaves." But soon many foreigners adopted American ways and raised their standards of living. Many held political offices. In Boston, New York, and Philadelphia, Irish voters were influential, and in St. Louis, Cincinnati, and Milwaukee anyone running

 Student Activity A: Differences between the North and the South

This chart summarizes the differences between the North and the South. After the students read Section 1, see how many of these differences they can find.

Debate Ideas

Have your students discuss and/or debate the following:

Slavery was only one of many causes for the Civil War.

The South should have been allowed to secede from the Union.

The American Civil War was inevitable.

On Civil Wars

How could Americans kill Americans? Brothers kill brothers? The most traumatic period in the nation's history cries out for an explanation. This chapter points the students to the answer, but they still need to think carefully about the issues that led Americans to kill their own people. The lessons from this period in U.S.

history will help students understand parallel events in the history of other nations, such as the Roman civil wars and the English Civil War. They also need to understand the American Civil War as a point of comparison for understanding modern civil wars that the UN sometimes gets entangled in. Knowledge of our own nation's civil war helps us to understand the deep feelings behind the warring sides in modern wars, and it also helps us to understand the folly of outside intervention in places such as the Balkans, Cyprus, and Rwanda.

for office had to consider the wishes of the German residents.

In the North owners of small farms, merchants, and increasing numbers of factory workers made up most of the population. Four-fifths of the nation's factories were in the North. Although most people were still farmers, mechanized agriculture helped them to produce food for nearby towns. Railroads carried food to the ever-growing cities and returned to rural areas carrying manufactured goods. Owners of factories, railroads, and other businesses and industries became the wealthy and influential people in northern society.

Differing Political Views

The differing economies and lifestyles produced differing political views as well. Generally the North favored a strong central government. Northerners tended to be more willing to pay higher taxes to provide local and state goods and services. The North also had more wage earners to help pay for such costs.

Many Southerners feared a strong central government. They still believed in Jefferson's ideal that the best government was local and state government. Little money was spent on local services because few of the Southerners lived in cities and towns where services such as police protection or city building projects were needed. Since education was considered a private matter, there were few public schools in the South at this time. Neither did most southern taxpayers wish to pay large amounts of taxes to the federal government for spending on improvements and benefits that often chiefly aided the more populous areas in the North.

The two sections also sharply disagreed about what level of government (federal or state) should possess more authority. Most Northerners believed that the Constitution was the nation's highest law under God and that the Constitution and federal law overruled any conflicting state and local laws. They based their view on Article VI of the Constitution.

Many Southerners disagreed, arguing that the federal government could not overrule the rights of the states. They emphasized the idea that government was an agreement between a ruling body and those ruled. When those rulers exceeded the power given to them by the people, the people had the right to nullify unacceptable laws. In this way states' rights could be upheld over national sovereignty or authority.

The South feared being in the minority, and every time a new state applied to join the Union, the South's fears resurfaced. Every new free state in the Union meant more votes against the southern views. If the North gained too large a majority, it might force the South into submission.

Another political issue dividing the North and South was the tariff. The North generally favored a high protective tariff to protect its industries from foreign imports. The South opposed it because it had little industry of its own and also because it needed foreign imports and trade to support its livelihood. The South was, in effect, being forced to pay the tariff to support northern industry.

In addition to the other differences, the issue of slavery was widening the rift between the North and the South.

SECTION REVIEW

1. What was the main economic focus of the South? the North?

2. What groups of people were most influential in northern and southern society?

 How and why did Northerners and Southerners differ in their views of government?

Other instances of appeal to this doctrine include the Virginia and Kentucky Resolutions (Chapter 9), the Hartford Convention at the end of the War of 1812 (margin note in Chapter 10), and South Carolina's Ordinance of Nullification and its accompanying threat of secession (Chapter 12).

Another issue that continually divided North and South was the conflict between industry and agriculture. The conflict was a major factor in differences over the National Bank. It also accounted for the tariff controversy—the desire for a high protective tariff by the North and the strong objection to tariffs by the South. This controversy became heated in 1828 when President John Quincy Adams signed the "tariff of abominations" (Chapter 11). The tariff of 1832, though slightly lower than the 1828 version, was still objectionable enough to provoke the Ordinance of Nullification (Chapter 12).

Central Versus Local Control
The question of whether public services should be administered centrally or locally is an important one, even today. Some of the services that are debated are education, welfare, health care, police and fire protection, and utilities. You and your students can probably think of other areas of debate, possibly ones that are discussed in your region of the country.

Article VI
Article VI of the Constitution states that the United States Constitution, together with laws and treaties made under its authority, are the supreme law of the land. Judges throughout the country are to consider the Constitution their final source of authority, even if the laws of the particular states in which they preside are contradictory.

Preview the outline of the chapter with students, reminding them that each of the five sections addresses part of the question "Why civil war?" As you look over the outline, ask the students to share what they already know. Section 1: differences in lifestyle, economy, and political views. Section 2: different viewpoints on slavery. Section 3: events that undermined the willingness of both sides to seek further compromise. Section 4: the event that caused the Deep South to leave (Lincoln's election). Section 5: the events that caused the departure of the Upper South (Lincoln's call for troops) and the later struggle for the loyalty of the border states. The last section also addresses the question "What advantages gave each side faith that victory was possible?" Without deep faith, civil wars do not usually last very long.

Section Review Answers

1. agriculture; industry (pp. 311-12)

2. northern—owners of factories, railroads, and other industries; southern—owners of large plantations (pp. 312-13)

 The North generally favored a strong central government. With its larger towns and domination by industry, the North wanted and could better afford public service programs. The South wanted more power for the states. There were few larger towns in the South, and Southern states did not want to pay for programs that would benefit mainly the North. (p. 313)

Objectives
Students should be able to
1. Explain how slavery in America was different from slavery in other countries.
2. Describe the way slaves were acquired and treated.
3. Contrast the Northern and Southern views of slavery.
4. Describe some of the black reactions to slavery.

Slavery: America's Great Debate

In Chapter 3 we learned about how slaves first came to America and how slavery developed there (see pp. 42-43). Although slavery is nearly as old as the human race, slavery in the United States was different from other instances of slavery in history in three ways. It was limited to the black race; it was usually a permanent condition for the slave; and slave traders seeking profits promoted it.

Slavery came about largely because of the need for labor, especially in the South. In that region many laborers were needed to produce the profitable crops of the region—tobacco, indigo, rice, cotton, and sugar cane. Few whites sought low-paying, hard field jobs on southern plantations when they could easily acquire land to farm for themselves. White landowners saw the forced labor of black slaves as a solution. In northern and western areas, farms were smaller, and large money crops had not developed. Not needing large numbers of field hands, and with immigrants to supply labor for many factories, the North did not use slaves, for the most part. Slavery was a terrible injustice, but it developed with little protest under the disguise of a "needed" and "acceptable" institution in early America.

By the 1830s, however, many Americans realized that slavery was not just another system of labor. The question of whether it was morally right or wrong became a great debate. Whites who depended on slavery defended the institution. Some justified slavery on religious grounds. They said that bringing the uncivilized slave to the New World helped him to be Christianized. Some praised it as "a positive good," as had a college professor, Thomas R. Dew, in 1832. He wrote that instead of being an evil, slavery was a positive good when compared to other labor systems. Dew used religious, historical, cultural, racial, and sociological arguments to support his "positive good" theory. John C. Calhoun and other Southerners used these arguments to defend slavery against rising attacks. Nonetheless, opposition to slavery increased as whites and free blacks exposed its wrongs.

How Slaves Were Acquired

Most slaves came from the nations on Africa's western coast. Some slaves were captured in raids and sold to traders. Some were prisoners of war captured by warring African tribes. These tribes were sometimes guilty of selling their enemies into slavery for personal profit. Men, women, and children were captured, chained together, and marched to the seacoast, where slave traders bought them with liquor and various utensils and trinkets. In early colonial days Europeans and New Englanders provided most of the slave ships that then carried the captives to the New World.

Slaves were treated inhumanly from the moment of capture, but perhaps the slave's worst experience was crossing the Atlantic to America. This crossing was called the **"middle passage."** (The first passage took the slave to the coast of Africa; the third passage involved the final sale to slave owners in America.)

Since slave traders knew that even under the best conditions many captives would die, they tried to pack their ships with as many people as possible. Crowded into shelflike decks, the Africans were then chained and shackled wrist-to-wrist and ankle-to-ankle. Poorly fed, these people usually received gruel and water twice a day. Disease spread quickly because of poor sanitation. Some captives broke down under the stress of the voyage and killed themselves and others. There is no way to estimate the number of Africans who died on the middle passage—it was at least one in seven or eight, but it may have been as high as one in four.

314

Materials

- Activities B and C from Chapter 16 of the *Student Activities* manual

- An anthology of historical documents containing Thomas Dew's argument in favor of slavery

- *The Narrative of the Life of Frederick Douglass, an American Slave* by Frederick Douglass

- *Free Indeed: Heroes of Black Christian History* (BJUP)

Student Activity B: Slavery: America's Great Debate

This prewriting activity helps students learn how to summarize information. In this case, they summarize the slavery issue.

Slave auctions had no regard for a slave's family relations. If the highest bid split a family, few dealers cared.

In 1808 the United States became the last major western nation to ban foreign slave trade. (See Article I, Section 9 of the Constitution.) Some slave smuggling did continue, but most new slaves after this time were the children of men and women already living in the United States. Most of the northern states had abolished slavery by the end of the War for Independence.

Some Southerners, moved by the ideals of American independence, spoke out against slavery. As early as the 1820s, a few Quaker-sponsored **emancipation** (ih man suh PAY shun) societies campaigned for gradual emancipation, or freeing of the slaves. Some also pushed for an overseas colony for freed American blacks. Low tobacco prices and worn-out soil caused some to predict that slavery was a dying institution. But the invention of the cotton gin and the opening of new fertile lands in the West revived the plantation economy and made slavery profitable again. When the first American census of the population was made in 1790, there were about 750,000 slaves in the United States. By 1860 the slave population had reached three and a half million; one out of every three Southerners was a slave.

The Northern Viewpoint

Since there was little slavery in the North, the practice had little direct effect on the region. Most Northerners in the early 1800s were not concerned with its existence in the South, either. The prospect that brought the issue of slavery to the attention of the North was its possible spread to new areas in the West. The North did not want more western

315

Student Activity C: Steps to War

This activity develops the students' understanding of the causes and effects that led to the Civil War. You may want to contrast the course of events with the nullification crisis discussed in Chapter 12 (Student Activity C). You can complete the chart in class, or the students can complete it on their own. The review questions can be used with your discussion of the last section or as part of your chapter review.

Pro-life Republicans dip back into the pre–Civil War era to support vigorous action against abortion. The Republican Party rose from the ashes of the Whig Party, which died because it refused to speak up on slavery. Alan Keyes, an outspoken opponent of abortion and a Republican candidate for president in 1996 and 2000, warned his party, "Those who are recommending that we pull the pro-life plank out of the platform are taking the party the way of the Whigs who advocated silence on slavery." Conservative journalist Cal Thomas quoted an 1860 election speech by Abraham Lincoln to prove that the Republican Party was founded to impose morality on society. After quoting Lincoln, he asked his readers to insert the word *abortion* for *slavery:* "You say that you think slavery is wrong, but you denounce all attempts to restrain it. Is there anything else that you think is wrong, that you are not willing to deal with as wrong? . . . [You say] we must not call it wrong in politics because that is bringing morality into politics; and we must not call it wrong in the pulpit because that is bringing politics into religion." Lincoln was condemning the same type of arguments that are used by pro-choice Republicans today.

Note that Lincoln was considered a moderate. Although he flatly denounced slavery as a moral wrong, he did not call for its abolition where it already existed. Most opponents of abortion simply want to undo the *Roe v. Wade* decision and allow states to make their own decisions about how to regulate abortion, as they did before 1973.

John Chavis and Lott Carey

Two other blacks of the early 1800s who had strong Christian testimonies were John Chavis and Lott Carey. Chavis was a free black; he was probably the first black to attend Princeton. He became a teacher and a Presbyterian minister. Carey went to Africa as a missionary after he gained his freedom.

states to gain the same interests and political views as the South.

Northern feelings also began to change with the growth of **abolitionism** (ab uh LISH uh niz um), a movement to do away with slavery completely. Abolitionists supported emancipation, either gradually or immediately. Some favored **compensated emancipation**, whereby the slave owner would be paid for the loss of his slave. One of the most vocal and militant abolitionists, **William Lloyd Garrison,** began a newspaper in Boston called the *Liberator*. Garrison strongly advocated immediate abolition of slavery without compensation.

While most Northerners embraced antislavery views, they were not willing to give blacks an equal place in society. Few northern states allowed free blacks to vote or offered them public education. Northerners also restricted blacks from many occupations and public offices, and they assigned them separate areas in many churches and other establishments. Some of the western states would not even let blacks settle within their borders!

The Southern Viewpoint

The more abolitionists attacked slavery, the more white Southerners rallied to defend it. Even those who were not slave owners supported it; some hoped one day to own slaves themselves. Because many of the South's businesses relied on cotton produced by slave labor, the prosperity of the entire region seemed to be dependent on the institution. Some whites might have been opposed to slavery, but they saw it as a necessary evil for keeping the cotton culture going.

On the other hand, struggling white farmers on the fringes of the Appalachians in western Virginia and North Carolina and some farmers in eastern Kentucky and Tennessee opposed slavery. Ownership of slaves gave the large plantation owners most of the influence

Bond Slave of Jesus Christ

John Jasper was the youngest of twenty-four children. He was born on a plantation in 1812 to parents who were both slaves. His mother was the main spiritual influence in his life. After his salvation, Jasper said of his mother, "She gave me to God before I was born, prayed me into glory when I was a wild, reckless boy. Prayed me into preaching the Gospel."

Jasper was saved on July 4, 1839, seven months after he learned to read by studying with a fellow slave. For Jasper that day became not only a day to celebrate the nation's independence but also a day to celebrate his own independence from the bonds of sin.

When Jasper's master heard the news of his salvation, he said, "John, your Savior is mine, and we are brothers in the Lord." Jasper was given the day off to "go and tell it." Jasper did just that. For forty years, God used John Jasper to preach the gospel, first as a slave and later as a free man.

As a free black preacher, Jasper started a church in Richmond, Virginia, with nine people meeting in a stable. Soon, however, this handful became a thriving church of over a thousand members. When white people came to hear him preach, they usually sat in a separate section in the balcony. Jasper would joke, "Now, look'a here, you all white people, you keep over in your section. Don't get in the places of the regular customers."

Freed from slavery and freed from sin, John Jasper became a bond slave for Christ. One of Jasper's church members said of him, "He always thought of hisself as the servant of King Jesus. That was a slavery that he liked and never wished to get free from it."

 Critique Thomas R. Dew's "Positive Good" Theory

Have students critique Thomas R. Dew's argument in favor of slavery (or one of John C. Calhoun's speeches on the same topic). These documents are included in many anthologies of U.S. history, and excerpts are available on the Internet. Analyzing these arguments gives the students an opportunity to investigate logical fallacies. Of particular interest are the arguments in behalf of slavery based on the Bible. Can the students think of any evils today that are justified in the name of the Bible?

 Autobiography of a Freed Slave

If you did not previously have time to read the autobiography of a slave in Chapter 3 (see page 42), you can do so now. It includes Olaudah Equiano's "middle passage." Students are sure to be moved by selections from the poignant autobiography *The Narrative of the Life of Frederick Douglass, an American Slave,* beginning with his lack of knowledge about his age

and his separation from his mother in infancy.

Pastors of Former Slaves

Free Indeed: Heroes of Black Christian History tells the story of Daniel Payne, a black man who was free at birth and became a strong abolitionist and an educator of the black race before, during, and after the Civil War.

"John Jasper" is the story of a slave who was freed at the end of the Civil War and who preached to many.

in state government. Many people from these highlands would later side with the North on the issue of slavery.

Treatment of Slaves

Slaves were treated differently from plantation to plantation. Since slaves were an economic investment, keeping them fit and treating them well made sense. They were generally assured of receiving food, clothing, and shelter, and care in childhood and old age was expected. The slave's food was plain like that of poor white Southerners. Cornmeal mush or cornbread, fatback (fat pork from the back of a hog), beans or field peas, and vegetables from the slaves' own gardens composed their staple diet. Slaves who did their work well were occasionally rewarded with an extra day off, better food, or even a little cash. Owners also used the promise of a bigger Christmas celebration or a marriage to someone on a nearby plantation to motivate the slaves. Some slaves became almost like members of the master's family. As a rule, house slaves were treated better than field slaves, and the smaller the plantation, the closer the slaves were to their master. Nonetheless, they were still a people with no basic rights other than those granted by their masters.

Slaves had no legal assistance in cases of mistreatment, and there is no question that some of them were badly treated. Some white masters treated their slaves little better than farm animals. Public whippings for laziness and disobedience sometimes took place. Slaves who were continual troublemakers might be sold to another plantation. Such a sale meant a forced parting with friends and loved ones. The typical slave was sold at least once in a lifetime. Especially dreadful was being "sold down river" (down the Mississippi) to sugar plantations. Cutting sugar cane was extremely hard work; some people were actually worked to death.

Black Responses to Conditions on Plantations

Obviously slaves were not slaves by choice. Strict slave codes in every southern state kept blacks in bondage. In some states even if a slave gained his freedom, he was not allowed to stay in the state.

The Underground Railroad—Hundreds of slaves ran away from their masters to find freedom. The **"Underground Railroad"** offered blacks who could reach the border states a reasonably good chance to escape. This "railroad" was actually a network of people who aided runaway slaves. These "conductors" hid the slaves by day from captors. Then they aided their night travels to the next stop, where others on the escape route helped the runaways move farther north. When the Fugitive Slave Law of 1850 required northern states to return runaways, the "railroad" extended its route. Ontario, Canada, became the final destination for many people seeking freedom.

Slave Rebellions—Some slaves, such as Nat Turner in Virginia and Denmark Vesey (VEE zee) in South Carolina, led revolts. All of them failed, and the blacks involved were hanged. While the hangings made other slaves less likely to rebel, the revolts panicked the whites. They slept with guns and enacted even stricter laws to control the blacks. Several southern states even made it illegal to teach slaves to read and write. They feared that ideas of revolt would spread uncontrollably if blacks possessed these skills.

Black Leaders Against Slavery—Among the blacks who worked against slavery in the troubled years before the Civil War were **Frederick Douglass** and **Harriet Tubman.** Douglass, the leading black abolitionist, escaped from slavery in 1838. A talented speaker, he lectured against slavery in the North and in Britain. Douglass used money that he made from speaking engagements to

317

Traveling to Freedom
Many of the fugitive slaves who traveled the Underground Railroad were men between the ages of sixteen and thirty-five. The Railroad had little organization in the South, so slaves traveling there had to find their own way. A common method of navigation was following the North Star. Another method involved looking for tree moss, which grows only on the north side of trees.

Once they reached the region of Railroad activity, the fugitives could anticipate more assistance. Railroad stations were generally ten or more miles apart. Slaves could identify stations in several different ways. Some were a candle in a window, a lantern in the front yard, a drinking gourd (symbolizing the Big Dipper, which points to the North Star), or a quilt containing the color black hung on a clothesline. Station conductors gave the fugitives food, clothing, and shelter during the day; at night they either told them how to get to the next station or actually took them there.

Nat Turner's Rebellion
In the early morning hours of August 22, 1831, Nat Turner led the bloodiest slave revolt in Southern history. By the time he and his followers were stopped in their path of killing, approximately sixty white males and females of all ages had been slain. In the unrest that followed the revolt, approximately two hundred blacks lost their lives. Some of the slain were guilty of participation in the massacre, but many more were innocent victims of frenzied fear and wrath on the part of some whites.

Nat Turner lived in Southampton County in Virginia. He was an extremely bright young man who learned to read at an early age. His first master encouraged him to study the Bible.

Turner was never treated especially harshly, yet he had the desire for freedom rooted deep within. His mother hated being a slave; his father had escaped to free-

---

Should Christians Support Civil Disobedience?

The citizens who supported the Underground Railroad practiced civil disobedience. Discuss whether they were right to do so. If slavery took place today, would it be right for a Christian to aid in the Underground Railroad? Some pro-life activists use the same argument to justify breaking the law in order to save the lives of unborn babies.

Educated Slaves

Explain to your students why the South might have forbidden education to blacks. Remind your students that both Nat Turner and Denmark Vesey were intelligent, educated men. How did their level of education give them more power among their people?

Compare Pro-Life Views

Discuss the common pro-life views about the best way to end the evil practice of abortion. At one extreme are radicals who bomb clinics, but at the other extreme are politicians who say they dislike abortion but merely hope it goes away. Abolitionists were divided into similar extremes. (See the discussion in the margin on page 316.) Note that Randall Terry justified civil disobedience based on his modern translation of Proverbs 24:11: "Rescue those unjustly sentenced to death."

dom. Turner expected that perhaps he would be given his freedom because of his unusual intellectual abilities. Instead, he was kept in the fields, performing backbreaking labor. He was a hard worker and generally gave no cause for complaint, but the seeds of rebellion were germinating in his mind. He began to withdraw from people and to fast for long periods of time. He became obsessed with the Old Testament prophets and the idea of the Day of Judgment. He claimed to have received visions from the Lord that he interpreted as signaling imminent judgment. He came to believe that he was to be involved in bringing about this judgment, and he gained a following through his persuasive speaking.

The question of when he should act was troubling to Turner, but he felt that he had received his sign when there was an eclipse of the sun in February 1831. Turner and a few followers planned an attack on Independence Day, but sickness and nervousness prevented them from carrying it out. Then on August 13 the sun again provided a sign. It grew dim, seemed to be changing colors, and then appeared to have a black spot. Turner knew that he must act; he led his men out early on the morning of August 22. He had only a small number of men but expected many more to join him when news of the rebellion spread.

The gruesome rampage did not last long. Most of the participants were killed or apprehended by the next day. Turner himself stayed at large in the county until October 30. Upon his capture he was sentenced to death and then hanged on November 11.

Former slave Frederick Douglass used money raised from speaking engagements to help escaped slaves.

help other escaped slaves. He also wrote an influential autobiography entitled *The Narrative of the Life of Frederick Douglass.* Douglass risked his freedom because the book told the name of his former master. To escape possible reenslavement, Douglass fled to England where sympathetic people bought his freedom from his master. When Douglass returned to the United States, he published an antislavery newspaper. His newspaper, the *North Star,* also supported women's rights.

After much abuse at the hands of her master, Harriet Tubman escaped from slavery in Maryland in 1849. Aided by Quaker friends, she returned to slave territory nearly twenty times to help runaway slaves. During these ventures she guided about three hundred blacks, including her own parents, whom she freed in 1857, along the Underground Railroad northward. Through a book about her life, Harriet Tubman became known as the "Moses" of her people.

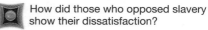

SECTION REVIEW

1. What three characteristics distinguished American slavery?
2. Describe the "middle passage."
3. Contrast the northern and southern viewpoints on slavery.
4. What was the "positive good" theory concerning slavery?

How did those who opposed slavery show their dissatisfaction?

Final Eruptions of the Slavery Issue

The nation had attempted to deal with the spread of slavery at different times. However, attempts such as the Missouri Compromise and the Compromise of 1850 never really solved the problem. All they did was postpone facing the problem.

Harriet Tubman

Section Review Answers

1. It was limited to the black race, was usually a permanent condition, and was promoted by slave traders seeking profits. (p. 314)

2. For crossing the Atlantic to America, slaves were packed tightly into the lower decks of ships, chained together, and fed sparingly. Poor sanitation led to disease. Many died or took their own lives. (p. 314)

3. Northerners believed slavery to be an injustice and advocated emancipation. Southerners grew increasingly defensive as their way of life came under attack. They believed slavery to be acceptable, necessary, and perhaps even a "positive good." (pp. 314-16)

4. Dew's "positive good" theory said that compared to other labor systems, slavery could be considered beneficial. He supported his view with religious, historical, cultural,

racial, and sociological arguments. (p. 314)

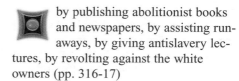 by publishing abolitionist books and newspapers, by assisting runaways, by giving antislavery lectures, by revolting against the white owners (pp. 316-17)

Uncle Tom's Cabin

The plight of slave families and runaways was brought to public attention in a unique way in 1852. **Harriet Beecher Stowe,** a preacher's daughter from Connecticut, lost a young son to cholera in 1849. Believing she now understood how slave mothers felt when their children were taken from them, she vowed to do something on their behalf.

Since the Stowe family had lived for a while in Cincinnati, Ohio, across the Ohio River from the slave state of Kentucky, Mrs.

Concerned women like Harriet Beecher Stowe and Harriet Tubman (opposite) helped lead the fight against slavery.

Stowe had glimpsed something of slavery and the plight of fugitive slaves. From 1850 to 1851 she submitted a novel in installments to the *National Era,* an antislavery paper. When the novel was released in book form, as *Life Among the Lowly, or Uncle Tom's Cabin,* 300,000 copies sold within a year. Although the book seems emotional and artificial by today's standards, ***Uncle Tom's Cabin*** became one of the most influential pieces of literature ever written. The story reached an even wider audience when performing troupes of actors toured the country enacting it. Soon the tragic sufferings of Little Eva and of the slaves Uncle Tom and Eliza were tugging at the heartstrings of readers and audiences. The novel rallied antislavery opinion in the North, but its implication that southern society was evil angered Southerners. The book was banned in the South.

The Kansas-Nebraska Act

When Kansas and Nebraska sought acceptance as new territories, the government again faced the slavery issue. Senator Stephen Douglas applied the idea of popular sovereignty to these territories in 1854. The Illinois senator designed a compromise that would allow the settlers in western lands to decide for or against slavery for themselves. Feelings ran so deep, however, that the bill produced rifts in the existing political parties. As soon as the **Kansas-Nebraska Act** passed, both proslavery and antislavery groups urged their supporters to go west. Naturally the two sides clashed, especially in Kansas, where open fighting took place between those supporting each side. The territory soon earned the nickname Bleeding Kansas. The bloodshed there was a foretaste of what was to happen nationwide.

The Founding of the Republican Party

By 1852 the Whig Party had split into two factions over the slavery issue—the Cotton Whigs and the Conscience Whigs. After the passage of the Kansas-Nebraska Act, the Cotton Whigs joined with southern Democrats because of their stand for slavery. The Conscience Whigs and northern Democrats, angered by the Kansas-Nebraska Act, now joined with Free Soilers, those against the spread of slavery to new lands. In 1854 these antislavery groups formed a new political

319

SECTION 3

Objectives

Students should be able to

1. Describe the effect of *Uncle Tom's Cabin* on the nation.
2. Explain the Kansas-Nebraska Act and its effect in Kansas.
3. Name the political party that grew out of antislavery views.
4. Explain the Dred Scott decision and its effect on the nation.
5. Describe John Brown and his activities.

Polarizing Attitudes

Notice that each issue discussed in this section had a major role in polarizing attitudes in the United States before the Civil War. Antislavery emotions were stirred by *Uncle Tom's Cabin,* the Dred Scott case, and John Brown's activity. As more and more anger and hatred were fixed on the South, southern fears and defenses grew accordingly. Other events fueled this polarization and the South's growing fear that it would be forced into subjection.

Harriet Beecher Stowe

Harriet Beecher Stowe could claim a strong religious heritage. Her father, brother, and husband were influential religious leaders of the nineteenth century.

Besides her several books, Harriet also wrote a few hymns: "Abide in Me, O Lord," "Still, Still with Thee," "That Mystic Work of Thine," and "When Winds Are Raging." Most of these were published in *Plymouth Collection of Hymns and Tunes,* a book her brother put together.

Uncle Tom's Cabin

Considering the circumstances surrounding the publication of *Uncle Tom's Cabin,* its success was phenomenal. The first day it was on the market, it sold three thousand copies. At the end of the first year, it had sold three hundred thousand copies. Eventually three

SECTION 3

Materials

- *American History in Verse* by Burton Stevenson (BJUP)
- Charles Ludwig's *Champion of Freedom* (1987)
- Harriet Beecher Stowe's *Uncle Tom's Cabin*
- Books on John Brown or Bloody Kansas.

Poetry Corner

You will find many poems on the events leading up to and including Fort Sumter in Burton Stevenson's *American History in Verse* (BJUP).

"The Kansas Emigrants" (John Greenleaf Whittier)

"Brown of Osawatomie" (John Greenleaf Whittier)

"Lincoln, the Man of the People" (Edwin Markham)

"Sumter" (Henry Howard Brownell)

Pages from U.S. History

Have the students read silently the selection from Harriet Beecher Stowe's account of the publication of *Uncle Tom's Cabin* on page 310. Then have them answer the questions.

Teaching History Through Literature

A compelling biographical novel of Harriet Beecher Stowe and the influence of her most noted work is Charles Ludwig's *Champion of Freedom* (1987).

million copies were in circulation. The book was translated into twenty-two different languages.

Josiah Henson

Stowe based much of her novel on the life of a slave named Josiah Henson who wrote an autobiography that detailed his hardships as a slave. Stowe used this information to create Uncle Tom.

Kansas and Nebraska Territories

Stephen Douglas was interested in establishing Kansas and Nebraska as territories because of their relationship to a central transcontinental railroad route. Douglas believed that a railroad route through the middle of the country would benefit his state of Illinois, but such a route could not be built until the land through which it would run was organized into territories.

An impediment in the process of organization was the issue of slavery. Douglas proposed popular sovereignty as a compromise. Southerners pointed out that the territory in question fell north of 36° 30', the area designated by the Missouri Compromise as free. They insisted that the Missouri Compromise would have to be declared void if the Kansas-Nebraska Act were to succeed. Douglas finally agreed, to the strong objections of Northern states.

In introducing the bill, its supporters expected that the more northern of the two territories, Nebraska, would reject slavery while the more southern, Kansas, would accept it, thus maintaining the balance between free states and slave states. Instead, Kansas became the site of a great conflict.

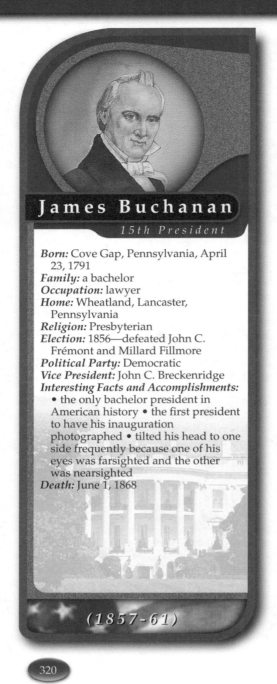

James Buchanan
15th President

Born: Cove Gap, Pennsylvania, April 23, 1791
Family: a bachelor
Occupation: lawyer
Home: Wheatland, Lancaster, Pennsylvania
Religion: Presbyterian
Election: 1856—defeated John C. Frémont and Millard Fillmore
Political Party: Democratic
Vice President: John C. Breckenridge
Interesting Facts and Accomplishments:
• the only bachelor president in American history • the first president to have his inauguration photographed • tilted his head to one side frequently because one of his eyes was farsighted and the other was nearsighted
Death: June 1, 1868

(1857-61)

320

party, the **Republican Party**. The party grew with startling speed, electing Congressmen its first year. In 1856 John C. Frémont became the first Republican to run for president. He was defeated, however, by the Democratic candidate, **James Buchanan.**

The Dred Scott Decision

For three years after the Kansas crisis, the nation experienced a relative calm. But two days after President Buchanan took office in 1857, the quiet ended when the question of the legal status of slavery in the territories came before the Supreme Court.

At stake was the freedom of an elderly black man, **Dred Scott.** Scott, born a slave, was owned by an army doctor, John Emerson of Missouri. Emerson took Scott with him to military posts in the state of Illinois and to the Wisconsin territory, where slavery was outlawed. In 1838 Scott returned with Emerson to Missouri. After Emerson's death, local antislavery lawyers helped Scott sue Emerson's heirs for his freedom on the grounds that living on free soil had made him free. Finally the case reached the Supreme Court, where the chief justice at that time was Roger B. Taney, a Southerner.

The majority of the court ruled against Scott, and Taney stated that since Scott was a slave and black, he was not a citizen. Hence, he had no right to sue in the nation's courts. Further, Taney ruled that Scott was not free as a result of having lived on free soil. Taney reasoned that the Fifth Amendment forbade the government from depriving a person of life, liberty, or property without due process of law. He ruled that the Missouri Compromise had deprived citizens north of 36° 30' of property, their slaves, and was thus invalid.

The consequences of the **Dred Scott decision** were serious. The South temporarily rejoiced in the fact that slavery had been upheld and could lawfully expand into new

---

An alternative activity is to have the students read *Uncle Tom's Cabin* and explain why the novel had such a profound impact. At a minimum, consider reading the key scene when Eliza carries her child across the Ohio River to safety in Chapter 7 (after discovering that her child is to be sold). One reason that the novel is so powerful is that the slaves are Christians. The patience of Tom, who is trying to honor Christ in his life, makes the evil lashes of Simon Legree all the more terrible.

The Straw That Broke the Camel's Back

Discuss each of the headings in this section. Ask the students to summarize how each event contributed to the final split of the Union. Who were the "actors" in each of these events. Discuss their motives. Did any of them foresee that their actions might contribute to a civil war? *(Except for John Brown, none of the actors in the events were hoping for a civil war. In fact, Stowe opposed war.)* The purpose of this discussion is to reinforce that God is in control of

events, and no individual can possibly foresee the final consequences of his actions.

Newspaper Broadsides

Assign different students to be reporters on events in this chapter. Some students should write for Garrison's abolitionist *Liberator,* and others should write for the *Charleston Gazette,* a fiery Southern publication. The articles should be somewhat inflammatory to reflect the divergent views. Topics include Nat Turner's rebellion, the success of *Uncle Tom's Cabin,* passage of the Kansas-

Dred Scott became the focus of attention when the Supreme Court handed down a proslavery decision.

territories. The Supreme Court, however, had made the national conflict more serious. Politically the decision wrecked any chance for future political compromise. The Republican stand against the spread of slavery into new territories had suffered a setback, but antislavery forces were not to be quieted. Now the question of slavery expansion lay in the hands of the new settlers who would vote on it. No one knew whether the North or the South would be willing to abide by the outcome in the West.

Loss of the Compromisers

Compromise to solve problems became even less likely after the men who had accomplished it in earlier years died. Henry Clay, John C. Calhoun, and Daniel Webster, giants of the first half of the century, were all dead by 1852. Most of their successors had less experi-

ence, less wisdom, and less patience. Men such as Millard Fillmore, Franklin Pierce, Stephen Douglas, and James Buchanan were not strong enough leaders to provide needed and acceptable solutions to the nation's problems.

John Brown: Slavery's Avenger

One settler who set out for Kansas to aid antislavery forces was **John Brown**. Although Brown's mental state has been questioned, his hatred for slavery cannot be denied. While most abolitionists sought peaceful means to end slavery, Brown saw violence as the only effective method for dealing with the issue. He wanted to do great harm to slaveholders, to "smite them for God." Brown used Scripture wrongly to justify his acts. He often quoted Hebrews 9:22—"Without shedding of blood is no remission"—implying that the verse meant that slaveholders would pay for the sin of slavery with their blood. In spite of the violence of his message, Brown won a following. "Wherever he spoke, his words commanded earnest attention," said Frederick Douglass. "His arguments seemed to convince all; his appeals touched all, and his will impressed all." Brown's bearing and dignity seemed to wash away all questions about his purposes.

Brown's first effort in his war against slavery was waged at Pottawatomie (paht uh WAHT uh mee), the center for proslavery efforts in Kansas in 1856. For no apparent reason, Brown and four of his seven sons murdered five proslavery men in one night of terror, adding to the turmoil of "Bleeding Kansas."

Then in the late 1850s, Brown began planning his most daring move against slavery. For several months he tried to stir up backing for his efforts, but rumors of the nature of his plans caused several abolitionists to withdraw their support. In the summer of 1859, Brown armed a small band, including four of his own

John Brown and Slavery

Regardless of the final assessment of John Brown's character, one must admit that he was unwavering in his dedication to the cause of abolition. Long before the massacres in Kansas and Harpers Ferry, Brown was championing the cause of freedom for the slaves. He actively sought to assist runaways and lived for a time in a community of freed blacks.

Brown settled near Osawatomie, Kansas, in October 1855, in the middle of the "Bleeding Kansas" turmoil. Proslavery forces raided Lawrence, a free-soil settlement, in May 1856. Possibly in response to that event, Brown and his sons killed five men at Pottawatomie, a proslavery settlement. After this massacre, Brown led attacks against proslavery armed forces. At one point, he made a raid into Missouri and led out a band of slaves to Canada. All of these activities whetted Brown's appetite to free slaves on a large scale.

The Raid on Harpers Ferry

John Brown began his long-anticipated uprising against slavery in October 1859. From his rented farmhouse in Maryland, he and his followers (including thirteen white and five black men) crossed over the Potomac River into Virginia. Brown's plan and belief was that he and his men would hold Harpers Ferry, including the bridges over the Potomac and Shenandoah Rivers that gave access to the town, for two days while scores of slaves left their masters and joined Brown's troops. The swelled ranks would then continue across the countryside, freeing slaves as they went.

Events did not culminate as Brown had hoped. He entered the town on October 16 and seized control of the federal armory there. His men worked to cut off access to the town and seized hostages. They set up their headquarters in the fire engine house of the armory complex. Then began Brown's downfall. He was expecting droves of slaves to flock to his side, but they never did. He was also

321

Nebraska Act, the founding of the Republican Party, the Dred Scott decision, the deaths of John C. Calhoun and Daniel Webster, and John Brown's raid and hanging. Have the students read their reports aloud, and then have the class discuss the different reporting styles.

Books on John Brown or Bloody Kansas

Display pictures and read excerpts from a library book on John Brown or Bloody Kansas. To help the students understand the fear and agitation created by this terrorism,

compare those events to modern incidents of bombings, terrorism, and school shootings in America.

Was John Brown Crazy?

John Brown is one of those complex figures from history that is either ridiculed as a lunatic or revered as a saint. His violence makes it easy to understand why some would call him crazy, but ask the students to explain why others followed him. Help the students to understand that it is all right to be passionate about a just cause, but uncontrolled passion about one issue can twist

a man's thinking. Some of John Brown's writings sound convincing, but they fail to recognize God's sovereignty. "Vengeance is mine," says the Lord (Rom. 12:19). Discuss some moral issues today that lead to twisted thinking. For example, some right-to-life groups condemn programs to reduce welfare as immoral because they might encourage women to seek more abortions.

underestimating the ability of the Virginians to stop him. Realizing that there was not an immediate response from the local slave population, Brown could have attempted to escape. Instead, he insisted on remaining where he was, giving time for local militia to cut off all escape routes. Federal troops were on the scene by the evening of October 17. They stormed the engine house the next morning, killing some of the insurgents and taking the rest into custody. Several men were executed in Charlestown, Virginia, as Brown himself was on December 2.

SECTION 4

Objectives
Students should be able to
1. Describe the position and the men involved in the 1860 election.
2. Name the winner of the 1860 election.
3. Describe the formation of the Confederacy.

Southern Democrats
The Southern Democrats called their branch of the party the National Democratic Party.

---

sons and two slaves he had freed. His plans were to raid a federal arsenal, or storage place for weapons, at Harpers Ferry, Virginia. On October 16, 1859, Brown and his twenty-one-man army rode into Harpers Ferry. They caught the watchman at the arsenal by surprise and took prominent local slave owners as hostages. Brown thought this action would stir slaves into rebellion. He hoped that thousands of slaves would revolt and rally to him; no such revolt occurred.

Brown allowed word of his takeover at Harpers Ferry to leak out. Soon local militia had blocked all the escape routes from the town. Colonel **Robert E. Lee** and J.E.B. Stuart arrived with federal troops the following day.

Brown refused to surrender. In the military action that followed, Brown was injured and two of his sons were killed. Only ten days after his capture, Brown faced trial. Before and during the trial he won many admirers. The Virginia jury, however, convicted him of murder, and he was hanged. Southern whites now feared a slave revolt more than ever. Although the revolt Brown hoped for never came, his actions did have a profound and far-reaching effect. Brown's trial and death made him a martyr for the antislavery cause. Soon Yankee soldiers marched off to war singing "John Brown's body lies a-mouldering in the grave, . . . His soul goes marching on."

SECTION REVIEW

1. What famous novel prompted a wave of sympathy for the abolitionist cause? Who wrote the novel?
2. The clash over slavery in Kansas led to what nickname for that territory?
3. What issue united the groups that formed the Republican Party?

---

4. Where did John Brown direct his attack to end slavery?

 What was the significance of the Dred Scott decision?

The Election of 1860 and Secession
The Election of 1860 was to have great consequence on the nation. The turmoil was displayed in the disruption of traditional ties in the political parties. The new regional bonds that formed were to remain for decades to come.

A Republican Victory
The South was clearly worried about the election of 1860. Southern extremists, called **fire-eaters,** threatened **secession,** to leave the Union, if the Republicans won. The views of the Republicans on almost all issues were in opposition to the interests of the South. Not only views on slavery but also positions on states' rights and the tariff were placing the Republicans at odds with most Southerners.

The best chance for defeating the Republicans lay in the Democrats' picking a moderate candidate acceptable to both the South and the North. Illinois Senator Stephen Douglas was such a moderate. But in 1860 fire-eaters, who had undue influence, thought him their enemy. Rather than uniting to stand behind Douglas, the southern Democrats left the nominating convention. Their split foreshadowed the Civil War. The divided party led to a divided nation. The Democrats no longer accepted "compromise" presidents like Pierce or Buchanan. While the northern Democrats nominated Douglas, the Southerners chose **John C. Breckenridge** of Kentucky. Their **platform** (statement of what they stood for politically), based on the Dred Scott decision, called for Congress to enact a federal slave code to protect slavery in all the territories.

Section Review Answers
1. *Uncle Tom's Cabin;* Harriet Beecher Stowe (p. 319)
2. Bleeding Kansas (p. 319)
3. opposition to slavery or to its spread (pp. 319-20)
4. Harpers Ferry, Virginia (pp. 321-22)

 It said that slaves were property, not citizens. With that decision it rejected the Missouri Compromise, saying it would deprive citizens north of 36° 30' of their property, and made future compromise nearly impossible. (pp. 320-21)

SECTION 4
Materials
• Historical atlas (U.S.)

A campaign banner from the election of 1860.

With the Democrats divided, the Republicans had real hopes for victory. In an effort to keep the Union intact, they chose a moderate rather than an abolitionist or Free Soiler. Their choice was an Illinois lawyer, **Abraham Lincoln.**

In the Illinois senate election in 1858, Lincoln had challenged Stephen Douglas, the Democratic candidate, to a series of seven debates. Although Douglas won the election, the debates gave Lincoln and his views public exposure. Although Lincoln was not an abolitionist and was not opposed to slavery where it already existed, he was against the spread of slavery to new territories. This stand, however, was not acceptable to the southern fire-eaters.

The Whigs from the border states of Delaware, Maryland, Virginia, and Kentucky were not eager to leave the Union. They decided to pick an alternate candidate, **John Bell** of Tennessee, who stood for staying in the Union. Their party was called the Constitutional Union Party. They were trying to buy time, hoping that the fire-eaters would see there was no real future in their position.

Southerners believed that a Lincoln victory would put southern states at a disadvantage in Washington and might spark more raids like John Brown's. They said that if Lincoln were elected, they would leave the Union and form their own nation. President Buchanan did nothing to discourage them.

Lincoln carried the northern and western states, enabling him to win more popular votes than any other candidate. Douglas came in second in popular votes, followed by Breckenridge and Bell. Lincoln's victory, however, was far from overwhelming. Douglas and Bell's vote total exceeded that of Lincoln's, and combined with the Breckenridge vote, these candidates won over sixty percent of the vote. In addition, Lincoln had failed to carry a single southern state or border state. The circumstances of the election put Lincoln at a disadvantage. No one knew what side the border states would take in the secession controversy. If Lincoln had been able to take office right away, however, he might have been able to save the Union.

The Confederacy Takes Shape

Fearing that its rights as a state could not be maintained, South Carolina voted to leave the Union on December 20. The nation waited for President Buchanan to react. Although he believed secession was illegal, he was unwilling

Seceding States

South Carolina and the other seceding states recognized that Lincoln's victory would signal a bolder attack by Northerners on the South and its "domestic concerns." Lincoln had declared that the Union must be preserved and that it could not "endure permanently half slave and half free. . . . It will become all one thing or all the other." Logically, the South recognized that the nation would not become "all slave," and therefore its livelihood was in peril. Southerners believed that the Declaration of Independence and the Constitution had left them with the option of seceding, and the North would have to prove otherwise by force. After the war Jefferson Davis summarized the South's position by saying, "No alternative remained except to seek the security out of the Union which they had vainly tried to obtain within it. The hope of our people may be stated in a sentence. It was to escape from injury and strife in the Union, to find prosperity and peace out of it."

323

"Folly" of Party Splits?

On rare occasions in U.S. history, parties have split and fielded separate presidential candidates. Can the students remember an example of this? *(In 1824 most candidates were elected by state legislatures [pp. 225-26]; in 1836 the Whigs selected several candidates and lost to the Democratic-Republicans [p. 246].)* Students will be seeing other examples of party splits and their consequences.

In each case of a party split, the opposing party has won. So is it worth it for parties to split? The only value of parties is to represent common views, and when people's views diverge too much, then there is no point in their staying in one party. In the end, parties must either appease the divergent view or run the risk of losing power and allowing a third party to take preeminence.

The Constitution of the Confederacy

When representatives of the seceding states met at Montgomery, Alabama, they immediately wrote a provisional constitution that would set up a temporary government. A smaller committee then met to write a permanent constitution. The constitution, with a few minor adjustments, was passed and adopted by the Montgomery Convention on March 11, 1861. The delegates signed it on March 16, and it then had to be presented to the states for ratification.

The constitution for the Confederacy was very close to the United States Constitution. Most of the differences can be traced to Southerners' dissatisfaction with certain sections of the original document. Many reflect the South's concern for states' rights. Following are some examples of ways in which the Confederate Constitution was different from that of the United States.

The president of the Confederacy would serve for six years but be limited to one term. The constitution provided for a national Supreme Court, but one was never established, partially because the Confederate Congress could never agree on whether a Supreme Court should be able to overrule the decisions of state supreme courts.

Four critical provisions protected slavery in the new nation. First, slaveholders had the right to take their slaves unmolested into any other state (see Dred Scott case, where a slave sued for freedom). Second, the fugitive slave provision was made more extensive. Third, the Confederate government was granted the right to acquire territory, and slavery was automatically protected in any new territory. Fourth, any new states admitted to the Confederacy must be approved by two-thirds of the House of Representatives and the Senate (with the Senate voting by states). The last provision was the compromise that resulted from a heated debate over the admission

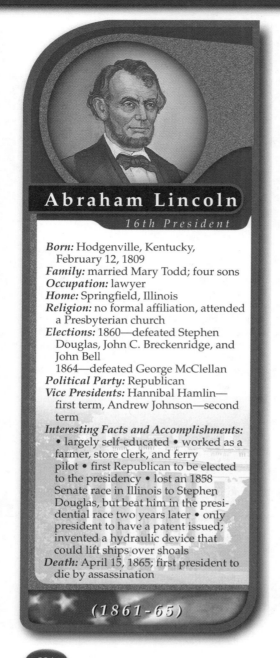

Abraham Lincoln
16th President

Born: Hodgenville, Kentucky, February 12, 1809
Family: married Mary Todd; four sons
Occupation: lawyer
Home: Springfield, Illinois
Religion: no formal affiliation, attended a Presbyterian church
Elections: 1860—defeated Stephen Douglas, John C. Breckenridge, and John Bell
1864—defeated George McClellan
Political Party: Republican
Vice Presidents: Hannibal Hamlin—first term, Andrew Johnson—second term
Interesting Facts and Accomplishments:
• largely self-educated • worked as a farmer, store clerk, and ferry pilot • first Republican to be elected to the presidency • lost an 1858 Senate race in Illinois to Stephen Douglas, but beat him in the presidential race two years later • only president to have a patent issued; invented a hydraulic device that could lift ships over shoals
Death: April 15, 1865; first president to die by assassination

(1861-65)

to use his influence or force to halt it. Instead he left the problem for Lincoln to face.

But before Lincoln could take office, other southern states called conventions.

Mississippi, Florida, Alabama, Georgia, Louisiana, and Texas all followed South Carolina's example. South Carolina summoned the other slaveholding states to a convention held in Montgomery, Alabama, on February 1, 1861.

Delegates from these seven states formed the **Confederate States of America.** They wrote their own constitution. It was like the American Constitution, except that it recognized the "sovereign and independent character" of the states and guaranteed states' rights. It also promised that no law against slavery could ever be passed, allowed cabinet members to take part in legislative debates, and gave the president a single six-year term.

Next, the Confederacy had to choose its leaders. Fire-eaters chose moderates, hoping to win the support of Southerners who were still unsure about splitting from the Union. **Jefferson Davis** from Mississippi became president. Alexander Stephens, a Georgian who had firmly opposed secession, took the vice-presidency.

The Confederacy sent out commissioners seeking to increase the size of the Confederacy. But the border and upper southern states took a "wait-and-see" position.

SECTION REVIEW

1. Name the four presidential candidates in 1860 and their parties.
2. What was Lincoln's attitude toward slavery?
3. Which state was the first to leave the Union?
4. Who became president of the Confederacy?

 What generally was the political position of the men chosen for leadership in the Confederacy? Why were they chosen?

 ### Identify the Border States

The allegiance of the border states was arguably the most decisive issue in the course of the Civil War. Refer the students to the map of border states on page 327. Explain how these states differed from the other states economically and politically. Point out the results of the pivotal 1860 election: Breckinridge won Maryland; Douglas won New Jersey and Missouri; and Bell won Kentucky, Virginia, and Tennessee. (If you have a U.S. historical atlas, show the election results on a political map.) Lincoln had to act wisely

because volatile public opinion could swing rapidly in the border states, which did not vote for him.

Look closely at the geography of the South on the relief map on page 333, and look at the relative location of states on the map on page 327. Ask the students to identify the geographic importance of each border state in the event of a war. *(Kentucky provided access to the Ohio River—a crucial trade route; Missouri bordered Illinois and the upper Missouri-Mississippi River; and Maryland bordered the federal capital.)* It can be argued that Lincoln ensured

Northern victory by successfully maneuvering to keep the border states in the Union.

Section Review Answers

1. Stephen Douglas—Democratic (Northern), John C. Breckinridge—Democratic (Southern), Abraham Lincoln—Republican, John Bell—Constitutional Union (pp. 322-23)

2. He did not oppose it where it was, but he was against its spread. (p. 323)

of new states. Some feared that free states would want to join the Confederacy, and the free state/slave state controversy that disrupted the Union would be renewed. The answer to this dilemma was making a rigorous approval process in Congress a prerequisite for admission into the Confederacy.

Finally, the process for amending the constitution was simpler in the Confederacy. Only three states had to request a change in order for a national convention to be called. (Two-thirds of state legislatures must suggest an amendment in the U.S. Constitution.) And just two-thirds of state legislatures or conventions had to ratify the amendment (as opposed to three-fourths with the U.S. Constitution).

SECTION 5

Objectives
Students should be able to
1. Describe the situation that led to the firing on Fort Sumter.
2. Explain the way the border states were kept in the Union.
3. List the North's advantages as it entered the war.
4. List the South's advantages as it entered the war.

Fort Sumter, Charleston Harbor, April 1865; Inset: Fort Sumter today

Fort Sumter and War

The South, realizing that the Union had been formed as a voluntary organization of the states, believed that it could withdraw its membership in the Union by secession to form the Confederacy. Lincoln believed that secession was not possible—the Union was permanent, and no state could pull out once it had joined. The Civil War resulted to determine whether the South's view or President Lincoln's view of the Union would prevail.

On March 4, 1861, Abraham Lincoln took office. In his inaugural address he appealed to the people, "In your hands, my dissatisfied fellow-countrymen, and not in mine, is the momentous issue of civil war." Lincoln held that the Union was still whole; it was, he held, indivisible and indissoluble (not able to be dissolved or split up). He hoped to reconcile the sections, but he would fight, if he had to, to preserve the Constitution and the Union. He stated that he would use the power of govern-

ment "to hold, occupy, and possess the property and places belonging to the government."

By property Lincoln meant the two federal forts in the South where the Stars and Stripes still flew: Fort Pickens at Pensacola, Florida, and Fort Sumter in South Carolina's Charleston harbor. To retain control of these forts, however, it would be necessary to send them supplies.

Firing on Fort Sumter

In January South Carolina had already shown it was unlikely to allow the government to land supplies at the fort. When a merchant ship, *The Star of the West,* approached **Fort Sumter** with supplies and troops, it was fired on and was turned away.

Lincoln reasoned that if he let the Confederates have Fort Sumter, he would have to invade the South to preserve the Union, and an invasion would probably drive the border states into the Confederate fold. The South might react to the Union's keeping its hold on

325

Moderates were chosen to lead the Confederacy; moderate leaders tend to draw greater support since they do not hold strongly to controversial opinions. The Confederacy chose moderate leaders to increase its support among Southerners. (p. 324)

SECTION 5

Materials
- Bibles
- *Scenes from American Church History* (BJUP)
- Student Activity: Case #3—The Search for King Cotton from Chapter 16 of the *Student Activities* manual

Political Strategy—You Are There

You have an opportunity to test the students' reasoning skills by asking them to rethink the issues that Abraham Lincoln faced during the crisis that precipitated the Civil War. None of his decisions were easy, and his choices were not obvious.

Many American presidents have faced such crises at momentous times in the nation's history (e.g., the Berlin airlift, the Cuban missile crisis, and recent crises in the Balkans). Presidents must carefully weigh

Washington Peace Conference

The Washington Peace Conference is not often mentioned, but it does illustrate the truth that not all of the states in the South were initially eager to secede from the Union. While the states of the Deep South were planning a convention to discuss secession in Montgomery, Alabama (see previous section), the Virginia legislature called for a conference in Washington, D.C. to discuss peace. Both groups convened on February 4, 1861. Twenty-one of thirty-four states of the Union attended the Washington Peace Conference. The former president John Tyler chaired the conference, and a series of proposals was drawn up for presentation to Congress. Unfortunately, the secessionists in Montgomery and the Republicans in the United States Congress were so far apart by February 27, when Congress received the proposals, that the prospects of a peaceful settlement were slim.

Kentucky

Kentucky's decision to remain in the Union was aided by the fact that Lincoln did not send troops into the state until after the Confederacy had "violated Kentucky's neutrality" by sending in troops first.

Fort Sumter in one of two ways: either by rejoining the Union or by shelling the fort. If the Confederates shelled Sumter, they would be the ones who started the war. Then if Lincoln had to call for federal troops to quell the rebelling Confederates, his action could be defended.

Lincoln sent a note to F. W. Pickens, the governor of South Carolina, telling him that a supply ship but no troops would be coming to Sumter. (Lincoln chose to write Pickens, the lawful governor of the state, rather than Jefferson Davis. He held that writing Davis meant recognizing the Confederacy.) Pickens contacted Davis, who gave orders to prevent all efforts to resupply Fort Sumter. When the federal supply ship came to Charleston harbor on April 12, 1861, the batteries (rows of guns) in Charleston harbor fired on the fort. After enduring a forty-hour Confederate bombardment, the Union troops surrendered the fort.

Across the Confederacy church bells rang and people celebrated. A pastor in Charleston confidently told his flock, "Providence is fast uniting the whole South in a common brotherhood of sympathy and action, and our first essay in arms has been crowned with perfect success."

The Call for Troops

Lincoln, meanwhile, sent out a call for 75,000 troops. Any reluctant border or southern states now had to take sides. Davis was especially eager to have Virginia join the Confederacy because it was the South's richest and most populous state. Virginia joined, as did Arkansas and Tennessee, although neither was especially eager to do so. Since North Carolina was now encircled by Confederate states, it was forced to join the Confederacy.

The people in fifty counties of western Virginia had long resented the tidewater area's greater influence in their state. This was their chance to strike back. They boldly set up their own state government and sought statehood. Since Virginia had left the Union, they held that they hardly needed her permission to become a state. In 1863 West Virginia came into the Union.

Lincoln took action to keep the four border slave states (Kentucky, Missouri, Delaware, and Maryland) in the Union. People in these states were divided in their loyalties. Some favored secession while others wanted to stay in the Union.

If Kentucky had become Confederate (and it did have a Confederate governor for a time), the North's access to the Ohio River would have been threatened. Its population, lukewarm to the Confederacy, was kept in the Union through persuasion and force. In Missouri, Union troops moved to key areas, preventing secession there. Missourians against the Union were carefully isolated and ignored, except when ruffian bands carried on warfare within the state.

There was little concern about Delaware, whose culture and location aligned her with other Middle Atlantic States more than with the South. But Maryland presented a real problem. If it joined the Confederate camp, Washington, D.C., could end up there too. Lincoln sent federal troops to Maryland and then closed bridges to keep others out. Potential Confederate leaders were held against their will. Lincoln justified his actions, the use of martial or military law, since a grave emergency existed. Maryland had little choice but to stay in the Union.

Northern Advantages

Looking at the resources available to the North and the South, it's obvious that the North had a great advantage. The North had both the means and the manpower to industrialize. This tremendous industrial capacity was the Union's most significant advantage, even more so as the war wore on.

complex options and their potential consequences. Mistakes can be catastrophic. Good citizens must support their government with wisdom and logic as they face these crises.

1. After his election and the secession of the seven lower states but before he was sworn into office, what did Lincoln do? What other options did he have, and why did he not choose them? *(He said nothing; he could have voiced his opinion and tried to work closely with Buchanan and Congress, but he did not want to suffer political fallout from any mistakes or catastrophes that might arise.)*

2. After taking office and recognizing Confederate intentions to take Sumter, what did the president do? What other options did he have, and why did he not choose them? *(He sent supplies but not troops and wrote the governor; he could have been belligerent and protected the fort with more troops and armed ships, but he wanted to put the first seven Confederate states in a bad light among all the other states.)*

3. The states of the upper South did not want to leave the Union even after the firing on Fort Sumter, but the lower states intended to fight to keep out of the Union. What did the president do? What other options did he have, and why did he not choose them? *(The president called for troops to put down the rebellion; as a direct result of this momentous*

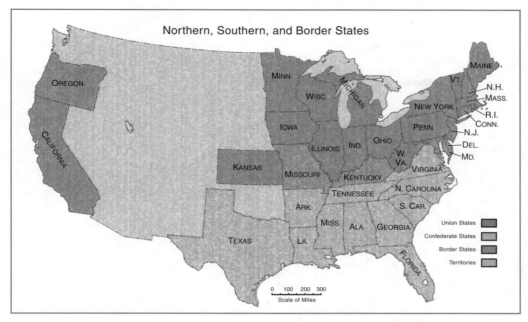

Northern, Southern, and Border States

OREGON — CALIFORNIA — MINN. — WISC. — MICHIGAN — IOWA — ILLINOIS — IND. — OHIO — W. VA. — KANSAS — MISSOURI — KENTUCKY — TENNESSEE — ARK. — MISS. — ALA. — GEORGIA — TEXAS — LA. — FLORIDA — N. CAROLINA — S. CAR. — VIRGINIA — MD. — DEL. — N.J. — CONN. — R.I. — PENN. — NEW YORK — MASS. — N.H. — VT. — MAINE

Union States
Confederate States
Border States
Territories

0   100   200   300
Scale of Miles

The South produced only ten percent of the nation's manufactured goods and had only 110,000 industrial workers. The North, meanwhile, had 120,000 factories. Consequently, the South had to buy overseas what it could not produce at home. Only at the outset of the war would she have the capital and the freedom to do this. The lack of southern sea power to maintain its trade routes would soon greatly hinder its war effort. In addition, the North was adding 300,000 immigrants a year to its population, almost as many as the total number of northern troops killed in the entire war.

Why the South Stood a Chance

With so many disadvantages, why did the South believe it could win? First, the southern goal was a simple one: to set up and to maintain a separate independent nation, the Confederate States of America. To do this, the South did not need to conquer the North; it had only to defend its own territory. Also, the

South was immense. The North would need long supply lines to attack and hold so vast an area.

Second, the average Southerner was more deeply involved in the war than was the average Northerner. The Southerner was fighting for his home and way of life. The Northerner, perhaps an immigrant, was supposedly "fighting for the Union." The North would lose if its people lost the desire to stay on the offensive. It could win only when it destroyed the Confederate desire and ability to fight.

Third, the Confederacy believed it would get foreign help. Since it was the source of much of Britain's cotton, the Confederacy believed that the British would be at least sympathetic, if not supportive.

Fourth, the South had an almost endless coastline. Even though the Confederacy had no real navy at the start, the North would need thousands of ships to block the entire coast from supply ships.

327

---

decision, political opinion in the upper South swung completely on the side of secession. Lincoln could have let the lower states go and made new overtures of peace, hoping that the weak nation would die on the vine, but he had made his position clear that no state could legally leave the Union, so he acted aggressively even though it made reconciliation less likely.)

4. The border states still did not want to leave the Union, but they refused

to fight against the South. What did the president do? What other options did he have, and why did he not choose them? *(The president took each state case by case, waiting until the last minute to send troops and letting the South act as the aggressor. He could have taken all the border states immediately by force, but he feared that they would swing to the South just as the states of the Upper South had done.)*

Comparisons to Israel's Civil War

The following could be used as an enrichment exercise. Have the students read the account of Israel's first civil war when David became king and was opposed by Saul's son (II Sam. 2:1–5:5). Note the jealousies between the twelve independent tribes (or "states"), the division of the nation between the north and the south, the length of the revolt (David's 7½ years in Hebron, 2:11), and David's efforts to reunite the people. Students need to understand that the division between the north

General Robert E. Lee

Robert E. Lee, the son of Lighthorse Harry Lee, a hero in the War for Independence, went to West Point. There Lee's behavior and academic excellence soon placed him at the top of his class. During the Mexican War Lee distinguished himself for bravery and leadership. After the Mexican War, Lee continued in the service, and while home in Virginia on leave, the army called on him to lead the small force that recaptured Harpers Ferry from John Brown and his group of fanatics.

When the Civil War broke out, Lee had a choice to make. His stand on slavery was well documented: "Slavery as an institution is a moral and political evil in any country." Yet he was a loyal Virginian. His dilemma was increased when he was offered the position of commander-in-chief of the Union army. Torn between loyalties, Lee decided for Virginia and was appointed commander of the Army of Northern Virginia. His methods were unconventional but brilliant. Constantly outnumbered, he managed time and again to defeat the northern armies. Only the tenacity of U. S. Grant and the Union's numerical supremacy in men and equipment eventually defeated Lee.

After the war Lee accepted the presidency of Washington College—now Washington and Lee. His presidency was an enormous success as the college grew and prospered. He was buried at a site on the university campus. The South greatly loved and honored him; the North also highly esteemed him. He is, perhaps, history's most admired losing general.

In 1960 as Dwight D. Eisenhower's second term neared its end, the president received a critical letter from a citizen. The citizen was upset that a picture of Robert E. Lee, a Confederate, was included among the Eisenhower mementos in the White House. Eisenhower had gained an interest in Lee as a fellow graduate of West Point. This was Eisenhower's reply to the citizen.

The White House
Washington, DC
August 18, 1960

Dear Dr. Scott:

General Robert E. Lee was, in my estimation, one of the supremely gifted men produced by our nation. He believed unswervingly in the constitutional validity of his cause, which until 1865 was still an arguable question in America; he was a poised and inspiring leader, true to the high trust reposed in him by millions of his fellow citizens. . . .

From deep conviction, I simply say this: A nation of men of Lee's calibre would be unconquerable in spirit and soul. Indeed, to the degree that present-day American youth will strive to emulate his painstaking efforts to help heal the nation's wounds once the bitter struggle was over, we, in our time of danger in a divided world, will be strengthened and our love of freedom sustained.

Such are the reasons I proudly display the picture of the great American on my office wall.

Dwight D. Eisenhower

328

---

and the south continued, and the ten northern tribes "seceded" after Solomon's death, and God commanded the new king to let them go (I Kings 12:24).

Could We Fight a Civil War Today?

Ask the students whether any issue, such as abortion, could lead to a civil war in America today. Another point of interest is whether Americans would have the strength of character to endure the horrors and hardships of war to defend a principle. With the decline in morals, this is an open question. Would Americans have the strength of character to fight another world war in defense of freedom?

Counting the Cost

Every wise nation counts the cost before starting a war (Luke 14:31-32). The text lists five reasons that the South went to war. Can the students think of five reasons that it was wise for the North to go to war? What are five reasons against going to war that each side should have considered?

Divide the students into two groups—North and South—and ask them to look at the maps of the states and evaluate their best strategy for victory. Ask them to condense their ideas into three points. When they are finished, point them to the actual strategies that the two sides adopted (listed on page 339 in Chapter 17).

Lee, the Christian

More information about Robert E. Lee's Christianity is available in "Robert E. Lee: Christian, Soldier, Gentleman" by Craig Jennings *(Scenes from American Church History)*.

Fifth, the Confederacy believed its soldiers were better. Confederates had little respect for Yankees as fighting men, and the South did have better commanders, at least in the beginning. Most of the Confederate officers were well trained; many were West Point graduates. And no one argued about Robert E. Lee's abilities. Lee had been Lincoln's first choice to be commander-in-chief of the Union armies. But because he believed that his duty was to his native state of Virginia, Lee declined. President Lincoln, on the other hand, had to go through seven different commanders before finding the one who could win the war, Ulysses S. Grant.

SECTION REVIEW

1. What state in particular did Jefferson Davis want to join the Confederacy?

2. What were the four key border states?

3. What was the Union's most significant advantage?

4. What factors gave the South a fighting chance despite the North's advantages?

 Why did Lincoln feel he must hold on to Fort Sumter?

SUMMARY

Political issues of the early 1800s came to a boil in the 1850s. The North's and South's differing views on states' rights, the tariff, slavery, and other topics led to great controversy. When Abraham Lincoln won the 1860 election for the Republicans, the South lost hope for a continued federal government tolerant of its views. The South then broke its ties with the Union by seceding. Whether the South could secede from the Union was the issue that would pull the nation into the Civil War. With the firing on Fort Sumter in April of 1861, the war had begun.

329

Section Review Answers

1. Virginia (p. 326)

2. Kentucky, Missouri, Delaware, and Maryland (p. 326)

3. its tremendous industrial capacity (p. 326)

4. had only to defend itself, deep personal concern, expected foreign help, assumed its long coast would allow the delivery of supplies, good military leadership (pp. 327, 329)

 If he gave up the fort, he would have to invade the South to preserve the Union, giving the appearance of aggression. Holding on to the fort might convince the South to reenter the Union. If the South attacked, Lincoln could then respond in self-defense. (pp. 325-26)

Chapter Review Idea

History Skills: Facts and Speculation

The History Skills activity at the end of the chapter tests students' comprehension of the key facts given in the chapter. The activity would make a good chapter review.

Chapter Review

People, Places, and Things to Remember

middle passage	*Uncle Tom's Cabin*	secession
emancipation	Kansas-Nebraska Act	John C. Breckenridge
abolitionism	Republican Party	platform
compensated emancipation	James Buchanan	Abraham Lincoln
William Lloyd Garrison	Dred Scott	John Bell
Underground Railroad	Dred Scott decision	Confederate States of
Frederick Douglass	John Brown	America
Harriet Tubman	Robert E. Lee	Jefferson Davis
Harriet Beecher Stowe	fire-eaters	Fort Sumter

Review Questions

Choose the correct name or term for each blank in the paragraph below. Not all will be used.

Middle Passage	John Brown
emancipation	Frederick Douglass
abolitionists	William Lloyd Garrison
compensated emancipation	Dred Scott
Underground Railroad	Harriet Beecher Stowe
Uncle Tom's Cabin	Harriet Tubman

As the problem of slavery troubled America, (1) began to work to put an end to slavery. They wanted (2) for the slaves, although some supported the idea of (3), reimbursing the slaveholders for their loss. (4) was a vocal supporter of abolitionism in Boston where he published a paper called the *Liberator*. Other abolitionists helped runaway slaves follow the (5) to freedom in the North or in Canada. (6) was an escaped slave who helped many other slaves follow that route. Another influence against slavery was the book (7), written by (8). (9), a black abolitionist, also spoke out against slavery in speeches and publications. The most daring antislavery action was probably that taken by (10), who tried to spark a slave rebellion by capturing a federal arsenal.

Make two columns on your paper: the United States of America and the Confederate States of America. Then answer these questions for each.

11. Who became its president in 1861?

12. Who was its leading general?

13. What advantages did it have as the war began?

14. What disadvantages did it have as the war began?

Questions for Discussion

15. Why was slavery a difficult problem for Americans to deal with?

16. What do you suppose would have happened if southern Democrats had supported Stephen Douglas in the 1860 election? Why?

330

Chapter Review Answers

1. abolitionists (p. 310)

2. emancipation (p. 310)

3. compensated emancipation (p. 310)

4. William Lloyd Garrison (p. 310)

5. Underground Railroad (p. 311)

6. Harriet Tubman (p. 312)

7. *Uncle Tom's Cabin* (p. 312)

8. Harriet Beecher Stowe (p. 312)

9. Frederick Douglass (p. 312)

10. John Brown (pp. 315-16)

11. Abraham Lincoln (USA); Jefferson Davis (CSA) (pp. 324-25)

12. Ulysses S. Grant (USA); Robert E. Lee (CSA) (p. 329)

13. more industry, people, railroads, and money and a larger navy (USA); defensive position, deep personal concern, expectation of foreign help, extensive coast, good military leadership (CSA) (pp. 326-29)

14. offensive position, lack of motivation, ineffective military leaders (USA); very few industries or factories, lack of sea power, fewer people (CSA) (pp. 326-27, 29)

15. Answers will vary.

16. Answers will vary. Douglas would probably have won and would likely have sought a compromise.

History Skills

Facts and Speculation

History books give many facts (what actually occurred). They also offer speculations (guesses about what might have happened under different circumstances). Read each statement below. Decide whether it is a fact or a speculation.

1. Slavery would have died out in the South if the cotton gin had never been invented.
2. Southern professor Thomas R. Dew argued that slavery was "a positive good" compared to other labor systems.
3. By 1860 one out of every three Southerners was a slave.
4. The United States was the last major western nation to ban foreign slave trade.
5. Gradual emancipation would have been a workable solution to the slavery issue.
6. The great compromisers Clay, Calhoun, and Webster would have been able to prevent the Civil War had they lived.
7. After the Dred Scott decision, no peaceful solutions to the slavery issue were possible.
8. John Brown made a mistake when he expected thousands of slaves to rally to him at Harper's Ferry.
9. During the presidential election of 1860, Southern Democrats voted for John C. Breckenridge.
10. If Lincoln had been able to take office right away in 1860, he would have been able to avoid a civil war.
11. Lincoln refused to write to Jefferson Davis because he did not want to recognize him as the president of the Confederacy.
12. If the North had fired the first shots of the Civil War, the border states would have joined the Confederacy.
13. North Carolina was forced to join the Confederacy because it was surrounded by Confederate states.
14. West Virginia held that it did not need Virginia's permission to become a state because Virginia had left the Union.
15. Robert E. Lee became a commander in the Confederate army even though he considered slavery an evil institution.

 331

History Skills

1. speculation
2. fact
3. fact
4. fact
5. speculation
6. speculation
7. speculation
8. fact
9. fact
10. speculation
11. fact
12. speculation
13. fact
14. fact
15. fact

Location

The South includes Alabama, Arkansas, Florida, Georgia, Kentucky, Louisiana, Mississippi, North Carolina, Oklahoma, South Carolina, Tennessee, Texas, Virginia, and West Virginia. With the exception of Kentucky, Virginia, and West Virginia, the entire region lies below the 34th parallel (latitude). All but five states border either the Gulf of Mexico or the Atlantic Ocean. The Rio Grande separates the region from Mexico in the West, while the remaining western border is shared with the state of New Mexico.

Climate

A humid subtropical climate dominates the region. Hot, humid summers end in mild winters, except at the southern tip of Florida, where the tropical climate keeps the weather warm all year round. Sufficient rainfall and warm temperatures give the region an extended growing season. In the late summers, hurricanes that start over the Atlantic Ocean or Gulf of Mexico sometimes blow over the region, causing extensive damage.

Topography

The Atlantic and Gulf Coastal Plains run along the entire coastline and join the Interior Plain along the Mississippi River valley. West of the Atlantic Coastal Plain, the Piedmont rises to meet some of the highest mountains of the Appalachian Range. In northwestern Arkansas, Oklahoma, and the western two-thirds of Texas the elevation rises. It increases first in Arkansas, where the Arkansas River splits the Ozark Mountains and the Ouachita Mountains, and again farther west into the Great Plains and Rocky Mountains.

Natural Resources

Variety is the word that best describes the South. With wide, fertile plains and a mild climate, the region has had great success in large agricultural efforts. The type of agriculture varies greatly. Kentucky, North Carolina, and Virginia are the leading states in the tobacco industry. South Carolina, Georgia, and Alabama turned to the production of peanuts, soybeans, and peaches (as well as other fruits) after cotton and rice had leached many nutrients from the soil. Once known for its swamps, Florida has become a tropical oasis complete with year-round vegetable farms and citrus groves. Across Mississippi, Louisiana, Arkansas, Oklahoma, and much of Texas, small farmers send their cotton, soybean, and vegetable harvests to factories that process and then send the crops to the busy ports along the Mississippi River. Along the Gulf of Mexico, oil and natural gas fields have boosted the economies of Texas and Louisiana. Where the terrain changes to dry plateaus in Texas, cattle roam on rangelands that remind visitors of the Wild West and a time past.

Geography and Culture

Religion is an important part of Southern culture. Many black churches became meeting places in the 1960s for blacks who fought for civil rights. The region has made great strides in equal rights issues over the past several decades, but old wounds are sometimes hard to heal. Prejudiced beliefs sometimes take generations to pass away. The entire South generally shares a conservative political outlook. Conservative views probably go back to the pre–Civil War years with the rejection of central government control and intervention in state matters. Such views also come from the small-town focus of the region. Family connections are important, and cousins, aunts, uncles, and grandparents may all live in the same community. The lack of large cities in much of the region makes Southerners less worried about some of the social issues confronted by the people of the Northeast.

Eloquence and education are marks of southern gentility. Elegant homes and gardens, refined accents, and polished etiquette go hand in hand with the "Y'all come back now" hospitality for which the region is best known.

332

 Student Activity: Case #3— The Search for King Cotton

The map adventures of Sir Vey continue with this humorous look at the geography of the South.

What Was It About?

Have your students read the page and answer the following questions.

- What gives this region an extended growing season? *(sufficient rainfall and warm temperatures)*

- What severe weather pattern sometimes causes great damage in the South? *(hurricanes)*

- What word best describes the region, especially its agricultural production? *(variety)*

- What factor has played an important part in the South's culture? *(religion)*

- Why is the South less interested in some of the social issues that the Northeast focuses on? *(because it has been a region of small towns and few big cities)*

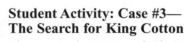

Using a Map

Use this map to find the following information.

- the name of the state that borders Mexico *(Texas)*
- the city that is 90° W and 30° N *(New Orleans)*
- the city that is farthest south in the region *(Key West, Florida)*
- the three states whose eastern borders lie in the Appalachian Mountain system *(Tennessee, Kentucky, West Virginia)*

- the distance between Savannah, Georgia, and Dallas, Texas (estimate to the nearest hundred miles) *(900 miles)*

Essay Idea

Write the following sentence on the overhead.

The South would be a perfect place to live for someone who is interested in _____.

Have your students fill in the blank with a word that names an occupation or hobby (such as *hiking*). Then have them use the sentence as a topic sentence for a one-paragraph essay about the South. They may use information from the text or implications from the map to support their topic sentence.

The Civil War

Goals

Students should be able to
1. Define and use the basic terms from the chapter.
2. Review the chronology of events from the Civil War.
3. Identify major battles and leaders in the war.
4. **Analyze the reasons for and effects of the Civil War.**

Gettysburg

Gettysburg National Battlefield commemorates the bloodiest battle of the Civil War. Over forty-five thousand casualties (killed, missing, wounded, and captured) were claimed in three days of fighting.

Chapter Motivation

Ask the students what they know about the Civil War and which side they think was right. Remind them that on both sides there were godly people who believed they had God's blessing in the battle. As they read the chapter, the students should look for information that presents viewpoints that differ from theirs.

Materials

SECTION 1
- Activities A and C from Chapter 17 of the *Student Activities* manual
- A Civil War novel
- A book of Mathew Brady photos
- Board games or computer games based on the Civil War

SECTION 2
- Activity B from Chapter 17 of the *Student Activities* manual
- Special speaker: a Civil War historian
- Video: *Red Runs the River* (available from BJUP)

SECTION 3
- No materials

SECTION 4
- Plans for a field trip to a Civil War site or pictures of Civil War sites
- Civil War documentary video

A s war loomed ahead after the election of Lincoln in 1860, Senator John Crittenden of Kentucky led one last vain attempt to preserve the Union peacefully. Despite his passionate pleas and stirring speeches, Crittenden's compromise plan failed to win enough support to pass the Senate. The defeat became doubly bitter for Crittenden when his own family divided over the issue of secession. His son George became a major general in the Confederate army, while his son Thomas became a major general in the Union army. After George took his stand with the South, a newspaper editor who opposed Crittenden roundly criticized the senator for his son's action. The editor must have been embarrassed a short while later, however, when his own son went south to join the Confederacy.

All through the country families split over the war. Brother sometimes fought against brother and father against son in the four years of bloody conflict. In his plea for the Union, Lincoln echoed Jesus' words in Matthew 12:25—A "house divided against itself shall not stand." When families fought against each other, what hope could there be for the nation?

334

CHAPTER 17	Lesson Plan Chart		
Section Title	**Main Activity**	**Pages**	**Time Frame**
1. Gearing Up for War	Student Activity A: Civil War	334-39	1-2 days
2. Marching into Battle	The Chronology of the Civil War	340-42	1-2 days
3. Controlling the Waters	The Unglamorous Side of War	342-45	1-2 days
4. The War in the East	Documentaries on the Civil War	345-47	1 day
5. The War of Attrition and Destruction	The Emancipation Proclamation	348-52	1 day
6. Appomattox and Aftermath	Discuss Bitterness Between Regions	353-57	1-2 days
Total Suggested Days (including 1 day for review and testing)			7-11 days

SECTION 1

Materials

- Activities A and C from Chapter 17 of the *Student Activities* manual
- A Civil War novel
- A book of Mathew Brady photos
- Board games or computer games based on the Civil War

Gearing Up for War

The firing on Fort Sumter in April of 1861 ignited the flame of civil war between North and South. Billy Yank and Johnny Reb were soon to struggle through the triumphs and tragedies of four years of bitter conflict. Not only the soldiers but also many civilian Americans came to know the hardships and the death and destruction that were part of this war to save the Union.

Turning Men into Soldiers

Thousands of young recruits, responding to the patriotic fervor, joined the armies. Union recruits poured into Washington, D.C., or newly built camps in the West. At the same time southern patriots were gathering in Confederate camps.

Life in the camps, however, was far from exciting. A soldier spent sixty-five percent of his time in camp, thirty percent marching or bivouacking (BIV wak ing; camping temporarily in the open air), and only five percent of his time fighting. Some soldiers assigned to forts never fired a shot.

At the beginning of the war, both sides relied totally on volunteers. But soon volunteers became too scarce to supply the needed troops, and thus both Lincoln and Davis resorted to drafting men to fill their armies.

Raising Northern Forces—President Lincoln's Fourth of July message in 1861 called for 500,000 volunteers to enlist for three years. The next year Congress called "all able-bodied male citizens between the ages of eighteen and forty-five" into state militias. At this point drafting soldiers was a state function. Most of the states also offered a large sum of money, a bounty, for those who joined.

In March of 1863 Congress passed a law for drafting a national army. The North had a harder time motivating the people to join its forces. While the South could appeal to the men to protect their own land and honor, the North's cause of fighting to preserve a nation was not so personal. This lack of personal concern for the northern cause led many northern men to join the army halfheartedly.

All men between the ages of twenty and forty-five were subject to regular army service. Those who were physically or mentally unfit were exempted, as were certain officeholders. A draftee was also allowed to hire a substitute or to pay $300 for an exemption. (Recent immigrants, who were not subject to the draft, often served as substitutes to earn money.) The system did not work well. At first over twice as many men bought substitutes as actually entered the army. Others ran away from service. Furthermore, the law caused ill will. Believing that the new draft law was unfair, penniless Irish immigrants, already harmed by runaway wartime inflation, rioted for four days in New York City. The rioters' hatred was vented on local blacks. The mob resented that they were being drafted to free the blacks while blacks stayed home. Most of the 128 people killed in the riot were black.

Raising Southern Forces—The South had more of a fighting spirit than the North. Furthermore, some of West Point's best students joined the Confederate command, providing able leadership for that army.

At the outset the South had no problem getting enough men to fight. In fact, there were more volunteers than the South could equip and train. But such enthusiasm was short-lived. When the first one-year enlistments were up and no special benefits were offered, the number of recruits declined. In April 1862, the South had to resort to drafting all men aged eighteen to thirty-five. Later the upper limit was extended to fifty, and men up to sixty-five could be placed in a home guard.

The southern system was not foolproof either. There were so many ways to get out of war duty that a War Department clerk joked: "Our Bureau of Conscription ought to be

335

- Copy of the Gettysburg Address

SECTION 5
- Copy of the Emancipation Proclamation

SECTION 6
- Activities D and E from Chapter 17 of the *Student Activities* manual

SECTION 1

Objectives
Students should be able to
1. Describe the recruitment and activities of soldiers as the war began.
2. Compare the civilian preparations and sacrifices for war in the North with those in the South.
3. List the modern aspects of the Civil War.
4. Describe the main goals involved in the Union and Confederate strategies.

Crittenden's Compromise
John Crittenden's attempt to obtain a compromise and avoid the war involved a reinstatement of the Missouri Compromise boundary for slavery and a constitutional amendment that would guarantee slavery forever where it already existed. The compromise was strongly opposed by Lincoln and the Republicans.

Difficulties in Raising Armies
Although volunteers rushed to join both armies at the beginning of the war, both sides eventually had to resort to the draft. In the North when more soldiers were needed, each state was given a quota. If the volunteer regiments did not meet the quota, a draft was held. Extreme efforts were made to raise as many volunteer regiments as possible to avoid the unpopular draft. Often cash incentives lured men to join. Some opportunists signed up, collected their bounty, deserted, and joined up again under a different name. Experienced soldiers would often watch the roll call for enlistees who forgot their "name."

Student Activity A: Civil War

This map activity gives a visual overview of events described in this chapter. You may want to assign it on the first day that Chapter 17 is taught. After the students complete the map, consider discussing it in conjunction with the History Skills activity "Geography in War" on page 359 of the student text. Geography and history are closely entwined in this chapter.

Teaching History Through Literature

Read excerpts from a Civil War novel to prepare for the chapter. There are several good Civil War novels for eighth graders. Among these are Bruce Catton's *Banners at Shenandoah* (1976) about a young boy's adventures in the Union cavalry and *Across Five Aprils* (1964) by Irene Hunt about a nine-year-old boy's difficult decisions during this time of political and social upheaval. A good biography is *Abraham Lincoln* (1976) by David R. Collins. Such outside reading is often a student's most memorable experience during the entire school year.

When the draft was called, many found ways to escape service. The most popular method was for wealthier men to pay a commutation fee or to hire a replacement. These replacement soldiers were usually inferior since many were serving only for the money. Drunks, new immigrants, and even residents of insane asylums were all targeted as replacements. Another method to avoid the draft was to suddenly develop a medical condition disqualifying the draftee for service. A few shady doctors provided the excuse, if the draftee provided the cash.

Wealthier men used these loopholes to avoid serving, which meant the main burden of service fell on the poorer classes. Throughout the war, draft riots broke out in places such as Ohio, Illinois, and Massachusetts. The worst riot, however, came in 1863 in New York City. Most of the rioters were Irish immigrants who feared that blacks would take their jobs while they served in the army. As a result blacks were especially targeted. A mob burned down a black boarding house, a black church, and a black orphanage. They also killed a couple of veteran soldiers and beat up the chief of police. Finally, military units fresh from Gettysburg arrived and restored order. In the fighting, one hundred or more people were killed.

Although the South did not experience the draft riots as North did, they still had the problems of inferior soldier replacements and deserters. In 1861 the Confederacy declared conscription into the army for all men between eighteen and thirty-five. Their service would last until the war was over.

called the Bureau of Exemptions." The most disputed feature of the law was the so-called "Twenty-Negro Law," which exempted any planter or overseer with more than twenty slaves. Its supporters claimed that these men were needed at home to keep the blacks from rioting. But poor Southerners who were drafted resented this exemption for the rich. Understandably, when the southern army began losing, getting recruits became even more difficult.

Blacks in the War—As early as 1861, Indiana blacks offered to serve the Union. Since blacks were fighting for freedom for their own people and being captured would mean almost certain enslavement, they had good reason to fight hard, harder perhaps than some whites. Yet it wasn't until after the Emancipation Proclamation was issued and the number of northern recruits dwindled that blacks were allowed to join the army.

Black soldiers, however, were not treated the same as white soldiers. Until 1864 black soldiers served at lower wages than white soldiers. Blacks also had medical care far below the norm. As a result the death toll for blacks ran thirty-seven percent higher than that of the whites. Blacks were also given the most mundane tasks. Because Northerners were unsure of how well blacks could lead, no blacks were appointed as officers. Instead, black regiments had white officers.

In the South blacks served in the army in noncombatant (nonfighting) positions such as

Many escaped slaves joined the Union Army to help fight for the freedom of all slaves.

cooks, wagon drivers, laborers, and personal servants to officers. By March of 1865, however, when there was an extremely severe manpower shortage, the Confederate Congress passed a bill to draft 300,000 blacks. The first two black companies astounded southern whites with their skill at arms. But no blacks fought for the Confederacy; the southern war effort ended before blacks could take the field.

Civilian Preparations

The Civil War was a total war; it involved both the military and civilians. Hardly anyone escaped at least some of its effects.

In the North—The North had begun to widen its industrial base even before the war. The North drew its workers from among women, who were new to the work force, and from a pool of 800,000 immigrants who came to America between 1861 and 1865. When war came, uniforms, boots, shoes, hats, blankets, tents, rifles, swords, cannon, revolvers, ammunition, wagons, canned foods, lumber, shovels, steamboats, and surgical instruments all went from northern factories into the war effort.

Industrialism also had a positive effect on farm production. Even though thousands of men left their farms to fight in the war, farm production did not decline. Instead, as the demand for food products increased, farmers began to mechanize. As many harvesters, reapers, and mowers were bought in one year as had been bought in

Civil War Mobile

Design a mobile with symbols from the era. Design your own symbols and historical allusions to the era. Have each student explain in writing what each piece represents and why he chose it.

Civil War Scrapbook

Make a historical scrapbook on the Civil War. It should be illustrated and should include a cover, a table of contents, sections, information about people and battles, maps, and a bibliography.

Student Activity C: Northern Advantages During the Civil War

This graphing activity reviews the Northern advantages during the war and teaches students how to make pie charts.

the previous decade. In addition to feeding the Union army, these farms began to feed Europeans. For example, forty percent of England's wheat and flour now came from the North.

The war also made private volunteer groups stronger. Private groups, sometimes called commissions, helped to purchase medicines and to supply Bibles and other reading materials. These commissions sent money home to a soldier's family and even secured food, shelter, and clothing for slaves who had fled from behind Confederate lines.

In the South—In the first months of the war, life changed little for most Southerners. Confident of their cause, they believed they would win and win quickly. Early victories at Fort Sumter and Bull Run seemed to confirm that belief. As the war continued, however, life began to change. The Union navy kept many needed imports from arriving in the South, and the small number of southern factories could not produce enough materials to supply the South and its armies. Soon there were severe shortages of some goods. Southerners also had to pay high prices for what goods they could get. Coffee, tea, sugar, butter, lard, flour, and fresh fruits became expensive. Then such things disappeared altogether, along with household items such as candles and oil.

Substitutions became common. Okra seeds, rye, sweet potatoes, and even peanuts were used to make coffee. As the need for medicines grew, the woods became the South's medicine chest. For example, Southerners could no longer import quinine to treat malaria, a disease that was a problem in swampy areas; so a less effective mixture of red pepper, table salt, and tea took its place.

Since cotton could be neither sold nor eaten, Jefferson Davis waged a crusade to get planters and farmers to grow corn. One Georgia newspaper said: "Plant corn and be

Young men such as Private Edwin Francis Jemison sacrificed their lives in the Civil War.

free, or plant cotton and be whipped!" *Corn* and *patriotism* became synonyms.

Farmers and planters often struggled more than others. The Confederate government took livestock, mules, horses, and carriages as well as tools and buckets for the war effort. Southerners had to use what they had available or do without. The longer the war lasted, the greater was the sacrifice required.

As real and counterfeit currency flooded the South, inflation occurred. Prices soared. By 1864 bacon sold at twenty dollars a pound and flour for one hundred dollars a barrel. Some people used a barter system, trading goods for food. To fight inflation and provide needed war materials, the South used **taxes in kind.** Such taxes required the producers to send one-tenth of their products—hogs, corn, or whatever—directly to the Confederacy.

Southern farmers did produce enough food. But hampered by a poor transportation system, they could not always get it to those who needed it.

337

Common Terms of the War
Make sure your students are familiar with some of the common terms associated with the war, such as the colors blue and gray. Most of the Northern soldiers wore blue uniforms. Many Confederate soldiers wore gray, at least at the beginning of the war. By the end of the war, however, many Southern soldiers were wearing whatever clothing they could find because Confederate supplies had been depleted. Northerners were commonly called "Yankees." "Billy Yank" became the standard name for any Northern soldier, while a Southern soldier was often called "Johnny Reb."

Railroads and the War

One technological development that made the Civil War a modern war was the railroad. At the outset of the war, the North had a considerable advantage in this area of technology. Two-thirds of all the railroads in America were in the North, and those in the South were of inferior quality. An industrial base in the North also allowed it to build new lines when needed. In contrast, no new line was manufactured in the South. When it needed more tracks, the material was taken from less-used side-tracks.

The advantages railroads provided were tremendous. Not only could food and supplies be brought quickly to the front, whole armies could be moved. Throughout the war, the North was able to shift soldiers from east to west when they were needed. Railroads could also provide the quick communications needed to coordinate attacks. Although the telegraph was already in use, lines could be cut or tapped. On a few occasions, trains were even used to meet direct military objectives. Armored cars with artillery on them bombarded the enemy. Abandoned cars were sent to ram enemy trains or were set on fire and rolled over bridges to burn down the whole structure.

The true value of railroads is shown by their connection to military objectives. In many instances armies were directed to protect or destroy railroad lines. Colonel John Singleton Mosby of the Confederacy was known for his daring raids behind the Federal lines. He left a trail of destroyed rails and trains. Sherman cut into the heart of the South by capturing Atlanta, a main railroad hub. In the closing days of the war, the North cut off Richmond by capturing Petersburg, which supplied the city by rail. As the war continued, the South's main problem was not a lack of provision so much as a lack of transportation to get provisions to the troops.

Military Methods

Because of the development of industry and technology and because of improved weapons, tactics, and strategies, the Civil War was really the first modern war.

Modern Warfare—For the first time the army was able to use the railroad to move goods and soldiers from place to place. In addition, the government could use the telegraph for its communications. Almost every evening before President Lincoln went to bed, he walked over to the War Department to read the war dispatches from the front lines. The telegraph helped him to make military decisions and to stay in close contact with his generals.

Mines, trench warfare, wire barricades, and other methods of fighting or hindering the enemy were put to use. Rifled guns and cannon were also used. These weapons spin the bullet or shell as it is fired to give it a straighter path, thus making it more accurate in hitting its intended target.

Tactics of the war progressed on land, in the sea, and also in the air. Much use was made of cavalry (mounted troops) for reconnaissance, or information gathering. On the sea, ironclad ships proved their superiority in warfare. The fight between the **Monitor,** a Union ironclad, and the **Merrimac,** a Confederate ironclad, was decisive in the future of fighting vessels. Balloons were first used in the Civil War for observing troop movements. In that way aerial reconnaissance began even before the invention of the airplane.

Images of the Civil War, its death and destruction, linger with us today because of another innovation of that time—photography. Photography had developed twenty years before, but its use had been limited. Only a few photographs were taken of wars in the 1840s and '50s. In addition, the complicated processes and the large expenses involved in early photography prohibited its common use.

By the time of the Civil War, however, photography was becoming less expensive

Union soldiers sit on the deck of the "victorious Union gunboat, Monitor."

The "First Modern War"?

The Civil War has been called the "first modern war." Based on their reading, the students should discuss aspects of this war that made it a modern war. *(railroad for movement of troops, telegraph for communication, mines, trenches, wire barricades, rifled guns and cannons, ironclad ships, balloon observation, photography, and— not mentioned in the text—a submarine)* Discuss how each of these advancements might change strategy and tactics.

Also discuss the fact that American generals did not have any books or examples to follow on modern warfare. Instead they followed classic lessons about warfare, and the more enterprising generals learned to improvise. Even Stonewall Jackson showed clear evidence of learning as he went. One of the most significant lessons of the war was the advantage of defense and the bloody effects of a massed charge. Another significant aspect of this modern war was the idea of "total war," with everyone in the country somehow involved in the war effort, particularly in the South. It is often said that the close of the Civil War around the trenches of Petersburg (outside Richmond) became the opening chapter of the Great War. Nevertheless, Germans in the latter half of the nineteenth century showed no interest in studying America's Civil War because they considered it a war of "armed mobs," not professional modern armies.

A Book of Brady's Photos

Find a book of Mathew Brady's photos to show to the class. Be sure to point out significant pictures from the major battles. Explain why no one is smiling in any of the pictures. (It was a tradition because no one believed the war was a happy event.)

and more common. Many soldiers had their pictures taken for their families or sweethearts. Photographers also followed the troops and captured images of war. One of these photographers was **Mathew Brady,** who kept his darkroom with him in a horsedrawn wagon. His many scenes of the war continue to offer revealing glimpses of that time of conflict.

Northern and Southern Strategy—As the South faced the task of making the North accept its independence, the North proceeded to show the South that the Union would not be dissolved. As each side approached its objective, it developed a strategy for winning the war that consisted of a few basic goals. Whichever side could accomplish its goals would emerge as the victor.

Mathew Brady specialized in taking Civil War photographs such as this one he titled "Between Decks."

Confederate Strategy

1. Break the blockade.
2. Gain recognition from Britain and France. Cut off cotton shipments to Britain so that it would recognize its dependence on the South.
3. Fight a defensive battle.

Union Strategy

1. Impose a naval blockade to shut off southern ports from foreign trade and thus strangle the Confederate economy.
2. Take control of the Mississippi River, splitting the Confederacy in two and cutting off the states west of the Mississippi from their sister states.
3. Take Richmond, the new Confederate capital.
4. Protect Washington, D.C.

SECTION REVIEW

1. Why was the draft initiated?
2. What are "taxes in kind"? Why did the South go to this system?
3. List several factors that made the Civil War the first "modern war."

 Compare and contrast the northern and southern war strategies.

War Games

There are many excellent board games and computer games based on the Civil War. The best board game on the strategy of the whole war is Victory Games' *Civil War*. The best computer game on the major battles is Sierra's *Civil War Generals II*. A sequel on grand strategy, *Civil War Generals III,* was released in 1999. These games take quite some time to learn, but the lessons about history can be valuable.

Section Review Answers

1. because volunteers became too scarce to supply the needed troops (p. 335)
2. taxes paid in products (one-tenth of total output) rather than in currency; to fight inflation and provide needed war materials (p. 337)
3. quick transportation and communication; more sophisticated weapons and fighting methods; use of advanced land (cavalry), sea (iron-clads), and air (balloons) fighting strategies; preservation of war scenes through photography (p. 338)

 The North wanted to impose a coastal blockade, which the South wanted to break. The North wanted to cut off all foreign trade forcibly to destroy the South's economy; the South wanted to stop cotton shipments to Britain voluntarily to force recognition. The North planned offensive moves; the South intended simply to defend itself. (p. 339)

The Face of War

Unlike any prior war, the American Civil War was captured on film for future generations to see. Photography was still in its infancy when the war began. The amount of time for an exposure to be made was at least a few seconds. This limited photographers to taking pictures of individuals posing for the camera. Any action shots would have blurred badly and been unrecognizable.

Objectives

Students should be able to
1. Describe the activity and results of the first battle of Bull Run.
2. Explain the way McClellan was defeated in the Seven Days' Battle.
3. Describe the activity and results of the second battle of Bull Run.

Jackson's Nickname

Brigadier General Barnard Bee of the Confederacy died in the first battle of Bull Run, but before he did, he uttered some of the most famous words about a famous man. As he attempted to inspire his Confederate troops to fight, Bee saw Brigadier General T. J. Jackson nearby. Jackson's Virginians were holding a hill near the center of the Confederate line. Bee called to his own men, "There is Jackson standing like a stone wall! Rally behind the Virginians!" Forever afterwards Jackson would be known as "Stonewall" Jackson.

Misconceptions of War

Congressmen, ladies, and other people from Washington expected to be able to picnic and watch the battle of Bull Run as if it were a sporting event. Southern soldiers expected to whip the Yankees, win the war, and be back home in time for harvest. Northern soldiers had similar expectations, yet the battle actually served as only a small preview of the horrors of war, and it set the stage for a long and exhausting struggle.

Battle Names

Several battles of the war are commonly known by two names. This usually resulted from the Northern practice of naming a battle for the nearest feature, such as a creek or a church, and the Southern practice of naming a battle for the nearest town. Therefore Bull Run was named by the North for a nearby creek, as was Antietam. The South's names for these two battle sites were

Marching into Battle

The fervor for war was on. After the attack on Fort Sumter, Northerners were eager for something to happen. But the Union Army, under seventy-five-year-old Winfield Scott, was made up of rough, untried recruits. Since many Northerners believed they had a decided edge and could win the war and be home before harvest, the pressure to attack Richmond grew greater. Richmond, the Confederate capital, lay only about one hundred miles away from Washington, D.C. The press cried "On to Richmond!" so loudly and so often that Congress soon joined the refrain.

First Battle of Bull Run

In July 1861, the Union army moved south, now led by General **Irvin McDowell,** a good strategist from West Point. A Confederate force was encamped twenty miles to the south of Washington, D.C., at Manassas, Virginia, and McDowell planned to capture it. Congressmen, their wives, and northern journalists followed McDowell's forces down the Centreville Turnpike to admire "the greatest army in the world."

The Confederates learned of this advance, and Jefferson Davis ordered General Joseph E. Johnston to leave the Shenandoah Valley and come to aid the troops at Bull Run Creek.

At the outset Union troops fought well. The Confederate Army gave ground and appeared to be retreating. But the brigade under the command of **Thomas Jackson** stood fast against the attack. (This action won Jackson the nickname "Stonewall.") Newly arriving Confederate troops then staged a southern counterattack, which forced the Union to retreat. The orderly retreat turned into a rout when a small Confederate force attacked some troops on the turnpike and they panicked. Instead of having supper in Richmond, the Union soldiers threw down their guns and canteens and ran for

Confederate soldiers ride to the battle of Petersburg, Virginia, in this reenactment.

Washington. Dazed Congressmen and reporters joined the exodus. In the resulting chaos, Washington was left unprotected, but the Confederate forces were just as disorganized as the Union troops, and they could not follow up their great victory.

Results of the First Battle

The **battle of Bull Run** (also called Manassas) affected both sides. The North realized that its troops were not yet ready to fight.

George B. McClellan was called to the White House, where Lincoln placed him in charge of all federal troops protecting Washington and told him to forge a new army to take Richmond. McClellan soon turned the army into a well-drilled machine. The troops sang, "For McClellan's our leader, he is gallant and strong! For God and our country, we are marching along." Meanwhile, the South had won so easily, just as Southerners had expected, that Bull Run made them overconfident.

Hesitation and Loss for the North

The North's goal of taking Richmond proved to be difficult. Slow progress in this "War in the East" frustrated Lincoln and most of the Union. Although McClellan claimed he

---

SECTION 2

Materials

- Activity B from Chapter 17 of the *Student Activities* manual
- Special speaker: a Civil War historian
- Video: *Red Runs the River* (available from BJUP)

Student Activity B: Major Battles

This chart summarizes the major battles in the Civil War. Students can fill in the portions they study each day, or you can help them complete the chart when you reach the end of the chapter.

The Chronology of the Civil War

Overview the organization of the chapter with your students. Explain that the Civil War is a complex period of history with many battles and events. Sorting out all of the details would require hours of study and meditation. A strict chronological study has advantages. But the reader also needs to see the flow of events in the three distinct fronts of the war: the eastern front, the western front, and the "home front." This textbook combines both approaches in six sections.

Section One: **home front,** including the *Monitor* vs. *Merrimac* (March 8-9, 1861)

Section Two: **eastern front** from the beginning of the war to the second battle of Manassas (Aug. 29-30, 1862)

Section Three: **western front** from the beginning of the war to the fall of Vicksburg (July 4, 1863)

Section Four: **eastern front,** picking up where Section Two left off and bringing it

needed more men and more time, Lincoln decided that McClellan had had enough time to ready the army.

McClellan finally tried a new approach. His army sailed down the Potomac River around the Virginia peninsula and debarked between the James and York Rivers. Since the Confederacy had spent less time fortifying that area, McClellan chose to attack there.

Joseph E. Johnston, the Confederate commander, was caught totally off guard. That should have been to McClellan's advantage, but McClellan, believing he needed more men to win, stalled.

McClellan's troubles were only beginning. Because the Confederate commander, Johnston, was wounded in an indecisive battle at Fair Oaks, the Confederacy got a new commander for the Army of Northern Virginia, Robert E. Lee. Although his troops were outnumbered, Lee knew his men, his resources, and the area. In seven days (hence the name Seven Days' Battle), Lee attacked McClellan in six different places and drove the Union army back. McClellan had been nine miles from Richmond on June 25. Seven days later he was back again where he had started, at the tip of the peninsula.

General George B. McClellan (fifth from the left) and his staff

Back to Bull Run

Lincoln quickly changed Union commanders and ordered McClellan back to Washington to join John Pope in a new land attack. But Lee decided the Confederacy could beat Pope before he gained strength.

Lee left half his force in Richmond and sent the other half north to keep John Pope busy. Meanwhile, J.E.B. Stuart, a dashing cav-

A portrait of Confederate generals Thomas J. "Stonewall" Jackson, Joseph E. Johnston, and Robert E. Lee

alry officer, raided Pope's headquarters while Pope was gone. Seeking revenge because his favorite hat had been lost to Yankees in a skirmish several days before, Stuart collected Pope's war chest of $300,000, his dress coat, and the dispatch book that told where Union forces would be going. Of course, this gave Lee the offensive advantage he needed.

As the armies of the North and South converged, they took their stand once more on the battlegrounds of Bull Run. Stonewall Jackson's foot soldiers raced to aid Lee,

341

Manassas and Sharpsburg. The North named Shiloh for a church on the battlefield, while the South called it the battle of Pittsburg Landing.

Quaker Guns
The Confederates may not have always had military equipment, but they often made the Union think they did. One reason for McClellan's cautious approach toward Richmond was "Quaker guns." Named for the Quakers' nonviolent beliefs, these were logs painted black or blackened by fire. They were placed on wagon wheels and placed into position like cannons. From a distance it was hard to tell whether they were real cannons or not, and it could be costly to find out. Occasionally a real cannon was placed among the Quaker guns. An attacker would have to decide if the one gun firing meant the others were fakes or if it was just measuring distance in preparation for a full barrage. Although Quaker guns were used in several places, they brought the biggest embarrassment to McClellan at Centreville.

The Element of Timing
The second battle of Bull Run demonstrated Lee's ability to know when to strike. Dissatisfied with McClellan's lack of progress, Lincoln made Henry Wager Halleck general in chief of the Union armies. Halleck decided the best plan was to pull back McClellan's and Pope's forces and unite them near Washington for a grand assault on the Confederate capital. If McClellan and Pope had united, they certainly would have outnumbered Lee, but Lee had other plans.

When McClellan began to withdraw his forces, he lessened Lee's pressure to protect Richmond. Thus, the Confederate general had a short amount of time to focus his attack on Pope before the Union armies united. In a daring move, Lee divided his force in two. One part, under Stonewall Jackson, moved northwest and attacked Pope's supply base. By the time Pope's forces got there, Jackson was gone. Pope's troops finally

up to the battle of Gettysburg (the same time as Vicksburg)

Section Five: **all fronts** after Vicksburg and Gettysburg to the election at the end of 1864

Section Six: **final events** in the destruction of Lee's army in the east

An eighth-grade study of the Civil War should focus on the difference between the eastern and western fronts and the significance of the important battles. An understanding of the full chronology and the

relationship of events to each other must come with time.

Enrichment Exercise: Time Line

Assign a student to create a poster showing the chronology of events during the Civil War, splitting events into three rows: the eastern front, the western front, and the home front.

Speaker on the Civil War

If your area has a Civil War historical society, invite a representative to speak to your class and to share some artifacts from the Civil War. Often these speakers are reenactors and will be glad to dress in full uniform. If your area does not have a historical society, it probably does have a few reenactors who would be glad to help—at least they can talk to students about their experiences reenacting Civil War battles.

caught up with Jackson at the site of the first battle of Bull Run. Pope attacked Jackson and anticipated a victory by the next day—but again time was the critical factor.

The other half of Lee's forces, under Major General John Longstreet, showed up on the battlefield the next day. While Pope was busy with Jackson, Longstreet attacked his flank. The result was a major victory for the Confederacy. Once again the Union army retreated from Bull Run toward Washington.

SECTION 3

Objectives

Students should be able to

1. Describe the Union blockade and the Confederacy's activity to overcome it.
2. Name the Union general who successfully led the North to control the Mississippi River.
3. Identify the last Confederate stronghold on the Mississippi River to fall into Union hands.

The C.S.S. *Alabama*

The most famous of the southern blockade-runners was a British-built ship, the C.S.S. *Alabama,* which was captained by Raphael Semmes. In 1863 the *Alabama* captured and burned thirty-six Yankee ships. Its raids put fear into Union sailors. After many months at sea, the *Alabama* went to a French port for repairs. While it was there, a Union ship attacked and sank the blockade-runner. In 1871 the United States pressed Britain to accept responsibility for the damage that the *Alabama* and other British-built Confederate raiders had caused during the Civil War. Britain paid the United States $15 million for its failure to exercise "due diligence" over its shipyards.

covering sixty-two miles in less than forty-eight hours. The two-day fight, the **second battle of Bull Run** (Manassas Junction), ended with the Union troops back in Washington. Jackson said that the day had been won "by nothing but the blessing and protection of Providence." A disgraced Pope was sent off to Minnesota to fight Indians, and he was replaced by McClellan, who was now given a second chance.

This was probably the high tide of the Confederacy. Lee had defeated the army that faced him and the relief army that had come to aid them and had successfully switched the locale of fighting from Richmond back to Washington where it would do more damage to the Union than to the Confederacy.

SECTION REVIEW

1. What key city was the Union army striving to conquer?
2. What Confederate commander kept his men from retreating at the first battle of Bull Run?
3. How did each side respond to that Confederate victory?
4. What exceptional Confederate leader overcame McClellan in the Seven Days' Battle?
5. What battle was probably the high tide of the Confederacy?

 What proved to be a major flaw in McClellan's leadership?

Controlling the Waters

Two goals of the Union forces involved shutting off the South's major water transportation links. The North achieved these objectives with a minimum of delay and a better demonstration of leadership.

The Union Blockade

On April 17, 1861, only a few days after the fall of Fort Sumter, the Confederacy permitted privately owned ships to be outfitted to capture Union vessels. Two days later Lincoln issued orders for a naval **blockade** of the southern coast from South Carolina around to the Mexican border. Later he extended it northward to the Potomac River. Because of the shortage of ships, however, it was difficult at first for the Union to maintain a successful blockade. But the Secretary of the Navy began a giant ship-buying program, leasing or purchasing just about anything big enough to be armed. Once ready, the North concentrated the blockade on ten major southern ports, each of which had inland connections by rail or river.

The South tried to overcome the blockade with **blockade runners.** Because the runners had shallow drafts (little of the ship extended below the water line), they could dart into shallow inlets for cover. Since the Union ships needed deeper water to operate, they could not follow them. Runner ships had low profiles and were usually painted dull gray to blend with the seas. Most of them were steam-powered, and some could do eighteen knots (27 m.p.h.), enabling them to outrun any Union vessel. Their powerful engines burned hard coal because its smoke was less noticeable. The easiest ports for blockade runners were those with more than one outlet, such as Wilmington, North Carolina. From these ports the outbound runners, loaded with cotton, usually headed south to British-held islands; Bermuda and the Bahama Islands were only about three days away. The goods were then shifted to ocean-going freighters that flew the flags of neutral countries. To overcome their ship and manpower shortage, the Confederates hired British ships and young captains from the Royal Navy. The chance for wealth made it worth the risks; a captain could

 ***Red Runs the River* Video**

Red Runs the River, produced by Unusual Films (Bob Jones University), traces the influence of Gen. Stonewall Jackson on the profane Gen. R. S. Ewell. This classic Christian film depicts the two battles at Bull Run.

Section Review Answers

1. Richmond (p. 340)
2. Thomas "Stonewall" Jackson (p. 340)

3. The North received a new general and grew more disciplined through increased training. The South became overconfident. (p. 340)
4. Robert E. Lee (p. 341)
5. the second battle of Bull Run (p. 342)

 an unwillingness to act that wasted opportunities to advance (p. 341)

SECTION 3

Materials

• No materials

make $5,000 in gold for one round trip, and the lowest crewman, $250. The Confederates made more than 8,500 successful trips through the blockade. Even in the closing months of the war, there was an even chance of evading the blockade.

In 1861 the chances of slipping through the blockade were high. Nine of every ten southern ships got through. But as the months went by, the Union increased its efforts. As various ports fell into Yankee hands, the blockade had more land bases to make it even more successful. In the spring of 1865, thirty-five fully laden runners carrying $15 million worth of goods sat in Nassau harbor with no ports of call open on the southern coast. Their provisions would never reach the starving South.

Although its effective rate at the war's end was only fifty percent, the blockade took a huge toll on the Confederacy. In three years the South went from exporting ten million bales of cotton a year to shipping only one million bales. Drained of income, the South had to issue money backed only by faith in its cause. Its credit was undermined, and the foreign products it desperately needed became nearly unattainable, its foreign trade decreasing by two-thirds. While the outcome of the war was not decided on the blockade line but on the battlefield, it would have been a far different war if the Union navy had not guarded the southern coast.

Taking the Mississippi

The "War in the West" centered on the North's goal of gaining control of the Mississippi River. With control of the river, the North could separate Texas, Arkansas, Louisiana, and their resources from the rest of the Confederacy. They could also eliminate southern use of the important riverway and take advantage of its transportation opportunities for the Union. Instrumental in achieving

Ulysses S. Grant helped lead the Union Army to gain control of the Mississippi River.

this goal was the leadership of a Union officer named **Ulysses S. Grant.**

Gaining the Upper Mississippi—Grant, who had given up soldiering earlier and had since failed at farming and business, rejoined the army in Illinois. He believed that the key to success west of the Appalachians was control of the Tennessee and Cumberland Rivers. (These rivers emptied into the Ohio River, which in turn flowed to the Mississippi.) Leaving Cairo, Illinois, he and his troops moved down to the Tennessee border and captured two forts, Fort Henry and Fort Donelson. These forts defended the key waterways, and their fall, followed by the capture of Corinth and the battle of Shiloh in April 1862, meant that the Union had control of the upper Mississippi and access to points south. The capture of these forts also made Grant a hero.

Gaining the Lower Mississippi—Next on the Union war agenda was gaining control of the lower Mississippi to prevent Confederate use of it. Two Confederate forts on a peninsula guarded the river. The Confederacy had also

343

The Unglamorous Side of War

Play the name game. Ask students to name the first five things that pop into their head when they hear the name "Civil War." They may say some of the generals or land battles, but it is very unlikely that they will mention any of the events mentioned in this section.

As the first modern war, the American Civil War was a "total war." Total wars have an unglamorous side: the need to starve the enemy nation of goods and supplies. Ask the students which of the four points in the Union strategy (page 339) are covered in

their reading for this section. *(one and two—the blockade and the conquest of the Mississippi)* The work of each ship was as vital as the work of any regiment. Also, the siege of Vicksburg was as important as any victory on the open battlefield (and perhaps more so).

Mapping Vicksburg

The map on this page displays the route of Farragut, who moved north on the Mississippi, and the overall route of the Northern forces that followed the Mississippi southward to Vicksburg. Trace Grant's separate and significant campaigns as he approached Vicksburg. Grant took overall command in the western theater of operations in July 1862.

The Vicksburg Key

Lincoln once said, "The war can never be brought to a close until that key is in our pocket." The key he was referring to was Vicksburg. Located on the eastern side of the Mississippi, Vicksburg stood as the Confederacy's last major stronghold on the river. Lincoln knew that if it could be taken Arkansas, Texas, and Louisiana would be completely cut off from the rest of the Confederacy. Victory would also restore commerce in the river-dependent Ohio and northern Mississippi valleys. Unfortunately for the Union, the Confederates were also aware of Vicksburg's importance. Eight forts, lines of trenches, and Confederate forces under Major General John C. Pemberton surrounded the city. Swamps to the north of the city made any attack there almost impossible. The best chance for Union victory was to approach the city from the east.

Ulysses S. Grant was the Union general in charge of the Vicksburg campaign. Before focusing on taking Vicksburg, he made several attempts to bypass the city.

Grant finally decided that Vicksburg would have to be taken from the east. But to get into position, he would have to move his men across the Mississippi. Leaving Sherman's force north of Vicksburg, Grant moved most of his forces down the western side of the Mississippi south of the city. A Confederate bombardment prevented him from crossing the river where intended, but he found an unprotected area farther south. Now it was a matter of moving to the east of the city. The only prob-

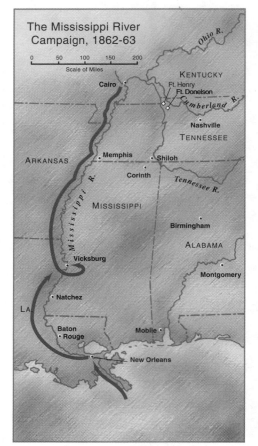

The Mississippi River Campaign, 1862–63

stretched two huge link chains across the Mississippi. The chains would be lifted to permit Confederate vessels to pass by and then lowered to snag any others that might try.

David Glasgow Farragut, a naval officer, devised a plan that with the aid of a land force, led by General Benjamin Butler, would take New Orleans. Farragut decided to bypass the forts and head for New Orleans. Under cover of night, an advance party unhooked the chains, and Farragut's fleet slipped past the forts despite heavy fire from the Confederates. Once past the forts, he scattered and disabled the Confederate fleet. New Orleans fell two days later. Butler's troops remained there to keep it under Federal control.

The Union navy then began moving up river, occupying first Baton Rouge, Louisiana, and then Natchez, Mississippi. By July of 1863 the Federals had won control of the entire Mississippi River, except for a small area around Vicksburg, Mississippi, a prime Union target.

Vicksburg—Control of the Mississippi eluded the North because the Confederacy held **Vicksburg,** built high on the bluffs overlooking the river. Six times Confederate General John C. Pemberton had repelled Union attacks on Vicksburg, each time inflicting heavy Union casualties.

Grant sought a new angle of attack. He designed a strategy that broke his army away from its own supply line. Grant announced his forces would "carry what rations of hard bread, coffee, and sort we can, and make the country furnish the balance." In a move that shocked Pemberton, Grant moved east to cut Confederate rail access to Vicksburg. Pemberton moved to cut off Grant's supply line only to find Grant had none. When Pemberton returned to Vicksburg, he was caught in a trap without an escape route. Now Grant could starve out Pemberton in the city. For six weeks, around the clock, the Union shelled Vicksburg. Short of goods, the people resorted to eating mules, rats, and even their own pets. Finally, with no food and no hope of relief, the Confederates surrendered Vicksburg. The date was July 4, 1863. It had taken Grant eighteen months to capture the Mississippi. A rising Union commander, William T. Sherman, had called it the "spinal column of America."

SECTION REVIEW

1. Why was it initially difficult for the Union to maintain a successful naval blockade?
2. What did Grant believe to be the key to military success west of the Appalachians?
3. What Union naval officer was responsible for breaking through the Confederate chain in the lower Mississippi?
4. What was the last Confederate stronghold on the Mississippi River? On what date did it fall to Union troops?

 Why did the North want to shut off the South's water links?

The War in the East

While Grant found quick success in the West, the Union forces slowly moved from defeat to victory in the East. In September of 1862, Lee decided to take the offensive and move into Maryland, hoping to free it from Union control. Since it was early fall, the move would also free farmers in the rich granary of the Confederacy to harvest their crops. Moreover, Lee had reason to believe that a successful southern offensive would bring Britain in on the Confederate side.

Antietam

Lee divided his army, sending Jackson into the Shenandoah Valley. J.E.B. Stuart's cavalry was left behind to halt any Union attempts at pursuit. McClellan would have had little idea where Lee had planned to attack had it not been for an amazing discovery.

When McClellan was moving across an area recently vacated by Confederates, a Union corporal and a sergeant picked up three cigars. Wrapped around the cigars was a dispatch from Lee that a courier had lost, giving Lee's location and making it obvious that his army was divided. Using the information, McClellan moved to force Lee into a battle before Jackson could reach him. Lee found

out about the lost dispatch less than twenty-four hours later and planned to pull back across the Potomac and change his strategy. But on September 17, 1862, McClellan's forces made massive attacks on Lee's lines. In one long, ghastly day, three battles were fought. Just before dusk, though, Lee's reinforcements arrived. With one more attack McClellan might have defeated Lee, but the attack never came, only a stalemate. Rather than renewing the attack at daybreak, McClellan waited, permitting Lee to engineer an orderly retreat across the Potomac back into the safety of northern Virginia.

Since the Confederacy did not win at **Antietam** (an TEE tum), Britain stayed out of the war. Since the Union did not lose, Lincoln used the occasion to issue the Emancipation Proclamation.

Fredericksburg

Ambrose Burnside, the dashing officer Lincoln picked to replace McClellan, had no better success than his predecessor. On December 13, 1862, Burnside drove his refitted army across the Rappahanock to attack Confederates entrenched at Fredericksburg. Wave after wave of men failed to dislodge the Confederate forces, and the Union lost twice as many men as the Confederacy. Union morale dipped to the lowest point of the war. In twenty months the North had organized a grand army; yet no general seemed to be able to win with it. Lincoln now sent for "Fighting Joe" Hooker.

Chancellorsville

Hooker, with 130,000 men, now decided to strike Lee's army of 60,000 by going west to **Chancellorsville.** The Union forces had an overwhelming advantage not only in numbers of men but also in supplies. An overconfident Hooker boasted, "May God have mercy on General Lee, for I will have none." Since the isolated crossroads was within easy reach of

lem was that Confederate troops in Jackson, Mississippi, might attack Grant's rear, so he moved on them first. Grant swept up toward Jackson, defeating Confederate forces at Fort Gibson and at Raymond. Next he attacked Confederate Joseph E. Johnston's forces at Jackson. While he was doing that, the Confederate forces at Vicksburg left the city to aid Johnston. They were too late. Johnston retreated north before Pemberton could help him.

Grant turned his forces and headed east toward Vicksburg. At Champion's Hill he defeated Pemberton, who quickly moved the rest of his forces back toward Vicksburg. The next day, Grant engaged Pemberton's rear guard and inflicted another costly defeat. By the time Grant reached Vicksburg, he was confident that the city would soon be in his hands. However, the Confederates were not ready to surrender. The siege of Vicksburg began on May 19 and lasted almost seven weeks. Pemberton finally surrendered on July 4, 1863. One Confederate chaplain said, "We surrendered to famine, not to them."

SECTION 4

Objectives
Students should be able to
1. List three reasons Lee moved his forces into Maryland.
2. Describe the circumstances of the battle of Antietam.
3. Explain the good and bad results of the battle of Chancellorsville for the South.
4. Describe the circumstances and results of the battle of Gettysburg.

Section Review Answers

1. because of a shortage of ships (p. 342)
2. control of the Tennessee and Cumberland Rivers (p. 343)
3. David Glasgow Farragut (p. 344)
4. Vicksburg; July 4, 1863 (p. 344)

 If the South's water links were closed, then ships could not bring food, weapons, and supplies to Southern troops. The South would also be

unable to export cotton and raise money to continue fighting the war. (p. 343)

SECTION 4

Materials

- Plans for a field trip to a Civil War site or pictures of Civil War sites
- Civil War documentary video
- Copy of the Gettysburg Address

Visit a Civil War Site

The National Park Service maintains eleven national battlefields, nine national

military parks, three national battlefield parks, along with several historic sites, historical parks, and memorials. A field trip to one of these parks would pay rich dividends, particularly if your class focuses a few days on the background of that battle or event from the Civil War. If you cannot take your class, at least show pictures from a visit you have taken or ask a student who has visited to share his experiences, pictures, and other materials.

Stonewall Jackson

Jackson's courage, his fighting ability, and his brilliant strategy had made him an extremely important leader for the South. Lee had such confidence in his ability that he remarked that the South would have won at Gettysburg if Jackson had been there. Much more important than Jackson's reputation as a soldier, however, was his reputation as a Christian. He was known as a man of faith and prayer. His sincere testimony had a profound effect on his men and on all those who knew him. Encourage your students to read a biography of his life.

The Minie Ball

The brutality of the American Civil War was augmented by major changes in guns and bullets. Prior to the Civil War, soldiers marched into battle in tight formations, firing massed volleys at the enemy and then breaking into bayonet or saber charges. The minie ball soon made these tactics outdated and suicidal.

Basically, the minie ball took advantage of an earlier invention—the rifled barrel. This type of barrel had spiraled grooves that sent a bullet spinning farther and on a more precise path. The problem was that the bullet had to fit snugly enough in the barrel to make use of these grooves. Soldiers would have to cram the bullet down into the barrel with a piece of equipment called a ramrod. Some rifles even came equipped with small mallets. All this work took time and was difficult to perform in the midst of battle. A Frenchman named Claude-Etienne Minié developed a solution to the problem.

His bullet had a cylindrical shape and a rounded tip. Like earlier bullets, it had grooves on its side to catch those in the rifled barrel. What made the bullet distinctive was its base. Minié left part of the base hollow and inserted a cup-shaped piece of iron here. When the gunpowder behind the bullet exploded, it pushed this cup forward. The cup pushed the sides of

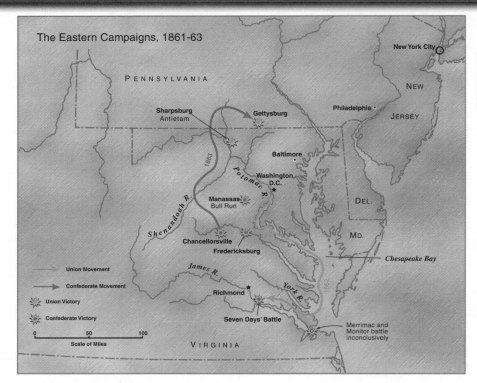

The Eastern Campaigns, 1861-63

Union Movement
Confederate Movement
Union Victory
Confederate Victory

Scale of Miles
0   50   100

Richmond, Lee risked a bold initiative. He split his army again and caught the Union by surprise. The battle, considered by many to be Lee's finest, raged for five days, and the fifth Union offensive for Richmond then failed.

Although the Confederate victory was probably the finest of the war, it cost the South dearly. The evening after the first day of battle, Stonewall Jackson was mortally wounded by some Confederate guards. In the darkness they failed to recognize Jackson, who was out scouting for information. When Lee heard of Jackson's wounds and the necessary amputation of his left arm, Lee sent word for Jackson to "make haste and get well, and come back to me as soon as he can. He has lost his left arm, but I have lost my right." However, Jackson died within the week. It was a loss that Lee

Confederate soldiers lie dead behind the "terrible stone wall," where they withstood wave after wave of Union assaults during the battle of Fredricksburg.

346

Documentaries on the Civil War

To liven up your discussion of the Civil War, consider including selections from a documentary on the war. The most famous of these is Ken Burns's PBS documentary, which is available on videocassette. Show selected battles.

and the Confederacy felt keenly. Because of his skill and unselfish cooperation, Jackson had been worth as much as many regiments to the Confederate cause.

Gettysburg

Buoyed by victory, Lee decided on a bold advance into Pennsylvania. This was his second and last invasion of the North. Lee believed that northern support for the war would be lost if he captured a northern city like Harrisburg or Baltimore. He also thought that it would make Lincoln pull some troops out of the campaign along the Mississippi River and lessen pressure there. Lee also hoped his famished army could be resupplied as they passed through lush Pennsylvania farmlands.

Lee's Hopeful Advance—Lee started north early in June, going up the Shenandoah Valley, across the Potomac, across western Maryland, and then into Pennsylvania. Even with ninety thousand men, Hooker was unable to stop Lee. In desperation, on June 28, Lincoln gave the army its fifth commander that year, George Gordon Meade. Although shy and scholarly, Meade was well qualified.

On July 1, Lee's advance troops came to a small town called **Gettysburg,** where they stopped to buy some badly needed shoes. There they unexpectedly met a Union scouting party. Both armies quickly pulled up to fight from two ridges. The Confederates were on Seminary Ridge; the Union forces stood on Cemetery Ridge about one mile away. At the southern end of Cemetery Ridge were two rocky points called Round Top and Little Round Top.

On the first day of the three-day battle, Lee's troops forced the Union lines back but did not break them. The next day, July 2, Lee attacked on the left end of the Union line near the Round Tops but was beaten back. That night Lee planned an attack on the Union center.

A Bitter Defeat for the South—The attack on July 3 began with the heaviest bombardment the South could deliver. Between one and two o'clock in the afternoon, fifteen thousand Confederate troops under General George Pickett gave the bloodcurdling "rebel yell" and charged across an open, mile-wide wheat field. Union firepower was murderous, and thousands of Pickett's men were killed in the courageous effort. "Pickett's charge" failed to break the Union lines.

Lee waited on July 4, poised for a counterattack that never came. Meade chose not to send his tired men across that open field. Thus he missed a golden opportunity to capture Lee and his forces. The next day Lee and his tattered troops rode back into Virginia in a torrential downpour. The Confederates and their baggage train were spread out over seventeen miles but returned without the slightest harassment from the Union army.

With Lee back in Virginia, the Union had no choice but to attack there. Since Meade showed no desire to follow through, Lincoln promoted a new general above him. On March 2, 1864, Lincoln brought Ulysses S. Grant from the West and made Grant his supreme commander. **William T. Sherman** took Grant's place in the West.

SECTION REVIEW

1. What discovery prevented Lee from winning at Antietam?
2. What valuable Confederate leader was mortally wounded during the battle of Chancellorsville?
3. Who led the famous Confederate charge at Gettysburg?
4. Who became supreme leader of the Union forces following the battle of Gettysburg?

 What would have been the benefit to the South of opening conflict in northern territory?

the bullet outward so that it would grip the barrel's grooves and start spinning. Ironically, the French did not adopt Minié's bullet idea. Instead, the British paid him twenty thousand pounds to use it with their Enfield rifles.

In the Civil War, 90 percent of battlefield wounds were caused by minie balls. However, most were not true minie balls but an American variation. In the 1850s James H. Burton, a master armorer in the U.S. Army, lengthened the bullet and thinned the walls of its base. The result was a bullet that did not need the iron cup insert and that could be mass produced quickly.

On the battlefield, the minie ball changed everything. Rifle fire was accurate up to four hundred or five hundred yards. Often men marching toward each other never got close enough for the bayonet charges of old. Artillery units were moved behind the rest of the troops because of the long-distance accuracy of the minie ball. Cavalry units also started to use short-barreled rifles called carbines rather than sabers. After the Civil War, armies began to fight more and more in trenches, which provided cover from accurate weapons of war such as the minie ball.

The Turning Point of the War

Ask the students to identify the battle that they think is the turning point of the Civil War and to defend their answers. Remind them that the text suggested on page 342 that the second battle of Bull Run was the "high tide of the Confederacy." Which battle turned the tide and made Union victory a near certainty? *(The best choices are the battles of Antietam and Gettysburg, although historians have suggested several other battles as well. A person's answer says much about his understanding of the issues of the war that led to the Union victory. Note that Lincoln issued the Emancipation Proclamation after Antietam, ensuring that Britain would stay out of the war.)*

Memorize Parts of the Gettysburg Address

Consider having students memorize the key portions of Lincoln's Gettysburg Address, one of the three fundamental documents on America's political philosophy. At a minimum include the first sentence and the end of the last sentence. Every American should recognize where these words came from.

Section Review Answers

1. a lost dispatch found by McClellan's men that disclosed Lee's location and his divided forces (p. 345)
2. Stonewall Jackson (p. 346)
3. General George Pickett (p. 347)
4. Ulysses S. Grant (p. 347)

 The South hoped that Northern support for the war would diminish, that pressure on the Mississippi River would let up, and that Northern farms would provide supplies. (p. 347)

Objectives

Students should be able to
1. Explain the purpose and effects of the Emancipation Proclamation.
2. Describe the way the North carried on a war of attrition through the activities of Sheridan and Sherman.
3. Name the candidates in the 1864 election and explain the results of the election.

Emancipation Proclamation

Notice that the North technically was not fighting a war to free the slaves before the Emancipation Proclamation. Many people perceived the war to be against slavery, but the stated purpose was simply to preserve the Union. On the other hand, the South did not consider itself to be fighting to preserve slavery but rather to preserve states' rights and the integrity of their states and the Confederacy. This is borne out by the fact that most of the men who fought for the South were not slaveholders, and many did not approve of slavery. The Emancipation Proclamation, however, changed the outlook of many people toward the war, encouraging Northerners to fight for the new cause and discouraging Southerners who were against slavery.

Copperheads

Throughout the Civil War, Lincoln faced opposition from anti-war Democrats known as Copperheads. Their name came from critics who likened them to copperhead snakes, always ready and willing to strike. Instead of fighting the critics, the Copperheads kept the title and wore copper lapel pins showing the head of liberty.

Their opposition to Lincoln came in part as a response to early Union defeats and general war weariness. Some thought that vic-

The War of Attrition and Destruction

Many Northerners, tiring of the war, wanted a negotiated peace. Lincoln and his cabinet planned definite steps to bring the war to a victorious end. They believed that freeing the slaves, destroying southern property, and winning the presidential election of 1864 might all help end the war.

Freeing the Slaves: The Emancipation Proclamation

President Lincoln had brought the nation into a war to preserve the Union, not to free the slaves. However, as the war continued, it became obvious that ending slavery was necessary. The war-weary North needed a new cause to revive its fighting spirit, and so the proclamation was an important political move for Lincoln. In 1862 Congress had abolished slavery in Washington and in the new territories. Then in September 1862 Lincoln issued his **Emancipation Proclamation,** not to take effect until January 1, 1863. Even then it would free slaves only in Confederate-held areas, not in the border states or any other areas then under federal control. Also, if any Confederate states quit fighting before January 1, they could keep their slaves. Not one state, however, quit.

348

The Gettysburg Address

The battle at Gettysburg left thousands of dead soldiers who could not be returned to their homes for burial. Instead they were laid to rest on the battlefield at Gettysburg, where they had fought and died. President Lincoln came to dedicate the new cemetery there and delivered one of the shortest but most memorable speeches of all time:

Four score and seven years ago our fathers brought forth on this continent, a new nation, conceived in Liberty, and dedicated to the proposition that all men are created equal.

Now we are engaged in a great civil war, testing whether that nation, or any nation so conceived and so dedicated, can long endure. We are met on a great battlefield of that war. We have come to dedicate a portion of that field, as a final resting place for those who here gave their lives that that nation might live. It is altogether fitting and proper that we should do this.

But, in a larger sense, we cannot dedicate—we cannot consecrate—we cannot hallow—this ground. The brave men, living and dead, who struggled here, have consecrated it, far above our poor power to add or detract. The world will little note, nor long remember what we say here, but it can never forget what they did here. It is for us the living, rather, to be dedicated here to the unfinished work which they who fought here have thus far so nobly advanced. It is rather for us to be here dedicated to the great task remaining before us— that from these honored dead we take increased devotion to that cause for which they gave the last full measure of devotion— that we here highly resolve that these dead shall not have died in vain—that this nation, under God, shall have a new birth of freedom—and that government of the people, by the people, for the people, shall not perish from the earth.

SECTION 5

Materials

• Copy of the Emancipation Proclamation

The Emancipation Proclamation

Copy the text of the Emancipation Proclamation onto an overhead for the class to read. Discuss the provisions of the proclamation and the politics involved. Did it go far enough? Was it only political rhetoric?

(An online transcript of the Emancipation Proclamation is available through the National Archives website.)

Politics and War

Every war that the students study has a political side that has a direct bearing on the course of the war. It is impossible to understand modern conflicts without understanding how public opinion affects military decisions. Lincoln had to issue his Emancipation Proclamation after a military victory lest it appear to be the last cry of a defeated country. He also had to choose his wording to have maximum effect without offending political supporters in the Union's border states.

Another political side to the war was the ever-present concern about "the next election." Generals in both the South and the North did everything they could to affect the outcome of the election—the South wanted the Northerners to be too war-weary to continue, while the North wanted to hand the nation some encouraging victories. Can the students think of any other examples of the impact of public opinion in wars they have already studied or will study? (*During World War II, the Japanese assumed that a few quick victories would make the Americans weary of war and sue*

Lincoln reads the Emancipation Proclamation before his cabinet.

Encouraging the Confederacy to give up was but one reason for issuing the proclamation. It also gave the Union a positive, measurable goal. Instead of merely fighting for the Union, Northerners were now waging war "to make men free," in the words of Julia Ward Howe's new "Battle Hymn of the Republic." Third, since they would be fighting to end slavery, blacks were now given a real reason for joining the fight. More than 190,000 blacks fought on the Union side. Fourth, the proclamation hurt the South's war efforts because many slaves left their masters. As the word spread that slaves who reached northern lines would be freed, thousands deserted. Moreover, the proclamation paved the way for public acceptance of the total end of slavery, which came with the Thirteenth Amendment. Finally, it helped prevent Britain from entering the war on the South's side, because most of the British people opposed slavery.

Destroying the South

A war of attrition meant wearing down the South until it was too poor, too tired, and too hungry to fight. While the blockade cut off foreign supplies from the Confederacy, and Union control of the Mississippi prevented further aid from the West, Union armies now began to destroy provisions in the very heart of the Confederacy.

Sheridan in the Shenandoah Valley— Since Lee was aware of northern war weariness, he sent Jubal Early and his cavalry north. Although Lee did not expect Early to win any major battles, he hoped to create some anxiety. From his base in the Shenandoah Valley, Early's men raided Maryland farms, stealing livestock. In July 1864, Early and his men rode to the outskirts of Washington. This action did keep some of Grant's troops in Washington for protection and out of the fight against Lee.

But Early's raid led Grant to make a decision that had a grave effect on the South. Grant decided to send **Philip Sheridan** to close down the Shenandoah Valley once and for all. Grant told Sheridan, "Leave nothing to invite the enemy to return. Destroy whatever cannot be consumed. Let that valley be left so that crows flying over it will have to carry their own rations."

Sheridan complied with grim efficiency. He not only defeated Jubal Early's outnumbered army three times but also laid waste to the valley that had fed Lee's army for three years. Sheridan's men rode out of nowhere, killing farm livestock and striking terror. They burned houses, barns, and crops. More than any one single battle, Sheridan's destruction marked the end of Lee's army. Now Lee's men lacked not only weapons but also food.

Taking Tennessee—Before Grant had been called to take control of the Union army, he had led his men from the Mississippi River eastward toward Chattanooga (chat uh NOO guh). There the Union general William S. Rosecrans had taken control of the city.

The Confederate forces, however, had moved south to Chickamauga (chik uh MAH guh), Cherokee for "river of death." Lee sent eleven thousand men to assist the Confederate commander, Braxton Bragg. Lee had no intention of letting the heartland go without a fight. On September 19, 1863, Bragg launched a

tory was unachievable and that peace was a greater goal than union among the states. However, deeper issues were also at stake. In particular, the Copperheads opposed Lincoln's extreme use of presidential power. Justifiably, they thought his suspension of habeas corpus was unconstitutional and an abuse of power.

Although the Copperheads aimed to defeat Lincoln politically, others turned to more violent methods to make their point. Secret societies, such as the Order of American Knights and the Sons of Liberty, devised plots to start fires and rob banks in the North. They believed that the North would surrender sooner and that peace would be achieved if they supplied the South with cash.

As the 1864 election approached, it appeared that the Copperheads would be victorious. Union armies were making little progress, and more and more soldiers were dying in prison camps. However, timely victories by Sherman and Sheridan helped to restore Northern confidence that the war would be won. Lincoln also ensured the vote of one of his biggest supporters—the army. Some soldiers were allowed to vote in camp, while others were furloughed and returned home to vote. However, the victory was also aided by the Copperheads' choice for president. They chose George B. McClellan, the Union general whom Lincoln had earlier dismissed from leading the Northern army. McClellan had leadership ability; he had war victories; but he also had different views from those of the Copperheads. McClellan was never quite willing to embrace the peace platform. This division weakened the party's chances of winning the election.

349

---

for peace before the United States could put its industrial muscle to work. Also, the Communists in North Vietnam based their strategy on simply wearing down public support for the Vietnam War, and their strategy worked.)

Scorched-Earth Policy

Ask the students if Sheridan's action reminds them of any other war. Remind them that they learned in World Studies (seventh-grade Heritage Studies) that the Russian people practiced a scorched-earth policy as they retreated before the German people.

Compare the effects of Sheridan's and the Russian people's actions. Were they effective against the enemy?

hard counterattack that forced the Union forces to retreat to Chattanooga. Things looked grim for the northern army while they were isolated there.

Then Grant and Sherman arrived. Union forces opened up the Tennessee River to get food in. On November 23 Grant gave the orders to attack. Sherman struck the Confederate right flank on Missionary Ridge while another force attacked Lookout Mountain. The combined Union armies dislodged the Confederates and regained Chattanooga. Their efforts cleared Tennessee of Confederate forces, sending Braxton Bragg south into Georgia.

Sherman's March to the Sea—Confederate troops lodged in north Georgia hoped to ride west into Alabama and slide back into Tennessee to attack Sherman again. Grant, leaving the western command to Sherman, told him to go after the Confederate army, to "break it up, and to get into the interior of the enemy's country as far as you can, inflicting all the damage you can." And that Sherman did.

Moving southeast into Georgia, Sherman met staunch resistance from General Joseph Johnston. In a series of brilliant moves, Sherman attacked the flanks, or edges, of Johnston's troops. Every time Johnston was ready to take a stand, Sherman threatened to sweep around him, forcing Johnston to retreat still farther. Finally, however, Johnston took his stand at Kennesaw (KEN ih saw) Mountain, and the Union troops could not assault his defenses. Sherman then threatened the rear, forcing a retreat.

When Jefferson Davis became impatient with Johnston's slowness, he foolishly replaced him with the less able John Bell Hood. Hood lost heavily in Atlanta and by September 1 realized he could save his army only by evacuating the city. Sherman was more than willing to have Atlanta, a major railroad center whose loss devastated the southern cause.

Sherman saw, however, that keeping Atlanta might not be to his advantage. After all, he was now in the heart of the Confederacy and had moved far away from his supply base in Tennessee. His supplies were coming in by rail on a one-hundred-mile line that could easily be cut, placing his own men in grave danger.

Sherman, though, saw a way to change danger into triumph. Although Hood had already destroyed the supplies in Atlanta, Sherman got Grant's permission to destroy the city and leave only ruins behind. The civilians were told to leave, the city was torched, and Sherman cut the railroad back to Chattanooga. Thus he kept the Confederates from using it to counterattack him.

On November 10, 1864, Sherman's army moved out of Atlanta quickly to avoid fighting another major battle. Sherman divided his army into four groups and sent them toward Savannah on four roads across a sixty-mile-wide band of Georgia. They carried maps that carefully marked every village, path, and plantation. Their orders were "to forage liberally on the country during the march," keeping a ten-day supply on hand at all times. What was not needed was to be destroyed.

In the years since, many have wondered why Sherman was so destructive. Simply put, Sherman destroyed what was left to make it impossible for the Confederate army, now back under Johnston's command, to chase him. Second, this area of the Confederacy had yet to be physically affected by the war. By destroying the spirit and resources of this area, Sherman hoped to press Davis and the Confederates into surrendering more quickly. Finally, Sherman was under orders from Grant to destroy the area.

Sherman's orders stated, "Soldiers must not enter the dwellings of any inhabitant or

Mathew Brady's photo of Chattanooga in 1864 shows army tents in the foreground.

commit any trespass" unless local bushwhackers molested them. Since the locals almost always did, wholesale destruction resulted. Confederate and Union deserters, called **bummers,** added to the problem, following the army and pillaging. Sherman did not attempt to stop them. As a result, Sherman's **March to the Sea** did cause a great deal of bitterness. To generations of Americans not accustomed to war, this was war at its worst.

By December 10 Sherman's men had reached the port city of Savannah. The city fell easily; now supplies could not come by sea. Sherman presented Savannah to Lincoln as a

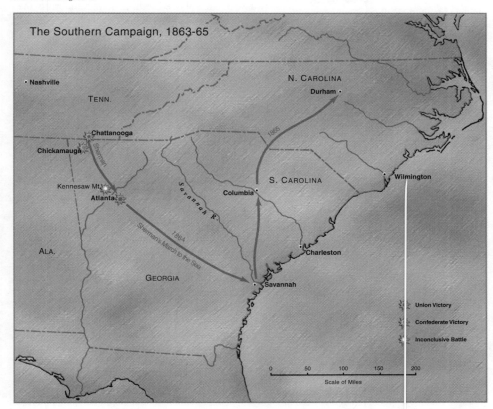

The Southern Campaign, 1863-65

351

Christmas present. Six weeks later he turned north to march across the Carolinas. His men devastated this area also. Sherman hoped to be able to join Grant in the final effort to defeat Lee.

The Election of 1864

Lincoln faced reelection in the fall of 1864. On August 23, 1864, Lincoln told his cabinet that he did not believe he would be reelected. Journalist Horace Greeley wrote that nine-tenths of all Americans were "anxious for peace, peace on almost any terms." The former Union general George McClellan,

Mathew Brady took this photograph of President Lincoln in February 1864.

who was running on a peace ticket, was Lincoln's opponent in the race.

Radical Republicans believed Lincoln was being too generous with the South, and northern Democrats criticized him at every turn. Yet they really could not see anyone else who could do better. Although he had not yet been able to end the war, he could not be faulted for lack of political skill. Lincoln used government jobs to increase his support; he picked cabinet members to appeal to different parts of the country and differing factions. He even picked a new running mate, a Southerner from Tennessee named **Andrew Johnson,** who, he believed, could help him bring the South back into the Union more easily. Lincoln's experience also had taught him how to win political fights without making personal enemies of those he defeated. He was a man of force, ability, and vision.

The American public sensed this more than did the politicians. Lincoln also had some men who helped to turn the tide for him. Their names were Sherman, Sheridan, and Farragut. Their victories in the fall of 1864 increased Lincoln's popularity and ensured his win over McClellan.

SECTION REVIEW

1. What were the provisions of the Emancipation Proclamation?

2. Near what Tennessee city did Union forces attack and send Confederate troops south into Georgia?

3. Who ran on the "peace ticket" in the 1864 election?

4. Why did Lincoln choose Andrew Johnson as his running mate?

 What was the general strategy behind Philip Sheridan's Shenandoah Valley campaign and William Sherman's March to the Sea?

Section Review Answers

1. It would free the slaves in Confederate-held areas still fighting on January 1, 1863. (p. 348)

2. Chattanooga (pp. 349-50)

3. George McClellan (p. 352)

4. because he believed that Johnson, a Southerner from Tennessee, could help bring the South back into the Union more easily (p. 352)

 to destroy as much of the countryside as possible with the idea that physical want would destroy the Confederate will to fight (pp. 349-50)

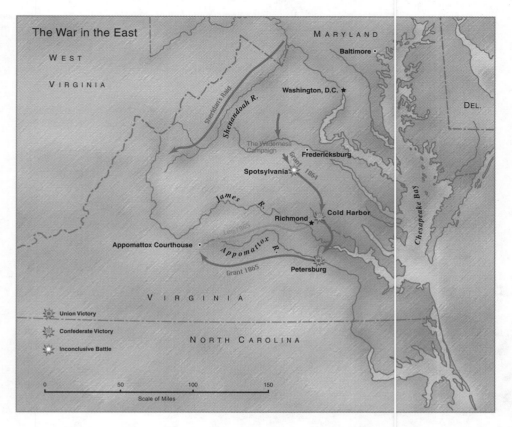

The War in the East

WEST VIRGINIA

MARYLAND

Baltimore

Washington, D.C. ★

DEL.

Fredericksburg

Spotsylvania

Richmond

Cold Harbor

Appomattox Courthouse

Petersburg

VIRGINIA

NORTH CAROLINA

Chesapeake Bay

☀ Union Victory

☀ Confederate Victory

☀ Inconclusive Battle

0   50   100   150
Scale of Miles

SECTION 6

Objectives
Students should be able to
1. Describe the way Grant finally pressured Lee to surrender.
2. Name the place where Lee surrendered.
3. Explain why the Civil War was so devastating for the country.
4. Describe the assassination of Lincoln.

Cold Harbor
The attack at Cold Harbor was a big mistake for Grant. He lost about twelve thousand men (killed and wounded) there in a half-hour of battle. Lee lost only about fifteen hundred. But Grant's army had the reinforcements and supplies to continue the campaign.

Appomattox and Aftermath

By May of 1864, Grant was ready to open a new Virginia campaign. His army moved into a heavily wooded area west of Fredericksburg called "The Wilderness." There Grant hurled a force of 100,000 men against Lee's smaller army. Although Grant suffered heavy losses, he knew he could replace his men while Lee could not. Grant believed that if he pressed Lee's army long enough and prevented Lee from maneuvering to fight him, he could wear Lee down and win.

The Road to Richmond

Despite his losses, Grant rebounded, moving east and then south. Lee marched all night to head him off and caught him at Spotsylvania Courthouse. But Grant moved south again, and Lee had to throw himself and his troops between the Union army and Richmond. Grant lost more men at Cold Harbor (the dead covered five acres of ground), but his advance continued. By now Yankee newspaper editors were calling the North's leading general "the butcher." In one month he had lost more than 50,000 men. But Grant was wearing Lee down. He had no

353

SECTION 6

Materials

• Activities D and E from Chapter 17 of the *Student Activities* manual

Questions No One Ever Asks

Can the students find anything odd about the South's conduct in the last few months of the war? One question is "Why did the South keep fighting?" Obviously, their cause was lost. Lincoln was reelected, and Grant was not going to give up. It seems that Lee recognized that the cause was lost,

but he made it clear that surrender was a political decision for congressmen to make, not a military decision. Apparently, no one in the Confederate government had the courage to make this politically unpopular decision.

Petersburg

Grant tried to shorten the siege of Petersburg by tunneling under the city's barricades. His men placed four tons of powder at the end of the tunnel and blew a big crater to open the city. Union troops tried to move in through the tunnel, but they piled up in "the Crater," where about four thousand men were killed or captured. The failure of this tactic forced Grant to continue the siege.

Appomattox Courthouse

Appomattox Courthouse was the county seat of Appomattox County, Virginia. Sometimes people refer to the site of surrender as simply "Appomattox."

Canadian Confederation

While the American Civil War obviously affected the United States, it also had consequences for Canada. At the time of the Civil War, Canada was known as British North America. Britain had already granted the Canadian colonies a measure of self-government, but they were still not united.

During the war Britain remained officially neutral, but sentiment and industrial interests influenced the British to favor the South. The North was well aware of British interest and looked on Britain and Canada with distrust. There was legitimate reason for concern. On a couple of occasions, Confederates used positions in Canada as a base from which to raid towns or ships in the North.

Canadians also had a deep fear and mistrust of the North. Many feared that if the North won the war its next step would be to annex Canada. The annexation issue was used to gain support for the Republicans in the 1864 election. A military operation in Canada would also have kept the Northern army occupied after the Civil War had ended, thereby preventing them from stirring up trouble at home.

However, two years after the end of the Civil War, Canada became a Confederation. Although many factors brought about the decision,

thought of changing his plans: "I intend to fight it out on this line if it takes all summer." Lincoln told his cabinet, "I cannot spare this man. He wins."

In June 1864, Grant crossed the James River, planning to attack Richmond from the south. To do this, the Federals needed to take Petersburg. Lee came to Petersburg's rescue. Grant settled in for a siege that did not end until April 1865. Eighteen trainloads of supplies came daily to Grant's aid while Lee's troops had less and less. The battle for Petersburg went on, and the South lost four thousand men but did not retreat. Lincoln told

A modern reenactment of the battle of Petersburg looks green and bright compared to the reality of an artillery stockpile outside of Richmond, Virginia, in 1865.

Grant, "Hold on with a bulldog grip and chew and choke as much as possible."

By March 1865 Lee realized he could not hold out much longer. On April 2 Lee moved the 54,000 men left in his army away from Petersburg. He hoped to lure Grant into open country and to neutralize Union numbers with superior tactics. But, outnumbered more than two to one, Lee had to fall back.

Surrender at Appomattox

Lee feared having his army trapped in Richmond. He decided to destroy Richmond and bolt west. Johnston's army was in upper North Carolina, and Lee's last hope was to link with it for one last stand, but Sheridan blocked Lee's retreat to the Blue Ridge Mountains. On April 9, 1865, near Appomattox (ap uh MAT uks) Courthouse, the Confederacy made one final hopeless attack on Grant's line, hoping to buy time. When it failed, Lee asked for terms of surrender.

Only half of Lee's men had arms to stack when they laid down their weapons at **Appomattox.** Some were barefoot, and most were hungry. With a nation to be reunited, Grant had been told to offer Lee generous terms. Officers could keep their revolvers and swords. Because horses were needed for farm work, the men were allowed to keep them. A local printer stayed up all night to print parole certificates. No prisoners would be kept. As soon as the soldiers signed a pledge not to take

Grant accepted Lee's surrender at the McLean House at Appomattox Courthouse.

the Civil War was one of them. Canadians believed that as a united country they would be better prepared for acts of aggression by the United States. The system of government the Canadians decided upon was also a reaction to the Civil War. It guaranteed a stronger central government that would make state/ province rights less of an issue.

up arms again, they would be given enough provisions from Union supplies and captured Confederate supplies to get them home.

Since Lee's army was the keystone of the Confederate army, it was only a matter of time until the more scattered units surrendered. On April 18 Joseph Johnston surrendered to Sherman at the Bennett House in Durham, North Carolina. The last group of Confederates to receive the news, in Texas, gave up early in May.

Counting the Casualties

The Civil War was the most destructive war America has ever experienced. About one-third of the approximately two million men who served in it were killed, injured, or captured. Practically every family lost at least one member or close friend in the war. In the South one-fourth of all manpower of military draft age never returned from war. By contrast, in World War II only one in sixteen was lost.

There had been great destruction of personal property, especially in the South. Unlike any other war since then, the Civil War was fought on America's own soil. Ruined homes, roads, businesses, and farmland were some of the material losses.

In addition, the war left deep bitterness. Mutual distrust and even hatred lingered between the North and South for decades, because each blamed the other for losses or problems.

Lincoln's Assassination

There was still one casualty to come. It affected both sides, the South perhaps more than the North. On Good Friday, April 14, 1865, President and Mrs. Lincoln went to

355

Discuss Bitterness Between Regions

As they finish the chapter, ask the students to list some of the decisions and actions that led to so much bitterness for the next century between Southerners and the rest of the nation. The South resented (1) the wanton destruction during Sherman's March to the Sea and Sheridan's raid, (2) the unparalleled loss of life and property, and (3) the new Republican state governments that were imposed (discussed in the next chapter). The North resented (1) the Southerners' decision to rebel, (2) the loss of life, and (3) Southern resistance to civil rights for blacks (next chapter).

Explain that such momentous sacrifices do not just disappear from the nation's memory. What keeps those memories alive today? *(national monuments, books, films, historic societies, reenactments, etc.)* Students will see how the Civil War had ramifications for over a century. The "Solid South" became a solid voting bloc. The Southern states, once the richest in the Union, collapsed economically and did not begin to recover for another half century.

Also, explain that other nations that have endured civil strife, such as those in the Balkans, do not easily forget. Discuss why many Southerners show more interest in the Civil War than those in other parts of the country. *(Southerners have always honored family and traditions, and it is impossible for them to think of their past without thinking of the Civil War. The war reminds Southerners of heroism and disappointment.)*

Larger Action and Reaction

Lincoln's assassination was actually part of a larger plot to also kill Vice President Andrew Johnson, Secretary of State William Seward, and Ulysses S. Grant. John Wilkes Booth settled on this plan after an initial scheme to kidnap the president failed.

Although Booth was a Southern sympathizer and had helped smuggle medical supplies there, he never fought for the South. This fact bothered him so much that he even referred to himself as a coward. As the war closed, Booth determined to help the South and win personal fame in one bold stroke. At first he and his followers, Lewis Powell and George Atzerodt, decided to kidnap Lincoln, take him south, and hold him ransom to win favorable postwar conditions for the South. However, the plot was unsuccessful.

After Lee's surrender at Appomattox, Booth became more desperate. He now plotted to kill Lincoln while Atzerodt killed Andrew Johnson and Powell killed William Seward. On April 14 the plot went into action—sort of. Atzerodt got scared and never tried to kill Johnson. Powell was a little more successful. He stabbed and seriously wounded Seward after forcing his way into the sickroom where the secretary of state was recovering from a carriage accident.

The major goal was accomplished, though. Booth shot Lincoln and fatally wounded him. In his escape he leaped to the stage and broke his leg, but he managed to hobble to his horse and ride away. Almost two weeks later, he was surrounded in a barn and died from a gunshot wound. Powell, Atzerodt, and six other people were charged with conspiracy in the action. All were found guilty, and four were hanged.

Ironically, Booth's actions hurt the South more than they helped it. Despite the lack of evidence, some people believed Booth was part of a Confederate conspiracy and called for tougher terms with

---

A Letter of Consolation

The Civil War took a terrible toll on the lives of America's young men. One powerful example of the suffering endured by the mothers of soldiers was a poignant letter of condolence written by President Lincoln to a bereaved mother in Massachusetts.

Dear Madam,

I have been shown in the files of the War Department a statement of the Adjutant General of Massachusetts, that you are the mother of five sons who have died gloriously on the field of battle.

I feel how weak and fruitless must be any word of mine which should attempt to beguile you from the grief of a loss so overwhelming. But I cannot refrain from tendering to you the consolation that may be found in the thanks of the Republic they died to save.

I pray that our Heavenly Father may assuage the anguish of your bereavement, and leave you only the cherished memory of the loved and lost, and the solemn pride that must be yours to have laid so costly a sacrifice upon the altar of Freedom.

*Yours very sincerely
and respectfully
A. Lincoln*

Mrs Bixby
Boston Massachusetts

Ford's Theater to attend a play. An actor who was also a fanatical Confederate sympathizer slipped into the president's box while the guard was away. **John Wilkes Booth** then shot Lincoln in the back of the head, and President Lincoln died the next morning. Booth was later trapped in a barn in Virginia. The barn was burned, and Booth either took his own life or was shot by one of his pursuers.

No one really knows what would have happened in the postwar years had Lincoln lived. However, Lincoln's second inaugural address had stressed "malice toward none,"

and his stated terms for reentry of the Southern states were quite generous. One writer said that Booth's "trigger finger had done the South more harm than all the lawless bummers in Sherman's Army."

Lincoln's funeral train retraced the route that had taken him to Washington only a little more than four years earlier. He was buried in his hometown of Springfield, Illinois, on May 4, 1865. After the nation laid a president to rest, it soon awakened to problems it had never faced before. These problems would challenge our nation for a century.

SECTION REVIEW

1. What was Grant's reason for continuing his pursuit of Lee despite the heavy losses Grant was suffering?

2. What strategic city did the Union soldiers need to take before attacking Richmond?

3. Where did Lee and his men lay down their weapons?

4. Who assassinated President Lincoln?

 Why is the Civil War called the most "destructive war Americans ever experienced"?

356

356   Chapter 17

Arlington National Cemetery

Across the Potomac River from Washington, D.C., stands a stately columned mansion on a hilltop. That mansion is the Arlington House, once called the Custis-Lee Mansion. Today the mansion is more often associated with Arlington National Cemetery, the site it overlooks, than with the families who once lived there.

In 1669 Governor Berkeley of Virginia deeded six thousand acres of land to a ship's captain. This was his pay for bringing over a shipload of colonists. Later the land was purchased by John Parke Custis, a son of Martha Washington by her first marriage. His granddaughter, Mary Ann Randolph Custis, married Robert E. Lee at the family mansion in 1831. In time Mary inherited the mansion and the surrounding lands.

When Mrs. Lee and her four children fled Arlington in 1861, the mansion fell into federal hands. Because of delinquent taxes, United States commissioners purchased the land in 1864. (Mrs. Lee had tried to pay the $92.00 due plus a fifty percent penalty, but her emissary was sent back with the message that she would have to pay the taxes in person. As a result the government took the mansion.)

Washington's many hospitals had become crowded with wounded men. Because of poor medical conditions, many died. Some place was needed to bury them. Quartermaster Montgomery C. Meigs suggested that the grounds around Arlington be dedicated as a

national cemetery so as to prevent Lee from ever returning to his family's home. Meigs even came up personally to ensure that the graves were placed as close to the house as possible. The burials were made throughout the war.

In 1866 the bones of 2,111 unknown Union soldiers were gathered from the battlefields of northern Virginia, brought to Arlington, and buried in a single mass grave right beside Lee's rose garden.

After the war Robert E. Lee's eldest son sued to regain his estate, and the Supreme Court ruled that it should be restored. But because thousands of soldiers were now buried on the estate, he settled quickly with the government for $150,000. Arlington National Cemetery was left to become America's most prestigious military cemetery.

the South. Other members of the government had been advocating toughness already and found less opposition with Lincoln out of the way. Booth's bullet ensured that Reconstruction would be harsh for the South.

SUMMARY

The Civil War began in 1861 between the North and the South. Although greatly outnumbered and lacking in materials, the Confederate armies successfully kept the Union armies from victory for four years. Eventually, however, the northern forces wore down the South's ability to fight until Lee finally surrendered to Grant in 1865. Four years of devastating struggle left much of the South in ruins and the nation in need of healing.

357

Student Activity D: Abraham Lincoln

You can use this trivia game to re-view the life of this great man, whose deeds and influence spread across several chapters of U.S. history. It is crucial that the students use the index to find the trivia. You can use this activity in several ways, depending on the needs of your class: take time to complete it in class, assign it as homework, or make it extra credit. Be aware that this activity takes a long time to complete.

Student Activity E: Types of History

This activity lists key facts that the students need to review from the chapter. The activity helps the students break down Civil War information into four types of history: military, political, economic, and social.

Chapter Review

People, Places, and Things to Remember

taxes in kind	blockade	Emancipation
Monitor	blockade runners	Proclamation
Merrimac	Ulysses S. Grant	Philip Sheridan
Mathew Brady	David Glasgow Farragut	bummers
Irvin McDowell	Vicksburg	March to the Sea
Thomas Jackson	Antietam	Andrew Johnson
battle of Bull Run	Chancellorsville	Appomattox
George B. McClellan	Gettysburg	John Wilkes Booth
second battle of Bull Run	William T. Sherman	

Review Questions

Identify the following.

1. The fall of this city in the West gave the Union control of the Mississippi.
2. This is the name given to Sherman's devastating trip through the South.
3. This one location was the site of two early battles won by the South.
4. These two ironclad ships fought a major naval battle during the Civil War.
5. Lee surrendered at this site.
6. This man shot Lincoln.
7. Lincoln hoped to make Union soldiers more willing to fight by issuing this document to free the slaves.
8. This man was a famous Civil War photographer.
9. This Pennsylvania battle was an important Union victory.

Identify each of the following men as Union or Confederate leaders, and then write a statement describing each man's role in the war.

10. Philip Sheridan
11. Thomas Jackson
12. Ulysses S. Grant
13. George B. McClellan
14. Robert E. Lee
15. William T. Sherman

Questions for Discussion

16. How did the first battle of Bull Run show that the people misunderstood what the war would be like?
17. Why did the North win the war?

Chapter Review Answers

1. Vicksburg (p. 344)
2. March to the Sea (p. 351)
3. Bull Run (Manassas) (pp. 340, 342)
4. *Monitor* and *Merrimac* (p. 338)
5. Appomattox (p. 354)
6. John Wilkes Booth (p. 356)
7. Emancipation Proclamation (p. 348)
8. Mathew Brady (p. 339)
9. Gettysburg (p. 347)

10. Union; raided the Shenandoah Valley, destroying Confederate farms (p. 349)
11. Confederate; rallied his retreating troops at Bull Run and became a key associate for Lee (pp. 340, 346-47)
12. Union; the last Union commander, broke Confederate control of the Mississippi and forced Lee to surrender (p. 343)
13. Union; known for hesitation to attack (pp. 340-41; 345-46)

14. Confederate; supreme commander, used brilliant strategy to defeat the larger Union army in battle (pp. 340-42)
15. Union; made destructive March to the Sea through the South to destroy remaining supplies and resistance (pp. 350-51)
16. Answers will vary. Spectators went out to watch the battle. Soldiers from both sides thought they would win quickly. Everyone discovered

History Skills

Geography in War

Answer these questions with the help of the text and the maps on pages 327, 339, 343, 346, 351, 353, and 646-45.

1. What mountain range separated the armies in the East and the West?

2. What river divided the Confederacy? How many states in the West were cut off when the Union captured this river?

3. What two important rivers run past Fort Henry, Grant's first objective in the West?

4. Rivers were important in supplying armies. After looking closely at the geography of Tennessee, guess why most of the fighting in the West took place there.

5. What geographic feature protected Vicksburg from Union attacks? (Because other cities on the Mississippi lacked this advantage, they were easily captured.)

6. What river, emptying into Chesapeake Bay, protected Washington from direct attack?

7. Based on the map scale, how many miles separate Washington and Richmond? In what state did most of the fighting in the East take place? Why?

8. What valley did Lee move through in 1863 and Sheridan in 1864?

9. The states of Alabama and Florida did not see as much action as other Confederate states. Look at their location. Why do you think they avoided major campaigns?

Think About It
There was more fighting in Missouri than almost any other state. Yet neither side paid much attention to it. Why? (Examine its location and the strategies listed in the text on page 339.)

---

that war was deadly. The conflict would not be decided in a day.

17. Answers will vary. They had more men, money, and supplies. Eventually these advantages wore down the South and forced it to surrender.

History Skills

1. Appalachians

2. Mississippi; three

3. Cumberland and Tennessee

4. Two major rivers that fed the Mississippi ran through Tennessee. This Confederate state was also next to the Mississippi. Armies moving south from Cairo needed to control this area.

5. Vicksburg had high bluffs overlooking the Mississippi.

6. Potomac

7. about 100; Virginia; each side fought to protect its own capital and to attack the other's

8. Shenandoah

9. These states were far away from the strategic objectives of the North. Alabama, in particular, was wrapped in a "blanket" of states.

 Missouri was far away from the Union's strategic objectives.

War's Devastation

President Lincoln was no doubt shocked by the devastation he saw when he rode into Richmond, Virginia, after the defeat of Lee's Army of Northern Virginia in April 1865.

Chapter Motivation

Imagine with your students how difficult it would be if your city had a civil war. One part of the city wants everyone to stay together; the other part of the city wants to form a completely new city. Your part wins the war and now has the difficult task of healing the division. Think how hard it would be to come back together as a cohesive unit. Talk about problems that would occur between the two sections. Tell your students to look for successes and failures in managing Reconstruction in the South. Have them especially look at how easy it is for greed and corruption to enter government processes.

Materials

SECTION 1
• No materials

SECTION 2
• Activity A from Chapter 18 of the *Student Activities* manual

18

Reconstruction

Just weeks before the end of the weary conflict and his own tragic death, Lincoln had given his second inaugural address. Expressing his desire for the future of the United States, he said, "With malice toward none; with charity for all; with firmness in the right, as God gives us to see the right, let us strive on to finish the work we are in; to bind up the nation's wounds; to care for him who shall have borne the battle, and for his widow, and his orphan—to do all which may achieve and cherish a just, and a lasting peace, among ourselves, and with all nations."

But as the Civil War ended and time progressed, more malice and less charity appeared than Lincoln would have liked. The wounds of the war were deep, and it would take years, even decades, before they would begin to heal. Some scars would linger for over a century.

Reconstruction and the South

The time following the Civil War is called **Reconstruction.** This was the time of reuniting the nation and attempting to solve the South's postwar problems.

The South's Need for Reconstruction

For many Northerners, life following the war changed little from life before the war. The North had lost thousands of men, and it felt that wound deeply, but industry had pro-

360

CHAPTER 18	Lesson Plan Chart			
Section Title	**Main Activity**	**Pages**	**Time Frame**	
1. Reconstruction and the South	It's Not Easy Being President	360-62	½ -1 day	
2. Presidential Reconstruction	Student Activity A: Time Line of Reconstruction	362-65	1-2 days	
3. Radical Republicans Take Over Reconstruction	Report on an Early Black Leader	365-72	2-3 days	
4. Bourbon Reconstruction Begins	Stealing Votes in America	373-76	1 day	
5. Recovery in the South	Teaching History Through Literature	376-79	1-2 days	
Total Suggested Days (including 1 day for review and testing)			6½-10 days	

gressed. Immigration continued to add to the northern population. Only a minor amount of northern property had been damaged in the war, so returning soldiers could go back to their farms or jobs with little hindrance.

The situation in the postwar South, however, was entirely different. Not only had it lost many of its young men, but it also had lost its slaves. Thus its labor force was entirely disrupted, and no great wave of immigrants came to add to the working population.

In addition to lost lives, the South had suffered severe property damage. Many of its major cities—Atlanta, Columbia, and Richmond—lay in ruins. Many of the South's fields had been stripped bare, and its livestock confiscated or destroyed. Homes, businesses, and railroads had been demolished. After the

war little remained with which the South could rebuild.

Not only was the South's plantation system dead, but also the money that remained was worthless. The South had almost no U.S. currency, and the paper Confederate money had no value. The South was bankrupt, and its accustomed means of making its living had been destroyed.

The freed slaves, or **freedmen,** were another problem for the South. No longer controlled under slavery, over four million blacks were free to live in the South. They needed jobs for support, but white Southerners had no money to pay them. Neither were the freedmen particularly eager to return to the same work they had done as slaves. Slaves had been vital to the South's economy before the war, but the freedmen lacked an important role in the postwar South. Yet they were there, and they had to be given a place in southern society.

The South not only suffered great loss of property but also was unable to pay for rebuilding with the worthless Confederate money (top).

361

SECTION 3
• *Free Indeed: Heroes of Black Christian History* (BJUP)

SECTION 4
• No materials

SECTION 5
• *Roll of Thunder, Hear My Cry* (1976) by Mildred D. Taylor
• Activity B from Chapter 18 of the *Student Activities* manual

SECTION 1

Objectives
Students should be able to
1. Define Reconstruction.
2. Explain why the South needed Reconstruction.

Battered Bridge
The ruins shown on this page are from Harper's Ferry, Virginia. A part of the Baltimore & Ohio railroad, this bridge was destroyed and rebuilt nine times during the war.

Bitter Feelings
The students should remember that the deep feelings regarding the Civil War did not result solely from the four years of military fighting or the defeat of the Confederacy. Many came from the following years of "political war" that decided how a conquered South and its people should be treated.

Rehearsal for Reconstruction
In November 1861 a Union force captured the island of Port Royal off the South Carolina coast. The Southern whites who owned the land on the island had fled, but they left behind about ten thousand slaves. Secretary of the Treasury Salmon P. Chase launched the "Port Royal Experiment" to develop policies and procedures for the care of the blacks and the property of the island. The experiment has been called a "rehearsal for Reconstruction." Not only did Union forces remain on the island throughout the war, but Northern missionaries and other volunteers joined them to try to help the blacks build a new life for themselves. Unfortunately, many of the

Debate Idea

Have your students discuss and/or debate the following:

Booth made the South's problems worse by assassinating Lincoln

It's Not Easy Being President

President Johnson was thrown into a complicated national crisis that had no precedent in American history. Divide the students into groups. Have each group represent the new president on the first day of his job. They must plot out their plans for the next four years in reconstructing the South by summarizing (1) their goals, (2) their challenges, and (3) their solutions. This activity will make the students think like the people of the times and understand the drama before them. After they have examined the possibilities, they can better evaluate the actual course of events that is described in the chapter.

Goals: replace the South's plantation economy, rebuild the South's cities and industry, give freedmen jobs and political power, re-establish state governments, open Congress to Southern senators and representatives, punish rebel leaders, ensure the long-term submission of Southern states to federal authority, restore the constitutional balance of powers between the president and Congress

Challenges: resistance of Southern whites, inexperience of the uneducated freedmen, harsh demands of Radical Republicans, Southern poverty, dangers of lawlessness, unequal distribution of land

Solutions: maintain delicate balance between federal oversight of change and eventual restoration of the South's control of its

soldiers and some other Northern opportunists bought up the confiscated land for their own profit and left little opportunity for the blacks. After the war the former Southern owners regained their lost lands, and the blacks there continued in poverty. The blacks gained little from the experiment except for some educational aid. The Reconstruction of the entire South that followed met some of the same problems that appeared in this rehearsal.

SECTION 2

Objectives

Students should be able to
1. Describe Lincoln's Ten Percent Plan.
2. Name the bill that Congress tried to pass in reaction to Lincoln's plan.
3. Compare Johnson's plan for Reconstruction to Lincoln's and to Congress's.
4. Explain the position of the Radical Republicans.

Ten Percent Plan

When Lincoln announced his Ten Percent Plan, he had more than Reconstruction on his mind. The plan was also intended to shorten the war by weakening the South's will to fight. If even ten percent of a state's voters took the oath, it would reduce the state's military manpower.

Many abolitionists criticized the plan because it neither gave blacks the vote nor promised equality. In fact, some labeled the governments proposed by the plan as "inverted pyramids." Only a few thousand voters would make decisions for the state while both blacks and disloyal Southerners would be excluded from the political process. It guaranteed unrest in Reconstruction.

Radical Republicans

Unlike Lincoln and Johnson, the Radical Republicans were appalled by the South's attitudes toward the dissolution of the Union and its idea that the Constitution granted the right of secession.

In addition to these problems was the need for the South to reestablish its state governments. Those governments in control during the Confederacy had been thrown out by the Union's victory. New governments had to be formed, and they in turn would have to deal with the conditions in the South.

All these problems of the postwar South were a major concern of the federal government. Presidents, Congress, and the states themselves would argue over their powers to control the methods of solving these problems of Reconstruction.

Phases of Reconstruction

Reconstruction is usually considered to be the twelve-year period from 1865 to 1877. During that time the federal government directly supervised the rebuilding of the South. In a larger sense, however, Reconstruction continued at least until the turn of the century as southern state governments continued to deal with the special problems of their region. According to the influences guiding Reconstruction policies, this larger period divides into three phases:

Phase 1 (1865-67):	Presidential Reconstruction or Self-Reconstruction
Phase 2 (1867-76):	Congressional Reconstruction or Radical Reconstruction
Phase 3 (1877-1900):	Bourbon Reconstruction or Redeemers' Reconstruction

---

SECTION REVIEW

1. What was the postwar era called?
2. What was the purpose of this era?
3. What were its three phases?

 How was the economic situation after the war different in the South from what it was in the North?

Presidential Reconstruction

For just a short time, Presidents Lincoln and Johnson directed the process of Reconstruction; this was the time of **Presidential Reconstruction.** Even before the war had ended, President Lincoln had developed a plan for bringing the seceded states back into the Union. Lincoln believed that the southern states, by illegally trying to secede, had committed an act of rebellion and had started an insurrection. As the commander in chief, his duty had been to quell their insurrection. Once this was done, he had the power given him under the Constitution to pardon their wrongdoing.

Lincoln's Ten Percent Plan and Congress's Reactions

In December 1863, Lincoln announced his **Ten Percent Plan** to reconstruct the areas of the South that had already come under Union control. This plan offered pardons to former Confederates who would swear an oath to support the Constitution and the Union. When ten percent of the registered voters in 1860 in any state had taken the oath, the state could form a new government and be restored to the Union. They could even get seats back in Congress and elect senators and representatives. By the spring of 1864 three occupied states (Tennessee, Louisiana, and Arkansas) had met these "easy" terms and were ready to reenter the Union.

Radical Republicans Object—Lincoln's plan, however, met resistance from a group of Republicans known as **Radical Republicans.** They believed that the plan treated the South too kindly. They wished the South to be treated as a conquered foreign nation, not as erring brethren. They were not ready to forgive the South for the war. According to these Radical Republicans, the South should be punished severely or all the sacrifices of war

---

own affairs, make demands clear and allow the South as much leeway as possible as long as it works toward meeting those demands

Section Review Answers

1. Reconstruction (p. 360)
2. to reunite the nation and to attempt to solve the South's postwar problems (p. 360)
3. Presidential Reconstruction or Self-Reconstruction (1865-67), Congressional Reconstruction or Radical

Reconstruction (1867-76), Bourbon Reconstruction or Redeemers' Reconstruction (1877-1900) (p. 362)

 The Northern economy actually grew after the war. Industry increased, and property loss was small. Returning soldiers could go right back to work, and immigrant laborers helped to replace workers lost in the war. But the Southern economy was devastated. Severe property damage kept soldiers from returning immediately to farming. Immigrants were not interested in the South,

and freed slaves had to find a new place in society and the economy. (pp. 360-61)

SECTION 2

Materials

• Activity A from Chapter 18 of the *Student Activities* manual

would be worthless. They also believed that if Southerners were let off too easily, they would try to regain the influence they had possessed before the war. Although a minority, the Radicals won moderate Republicans to their side. Because the Radicals and moderates did not wish to see Confederates back in Congress before the war ended, they refused to let the three states back into the Union under the president's plan.

The Radicals also reacted to Lincoln's use of executive (presidential) powers during the war. Since war created many emergencies, the president had made decisions without asking Congress. The Emancipation Proclamation, for example, had not received the approval of Congress. The Radicals believed that Lincoln had gone beyond his powers as president.

The Wade-Davis Bill—In 1864 Congress responded with its own Reconstruction plan, the **Wade-Davis Bill.** Under this plan a state could reenter the Union when fifty percent of the state's registered voters in 1860 had taken the oath of allegiance. In addition, those who wished to vote or help govern their states had to swear that they had never supported the Confederacy voluntarily. The states also had to abolish slavery and repudiate (rih PYOO dee ATE; refuse to pay or acknowledge) their debts and their acts of secession.

The Wade-Davis Bill passed both houses. Congress was letting the president know that it alone, not the president, would be the judge for state readmissions and reseating members of the legislative branch. In turn, Lincoln let Congress know he disagreed. Rather than

Andrew Johnson faced the incredible task of trying to rebuild the nation.

vetoing the bill by sending a formal message to Congress listing his objections, Lincoln killed the Wade-Davis Bill by pocket veto (See page 141.)

The conflict between Congress and Lincoln had not yet been resolved when Lincoln was shot. Andrew Johnson was left to battle with Congress for control of Reconstruction.

Andrew Johnson Takes Over

Vice President Andrew Johnson had been born in poverty in North Carolina. His wife, who was a teacher, had taught him to read and write. After moving to Tennessee, Johnson held his first political office. He moved up the local and state ladders to become a congressman and a senator. When Tennessee seceded in 1861, Johnson opposed its action and was the only southern senator who did not resign his Senate seat. President Lincoln named him military governor of Union-held areas of Tennessee and later chose him as his running mate. Johnson's outspokenness (he once said that Jefferson Davis and other leading Confederates should be hanged) won him the support of Radical Republicans.

When Johnson took over the presidency, Congress was out of session. Since he did not reconvene Congress, he had from April through December to state his ideals and to put them into effect without its interference. Johnson shared Lincoln's belief that it was impossible for a state to secede. Thus, Confederate states were still in the Union. Even so, Johnson believed individuals in the states had left the

Wade-Davis Bill
Notice that the Wade-Davis Bill would have required all Southern voters to swear that they had never supported the Confederacy voluntarily. This would have prevented almost all Southerners from voting except blacks and people who were "traitors" to the Confederacy. Therefore, such a restriction would have been especially repugnant to the South and would have caused greater bitterness.

Democrat or Republican?
Johnson was a Democrat from Tennessee, but he became vice president on a Republican ticket. For this reason he is sometimes listed as a Democrat and sometimes as a Republican. This political situation did not help win Johnson friends among the Radical Republicans or the Southern Democrats.

363

Student Activity A: Time Line of Reconstruction

This chart summarizes the key events in the era of Reconstruction. Students can complete the chart as they read through the chapter, or you can help them complete the chart as part of your lecture.

What If Lincoln Had Led Reconstruction?

If Lincoln's bodyguard had been on duty outside his door at Ford's Theater, Lincoln probably would have lived. But God has a purpose for the rise and fall of

leaders. Ask the students to evaluate the consequences of God's allowing Johnson to become president and then lose control to the Radicals. *(A century of Southern hardships and bitterness may have been alleviated, but the South may also have blocked the introduction of civil rights. The Lord allowed the power of the presidency to be tested but not broken.)*

Joint Committee on Reconstruction

The three major conclusions of the Joint Committee were as follows:

I. That the States lately in rebellion were, at the close of the war, disorganized communities, without civil government, and without constitutions or other forms, by virtue of which political relations could legally exist between them and the federal government.

II. That Congress cannot be expected to recognize as valid the election of representatives from disorganized communities, which, from the very nature of the case, were unable to present their claim to representation under those established and recognized rules, the observance of which has been hitherto required.

III. That Congress would not be justified in admitting such communities to a participation in the government of the country without first providing such constitutional or other guarantees as will tend to secure the civil rights of all citizens of the republic; a just equality of representation; protection against claims founded in rebellion and crime; a temporary restoration of the right of suffrage to those who had not actively participated in the efforts to destroy the Union and overthrow the government, and the exclusion from positions of public trust of, at least, a portion of those whose crimes have proved them to be enemies to the Union and unworthy of public confidence.

Union, and they, rather than the states, deserved to be punished.

Johnson's Plan—Johnson began by offering **amnesty,** or group pardon, to Southerners who willingly took a loyalty oath to the Union. However, he excluded those whose taxable property was over $20,000. These people, mostly former planters, had to apply to him for a pardon. Unpardoned Southerners were unable to vote, hold office, or get back any property seized by the federal government.

Next, Johnson's plan provided for presidential appointment of provisional state governors to hold state conventions. Such state bodies would draft new state constitutions that repudiated Confederate debts and ratified the **Thirteenth Amendment,** the recent Constitutional amendment that had abolished slavery. When a state had taken this action and fifty percent of its voters had sworn loyalty, Johnson assumed Congress would readmit it.

By winter all of the former Confederate states except Texas had met most of Johnson's terms. But South Carolina refused to repudiate its war debt, Mississippi did not ratify the Thirteenth Amendment, and not one southern state offered voting rights to blacks. When Congress convened, it refused to seat southern representatives. Instead, moderate and Radical Republicans in the House and Senate formed their own Joint Committee on Reconstruction. They would determine whether the southern states were really reconstructed. Unsurprisingly, they decided they were not.

Republicans React to the "Johnson Governments"—Several things offended northern Republicans. First, when southern states held their state and local elections, they voted former Confederates into office. Second, many Radicals and others believed that the government should take southern lands and divide them among the newly freed slaves, but this was not done.

Third, because most of the South's representatives and senators were Democrats, Republicans realized that seating them might cost them their power. The Republicans would be in the minority if northern Democrats sided with the Southerners to outvote them.

Fourth, some believed that the cost of the war could be justified only if black Americans received full rights of citizens. "We must," one said, "see to it that the man made free in the Constitution . . . is a free man indeed . . . and that he walks the earth proud and erect in the conscious dignity of a free man." When the Joint Committee held hearings early in 1866, it found out that instead of being granted more rights, the former slaves were being denied them through **black codes.**

Black Codes—The black codes established after the war in the South were much like the old slave laws, although they did allow a few new basic rights. Black codes allowed blacks to sue, to be sued, and to testify in courts. They were also entitled to legalize their marriages and to marry within their own race. They could now buy, own, and transfer property. But in trying to control the large population of freed blacks, the codes were very restrictive. They placed blacks in an inferior position to whites, making them, in essence, second-class citizens. The codes were in some ways a replacement for slavery.

In some states, for example, blacks were allowed to work only as domestic servants and farmers. Some codes forbade blacks to live in towns or cities. Hence it seemed that the codes condemned many blacks to do the same field work they had done in slave days. Blacks who wanted to practice trades or do anything besides farming had to be apprenticed and often had to get licenses. Since few blacks had money, this closed trade doors to them. Blacks not usefully employed could be arrested for vagrancy (wandering around with no job). Blacks who could not pay fines for vagrancy

How Could Anyone Support Black Codes?

Like slavery, Reconstruction raises difficult questions about the basic tenets of democracy and majority rule. The South needed to make radical changes, but who should have the power to make the difficult choices? In a republic, the majority gets to make the laws. Southerners chose to adhere to prejudices embodied in old slave laws. Today it is hard to understand how anyone could support such demeaning laws, and it is easy to understand why Northerners were so upset and demanded that the federal

government intervene. But a historian must learn to be objective.

Divide the class into Radical Republicans and Southern Democrats. Ask the Democrats to give arguments to justify the black codes. The Republicans should be prepared to challenge these views. Note that the issue is not necessarily whether the black codes were right but whether it is proper for the federal government to intervene in state affairs when the state goes against national opinion. In other words, should states have the right to "be wrong" or "make mistakes" when the rest of the nation disagrees with

them? If states do not have this freedom, then what checks the power of the federal government when it makes mistakes?

or other crimes could be hired out to anyone who would pay their fines. Southern states forbade blacks to carry arms, and some codes told them where they could or could not own property. Southerners held that the black codes prevented the chaos that could have come from freeing four million slaves at once.

***Johnson's Response to the Radicals*—** Although Johnson had worked hard to overcome poverty and a lack of formal education, he did not have the ability to be a strong but sensitive leader for the nation at that time. He was firm in his positions on Reconstruction, and when his policies were defied, he stubbornly refused to change and lashed back at those who opposed him. His stubbornness often forced his foes into harsher positions. Because Johnson refused to give any ground, his inflexibility disheartened moderates and drove them into the Radical camp. Soon, with the majority of Congress united against Johnson, Presidential Reconstruction was coming to an end.

SECTION REVIEW

1. How could Confederate states be restored to the Union under Lincoln's Ten Percent Plan?

2. How did Congress's plan differ from Lincoln's?

3. Who assumed the presidency after Lincoln's assassination?

4. The black codes might be said to have replaced what former southern institution?

 How could Johnson have improved his handling of Reconstruction?

Radical Republicans Take Over Reconstruction

Radical Republicans in the House were led by **Thaddeus Stevens** of Pennsylvania and Senate Radicals by **Charles Sumner** of Massachusetts. After refusing Southerners

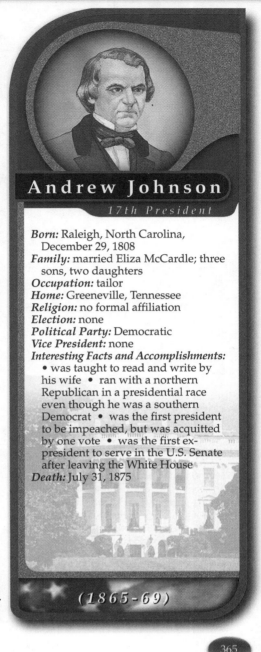

Andrew Johnson
17th President

Born: Raleigh, North Carolina, December 29, 1808
Family: married Eliza McCardle; three sons, two daughters
Occupation: tailor
Home: Greeneville, Tennessee
Religion: no formal affiliation
Election: none
Political Party: Democratic
Vice President: none
Interesting Facts and Accomplishments:
• was taught to read and write by his wife • ran with a northern Republican in a presidential race even though he was a southern Democrat • was the first president to be impeached, but was acquitted by one vote • was the first ex-president to serve in the U.S. Senate after leaving the White House
Death: July 31, 1875

(1865-69)

365

Objectives
Students should be able to
1. List and describe the important amendments and legislation passed during Radical Reconstruction.
2. Identify and describe the circumstances of Johnson's impeachment.
3. Name two of Johnson's achievements in foreign affairs.
4. Name the president who followed Andrew Johnson.

Section Review Answers

1. by having ten percent of the registered voters in 1860 take an oath to support the Constitution and the Union (p. 362)

2. Congress wanted fifty percent of voters to take the oath, new voters to swear they had not voluntarily supported the Confederacy, the abolition of slavery, and repudiation of Confederate debts and secession. (p. 363)

3. Andrew Johnson (p. 363)

4. slavery (p. 364)

If he had shown some willingness to compromise rather than stubbornly maintaining his positions, he might have improved his relationship with the Radical Republicans or at least kept the moderates on his side. (p. 365)

SECTION 3

Materials
• *Free Indeed: Heroes of Black Christian History* (BJUP)

Freedmen's Bureau

Officially known as the U.S. Bureau of Refugees, Freedmen, and Abandoned Lands, the Freedmen's Bureau faced presidential opposition from the beginning. Johnson claimed that it violated the Constitution for several reasons. First, it made the federal government responsible for the care of impoverished people. Second, it was passed into law by a Congress in which eleven states did not have seats. Johnson, like Lincoln, believed the Confederate states had never really left the Union. Johnson also criticized the bureau's vague definitions of "civil rights and immunities."

Despite Johnson's opposition, the Freedmen's Bureau went to work. Major General Oliver Otis Howard was appointed as its commissioner. Between 1868 and 1872, when it was abolished, the Bureau established more than one thousand schools for blacks and spent over $400,000 for teacher training. Although it had its own courts for cases involving freedmen, they were poorly organized and provided little justice. When the bureau was abolished in 1872, its unfinished work was carried on by the Freedmen's branch of the Adjutant General's Office.

Visit the Freedmen's Bureau Online at **www.freedmensbureau.com**.

Balance of Power

Note that when a two-thirds majority of the House and Senate are opposed to a president's views, they have the power to have their way in all legislation, and the president becomes almost helpless. Of course, the Supreme Court still has the power to declare laws unconstitutional, and therefore it provides a check against too much power.

Fourteenth Amendment

The Fourteenth Amendment played a key role in the debate over three key legal issues. The first was civil rights. The amendment guaranteed equal protection of the law for everyone. This provision was tested by the case of

Charles Sumner and Thaddeus Stevens led the Radical Republicans against President Johnson.

entrance into the House, they then took action to ensure that the legislative branch, and not the executive, would control Reconstruction. However, President Johnson could and did use his power to veto their acts. The president retained his power until February of 1866, when the Radicals gained control of two-thirds of both houses of Congress and could override his vetoes.

Radical Republican Legislation

While Radical Republican strength grew in Congress, several pieces of legislation were brought forward to fight against the black codes and to aid the freedmen in the South.

The Freedmen's Bureau—In March of 1865 Congress had passed laws to set up a short-term agency to provide aid for refugees. The **Freedmen's Bureau** was the first federal relief agency ever established. It issued rations of surplus army food and clothing to freed slaves and to poverty-stricken whites. It also sent agents into the South to establish schools and hospitals for blacks of all ages. The bureau tried to locate jobs for the freedmen and to prevent employers from exploiting them. Because Congress assumed that state governments would soon be able to provide relief services, the bureau was to be federally funded for only one year. Since Congress refused to recognize the new state governments, it voted to keep the bureau going and even to extend its powers. President Johnson vetoed two versions of the bill, but the Republicans united to override his veto the second time. The Freedmen's Bureau then continued its work.

The Fourteenth Amendment—Next, Congress voted to give blacks legal citizenship through the Civil Rights Act of 1866. Because Johnson believed that the Constitution gave the states power over citizenship, he vetoed the act, but Congress passed it over his veto. However, Congress still feared that it would be declared unconstitutional. In June of that year Congress solved the problem of granting blacks citizenship by proposing the Fourteenth Amendment. The longest amendment to date, the **Fourteenth Amendment** was, and still is, significant.

First, the amendment made all persons citizens of both the United States and of the states where they resided. It also prohibited

Lessons from the First Federal Relief Agency

The Civil War marked a turning point in the nation's history in more ways than the end of slavery. It ended the nip-and-tuck struggle between the states and the federal government over power. Forever after, the federal government reigned supreme, and its size grew unabated. This period is full of warnings for future generations about the potential dangers of this new federal power. Among the many modern policies attributed to the war is the first income tax (and the first complaints about unfairness and wrongdoing by tax officers). Another warning sign was the abuses under the Freedmen's Bureau, a precursor to the New Deal programs under Franklin Delano Roosevelt. While the bureau did a valuable service in helping starving people and protecting freedmen, it had a dark side common to any federal program that spends a lot of money. For one thing, the Radical Republicans used the bureau to "buy votes." Anytime the government hands out benefits, it gets political support from grateful recipients of the aid. Another dark side of the bureau was graft. With so much money and power, it was impossible to effectively oversee how the money was spent. Another danger of the bureau was its function to redistribute confiscated and "abandoned" land. The redistribution of wealth is a basic tenet of socialism and a temptation in federal relief programs. Discuss these problems with your class and have them share any other examples of big government and its abuses.

The Plight of Robert E. Lee

Robert E. Lee, who had served as commander in chief of the Confederate army, was one of many Confederate soldiers and leaders affected by the government's policies for Reconstruction. Since he had served in the Confederacy, Lee had lost his American citizenship.

After the surrender Lee applied for pardon and restoration of his citizenship. General Grant endorsed his request and sent it on to President Andrew Johnson. Although Lee was not aware of it, he was also to have taken an oath of allegiance. On October 2, 1865, when he was sworn in as president of Washington College, Lee took that oath. Proof of the oath-taking was then sent to Washington. President Johnson had the power to issue pardons and restore citizenship until 1868. Either Johnson never received the oath or he chose not to sign it (perhaps because Grant, whom he saw as a political rival, had made the request).

In 1868 the Fourteenth Amendment changed the system. Congress was allowed to pardon Confederates who had lost their citizenship by a two-thirds vote of each house.

Treason charges against Lee, his sons, and fourteen other Confederates were dropped in 1869. Yet he died in 1870 without regaining his citizenship.

In 1971 a historian rediscovered Lee's petition among some Civil War papers in the National Archives. The Virginia State Senate asked Congress to pass a resolution restoring Lee's citizenship posthumously (POSS chuh mus lee; after his death). In April 1974 the Senate approved his request and by June the House had concurred. One-hundred ten years after he had lost his citizenship, Lee's status as a man without a country ended.

any state from depriving a person of his life, liberty, or property without due process of law (a proper trial). Moreover, a state could not deny equal protection of its laws to any person under its jurisdiction.

Second, a state's representation in Congress would be based on its whole population. This provision meant that blacks were no longer to be counted as three-fifths of a person. States that denied voting rights to blacks could have the number of representatives they had in Congress reduced.

Third, those who had engaged in insurrection or rebellion against the United States would be barred from voting or holding office unless Congress specifically pardoned them by a two-thirds vote. Finally, Congress refused to assume Confederate debts or accept claims for any costs of freeing the slaves.

When ratified, the amendment would cancel black codes in the southern states as well as laws against blacks in some midwestern states. President Johnson urged southern states to vote against it. He held the amendment to be an invasion of states' rights. He traveled in the North and Midwest to give speeches against Radical Republicans running for the 1866 Congressional elections. Johnson's tour cost him support. His audiences rudely heckled him. Instead of ignoring them, Johnson lost his temper. Some people had rejected his plan for Reconstruction already because they feared it would put former Confederates back into power. Now many more were skeptical of his leadership.

When Congress convened in 1867, Reconstruction was wholly in Radical hands, and the phase of **Radical Reconstruction** had begun. By 1868 enough states had ratified the Fourteenth Amendment to put it into effect.

Further Radical Reconstruction Rule

Beginning in 1867 the Radical Republicans in Congress put their program into

367

Plessy v. Ferguson (1896). Railroads in Louisiana offered blacks and whites "separate but equal" accommodations. A black man challenged this practice in court, but the Supreme Court upheld it. It decided that separating the races did not imply that one was inferior; therefore, both were receiving the equal protection of the law. However, in 1954 the Supreme Court changed its mind in *Brown v. Board of Education of Topeka*. In this case it ruled against segregated schools, deciding that separate institutions were "inherently unequal." Affirmative action is another civil rights issue for which justification has been sought from the Fourteenth Amendment. In an 1880 case, Justice William Strong affirmed that the Fourteenth Amendment was intended to protect the civil rights of blacks but qualified that the protection was from actions that would harm them. Some suggest that his opinion supports the idea that separation favorable to blacks, as in preferences assigned as the result of affirmative action, might be acceptable.

A second legal issue was the regulation of business. It grew out of cases involving a meatpacking company that was granted a monopoly by the state of Louisiana. A group of white butchers sued on the grounds that the state was depriving them of property without the due process of law (another clause of the amendment). The Supreme Court decided in the late 1800s that the clause applied only to slaves, but one justice wanted to broaden the definition to include companies. His view was later adopted, and the amendment was cited as a protection for companies from regulation by states.

A third legal issue was the nationalization of the Bill of Rights. As the Constitution was originally written, only the federal government was required to protect the rights listed in the Bill of Rights. In *Adamson v. California* (1947), Justice Hugo Black stated his opinion that the Fourteenth Amendment was intended to apply

The Lessons of Obstinacy

Johnson's administration is a lesson in the impact of obstinacy. The Bible teaches the value of soft words and the folly of stubbornness. Note the negative impact of Johnson's campaigning during the 1866 elections—his anger helped his enemies. Even if he was right in his views, Johnson's attitude turned the moderates against him and helped the Radicals to pass their program and to impeach him. If possible, make parallels to modern examples of obstinate leaders who end up helping their enemies and hurting themselves.

the Bill of Rights to the states. In other words, the rights that the Constitution required the federal government to protect must also be protected by the states. Black's view was not adopted across the board, but certain key rights were nationalized as he proposed.

Martial Law

Note that the Reconstruction Act of 1867 placed the South under martial law as if it were a conquered foreign nation. This action, which embittered the South, was totally contrary to Lincoln's (and Johnson's) view that the South had never left the Union.

Carpetbaggers and Scalawags

Corruption was a major problem in the South during Reconstruction. Although some carpetbaggers and scalawags had a sincere interest in reforming the South, personal interest was often a greater concern. South Carolina's government gives a prime example of this corruption. During Reconstruction more than $200,000 was spent on furniture for the State House. The value of the furniture was no more than $18,000. Bills also approved large sums of money for chairs, mirrors, and food.

Corruption was not limited to the South, however. The state legislatures of Pennsylvania and New York were also filled with corrupt practices. In fact, Northern graft operations were even more organized. Corruption reached the highest levels during the Grant administration.

effect with great speed and little resistance. When the president vetoed their legislation, Congress quickly overrode his vetoes.

Reconstruction Act of 1867—The **Reconstruction Act of 1867** went far beyond the controls Lincoln and Johnson had wished to place on the South. This radical legislation put the area under military rule or "martial law," thus sending in the army to make sure that the South complied with the wishes of Congress. Naturally, Southerners resented this military occupation.

First, the act cut the South into five military districts, each ruled by a Union general. Second, it gave blacks the right to vote and hold office. At the same time the act denied voting rights to those who had served in the Confederacy. Third, southern states wanting to reenter the Union were to hold open conventions with both black and white voting delegates. These conventions were to draw up new state constitutions using the guidelines given by Congress. The act also required the states to submit their documents to Congress for approval. Finally, to return to the fold, states would be required to ratify the Fourteenth Amendment. When these requirements were met, the troops would be withdrawn.

Scalawags and Carpetbaggers in the South—Few former southern leaders were eligible to hold public offices, because they had lost their citizenship by serving the Confederacy. And since Congress had opened politics to blacks by its Reconstruction acts, southern politics now underwent great change. New groups now took command of the South.

Northerners who came south to assist in Radical Reconstruction were called **carpetbaggers.** (They were supposed to have come south carrying their possessions in small suitcases made from pieces of carpet.) Most car-

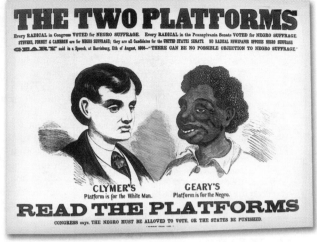

During Reconstruction some politicians used posters such as the one above to play upon the white voter's fears about blacks.

petbaggers were opportunists who came south seeking financial or political gain. Of course, Southerners resented them. A few carpetbaggers, however, were sincere men who came because they wanted to help the freedmen change the South. Some were Union soldiers who liked what they had seen of the South and decided to stay. Carpetbaggers took control of Southern politics for a while, but they also brought needed investment capital to a ravaged South.

White Southerners who supported Radical Reconstruction received the derisive name of **scalawag.** Some had been Unionists during the war and had no reason to change after. Others endorsed Radical Reconstruction because they honestly believed it was in the

Unjust Stereotypes

Talk to your students about the poster on this page. Discuss how the artist is playing to fears of the white people. How has the black man been portrayed? *(sloppy, ignorant, sleepy-eyed)* How is the white man portrayed in contrast? *(sensitive, intelligent looking, neatly dressed)*

Plans for Reconstruction

Make a simple chart comparing the Reconstruction Act of 1867 to previous plans for Reconstruction (the Ten Percent Plan, Johnson's Plan, and the Wade-Davis Bill). Compare the percentage of voters swearing an oath, the conditions for pardons, and extra conditions newly admitted states must accept. (See Activity B in the *Student Activities* book.)

South's best interest. Some scalawags were prewar Whigs seeking a new party since theirs had collapsed. However, there were scalawags who did deserve their bad name. Many were those who saw a chance to get ahead with the help of Radical Republican support and military protection. Most Southerners looked upon scalawags as traitors.

Although they did not control the government in any state, black freedmen did gain office in every southern state. Unfortunately, since blacks had no earlier political experience, they were sometimes more susceptible to improper influence. Radical Republicans often used the black officeholders as puppets for their purposes. Some of the blacks were bribed to promote the interests of carpetbaggers and scalawags. Since southern whites already resented their former slaves, they were especially critical of any black corruption. Most of the blacks who held national political offices—for example,

The House impeachment council that brought charges against President Johnson

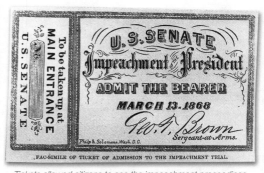
Tickets allowed citizens to see the impeachment proceedings.

Mississippi senators Hiram H. Revels and Blanche K. Bruce, and South Carolina's Robert Smalls—were well educated. Many blacks elected to offices served with dignity.

Congress Impeaches Johnson

Although the Congress passed its Radical legislation over Johnson's veto, he still enforced the laws that were passed. He carried out the laws because this was his constitutional duty. The Radical Republicans, however, were still unhappy with him and sought ways to limit what power he had. One executive power is to appoint officials. The Radicals feared that Johnson would remove those officials sympathetic to their views and replace them with his own men. Therefore, they passed the **Tenure of Office Act** in 1867. This act made it illegal to remove any presidential appointments approved by the Senate unless the Senate also approved their dismissal.

369

Black Christian Leaders

Several black Christian leaders upheld the dignity of their race after the Civil War. One was Matthew Anderson, whose story is told in the article "Matthew Anderson" in *Free Indeed: Heroes of Black Christian History*. The article "Charles Tindley" covers the life of another Christian worker at the beginning of the twentieth century. Four of the popular hymns he wrote are included. Another account of a great hymnwriter is "Charles Price Jones," who helped found the Holiness movement at the turn of the century.

Report on an Early Black Leader

Assign each student to give an oral report on one of the Southern black leaders during the era of Reconstruction. Hiram H. Revels, Blanche K. Bruce, and Robert Smalls are mentioned in the text. There were twenty-two blacks elected to Congress between 1879 and 1901.

God's Providence in the Abuse of Power

One of the recurrent themes in U.S. history is the growth of federal power and its abuses. The Founding Fathers' greatest concern in the establishment of a new federal government was the rise of tyranny. Each new power that the federal government assumes brings tyranny that much closer. But as in all other facets of human government, God uses this tyranny to accomplish His purposes.

Ask the students to discuss the ways that the Radical Republicans abused power and the good that came from it. *(They imposed their will on Southern governments; they attempted to remove the president; and they tried to maintain their power by keeping*

New Appointments

Andrew Johnson was eager to remove the radical secretary of war, Edwin Stanton, from his Cabinet. Stanton seemed to be working more against Johnson than for him. Johnson first tried to put Ulysses S. Grant into Stanton's position, but the Senate would not approve the appointment. Then Johnson fired Stanton outright and appointed Adjutant General Lorenzo Thomas to fill his post. Nine of the eleven articles of impeachment from the House were based on this action.

Opposition to Impeachment in the Senate

Of the nineteen who voted against conviction in the Senate, seven were Republicans. Six were against impeachment from the start, but Edmund G. Ross of Kansas was undecided. Knowing that Ross was wavering, supporters of the impeachment proceedings threatened him with everything from loss of his seat in the Senate to loss of his life if he did not vote their way. Despite the pressure, Ross became persuaded that the charges were unfounded and voted against the impeachment articles. Johnson remained in the presidency, but neither Ross nor any of the other Republicans who voted against impeachment were ever reelected to the Senate.

Grover Cleveland and the Tenure of Office Act

It was President Grover Cleveland in 1887 who declared that only the president had the power to remove his own appointees. The Supreme Court agreed with him and declared the Tenure of Office Act unconstitutional.

Johnson in the Senate

Six years after Johnson left the presidency, he was reelected to the Senate from the state of Tennessee. He served only a small amount of his term, however; for he died in the same year that he took office (1875).

Johnson tested the law by removing from office **Edwin Stanton,** Lincoln's holdover secretary of war. (Stanton had never upheld Johnson's views and now openly sided with the Radicals.) Stanton refused to leave. He barricaded himself behind his office doors, accepted food through the windows, and cooked for himself. He even slept in his office. Congress now believed it had grounds for impeaching, or bringing charges against, Johnson so that they could remove him from office. (See page 149.) In presidential impeachments the Constitution says that the House of Representatives is to file the charges; the Senate then serves as the trial court, and the chief justice of the Supreme Court presides as the judge. A two-thirds vote is required to remove the president. The basis for removal is "conviction of treason, bribery, or other high crimes and misdemeanors." A congressional committee did not believe President Johnson was guilty of such crimes, but the Radicals pressed on.

On February 24, 1868, the House voted to impeach Johnson. The president's trial under Justice Salmon P. Chase began March 13 and lasted until May 26. Johnson himself never attended the trial. He believed he had done nothing wrong and that his attendance would lend credence to his accusers' cause. Senators sold tickets to the affair, and at times the trial rivaled a theater performance.

Senators could not agree on whether the Tenure of Office Act was constitutional. Even if it had been, they did not know whether the act applied in Stanton's case. Stanton, after all, had been Lincoln's appointee before the Tenure of Office Act had been passed. The real issue was that Radicals were trying to get rid of the president because they disagreed with him politically, not because he was guilty of a crime. Removing a president for political reasons would have set a dangerous precedent.

Some senators saw this danger, and others knew that if Johnson were removed, Ben Wade, an extreme radical, would be named the next president. Wade's views on public finance, labor, women's suffrage, and blacks were too shocking for most Americans to accept at that time.

When the final vote was taken, thirty-five Senators voted to convict the president; nineteen voted against. This was one vote short of the total needed to remove Johnson. Johnson finished his term; the presidency was preserved. But Johnson's reputation was never the same. Years later, however, the Supreme Court completely cleared Johnson of any blame by declaring the Tenure of Office Act to be unconstitutional.

Johnson's Achievements in Foreign Affairs

Although Congress had kept Johnson's policies at home from working well, his

Secretary of State William Seward's "foolish" purchase of Alaska proved to be a great bargain.

Southern Democrats out of Congress. However, the freedmen received new protections under the Fourteenth and Fifteenth Amendments.)

Abuse of power is often the consequence of "abuse" of freedom. When businesses, people, and governments resist good changes, God often uses the central government to force them to make the changes. Students will see this happen again when Congress stepped in to help labor unions because businesses refused to make common-sense changes on the behalf of workers. While conservatives decry the use of federal power to limit the freedom of businessmen to run their businesses and to dispose of their property freely as they choose, God used this power as a check on human greed. In the same way, he has used federal power as a check on racial prejudice.

The Lowest Point in American History

Ask students to name the "lowest point" in American government that they have read so far. In other words, what is the most embarrassing action that the U.S. government has taken so far in the nation's history?

Without a doubt, the impeachment of Johnson should be included on any list of low points in government history. Discuss the reasons for this action, the dangers it posed, and the lessons we can learn today about the founders' wisdom in creating checks and balances between the legislative and executive branches. Can the students name any other low points in U.S. history that are yet to come? *(Three examples are the scandals under Grant, the resignation of Nixon, and the impeachment of Clinton.)*

achievements in foreign affairs were noteworthy. **William Seward,** his talented secretary of state, ably directed his foreign policy.

In 1864 Napoleon III, the emperor of France, had violated the Monroe Doctrine by setting up Austrian Archduke Maximilian (mak suh MIL yun) as the puppet emperor of Mexico. Since the Civil War occupied America's attention at the time, Lincoln and Seward only reprimanded the French for their actions, but they could not send troops to evict Maximilian. In 1866, however, President Johnson moved against the French. He sent fifty thousand veteran troops to the border, and their presence forced the withdrawal of French troops.

Seward was also an expansionist. He signed a treaty of friendship and commerce with China in 1868. In 1867 he secretly negotiated a treaty with Russia to purchase Alaska for $7 million. When President Johnson sought Senate approval, cries of "Seward's Folly," "Johnson's Polar Bear Garden," and "Frigidia" flooded the press. But within ten days the treaty went through by a thirty-seven to two vote. Years later this purchase would prove to be a great bargain for the United States.

President U.S. Grant

By 1868 Andrew Johnson had lost almost all influence in the Republican Party. For their presidential candidate in the election, the Republicans chose Ulysses S. Grant. The Democrats were still hampered by their ties to the old Civil War issues and by the Radical Republican takeover of the South, the party's former stronghold.

Even so, Grant only narrowly defeated the Democratic candidate, New York's governor Horatio Seymour. The support of a half-million new black voters helped bring about the Republican victory.

An 1868 campaign banner for the Republicans

The Fifteenth Amendment—Once in office Grant disappointed the Radicals. He did reward black support, however, by calling for the passage of the **Fifteenth Amendment.** This amendment kept states from denying the vote to any person "on account of race, color, or previous condition of servitude." (See

Purchase of Alaska

By the mid-nineteenth century, Russia was ready to get rid of its Alaskan territory. First, Britain and America were starting to push up from the south, and Russia was not eager to defend the territory militarily. In addition, Russia was not receiving adequate profits to convince it of the land's worth. Fur trading, formerly the principal source of revenue from the territory, had declined. Russia was just coming out of the Crimean War in need of funds for its treasury, and Alaska seemed to be a worthless drain on the nation's resources.

William Seward was so eager to purchase the Alaska territory that he began negotiations with the Russians before receiving authorization from the president. His preliminary offer to Russia was $5 million, but he found to his surprise that Congress was willing to offer $7 million. Despite the offer and the fact that the treaty passed by a substantial margin, Congress was not especially excited about the purchase. The treaty was passed in 1867, but an appropriation for the money was not approved until July 1868.

Later generations would praise Seward, though. He had acquired an area that was two times the size of Texas. And in that area was a wealth of natural resources that began to be unearthed in 1896 with the Klondike gold strike.

371

Do Good Generals Make Good Presidents?

Ask the students to name as many presidents as they can who were former generals. *(George Washington, Andrew Jackson, William Henry Harrison, Zachary Taylor, Ulysses S. Grant, Rutherford B. Hayes, Dwight D. Eisenhower)* Did any of these generals make good presidents? Why is it often easy for generals to get elected? *(name recognition and respect; note that Colin Powell was a popular choice for president after his victory in the Gulf War)* Why do good generals often make bad

presidents? *(They are used to giving orders, not making compromises and deals to please their supporters.)* Why do Americans keep electing war heroes? *(ignorance of history and an idealistic view of men)*

When "Special Interest Groups" Run the Government

Ask the students whether they see any connection between Reconstruction and Grant's scandals. What aspects of Reconstruction opened the door for corruption to spread so rapidly? *(Men's hearts are evil and prone to greed, and corruption*

seems to spread whenever the government spends money without political checks on its power.) The Radical Republicans controlled Congress; the president was passive; and large amounts of money were spent on new programs. Before the Civil War, political rivalries and limited government revenue restrained corruption.

Discuss any recent financial scandals related to the government. Is there any way to limit such abuse of power? Obviously, the easiest way is to make drastic cuts in federal spending. Then special interest groups have less to influence.

Scandals

Two of the most noteworthy scandals of the Grant administration were the gold conspiracy and the Crédit Mobilier scandals. Jay Gould and James Fisk received aid from the Grant administration as they gained control of much of the country's gold and then drove the price up to make huge profits. Vice President Colfax and members of Congress participated in the Crédit Mobilier scheme, whereby they owned stock in the construction company that received contracts from the Union Pacific Railroad. The government granted public funds for the railroad construction, and the politicians received large dividends from their Crédit Mobilier stock in return.

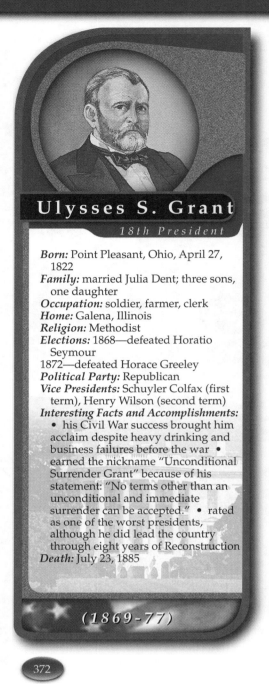

Ulysses S. Grant
18th President

Born: Point Pleasant, Ohio, April 27, 1822
Family: married Julia Dent; three sons, one daughter
Occupation: soldier, farmer, clerk
Home: Galena, Illinois
Religion: Methodist
Elections: 1868—defeated Horatio Seymour
1872—defeated Horace Greeley
Political Party: Republican
Vice Presidents: Schuyler Colfax (first term), Henry Wilson (second term)
Interesting Facts and Accomplishments:
• his Civil War success brought him acclaim despite heavy drinking and business failures before the war • earned the nickname "Unconditional Surrender Grant" because of his statement: "No terms other than an unconditional and immediate surrender can be accepted." • rated as one of the worst presidents, although he did lead the country through eight years of Reconstruction
Death: July 23, 1885

(1869-77)

372

pages 160-61.) Passage of the amendment kept Republicans in power by giving them more votes in northern states that still had antiblack laws. Since the southern states still had Republican governments that favored the blacks, the Fifteenth Amendment was ratified in less than a year. It took effect in 1870.

Grant was sympathetic to the plight of the South, and he limited the number of federal troops there. Six states—Alabama, Arkansas, Florida, South Carolina, North Carolina, and Louisiana—had been readmitted to the Union by the summer of 1868. (Tennessee had been readmitted in 1866.) Four remaining states—Georgia, Mississippi, Texas, and Virginia—held out until 1870. By the time they sought readmission, they were also required to ratify the Fifteenth Amendment.

The Grant Scandals—Ulysses S. Grant served two terms as president. Unfortunately he showed that a good general does not always make a good president. Both of Grant's terms in office were marked by political corruption. The corruption, largely the result of greed, was not the president's doing and existed on national, state, and local levels. But when the corruption was uncovered, the president allowed the dishonest to resign rather than face prosecution. He believed that prosecution would only divide the nation further. To distract the voters from the scandals, the party appealed to people to unite against the ex-rebels. Reviving these ill feelings, however, was not what the country wanted. The Radical Republicans, with their fierce hatred for the South, were losing power.

SECTION REVIEW

1. What was the first federal relief agency? What groups did it assist?

2. The basic purpose of the Fourteenth Amendment was to provide what for blacks?

Grant's Legacy, Good or Bad?

Discuss the ingredients of a man's reputation. Since all men have a sinful nature, what allows them to keep a good reputation in spite of their wrongs? Name some Bible characters and ask students to name the events that are associated most with their legacy: Noah, Saul, David, Solomon, Peter, and Paul. In each case these men did great wrongs as well as great good. Why do some keep a good reputation and not others? What reputation does Grant have? *(a good general and a terrible president)* Why is he generally well thought of? *(He was a hum-*

ble man; he overcame great obstacles to become commander of all Union armies; and—though it is not mentioned in the text—he fought a noble fight against cancer to finish writing his memoirs.) The lesson for us is that believers can overcome the embarrassment of the past.

Section Review Answers

1. the Freedmen's Bureau; freed slaves and poverty-stricken whites (p. 366)

2. citizenship (p. 366)

3. military rule or "martial law" (p. 368)

4. scalawags—Southerners who supported Radical Reconstruction, carpetbaggers—Northerners who went south to assist in Radical Reconstruction, freedmen—former slaves (p. 68)

5. Edwin Stanton; the Tenure of Office Act (pp. 369-70)

6. He forced the withdrawal of French troops from Mexico, signed a treaty

SECTION 4

Objectives
Students should be able to
1. Identify Bourbon Reconstruction.
2. Describe the circumstances of the disputed election of 1876.

Why Bourbon?
Bourbon was a nickname used to denote a politician who was so conservative that he clung to outmoded ideas. Its primary use was with the Southern Democrats of the late 1800s.

3. What type of system did the Reconstruction Act of 1867 establish to enforce Congress's will in the South?

4. Who were the scalawags, the carpetbaggers, and the freedmen?

5. The conflict between Johnson and the Radical Republicans came to a climax when Johnson attempted to remove whom from office? His action was said to be a violation of what law?

6. What significant contributions did Johnson make in foreign affairs?

7. Who won the election of 1868?

 What potential danger did Johnson's impeachment trial pose for our system of government?

Bourbon Reconstruction Begins

Even while Grant was still in office, views toward Reconstruction were changing. Many Republican supporters were beginning to think that abandoning blacks and Southerners might be better than losing the whole country to the turmoil of Radical Reconstruction. They believed that peace in the South would certainly be better for business. The country was sick of bitter controversy and scandal. These attitudes paved the way for **Bourbon Reconstruction,** reconstruction led by conservative Southerners, or "Redeemers."

Liberal Republicans in 1872 persuaded Congress to pardon the remaining former Confederate leaders. A General Amnesty Act in 1872 pardoned all but a few hundred Confederate leaders. Those who had held federal offices at the time of secession were

An 1876 campaign banner for the Democrats

among those excluded. This action would allow many former southern leaders to regain their influence in government.

Although the blacks had gained rights on paper, the white Southerners did not find it easy to accept the changes that made blacks their legal equals. While blacks and Radicals were able to hang on to offices for a while, they soon found they could not match the organization and experience of Southerners who now sought to "redeem the South" from

373

---

of friendship and commerce with China, and purchased Alaska. (p. 371)

7. Ulysses S. Grant (p. 371)

 The charges against Johnson were really political, not criminal. If he had been convicted, the precedent of removing officials for political differences would have been set, upsetting the balance of power between branches. (p. 370)

SECTION 4

Materials
• No materials

Shifts in the Political Winds
The Reconstruction era shows how quickly political winds can shift. Voters get tired of controversy, turmoil, and scandal. Eventually, they will sacrifice principle in the interest of peace and getting "back to business as usual." Discuss whatever political debate is on the front pages of the newspaper today in America, and warn the students not to get so caught up in the heat of the moment that they lose sight of the fact that public opinion is sure to change someday and possibly soon. What is true in national politics is also true on a personal basis. Our job as Christians is to advocate what is right, no matter which way the political winds are blowing.

Rutherford B. Hayes

Rutherford B. Hayes was a man of honor and humility. He fought with distinction in the Civil War. He was wounded four times and had a horse shot out from under him four times. When supporters wanted him to run for Congress during the war, he agreed but refused to campaign since he felt that his first duty was to his regiment.

After a term in Congress and three terms as governor of Ohio, Hayes was selected as the Republican candidate for president. Still he did not become puffed up with his success. He did not believe that he would win the election. (He had good grounds for his belief. The Democrats had experienced a renewed surge of power in the midterm election of 1874, and their strength had increased even more since then.) When the first returns on election night indicated a victory for Tilden, Hayes went to bed, unaware of the maneuvering that was to follow.

Before he took office, Hayes declared that he would seek only one term. He wanted to reform the civil service system, and he knew that he could pursue his agenda more easily if he were not seeking re-election. He stuck to his promise of choosing workers because of their merit. In fact, he made his own party angry by choosing a capable ex-Confederate for his Cabinet. Congress did not accept the changes in the civil service that Hayes wanted, but he did pave the way for those reforms to be reintroduced and passed in the future.

Technology in the White House

Rutherford Hayes had the opportunity to welcome at least two major inventions to the White House. Thomas Edison brought his phonograph for the president to inspect. And a telephone was installed for the first time in the executive mansion. The problem with having a telephone at this time was that not many others in Washington had telephones, so there was no one to call.

black rule. Southern states began the process of turning out blacks and Republicans and replacing them with southern Democrats. It was only in areas still occupied by Federal forces that Republican governments held on a bit longer. Grant, meanwhile, became more and more reluctant to send troops into the South to keep Republicans in power.

The Disputed Election of 1876

Since the Grant administration had been marred by one scandal after another and since corruption existed in some state and local governments as well, both political parties chose honest reformers as presidential candidates in 1876. When the results came in, Democrat **Samuel J. Tilden** of New York won the popular vote. He also had an electoral college vote of 184, compared to 165 for **Rutherford B. Hayes,** his opponent. But the votes of three southern states occupied by Federal troops—Florida, Louisiana, and South Carolina—were disputed. If the Democratic votes from those states were counted, Tilden would win easily. But if the Republican votes were accepted, Hayes would win, 185 to 184.

This was an unusual situation. Whose electoral votes should be counted? Finally Congress appointed a special electoral commission. Five senators, five representatives, and five Supreme Court justices were picked for the commission. Seven of the commissioners were Republicans; seven were Democrats. Justice David Stevens was an independent. But he resigned rather than cast the deciding vote. His replacement, a Republican, voted to accept the Republican ballots, making Hayes the president.

The Hayes Presidency

Even though the Republicans won in 1876, the election was the final blow to the harsh Reconstruction of the Radicals. Rutherford B. Hayes had sought the support of southern whites, who favored his economic

Lemonade Lucy

Lucy Ware Webb Hayes was popular throughout her life for her moral uprightness and charity. When Lucy was only two, her father died while on a trip to Kentucky to arrange for the freeing of his slaves. Lucy's mother was a woman of strong convictions, and she shared them with her two sons and daughter. Lucy was trained in religious schools along with her two older brothers; she later attended Wesleyan Women's College (the first chartered college for women in the United States) at age sixteen and graduated with honors. Her commencement essay, entitled "The Influence of Christianity on National Prosperity," was read at her graduation.

The young lawyer Rutherford B. Hayes was attracted by Lucy's beauty as well as by her reputation for religious devotion and intelligence. One year after her graduation, the two were engaged; and on December 30, 1852, they were married. She encouraged him as he defended fugitive slaves in court. In 1856 he first made a public stand against slavery by joining the new Republican Party. With the coming of the Civil War, he believed it was his duty to join the Union army. Lucy did not discourage him, and when he was wounded in September of 1862, she joined him at the battlefront to nurse him back to health. Whenever she visited the Twenty-third Ohio Regiment, which he commanded, she spent much time encouraging the sick, writing for them, and tending to their needs. The grateful soldiers affectionately called her "Mother Lucy."

While still serving in the army, Hayes was elected to Congress. He served there from 1864 until he was elected the governor of Ohio in 1867. During his three terms in the Governor's Mansion, Lucy proved to be a perfect hostess and tremendous support to her husband. She was especially active in community services, and by her labors the Home for Soldiers' Orphans was started at Xenia, Ohio, in 1869. She and her husband remained aloof from the scandals and waste of the Grant administration. When Hayes was elected president in 1877, he brought with him a wife who was well prepared for her role as First Lady.

From the day of the inauguration, Lucy set a new trend of modesty and dignity in Washington. As the first First Lady with a college

---

Stealing Votes in America

Often Americans act shocked by the rampant cheating in Third World elections. But U.S. history proves that this country is not free from cheating. In fact, in the 1872 election, cheating "threw" the presidential election. The final results had nothing to do with the people's votes because the counting of ballots could not be trusted. Can the students recall what other election was unfairly thrown to a candidate, despite popular desires? *(the "corrupt bargain" of 1828, p. 226)* Why do Americans have such faith in their balloting? *(Voting reforms, such as*

the secret ballot, are discussed in later chapters; in addition, votes are a matter of public record and can be tested by bringing the results to court.)

degree, she was hailed as a "new woman" in a new period of American history. The couple continued to have receptions and balls, but they were much more modest than the extravagant ones of the previous administration. The Hayes family was wholesome and God-fearing. The daily routine included after-dinner family gatherings in the Red Room to sing popular ballads and hymns. Afterward they retired to the Blue Room for family devotions and prayer.

The most noted trait of Lucy's stay in the White House was her insistence on abstinence from all gambling and liquor and from most dances. She was labeled as "Lemonade Lucy" and was criticized when she would not allow alcoholic beverages in the White House. But she was so gracious about her views that she gained the respect and good-humored support of the Washington officials. Her popularity did much to improve the popularity of her husband.

Two events during Hayes's administration are popular stories from White House lore. On Sunday, December 30, 1877, the couple held their twenty-fifth wedding anniversary in the Blue Room. Lucy dressed up in her original satin gown, many of the original guests were present, and the original minister led them in a renewal of their wedding vows. After the ceremony the two youngest children were baptized. The other event came on the following Easter, when Lucy came to the rescue of some children who were egg-rolling on Capitol grounds. When some Congressmen told them to leave, Lucy invited the children to the White House lawn. A similar invitation for Easter egg rolling has been given every year since.

Rutherford B. Hayes
19th President

Born: Delaware, Ohio, October 4, 1822
Family: married Lucy Ware Webb; seven sons, one daughter
Occupation: lawyer
Home: Spiegel Grove, Fremont, Ohio
Religion: no formal affiliation
Election: 1876—elected by an electoral commission over Samuel J. Tilden in a disputed election
Political Party: Republican
Vice President: William A. Wheeler
Interesting Facts and Accomplishments:
  • took oath of office privately and had no inaugural parade or ball because of national turmoil over his disputed election • first president to visit the Pacific Coast (1880) • had the first telephone installed in the White House • his wife was the first president's wife who was a college graduate; she received the nickname "Lemonade Lucy" because she served lemonade instead of liquor at White House receptions
Death: January 17, 1893

(1877–81)

375

Literature of the Period

Two popular and influential books were published during Hayes's presidency. One was *Uncle Remus: His Songs and His Sayings.* Joel Chandler Harris, an author and journalist from Georgia, wrote the Uncle Remus stories. He spent four years of his youth working as a printer for a plantation owner who published a newspaper. During that time he not only received encouragement to write but also made the acquaintance of the plantation slaves, learning their habits, their speech, and their stories.

Harris's Uncle Remus is a former slave who works for a Southern family. He tells animal fables to the young son of the family. The main characters in the fables are Brer Rabbit, Brer Fox, Brer Bear, and Brer Wolf; the small but clever Brer Rabbit usually defeats the larger animals. Besides entertaining, the books taught about Southern culture and ideology. Uncle Remus was so popular that Harris published two more collections of his stories. He also wrote other books about life in the South during and after the Civil War.

The other book was *Ben-Hur* by Lew Wallace. Wallace served in both the Mexican and Civil Wars. He was a major general in the Union army in the latter conflict. Also having experience as a lawyer, he was chosen as an observer at the official ballot counting in New Orleans and Florida for the disputed election of 1876. President Hayes chose him to be governor of the New Mexican territory, and President Garfield appointed him official representative of the United States to the Ottoman Empire.

Wallace was inspired to write *Ben-Hur* after a discussion with an outspoken atheist, Colonel Robert Ingersoll. Wallace had had some limited religious training, but he found that he had no responses to Ingersoll's arguments. This discovery led him to a study of the Bible and eventually to the writing of *Ben-Hur.* Wallace said that he was converted to Christ long before he finished writing the book, which tells about a first-century Jew and his journey to Christ. This was not Wallace's only book, but it was certainly his most popular. It was the best-selling novel of the nineteenth century and has never gone out of print.

Hayes's Economic Policy

Hayes had hoped that introducing moderation into government would ingratiate Republicans with Southern whites. His hopes were disappointed, however; he was unable to convince even conservatives in the South to join the party of Radical Reconstruction. But he did find those who agreed with his economic policy. He held staunchly to a conservative position. Despite requests from businessmen and farmers for the government to issue more paper and silver money, Hayes pushed for maintaining the gold standard as a means of keeping the currency strong and preventing inflation from rising.

SECTION 5

Objectives

Students should be able to
1. Describe the sharecropping system that developed in the South.
2. Explain how industry began to grow in the South.
3. Explain why the South became the *Solid South.*
4. Identify the Ku Klux Klan and explain how Congress reacted to it.

Cotton Production

The South damaged itself economically by focusing too much on the production of cotton. Cotton was a popular crop since it brought instant cash. Landholders often required their sharecroppers to grow cotton; local merchants did the same with farmers who sought loans. Cotton production, which had drastically diminished during the war, boomed back to new heights.

---

policies. To gain their support, he embraced policies that were to their liking. Undoubtedly southern Democrats chose not to dispute his election because he had promised the South the freedoms it wanted. However, Hayes soon found that he had bargained away most of his presidential power. By the time he saw the real picture, it was too late to change his position.

Once in office Hayes pleased the Democrats more than he did his own party. In April of 1877, a month after taking office, Hayes withdrew the last federal troops from South Carolina and Louisiana. With troops no longer supervising elections, Democratic governors soon replaced the Republicans in power. With the military gone and with white southern Democrats back in control in the southern states, Reconstruction now followed the dictates of these state leaders.

SECTION REVIEW

1. What did the General Amnesty Act do?
2. What action did President Hayes take to please Southerners?

 What was unusual about the 1876 election?

Recovery in the South

While government tried to deal with the South's problems during the phases of Reconstruction, many unusual features developed in southern life. The South's people, economy, and political organization were molded by the pressures of Reconstruction.

Economic Aspects of Reconstruction

Because the Civil War had destroyed the South's plantation system, the freedmen were at once without jobs. Some hoped that the government would take over the old plantations and from them give every freed slave forty acres and a mule. Although some politi-

---

cians supported such a plan, it never came to pass. While southern farmland needed laborers to grow its crops once again, there was no money to pay hired hands. To meet the needs of southern agriculture under such conditions, **sharecropping** became common.

Sharecropping—Blacks and poor whites became involved in this new economic system. Sharecroppers farmed small plots owned by planters and paid their annual rent for the use of the land with a part, or share, of their crop. Since sharecroppers had little money, especially at the beginning of the season, they borrowed for seed and provisions. Often the landlord was their creditor and owned the local store. When the harvest came in, the sharecropper squared up. If the sharecropper broke even, he was fortunate. He often started the next season in debt, however. The average sharecropper showed a profit only two years out of twenty-five. As a result the sharecropper was locked into a cycle of debt and poverty. The chances of breaking out of it were small indeed. Under such conditions, having the right to vote meant little. Most sharecroppers were more concerned about putting food on the family table.

Industry—During Reconstruction the Industrial Revolution finally reached the South. The Southerners had little money for industry, but many Northerners had capital and were eager to make profitable investments. These men saw the South as a place of opportunity. Consequently railroads, steelmaking, and the textile industry all expanded widely. As the need for laborers increased, Southerners moved from rural areas to factory towns and cities. The South's economy began to boom. By 1890 Southerners and Northerners spoke hopefully of a "New South" that would rival the North as an economic force.

One feature of southern industry was the **mill town.** Mill towns had some of the same features as plantations. The owner or investors

---

Section Review Answers

1. pardoned all but a few hundred Confederate leaders (p. 373)

2. He withdrew the last federal troops from South Carolina and Louisiana. (p. 376)

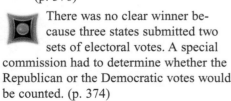 There was no clear winner because three states submitted two sets of electoral votes. A special commission had to determine whether the Republican or the Democratic votes would be counted. (p. 374)

SECTION 5

Materials

- *Roll of Thunder, Hear My Cry* (1976) by Mildred D. Taylor
- Activity B from Chapter 18 of the *Student Activities* manual

History Skills: Solving the South's Postwar Problems

The "History Skills" activity at the end of this chapter requires students to synthesize the information in this chapter. This is a difficult, controversial period in American history, and the activity requires students to think through some of the difficulties that the country faced.

built the housing, usually identical rows of houses near the factory site. The mill owners often built towns with churches and other community needs such as stores and doctors' offices. Often the workers bought needed items like food and clothing from company stores. Generally, employers in the textile industry hired whole families. Manufacturers of machines lowered the heights of their looms so that children could work them.

Political Trends

The prosperity of the nation through most of the era helped the Republicans control the presidency and usually Congress during most of the Reconstruction years. Stirring up war hatreds, or "waving the bloody shirt," also helped them stay in power, because Republicans were associated with winning the war and with freeing the slaves. The Republicans made inroads right after the war as the vote was given to blacks for the first time and ex-Confederate whites were barred from the polls. But when southern "Redeemers" got their power back, the Republican Party declined dramatically in the South.

Because Southerners generally blamed the war and the hardships of Reconstruction on the Republicans, the South aligned itself with the Democratic Party. For a century the South voted solidly for Democratic candidates almost without exception. Sometimes when people referred to the South's strong support of the Democratic Party, they called it the Solid South.

In 1866 a secret organization, the **Ku Klux Klan,** was founded to frighten blacks and whites sympathetic to black interests in order to keep blacks away from the polls. Their least offensive tactic was to boycott businesses and force them to close. More unsavory were Klansmen dressed as white-hooded ghosts who rode through black communities at night, erecting burning crosses and even beating or killing blacks who tried to exercise their civil rights.

The Ku Klux Klan tried to prevent blacks from exercising their political rights.

Unfortunately, the demand for cotton was not rising. When Great Britain was cut off from the South during the Civil War, it turned to India, Brazil, and Egypt to fill the void left by its major cotton supplier. These new suppliers not only solved the immediate crisis but also continued their trade with Britain after the South resumed production. The combination of foreign competition and increased domestic output pushed cotton prices down. The depressed cotton market hurt independent farmers and sharecroppers alike.

Social Adjustments of Blacks

Emancipation opened up a whole series of social issues. Faced with the prospect of freedom, blacks had many decisions to make about how they would live. First, they had to decide where they would live. Whether or not to stay on the old plantation was often a matter of the treatment received while under slavery. Even if a family decided to stay, they were likely to move out of the old slave quarters into their own place, perhaps back in the woods. Communities for freed blacks were also popular.

Second, freed slaves had to decide how to spend their time. Education was a major interest to blacks of all ages. Basic grammar schools sprung up throughout the South. Many agricultural laborers paid one-tenth of their income (about $1.00 or $1.50 a month) to send their children to these schools. Higher education was also a concern. The black community needed leaders for the future, so schools were established to train preachers, teachers, and other professionals.

Third, freed slaves had to decide how they would run their families. A first step in getting a family life established was to reunite those who had been separated. Many husbands and wives and parents and children went to great lengths to find each other. Once they were reunited, families began to look for more traditional roles. Black women wanted to stay at home rather than work in the fields, and

Teaching History Through Literature

Newbery medal winner *Roll of Thunder, Hear My Cry* (1976) by Mildred Taylor portrays a black sharecropping family in Mississippi during the 1950s. Some disturbing elements (e.g., burnings) need to be discussed in class. You may want to read portions of this compelling book to your class. It can also be assigned for reading later in conjunction with the civil rights movement in Chapter 28.

parents wanted to keep their children from forced labor.

Finally, freed slaves had to decide how they would worship. Most worshiped separately from whites. Once it was no longer illegal, blacks established a number of their own churches, mostly Methodist and Baptist.

Ku Klux Klan

The Ku Klux Klan was founded in 1866. A group of Confederate veterans met at Pulaski, Tennessee, to establish a social fraternity. The name they adopted came from the Greek word *kyklos,* meaning "circle" or "band," and the English word *clan.* Although the group seemed rather innocent at first in its tactics (e.g., pretending to be ghosts), it took on a more sinister tone when its members (or those posing as members) turned to violence. Its goals were to defeat Radical Republicans in the South and to suppress blacks.

Some believe that the burning of a cross was not a practice of the earliest Klan but was introduced by *The Clansman,* a novel by a North Carolina minister and writer, Thomas Dixon. In the book several Klansmen are preparing to take vengeance for the death of a young woman. They copy an old Scottish rite known as the Fiery Cross. After they burn wood fashioned into the shape of a cross, they send the burnt cross around to various villages, calling their fellow Klan members to action.

Civil Rights

The Fourteenth and Fifteenth Amendments, along with the Civil Rights Acts of the 1860s and 1870s, may be considered additional attempts to guarantee blacks their civil rights. These acts and amendments provided a solid framework of laws to protect civil rights, not only for blacks but for all Americans. These acts were overlooked or unheeded, however, for nearly a century. The failure to deal with these issues in the 1800s caused the country to face even greater trials when the abuses were brought to light in the mid-1900s.

Southern moderates and many Northerners were upset by the Klan's activities. Congress passed two acts in 1870 and 1871, the Force Act and the Ku Klux Klan Act, to deal with Klan abuses. The acts outlawed the use of force to prevent people from voting and gave President Grant the power to place federal troops in polling places to ensure everyone's voting rights. The Klan was officially disbanded, but in reality it went underground.

Civil Rights

Congress passed two acts to give blacks citizenship and all of its privileges or civil rights. The Civil Rights Act of 1866, noted earlier, had granted freedmen the same rights and legal protection as whites regardless of local laws. A second act, the Civil Rights Act of 1875, guaranteed equal accommodations in public places, such as inns and theaters. It also said blacks could serve on juries. However, the bill did not provide any means of enforcing its provisions. The Supreme Court further weakened the legislation when in 1883 it declared the social provisions of the bill to be unconstitutional.

As the years passed, concern for the rights of the blacks lessened. The Civil Rights Acts were no longer enforced, although they did serve as precedents for the civil rights acts passed in the twentieth century. In the meantime blacks found little political equality.

Reforms in the South

Before the war the South had collected few taxes for public purposes. After the war both taxes and spending increased. Many people were critical of the high spending of southern governments, but in many instances the spending was justified. For the first time southern states began providing free public education. Prison systems were improved. Care for mentally and physically handicapped people developed, and imprisonment for debt was abolished.

Reconstruction Evaluated

Reconstruction was generally not a happy time for anyone. Northerners were not satisfied with its processes or results, and many Southerners remained bitter. The Civil War and Reconstruction had caused the South to change economically and socially. However, not all the changes were ushered in smoothly. While many social advances were later lost, a foundation for future change had been laid in the postwar years.

Some critics believe that Reconstruction was unduly hard on the South. Radical Republicans had gone the furthest treating the South more as a foreign nation than a part of the United States. However, any attempt to rebuild the South would have been difficult considering the political, economic, and social devastation of the region.

Other critics believe Reconstruction did not go far enough. While on paper it ensured civil rights for blacks, those rights did not become permanently established during Reconstruction. The granting of such rights was a major step, but few whites even in the North were willing for blacks to gain significant social and political power. Reconstruction left many social, political, and economic problems for future generations to solve, but it also began the legislation and set an example for present Americans to follow or improve.

Reconstruction's chances for success were limited still further by great changes that America was undergoing at the same time. America was industrializing, and the industrial age brought a whole new set of problems. In both Reconstruction and the industrial era, people tried to solve these problems in new ways. Sometimes the solutions proposed were

Like No Other Rebellion in History

Students should learn every aspect of the American Civil War, from beginning to end, as a point of comparison with other civil wars throughout history and in other countries today. Just as the American Revolution was followed by years of turmoil, so too were the years following the Civil War. Perhaps the most amazing aspect of America's Civil War is that no heads rolled in the aftermath. As one historian has said, "Probably no large-scale and unsuccessful revolt has ever ended with so little head-rolling." No leaders were hanged for

political offenses, although the commander of the infamous Andersonville prison was hanged for murder.

What Next?

The end of this unit on the Civil War is an important place to pause, looking back and looking ahead to the remaining eras of U.S. history. Look over the outline of the book, particularly the titles of the remaining chapters. Ask the students to summarize the nation's main concerns in the previous chapters. Now that slavery was dead and interest in the South was gone, where would

the nation direct its energies? It is often said that people need an enemy to fight, a cause to win. What would become the next great cause, the next great enemy? Note that the industry of the nation, so long distracted by internal division, now exploded with productivity. But the Industrial Revolution also introduced new enemies to conquer, such as labor demands and immigration. Now that the nation's borders were complete (except for Hawaii), it also had to decide its role in the changing world, where imperialism was the order of the day. Help

merely experiments. When they did not work, they should have been discarded.

Unfortunately, when the people of a country fail to assume their responsibility, government moves in. Some of the problems of Reconstruction should have been solved first by individuals willing to follow biblical precepts on how to treat others. Some problems could have been solved by churches or private groups. But when they were not solved these ways, the federal government moved in. And life for Americans was really never the same again, as federal government powers began to increase.

SECTION REVIEW

1. How did sharecropping get its name?
2. In what kind of community did southern factory workers sometimes live?
3. What was the purpose of the Ku Klux Klan?
4. Why did civil rights legislation of the late 1800s bring little real change for blacks?

What answer could be made to the charge that Reconstruction went either too far or not far enough?

SUMMARY

At the end of the Civil War the South's government, economy, and society were in disarray. Because of its condition, the South needed a time of reconstruction. The Reconstruction did not come easily or smoothly, however, because of conflicting policies and desires in the nation. Presidents Lincoln and Johnson tried to restore the South quickly and with little punishment. Radical Republicans in Congress opposed these lenient policies and determined to make Reconstruction follow their strict guidelines. Eventually the Radicals lost their control, and Southerners were able to finish Reconstruction on their own terms.

students to see how these subjects became the natural topics of the next chapters.

Section Review Answers

1. Sharecroppers farmed small plots owned by planters and paid rent with a share of their crops. (p. 376)
2. mill towns (p. 376)
3. to frighten blacks and whites sympathetic to black interests away from the polls (p. 377)
4. It provided no measures for enforcement; the Supreme Court declared sections unconstitutional; and time eased pressures for reform. (p. 378)

Reconstruction was difficult, yet no recovery from war would be completely painless. On the other side, though racial equality did not become a reality at this time, important legislative steps set precedents for future action on civil rights. (p. 378)

Chapter Review Ideas

Student Activity B: Problems in the Presidency
This matching activity reviews the main terms and events associated with each president in the chapter.

Student Activity B: Plans for Reconstruction
This chart summarizes the four plans to reconstruct the South.

Chapter Review

People, Places, and Things to Remember

Reconstruction	Thaddeus Stevens	Edwin Stanton
freedmen	Charles Sumner	Fifteenth Amendment
Presidential Reconstruction	Freedmen's Bureau	William Seward
Ten Percent Plan	Fourteenth Amendment	Bourbon Reconstruction
Radical Republicans	Radical Reconstruction	Samuel J. Tilden
Wade-Davis Bill	Reconstruction Act of 1867	Rutherford B. Hayes
amnesty	carpetbaggers	sharecropping
Thirteenth Amendment	scalawag	mill town
black codes	Tenure of Office Act	Ku Klux Klan

Review Questions

Match each item with the corresponding man.

1. Ten Percent Plan
2. impeached president
3. secretary of war
4. Alaska purchase
5. presidential scandals
6. withdrew the last federal troops from the South

  a. Ulysses S. Grant
  b. Rutherford B. Hayes
  c. Andrew Johnson
  d. Abraham Lincoln
  e. William Seward
  f. Edwin Stanton

Unscramble these letters to find the names of groups involved in Reconstruction.

7. TARGEBACSPREG (Northerners in the South)
8. DEFEMERN (slaves no longer)
9. PRORRASHECEPS (poor farmers)
10. GACLASAWS (despised Southerners)

Match the following legislation and amendments with their effects.

11. Thirteenth Amendment
12. Fourteenth Amendment
13. Reconstruction Act of 1867
14. Tenure of Office Act
15. Fifteenth Amendment

  a. made all persons citizens
  b. used to impeach Johnson
  c. abolished slavery
  d. gave blacks the vote
  e. put the South under military rule

Questions for Discussion

16. Why is Reconstruction a good name for the time following the Civil War?
17. How might Reconstruction have been different if Lincoln had lived?

380

Chapter Review Answers

1. d (p. 362)
2. c (p. 370)
3. f (p. 370)
4. e (p. 371)
5. a (p. 372)
6. b (p. 376)
7. CARPETBAGGERS (p. 368)
8. FREEDMEN (p. 361)
9. SHARECROPPERS (p. 376)
10. SCALAWAGS (p. 368)
11. c (p. 364)
12. a (p. 366)
13. e (p. 368)
14. b (p. 369)
15. d (p. 371)
16. Answers will vary. The South (its homes, businesses, and government) was being rebuilt after its destruction in the war.
17. Answers will vary. He might have had the power to prevent the Radical Republicans from taking control. If the South had accepted his generous proposals, the results might have been less painful and the recovery more complete.

History Skills

Writing a History Paper

Writing an essay for a history class will be much easier if you follow some basic procedures. The first step is to break the topic down into logical parts. Let's go through an example together. Suppose the essay topic is "The United States had difficulty trying to solve the South's problems following the Civil War." How can you break down this topic? A good approach is to discuss each major problem separately. A possible outline appears below.

 I.   The South needed to raise money to meet basic needs for food, services, and industry.

 II. The South needed to give freedmen a new place in a changed society.

 III. The South needed to establish new state governments.

After you choose a basic outline, you need to decide what things to discuss under each main point. Northerners and Southerners had completely different ideas about how to solve each problem. Perhaps under each point you could discuss (A) the solutions adopted by the federal government and Northerners, and (B) the solutions later adopted by Southerners. Your discussion under each main point would look something like this:

 I.   The South needed to raise money to meet basic needs for food, services, and industry.
    A. Northern ideas
    B. Southern ideas

Now all that is left for you is to fill in the details! Look for key terms and concepts. Below is a list of the key terms under each main point in the outline:

 I.   The South needed to raise money to meet basic needs for food, services, and industry.
    A. Northern ideas: the Freedmen's Bureau
    B. Southern ideas: mill towns

 II. The South needed to give freedmen a new place in a changed society.
    A. Northern ideas: constitutional amendments, civil rights acts
    B. Southern ideas: black codes, the Ku Klux Klan, sharecropping

 III. The South needed to establish new state governments.
    A. Northern ideas: the Reconstruction Act of 1867, carpetbaggers
    B. Southern ideas: scalawags, Redeemers, and the Solid South

Write a short paragraph on each of the main ideas above (three paragraphs). To complete your essay, write a brief introductory paragraph stating your topic. Then write a brief concluding paragraph. Ask your teacher for help if you do not know how to write an introduction and conclusion.

History Skills

Answers will vary. Most students will need to follow the outline provided. Motivated students may want to tackle a more challenging subject on their own. You may want to make the English teacher aware of your project and check to see what they have already learned in English class.

Nearly one hundred years after the Civil Rights Act of 1866 was passed, civil rights gained national attention again. Various groups within the nation pressed for legislation that would provide for actual social changes. The following people represent several of these movements. As you read about them, consider the issues they fought for and the methods they used. Were they fighting for good causes? Did they use methods that would be acceptable to Christians? How should Christians respond to these issues?

Hispanic Rights: Cesar Chavez (1927-93)

Cesar Chavez was born near Yuma, Arizona, and grew up migrating across the Southwest with his family. Like other Hispanic migrant workers, he made less than minimum wage and had to endure life in pitiful work camps. After serving in World War II, Chavez began working in an apricot field near San Jose. It was there that he became involved with an organization called the Community Service Organization (CSO). Chavez eventually became its general director and dreamed of uniting farm workers and helping them fight against poor work conditions. He later resigned and formed his own National Farm Worker's Organization. In 1966 he merged his organization with another union to form the United Farm Workers (UFW).

To fight for higher pay, family health coverage, and pension benefits, Chavez used the same nonviolent tactics of Gandhi and Martin Luther King Jr. One of his most successful methods was the boycott—refusing to buy from, sell to, or deal with a company. In 1965 he organized a boycott against grape growers around Delano, California. By 1970 most growers had signed contracts with the UFW. Another method he used was the fast. Chavez held a thirty-six-day fast in 1988 to protest the use of poisonous pesticides where grape workers worked. Despite his death in 1993, the UFW has continued Chavez's fight for Hispanic workers' rights in America.

Native American Rights: Russell Means (1939-)

Born in 1939, Russell Means grew up on the Pine Ridge Indian Reservation near the Black Hills of South Dakota. In 1969 he joined an Indian rights group in Minnesota called the American Indian Movement (AIM). He soon became its first national director. In February 1973 Means led two hundred members of AIM to declare their own nation at Wounded Knee, South Dakota. Federal marshals arrived, and an armed standoff began. By its end on May 3, two Indians had been killed and one marshal seriously injured. Means and the other protesters surrendered after the government promised to discuss the Indians' grievances.

The Wounded Knee standoff marked a high point in Means's career. He continued working with AIM, ran for United States president in 1987, and launched a successful Hollywood career in the 1990s. However, some members of AIM sought to separate the organization from Means. They believed he was portraying Indians falsely in the movies. The differences between AIM and Means became greater when he was charged with battery against his father-in-law. Respecting one's elders is highly valued in the Indian community, and Means had gone too far. AIM continued without him.

Women's Rights: Betty Friedan (1921-)

Betty Friedan was born in Peoria, Illinois, and grew up in a Jewish family. She attended Smith College, majored in psychology, and edited a campus magazine covering social issues. Although offered a scholarship to get a Ph.D. at Berkley, she turned it down believing that if she accepted it, she wouldn't have time to get married and start a family. Instead, she became a reporter for the Worker's Press in New York. While working there she began to notice discrimination against women in the workplace.

Friedan married in 1947 and started a family. After she requested time off to have her second baby, the newspaper fired her. Friedan became a housewife, but she was never content. She surveyed some of her college friends and found that many of them were dissatisfied as well. They wanted to have families but also have careers

382

outside the home. Friedan expressed her ideas in a book called *The Feminine Mystique*. The book was an instant success among liberals, and Friedan soon became a leading spokesperson for women's rights. In 1966 she helped found the National Organization for Women (NOW) and was named its first president.

Friedan fought for changes such as equal pay for women in the work force and legalized abortions. Not all women in NOW supported Friedan though. Some believed she was going too far. Others thought she was not going far enough. Friedan divorced in 1969 and retired from NOW's presidency the following year. She continued to focus on political reform and became an active member in the women's liberation movement.

Black Rights: Malcolm X (1925-65)

Malcolm Little was reared in Omaha, Nebraska, in an environment of social turmoil. His home was burned by members of the Ku Klux Klan, and his father, a black Baptist minister, was killed by racists when Malcolm was six. At fifteen he dropped out of school and got involved in crime. In 1946 he was convicted of a petty burglary and sent to prison. While there he joined the Black Muslim faith (Nation of Islam). Upon his release he dedicated himself to his faith and became one of its leading spokespersons. He also changed his last name to "X," rejecting "Little" because the name was given to his ancestors by their slave masters.

Malcolm skillfully described the racial conditions of the United States and denounced the white man. Although it appeared he would become the Nation of Islam's second leader, disagreements with the leader, Elijah Muhammad, led Malcolm to form his own religious organization—the Muslim Mosque. After a pilgrimage to Mecca in 1964, he publicly denounced racism and envisioned world brotherhood. However, he still promoted the use of violence. Other groups soon made Malcolm the target of their attacks. While preparing for a speech in New York, Malcolm X was assassinated by three Black Muslims. Since his death, he has continued to be a powerful symbol of the black civil rights movement.

Henrietta's plans for a passive resistance demonstration were quickly foiled.

Growing to Meet Challenges

Unit Five

As the nation expanded from sea to sea and the population grew within the cities, new problems arose that stirred the emotions of concerned people. But instead of turning to God for help and accepting responsibility for their problems, people turned more and more to the government. Well-meaning politicians were only too happy to expand government powers and control to try to answer the needs. Unfortunately, bigger government only caused bigger problems.

 Trouble in Paradise

On a map of the nation, show pictures appropriate to different regions: gold miners in the West, the Chinese working on the railroad or in conflict with Californians, immigrants in crowded tenement houses in New York City, union workers striking in Chicago, women marching for suffrage, outlaws in the West, and so on. You may refer to this bulletin board throughout your teaching of the unit.

Materials

You will need the following special materials for your teaching of Unit Five.

- *Student Activities* manual for THE AMERICAN REPUBLIC for Christian Schools (Second Edition)
- *Free Indeed: Heroes of Black Christian History* (BJUP)
- Special speaker: a model train enthusiast
- The board game Rail Baron (Avalon Hill)
- The latest issue of *Forbes* magazine on the 400 wealthiest people in America (or a list downloaded from **www.forbes.com**)
- Books that include works by Bret Harte
- CD, cassette, or other recording with songs of the West
- A map showing western lands owned by the federal

384

1876: Relationships between Indians and frontier settlers were often tense, requiring frequent intervention by the United States Cavalry. The most famous Indian battle was at Little Big Horn, where Colonel George A. Custer and his men were all killed.

1912: Theodore Roosevelt, a strong supporter of progressive reforms, chose to run for president from the new Progressive Party.

Unit 5	Lesson Plan Chart		
Chapter Title	**Main Goal**	**Pages**	**Time Frame**
19. Industrialism	To analyze the issues that affect an emerging industrial society	387-407	5½-9 days
20. The Last Frontier	To identify "profit" as the main motive for frontier settlement	408-29	6-10 days
The West	To identify the social and geographic features of the West	430-31	½-1 day
21. America and the World	To analyze how the decisions of the late 1800s created America's continuing conflict over foreign policy decisions	432-49	5½-7 days
Immigration	To summarize the effects of immigration on American society	450-51	½-1 day
22. Progressivism	To identify progressivism as a new role for government and explain how it was able to so quickly change the thinking of the nation	452-71	5½-9 days
Total Suggested Days			23½-37 days

1800s: Rescue missions reached out to "rescue" the people of the inner cities from their sin.

1869: The Union Pacific and Central Pacific railroads met at Promontory Point near Ogden, Utah, on May 10. The transcontinental railroad moved settlement of the West forward at a rapid pace.

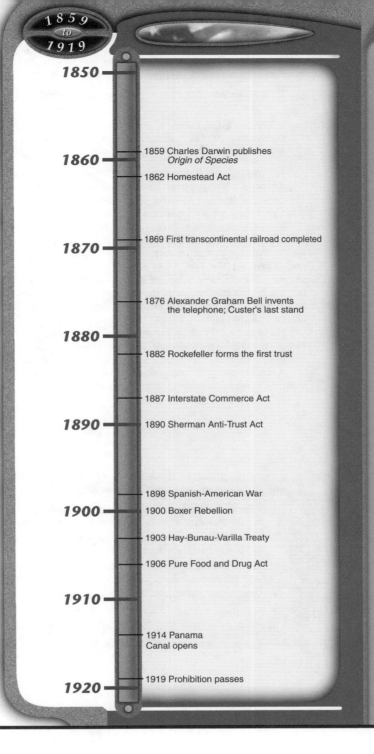

1859 to 1919

1850

1860 — 1859 Charles Darwin publishes *Origin of Species*
— 1862 Homestead Act

1870 — 1869 First transcontinental railroad completed

— 1876 Alexander Graham Bell invents the telephone; Custer's last stand

1880
— 1882 Rockefeller forms the first trust

— 1887 Interstate Commerce Act

1890 — 1890 Sherman Anti-Trust Act

— 1898 Spanish-American War
1900 — 1900 Boxer Rebellion

— 1903 Hay-Bunau-Varilla Treaty

— 1906 Pure Food and Drug Act

1910

— 1914 Panama Canal opens

— 1919 Prohibition passes
1920

- government (available from the U.S. Geological Survey)
- Special speaker: a rancher or farmer
- *North American Indians* by David Murdoch (Eyewitness Books)
- October 1992 issue of *National Geographic*
- *GEOGRAPHY for Christian Schools,* Second Edition (BJUP)
- Biography of D. L. Moody
- *Scenes from American Church History* (BJUP)
- *American History in Verse* by Burton Stevenson (BJUP)
- February 1998 issue of *National Geographic*
- Special speaker: a rescue mission worker or director
- Biography of Billy Sunday

Time Out

Ask the following questions about the time line. Have your students give the event and the date.

- What four events show the government's intervention to solve problems? *(the Homestead Act, 1862; the Interstate Commerce Act, 1887; the Sherman Anti-trust Act, 1890; the Pure Food and Drug Act, 1906)*

- People were easily able to travel from one end of the nation to the other because of

what? *(the completion of the first continental railroad in 1869)*

- What was the treaty that ended the Spanish-American War? *(the 1903 Hay-Bunau-Varilla Treaty)*

- Which event do you think changed people's thinking about religion and life most? *(the 1859 publishing of Charles Darwin's* Origin of Species*)*

The Death of Rodriguez

Yellow journalism in Hearst's New York Journal created sympathy for the Cuban rebellion. On January 19, 1897, Richard Harding Davis, America's most popular war correspondent, watched the predawn execution of a twenty-year-old Cuban rebel, Adolpho Rodriguez.

He had a handsome, gentle face of the peasant type, a light, pointed beard, great wistful eyes, and a mass of curly black hair. He was shockingly young for such a sacrifice. . . .

The officer of the firing squad hastily whipped up his sword, the men . . . leveled their rifles, the sword rose, dropped, and the men fired. At the report the Cuban's head snapped back almost between his shoulders, but his body fell slowly, as though someone had pushed him gently forward from behind and he had stumbled. . . .

He sank on his side in the wet grass without a struggle or sound, and did not move again. . . .

At that moment the sun, which had shown some promise of its coming in the glow above the hills, shot up suddenly from behind them in all the splendor of the tropics, a fierce red disk of heat, and filled the air with warmth and light. . . .

The whole world of Santa Clara seemed to stir and stretch itself and to wake to welcome the day just begun.

But as I fell in at the rear of the procession and looked back, the figure of the young Cuban, who was no longer part of the world of Santa Clara, was asleep in the wet grass, with his motionless arms still tightly bound behind him, with the scapular twisted awry across his face, and the blood from his breast sinking into the soil he had tried to free.

1. In the first paragraph, what word does the report use for execution? Does the report's description of the peasant create sympathy for him?

2. In the second paragraph, how does the officer perform his duty? Does this description create sympathy for him?

3. Do the two paragraphs about the sun and the town tell anything about the execution? Why does the report include these details?

4. What do the last seven words imply about the reason for the peasant's execution?

The Death of Rodriguez

1. sacrifice; yes, with descriptions such as "gentle face, wistful eyes, shockingly young"

2. hastily; no, it gives a sense of unconcern, cold stoicism

3. The execution was performed early in the morning; it may have been done early so that people would not know or be outraged.

4. He was rebelling against a government that was oppressing the people.

Have your students write a three-sentence description of how this narrative makes them feel. Then talk about why the author wrote it that way and what he was trying to achieve.

19

Industrialism

Goals

Students should be able to
1. Define and use the terms from the chapter.
2. Understand the impact of immigration on industry in America.
3. Summarize the effect of transportation and technology on industry.
4. **Analyze the issues that affect an emerging industrial society.**

Early Industrialism

The nineteenth century saw the United States emerge as a major industrial power, as is demonstrated by this iron works that was in operation in 1865.

Chapter Motivation

Unit 5 covers a transitional period in American history. To help the students recognize what the transition was *from,* ask them to describe the typical American and the typical way of life before the Civil War (covered thoroughly in Chapters 13-14). How is the typical American different today? What major changes had to take place to produce this change? Also list some characteristics of Americans, both good and bad, that have not changed. *(industrious, self-confident, democratic, open to change, idealistic)*

This chapter focuses on the end of an agricultural society and the rise of an industrial society. The next chapter examines the passing of the American frontier and the last icons of the typical "frontier spirit"—miners, homesteaders, cowboys, and Indians. The last two chapters in this unit describe two other major changes in America: its bigger role in world politics (Chapter 21) and progressive ideas in society and government (Chapter 22).

When the United States entered the nineteenth century, it was a quiet land with family farms, small villages, and a few small cities on the Atlantic coastline. By the end of the century, however, crowded cities, busy factories, and mechanized farms stretched across the country. At the dawn of the twentieth century, the United States was on its way to becoming the greatest industrial nation in the world. Capitalism, America's economic system, along with new industrial techniques and American ingenuity, was providing people with a host of products that made life easier. At the same time, America's population was swelling. The population in 1800 was less than 5.5 million. The 1870 census counted 40 million, and by 1910 the population had reached 92 million. Immigration was the biggest single reason for that growth, though the birthrate was high as well. Not only the population but also the size of the country increased. In 1800 there were only sixteen states in the Union, but a hundred years later there were forty-five.

The late nineteenth century was a time of growth for the nation, especially for its industries. The land and its people were uniquely suited for its large industrial building projects.

387

CHAPTER 19 Lesson Plan Chart			
Section Title	Main Activity	Pages	Time Frame
1. Materials and People	Student Activity B: Railroads, Resources, and Immigrants	387-92	1-2 days
2. Transportation and Technology	Questions People Never Ask	392-96	1-2 days
3. New Ways of Doing Business	Biggest Businesses Today	396-98	½-1 day
4. Effects of Industrial Expansion	Modern Economic Issues	398-405	2-3 days
Total Suggested Days (including 1 day for review and testing)			5½-9 days

SECTION 1

Materials

- Activities A and B from Chapter 19 of the *Student Activities* manual

- *Free Indeed: Heroes of Black Christian History* (BJUP)

Materials

SECTION 1

Objectives

Students should be able to
1. Describe some of the changes in America during the nineteenth century.
2. List some of America's natural resources that aided the growth of industries.
3. Describe American immigration during the nineteenth century.

Frederick Weyerhaeuser: Timber Supplier

Most early settlers could cut enough trees in their area to build their homes. In the late 1800s, however, the demand for timber increased as settlers moved onto the treeless plains and as railroad tracks needed wooden ties.

Frederick Weyerhaeuser (WIE ur HOU zur) was a young German immigrant working for day wages in a Rock Island, Illinois, sawmill. In 1860 Weyerhaeuser and his

Mining towns rose up overnight only to be deserted when the mine played out.

Materials and People

The United States was able to undergo such rapid changes for a variety of reasons. No single factor could have produced such change by itself. Two of the resources that helped the United States to produce goods for itself and the world were its supplies of raw materials and its labor force.

Natural Resources

One key to American industrial growth was its abundant natural resources. God endowed the nation with fertile soil and almost all the raw materials needed for important industries. After the purchase of Alaska in 1867, little geographic growth occurred. Hawaii, Puerto Rico, and a few other areas were added. Yet the resources grew as new minerals were discovered and previously inaccessible regions were opened by new means of transportation.

Great lodes of gold, silver, and copper were found in the Rocky Mountains, the Far West, and Alaska. After the Civil War, thousands of miners and businessmen streamed into the sparsely settled West. Towns with exotic or unusual names like Eureka, Paradise, Coarsegold, Sloughouse, Dinkey Creek, and Whiskeytown flourished briefly near the rich ore veins. When the ore was gone, most miners moved on, leaving behind some ghost towns. But some stayed in the West and found new ways to earn their living.

The rich iron ore deposits of northern Minnesota, the Mesabi (muh SAH bee) and Cayuna (kuh YOO nuh) ranges, provided raw materials for the growing iron and steel industries. Discovery of petroleum fuel resources added to America's wealth of natural resources. Tremendous coal deposits also provided an important fuel. And another source of energy, water power, would soon help the nation to produce electricity.

388

Student Activity A: Topic Sentences for "Materials and People"

This prewriting activity teaches the importance of topic sentences in the structure of historical narratives. The activity reinforces the flow of main ideas in the first section of the chapter.

Another important American resource was its timber. Vast forests covering the Northwest and other areas of the country supplied timber for lumber, pulp, and other uses.

Immigration Provides Labor

Developing industries need workers. Most of the American population was hard at work in the 1800s. Yet, for the country to expand its industrial production, it needed even more. The growing tide of immigrants met America's need for laborers.

Immigrants Come to America— Before 1880 most of the immigrants came from northwestern European countries like Britain, Ireland, Germany, or the Scandinavian countries, and they were largely Protestant. Although immigrants continued to come from those countries, a greater proportion now came from eastern and southern European countries, and they were often Roman Catholics. Italians, Turks, Greeks, Slavs, Hungarians, and Rumanians all flocked to America. From northern Russia came Russians, Poles (Poland was then part of Russia), Finns, and Jews. Other immigrants came from Russia's Baltic States—Estonia, Latvia, and Lithuania. Between 1890 and 1914, the largest single group of immigrants was the Italians.

Most Europeans crossed the Atlantic by the shortest and cheapest routes. Many traveled first to Liverpool, England, or to Bremen or Hamburg, Germany, where the major steamship companies were located. Steamship companies often used freighters to carry passengers over to the United States and then carried raw materials or manufactured goods back to Europe. The cheapest tickets gave travelers space in steerage, the noisiest, most crowded part of the ship, located underneath the deck and near the engine and rudder.

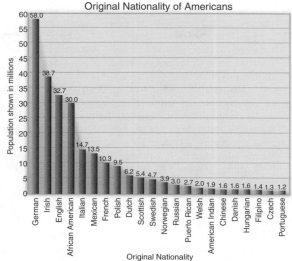

Original Nationality of Americans

Passengers brought their food with them in their bundles. Seasickness or disease often made the voyage a miserable experience, and some immigrants lost their lives. People from different walks of life were thrown together under strange conditions. In addition, many came from different countries and spoke different languages.

Some immigrants had been recruited in their homelands by agents of various American companies in need of laborers. It was common for companies to make contracts with immigrants. The companies agreed to pay their fares if the immigrants would agree to work a specified length of time for the employer. Other immigrants used most of their life's savings to come to America. Still others had their trans-Atlantic tickets and even their rail tickets from the port where they landed paid for by relatives who had come earlier.

Employers eagerly hired immigrants. Because the recent immigrants were usually happy just to have a job, they were generally willing to work for cheaper wages than other

389

brother-in-law, Frederick Denkmann, pooled their earnings, borrowed some money, and bought the sawmill.

Weyerhaeuser expanded the operation northward. Unlike some heads of corporations, Weyerhaeuser was always willing to share the responsibilities with a large circle of capable men. He rarely held more than a 15-20 percent interest in any company, yet his partners took his advice because his past decisions had brought great profits. Weyerhaeuser's most innovative operation was a sales company that served as a nationwide wholesaler, handling sawmill products from more than twenty firms. The Weyerhaeuser Sales Company eventually became the world's largest lumber company.

When the forests of the Great Lakes had fallen to ax and saw, Weyerhaeuser sought land elsewhere. James J. Hill, the railroad baron who lived next door to him in St. Paul, Minnesota, sold him nine hundred thousand acres of timberland in the Pacific Northwest for $5.4 million dollars. The value of the land soon quadrupled, and the company moved its headquarters to Tacoma, Washington, where it remains active today.

Weyerhaeuser's giant firms were often criticized because of their methods. His company cut timber, milled it, and then left or sold the scarred land. Vast forests were available at the time, and the company acted in response to public need and to the public policy of that day. Reforestation and conservation have replaced this practice of "cut and run." Innovative uses for wood byproducts also lead to much less waste today.

History of the Immigration and Naturalization Service

As the United States has changed and grown, so have its views on immigrants and its methods of handling them. Immigration first became a federal concern in 1864. Desiring to encourage immigration, Congress created the position of

Student Activity B: Railroads, Resources, and Immigrants

Students should complete the map activity for this chapter early so that they can visualize the places described in the text.

Compare Colonial Settlers and Immigrants

Ask the students whether it is fair to call immigrants "the next generation of settlers." In other words, did the immigrants face the same kinds of challenges as the first Pilgrims and settlers who arrived from

England? If so, then it seems reasonable to argue that they have earned an equal place in America by the sweat of their brow. It was not much easier for them to adjust than for the first settlers.

Commissioner of Immigration within the State Department. However, the states still had control over their own immigration affairs, so it was difficult for the commissioner to create one unified national policy. The position went defunct in 1868, but in 1891 the federal government again stepped into the immigration picture by establishing the Bureau of Immigration under the Secretary of the Treasury. From this point on, the federal government had the final authority over immigration affairs.

The courts originally handled naturalization, the process of becoming a citizen. It came under the authority of the executive branch in 1906. Immigration and naturalization issues were permanently joined in the Immigration and Naturalization Service (INS) under the Labor Department in 1933. The INS reached its final home at the Justice Department in June of 1940. Because of the looming threat of war at that time, the government wanted to have stronger control over the activities of foreigners entering the country.

Since the Second World War, one major concern has been preventing illegal immigrant workers from operating in the country. Another concern is refugees. Though the United States places a cap on the number of immigrants it receives each year, people who are fleeing desperate circumstances are considered in a different category. The INS reports that since 1965 the major source of immigration has shifted from Europe to Latin America and Asia. For more information, see **www.ins.usdoj.gov**.

Americans. Moreover, immigrants who complained risked losing their jobs. There were always newcomers waiting to be hired. Employers also liked hiring immigrants because most were hard working and reluctant to join the labor unions.

Ellis Island and Ports of Entry—The largest number of European immigrants came to America by way of New York harbor. Many were registered there at **Ellis Island.** It served as a temporary stopover for incoming immigrants who used its beautifully designed great hall, dining room, and hospital. Those who looked healthy enough to hold a job and who could prove they had the means to reach distant destinations usually took the ferry to New Jersey and rode a train inland. Others entered New York City totally bewildered. Public Health Service doctors assisted the immigrants who were ill. If they could be cured, they were treated and sent on their way as soon as possible. The immigrant center at Ellis

Island operated from 1894 to 1943 and handled the entry of more than seventeen million immigrants. Often immigrants feared being turned back at Ellis Island, but of the millions who came, the total number rejected was under two percent.

Some immigrants landed in Montreal; others, especially the Irish, came to Boston. New Orleans was a port of entry for many immigrants planning to go to the Midwest or the Far West.

Immigrants often settled in neighborhoods of cities where others of their nationality lived. Some of these neighborhoods came to be known by such names as "Chinatown" or "Little Italy." In later years, after immigrants learned the language and saved enough money, many moved on to other areas of the city or suburbs and left the inner city to be occupied by newer immigrants.

Immigrants Work to Build America—While immigrants came from many lands,

Ellis Island was the first stop for immigrants coming into America by way of New York City.

Ireland provided a large share in the 1800s. In the 1840s a potato blight spread slowly across Europe. The plant disease devastated Ireland, where the potato was the major farm crop and food. One-eighth of Ireland's population starved to death or died from diseases caused by malnutrition. Another three-eighths of the people, three million in all, left Ireland. Many of them came to the United States, primarily to Boston and New York City.

The Irish played important roles in the construction of America's canal and railroad systems. An early group of Irish immigrants provided the muscle to build the Erie Canal. Crews of Irishmen were also responsible for laying the track for western railroads. The Irish took these jobs despite a high risk of injury because they saw them as a means to escape their poverty.

Some Irishmen sought altogether different work. Because of previously unstable circumstances, they sought more stable jobs in civic service. Men became police or firemen, and Irish women became schoolmarms and domestic servants.

China also provided many immigrants for America. Because American ships were involved in the China trade, news of the discovery of gold in California soon reached China. Since China was overpopulated and her people faced flood and famine, the Chinese were easily attracted to America. Opportunities of the California gold rush brought them in great numbers. As was frequently the case with immigrants, the men came first. Once they had attained their riches, they hoped to return to China and find wives. Instead of mining for gold themselves, many of the Chinese founded businesses such as restaurants and laundries, providing needed services for others. Later, Chinese workers were hired to build western sections of the transcontinental railroad.

James A. Garfield
20th President

Born: Orange Township, Ohio, November 19, 1831
Family: married Lucretia Rudolph; two daughters, five sons
Occupation: carpenter, teacher, lay preacher
Home: Lawnfield, Mentor, Ohio
Religion: Disciples of Christ
Election: 1880—defeated Winfield Hancock (Democrat), James B. Weaver (Greenback-Labor), and Neal Dow (Prohibition)
Political Party: Republican
Vice President: Chester A. Arthur
Interesting Facts and Accomplishments:
• could write with either hand (ambidextrous) • had been a lay preacher and as such was the only preacher to become president • exposed fraud in the Post Office Department and attempted to clean up some of the corruption in government
Death: Died September 19, 1881, after being shot on July 2 by a disappointed office seeker, Charles Guiteau

(1881)

More on Immigration
For more on immigration see pages 450-51.

391

 Immigration, Good or Bad?
Discuss any modern debates on immigration now raging in state capitals or in Washington, D.C. The issue has always been whether to limit the number of immigrants. Both sides of the debate rummage through the past to find support for their positions. Based on their reading in this chapter, the students should list the arguments that both sides might have given during the debate over the pros and cons of the Exclusion Act of 1882 (page 392). Note that the change in the ethnic background of the immigrants was one of the major matters of concern. Immigration is covered in more detail in the special feature on pages 450-51. God told the Hebrews to love foreigners and treat them well (Exod. 22:21; Lev. 19:33), and He even expected the heathen nation of Moab to accept outcasts from other nations (Isa. 16:3-4).

Objectives

Students should be able to
1. Explain the need for and the hazard of railroad consolidation.
2. Describe the growth of America's railroad network in the late 1800s.
3. Name two important inventors of the late 1900s and explain the significance of their contributions to technology.

Chinese immigrants continued to come, and as long as jobs were available, Americans did not object too much to their arrival. But when financial panics came, hostility grew. Californians claimed that the Chinese, who were willing to work for lower wages, were getting the jobs that whites deserved. They soon influenced politicians to pass the **Exclusion Act of 1882,** which cut off all legal Chinese immigration except for a few hundred per year. This act was passed over the veto of President Chester Arthur, who had assumed office after the assassination of James Garfield in 1881.

Northern Europe also sent many of its people to America. Political and religious unrest swept the German states during the 1840s. When the revolutions failed, people left that land. Many of these people had been landowners in Europe, so they had enough money to buy land in the United States when they arrived. They often settled in the farming areas of America's heartland, such as in Wisconsin. Others found work as lumberjacks in the northern woods, and then they bought farmland soon after.

Scandinavians—Norwegians, Swedes, and Finns—also came to America. They tended to settle whole towns or counties in Iowa, Minnesota, Wisconsin, and the Dakotas. They had their own newspapers and started their own colleges. Most were Lutheran and had come to America in protest of the policies of their churches back home. Some Swedes, Norwegians, and Finns worked in logging camps; others worked in the iron mines of northern Minnesota and the copper mines of Michigan.

The people of these and other ethnic groups contributed greatly to the American way of life. Inventions, works of literature and music, designs, and customs came with the immigrants. America would not be what it is

today without the contributions these citizens made to the developing culture of the nation.

SECTION REVIEW

1. What was the biggest single reason for the growth of the American population in the nineteenth century?
2. What were two of the factors that helped the industries of the United States to grow?
3. After 1880 many immigrants came from what regions of Europe?
4. Where did many European immigrants go first to be registered?
5. What piece of legislation attempted to limit Chinese immigration?

 Why did established Americans sometimes object to immigrants?

Transportation and Technology

Two more American resources that helped the land's industries grow were its transportation networks and its technological developments. Promoting the development of these features became an important goal for the country.

Transportation and the Railroads

While steamships were improving transportation for trade with foreign countries, the railroads made it possible for America to conquer its immense territory. Railroads also moved America's raw materials to distant factories and distributed the manufactured goods to ready markets.

By 1860 there were 30,626 miles of track, but almost all of it was in the East. There were still no railroad bridges across the Hudson, Ohio, or Mississippi Rivers. In addition, since different companies built the railroads, they failed to use a uniform gauge (width) of track. Different gauges kept lines from connecting, prohibiting transportation from area to area

392

 "Immigrant" Samuel Morris

Immigrants came from many places and for many reasons. "Samuel Morris" is the story of an African prince who came to study in order to return and teach his native family and tribesmen of Christ. This story can be found in *Free Indeed: Heroes of Black Christian History.*

Section Review Answers

1. immigration (p. 387)
2. its supplies of raw materials and its labor force (p. 388)

3. eastern and southern Europe (p. 389)
4. Ellis Island (p. 390)
5. the Exclusion Act of 1882 (p. 392)

 Especially during times of financial difficulty, they felt that immigrants took work away from native-born Americans. (p. 392)

SECTION 2

Materials

- Activity C from Chapter 19 of the *Student Activities* manual
- A model train
- Special speaker: a model train enthusiast
- The board game Rail Baron (produced by Avalon Hill)

unless goods were transferred from one line to another. Such problems made it difficult to travel by rail or to send freight long distances. Chicago and New York had rails between them, but passengers and cargo had to change cars six times en route. The Civil War made the problems obvious and stimulated the building of more track and the development of more efficient and economical systems.

Consolidation Helps the Railroads—One means of making railroads more efficient and more economical was **consolidation,** combining small lines. Sometimes this was done through the friendly purchase of one company by another, but more often it was the result of ruthless pressure. Several men sought to gain control of large railroad networks. **Cornelius Vanderbilt** had the vision of connecting the Great Lake states to New York City by rail. He forced all his competition to sell out and gained a railroad empire. J. Edgar Thompson secretly bought up small lines in Pennsylvania and Ohio. Once he had a base, he cut his rates and drove his rivals out of business. Then he raised his rates.

Other men tried to make fortunes as they built railroad empires. Although small railroads were often hurt by the consolidation, the process did help the nation acquire an efficient railroad transportation network.

Government Policy Aids Railroad Building—A second factor leading to the development of a railroad system was government policy. Lincoln and the Republican Party supported the idea of a transcontinental railroad. The outbreak of the war caused Congress to agree, and it chartered the **Union Pacific** and **Central Pacific** railroads in 1864. These two lines—the Union Pacific building westward using Irish workers and war veterans, and the Central Pacific building eastward using Chinese laborers—were linked on May 10, 1869. The official wedding of the rails took place at Promontory Point near Ogden, Utah,

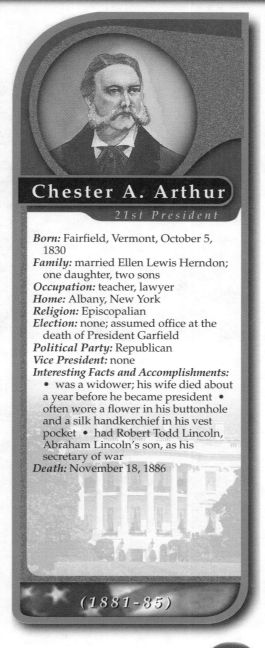

Chester A. Arthur
21st President

Born: Fairfield, Vermont, October 5, 1830
Family: married Ellen Lewis Herndon; one daughter, two sons
Occupation: teacher, lawyer
Home: Albany, New York
Religion: Episcopalian
Election: none; assumed office at the death of President Garfield
Political Party: Republican
Vice President: none
Interesting Facts and Accomplishments:
- was a widower; his wife died about a year before he became president • often wore a flower in his buttonhole and a silk handkerchief in his vest pocket • had Robert Todd Lincoln, Abraham Lincoln's son, as his secretary of war
Death: November 18, 1886

(1881–85)

393

Standard Gauge
The Union Pacific Railroad used a gauge (distance between the rails) of four feet, eight and one-half inches. This became the standard gauge for railroads in the later 1800s, and thus locomotives and rolling stock could move freely from one line to another. Two other important developments for railroads in the same era were the sleeping cars and other passenger cars, developed by George Pullman, and the air brake, devised by George Westinghouse.

Lorenzo Coffin
One of the early leaders in the fight for railroad safety was Lorenzo Coffin, a farmer from Iowa. After watching a brakeman lose two fingers while attempting to join two railroad cars, Coffin began to lobby for Westinghouse's air brakes as well as a safer method of coupling cars. For more information on Coffin, see *BIBLE TRUTHS for Christian Schools: Level C, Lessons from the Early Church* (BJUP), p. 76, and Richard F. Snow, "Lorenzo Coffin," *American Heritage* magazine, October 1979, pp. 98-99.

Chinese Laborers
Of all the decisions James Strobridge made as head of construction for the Central Pacific Railroad, one of the most potentially devastating was his refusal to hire Chinese laborers. Fortunately, for the completion of the railroad and the security of his job, he was forced to change his mind. White laborers did not want to continue the backbreaking work of railroad building when gold mines presented the tempting possibility of quick riches. So Strobridge had to accept what laborers were available.

The Chinese did not take long to prove their worth. They were soon grading railbeds that were bigger and better than those the white crews had graded. They became legendary for the speed and quality of their work. Approximately ten thousand Chinese worked on the railroad, some coming from

Student Activity C: Trivia Game: Railroads

You can use this trivia game to review the place of railroads in U.S. history. It is crucial that students use the index to find the trivia. You can complete the activity in class, assign it as homework, or make it extra credit. Consider using this activity in conjunction with other discussions of the railroad's honored place in American lore. Why do students think Americans are so fascinated with trains?

Display Model Trains

Bring in a model train or ask interested students to help you set up model trains from their homes. If you find a parent who is a model hobbyist, let him explain the basis for his fascination with trains and share some of the things he has learned. Perhaps someone from a local hobby shop would be willing to help you as well.

California and some directly from China. More than twelve hundred of those were killed on the job.

James J. Hill's Northern Pacific

Because it was built without any federal land or federal funds, the most unusual railroad of the late 1800s was probably the Great Northern Railroad owned by James J. Hill. He had begun his career as a clerk for a steamboat line. In 1865 he started his own business as a salesman, and five years later he used his savings to buy a little steamship named the *Selkirk*.

Next, with the help of a state land grant, Hill bought the almost defunct St. Paul and Pacific Railroad. By January 1879, he had connected St. Paul, Minnesota, to Winnipeg, Canada. The sale of grant lands alone brought him $100,000 a month, not to mention the money he made from shipping rich grain harvests on his line.

In 1893 his line finally reached the Pacific. When a financial panic in 1893 toppled the Northern Pacific, Hill bought it too. In 1901 he bargained with J. P. Morgan to buy half the stock of another line, the Burlington and Quincy, that ran to Illinois. This meant that his railroads now linked the West Coast with Chicago, St. Louis, Omaha, and Denver.

Some people hated Hill, claiming he had gained his wealth unjustly at the expense of loggers, miners, and farmers. But others praised him as the man who unlocked the wealth of the Great Northwest.

Bell: Communication Pioneer

Alexander Graham Bell taught teachers of the deaf. As a result of his interest in technical devices to help the deaf, he envisioned the possibility of uniting two hearing aids. Thus, he invented the telephone.

The public found Bell's device fascinating. Yet when Bell sought to market it, no company showed any interest. Western Union, the most logical vendor in the communications industry, ignored him.

The celebration at Promontory Point marked the completion of the first transcontinental railroad.

a short distance from the Great Salt Lake. The Central Pacific had faced the trial of crossing the steep Sierra Nevada range. The Union Pacific gang had its problems, too. Because of a lack of wood, most of their ties had to be shipped long distances. A lack of water and the danger of attacks from fierce plains Indian tribes also hindered their work.

The federal government not only gave financial aid to the railroad builders but also provided the builders with land. In 1862 and 1864 Congress developed a new land grant system. Each railroad got a strip of land

The Union Pacific offered passage from Omaha to San Francisco in four days.

four hundred feet wide for the right of way for its tracks. It also received two sections of land on alternating sides of the tracks. The railroad could do whatever it wanted with the 1,280 acres of land it was given for each mile of track it laid. The railroads held on to some lands. More often than not, they sold the lands next to their tracks to eager settlers. The money from the sales helped pay for building the railroad.

The government's Homestead Act of 1862 also helped railroads. The alternate sections of land owned by the federal government were sold at low prices or made

Questions People Never Ask

Americans did not universally applaud the idea of a transcontinental railroad funded by federal loans and lavish grants of public lands. The transcontinental railroad was the first major business endeavor funded by federal subsidies. No one asks any more, "Was it a wise decision?" In weighing the answer to this question, students should consider the consequences of the deal—the giveaway helped to create a monopoly that would later gouge the poor and use its wealth to corrupt politicians; the original tracks were poorly laid just to get the federal money as quickly as possible. Note also that the rapid expansion heightened tensions with the Indians.

A common argument in support of a government subsidized railroad is that the poor regions of the frontier could not have funded the railroads on their own. But it can be argued that the vast railroad network in the Northeast was not built with federal money. If given time, private enterprise will do a better job, more efficiently and less expensively. A vital lesson in the study of history is to examine events objectively. By making parallels to modern complaints about government inefficiency and mismanagement, students can apply their knowledge of human depravity to help them ask the questions that people do not want to ask.

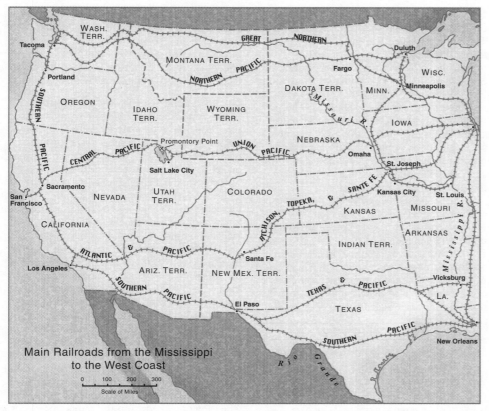

Main Railroads from the Mississippi
to the West Coast

0   100   200   300
Scale of Miles

available free under the Homestead Act. Thus even more settlers and land speculators came into the region by means of the new railroad lines.

Building Other Lines—Because the men investing in railroads were accumulating enormous wealth, other people soon sought railroad land grants of their own. In 1864 Congress approved generous land grants for building a railroad linking Lake Superior and the Pacific Ocean. The Northern Pacific line, finished in 1883, joined Duluth, Minnesota, to Portland, Oregon, and also to Spokane and Tacoma, Washington.

In 1884 the Atchison, Topeka, and Santa Fe Railroad provided a more southerly route. The Texas Pacific Railroad built across Texas linked to the Southern Pacific at El Paso, Texas. When this route was finished, New Orleans was linked by rail with Los Angeles and San Francisco. Another transcontinental line was built with private funds by **James J. Hill.** His **Great Northern Railroad** included extensions into Canada to help provide transportation for farmers there.

Technology

Another important ingredient in American industrialization was technology—scientific

They could have bought the telephone for a mere $100,000 and made millions over the years.

Early phone systems were local ones. In 1892 the Bell Telephone Company formed the first long-distance telephone network, the American Telephone and Telegraph Company. AT&T held almost total control of the communications industry until 1985, when the federal government forced it to break up into smaller units.

Edison: Electricity Pioneer

In 1878 Edison began experimenting to find a way to manufacture light bulbs. Edison applied the work ethic to invention, saying, "There is no substitute for hard work. Genius is one percent inspiration, and ninety-nine percent perspiration." After thousands of experiments, Edison tried carbonizing (burning) cotton threads. In October 1879 he made a bulb that burned forty hours. In 1882 he opened the first commercial electrical station. It sold electricity to eighty-five customers and kept four hundred new electric lights burning.

By the time he died in 1931, he owned more than a thousand patents. Most were improvements on existing inventions or processes. But a few—the alkaline storage battery, the movie projector, and the phonograph—were innovations that led to whole new industries.

395

Play the Board Game Rail Baron

Avalon Hill's board game Rail Baron gives students an enjoyable insight on the nation's railroad network. Similar to Monopoly, this game allows students to build their own networks of intercontinental railroads (using historical lines) and to build the greatest fortune. The game is time-consuming, lasting up to four hours, but it gives students a new appreciation of the nations' rail lines.

Objectives

Students should be able to
1. Define capital (in the economic sense).
2. Name three kinds of business organizations and describe the benefits and limitations of each.
3. Explain the way corporations obtained money to expand industry.
4. Define a trust.

Andrew Carnegie: Steel

Carnegie's parents were penniless Scottish immigrants. Carnegie himself had spent his childhood as a bobbin winder in a textile factory, earning only twelve and one-half cents a day. In America he got a job as a railroad telegraph boy. Because he acted quickly to prevent an accident and kept traffic moving in his boss's absence, he was promoted.

Carnegie saved his money and looked for ways to invest it. He believed that steel would be needed to build America. Carnegie got his foot in the door in the steel industry when he invested in the Keystone Bridge Company. Its steel bridges were stronger and easier to construct than wood bridges and soon replaced them.

Carnegie then started his own steel company, and new uses for the product made his business boom. Structural steel was soon used to build large buildings and even skyscrapers. Barbed wire replaced wooden fences. Wire nails took the place of forged nails. Railroads used steel for rails and railroad cars.

Carnegie was the first captain of industry who viewed productivity and wealth as a means to achieve social goals. He did not believe that his business success resulted just from his ability to beat the competition. He believed that America's industrial supremacy was also the result of the triumph of its form of government over a monarchy.

---

inventions and improved methods for industry. The Yankee ingenuity at the dawn of the nineteenth century had, by the century's end, turned into a remarkable ability to innovate. Some inventions, like **Alexander Graham Bell**'s telephone, led to whole new industries and big changes in American life. Other simple inventions—rivets for points of stress in Levi Strauss's blue jeans, for example—although minor, remain useful even today. The number of patents issued by the patent office shot up, averaging more than 21,000 a year through the 1880s and 1890s.

The increased use of electricity was especially beneficial to the advancement of both industry and technology. **Thomas Edison** promoted the generation of electricity for practical uses and also invented many electrical appliances. His incandescent light (light bulb) was among the most important. Hundreds of other inventors also made important contributions to American industry.

SECTION REVIEW

1. Give three reasons for the difficulty of traveling long distances by rail.

2. What regions of the country did Cornelius Vanderbilt connect with his railroad empire?

3. What did the federal government give railroad companies to aid their building?

4. Name two key inventors of the period and the inventions for which they are best known.

 What could be the potential danger(s) of railroad empires?

New Ways of Doing Business

America's industries grew in size and produced more and more during the late 1800s. Competition, new technology, and better management helped to bring about this industrial growth. Companies were constantly looking

for ways to improve their production, but improvements often required investment money or **capital.** To meet this financial need and other legal needs, businesses began to find new ways to organize and obtain capital.

Corporations for Increased Capital

In America's early years most businesses were either **sole proprietorships** or **partnerships.** Sole proprietorships were businesses owned by one person, while partnerships were owned by two or more people. Both worked well for small-scale operations. Proprietorships had the advantages of catering to individual needs. The owner got all the profit, but he also absorbed all the losses and often lacked the funds to expand his business.

Partnerships had the distinct advantage of increasing capital in a business and of sharing the losses of the business. **Andrew Carnegie** built a huge steel empire with the help of multiple partners. They provided him with expertise in areas about which he knew little. He suggested that the epitaph on his tombstone should read: "Here lies a man who was able to surround himself with others far wiser than he." However, a big disadvantage of sharing the responsibility for all losses in a partnership was that those losses must be shared even when they resulted from the faults or failures of just one partner. It could lead to the financial ruin of all the partners unless protective measures were taken. Other disadvantages were that all the partners had to participate in the business's legal dealings, and if one partner died or pulled out, the partnership ended.

Another way to organize a business is to incorporate, a method that became very popular in the late 1800s. A **corporation** is formed when a business gains a legal charter and sells stock to many individual investors. Although the stockholders are essentially the owners, they can lose only the amount they invested in the stock if the corporation fails. If the busi-

---

Section Review Answers

1. Most track was in the East. There were no railroad bridges across the Hudson, Ohio, or Mississippi Rivers. And track width varied from one set of tracks to another, preventing trains from traveling freely across the land. (pp. 392-93)

2. the Great Lake states and New York City (p. 393)

3. financial aid and land (p. 394)

4. Alexander Graham Bell—the telephone, Thomas Edison—the incandescent light (and other uses for electricity) (p. 396)

 Large companies, having driven smaller companies out of business, might then raise their rates. This monopoly could hurt the consumer as well as the small businessman. (p. 393)

SECTION 3

Materials

- Activity D from Chapter 19 of the *Student Activities* manual

- Latest issue of *Forbes* magazine on the four hundred wealthiest people in America (or a list downloaded from **www.forbes.com**)

- World almanac

ness makes a profit, the stockholders receive dividends, or payments from that profit. Moreover, a corporation is considered a "person" in the eyes of the law, and it can carry on legal dealings without all of its stockholders being present. Nor is its existence ended by the death of a manager or single stockholder.

Andrew Carnegie built a huge empire based on steel production.

Because of advantages like these, more and more executives sought to incorporate in the years after the Civil War. Steel, petroleum, and chemical manufacturers are but a few of the many who used the corporate form of business.

Sources of Corporate Money

Company executives realized that they needed large amounts of capital to finance the growth of their ventures. Some people with savings or other wealth became stockholders, buying stock with money that provided the corporation with capital. More capital, however, was raised in larger amounts from other sources.

The nation's banking system also helped provide industry with capital. As more Americans entered the work force and the number of businesses grew, the number of bank deposits increased. Banks invested their money in corporations to make more money and also offered credit to such corporations to cover the expansion of industry. Another large-scale source of capital came from life insurance companies that invested the premiums paid by policy holders.

Corporations Find New Ways to Organize

As the corporations grew larger, they needed better internal organization. America's early factories had employed few executives, usually just managers and bookkeepers. Most new large-scale operations, however, required more management. Thus, separate departments to handle each major phase of operations became normal. There were department heads for such responsibilities as purchasing, marketing, accounting, financing, and development. These specialized executives often helped to manage businesses more efficiently and profitably.

In 1882 oilman **John D. Rockefeller** and his associates formed the first **trust.** A trust combined several separate companies into one super-size corporation, such as Rockefeller's Standard Oil. The executives of the trust then had power to organize and manage all the companies involved as they wished. Other

Carnegie believed that along with wealth came responsibility. He was a steward, a wise caretaker, of the wealth he had gained. In an essay, "The Gospel of Wealth," Carnegie spoke on the duties of the wealthy. Carnegie believed each man had a responsibility to provide for his own family just as the Word of God teaches in I Timothy 5:8. Carnegie also believed that the wealthy had a duty to plunge wealth back into society. "The man who dies . . . rich dies disgraced. Surplus wealth is a sacred trust which its possessor is bound to administer in his lifetime for the good of the community."

397

Student Activity D: Ways of Doing Business

This chart summarizes the advantages and disadvantages of the different types of businesses discussed in the chapter. The "holding company" is not discussed until Section 4, but you can fill in that row while you are teaching Section 3.

Question of the Century—What Are the Keys to America's Industrial Success?

Why did the United States become the world's industrial giant? The answer to this question is the focus of the chapter. Ask the students to recall the keys to American industrial growth outlined in this chapter—natural resources, immigrant laborers, transportation networks, technological developments, new ways of doing business (corporations), and the competition of capitalism (in the next section). Other nations around the world ask themselves what made American industry so great because they would like to imitate its "keys to success." What do the students consider the most important key to success? *(Answers will vary.)* Is the United States likely to remain the world's industrial giant, or does another country have the keys necessary to surpass the United States?

The World's Richest People

Forbes magazine publishes an annual list of the world's richest people (also available on its Internet site). Make a photocopy of these lists from *Forbes* or download them from the Internet, and then discuss them in class. Note how the source of great income has changed as the cutting edge of industry has changed. Also raise issues about greed and the everpresent urge to become a millionaire. (The

John D. Rockefeller: Trust Innovator

During the Civil War, John D. Rockefeller, a bookkeeper in Cleveland, Ohio, was looking for an investment for his savings. Because he believed petroleum would have a role in America's growth, he invested in a refinery with a good profit record. He correctly guessed that the refinery business was the key to success in the oil industry. He also felt that small refineries were cutting profits and that such duplication was wasteful. In 1870, by acquiring the various refineries within his area, Rockefeller formed the Standard Oil Company. Rockefeller promised the railroads large-scale shipments in return for a reduction on his freight rates. On paper the railroad charged him the public rate, but they gave him a rebate or kickback for each barrel shipped. Rockefeller's methods, though not illegal at the time, were unfair.

Within two years, Rockefeller had gained control of one-fourth of the refining industry. By 1910, Standard Oil gained control of 90 percent of the nation's refineries and 92 percent of the crude oil supply from the Appalachians, the nation's major oil source at the time.

SECTION 4

Objectives

Students should be able to
1. Name and describe two pieces of legislation passed to regulate businesses.
2. Name two important unions of the era.
3. Explain the problem of materialism.

John D. Rockefeller and his associates combined several companies to form the Standard Oil Company.

industries followed Rockefeller's example and set up trusts of their own in the 1880s.

SECTION REVIEW

1. What is the difference between a proprietorship and a partnership?

2. Who built a huge steel empire by means of a partnership?

3. Name two sources of capital for corporations besides individuals.

4. What is a trust? Who formed the first business trust?

 What problems of a proprietorship or partnership does a corporation avoid? How?

Effects of Industrial Expansion

The growth of industries brought many changes to the way Americans lived and to the government's attention to industry.

Changing American Life

First, America's trade increased greatly. American foodstuffs and factory products found their way to distant parts of the world. This trade also helped to make many more products available to Americans.

Second, urbanization occurred. Immigrants swelled city populations. In addition, as farming mechanized and farm production increased, fewer farmers were needed. Farmers—or at least several of their children—often moved to towns and cities where work was available.

Industrialization emphasized urban problems. Pollution of air or water, overcrowding, and crime all became more obvious when concentrated in a single area.

Industrialism also meant that Americans began to have more leisure time. Machines freed people from some work, while other machines, labor-saving devices, made work easier. Americans soon found new ways to use the extra time. New spectator sports captured the public fancy. Others participated in already existing sports or tried the newly invented or popularized ones, such as bicycling, tennis, or basketball.

In addition, industrialism affected American family life. Some women had gone to work outside the home during the Civil War. A few continued to work after the war. Some were recruited to work in expanding industries. And because inventions made housekeeping easier, some women were finding time to take other jobs. The number of women in the work force would continue to grow in the years that followed, changing the lifestyle of more and more families.

Bible says in Proverbs 23:4 that it is wrong to set out to become wealthy, but wealth itself is not evil.)

Biggest Businesses Today

Look in a world almanac for the list of the one hundred leading U.S. businesses, along with the fastest-growing businesses (based on revenues). List the top ten or twenty-five businesses and discuss the categories they fall under. Which types of businesses have been around for over a century? What is the newest type of business?

Section Review Answers

1. A proprietorship is owned by one person; a partnership is owned by two or more people. (p. 396)

2. Andrew Carnegie (p. 396)

3. banks and life insurance companies (p. 397)

4. a combination of several companies into one super-size corporation; John D. Rockefeller (p. 397)

 It solves the need for capital by pooling the resources of a group of people. It avoids the potential for losing everything by limiting the amount of a person's loss to the amount of his investment. And it bypasses the legal problems involved in the loss of a partner by viewing the corporation itself as a person that can continue to live even if stockholders change. (pp. 396-97)

Americans Focus on Capitalism

The United States had been founded with a capitalistic economy. **Capitalism** is an economy in which people are free to invest in businesses and make profits on their investments. Businesses are owned by private citizens instead of the government, and anyone is allowed to go into business, competing with others. Generally, capitalism works well because it recognizes man's natural selfish desires. In competing for personal gain, businesses usually strive to sell good products or services so that the business can continue and grow. Poor products or services drive customers away. The competition among businesses, created by a capitalistic system, helped to bring Americans a high standard of living.

Nonetheless, industrialization revealed some weaknesses in the capitalistic system. The capitalistic system is not perfect, and man's evil nature caused some industrialists to run roughshod over their competitors. In some industries, workers labored long hours doing dangerous work at low pay while company owners became millionaires. The biblical idea that "the labourer is worthy of his hire" (Luke 10:7) was sometimes ignored.

At that time of rapid industrial growth, a philosophy that justified harsh actions became popular. Charles Darwin's theory of evolution was used to defend piling up wealth by any means one wanted. Darwin's theory said that there was a constant struggle in nature. Only the fittest members of the species would survive. Applied to society, this thinking was called **social Darwinism**. Social Darwinists showed little mercy and no recognition of human weaknesses. In industry, social Darwinists held that driving weaker competitors out of business was just a part of the struggle for survival. Making a profit, according to their philosophy, should be accomplished by any means possible, even if others were hurt.

The ageless principles of God's Word shed light on this thinking. God's Word does not justify taking advantage of the weaknesses of others, even our enemies, for personal gain. The Bible reminds us often of the need to show mercy and love. Some industrialists gained wealth but ignored the principles of God's Word. "He that oppresseth the poor to increase his riches . . . shall surely come to want" (Prov. 22:16).

Closely tied to capitalism was the idea of *laissez-faire* economics. Most Americans believed that the best way for a capitalistic economy to develop was without any government interference or regulation. Those who supported *laissez-faire* policies argued that government regulation would disturb the fine balance between supply of products and the public's demand for those products; the economy might be ruined. Yet because individual men and some companies did not take on the responsibility to make changes, to right wrongs, and to correct imperfections in the system, people put more and more pressure on the government to do so. Americans were growing fearful that large corporations were going to control the nation. They generally preferred that their elected representative in Congress would take that control instead.

America's Government Begins to Regulate Business

Thus another result of industrialism was governmental regulation of business. Although the regulation at the time was probably meant to be experimental and was not as extensive as today's, a precedent was set. Government regulation of business and industry grew ever after.

399

SECTION 4

Materials

- Newspaper and magazine articles on economic issues

The Role of Economic History

Understanding the development of America's businesses is just as vital to a study of U.S. history as understanding America's exploration and wars. Calvin Coolidge claimed, "The business of America is business." Ask the students to consider the value of understanding the economic history of the United States. For one thing, history provides valuable lessons to young people entering modern businesses. It also gives voting citizens guidance during elections and civic debates.

Modern Economic Issues

Gather articles from newspapers and magazines on the economic issues that are debated today. Compare and contrast these debates with the ones at the end of the nineteenth century. (Note pollution, shortages, and garbage.) Discuss any antitrust suits, such as those against Microsoft (discussed on p. 401) and tobacco companies in the late 1990s.

What labor issues are most often in the news? Have the labor issues changed? Explain why labor unions declined so rapidly during the prosperity of the 1980s and 1990s. New technology allowed more and more Americans to operate their own businesses. Also, labor unions grow when laborers are struggling financially, but they shrink when the economy is good.

A monopoly is the total control of a certain business or industry so that free trade is discouraged. A trust or a holding company, for example, creates a monopoly. This 1881 political cartoon depicts a monopoly as a snake threatening America's liberty.

The Interstate Commerce Act of 1887—Because the ruthless competition among railroads had hurt small shippers and western farmers, government first demanded regulation of railroad rates. The first law regulating industry, the **Interstate Commerce Act** of 1887, was a reaction to the unjust practices of the railroads.

Initially, states set up commissions to regulate the rates railroads could charge. Midwestern states like Illinois and Iowa provided strong enforcement, but in other states, like Massachusetts and Alabama, commissions gave only advisory opinions. Disputes grew as the rulings of some states affected railroad transportation in other states.

When the Supreme Court ruled that states could regulate railroads only within their own state boundaries and not those crossing state lines, Congress felt pressure to act. In 1887 the Interstate Commerce Act was passed. It directed railroads to set "reasonable and just rates." It also prevented railroads from charging more for short runs that involved little competition than for long runs involving stiff competion. An Interstate Commerce Commission was formed to examine complaints and take offenders to court.

But when the offenders came to court, the judges usually decided in favor of the railroads. Thus the ICC lost nearly every case filed from 1887 to 1906. Yet the act had an impact. It set a precedent for the government to organize other independent regulatory agencies. And in later years as the Supreme Court judges changed and reflected public opinion toward business practices more closely, court cases made more regulation effective. ***The Sherman Anti-Trust Act of 1890***—The public viewed trusts with suspicion. They felt that their size and power gave them an unfair edge that harmed free enterprise. Large trusts such as Rockefeller's had driven small companies out of business by lowering prices. Once the competition was gone, prices reached new highs. By 1880 both political parties promised to regulate trusts.

In 1890 under Benjamin Harrison's presidency, Congress passed the **Sherman Anti-Trust Act.** The act said, "Every contract, combination in the form of trust or otherwise . . . in restraint of trade or commerce . . . is declared to be illegal." But since "restraint of trade" was not defined and the courts still favored big business, the act had little effect at first. Its effects were also weakened when trusts devised ways to get around it. A new form of business consolidation, the **holding company,** came into being. The holding company gained control of companies by buying stock. While member companies retained their names, the holding company made decisions for them in the interest of the entire group, as if it were one giant corporation. The holding companies controlled the businesses as efficiently as the trusts had before them.

Abuses of Workers Lead to Labor Unions

The industrial era aided the rapid rise of labor unions. The abuses in some factories opened the door to unofficial and organized protests by the workers. Many began to organize in large groups or unions that could stand up against the management and ask for desired wages and working conditions. Although unions showed spurts of growth in this era, growth was often uneven. Competition for jobs among war veterans and immigrants plus

economic depressions in 1873, 1882, and 1893 hindered their growth.

The Knights of Labor—The **Knights of Labor** began in 1869 under the leadership of Uriah P. Stephens. Its goal was the formation of one big union for all workers, skilled and unskilled, men and women. It sought equal pay for men and women, an eight-hour day for workers, safety features, and compensation (payment for loss) for injuries occurring on the job. In the year 1879 Terence V. Powderly took over the union's leadership. He was against strikes and believed that the union should not take sides politically. The membership rose from 9,000 in 1879 to 115,000 by 1884. By 1886 the Knights had a membership of 700,000.

Unfortunately for the future of the union, 1886 was a bad year. In Chicago about 80,000 workers, mostly Knights, struck for an eight-hour day. The police killed several workers when things appeared to get out of hand. Some anarchists (people who refused to obey the laws) staged a protest rally soon after. The police moved in to break up the meeting and someone threw a bomb into the crowd, killing a policeman and six spectators. A riot ensued, in which eleven more people were killed. The Haymarket Square Riot, as it was called, hurt the unions because people then linked the union with violence. Membership dropped to just 100,000 in four years.

The American Federation of Labor—A second union, the **American Federation of Labor,** began in 1881. Its first president was a British-born cigar maker, **Samuel Gompers.** Gompers saw the problem in the structure of the Knights of Labor and set up his union on different lines. Only skilled workers could join; dues were high; women were not allowed. Workers joined local craft unions with those of the same skills. Local unions then affiliated or associated with state and

401

Microsoft Antitrust Suit
The Sherman Act did not lose its relevance with the passing of the Industrial Age. In fact, its effects continue to be felt in the business world today. In the 1990s, it was the basis for a lawsuit by the Department of Justice against the computer industry's Microsoft Corporation.

Microsoft attracted attention by attaching its Internet Explorer web browser to its Windows operating system. The Justice Department said that Microsoft was trying to use an already illegal monopoly in the operating systems market to establish a monopoly in Internet browsers. The thought was that if computer users received a web browser automatically with their operating system, they would not examine other products. That browser could then control a good portion of Internet traffic.

The Justice Department claimed that Microsoft was violating the Sherman Act in two points. First, the company had entered into agreements with computer manufacturers and service providers that required those companies to use Microsoft operating systems exclusively. Second, they had enforced their monopoly through the pressure of their power in the marketplace.

Two other large companies faced antitrust suits in the latter 1900s. AT&T was on trial from 1974 to 1982, at which time it agreed to stop certain activities in exchange for the dropping of all charges. IBM faced thirteen years of litigation, from 1969 to 1982. The case was finally dismissed, but the company did make some concessions that led to a freer computer market.

Views on Labor Unions
The American Federation of Labor and Congress of Industrial Organizations (AFL-CIO) is a voluntary federation of national and international labor unions. It was created in 1955 by a merger of the AFL and the CIO.

Debate Ideas

Have your students discuss and/or debate the following:

Organized labor has increased the dignity of the individual American worker.

The power to strike is critical to collective bargaining.

The labor union's accomplishments for the individual worker are overrated.

The federation is interested in acquiring good wages and benefits and more input at work for its members. It supports political activism and community service at home. It also wants to be influential globally in the promotion of its goals (e.g., ending child labor). It wants fairer treatment for all groups, regardless of their race, sex, sexual preference, or any other area of difference. For more information on the AFL-CIO, see **www.aflcio.org**.

A voice that speaks against labor unions is the National Right to Work Legal Defense Foundation. This organization works for people who do not want to be forced to join labor unions. It contends that labor unions have undue economic and political influence. Employees should not have to pay dues to support causes they do not agree with or pay fines for acts they committed while being forced into membership. They want to inform employees of legal decisions such as *NLRB v. General Motors Corp.*, which decided that workers could be forced to pay only "financial core" fees to unions. These fees support just those activities that involve bargaining for workplace issues (wages, benefits, and production decisions). For more information on the National Right to Work Legal Defense Foundation, see **www.nrtw.org**.

national groups. Each local union, however, made its own decisions and handled its own funds. The national group provided guidelines. This union also pushed for an eight-hour day and for **collective bargaining** (the right of unions to represent workers in negotiations with owners and managers). This union did use strikes, and its high dues were spent supporting the workers during strike times. A violent strike over a wage cut at Carnegie Steel's Homestead Plant in 1892 greatly hurt this union's attempt to organize in other industries.

Responses to Unions—Employers were often unsympathetic to unions and their demands. They wanted the right to bargain with workers individually and deplored strikes because they hurt production. Courts did not favor unions either and often issued **injunctions,** official court orders, to stop strikes. The local press usually sided with employers too. Since most of the papers made their money from local advertising, they could ill afford to anger their advertisers. The general public reacted negatively to unions because they associated labor aims, like the distribution of wealth and agitation by lower classes, with socialism. Some also opposed collective bargaining because it could deprive an individual of his own worth.

In 1893 a group of employers joined together to form the National Association of Manufacturers. Its aim was to counteract unionism. In 1900 the National Civic Federation was formed. Its leaders, Frank Easley and Marcus Hanna, believed that labor unions were here to stay. The choice then became what kind of union employers would work with. They discouraged anticapitalistic, socialistic, revolutionary unions and encouraged contact with conservative procapitalistic unions.

The Johnstown Flood: The Nightmare of 1889

One of the great disasters in American history occurred in Pennsylvania in 1889. The victims were inhabitants of the mining town of Johnstown and inhabitants of some smaller towns to its north. Over two thousand people died. The killer was a flood resulting from the breaking of an old, neglected earthen dam. To some, however, the killer was actually the negligence of a group of millionaires who owned the dam and refused to make repairs they knew were necessary. These wealthy families were too busy enjoying the lake resort and the hunting and fishing spot created by the formation of Lake Conemaugh (KAHN uh MAW), at the time the largest artificial lake in the world.

The lake was three miles long, one mile wide, and in places one hundred feet deep. It contained twenty million tons of water. The earthen dam, located fourteen miles from Johnstown and at an elevation four hundred feet higher than the town, was thirty-seven years old. It stretched three hundred yards wide and seventy-two feet deep. It was wide enough at the top for a two-lane dirt road. To keep the fish in the lake, the spillways had been closed off. The overflow valves had clogged because of neglect. The few repairs that had been made on the dam had been done by stuffing tree stumps, leaves, and straw into the numerous leaks that had developed since the dam's construction. Several engineers had warned the owners of the dam's deteriorated condition. One company had even offered to pay half the cost of repairing the structure. Yet nothing had been done.

The people in the towns below had become indifferent as well. They had heard so many times that the dam was breaking that they had lost all concern. No one could convince them that the dam would someday actually break. And if it did break, they did not believe that the result would be disastrous.

At 3:10 P.M. on May 31, 1889, it happened. After a number of heavy storms, the dam burst. In thirty-five minutes, all twenty

402

million tons of Lake Conemaugh came rushing down the valley in a wave forty feet high and traveling at forty miles an hour. At times it met an obstruction and the water piled higher, once up to ninety feet, and then it burst through again to rush down on the towns below. Along the way it picked up debris that became as deadly as the wall of water itself: twenty-nine locomotives weighing up to eighty tons each, other railroad cars, boiling hot water from the iron works, hundreds of miles of barbed wire from a factory, the bricks and lumber from crushed houses and businesses, along with trees and animals. Because of the debris, the water at the top of the flood wave moved faster than the water at the bottom. Engineers estimated that the crushing force caused by that difference in speeds was as great as the power behind the water flowing over Niagara Falls. Nothing could stand in its way.

Had it not been for the heroic efforts of many of the townspeople, many more lives would have been lost than actually were. Those who managed to escape the flood stood on the edge and hauled other people out. Some in buildings on the edge of the waters pulled others through windows to the safety of the buildings. Some people even leaped into the rushing waters to make rescues.

Every town along the flood's path was flattened. Finally, the waters were stopped at a bridge in Johnstown, where the debris piled up thirty feet high and covered sixty acres. Behind the debris, Johnstown had become a twenty-foot-deep lake. Then, to make matters worse, the debris caught fire. Some that had escaped drowning but were pinned in the rubble were

403

Department Stores

One development of the nineteenth century that fed Americans' desire for things was the transformation of shopping through the creation of department stores. Department stores offered everything from the practical to the most luxurious of goods, all under one roof. To lure customers inside, stores arranged attractive displays of merchandise in their windows. Once inside, customers would be eager to buy the vast array of items for sale.

Marshall Field of Chicago was one of the giants in this industry. His customers were treated like royalty, regardless—to his credit—of their financial status. Doormen greeted them as they entered the store, and hundreds of workers were available to wait on them and answer their questions. A tearoom offered a nice luncheon for weary shoppers. Company wagons delivered purchases, and unsatisfactory items could be returned. With these enticements, it is no wonder that the consumer was eager to buy.

killed by the fire. Nearly one thousand people were never found.

America and the world came to the rescue of the survivors. Clara Barton and her newly formed Red Cross reacted magnificently to its first major disaster. People from all over the world donated money and food to aid the needy. The millionaires who owned the lake did little except go into hiding to avoid the press.

In a remarkably short time, Johnstown was rebuilt and again became a thriving iron and steel town. A coroner's investigation held the dam's owners responsible for the flood, but few people sued and no one won a suit against the millionaires. The total damages, staggering in 1889, came to seventeen million dollars. None of the survivors would ever forget the tragic day when neglect and indifference brought a rushing wall of death into unprepared Johnstown, Pennsylvania.

The Dangers of Materialism

Another obvious result of industrialism was an increase in wealth, both nationally and individually. By the year 1900 the nation counted four hundred millionaires. The buying power of the average worker had increased by fifty percent over forty years. God's Word

Cornelius Vanderbilt's home displayed the extravagant luxury of the wealthy.

does not denounce wealth or money; instead, it denounces the love of money, its unwise use, and the envy and greed it can encourage. Christians are told to give God the first fruits of their labor. Sadly, in the industrial era as well as today, many Americans who had wealth were never satisfied. They wanted and sought more. Some of the rich competed with one another in showing off their wealth. **Materialism,** putting a higher value on money and possessions than Scripture and common

Report on the Richest People in America

Have students prepare written or oral reports on the richest people in America, either historical people or current people listed in *Forbes* magazine. The main object of the reports is for the students to understand how the people got their wealth, their attitudes about wealth, and how their wealth has affected them.

sense dictate, surfaced as an American problem. It was a problem that would appear repeatedly throughout the twentieth century.

SECTION REVIEW

1. List five major changes in America that resulted from industrial growth.

2. What is capitalism?

3. How was social Darwinism applied to industry?

4. What industry was regulated by the Interstate Commerce Act of 1887?

5. Why did labor unions emerge? Name two of the earliest ones.

 How did holding companies allow businesses to get around the legislation against trusts?

SUMMARY

The late 1800s was a time of great industrial expansion for the United States. Growing industries used the nation's resources, its labor supply, railroad networks, and developing technology to produce more and more. Businesses also used forms of organization such as incorporation, trusts, and holding companies to increase capital and grow more powerful. While industrial expansion was generally good for the country, it did allow some men to take advantage of others while amassing large personal fortunes. Fear of ruthless business practices aided the growth of labor unions and eventually prompted the beginnings of government regulation of industry.

405

Section Review Answers

1. Trade increased; urbanization occurred; urban problems became more noticeable; Americans had more leisure time; and family life changed as many women worked in factories. (p. 398)

2. an economy in which businesses are privately owned, competition is open, and people are free to invest and make profits (p. 399)

3. Profits are most important. Eliminating weaker competitors is just part of the struggle for survival. (p. 399)

4. the railroad industry (p. 400)

5. because of the abuses in some factories (in wages and working conditions); the Knights of Labor and the American Federation of Labor (p. 401)

 They allowed businesses to take over companies not by forming

trusts but by buying stock and controlling the companies as stockholders. (p. 401)

Chapter Review Idea

For homework or in class, have the students write ten questions from the text. The questions should include three *who* questions, three *what* questions, two *how* questions, and one *why* question. (You may want them to write the *who* and *what* questions on one piece of paper and the *how* and *why* questions on another piece.) When the students hand in their papers, have them stack the *who* and *what* pages in one pile and the *how* and *why* pages in another.

Divide the class in half by numbering off by twos. Have the "ones" move to one side of the room and the "twos" to the other. Decide which team will answer first. Explain that the *who* and *what* questions will be worth 100 points and the *how* and *why* questions will be worth 200 points. A wrong answer deducts fifty points. When the class period is over, the team with the highest number of points wins. Make sure that you finish with the side that began second. Ask the teams questions by working down the rows one at a time.

Chapter Review

People, Places, and Things to Remember

Ellis Island
Exclusion Act of 1882
consolidation
Cornelius Vanderbilt
Union Pacific
Central Pacific
James J. Hill
Great Northern Railroad
Alexander Graham Bell
Thomas Edison
capital
sole proprietorships
partnerships
Andrew Carnegie
corporation
John D. Rockefeller
trust
capitalism
social Darwinism
Interstate Commerce Act
Sherman Anti-Trust Act
holding company
Knights of Labor
American Federation of Labor
Samuel Gompers
collective bargaining
injunctions
materialism

Review Questions

Write the word that best completes each sentence.

1. A business owned by just one person is called a ___.
2. Businesses need large amounts of money or ___ to finance their operations.
3. The Interstate Commerce Act was intended to regulate some of the abuses in the ___ industry.
4. Union members wanted ___ so that the union could negotiate with owners and management.
5. Many of America's turn-of-the-century immigrants landed first at ___.
6. A ___ is an advantageous business organization assembled under a charter by individual stockholders.
7. A theory of ___ was used to support the idea that the biggest and best businesses would survive while others would fall.
8. Uriah P. Stephens first led an early labor union called the ___.
9. The ___ was legislation intended to break up the unfair advantages of trusts.

Match these men with their achievements.

10. Alexander Graham Bell
11. Andrew Carnegie
12. Thomas Edison
13. Samuel Gompers
14. John D. Rockefeller
15. Cornelius Vanderbilt

a. invented the incandescent light
b. formed a trust in the oil industry
c. consolidated railroads in the Northeast
d. invented the telephone
e. built a huge steel empire
f. president of the American Federation of Labor

Questions for Discussion

16. Should government place controls on industries? Explain your answer.
17. Can Christians be wealthy without being materialistic? Can Christians be materialistic without being wealthy? Explain your answers.

Chapter Review Answers

1. sole proprietorship (p. 396)
2. capital (p. 396)
3. railroad (p. 400)
4. collective bargaining (p. 402)
5. Ellis Island (p. 390)
6. corporation (p. 396)
7. social Darwinism (p. 399)
8. Knights of Labor (p. 401)
9. Sherman Anti-Trust Act (p. 401)
10. d (p. 396)
11. e (p. 396)
12. a (p. 396)
13. f (p. 401)
14. b (p. 397)
15. c (p. 393)
16. Answers will vary. Because men are sinful, employers will tend to take advantage of their employees, so some regulation is probably necessary. However, the government might abuse its power if given too much.
17. The answer to both questions is yes. Materialism depends not on income but on attitude toward income.

History Skills

What God Says About the Problems of an Industrial Society

As they adapted to the industrial age, Americans tended to ignore the Bible. Use your Bible to find what God says about (1) selfish employers, (2) angry employees, (3) government regulations, and (4) materialism.

A. Social Darwinists believed it was the duty of the strong to take advantage of the weak.

   1. What does God say employers owe employees (Luke 10:7)?

   2. How does God respond to those who oppress the poor (Prov. 22:16)?

   3. Who was told not to abuse their power to collect money (Luke 3:12-13)?

B. Gompers's AFL supported strikes, even though strikes sometimes became violent.

   4. What should be our attitude towards our wages (Luke 3:14)?

   5. Why should Christians honor their masters (I Tim. 6:1)?

   6. How should servants respond to cruel masters (I Pet. 2:18)?

C. The American public asked the government to solve their problems with industry.

   7. Where should men look for help (Jer. 17:5, 7)?

   8. What are the responsibilities of a ruler (Rom. 13:3-4)?

   9. What abuses are rulers prone to commit (Ezek. 45:9-10)?

D. Rich Americans replaced the true gospel with a false "gospel of wealth."

   10. What is the purpose of riches (Eph. 4:28)?

   11. What is the ultimate value of riches (Matt. 16:26)?

   12. How much wealth should we seek (Prov. 30:8-9)?

407

History Skills

A.

   1. fair wages

   2. with emptiness

   3. tax collectors

B.

   4. be content

   5. God's testimony

   6. serve with fear

C.

   7. the Lord

   8. minister good and execute judgment

   9. violence, spoil, injustice, exactions

D.

   10. to have to give to those who need

   11. nothing

   12. neither poverty nor riches

Wide-Open Spaces

The frontier's wide-open spaces beckoned young couples looking for land to claim by the sweat of their brow.

Chapter Motivation

Ask your students if they think that Americans today would go to an uninhabited planet to homestead if free or cheap land were being given away. Ask them to explain their answers. What other countries in the world would be more likely to have people take the opportunity to receive free land? *(China, India, and other heavily populated, agrarian societies)* Contrast American society today and American society in the mid-1800s.

Materials

SECTION 1

• Samples of gold and silver jewelry
• Bibles
• A collection of American short stories that includes works by Bret Harte
• Paper money from a board game
• Dry goods such as sugar, flour, rice, and oats (five pounds of each)

SECTION 2

• Activity A from Chapter 20 of the *Student Activities* manual
• CD, cassette, or other recording with songs of the West
• Books on outlaws and lawmen

The Last Frontier

The term *frontier* refers to the outer fringe of settlement. America's frontier had moved west gradually. First men, moved across the Appalachians and then on to the Mississippi River. The next frontier, however, had been the far West. The discovery of gold and rich lands on the West Coast had lured numbers of settlers west. At the same time, much of the land from the Mississippi River to the Great Plains and beyond the Rocky Mountains to the Great Basin was bypassed and remained unsettled until after the Civil War.

Western explorers and wagon trains crossing the plains and deserts believed that the hard soil was not fertile. The climate seemed unsuitable too. The winters were cold, and the summers almost unbearably hot. Even worse, rainfall was scarce. Many areas received less than twenty inches annually. The area could have made up for its lack of rainfall had a good water supply been available. But the flow of most of the rivers and the underground water supply rose and fell with the amount of precipitation. A further hindrance to settlement was the lack of trees on the plains. Not only would it be hard for settlers to get used to the glaring sun, but they also could not build the log cabins and wooden houses that had been their homes in the East.

As if the geography of the vast region were not enough to deter settlement, the Indians added to the risk. The land west of the ninety-fifth meridian of longitude (roughly

CHAPTER 20	Lesson Plan Chart			
Section Title	**Main Activity**	**Pages**	**Time Frame**
1. Gold and Silver Miners	Get-Rich-Quick Schemes	408-11	1-2 days
2. The Cowboys	Myth and Reality	411-19	2-3 days
3. The Homesteaders	Teaching History Through Literature	419-24	1-2 days
4. The Indians	Mistreatment of Aboriginal Peoples	424-27	1-2 days
Total Suggested Days (including 1 day for review and testing)			6-10 days

west of the first tier of states west of the Mississippi) was occupied by the Plains Indian tribes, and the Plains Indians were very warlike. Their lands had been invaded by eastern Woodland tribes who had been forced west by previous white settlement. The Plains Indians knew enough American history to realize that the eastern Indians had been cheated out of their land. These Plains Indians knew that white settlement meant being uprooted, and they were not about to give up the plains lands without a fight.

Despite these many discouragements to pioneers, the West would be settled. The building of the transcontinental railroad brought change to the Great Plains. With this new form of transportation, people and agricultural products could easily move across the grasslands. As the railroads crisscrossed the prairies, the vast herds of buffalo on which the

nomadic Indians depended declined. Railroad crews shot buffalo for meat, to prevent the buffalo from damaging the tracks, and for the sheer sport. This activity took away the Plains Indian's source of food, shelter, and clothing and made him a less formidable enemy.

New inventions and pioneer flexibility also aided the plains settler in his quest to conquer and adapt to the prairie environment. Although earlier writers had predicted it would take seventy-five to a hundred years to settle the remaining lands, by 1890 the frontier was closed. There were no more large tracts of land that had enough water available to make them useful for settlement. The frontier had been conquered largely by three groups of Americans who had sought its wealth and opportunity. They were the miners, the cattlemen, and the settled farmers.

Gold and Silver Miners

In 1848 the discovery of gold had drawn thousands to California. When the California gold fields had no more to offer, prospectors turned to other jobs or moved elsewhere to seek their fortunes. Some wandered into the mountain areas of the West that had known few explorers, and many were not disappointed by what they found. For about a generation these lands yielded new riches.

Riches in the West

There were several great strikes of gold and silver that brought miners into the West. The first was near Pikes Peak in Colorado. (Colorado was then part of the Kansas Territory.) Many prospectors raced across the prairie with "Pikes Peak or bust!" written on their wagons. This strike made few men rich, but it brought attention to the region.

A richer strike was made in northern Nevada. There James Finney and Henry Comstock mined gold. At ground level they made $5.00 a day. Two feet down, their take

Pioneers saw great herds of buffalo roaming the West.

- Art books containing art of the West
- A map showing western lands owned by the federal government (available from the U.S. Geological Survey)
- Special speaker: a rancher or farmer

SECTION 3
- Activity B from Chapter 20 of the *Student Activities* manual
- Historical novels about the Old West

SECTION 4
- Activities C and D from Chapter 20 of the *Student Activities* manual
- *North American Indians* by David Murdoch (Eyewitness Books)
- October 1992 issue of *National Geographic*

SECTION 1

Objectives
Students should be able to
1. Explain why the Great Plains, Rocky Mountains, and most of the Great Basin were not settled until after the Civil War.
2. Describe the development of mining towns.
3. Explain westerners' reasons for wanting money backed by silver.

The Lone Ranger
Fascination with the Old West continued into the twentieth century. Western movies, along with radio and television shows, created many legends for Americans. One of those legends, who appeared on both radio and television, was the Lone Ranger. Together with his friend, Tonto, the Lone Ranger triumphed over the bad guys in a weekly show.

The Lone Ranger's "real" name was John Reid. He was one of a group of six Texas Rangers who were after outlaw Butch Cavendish and his band. The Rangers were led into an ambush, and all but Reid were killed. He was wounded

---

Bring in Samples of Jewelry

Bring in some samples of gold and silver, and explain why these metals are so valuable (scarcity, beauty, durability).

Share Experiences with Panning

If you or any of the students have experience with panning or mining (at a tourist attraction, for example), share your experiences.

Get-Rich-Quick Schemes

Another trademark of Americans is their schemes to get rich quickly. Many Americans throw their money into

investments that promise fabulous returns. Ask the students whether they know any Bible verses on acquiring quick wealth (e.g., through gambling). (See I Timothy 6:6-10.)

Explain to the students that prudent businessmen and bankers usually made more profit from the gold than the miners. Even today, extracting raw materials from the ground is not nearly as profitable as wise investment of money in manufacturing and services. Countries with some of the greatest mineral reserves, such as the Democratic Republic of Congo, are some of the poorest, as different groups war over con-

trol of the mineral fields. But the countries that supply the expertise to manufacture goods from the products, such as Japan, are among the wealthiest countries. Abundance of natural resources is clearly *not* the main reason for America's economic success.

Read a Short Story

Bret Harte is perhaps the best-known author of short stories about the American West. Three frequently reprinted tales are "The Luck of Roaring Camp," "The Outcasts of Poker Flat," and "Tennessee's Partner." If you read one of the stories, be sure to discuss realism.

but recovered under the watchful care of his friend Tonto.

The two men fought out a battle with Butch Cavendish and then devoted the rest of their lives to righting injustice throughout the West. The Lone Ranger never accepted money from those he helped. He supported himself with the proceeds of a silver mine that he and his brother had discovered. The Lone Ranger was easily recognizable by his mask and white horse, Silver.

The Lumber Flume

Strong mine shafts were essential to the safety of a mine. Rotted timbers could easily cause a cave-in, so mine operators had a regular need for new logs to fix potential problems. Sawmills at the top of mountains often provided the logs needed by the mines in the earth below. A quick means of getting those logs from one place to the other was a lumber flume.

The flume was a chute through which water flowed. The logs were placed in the flume at the top of the mountain, and gravity carried them down through the water to the mine below, often at high speeds. Generally, it was an efficient way of getting the logs to where they needed to go.

An 1875 event foreshadowed a future use of the lumber flume. On a dare, reporter H. J. Ramsdell went with four other men for a wild ride down the flume in an improvised boat. Similar to a log ride in a modern-day amusement park, the flume carried the men down the mountain at breakneck speed. James Flood, one of the riders and part owner of the mine, declared that he would not make the trip again if he were given the entire mine.

rose to $20.00 a day. At a depth of four feet, they hit heavy blue-black sand. It had gold in it, but the gold did not seem as pure because it was being affected by a blue substance. They did not know what the blue mineral was, nor did they know that they had found the northern end of a rich lode, or deposit, of precious metal. Several weeks later someone else found out that the "blue stuff" was silver, nearly pure. Over the next thirty years the **Comstock Lode** yielded more than $400 million worth of

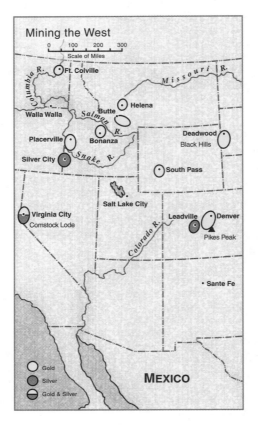

Mining the West

metal. (Fifty-five percent of the wealth from the lode was from silver; forty-five percent from gold.)

Farther north the Fraser and Columbia River valleys also yielded rich finds. Strikes in Idaho and Montana along the Bitterroot and Salmon Rivers attracted thousands of miners. Gold was discovered in Helena, Montana, in 1864 and also in Butte. In the 1880s copper mines were developed in Butte as well. The city is built over a vein one mile deep.

In 1876 two soldiers with prospecting experience discovered gold in the Black Hills of South Dakota, an area that was supposed to belong to the Indians. Fortune seekers soon invaded the area. Although the army had been sent to keep the whites out, it did not. When the government tried to buy back the land from the Sioux—land they had just given them in 1868—the Indians went on a rampage. Nevertheless, the miners got their claim, and the resulting **Homestake Mine** became the world's richest single gold mine.

Mining Camps and Boom Towns

Some miners came west alone, but for safety and for economy in buying supplies, mining guidebooks suggested four-man companies. Miners gathered into makeshift mining camps, living in tents or hastily constructed brush arbors. They staked claims quickly. To keep a claim, a miner had to work it one day out of every three. If a miner did not show up after ten days, someone else could take the claim. Of course the mining claims were not really official, since the miners did not own the land. They depended on claim societies that they had organized to protect their interests.

As more people came, businesses came with them. Supply stores and saloons were usually first. Soon after, a meeting would be called to plan a town. Streets were drawn out and a town name picked. Lots were drawn for

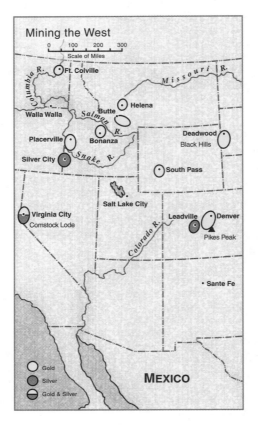

410

Discuss how literature often handles history and how historical fiction can become part of American history too.

Demonstrate Inflation with Paper Money

Bring in paper money from a board game, along with some dry goods (divided into twenty portions). Put a $1 price tag on each item. Call to your desk "store" three students to represent all of the people in the region. Give them each $5 worth of gold "certificates" (just enough for everyone to buy five items). Now let each of them make a purchase, one at a time. They can spend

their money as they wish. Notice that some items sell out while others are left. Ask the students how the shopkeeper would respond to the day's sales. *(He would mark up the price of the items that sold quickly, and he would mark down the price of the unpopular items so that he could sell them.)*

Now pretend that the government has made silver an acceptable form of money too. Give the three students ten dollars this time—five dollars worth of gold certificates and five dollars worth of silver certificates. Let each of them come to the store, one at a time, to make purchases.

After the first customer leaves, what does the shopkeeper notice? *(Half of his goods were sold.)* If he sees two more customers approaching his store, what is he likely to do? *(Lead the students to understand that a smart shopkeeper will quickly raise his prices on everything that is selling—perhaps more than doubling the prices, depending on how much he sells of an item.)*

This situation illustrates why the farmers were demanding silver minting and why the northeastern businessmen wanted only the gold standard. The farmers benefited by having more buying power, though the ben-

home sites. A church, a school, a miner's union hall, and processing mills for ore soon dotted the town's horizon. Where services were lacking, enterprising people could just about name their own fees. For example, one woman made $18,000 in one year just baking pies for the miners.

A few people made fortunes in mining. Many more made only a living. If the ore ran out or prices dropped, the mines closed down. Often miners, storekeepers, hotel owners, newsmen, and their families left when a mine closed. If everyone left, the empty buildings became weather-beaten over the years and were known as ghost towns. In addition to the mining towns, other ghost towns resulted from abandoned railroad towns, cow towns, lumber towns, and even farm towns across the West.

Silver and the Currency System

The mining of silver and gold aided the growth of the nation's economy. From before the Civil War until 1873, the government had minted both gold and silver coins. These coins were the nation's money during that time, along with greenbacks (paper money) printed during the war. When both the greenbacks and the silver coins were phased out, however, the money supply rested on its gold. The country was on the "gold standard."

Naturally, the price of silver plunged sharply once the government quit buying it for coins. Miners were disappointed by this action, and so were many other Westerners. The public began to pressure Congress for legislation that would put money backed by silver into circulation along with that backed by gold. They wanted more money (which would cause inflation) because they believed it would be easier for them to buy goods and to pay off old debts.

Finally in 1878 Congress passed the **Bland-Allison Act.** It set the price of silver at a 16:1 ratio (sixteen ounces of silver would be equal to one ounce of gold) and also required the secretary of the treasury to buy $2 to $4 million a month in silver at the market price. This silver was coined but only into token silver dollars that were still backed by gold in the treasury's vaults. Farmers, silver miners, and mine owners were not satisfied. When six new states having agricultural and mining interests came into the Union, supporters of the free coinage of silver had more leverage. They were able to force the issue, and by 1896 the Democratic Party supported free silver in its party platform.

SECTION REVIEW

1. List at least four reasons people were hesitant to settle the frontier.
2. What system of transportation encouraged the settlement of the frontier?
3. The discovery of what two metals drew thousands into the Great Plains territories?
4. Why did ghost towns emerge?

 Why did Westerners object to a "gold standard" for the nation's money supply?

The Cowboys

Cattlemen played an important role in developing the American West. Acre for acre, they were responsible for taming more of the new frontier than the miners or pioneer farmers, and they did so with a relish and a romance that have appealed to people ever since.

The era of the cattle frontier was short. Although the animals had roamed the Southwest since the Spanish explorers brought the first cattle to the New World, a large cattle industry did not boom until after the Civil War. The peak of cowboy activity came in the 1880s, and by the early 1890s most of the cowboy legend had passed into history,

411

Gold Standard
Describe the gold standard by explaining that every dollar in circulation was either an actual gold piece worth a dollar or other money that was backed by a dollar's worth of gold in the nation's treasury. In other words, the money in circulation was limited to the amount of gold either held by the treasury or circulated in coins. There was a fixed amount of money.

The "silverites" wanted to increase that amount by adding money backed by silver in a similar way to that backed by gold. Because the West had lots of silver from its mines, such an action would automatically make that region "richer."

SECTION 2
Objectives
Students should be able to
1. Explain why the cattle drives were begun.
2. Name two important cattle trails.
3. List reasons for the decline of the cattle industry.
4. Explain why cattlemen were opposed to sheep on the range.

---

efits were only temporary. The government today controls inflation by controlling how much money it prints. Both sides of the debate continue to use the same old arguments. Note that the Bible calls for a just/stable standard (Prov. 11:1; 20:23).

Section Review Answers
1. infertile soil; severe climate; scarce rainfall; few rivers and an inadequate underground water supply; no trees for lumber and fuel; and hostile Plains Indians (any four). (pp. 408-9)
2. transcontinental railroads (p. 409)
3. gold and silver (pp. 409-10)
4. When the ore ran out near a mining town (or the main business died out at other towns), people moved away, leaving the buildings to decay. (p. 411)

 If all the nation's money were backed by gold, the federal government would not need to buy silver, and miners would be devastated. Without silver-backed money, the currency supply would decrease. Westerners thought having more money available would let them buy more and repay debts more quickly. (p. 411)

SECTION 2
Materials
- Activity A from Chapter 20 of the *Student Activities* manual
- CD, cassette, or other recording with songs of the West
- Books on outlaws and lawmen
- Art books containing art of the West
- A map showing western lands owned by the federal government (available from the U.S. Geological Survey)
- Special speaker: a rancher or farmer

Dime Novels

Many of the major western legends won their fame or notoriety through the stories told about them in dime novels. Dime novels were serial stories that recorded the adventures, some true and some not, of various characters from American history and legend. The books got their name from their initial selling price.

Life After Crime

Emmett Dalton was not the only former desperado to successfully adjust to the life of an honest man. The former James-Younger gang produced three such men.

Frank James surrendered to the governor of Missouri shortly after his brother Jesse was murdered. When he was acquitted, Frank took up honest employment. He worked as a race starter, a theater doorman, and an organizer of a Wild West show. A former comrade, Cole Younger, joined him in this last venture.

After serving part of a prison term, Cole Younger was paroled in 1901. He sold tombstones and then insurance before joining with Frank James in the entertainment business. When their show broke up, he continued to travel, giving lectures against crime. Cole's younger brother Bob was on his way to living honestly and with distinction. He studied medicine with good success while he was in prison, but he died of tuberculosis in 1889, twelve years before his brothers were paroled.

The Outlaws: Men Who Reaped What They Sowed

Jesse and Frank James: Both had been Confederate raiders with a rebel leader named Quantrill. After the war they took up a career of robbing banks, trains, and stagecoaches in Missouri and other nearby states. Their gang included the four Younger brothers. They claimed that the Northerners drove them to their life of crime, and they gained many sympathizers who regarded them as modern "Robin Hoods" instead of the thieves that they were. Jesse, whom his friends called Dingus, was shot in the back by a "friend" who wanted the reward. He was thirty-four. Frank surrendered, was tried, and was acquitted because of a great deal of political pressure.

Billy the Kid: At the age of seventeen he became involved in the Lincoln County, New Mexico, cattle wars. He fought for an English gentleman, John H. Tunstall, who became a father-image to the young boy. When a crooked sheriff and his posse murdered Tunstall, Billy swore to get revenge, and he did. By the time he was eighteen, Billy was charged with twelve murders.

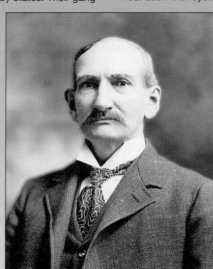

Frank James

Captured by a former friend, Pat Garrett, Billy murdered his two guards and escaped again. Garrett eventually found him again and killed him. He was only twenty-one years old.

Black Bart: He was called "the gentleman bandit." Primarily a stagecoach robber, he wore a flour sack with eyeholes as a mask, treated everyone with the best of manners, and left a poem at the scene of each crime. Bart was captured when a handkerchief he dropped at one job was traced to him, and his real name was discovered to be Charles Bolton. After his release from prison, Bolton disappeared.

The Dalton Gang: Most of their crime spree took place over an eighteen-month period. All the gangmen were in their twenties. While attempting to rob a bank at Coffeyville, Kansas, all except one were killed. The survivor, Emmett, had eighteen wounds. After spending fourteen years in prison, he married the girl who had waited for him. They moved to Los Angeles, where Emmett worked as a building contractor, a real estate man, and a movie writer. Outspoken in his condemnation of outlaws, Emmett died in 1937, a respected businessman.

412

Student Activity A: It's the End of the Trail

This prewriting activity gives students practice in editing their writing, looking for both stylistic and mechanical errors.

Songs of the West

Play some songs of the West for your students and discuss the images they reveal. The songs may include "Shenandoah," "Red River Valley," "Home on the Range," "Whoopie-Ti-Yi-Yo," "The Yellow Rose of Texas," and "Cool Water."

Dress-Up Day

Have the students dress up as characters from the Old West. Each should come prepared to share one unusual fact about the person he represents.

Books on Outlaws and Lawmen

Have the students close their books. Then ask them to name as many famous outlaws and gunslingers from the Old West as they can. Discuss what the students already know about these figures and where they got their information. Display books on the outlaws and lawmen of the West, and allow the students to look up information on these historical figures to distinguish truth from myth.

Bring in Collections of Western Art

Bring to class books containing works by Charles M. Russell, Frederick Remington, or Olaf Selter. You or your students might also bring in samples of (or pictures of) western décor, which is popular in many areas of the country today.

Jesse James

Harry Tracy: Tracy was the subject of one of the greatest manhunts in the nation's history. Being pursued throughout the state of Oregon, he could have escaped back to the hideouts in the West but seemed to relish the hunt. He stole a boat and sailed around Puget Sound, stole a train, had lunch with farmers and their families, joined the posses looking for him, called sheriffs on the telephone to tell them he was in town, and even helped do some of the work on the farms he visited. Eventually cornered by a group of farmers, Tracy killed himself.

leaving the dress and song to be copied and idealized by twentieth-century Americans. In the twenty-five short years that the cattle trade flourished, forty thousand men drove ten million head of cattle over a network of trails, most of which led north from Texas.

The term *cowboy* was a fitting one. Photographs of the era, and there are many, and artwork by such cowboy artists as Charles M. Russell, Frederic Remington, and Olaf Seltzer show faces of young men. Booking and arrest records from cowboy towns show that most were under twenty. Young cowboys spent a few years riding the range or trail and then usually married, settling down as farmers or ranchers.

A Wealth of Cattle

Following the Civil War, Texans began to realize that the growing herds of longhorn cattle on their lands would bring large prices at market. The Easterners were hungry for beef, and they had the money to buy the cattle. Since there were no railroads reaching to Texas, the only way to get the cattle to market was to walk them there.

The Cattle Trails—Cattle could be sold at a much higher price in the East than in the West. Steers cost $5.00 when fed on the open range on free public lands. It cost about one cent per mile to drive them north. There they could be sold for between $25 and $50 a head. To take advantage of such profits, cattlemen began to move herds across the Red River in 1866.

The closest railroad at that time reached to Sedalia, Missouri. But cowboys moving north on the Sedalia Trail did not find a warm welcome. For one thing, the cowboys had trouble driving the cattle through the forests and brush of eastern Oklahoma and southern Missouri. For another, cattle ticks clung to the Texas longhorns for hundreds of miles. The insects

413

A Life of Violence

For the few outlaws who reformed, there were many others who died the same way they had lived— violently. Though faced with the opportunity to change, these men persisted in their wicked ways. John Wesley Hardin is one example.

Hardin was born into the home of a Methodist preacher, and his father hoped that his son would follow him into the ministry. However, young Wesley showed more of an inclination for the pistol than the pulpit. He had a hot temper and was quick to act violently on his impulses. By age twenty-one, he had already committed several murders.

After an encounter that nearly cost him his life, Hardin tried to assume a new identity in Florida, but the law caught up with him three years later. In prison for seventeen years, Hardin eventually settled down to a wise use of his time. He studied theology and became the superintendent of the prison Sunday school. He also studied law and made preparations to take the bar. When he was released, he started a legal practice. But unfortunately he did not sever all of the ties to his former life. He kept company with the wrong crowd and was eventually murdered.

then fell off and attached themselves to stock in Oklahoma and Missouri. Those cattle lacked the immunity of the longhorns, and many animals died from outbreaks of Texas fever. Some laws were passed to prohibit the passage of Texas herds, but some people took matters into their own hands. They set up "shotgun quarantines" to keep the longhorns from passing through their lands.

In 1867 Joseph G. McCoy, a shrewd cattle broker from Illinois, built large corrals in Abilene (AB uh leen), Kansas. Using the railroad, which had just reached Abilene, he shipped cattle to the Chicago stockyards. This cut the distance of the long drives and freed the cattlemen from the dangers of armed farmers farther east. It also made the **Chisholm** (CHIZ um) **Trail** the busiest trail north.

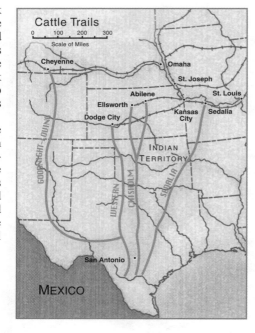

Huge herds of longhorn steers were driven along trails and then taken by train to Chicago stockyards.

414

The Chisholm Trail took its name from an Indian trader, Jesse Chisholm, who used the 225-mile trail not to move cattle, but to take supplies to Indian Territory (modern Oklahoma). Although cattle drives became common, they continued to meet difficulties. The trail ran through Indian Territory, and the Chickasaw Indians began levying a grazing tax of up to fifty cents a head on all the cattle driven through. Also, farmers near the trails began putting up fences to keep the cattle out. This meant less open range and fewer water holes for moving stock. Thus, the cowboys began to swing farther west before heading north. They connected with new railroad lines at Ellsworth and Dodge City, Kansas. The Ellsworth route was a cutoff from the Chisholm Trail. The trail to Dodge City was named the Western Trail.

Myth and Reality

Ask the students to try to summarize the elements in a typical western novel or movie: the strong, silent hero; the eastern teacher who falls for the hero; the bullying villain; the crime; the chase; the barroom brawl; and the showdown. Discuss some of the common myths described in the margin above and on the next page. Ask the students to identify modern examples of myth-making by Hollywood.

Two New Mexico ranchers looked for a southeasterly route that would allow them to drive their cattle to the Pecos River and then up the Pecos to the markets in Colorado. Many people thought such a trail to be impossible, primarily because of one stretch of eighty miles that had no water. Nonetheless, Charles Goodnight and Oliver Loving hired eighteen well-armed men, rounded up two thousand head of cattle, and set out for the Pecos in 1866. On the first trip they lost nearly four hundred cattle, but on their second trip they lost no cattle at all. By 1895 ten thousand head of cattle had taken the **Goodnight-Loving Trail** to western markets. The greatest danger along the route became Comanche Indians, who were on the lookout for free steak on the hoof. In fact, Loving, who had also opened the Shawnee Trail, was killed in an Indian raid on one of his drives.

The Cattle Drive—The heart of the cattle industry and the most important part of a cowboy's job was the trail drive. Getting ready for the drive took careful planning. A rancher or cattle buyer set out to gather a herd in the early spring. The ideal size for a herd was two thousand head of four-year-olds.

The **trail boss,** who was paid around $125 a month, was in charge of the men, equipment, and animals. It was his responsibility to get the herd to market safely. About eight cowboys were hired to work the herd at salaries ranging from $25 to $40 a month. Two were "point" men who rode in the lead. Two "swing" men and two "flank" men rode beside the herd and kept the stock from wandering off. Two "drag" men brought up the rear. Riding in choking dust, they had to keep any weak and tired stragglers moving along. The outfit was accompanied by a cook. He hauled the chuck wagon a mile or two ahead of the herd. Thus he could stop to have food ready for a tired crew. The cook's day could start as early as 3:00 A.M. and sometimes lasted until

The Lawmen: The Guys in the White Hats

Tom Smith: He served as the sheriff of Abilene, Kansas, before Wild Bill Hickock. Smith was actually the man who cleaned up Abilene, and he did it with his fists more than with his guns. He was widely respected by the citizens. He was killed when trying to arrest a homesteader.

Wyatt Earp: Wherever he was sheriff, Earp was not well liked. He and a brother and some friends killed three cowboys in the famous gunfight at the O.K. Corral in Tombstone, Arizona. Considered murderers by the townspeople, Earp and his group left town shortly thereafter. Earp died in 1927 at the age of seventy-one.

Bat Masterson: His first love was gambling, but he also served as a rider for the railroads. As sheriff of Tombstone, Arizona, for two years, he did an excellent job of maintaining the peace. Later he became a sportswriter in New York. Teddy Roosevelt made him a deputy U.S. marshal.

The Pinkertons: This detective agency hunted down and captured many criminals. They also established the first Rogues Gallery for identifying known outlaws. The Pinkertons also became known as strikebreakers and union infiltrators as well.

Bill Tilghman: Like Tom Smith, Tilghman used his guns only when he had to. He served as the U.S. marshal in Perry, Oklahoma, for thirty-five years. Tilghman was so well respected by even the outlaws and their gangs that one famous thief refused to let a henchman shoot Tilghman in the back because he was "too good a man." Tilghman was killed when he grabbed a gunman and asked a bystander to take the man's gun. The bystander did, and then he shot Tilghman.

- Most people in town were working, not leisurely milling around the streets or in the saloon.
- Most cowboys and gunslingers wore a sort of sombrero, borrowed from the Mexicans, not a Stetson or ten-gallon hat.
- No more than thirty-five thousand cowboys ever hit the cattle trail, and one-third of the cowboys were Mexican or black. Blacks have been excluded from popular accounts and western films, so they are almost ignored in the history of the West.

Old Blue

One of the most famous travelers on the Goodnight-Loving Trail was a steer named Old Blue. On every drive, one steer usually assumed leadership of the herd. A good steer who was not edgy or temperamental was a great asset to a trail boss. It was said that Old Blue knew the trail up to Dodge City better than his owner, Charles Goodnight. For eight years, sometimes twice a year, Old Blue would lead a herd down the trail to market. Supposedly, he never shied or stampeded. Old Blue was rewarded for his leadership abilities by being spared from the slaughterhouse; he lived to the ripe old age (for a steer) of twenty. Today his horns are on display in a museum in Canyon, Texas.

Private Eyes

Pinkerton's National Detective Agency, started in 1852 by Scottish immigrant Allan Pinkerton, grew quickly in popularity. By the time of its founder's death, it had offices in Chicago (its original headquarters), New York, Denver, Seattle, and Kansas City. Criminals throughout the country had a special name for the Pinkertons: the Eye. The nickname was drawn from the Pinkerton logo, an open eye, and the agency motto, "We never sleep." Because the Pinkertons did so much to establish the modern detective business, the term "private eye" came to be applied to all detectives.

415

Roundups

Before they could drive the cattle on the trail, cowboys had to round them up on the range. Cattle that were to be sent to market were rounded up in the fall. But the big roundup took place in the spring. This was the time to separate and brand new calves.

Before the invention of barbed wire made the separation of land practical, ranchers grazed their herds together on the open range. Brands were a necessity for identifying one's herd. As calves were born each year, they had to be added to the herd. The spring roundups gathered the cattle together while the calves were still with their mothers. Cowboys then branded the calves with the mark of their owners.

The roundup could take several weeks. It was a large-scale production and required careful planning. Hundreds of cowboys participated, all of them overseen by a wagon boss. A cook traveled with the group to feed the men, and wranglers took care of the horses (each cowboy had several fresh mounts).

A typical day involved rising before dawn, eating a quick breakfast of steak and coffee, and heading out on the horses. The cowboys would ride out in a circle several miles across. As they worked their way back in, they picked up all the cattle they could find. Some cowboys would branch out to search for stragglers while the group continued to move. The circle might contain a thousand cattle by the time the men had returned to their starting point. The calves then had to be sorted and branded. At sundown the men would gather for supper and within about an hour would be asleep.

midnight. A **wrangler** was usually the youngest of the hands and paid the least. He took care of the horses and the riding equipment.

The drive started at daylight and went until dusk or even later—if the trail boss couldn't find good grass and water. After dinner, a cowboy's work was still not done. At night there were four two-hour watches. Pairs of riders circled the herd, riding in opposite directions, on guard for any signs of trouble. Night riding was not only hated for its loneliness but feared because of its dangers. Almost all stampedes, the most frightening experience faced by a cowboy, started at night. The snap of a twig, the bolt of a jack rabbit, a strange smell, or a streak of lightning could set off a dreaded stampede. If a stampede could not be stopped quickly, the cowboys faced several days of gathering the scattered herd. Even worse, cowboys often died if their horses stumbled and they fell in the dust to be trampled by the herd.

The Development of the Meatpacking Industry

The continued success of the open-range cattle industry was assured for a time by the development of a new industry, meatpacking. Two men, **Philip Armour** and **Gustavus Swift,** led the way in making the meatpacking industry successful. Their success came because they were willing to try new ideas and ways of doing things.

Philip Armour left his Massachusetts home to build sluices (long boxes for separating ore) for California forty-niners. Becoming bored upon his return east, he went to Milwaukee, Wisconsin, where he became his brother's partner in a firm dealing in wholesale grains and provisions. Armour's business boomed when he contracted to sell barrels of meat to the Union armies. Before and during the Civil War, meat was usually slaughtered

locally because the only ways to preserve it for transport were by salting, drying, or pickling. Armour's meat packing operation during the war was a success, and after the war he realized that there would be a large market in the eastern cities for meat if it were shipped there in large quantities. The trail drives helped supply the cattle his business needed, and the railroads provided the transportation to the packing plants. Because the cattle were transported quickly and slaughtered almost immediately, they lost little weight during their journey and yielded large amounts of beef.

In 1875 Armour moved to Chicago and opened a packing plant. Hogs and steers moved down narrow wooden chutes to the slaughterhouse. On entrance, they were stunned by a hammer blow on the head. Slung up by the hind legs from a moving overhead belt, they moved past men who cut their throats, took out their organs, peeled off their hides and bristles, and cut up the meat.

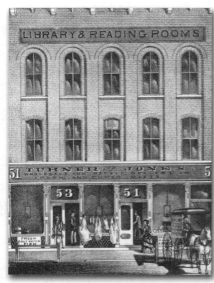

A meat market in the late 1800s looks quite different from a modern supermarket.

Armour also saw the possible value of using **by-products**—bones, hide, and other parts of the animal not generally used for meat. Since his company handled many thousands of cattle and hogs a day, it would be better to turn the by-products into something profitable than to discard them. Consequently, he hired chemists to find uses for them. The fat was used to make soap; bones to make glue, buttons, and fertilizer; and hides to make shoes and gloves. It was said that the meatpackers used "every part of a pig but the squeal."

Gustavus Swift believed there was a market for more fresh meat in his native Massachusetts. In 1875 he also set up a meatpacking company in Chicago, and he began shipping fresh meat across the country a few years later. The meatpackers knew that chilled meat, whether frozen in winter or chilled on ice in summer, stayed fresh as long as a month. With this knowledge, beef had been put on ice in a railroad car and sent to Boston in 1877. But since the meat had lain directly on the ice, it had discolored. Soon after, specially designed refrigerator cars with separate ice bins came into common use. Their ability to carry fresh meat long distances from the meatpacking plants boosted the industry.

The End of the Open Range

By the 1890s the open-range cattle industry was declining. The last long drive was in 1896. Many factors combined to cause this decline. One problem was a drop in meat prices. With the efficiency of production and the amount of meat produced, meat prices plummeted. Thus it became less profitable to raise livestock.

Overgrazing was also a problem. When more and more people became involved in the cattle industry, grazing grasses became shorter and more scarce. Overgrazing was a greater problem as the season wore on, particularly if there had been little rain. In the summer of 1885, especially dry ranges with short grasses left the herds in poor condition. With overgrazing, pure clear springs became stinking mudholes. Harmful weeds took the place of lush prairie grasses. Erosion turned cattle trails into ravines.

Even water could prove a danger to the cattle. Sometimes steers broke for water holes or rivers, and as they charged in on top of each other, some drowned. Some died while crossing rain-swollen rivers like the Colorado, the Brazos, the Red, the Washita (WOSH ih TAW), or the Arkansas. Deadly flash floods were frequent because the sun-baked prairie ground simply could not absorb all of the run-off from sudden thunderstorms.

Droughts and blizzards threatened the cattle as well. When water could not be found, both the cowboys and the cattle suffered terribly. Dehydration made the cattle unmanageable; some even went blind. Winter's cold could freeze the livestock to death if they were stranded in a blizzard without food or shelter.

The summer of 1884 brought severe drought; the winter that followed was the most severe of the century. A raging December blizzard laid a thick coat of ice and sleet over the thin grasses. Cattle drifted south until they reached a 170-mile-long fence that stockmen had built to end earlier feuding with farmers. There thousands of cattle starved or froze to death. More than 10,000 dead cows were found along the fence. Over fifty percent of the stock had died that winter, and the cattle that survived faced another severe drought the following summer. The cycle of drought and blizzard was repeated again in 1886-87. The weather in those years dealt the extensive cattle operations in the West a blow from which they did not quickly recover. President Grover Cleveland, although sympathetic with the plight of the cattlemen, wisely did not offer government aid. This forced American agri-

Refrigerator Cars

George Henry Hammond put ice in a railroad car to send fresh beef to Boston in 1877. But since the meat had lain directly on the ice, it had discolored. Soon after, a car with bunkers, ice tanks, and heat-proof doors was designed. Then a refrigerator car was designed that carried ice in V-shaped containers at the ends of the car. The design of the car helped circulate cool air through the ice container and into the boxcar. The ice tanks could be refilled on sidetracks along the route, usually every twenty-four hours. At first the railroads did not want to build refrigerator cars, so Swift and other meatpackers built their own. Fruits and vegetables were soon shipped using the refrigerator cars too.

Tin Cans

Another major revolution in food preservation in America was the tin can. Prior to innovations such as refrigeration and canned foods, food had to be eaten almost immediately, whether it was beef, dairy products, or fruits and vegetables. The Civil War created an urgent need for ways to keep food longer. Soldiers had to be fed. Consequently, the science of canning foods advanced significantly at that time.

Tin cans were a great asset to the cowboy on the trail. He was able to enjoy not only a greater variety of food but also better-tasting foods. Sometimes the foods even had medicinal value. For instance, if a cowboy had a can of tomatoes, he could drink the juice to settle a queasy stomach and rub the tomatoes across an open wound. Tomatoes could also help heal a horse's wounds. The one potential problem with a tin can—getting it open—was never a difficulty for a cowboy with a six-shooter.

417

Public Lands Today

The use of public lands remains a topic of heated debate between individuals, states, and the federal government. Currently, about half of western land is still owned by the government, and the Department of the Interior must decide on an equitable way to lease the land for private use by miners, ranchers, and lumber companies. Ask the students to find a recent article on this subject, or bring one in yourself.

Also bring in a map of lands owned by the federal government. Contrary to popular opinion, most of the land is not set aside as parks but is directed by the Bureau of Land Management (BLM). *GEOGRAPHY for Christian Schools* (Second Edition), page 190, shows the lands controlled by the BLM.

Grover and Frances Cleveland

Grover Cleveland received a great boost in popularity when he married Frances Folsom in the Blue Room of the White House on June 2, 1886. Though he had kept the event secret until just a few days before the wedding, once the word was out interest in the event soared. The press followed the movements of the couple closely, and the nation soon developed a sincere affection for its new first lady.

One reason for the secrecy of the courtship and marriage was the difference in the Clevelands' ages. President Cleveland was twenty-seven years older than his twenty-two-year-old bride. As he said himself, he was waiting for her to grow up. As her father's law partner, Cleveland had known Frances from her infancy. After her father's death (when Frances was eleven), Cleveland took charge of the estate and helped to supervise her education. Not until she entered Wells College did Cleveland pursue the relationship, however. With her mother's permission, he wrote letters to Frances. After Frances had graduated and taken a trip to Europe, the two were married.

Frances became one of the best loved of all the presidents' wives, and her children, two of whom were born in the White House, shared her popularity. From all accounts, the presidential couple shared a genuine love and affection.

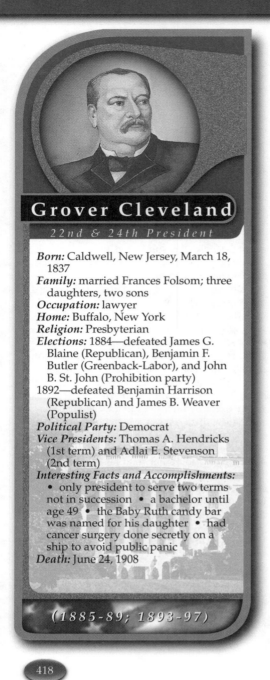

Grover Cleveland
22nd & 24th President

Born: Caldwell, New Jersey, March 18, 1837
Family: married Frances Folsom; three daughters, two sons
Occupation: lawyer
Home: Buffalo, New York
Religion: Presbyterian
Elections: 1884—defeated James G. Blaine (Republican), Benjamin F. Butler (Greenback-Labor), and John B. St. John (Prohibition party)
1892—defeated Benjamin Harrison (Republican) and James B. Weaver (Populist)
Political Party: Democrat
Vice Presidents: Thomas A. Hendricks (1st term) and Adlai E. Stevenson (2nd term)
Interesting Facts and Accomplishments:
• only president to serve two terms not in succession • a bachelor until age 49 • the Baby Ruth candy bar was named for his daughter • had cancer surgery done secretly on a ship to avoid public panic
Death: June 24, 1908

(1885-89; 1893-97)

culture to face its own problems and adjust to the needs of the market at that time instead of letting the government give it immediate help.

Indians and horse thieves also plagued the cowboy trails. Indians often demanded a toll of beef or horses. If the cowboys refused to pay the toll, the Indians would set off a stampede. Horse thieves and cattle rustlers hid along the trail. Stockgrowers' associations tried to rid the plains of such thieves by hanging or shooting them.

Sheep on the Range

One more problem for the cattlemen was the sheepherders. The vast vacant grasslands of the plains were as attractive to sheep owners as they were to cattlemen. In 1880 there were about 200,000 sheep in the northern mountain states and territories. By 1890 there were 1.5 million and by 1900, 15 million.

Cattlemen had reached the grasslands first. Now they eyed the "woollyback" invasion with anger. To the already overstocked ranges, sheep meant disaster. Cattlemen said that sheep ate grass down to the roots and then trampled what little grass was left behind, stripped the ground so that no new growth appeared until the next spring's rain, and fouled water holes, leaving a smell that made cattle refuse to drink.

As grass ran out and tempers grew short, the more numerous cowboys resorted to bullying, intimidating, and even attacking sheepmen and their flocks. Clubbing, shooting, torching, stampeding, and rim-rocking (driving sheep over cliffs) were all effective means of destroying herds. The murder of sheepherders was common too.

A combination of events lessened disputes: the winter of 1886-87 reduced the number of cattle that needed to be grazed; fencing began to divide range lands; some found that it was possible for sheep and cattle to share some of the same range lands.

Life on a Ranch

Most ranches today are relatively small and family operated. Few hire cowboys. Ask a local farmer or rancher (a friend or fellow church member perhaps) to discuss ranch life today and some of the changes since the nineteenth century. Perhaps he can also discuss reasons for entering that line of work (especially if it was based on romantic images he got from reading books or watching movies as a child). Another possibility is to have an adult (or student) describe his or her experiences at one of the dude ranches that have become popular vacation spots in America.

The Candlish Movable Home on the Range

Until the late nineteenth century, sheepherders slept on the ground on blankets. Home on the range was very bumpy and cold. But finally a Wyoming blacksmith came to the rescue. His name was James Candlish. In 1884 he took an old wagon and converted it into the first home on wheels. Open in the front, the wagon had a canvas flap to block the wind. In 1892 a hardware company came out with an improved model that had a stove with an oven, a window, and Dutch doors among other "conveniences." Soon most sheepherders, especially on the northern plains, were owners of their own home on wheels.

There, of course, were some diehards who thought the manufacturers were just trying to pull the wool over their eyes. Some sheep ranchers wouldn't even hire herders who used a wagon. The most legitimate complaint was that to return to his wagon each night the sheepherder had to herd his sheep back over land already grazed.

Nevertheless, for a vast majority of the sheepherders "home, home, on the range" came with wheels in what was the forerunner of the mobile home.

SECTION REVIEW

1. Where did most cattle trails start? How long did the cattle trade flourish?

2. List two trails that were used to herd longhorns from the South to the North.

3. List four reasons for the decline of the cattle industry.

 How was the cattle industry benefited by the meatpacking industry?

The Homesteaders

Rich lands and the promise of a better lifestyle lured people steadily west. Easterners who had farmed worn-out soil left for the West. They were joined by immigrants and Civil War veterans who were looking for a place to settle down. Even a few thousand freed slaves joined these other pioneers on the plains.

Conflict with the Cattlemen

As more and more farmers went west to stake claims on western public lands (the public domain), the acreage left for open-range grazing decreased. Because these homesteaders did not appreciate having their crops overrun by marauding livestock, they put up fences. Since wood for fencing was practically nonexistent, the invention of barbed wire gave farmers the fencing material they needed.

For a time cattlemen fought the homesteaders, cutting the fences and threatening the farmers. There were even some range wars. The cattlemen eventually changed their style. Rather than grazing their cattle on the public domain, they took up ranching on their own lands or land that they leased from the government or other owners.

Farmers on the Plains

The **Homestead Act** of 1862 opened western lands for free settlement. Although the 160 acres allowed to a homesteader was hardly enough to sustain a family in these areas, no one seemed to mind. A settler was supposed to build a 12' by 12' house with windows, have a well, improve the land, and live on the homestead for five years. If he met these terms, the land became his. To cheat on the homesteading terms, some built 12" by 12" houses or had a house on wheels with a

419

Mobile Homes

Americans continued to develop the sheepherders' idea of a home that was mobile. The concept began to be applied to recreation. Some early mobile homes were just cars loaded down with tents and as much camping paraphernalia as they would hold. Others were built specifically for the purpose of travel, with extra storage shelves or built-in beds. One camper was carved out of a huge log. Another looked like a fancy trolley car and contained fine furnishings.

Though some mobile homes were very nice, most were crudely constructed. Travelers in the late 1920s welcomed Arthur Sherman's two-wheeled, six-by-nine-foot trailer. It contained beds and cooking facilities and could be hitched to a car. One of the best things about the trailer was its price. Since the trailer was mass-produced, it could be sold at a price that the average family could afford.

Though mobile homes lost popularity during the Great Depression (camping out was not as much fun when many were "camping out" permanently), they came back into fashion when times got better. Bigger and better vehicles were in demand as Americans continued to earn more money and receive more vacation time.

SECTION 3

Objectives
Students should be able to
1. Explain why farmers sometimes fell into conflict with cattlemen.
2. Explain the significance of the Homestead Act.
3. Describe the settlement of Oklahoma.
4. List the problems and hardships faced by prairie farmers.

Glass Windows
The Homestead Act said that a pioneer family trying to prove up on a piece of land must have at least

---

Section Review Answers

1. Texas; twenty-five years (p. 413)

2. Sedalia, Chisholm, Western, Goodnight-Loving (any two) (pp. 413-15)

3. a drop in meat prices, overgrazing, drowning in rivers or flash floods, droughts and blizzards, Indians and horse thieves, conflicts with sheepherders (any four) (pp. 417-18)

 By finding new ways of preserving meat and of using cattle to their greatest profitability, meatpackers ensured that cattlemen would be able to sell their livestock. (pp. 416-17)

SECTION 3

Materials
- Activity B from Chapter 20 of the *Student Activities* manual
- Historical novels about the Old West

Student Activity B: Outlining Paragraphs

This outlining activity expands the students' outlining skills to include outlining the content within paragraphs.

one glass window in their house. Unfortunately for the settlers, it was very difficult to get glass on the frontier. Not everyone could afford such a luxury. To solve their problem, some families set up a system of sharing. They would pool their resources to buy one glass window and then pass it around. Each family would put up the window long enough for the inspector to check the house, and then they would store the window away to prevent its being broken before other families had the chance to use it. After the inspector left, a durable material would be nailed over the open window frame to protect those inside from the weather.

Homesteaders faced great obstacles to claim their land.

bucket of water on it rolled onto (and off) the land. Some lived on the land seasonally. This last practice was a legal option, however.

Settlers could also increase land holdings legally by outright purchase of as much as an extra quarter-section (a section was 640 acres) at $1.25 per acre. The smallest amount someone could purchase was forty acres. That would have cost the princely sum of $50.00, a large amount in those days. If a pioneer filed a timber claim and planted ten acres in trees, another quarter-section could be added to his holdings. In the first six months after the Homestead Act was passed, settlers gobbled up 224,550 acres of land in Kansas and Nebraska alone.

The railroads sold farmland too, at $2.50 an acre. They sent agents to Europe with millions of pamphlets and posters. Thus the news of cheap American lands circulated in Norway, Denmark, Germany, England, and Wales. The Nebraska and Dakota territorial legislatures also paid immigration bureaus to attract settlers.

The Morrill Land Grant Act of 1862 gave states thirty thousand acres of federal land for every representative and senator they had. Most of the states sold the land to speculators. They in turn sold it to lumber companies, mining companies, and farmers.

The Oklahoma Land Rush

You have read how the government moved the Cherokee and other eastern Indian tribes west in the 1830s. Five tribes from the Southwest, all farming tribes, also were moved to **Indian Territory** (Oklahoma). By the 1880s most of the desirable farmland in the West had been claimed. Then the white man began to look greedily at this Indian Territory.

The railroads, land-hungry white settlers, and speculators saw the opportunity to make some money and pressured the federal government to open up Oklahoma to white settlers.

In 1885 the government bought lands in the territory. President Benjamin Harrison announced that some of these lands would be opened to settlers at noon on April 22, 1889. The U.S. Army was on hand to keep the settlers out until the given hour. More than twenty thousand pioneers were poised on the border that day. At the sound of cannons, they raced across the border to claim their land. Those who made their way into the area in this land boom were called "Boomers." (Some had "jumped the gun" illegally and made their claim ahead of time. These people were called **Sooners**.) Some 1.9 million acres of land were claimed in a few hours. In the year 1893 another part of Oklahoma, the Cherokee Strip, was opened to settlement. Oklahoma gained territorial status in 1890, and in 1907 President Theodore Roosevelt welcomed the

Who Were the Best Settlers?

Ask the students to consider which type of settler was in the best long-term interests of the country: the miner, the rancher, or the farmer. In fact, each of these played a valuable part in the settlement of the West, and in many ways they needed each other. The "glue" that held the West together was the businessmen in the towns who provided the basic services that everyone needed, but the businessmen needed all types of customers in order to stay in business. The same is true today. No specific career is "better" for America than any other.

Recruitment Poster

Make a recruitment poster for the railroad lines to encourage Easterners and Europeans to go west.

"Sooner State" as the forty-sixth state in the Union.

Overcoming the Obstacles to Settlement

As the farmers settled on the plains in the later 1800s, they faced some of the same obstacles that cowboys and ranchers had faced. They faced some additional problems besides. The ways that the homesteaders overcame these difficulties are a tribute to their faith in God, their perseverance, and their ingenuity.

A Lack of Some Resources—Since trees were rare on the plains, wood had to be brought from other places. This made the log cabin both expensive and impractical. Some settlers began by living in sod dugouts braced by a few purchased boards. These dreary homes were little more than ditches dug into a hillside and covered with a roof of sod (grass and soil). The **sod house,** however, was a little more pleasant, and it became the classic dwelling on the prairie.

A sod house was drier, sturdier, and more comfortable than a dugout. The sod strips used to build it were twelve to eighteen inches wide, three inches deep, and two or three feet long. The sod blocks were staggered like bricks, grass side down, to form the thick walls of the house. Soddies, as such shelters were called, were warm in winter and cool in summer. Usually a lattice of willow branches was woven and covered with clay from a nearby creek bed for the base of the roof. Then sod shingles were laid over it. In heavy rains, however, such roofs leaked water like oversoaked sponges. Debris often fell from the roof, but pioneer wives hung cheesecloth below the rafters to catch the mud and bugs. Inside walls were whitewashed with a mixture of lime and sand. Tight construction was crucial, not just to keep out the cold but also to make snakes

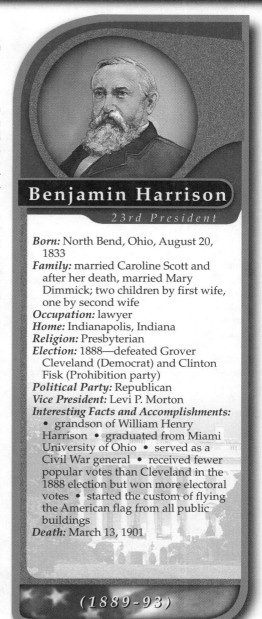

Benjamin Harrison
23rd President

Born: North Bend, Ohio, August 20, 1833
Family: married Caroline Scott and after her death, married Mary Dimmick; two children by first wife, one by second wife
Occupation: lawyer
Home: Indianapolis, Indiana
Religion: Presbyterian
Election: 1888—defeated Grover Cleveland (Democrat) and Clinton Fisk (Prohibition party)
Political Party: Republican
Vice President: Levi P. Morton
Interesting Facts and Accomplishments:
• grandson of William Henry Harrison • graduated from Miami University of Ohio • served as a Civil War general • received fewer popular votes than Cleveland in the 1888 election but won more electoral votes • started the custom of flying the American flag from all public buildings
Death: March 13, 1901

(1889-93)

421

Pioneer Housing

New homesteaders set up housekeeping in all types of shelters. Besides sod houses, they lived in caves, tents, and canvas homes. There were even cases of families living in the hollowed-out stumps of giant trees.

The day that a family started raising a log cabin was exciting. Construction often became a community activity. Neighboring men worked together cutting logs for the frame. Then they raised the frame into place by attaching ropes to the beams and pulling. Everyone took part in the chinking, filling the cracks between the logs with a material like mud or grass. Neighbors enjoyed food, conversation, and games in addition to their hard work.

Caroline Scott Harrison

As first lady, Caroline Scott Harrison, was the first to adopt a project or cause during her time in the White House. Her project was the renovation of the White House. It had fallen into disrepair and was in serious need of a face-lift.

Caroline wanted to do a complete overhaul, but she could not get the funds that such a project would have required. She was given an allowance for repairs, though, and she made the most of it. By the time she was through, the kitchen, flooring, and heating system were all new. Furniture and curtains had been replaced. The president's family had more than one bathroom. And, most exciting of all, the house was lit by electric lights. In the midst of this remodeling, Caroline found many old pieces of presidential china stored away. She brought them out and organized them into the start of the collection that now appears in the White House's China Room.

Samplers and Quilting

Make an authentic sampler or other piece of needlework (cross-stitch, crewel, etc.). Historical incidents can also be represented by stitching appliques or by carefully gluing felt shapes onto burlap.

Study different types of quilting and either make a small quilt (doll bed or crib size) or different types of quilt blocks. Have your student research quilting bees and explain their popularity.

Teaching History Through Literature

There are several good historical novels about the hardships of the Old West. *Giants of the Earth* (1927) by O. E. Rölvaag tells the story of an immigrant Norwegian family in South Dakota. The despair in the novel needs to be discussed in class. Other popular novels include *Shane* by Jack Schaefer, *A Lantern in Her Hand* by Bess Streeter Aldrich, and *Prairie Songs* by Pamela Conrad. Share selected excerpts with your class and discuss the experiences of the characters.

Steam-powered well-drilling rigs that looked much like oil derricks were available for hire in the later part of the century. Drillers often charged one dollar per foot to drill the wells, however, and because the water table in the Great Plains area was often deep, the well-drilling became very expensive for the poor farmer.

Desert Land Act

The Desert Land Act of 1878 permitted 640-acre homesteads for farmers who would pledge to irrigate the land. Many of these claims ended up in the hands of stockmen.

Barbed Wire Test

Even after Joseph Glidden had invented a practical version of barbed wire, many ranchers and farmers were not interested in buying it. They simply did not believe that it would work. To try to get over this barrier of disbelief, two barbed wire salesmen, John Warne Gates and Pete P. McManus, planned a demonstration of the product in a plaza in the city of San Antonio, Texas.

The men received permission to build a corral using barbed wire. They then arranged for a herd of cattle to be driven into the corral. To the amazement of the skeptical onlookers, the wire held when the cattle charged it. After a couple of encounters, the barbs on the wire convinced the cattle to stay in the corral. Sales of barbed wire shot up.

John Warne Gates later had a role in the establishment of the Texas Company (Texaco) and the American Steel and Wire Company, the first billion-dollar corporation.

Sod houses were common on the plains, but when wood was available, settlers sometimes built a sod-roofed house like this one.

and field mice unwelcome. Some sod houses were real works of art; a few, combined with some lumber, were two stories high.

The lack of wood also gave the farmers a couple of other obstacles to overcome. One was scarcity of fuel for fires. Until the railroads brought coal to heat prairie homes, corncobs, hay, and even manure served as fuel. Another problem was the lack of wood for the split rail fences commonly used back east. Although prairie farmers were generally glad their lands were not rocky, they did lack stones to be used for building purposes. There was no practical material for constructing fences until barbed wire was invented.

A sodbuster had to have an adequate water supply. Some settlers set out rain barrels or cisterns to collect rain. Some homesteaded near creeks. Most found water by digging wells, but wells had to be exceptionally deep to reach water in many areas of the dry plains. Even with wells, the farmers could not pump enough water by hand to water their stock and irrigate their crop land. The invention of the **windmill**, however, put the strong breezes of the region to this use.

Even wells or rivers could not necessarily irrigate many crops. Other means of overcoming this lack of water included raising crops that required less water or using dry-farming techniques, such as the use of mulch to protect what little moisture there was in the ground.

Help for the Prairie Farmers—The late 1800s brought many new and helpful developments for western settlers. One was barbed wire. Without wood and rocks, fences could not be built. And with cattle grazing contentedly in his corn and wheat, a farmer could not hope to prosper. Plain wire fences were tried, but they failed to hold up when herds pressed on them. Some farmers started thorn hedges, but it was often years before the hedges were high enough to do any good. In 1874 an Illinois farmer, **Joseph Glidden,** designed the first practical barbed wire. He used part of a coffee grinder to cut and coil small lengths of wire and then strung the barbs on by hand. Soon a machine was invented to do the work. Within a decade 120 million pounds of wire were being sold per year.

A Connecticut mechanic, David Halladay, perfected a windmill that helped farmers get water they needed for their family and stock. His device pivoted to face the wind and used centrifugal force to adjust the pitch of its wooden vanes. This feature allowed the windmill to withstand the pressure of high prairie winds. A crankshaft transferred the mill's rotary motion to force the pump to go up and down.

Railroads helped alleviate some of the transportation problems on the vast plains. Many lines built spurs (extensions) to the scattered towns to bring in needed goods and to carry out the farmers' harvests. The lines also made trips to other cities or regions easier.

American ingenuity helped the prairie farmer too. Heavier steel plows were designed to cut through the matted sod, and mechanical grain drills planted seeds of grain at the proper depth. The crops were harvested using a binder, an improvement on the reaper. Steam engines provided power for the larger inventions, and threshing crews often traveled through areas with this equipment for harvesting the crops of many farmers. The steam-driven tractor also appeared later in the century to aid the farmer.

Hardships of the Prairie Settler—Not only did the homesteaders have to overcome the lack of some needed resources; they also had to deal with many hazards of prairie life. One of these problems arose as more and more western lands were plowed. Especially in dry years, the wind blew tons of topsoil across the dry ground. It was impossible to keep a house clean since the dust settled everywhere. Outside the dust was blinding. Sadly, in addition to the inconvenience, the erosion of precious topsoil left much land infertile. In their eagerness to cultivate more land, settlers plowed up soil that God in His wisdom had given a protective layer of grasses. The grasses had prevented erosion and helped hold the moisture in the ground.

The prairie fire was another danger for the sodbuster. What little rain there was came in spring and early summer. As the season wore on, the grasses became dry. The smallest spark from a campfire or chimney or a stroke of lightning could turn the prairie into an inferno. When the flames were fanned by winds, the settler was powerless to stop the spreading fire. Damp clothing and blankets were used to beat out small fires. Sometimes farmers used the carcasses of slaughtered livestock, dragging them over the flaming grass. Backfires were lit to slow the progress of the flames. More often the only thing to do was to go inside the dugouts or soddies and pray. The heavy sod of the house and wet sheets over openings might protect people; but it could not keep the crops from going up in smoke.

Hailstorms did as much damage as fires. Crops were flattened, and little could be salvaged for harvest. Sometimes the settlers themselves were battered. Another one of nature's assaults on the prairie was the tornado. These small intense whirlwinds formed by severe thunderstorms destroyed everything in their paths. There were so many tornadoes on the plains that the region was called "tornado alley." For protection against such storms the sodbusters often dug root cellars. These cellars could be used for storing food, and they doubled as storm shelters when tornadoes threatened.

Large swarms of locusts and grasshoppers were an additional scourge. Swarming across the prairies in the 1870s, they devoured everything that grew. "Their fluttering wings," wrote the editor of the *Wichita City Eagle*, "looked like a sweeping snowstorm in the heavens, until their dark bodies covered everything green upon the earth." Accounts say the locusts covered the ground in a wiggling layer up to six inches deep. They ate crops, grasses, leaves, tree bark, leather boots, harness straps, and even fence posts and door frames. No one knew what caused the swarms to drop from the skies or what caused them to leave, but everyone feared them. Their arrival usually meant a two-year crop loss, because the locusts laid eggs that hatched the next year.

Barbed wire made it possible for prairie farmers to keep out hungry cattle roaming on the plains.

423

Spelling Bees

Being far away from the entertainment of eastern cities, pioneer communities became adept at creating their own amusements. One popular community activity was the school spelling bee.

Noah Webster's *Blue-Back Speller* made the spelling bee possible. First, it established standard spellings of words. Second, it grouped words together according to level of difficulty. This arrangement of progressively harder words was ideal for the organization of spelling bees.

On the frontier, competition between opposing teams was so exciting that the whole community wanted to share in the fun. Anticipation ran high to see whose child would be the local spelling champion.

A Sleighing Song

A favorite winter activity in many places was sleigh riding. Driving up and down the streets of the town with several other sleighs on a frosty winter day was great entertainment.

Sleighs also had potential for danger, however. If something moved into the path of the sleigh, the driver was in trouble because he would be unable to stop quickly. In addition, turning too sharply meant a tumble in the snow for everybody. Also, sleds glided over the snow so quietly that they were in danger of running into each other.

To remedy the potential of collision, sleighs started carrying bells. The bells were typically made of brass or bronze because those metals produced a rich sound. The bells not only increased the safety of the sleighs but also gave sleigh riding the happy sound celebrated in songs such as "Jingle Bells."

Why the Farmer's Hardships?

Ask the students to explain why farmers have had such difficulty throughout history—not just U.S. history—in getting fair treatment. The basic reason is that the farming industry is the exact opposite of a monopoly. Farming as a form of competition is called "perfect competition." Ask the students to make a list contrasting a monopoly and a farming business. (*There are many farmers; each product is essentially the same no matter who produces it; because there are so many farmers selling their crop, no individual farmer can control the price; and new farmers may enter farming with relative ease.*)

The farmer's inability to influence prices became even more pronounced with the advances in transportation and communication. In earlier days, farmers who were experiencing a drought could charge high prices to make up for their diminished crop, but with the advent of railroads, people in a drought-stricken region simply bought food from a different region, leaving local farmers in huge debt. This change raised a new, fundamental question for the American republic: in a free-market, capitalistic country, should the government intervene to help the farmer? The questions raised during the Populist movement are still being asked today.

Objectives

Students should be able to
1. Name the most famous Indian battle of the late 1800s.
2. Explain how the Indians were treated after they surrendered.
3. Describe the policies of the Dawes Act.

Custer

Custer is sometimes called a general and sometimes a colonel. This discrepancy results from the fact that he did obtain the rank of brevet general during the Civil War, but after the war he served at the rank of colonel in the cavalry.

Comanche

Each of the men who fought with Custer at the battle of Little Bighorn was killed. The only survivor of Custer's group was a horse named Comanche. Comanche was the horse of Captain Keogh, one of Custer's officers. Though he had seven arrows in his body when found, Comanche was nursed back to health at Fort Lincoln in the Dakota Territory. For the service he had rendered, Comanche was given free rein of the fort's grounds and the honor of being saddled for official military occasions (though he was never actually ridden again). After he died, Comanche was preserved and exhibited at the Museum of Kansas University.

Crazy Horse

For over fifty years, sculptors in the Black Hills of South Dakota have been working on a monument to honor Sioux chief Crazy Horse. Like nearby Mount Rushmore, the monument is carved out of the stone face of a mountain. Unlike Mount Rushmore, Crazy Horse is intended to be a three-dimensional, full-length statue depicting the Indian chief astride his horse and with an arm outstretched. The completed statue will be 563 feet high and 641 feet long. The head is 87 feet, and the arm will be nearly as long as a

Homesteads were often miles from a settlement. Because neighbors were few and the distances between homesteads great, loneliness was a problem. Of course, efforts were made to deal with loneliness. For example, pioneers made great efforts to go long distances to churches built in towns. Another link to the outside world was mail. After pressure by farmers, the post office began **rural free delivery** (RFD), making it cost no more to send a letter to a soddie than to send one across New York City. Mail-order catalog houses also began. The first, Montgomery Ward and Company, began in Chicago in 1872, and soon afterward, Sears Roebuck and Company started. These businesses offered settlers a wide array of products to be ordered from their catalogs. Most could be delivered to the door; some were shipped by rail to the nearest town for pickup. Farmers also formed their own social groups. The **Grange**, founded in 1867 by Oliver H. Kelley, a Minnesotan, began as a social organization. Later it became a political tool to promote the interests of farmers. It may even have encouraged the rise of the Populists, a political party that sought to help relieve farmers from some of their problems.

SECTION REVIEW

1. How did the homesteaders react to the cattle drives?
2. What major territory was the last to open to homesteaders?
3. What two important resources did homesteaders often lack?
4. What contributions did Joseph Glidden and David Halladay make to the improvement of prairie farming?
5. List at least five hardships faced by plains settlers.

 How did the federal government encourage the settlement of the frontier?

A romanticized lithograph of Custer's Last Stand reminds viewers of the hostility between the U.S. Army and Indians.

The Indians

The Indians who fought against the miners and cowboys fought against the settlers too. Frustrated and desperate over the loss of their lands and the destruction of the buffalo, some of the Indians were quick to fight back.

Indian attacks and uprisings were common during the latter part of the nineteenth century. The United States Cavalry often defended settlers and traders. Probably the best-known Indian battle of these Indian wars was at Little Big Horn in 1876. There Colonel **George Armstrong Custer** misjudged the strength and ferocity of a group of Sioux warriors. His defeat at Little Big Horn ("Custer's Last Stand") was led by **Crazy Horse** and Gall. **Sitting Bull,** who stayed behind the lines, was the medicine man who inspired the attack.

Section Review Answers

1. They put up fences to keep cattle out of their fields. (p. 419)
2. Indian Territory (Oklahoma) (p. 420)
3. trees and water (pp. 421-22)
4. Glidden—designed the first practical barbed wire, Halladay—perfected a windmill to help get water to the farmer's house and crops (p. 422)
5. dry and dusty conditions, erosion, fire, hailstorms, tornadoes, locusts

and grasshoppers, loneliness (any five) (pp. 423-24)

 by giving away or selling plots of land, some directly to settlers and some to railroads and states (p. 419-20)

SECTION 4

Materials

- Activities C and D from Chapter 20 of the *Student Activities* manual

- *North American Indians* by David Murdoch (Eyewitness Books)
- October 1992 issue of *National Geographic*

Student Activity C: Trivia Game: Indians

You can use this trivia game to review the history of the Indians, whose deeds spread across many chapters of U.S. history. It is crucial that students use the index to find the trivia. You can complete the activity in class, assign it as homework, or make it extra credit. Be forewarned that this activity takes a long time to complete. Consider

Sioux chief and medicine man, Sitting Bull

Indians Surrender

Plains Indian resistance ended as much from defeat in war as from the destruction of the buffalo herds on which they depended. Although the frontiersmen had little sympathy for the Indians, for many Easterners, who lived far from the conflict, the mistreatment of the Indians was inexcusable. In 1877 President Rutherford B. Hayes made a statement about this issue in his yearly national address. "Many, if not most, of our Indian Wars have had their origin in broken promises and acts of injustice on our part."

But recognition of the problem by Easterners did little to change reality for the Indians. The same year that President Hayes made his speech, the peaceful Nez Perce tribe of Idaho made a desperate attempt to avoid captivity on a reservation by fleeing to

Canada. The United States Cavalry caught up with the tribe forty miles from the border. Their leader, **Chief Joseph,** had little choice but to surrender to American troops.

By 1885 all but a few scattered groups of Indians had been forced onto **reservations,** tracts of land set aside for them. One such group was a rebel band of Apache Indians. Their leader Geronimo, who had been captured and then escaped from reservations several times, finally gave up in 1886.

In 1890, as final defeat for the Indian seemed apparent, the Dakota Sioux gathered for a Ghost Dance. The ritual celebrated a time when the Indians envisioned the earth would die and be reborn. The white men would go to

Apache warrior, Geronimo

football field. By way of comparison, the four heads on Mount Rushmore are each approximately 60 feet high.

Sculptor Korczak Ziolkowski started the project in the late 1940s and worked on it until his death in 1982. His family kept the work going, and the head was completed in 1998. Private donations and admission fees continue to finance the construction. Crazy Horse was never photographed in his lifetime, so the monument is intended to portray his spirit, not a strict likeness.

Chief Joseph's Surrender Speech

Chief Joseph's words at his surrender on October 15, 1877, are some of the most moving in the history of the U.S. mistreatment of the Indians: "Tell General Howard I know his heart. What he told me before, I have it in my heart. I am tired of fighting. Our Chiefs are killed; Looking Glass is dead, Ta Hool Hool Shute is dead. The old men are all dead. It is the young men who say yes or no. He who led on the young men is dead. It is cold, and we have no blankets; the little children are freezing to death. My people, some of them, have run away to the hills, and have no blankets, no food. No one knows where they are—perhaps freezing to death. I want to have time to look for my children, and see how many of them I can find. Maybe I shall find them among the dead. Hear me, my Chiefs! I am tired; my heart is sick and sad. From where the sun now stands I will fight no more forever."

425

---

using this activity in conjunction with other activities on the lore of the American Indian.

Reports on Indian Wars

Have students choose one of the Indian wars to report on. Make sure that at least one student reports on the battle of the Little Bighorn. American Heritage has published a book called *Indian Wars,* which gives all of the details any of the students would need.

Debate Ideas

Have your students discuss and/or debate the following:

Neither assimilation nor separation has been a satisfactory way of dealing with the American Indians.

American Indians are America's forgotten minority.

The treatment of the American Indians has been immoral.

Eyewitness Book

The Eyewitness Book *North American Indians,* by David Murdoch, is visually exciting. Show the students some of the old photographs and paintings and see how many of the famous Indian leaders they can name. Try to include some of the Indians they have studied so far.

Nuggets from *National Geographic*

The story of a famous Indian, Geronimo, is captured in the October 1992 issue of *National Geographic.* It is a biographical

Treatment of the American Indians

It is easy for us to look at the treatment of the American Indians and recognize the injustice that they faced, just as we look back at the injustice of slavery. We cannot change history, however. We can only do our best to live today in such a way that we treat all the people around us with a proper kindness. We must especially remember that the greatest need of all people is their need for the Savior. In every generation it is a Christian's responsibility to spread the gospel. That is the only permanently satisfying aid we can share with others.

Sioux warrior, Gall

another world; the Indians would then get their lands back. These strange ceremonies stirred fears among whites. On December 29, 1890, army troops sent to disarm the Indians panicked, and mowed down almost two hundred Sioux at Wounded Knee, South Dakota. This action proved to be the last of many Indian battles—the Indians were conquered.

Those Indians who had not resisted were made **wards** of the federal government. The government supported them with an annual payment system and placed them under federal protection. Missionaries often proved to be the Indian's best friends during this time of transition. They offered not only help for the physical needs of the Indian but also the gospel to meet his spiritual need. Un-

fortunately, the greed and malice of some other whites caused many Indians to reject the aid of the missionaries.

The Dawes Act

By 1887 pro-Indian sentiment was strong enough to force Congress to do something for the Indians. The **Dawes Act** of 1887 assumed that the Indian way of life would no longer work. Hence the Indian should be Americanized and assimilated (absorbed culturally) into the mainstream of American life. Under this act tribal unions were to be dissolved, and individual Indians were to receive lands and become self-supporting. Each head of a household was assigned 160 acres.

The reformers, mostly Easterners, did not understand the Indian's needs, however. First, most western Indians who were given lands had been hunters and traders, not farmers. Second, the lands the Indians had been allotted were very dry. Whites had given them to the Indians because they were undesirable for their own use. Such small plots of arid land could not sustain a family. Third, Indians were not used to the idea of private ownership of land, so the land deeds meant little to them. Also, their basic social units were the tribe and extended family (several generations of a family, including grandparents, aunts, uncles, and cousins). When these two units were broken down on the reservations, the Indian way of life suffered even more.

Defeated militarily, economically, and psychologically, the Indians became idle and often turned to alcohol. All too eager to make money, some greedy whites offered to buy Indian lands. Since Indians now owned the land personally, they had the option to sell it and often did. Not used to a money economy, however, the Indians were easily cheated. When oil was found on Indian lands, speculators bought up even more Indian land.

426

---

sketch of the famous warrior as well as a discussion of popular ideas of that day.

Mistreatment of Aboriginal Peoples

Since the flowering of the civil rights movement in the 1960s, Americans have become increasingly sensitive to the mistreatment of aboriginal peoples around the world. An *aborigine* (Latin, "from the beginning") is a member of the earliest known population of a region. As European civilizations conquered the world, they subjugated the aborigines and took their lands.

Spanish enslavement of Indians was an especially deplorable example of abuse. But America's own mistreatment of the Indians, unfortunately, was observed and imitated by other nations. The English depopulated Australia, for example, and the Afrikaners (Dutch descendants) instituted apartheid in South Africa.

The past wrongs against the Indians teach us many lessons. Injustice breeds bitterness, has lasting effects, sets a bad example, and becomes a permanent blotch on a nation's reputation. The citizens of a great nation must carefully weigh every decision

their country makes. Another lesson is that wrong decisions create virtually unsolvable problems for the future. There is no easy solution for the plight of the Indians today. They have already lost their homes and their historic means of livelihood. Liberals, beginning with Franklin Roosevelt, heaped federal aid on the Indians, while conservatives in the 1980s blamed the Indians' problems on their lack of private property and the federal government's socialistic programs. Conservatives helped to legalize gambling on the reservations as an alternative means of income.

426   Chapter 20

The Indian Today

By the late 1960s, Indian problems regained federal attention when Indian groups pressed for rights for Indians. Not all of the pressure has been peaceful, nor have all the motives involved been for the good of the Indians.

In 1970 the Nixon administration set up a policy of Indian self-determination. This allowed Indians to set up their own tribal systems on reservations. The federal government would assist them by providing housing and vocational training as well as money for economic development. The Department of the Interior also set up a new official to coordinate these programs for the Indians: the Assistant Secretary of the Interior for Indian Affairs.

During the 1980s Indian tribes that gave up land under questionable treaties in earlier centuries sued the federal government for the value of those lands. Although not much can be done to restore lands now owned by others, the Indians have called attention to their plight.

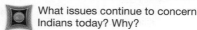

SECTION REVIEW

1. How did the Indians react to white settlers taking over their land?

2. What was probably the most famous Indian battle? Who was defeated during this battle?

3. Name four ways in which the Dawes Act failed to meet the needs of the Indians.

What issues continue to concern Indians today? Why?

Today's Indian

There is a special push on the part of many Indian tribes today to preserve the ways of the past. Some still live in their ancestral villages and craft traditional jewelry and ceramics. Others have resurrected tribal languages or ceremonies. Interest in native religion has increased dramatically.

The Native American Church of the United States is a product of that interest. It combines the beliefs of several different tribes with Christian doctrines and, in some cases, the use of peyote. Peyote is a cactus plant about the size of a small to medium potato. Parts of the plant have a hallucinogenic quality. Some church members take part in a peyote ritual that is said to have spiritual and medicinal value. Since peyote is a drug, its use is limited by law to designated religious practices.

The Native American Church is interested in promoting its religious liberty. Other issues that are of general interest to Indians today include recognition of tribes and their rights, restoration and preservation of important tribal sites, and financial advancement.

SUMMARY

Settlement had moved across the continent to the Pacific Coast before the Civil War, but the vast areas of the Great Plains and Rocky Mountains had been passed by. The dry climate, fierce Indians, and rugged terrain had discouraged early settlement. After the war, however, settlement in these regions began. Gold and silver brought miners, especially to mountain regions of the West. The demand for beef in the East prompted cattlemen on the plains to expand their herds and drive them to the railheads where they could be shipped to market. Farmers joined the cattlemen on the plains, attempting to raise their crops in the prairie soil. Although settlement was not dense on the plains or in the mountains, the advances of the miners, cattlemen, and farmers pushed the Indians off the land and onto reservations.

427

For the United States, which claims to be a nation of laws, the plight of the Indians raises many troubling questions. Is the United States obligated to pay reparations for the lands it took from the Indians in violation of its own treaties? If the United States does not honor its treaties, is the law really supreme?

The First Socialist Program in America

The federal aid program to the Indians is the first example of a massive federal welfare program. Some conservatives even argue that this debilitating welfare program lies at the heart of the Indians' history of problems on reservations. Discuss the pros and cons of this claim.

Section Review Answers

1. They took part in attacks and uprisings. (p. 424)

2. the battle of the Little Bighorn (Custer's Last Stand); George Armstrong Custer (p. 424)

3. Most western Indians had been hunters and traders, not farmers. Lands given to Indians were very dry. Indians had no experience with owning private property. And reservation life destroyed the traditional Indian social units—tribes and extended families. (p. 426)

Self-determination and land continue to concern Indians because these things were taken away from them through wars, treaties, and acts. (p. 427)

Chapter Review Idea
Student Activity D: People of the Last Frontier
This activity reviews the main terms associated with four groups—miners, cowboys, homesteaders, and Indians.

Chapter Review

People, Places, and Things to Remember

Comstock Lode	by-products	George Armstrong Custer
Homestake Mine	Homestead Act	Crazy Horse
Bland-Allison Act	Indian Territory	Sitting Bull
Chisholm Trail	Sooners	reservations
Goodnight-Loving Trail	sod house	Chief Joseph
trail boss	windmill	wards
wrangler	Joseph Glidden	Dawes Act
Philip Armour	rural free delivery	
Gustavus Swift	Grange	

Review Questions

Indicate whether each of the following would be most closely associated with the miners, the cattlemen, the homesteaders, or the Indians.

1. windmills
2. Chisholm Trail
3. Comstock Lode
4. wrangler
5. Ghost Dance
6. Dawes Act
7. "Pikes Peak or bust!"
8. Sooners

Who Am I?

9. I am the colonel killed at the battle of Little Big Horn.
10. I am the Nez Perce chief who sought refuge in Canada.
11. I am the Sioux medicine man.
12. I am the businessman who sold meat to the Union army.

Which term in each set does not belong with the others?

13. Chisholm, Comstock, Goodnight-Loving
14. ghost town, sod house, windmill
15. by-products, refrigerator car, wrangler

Questions for Discussion

16. Why can homesteaders, rather than miners and cowboys, be given more credit for actually settling the frontier?
17. How could the Indians have been treated differently during the settlement of the West?

Chapter Review Answers

1. homesteaders (p. 422)
2. cattlemen (p. 414)
3. miners (p. 410)
4. cattlemen (p. 416)
5. Indians (p. 425)
6. Indians (p. 426)
7. miners (p. 409)
8. homesteaders (p. 420)
9. George Armstrong Custer (p. 424)
10. Chief Joseph (p. 425)
11. Sitting Bull (p. 424)
12. Philip Armour (p. 416)
13. Comstock (pp. 410, 414-15)
14. ghost town (pp. 411, 421-22)
15. wrangler (pp. 416-17)
16. Answers will vary. They more often settled down to live permanently in an area. The others tended to move around.
17. Answers will vary.

History Skills

Analysis: Find the Related Words

In each row, decide which words are related to the first term and list them on a piece of paper. The number of related terms will vary from one to four. (The first answers are underlined for you.)

1.	*chief*	<u>Crazy Horse</u>	Custer	<u>Joseph</u>	<u>Sitting Bull</u>
2.	*cowboy*	Armour	Swift	Goodnight	Loving
3.	*outlaw*	Jesse James	Black Bart	Tom Smith	Emmett Dalton
4.	*lawman*	Joe Glidden	Wyatt Earp	Oliver Kelley	Jesse Chisholm
5.	*meat-packer*	Armour	Glidden	Halladay	Swift
6.	*inventor*	Glidden	Halladay	Chisholm	Custer
7.	*mining town*	Helena	Butte	Dodge City	Chicago
8.	*cow town*	Bonanza	St. Louis	Ellsworth	Abilene
9.	*cattle trail*	Western	Sedalia	Chisholm	Goodnight-Loving
10.	*mine*	Cheyenne	Grange	Comstock	Homestake

In each row below, decide the word that is least related to the other words. (The first answer is underlined for you.)

11.	cook	wrangler	trail boss	<u>ward</u>
12.	bones	hide	wagon	fat
13.	sheep	fire	tornado	hailstorm
14.	tractor	railroad	by-product	barbed wire
15.	silver	wheat	gold	copper
16.	drought	blizzard	overgrazing	reservation
17.	Iroquois	Apache	Sioux	Nez Perce
18.	Pecos	Pikes Peak	Bitterfoot	Black Hills
19.	cowboy	miner	president	homesteader
20.	steer	hog	windmill	sheep

History Skills

1. (answer given)
2. Goodnight, Loving
3. Jesse James, Black Bart, Emmett Dalton
4. Wyatt Earp
5. Armour, Swift
6. Glidden, Halladay
7. Helena, Butte
8. Ellsworth, Abilene
9. Western, Sedalia, Chisholm, Goodnight-Loving
10. Comstock, Homestake
11. (answer given)
12. wagon
13. sheep
14. by-product
15. wheat
16. reservation
17. Iroquois
18. Pecos
19. president
20. windmill

Location

The West includes the states of Montana, Wyoming, Colorado, New Mexico, Arizona, Utah, Nevada, Idaho, Washington, Oregon, and California. It extends the entire length of the country, bordered by Canada to the north and Mexico to the south. To the east are the Great Plains, and to the west is the Pacific Ocean.

Climate

The interior of the West is generally dry. To the south is desert. Farther north the land, though still dry, receives enough rainfall to support grass. Climate in the mountains varies according to altitude; the higher the elevation, the thinner and cooler the air. Even in the middle of a warm summer, the peaks of tall mountains might be snow-covered. Washington, Oregon, and northern California have marine west coast climates. Temperatures are generally mild throughout the year with cloudy, rainy winters and warm, sunny summers. Central and southern California enjoy mediterranean climates. Summers are warm and dry, while winters are mild.

Topography

Mountains dominate the landscape of the West. The Rocky Mountains are the largest range on the entire continent. Extending from northern New Mexico through northern Alaska, the Rockies are sometimes called the Backbone of North America. They serve as the Continental Divide, separating waters that flow into the Atlantic from those that flow into the Pacific. The Pacific Coast states have the Coast Ranges along the ocean and the Sierra Nevada (in California) and Cascades (in Oregon and Washington) farther inland. Between the mountain ranges on the coast is fertile farmland: the Central Valley in California, the Willamette Valley in Oregon, and the Puget Sound Lowland in Washington. Dry lands prevail between the coast and the Rocky Mountains. The Colorado Plateau extends into the desert southwest, and the Columbia Plateau dominates in the temperate northwest. These two plateaus are separated by the Great Basin, a bowl of low, rugged land. The Basin includes Utah's Great Salt Lake and California's Death Valley, the lowest (282 feet below sea level), hottest (often over 120° F), and driest (less than 2" of rain annually) spot in North America. The West ends in the edges of the Great Plains.

Natural Resources

Promise of great mineral wealth drew many settlers to the West in the 1800s. Though some veins of gold and silver have run out, the land still holds minerals. For example, Utah, Montana, and New Mexico are leading producers of copper. Oil has been found on the western slopes of the Rockies and off the coast of California. Forests and fish are major resources of the Northwest. Agriculture is abundant in the fertile valleys of California, Washington, and Oregon and in the irrigated plateau east of the Cascade Mountains. Because it is scarce, fresh water is one of the most precious resources in the West. The Colorado River in the south and the Columbia River in the north are crucial sources.

Geography & Culture

The West has always intrigued Americans and continues to do so today. The land offers spectacular scenery and exciting activities. Skiing, snowboarding, hiking, biking, climbing, and white-water rafting lure the adventure lover. Warm weather also brings many to the West. The film industry settled in southern California in the early 1900s to take advantage of the mild temperatures, sunny weather, and variety of scenery. Young people and retirees alike enjoy the relaxed atmosphere that comes with a year-round summer playground. Finally, the West reflects the independent spirit of the American pioneer. That spirit has led to the position of the West Coast as trendsetter. The West is an important part of America and is likely to become even more important as the region continues to grow.

Student Activity: Case #4— Taming the West

This is the last adventure of Sir Vey, who helps bring law and order to the West. The activity gives the students a humorous look at the geography of the region.

What Was It About?

- What causes the greatest variation in climate in the region? *(altitude)*

- What is sometimes referred to as the Backbone of North America? *(the Rocky Mountains)*

- What lies between the mountain ranges along the coast? *(fertile farmland)*

- What is the West's most precious resource? *(water)*

- What spirit has caused the West to be known as a trendsetter? *(the independent spirit of the American pioneer)*

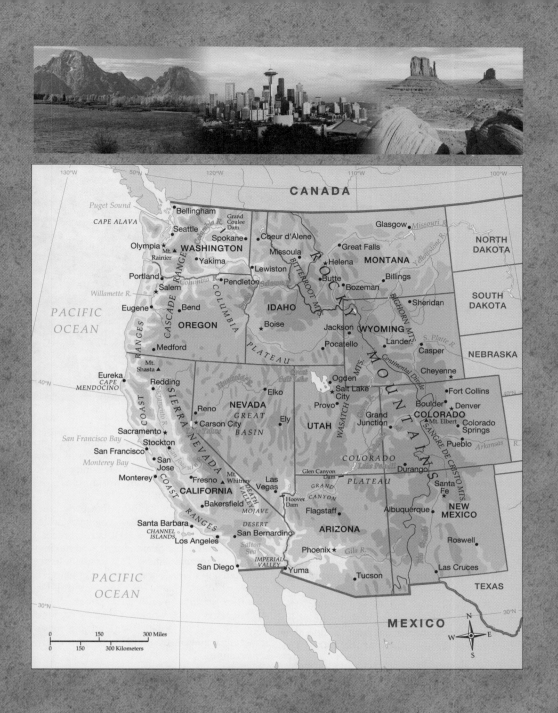

Using a Map

Use the map on this page to find the following information.

- the border of the region that is formed by the Pacific Ocean *(the western border)*
- the color that represents low elevation *(green)*

Which state would you be in if you were at

- the Grand Canyon? *(Arizona)*
- Death Valley? *(California)*
- the Grand Coulee Dam? *(Washington)*
- the Great Basin? *(Nevada)*

Writing Idea

Have each student choose one of the states in the region and write a two-paragraph advertisement to attract people to that state. The students will need to use the encyclopedia or other resources, such as the Internet, to find information.

America and the World

Throughout the nineteenth century America increased its population, built its industries, and expanded its settlement across the continent. As it grew, the United States had extended its influence and developed its strength. By the turn of the century, much of the world began to recognize that America was an impressive, new world power.

Imperialism in the Late Nineteenth Century

The Civil War and Reconstruction, the settlement of the frontier, and the development of new businesses had kept the attention of America through much of the 1800s. The United States showed little concern for foreign affairs that did not affect its borders or its people. This attitude of minding the country's own business and staying out of world politics is known as **isolationism.**

During the late 1800s, however, the United States saw that other countries were building world empires. Britain, France, Germany, and a few other nations were taking control of foreign lands. This **imperialism,** the extension of one's way of life over another people, brought many of these controlling countries greater wealth and power. Soon Americans began to wonder if their own country would end its isolationism and join these imperialist powers by building its own overseas empire.

Reasons for Imperialism

Aside from the prestige of building a large world empire, imperialist countries had several reasons for extending their control in other areas of the world. One reaon concerned military strength. Because taking control of foreign lands often required military force, an imperialist power could naturally be proud of its strong army. Empire building required a large and well-trained army ready to handle the needs of the empire and to defend against enemies. The military also gained important naval bases and army bases around the world in the lands it controlled. These bases increased the nation's strength as a world power.

Another major reason for imperialism was wealth. An imperialist country could regulate the trade and the development of natural resources in its colonies. The country could send its own businessmen to oversee the industries of the colony. It could hire the natives for very low wages and send the profits back to the mother country. The mother country could benefit from the products of the mines and plantations, and it could also make sure that the colony bought all its imported items from the mother country. Thus the imperialist country held every economic advantage over the colony. Sometimes the imperialist country took extreme advantage of the native people and their poverty and ignorance to keep them working for the benefit of the mother country. Such practices are called exploitation.

The final major reason for imperialist activity in the late 1800s was a desire to help the unlearned and poor peoples in undeveloped lands. Some people in the imperialist countries wished to teach the "uncivilized" peoples of the world how to read and write, especially in European languages. They wanted to extend the benefits of education and Western art and science to the natives of their colonies so that the natives could learn to live like Europeans.

Many imperialists wished to extend not only education but also food and health care to the hungry and sick. Helping poorer peoples who need food, medicine, education, or other assistance is called **humanitarianism.** British writer Rudyard Kipling spoke of the task of aiding the needy people of the world as the "white man's burden." This burden, or responsibility, motivated many western Europeans and Americans to take humanitarian aid and Christianity to lands in Asia, Africa, and the Pacific. Thousands of missionaries were recruited, and many sincerely spread the gospel of Jesus Christ. Others, lacking a personal knowledge of Christ as Saviour themselves, spread a "social gospel" which stressed the good works of humanitarian aid rather than salvation through Jesus Christ.

America's desire to evangelize foreign fields is exemplified by the work of the evangelist **Dwight L. Moody.** He had a profound influence on both American and British missions through his preaching and recruiting at many universities. Missions-minded American students were invited to a summer session at Moody's school in Northfield, Massachusetts, in 1886. In one month, one hundred students pledged themselves to be foreign missionaries. By the next summer session there were twenty-one hundred young men and women in attendance. In 1888 the Student Volunteer Movement was set up with the goal of "the evangelization of the world in this generation." Although it did not attain its lofty goal, its missionaries fanned out across India, Africa, China, and Japan. Sadly, within forty years even this group had strayed from preaching the Bible as God's truth and preached instead a social gospel.

433

- Biography of D. L. Moody
- *Scenes from American Church History* (BJUP)

SECTION 2

- Activities B and C from Chapter 21 of the *Student Activities* manual
- *American History in Verse* by Burton Stevenson (BJUP)
- February 1998 issue *of National Geographic*
- World map or globe
- Rudyard Kipling's poem "The White Man's Burden"

SECTION 3

- World map

SECTION 1

Objectives
Students should be able to
1. Define *isolationism* and *imperialism.*
2. Explain the reasons nations were building empires in the late 1800s.
3. Contrast the true gospel with the social gospel.
4. List the early imperial acquisitions of the United States.

Imperialism Versus Colonialism

The imperialism of the late 1800s can be contrasted with the colonialism of the 1500s to 1700s. That colonialism was usually intended either to establish a colony of people from the mother country in a new land or to collect the gold, spices, or other treasures of the land to bring back to the mother country. The imperialism of the late nineteenth century neither sought new land for the homes of colonists nor intended to strip the land of its treasures. Instead, it subjugated the natives of the land to work for the benefit of the mother country, developed industries and activities that could benefit the mother country, and tried to help the people of the land adjust to the culture and become like the people of the mother country.

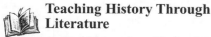

Student Activity A: American Imperialism

This chart summarizes the key events in the growth of the American "empire." Students can complete the chart as they go through the chapter, or you can complete it with them when you discuss the final section of the chapter.

Teaching History Through Literature

A good biography will give the students a feel for the life and times of D. L. Moody. BJU Press distributes *D. L. Moody*

by David Bennett and *D. L. Moody* by Faith Coxe Bailey.

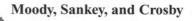

Moody, Sankey, and Crosby

D. L. Moody and his song leader, Ira Sankey, are written about in more detail in "Moody and Sankey" in *Scenes from American Church History.* Another story of a hymn writer is "Fanny Crosby: The Blind Poetess."

Journey Back in Time

At times during their study of U.S. history, the students will need an understanding of world conditions in order to understand events in America. Use a historical wall map or atlas to show the students the world on the eve of World War I.

As the students examine these maps, ask them to compare the world situation at the turn of the nineteenth century with the world situation today. This chapter is an ideal "case study" for students to test their thinking skills on foreign relations and diplomacy. The students need to understand that foreign affairs are never stable. Friends become enemies, and nations rise and fall.

British Empire

In the early 1900s the largest empire belonged to Britain. It was said that "the sun never sets on the British Empire" because it ruled countries across the globe—all or part of India, the Malay Peninsula, Canada, Australia, New Zealand, Africa, and the Pacific Islands. France was a strong imperial power as well, with holdings in Africa, Indochina, and the Pacific Islands. Belgium, the Netherlands, Germany, Italy, and Portugal also participated in the imperialist land grab.

Social Gospel

Impress on your students the fact that providing food, medical aid, and other care for those who are truly in need is a task Christians should perform. However, humanitarian aid is to no avail if people are not reached with the gospel. Those who preach the social gospel say that "Christian" people should help the needy with humanitarian aid, but they overlook the fact that the poor have a greater need that can be met only by salvation through the Lord Jesus Christ. The preachers of the social gospel overlook this fact usually because they have not recognized their own sin and need of Christ and because they expect their good works of humanitarianism to satisfy God.

New Role for the American Military

Keep in mind during this chapter that with all of America's involvement in the Caribbean and the Pacific in acquiring territories, investing money, building industries, and sending American citizens to oversee its interests, America's military policy changed. Before 1898 America had a standing army and navy only when they were needed. As a result, the United States was usually unprepared for military action. After the Spanish-American War, however, America's military forces became a permanent fixture. Their new role involved providing protection for land, American citizens, and investments overseas, but they

The Student Volunteer Movement was established as a result of Dwight L. Moody's faithful evangelism.

Arguments About American Imperialism

The United States saw the economic benefits and other advantages of empire building. By 1880 Americans were producing far more food and goods than could be sold at home. They were also looking for new supplies of raw materials, and some people wanted a stronger army and navy. As a result, Americans began to think about imperialism as an aid to their own country.

Some Americans were opposed to the nation's expansion. Since the United States was large and lacked few natural resources, it really did not need to acquire the raw materials of lands overseas as smaller countries did. Moreover, Americans opposed imperialism because it contradicted their ideals. Americans had fought for their own liberty. Could they now take away the liberty of foreign people? Some people were also concerned because exploitation of other peoples violates God's Word.

Other Americans favored expansion. First, some believed that the United States would become a second-rate nation if it did not build an empire. Second, America's supply of raw materials was not inexhaustible. New sources of raw materials might be needed. Third, new markets for America's manufactured products would be needed if the market at home became saturated. Fourth, the nation needed Pacific islands so that American ships traveling west could refuel. Fifth, the United States needed to extend its military power and position to protect itself from other countries.

America Acquires New Territory

The United States practiced imperialism when it purchased Alaska from Russia in 1867. Unlike all the land acquired before that time, Alaska was not connected to the other land areas of the United States. It was a "distant land" bought for America's benefit. As it turned out, Alaska proved to be very beneficial.

A gold rush in 1897 brought a flood of miners to the area around the Yukon River. The rush also boosted the economy of the United States. Later, silver, copper, and oil were found in Alaska to add to the nation's resources. Fishing became important to Alaska's economy; salmon fishing produced far more wealth for the area than gold ever did. In later years Alaska also became important for national defense. And, of course, Alaska did become the forty-ninth state when it joined the union in 1959. Yet when Alaska was purchased in 1867, no one realized that was the beginning of American imperialism.

Another advance toward America's world empire also took place in 1867 with a far

GEOGRAPHY for Christian Schools (Second Edition), pages 109-10, discusses terms, such as *world superpower, sphere of influence,* and *militarized states.* Students will have a better understanding of the remaining years in U.S. history if you give them a good foundation now.

America's Role in the World

The students have already studied foreign relations during the era of Manifest Destiny. Have them summarize American experiences and changes between the era of Manifest Destiny and 1900. *(The United States had settled its sectional divisions, the West had been won, and the rest of the world was threatening to cut off America's international trade by conquest.)* Why do the students think international issues again came to the forefront? *(Answers will vary.)*

A question now arose that Americans have never been able to answer satisfactorily: Now that the United States is a major world power with vital trade relations in both Asia and Europe, what role should it play? George Washington's policy of isolationism was easy to defend when the nation was a struggling minor nation hemmed in on the East Coast. But God does not raise up great nations in order for them to hide and ignore the problems of other nations. Students should study this chapter carefully to find historical lessons that will help them in resolving modern debates. More than choosing the best policy to meet the immediate needs, the students should strive to uncover the underlying principles that should guide a wise foreign policy.

The two basic options in foreign policy are isolationism and interventionism. If the

smaller acquisition than Alaska. American seamen had discovered Midway Island, located to the northwest of Hawaii, in 1859. Midway, however, remained a little-known Pacific outpost until it became the focus of a major battle for control of the Pacific Ocean in World War II.

Alaska and Midway aside, the first intentional imperial gain for the United States did not come until early in 1898, when Congress annexed the islands of Hawaii. American missionaries and businessmen had gone to the islands in the early 1800s. The large pineapple and sugarcane plantations built by the businessmen had taken advantage of the native Hawaiian workers. The Americans had also gained influence in the Hawaiian government. In 1893, they forced Hawaii's queen, Liliuokalani (lee LEE oo oh kah LAH nee), out of power, declared a republic, and asked the United States for annexation. President Cleveland, however, refused to purchase the islands because the queen had been removed from power illegally. But in 1898 President McKinley agreed to the purchase, and Hawaii became the first in a series of imperial gains for the nation.

SECTION REVIEW

1. Define *imperialism.*

2. What were the three major reasons for imperialism?

3. List at least three reasons for opposition to American expansion in the early 1900s.

4. What 1898 American acquisition in the Pacific started the country on its quest for an overseas empire?

 What shift in focus was manifested by some missionaries of this period?

The Spanish-American War

Along with adding Hawaii to its territories in 1898, America also entered a war that would greatly expand its overseas empire. Although a short and inexpensive war (as wars go), the **Spanish-American War** was an action of great consequence for American imperialism.

The island of Cuba, lying less than one hundred miles off the coast of Florida in the Caribbean Sea, was the source of America's quarrel with Spain. Although four centuries had passed since Cuba's discovery and the beginning of Spanish rule, this island nation had experienced only about a dozen years of well-run, peaceful, productive existence. Spain had allowed this colony to suffer from exploitation and poor government. The United States and other nations had tried to help the Cubans and had encouraged Spain to improve the situation, but little change occurred.

Causes of the War

As Americans watched the plight of their Cuban neighbors, conditions developed that encouraged them to do something to help.

Cuban Dissatisfaction—The Cubans had long been dissatisfied with conditions in their land. Many of the people suffered from poverty and cruel treatment. Several rebellions had erupted in the land, and in 1895 revolution again came to Cuba. The revolutionaries had three goals: terrorizing Cuba, destroying its livelihood (the sugar industry), and drawing the United States into the conflict. While fighting in Cuba, the revolutionary forces were smart enough to have agents in the United States who helped to raise money for the revolution and to feed the American press a steady diet of overblown incidents, all blamed on Spain.

The Yellow Press—The news that the revolutionaries wanted the Americans to hear was funneled to key newspapers. Many of these newspapers were themselves locked in deadly warfare to sell subscriptions. One way to increase sales was to subject the reading public

also became the policemen of the world.

Objectives

Students should be able to

1. Explain the long-term and immediate causes of the Spanish-American War.

2. Describe the course of the war.

3. List the areas that came under American control as a result of the war.

435

---

country accepts the need to intervene, then it must define the limits of intervention.

Section Review Answers

1. the extension of one's way of life over another people (p. 432)

2. to build military strength, to gain wealth from raw materials and trade, to help unlearned and poor peoples (p. 433)

3. America did not need the resources; America should not take away the liberty of these lands; America should not exploit other peoples (contradicted biblical principles). (p. 434)

4. the Hawaiian Islands (p. 435)

 Rather than preaching salvation through Jesus Christ, they emphasized good works that met physical needs only. (p. 433)

SECTION 2

Materials

• Activities B and C from Chapter 21 of the *Student Activities* manual

• *American History in Verse* by Burton Stevenson (BJUP)

• February 1998 issue of *National Geographic*

• World map or globe

• Rudyard Kipling's poem "The White Man's Burden"

Sugar and Politics

The profitable sugar cane plantations set up by American businessmen in Hawaii found a strong trading partner in the United States. In fact, Hawaiian exports were allowed into the country duty-free. Problems arose, however, with the passing of the McKinley Tariff of 1890. The tariff eliminated duties on all foreign sugar and, in addition, paid United States farmers two cents for each pound of sugar they produced. Thus, Hawaiian plantation owners lost the advantage they had held over other foreign markets and also faced the competition of cheaper domestic sugar. These owners pushed for Hawaiian annexation with the United States so that their sugar would be considered domestic rather than foreign. Statehood would allow them to compete successfully and turn a profit with their sugar cane.

San Simeon

William Randolph Hearst displayed his great wealth and extravagant tastes in his estate at San Simeon, California.

On the estate grounds, he established a private zoo with animals from all over the world, some caged and others roaming freely.

At the top of a large hill, he built La Casa Grande, a magnificent castle in the style of the Spanish Renaissance. He not only created an impressive exterior but also filled the inside of the house with an array of European art treasures, procured through diligent searching by Hearst and his agents and costing millions of dollars. One of the most outstanding rooms is the Refectory, where guests enjoyed the atmosphere of a medieval banquet hall, complete with massive dining table, tapestried walls, and rows of banners.

For family and guest recreation, Hearst built a huge climate-controlled indoor swimming pool as well as an elegant outdoor pool. Part of the architecture surrounding the outdoor pool is the

to a steady diet of sensational stories. They manipulated news stories, trying to make each one more exciting and attention-getting than the others, a technique called **yellow journalism.** Two powerful newspapermen facing off in this struggle were **William Randolph Hearst** (HURST), owner of the *New York Journal,* and **Joseph Pulitzer** (P*OOL* it sur) with the *New York World.* Unfortunately, some of what they reported was either inaccurate or greatly exaggerated. They knew that if they wrote about extremely poor conditions in Cuba and about Spain insulting the United States, they could stir up great interest in a growing conflict. Their reporting intentionally drove America toward war.

United States Sympathies—The humanitarian sympathies stirred by the news reports caused Americans to want to help. Many believed that the Cubans were oppressed by Spain. They wished that Cuba could obtain the freedoms and advantages that Americans enjoyed. Influenced by the press, most Americans favored helping the Cubans rid themselves of Spanish oppression.

American Investment—Another reason for United States interest in Cuba was that American businessmen had invested in Cuban sugar plantations and refineries. These investors feared that if the government stayed unstable and the terrorist acts continued, they might lose their money. The investors frantically pressured President **William McKinley** to protect their financial interests.

Immediate Causes—As tensions rose concerning the Cuban situation, two impor-

American journalist Joseph Pulitzer established an endowment to fund annual awards for excellence in journalism, literature, and music.

tant events took place that spurred the United States into action.

In February 1898 Hearst's *New York Journal* published a letter written by **Dupuy de Lôme,** the Spanish minister to the United States. The letter, to a personal friend of the minister, was never meant for publication, but it was stolen by Cuban rebels who gave it to the Hearst press. The letter described President McKinley as "weak and a bidder for the admiration of the crowd, besides being a common politician." At this time Americans held the presidency in such high esteem that they considered any criticism of the person holding the office as a national insult. The press demanded Spain be punished. De Lôme resigned, but the furor did not diminish.

Less than a week after the de Lôme letter, a second incident occurred. On February 15, 1898, an American warship, the **U.S.S. Maine,** anchored in Havana, Cuba, for an indefinite stay. The navy called it a goodwill mission, and Spain reacted appropriately. However, on February 15 at 9:40 P.M. the *Maine* mysteriously blew up. Two officers and 250 enlisted men died in the initial blast. Of course, the conclusion drawn by the yellow press was that Spain was responsible. There were other possible explanations, but Americans wished to blame Spain. The public yelled, "Remember the *Maine*!" and cried for action.

The president and Congress stalled briefly, but they issued a resolution that approved the use of force to end hostilities in Cuba and set up a stable government there. They

---

The Press, Public Opinion, and Comic Strips Too

Joseph Pulitzer, a Hungarian immigrant, had refined his journalistic trade in St. Louis with his powerful paper, the *St. Louis Post-Dispatch*. In 1883 he invaded New York City and bought out the dying *New York World*. Alert reporting, sensational stunts, and vivid pictures helped the *World* make a profit. Pulitzer was a crusader. No matter what the cause, he was able to drum up excitement and inspiration much as a bandmaster does with a band.

Editors across America studied his techniques and imitated them. His most successful imitator, William Randolph Hearst, copied him so well that Hearst soon became Pulitzer's chief competitor. Hearst had been given the *San Francisco Examiner* by his father. When he later inherited his father's millions, he enlarged his base and bought the *New York Journal*. He used some of his fortune to hire writers away from Pulitzer. When news was lacking, Hearst made his own news. He turned reporters into detectives to pursue criminals and made crime columns more exciting. He hired preachers to furnish religious material that would fire editorial controversy.

In 1897 Hearst challenged Pulitzer to a duel for subscribers. The battleground became events leading to the Spanish-American War. In 1897 artist-reporter Frederic Remington was ready to leave Cuba, believing that there was nothing of importance to report. Pulitzer is said to have cabled him: "Please remain. You furnish the pictures and I'll furnish the war." Hearst entered the journalistic battleground claiming that he was just doing his patriotic duty.

Smaller newspapers copied the style of Hearst and Pulitzer; their pages were filled with the same jingoism (extreme nationalism). Some thoughtful citizens were troubled when they realized that these journalists were not just reporting public opinion, but creating and controlling it. And the issue involved, entry into a war, was deadly serious. This was not the first time the American press had created rather than reflected opinion. But it had never happened before on such a wide scale.

Once this round with Hearst was over, Pulitzer quit the fight and decided to compete on a higher level. He turned his paper into a responsible journal. Although liberal, it did maintain high standards of journalism. He tried to raise standards for future journalists by endowing a School of Journalism at Columbia University in 1912. Hearst meanwhile created a chain of newspapers and bought magazines. He had political ambitions, but he was widely distrusted, and his ambitions were frustrated.

The Hearst press did leave a lasting legacy to journalism: the funnies, or Sunday comics. Trying to capture working-class families as readers, Hearst's Sunday *Journal* added an eight-page colored Sunday supplement in 1896. Hearst hired the artist who drew Pulitzer's "Yellow Kid" drawings away from him. The *Journal* then published the first real comic strip. Called the "Katzenjammer Kids," it was written by a cartoonist named Rudolph Dirks. Other comics included "Mutt and Jeff" and "Krazy Kat." Editors found that the funnies were the first part of the paper most people read. The funnies became a kind of American folk art expressing what some Americans thought or felt or at least what amused them.

---

reconstructed facade of an ancient temple.

Though Hearst spent $30 million on the estate, he still had not completed the house to his satisfaction when he died.

The Sinking of the *Maine*

Two other possible explanations for the sinking of the *Maine* are either that it was an accident or that it was the work of Cuban terrorists who wanted the act to create American anger toward Spain (as it did). No evidence has been found to prove the cause of the explosion, but historians generally agree that the Cubans had the most to gain and are the most likely culprits.

The Yellow Kid and Yellow Journalism

He started in 1895 as a minor character in the comic strip "Hogan's Alley." But the public liked him. He was named the Yellow Kid after he started appearing in a bright yellow nightshirt. Given his own comic strip shortly thereafter, he communicated with the audience by means of words written on the front of his shirt. New Yorkers were crazy about this youngster from their own streets.

"The Yellow Kid" appeared first as a comic strip in Joseph Pulitzer's *New York World*. Seeing its popularity, William Randolph Hearst hired artist R. F. Outcault to come and draw "The Yellow Kid" for his paper, the *New York Journal*. Not to be outfoxed, Pulitzer hired George B. Luks to continue to draw a Yellow Kid comic strip for the *World*. The intense rivalry that arose between the papers over the character led to the coining of the term "yellow journalism," which referred to any situation in which publishers tried to make their newspapers more exciting in order to compete for subscriptions.

"The Katzenjammer Kids"

"The Katzenjammer Kids" is the oldest comic strip still in syndication. Created in 1897 by Rudolph Dirks, the strip's chief characters, twins Hans and Fritz, continue to operate today with the help of a

437

---

no conclusive result is reached. Computer simulations show that either explanation is plausible.

Bias in the Media

Share recent examples of bias in the media or ask the students to give examples. Also discuss the media's influence on opinion. The media fabricate some "crises" merely by overreporting an incident.

Note that Pulitzer's decision to champion a "neutral" press was atypical for the era of yellow journalism. Perhaps never before had a reporter claimed to be neutral. Normally, reporters made their bias known ahead of time. For instance, one paper might be called the *Conservative Press* and another the *Liberal Press*.

Ask the students whether a "neutral" press is a worthy goal or whether it is even achievable. Everyone has a worldview that guides his selection of "important" and "relevant" facts. It is impossible to be completely neutral about facts. In fact, such a viewpoint assumes that God does not set an absolute standard for evaluating the truth. Rather than insisting that the modern media become "neutral," it might make more sense to demand that media declare their bias openly. Perhaps you can discuss the controversial *World* magazine, a full-color weekly like *Time* and *Newsweek,* which is attempting to apply a biblical worldview in its reports on public affairs. The editors are imitating early American journalists who were Christians. (See the magazine's mission statement at **www.worldmag.com**.)

"Red Flags" in Historical Narratives

Point students to the first sentence of the paragraph beginning "Many historians believe." Read the paragraph and ask the stu-

new artist, Hy Eisman. Unfortunately, the twins' activities often involve rebellion against authority, either at home or at school.

Comic strips became so popular in twentieth-century America that in 1935 William Randolph Hearst offered his weekend readers a thirty-two-page special comic section.

William Jennings Bryan

Though William Jennings Bryan never became president, it was certainly not for lack of trying. He ran three times for the presidency (and tried unsuccessfully another time for the Democratic nomination). During one election four different parties supported him as their candidate. However, his message of free silver and other reforms never drew enough voters to enable him to win an election.

Although he did not win the highest office, Bryan did serve two terms in Congress and was appointed secretary of state during Woodrow Wilson's administration. Bryan was a powerful orator. In his last years, he spoke and wrote prolifically for the cause of biblical truth, opposing evolution (see discussion of Scopes Trial, page 506) and championing a literal interpretation of the Scriptures.

McKinley's Civil War Service

William McKinley served the Union army in the Twenty-third Ohio Volunteer Infantry from 1861 to 1865. He saw considerable action and rose from the rank of second lieutenant to brevet major. His commanding officer was another future president, Rutherford B. Hayes.

McKinley's Secret to Political Success

William McKinley won elections to Congress, the governorship of Ohio, and eventually the presidency. He was a highly popular, successful politician. In the presidential election of 1896, he became the first candidate since 1872 to receive a majority of the popular votes. In 1900 he won the largest popular majority that any

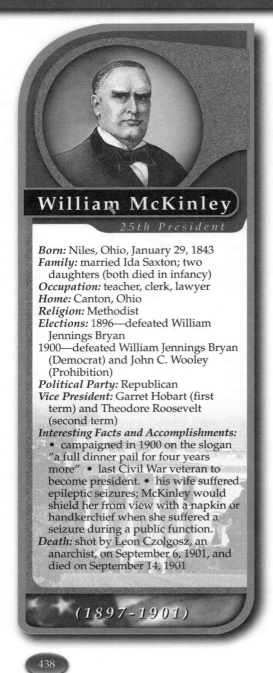

William McKinley

25th President

Born: Niles, Ohio, January 29, 1843
Family: married Ida Saxton; two daughters (both died in infancy)
Occupation: teacher, clerk, lawyer
Home: Canton, Ohio
Religion: Methodist
Elections: 1896—defeated William Jennings Bryan
1900—defeated William Jennings Bryan (Democrat) and John C. Wooley (Prohibition)
Political Party: Republican
Vice President: Garret Hobart (first term) and Theodore Roosevelt (second term)
Interesting Facts and Accomplishments:
  • campaigned in 1900 on the slogan "a full dinner pail for four years more" • last Civil War veteran to become president. • his wife suffered epileptic seizures; McKinley would shield her from view with a napkin or handkerchief when she suffered a seizure during a public function.
Death: shot by Leon Czolgosz, an anarchist, on September 6, 1901, and died on September 14, 1901

(1897–1901)

438

also added the **Teller amendment** to the resolution. It said that the United States had no intention of adding Cuba to its empire but desired only the independence of that land. This statement gave Americans confidence that further action would only help the Cubans, not further American imperialism.

Some believe that McKinley yielded to public pressure. McKinley believed Spain would never grant Cuba independence and that only independence would satisfy the American public. When Congress recognized Cuba's independence (even though Cuba did not have its own government at the time), Spain tried to uphold its honor by declaring war on the United States. And on April 25, 1898, the United States declared war on Spain.

Many historians today believe that United States involvement in the Spanish-American War was not justified. However, we need to remember that we are far removed from the feelings that Americans shared in 1898. It is much easier for us to pass judgment on events and motives of the past than it is to evaluate our own actions and motives honestly. As we study history, it is important that we not look at an event with only a modern, critical eye. We must also examine it in the context of the culture of that day, considering the information and attitudes we would have had if we had lived at that time.

Americans desired a better way of life for Cuba, and most honestly thought that the United States could help the Cubans achieve progress. As it turned out, however, their interest in Cuba opened the way for the expansion of American power and influence along with the problems of an empire.

Course of the War

The Spanish-American War was over in one hundred days. The United States was not really ready for a full-scale war, but the

dents to explain the reason for this statement. One of the joys of reading history is to read between the lines, to find the debates that rage between historians, and then to form opinions about them. Students need to be alert to different opinions. Any good history narrative will acknowledge differences of opinion.

Point out the list of anti-imperialists on page 441. Students need to recognize that the United States has never fought a war without public opposition. Often, the arguments against the wars remain open questions, and the students should consider which side of the argument they would have taken. Would they have sided with President McKinley, or would they have sided with Presidents Cleveland and Harrison?

After the destruction of the U.S.S. Maine, "Remember the Maine" became a call for action against the Spanish.

Spanish government and army were weak. The United States won every battle fought in this war.

Military Preparedness—Most of the fighting men came from the state's national guards. By late spring, troops had gathered at a military base in Tampa, Florida. Although the war would be fought in a subtropical area, many soldiers had been issued wool uniforms, and some cavalry troops lacked horses. But the invasion force sailed on June 14.

While the army fought bravely, and several regiments, such as the **Rough Riders,** gained special fame, the navy played the most important role. President Cleveland had approved a program to build a fleet of steel ships, and the ships now came in handy. More than anything, the navy's success showed that the United States had arrived as one of the world's great powers.

Battles of the Spanish-American War— Long before war was declared, Assistant

Theodore Roosevelt served as a colonel in the Spanish-American War and became a hero as the leader of the Rough Riders.

presidential candidate up to that point had received.

His political success was due in good measure to his personal traits. He was a very courteous man. He was also reasonable. He did not insist blindly on his own way but was willing to look at other sides of an issue. His goal was to bring all sides together. And his skill in compromise was such that he often did just that.

Rough Riders

Lieutenant Colonel Theodore Roosevelt, serving under Colonel Leonard Wood, led a company of soldiers in a successful charge up San Juan Hill in Cuba in 1898. The charge helped to pave the way for an American victory in the Spanish-American War. The men were given the name Rough Riders.

Earlier, the term *Rough Riders* described men who carried messages across the West in the days before the pony express. Buffalo Bill also used the name in his "Wild West Show and Congress of Rough Riders of the World." The Rough Riders who rode in the show were supposedly the top horsemen in the world.

When America declared war on Spain in 1898, the governor of the New Mexico territory offered to send a rifle brigade. His men became the largest contingent of the First United States Volunteer Cavalry. Because many of the cavalrymen had western associations, they were called "Rough Riders." Ironically, most of their fighting in Cuba was done on foot since transportation difficulties kept many of their horses in Florida.

After the Rough Riders of San Juan Hill won international fame, Buffalo Bill added a reenactment of their charge to his show. The deceased of the company were given a stone memorial at Arlington National Cemetery in 1908.

Art Propaganda

Discuss how the picture at the top of this page was a form of yellow journalism in art.

Secretary of the Navy **Theodore Roosevelt** sent secret orders to Commodore George Dewey, who was in Hong Kong with the American fleet in the Pacific. Roosevelt told Dewey to prepare for an attack on the Spanish fleet in the Philippines in case war broke out with Spain. The American force arrived in Manila on April 30 and met the Spanish fleet the next morning. By noon the **battle of Manila Bay** was over. No Americans died from wounds, though one engineer died from sunstroke. Spain lost 167 men and much of its fleet, and it was quickly defeated in the Pacific.

In the Caribbean, the American fleet was able to trap the Spanish fleet in the harbor at Santiago, which was then the capital of Cuba. American troops then came to storm their way to the city. The soldiers landed near Santiago and pushed the Spanish back to their defenses on San Juan Hill. Theodore Roosevelt's all-volunteer group, the "Rough Riders," was among the troops. Their famous charge up San Juan Hill helped defeat the Spanish on land while the Caribbean Spanish fleet lost every ship in a sea battle. On July 17 Santiago officially surrendered. The American army took Puerto Rico, another Spanish possession, without resistance on July 25.

When the war was officially over in August, fewer than four hundred American soldiers had died in battle or from combat wounds. Disease, however, took a far greater toll. Over five thousand died of typhoid, malaria, yellow fever, or other diseases.

The Treaty of Paris—The Spanish sued for peace and signed a truce on August 12, 1898. Spanish and American treaty commis-

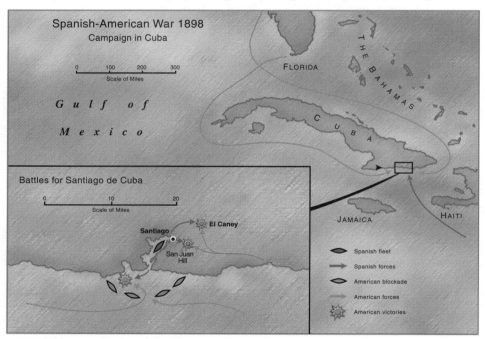

440

sioners met in Paris on October 1, and by December 10, 1898, a treaty had been worked out. Spain agreed to give up its claim to Cuba and also to cede Guam and the Philippines in the Pacific and Puerto Rico in the Caribbean to the United States. In return the United States gave Spain $20 million.

However, a great debate soon ensued in the Senate. Influential anti-imperialists, including Charles Francis Adams, Andrew Carnegie, former presidents Cleveland and Harrison, and authors Mark Twain and William Dean Howells, opposed the treaty. They said the treaty violated the principles of the Monroe Doctrine. Only when William Jennings Bryan, the leader of the Democratic Party, supported the treaty and promised Filipino independence did the Senate ratify the treaty by a margin of two votes.

More New Territories and Responsibilities

By the terms of the peace treaty the United States, like it or not, now had an empire and all the problems that came with taking care of one.

Governing Cuba—The Teller Amendment had promised Cuba its independence. But until Cuba was ready for independence, the United States supervised the government. In 1901 Congress passed the **Platt amendment,** which gave Cuba strict regulations for its new independent government. In effect this legislation kept Cuba from alliances with countries other than the United States, allowed the United States to oversee Cuba's financial affairs, and authorized the United States to send forces to Cuba to keep order. This arrangement was not exactly "independence." In addition, the United States was permitted to establish and keep a navy base in Cuba. The U.S. Navy still uses the base at **Guantanamo Bay** today.

Despite its reluctance to give up control of Cuba after the war, the United States did a great deal to help the island. The tropical disease yellow fever was a scourge in the Caribbean. A Cuban doctor, Dr. Carlos Finlay, believed the disease was carried by a certain type of mosquito. An American army doctor, **Walter Reed,** proved that Finlay was right. Major **William Gorgas** (GOR gus) and a crew of army engineers then drained the swamps and low-lying areas and succeeded in getting rid of the water where the mosquitoes bred. The United States also provided food and clothing for the poor and built roads, schools, railroads, and hospitals.

Puerto Rico—The United States gave Puerto Rico much of the same aid that Cuba received. Puerto Rico also got special economic considerations such as duty-free trade with the United States. This trade benefitted the sugar industry. Puerto Rico was also exempted from having to contribute to the United States federal treasury. In 1917 under the Jones Act, Puerto Rico became a territory with a governor appointed by the president and a two-house legislative assembly. In 1952, at Puerto Rico's request, it became a commonwealth, a freely associated part of the United States.

Governing the Philippines—Many Americans were skeptical about taking the Philippines, a land made up of over seven thousand Pacific islands. It would be hard for the United States to provide even the most basic government to rule the people of the entire area. Since the Filipinos were largely uneducated and had almost no experience in self-government, the United States would have trouble helping them set up a republican form of government. Opponents also held that annexing the Philippines violated the American ideal of liberty and might even be unconstitutional. Some even believed that the United States's presence in the Philippines

441

Platt Amendment
Under the provisions of the Platt Amendment, the United States sent troops into Cuba in 1906 and again in 1917.

Walter Reed
Dr. Walter Reed led a commission to study the problem of yellow fever in Cuba. Dr. Carlos Finlay believed that mosquitoes carried yellow fever, while others held that a bacterium caused the disease and that contaminated objects spread it. Dr. Reed set out to discover which theory was correct.

A group of soldiers and surgeons volunteered for the experiment. Reed divided the volunteers into two groups. The first group was exposed to the clothes and bedding of yellow-fever victims. The others were either bitten by mosquitoes or exposed somehow to infected blood. All of the men in the second group contracted yellow fever. Reed concluded that a virus caused the disease (this was the first time that a human disease was traced back to a virus) and that mosquitoes of the species *Aedes aegypti* spread it. Identification of the cause of the problem enabled the development of a solution.

Puerto Rico
As a commonwealth, Puerto Rico runs its own government under its own constitution, but its residents receive the benefits of United States citizenship. Puerto Ricans do not vote in United States presidential elections or pay federal income tax, but they do participate in activities such as military service and Social Security programs. Debate arises regularly among those who favor complete independence for Puerto Rico, those who would like to become a state, and those who wish to maintain their status as a commonwealth.

Locate Acquisitions on a Map
Use a globe or map to locate all of the lands that the United States acquired during the era of imperialism.

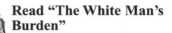

Read "The White Man's Burden"
The British Victorian poet Rudyard Kipling was living in Vermont during the Spanish-American War. He published the poem "The White Man's Burden" in *McClure's Magazine* in February 1899, days before peace was signed with Spain granting the United States control of the

Philippines. The pro-imperialist poem has been a source of controversy ever since. Theodore Roosevelt called it "rather bad poetry but good sense from the expansionist point of view." Read and discuss the poem to understand the motives behind imperialism. (Numerous copies can be downloaded from the Internet. Four verses are recorded in *WORLD STUDIES for Christian Schools,* Second Edition (seventh-grade Heritage Studies), page 339. Which motives, if any, were justified?

Emilio Aguinaldo

Filipino Emilio Aguinaldo, municipal official and lover of adventure, joined a secret revolutionary society in 1895 and began a quest to overthrow Spanish rule. He was highly skilled in battle and won a number of victories. In fact, he seemed so dangerous to the Spanish that they offered him a large sum of money if he would leave the country. He took the money and went to Hong Kong, planning to use the funds for a renewed revolt when the time was right.

When America invaded the Philippines, Aguinaldo saw his opportunity. He returned to the Philippines and led native troops in assisting the Americans. Their assistance helped contribute to an American victory but did not win them the independence they desired. Aguinaldo then led the people in revolt against the Americans, and the Filipinos declared themselves an independent republic.

The United States did not let this rebellion continue unchecked, but considerable manpower and resources were required to stop Aguinaldo's forces. Amazingly, when he was finally defeated, Aguinaldo swore allegiance to the United States and became a courageous patriot.

might involve the United States in a needless foreign war.

Nonetheless, President McKinley believed that if left to itself, the Philippines might be taken over by another major power or fall into anarchy. The land would also make a good base for trade with China, and American missionaries could go to help the Filipinos. McKinley's view won, and Congress decided to take over the islands.

The Philippines had long fought against Spanish rule, under the leadership of **Emilio Aguinaldo.** When the United States won the war, Aguinaldo and his followers hoped that the Philippines would be given their independence. The news of the takeover by the United States angered the Filipinos, and Aguinaldo and his forces went to work again. The United States then had to fight the rebels for two and one-half years to suppress the insurrection. This problem cost the United States far more time, military expense, and casualties than had the entire Spanish-American War.

The United States worked to prepare the Philippines for eventual independence by establishing a public school system to train Filipinos for citizenship. Hospitals, railroads, power plants, and greatly improved communication systems were also built. The islands were ruled for a few years by American governors. In the year 1934 the islands were granted commonwealth status. World War II

New responsibilities in Cuba, Puerto Rico, the Philippines, and elsewhere forced the United States to commit troops to the defense and administration of those lands.

442

The Burdens of Victory

Stress the lesson of this chapter—that foreign wars bring long-lasting commitments. A country's leaders should weigh the potential long-term costs carefully before going to war. (See Prov. 24:6.) Discuss any recent military actions that have brought long-term obligations. *(The Persian Gulf War, the invasion of Haiti, and the bombing of Kosovo committed the United States to contribute billions of dollars for rebuilding and defending the freed peoples.)*

What If . . .

Ask the students about their knowledge of Cuba, the Philippines, and Puerto Rico from previous classes, from news reports, and from missionaries. Fill in holes in their knowledge. Then ask them to consider how different the world would have been if the anti-imperialists had won the debate in Congress or if William Jennings Bryan had come out against acquiring these territories. Note the large part that the Philippines played during World War II, and note the eventual takeover of Cuba by Communists. Might these countries have taken a radi-

cally different course if the United States had not taken responsibility for them?

delayed Philippine independence, however, until July 4, 1946.

SECTION REVIEW

1. What were the two immediate causes of the Spanish-American War?

2. What did the Teller amendment state?

3. How long did the Spanish-American War last?

4. What were the provisions of the treaty that ended the Spanish-American War?

5. Who was Emilio Aguinaldo? Why did he cause problems for the United States?

 How did American journalists contribute to the outbreak of the Spanish-American War?

American Foreign Policy

As American interests widened in the late 1800s, United States foreign policy began to steer away from isolationism. The government was no longer careful to stay out of disputes between foreign countries if it was to America's advantage to become involved. If American trade and power could be advanced, the United States began to get involved in world affairs, especially those in Latin America and eastern Asia.

In Latin America

Ever since the Monroe Doctrine, the United States protected its American neighbors. In 1867 the United States drove French forces out of Mexico. In 1895 the U.S. forced Britain to allow American mediations of a boundary dispute between Venezuela and British Guinea. By 1900, the United States was ready to take its place as leader of the Western Hemisphere.

The Panama Canal—A first priority for the United States in Latin America was to build a canal. American naval officers had been pressing for the building of a canal across Central America. A canal would enable the few ships in the American fleet to defend both the Atlantic and Pacific coasts more easily. The Spanish-American War helped prove the point. It took two months to sail a warship from Puget Sound to the East Coast by way of the Cape Horn of South America.

The idea of a canal was not new. In 1851 the United States and England had signed a treaty to build an inter-ocean canal open to both nations. The construction of a canal, however, eventually fell to a French company headed by Ferdinand de Lesseps (LES ups), builder of the Suez Canal. The French chose a route across the Isthmus of Panama. But when the project took much longer than expected, the company went bankrupt. The United States then stepped in to take over the project.

Although the United States had considered an alternate route across Nicaragua, it decided to pursue the Panama canal. Since Panama was legally a part of Colombia, the United States now took steps to obtain the land from Colombia. The United States offered Colombia $10 million for the right to build the canal and an annual rental fee of $250,000. Colombia refused, holding out for $25 million.

Meanwhile, leaders in Panama wanted independence. America realized that if there were a revolt against Colombia, and Panama gained its independence, the new Panamanian government would gladly sell the United States rights for a canal. No time was wasted. Several American warships moved into positions off the coast on November 2, 1903. The next day Panamanians rioted and declared their independence from Colombia. When Colombia tried to send troops, American ships conveniently blocked the harbors. Then the rebels overcame the Colombian opposition within the country. On November 6, President Roosevelt used his presidential power to

443

SECTION 3
Objectives
Students should be able to
1. Explain why the United States wanted the Panama Canal and how it came to build it.
2. Compare Roosevelt's strategy for Latin American foreign policy with that of Taft and Wilson.
3. Describe the foreign activity in China at the turn of the century.

Ferdinand de Lesseps
Ferdinand de Lesseps was both a diplomat and an engineer. As the French consul in Cairo, Egypt, from 1833 to 1838, he became familiar with ideas for a canal that would join the Mediterranean and Red Seas. After his retirement from the diplomatic service, he pushed for the organization of the Suez Canal Company and supervised the canal's construction from 1859 to 1869.

After his triumph in Egypt, Lesseps sought a new challenge. In 1881 he formed the Interoceanic Canal Company to build a sea-level canal across the Isthmus of Panama. Engineering difficulties and financial troubles, including charges of mishandling funds, prevented his completion of the project.

Section Review Answers

1. anger over the de Lôme letter and anger over the sinking of the *Maine* (p. 436)

2. that the United States wanted Cuba to be independent, not part of America's empire (p. 438)

3. one hundred days (p. 438)

4. Cuba became independent, and Spain ceded Guam, the Philippines, and Puerto Rico to the United States for $20 million. (p. 441)

5. a rebel leader in the Philippines; because he wanted the Philippines to be given independence (p. 442)

 They wanted to report exciting stories to gain more readers, so they purposefully exaggerated events in Cuba to stir up conflict there. (pp. 435-36)

SECTION 3
Materials
• World map

Carter and the Canal Treaties

Nationalists in Panama believed that the area surrounding the Panama Canal—the Canal Zone—should belong to Panama, not to the United States. Anti-American riots in the area in 1964 led the United States to begin negotiations with Panama concerning the future of the Canal Zone.

Despite the objections of conservatives, Jimmy Carter felt in 1977 that the time had come to conclude a deal with the Panamanians. First, he feared that agitators might resort to violence, either seizing control of the canal or damaging it. Second, the locks of the canal were not big enough for new, larger ships. So the canal did not seem as valuable as it once had.

Carter negotiated two treaties. The first agreed to return the Canal Zone to Panama on December 31, 1999. The second maintained the right of the United States to continue its defense of the canal. The Senate approved both treaties but by small margins.

The Panama Canal continues to serve the world's ocean transport needs.

extend diplomatic recognition to the new nation of Panama.

On November 18, 1903, the United States signed the **Hay-Bunau-Varilla Treaty** with Panama. Negotiated by Secretary of State **John Hay** and Panama's new foreign minister, Philippe Bunau-Varilla (byoo-NOH va-REE-ya), the terms were generous. The United States received perpetual use of a ten-mile-wide strip of land. This "canal zone" would be controlled and fortified by the United States, and the canal built on it would be open to all nations on equal terms through payment of tolls. Eleven years later, the **Panama Canal** opened.

Theodore Roosevelt and the Big Stick— Theodore Roosevelt operated his foreign policy in Latin America with the same zest he showed in his charge up San Juan Hill. He summarized his policy by saying:, "I have always been fond of the West African proverb, 'Speak softly and carry a big stick, and you will go far!'" Roosevelt believed that the United States was the most important nation in the Western Hemisphere; in fact, he believed that this hemisphere was actually an American sphere of influence and that the Caribbean was an American lake. Roosevelt's foreign policy relied on America's military strength to persuade foreign nations to act properly, and this became known as the **"big stick" policy.**

In 1902, Britain, Germany, and Italy sent warships to blockade Venezuelan ports to collect unpaid loans. Venezuela asked the United States to intervene, and Great Britain asked Roosevelt to mediate. He eagerly obliged, but he saw the incident as a warning that European interests in Latin America were growing. This European presence was perhaps a possible violation of the Monroe Doctrine of 1823. Hence he made a new policy to clear up any misunderstanding: the **Roosevelt Corollary** to the Monroe Doctrine. In this statement the United States asserted the right to be an "international police power" in the Western Hemisphere. Whenever a country was guilty of long-term wrongdoing, the United States reserved the right to intervene.

What Makes a Great President?

Ask students what they think makes a great president. Most polls of historians list Teddy Roosevelt as a "near great" president. (The four "great" presidents are Washington, Jefferson, Lincoln, and Franklin D. Roosevelt—three of whom appear on Mount Rushmore.) Calvin Coolidge, who served during the Roaring Twenties, is usually relegated to the ranks of "below average." Nevertheless, Coolidge was the favorite president of President Reagan (whom many conservatives deeply admire). Why? Reagan considered a great leader to be one who was willing to serve the country's interests by keeping taxes low and government small. Historians like to pick presidents who were strong and assertive. But is an assertive president good for the republic? Evaluate Teddy Roosevelt. Was he great? You may want to wait until the next chapter to address this question.

Digging the Big Ditch

Building the Panama Canal was no easy task. The United States first attacked the problem of disease in the isthmus. Colonel William Gorgas and his workers made war on the mosquitoes that spread yellow fever and malaria and on the rats that carried the dreaded bubonic plague. By 1906 swamps had been drained and brush and grassy marshes eliminated.

An army engineer, Colonel George W. Goethals, supervised construction of the canal itself. Sixty-eight huge steam shovels hacked away. For seven years Goethals supervised 43,000 workers, 5,000 of whom were Americans. The final cost came to $400 million.

On August 5, 1914, the *Ancon* became the first ship to pass through the completed canal, saving almost seven thousand of travel. The formal opening of the canal, under President Woodrow Wilson, came on July 12, 1915. Most of the credit for completing the canal was claimed by Theodore Roosevelt. "If I had followed traditional, conservative methods," he said in 1911, "the debates on it would have been going on yet; but I took the Canal Zone and let Congress debate: and while the debate goes on, the Canal does also."

One of Teddy Roosevelt's hobbies was big-game hunting. This room at Sagamore Hill displays some of his trophies.

Because of Roosevelt's policy, the United States would send forces to Cuba, Venezuela, the Dominican Republic, Haiti, Nicaragua, Guatemala, and Mexico throughout the next sixty years. Although the policy kept European powers out of Latin America and made Americans happy by protecting their financial interests, some Latin Americans began to regard the United States as an unwelcome powerful neighbor, "the colossus of the North."

Dollar Diplomacy and Moral Diplomacy—Roosevelt's successors modified his policy slightly. **William Howard Taft** substituted dollars for bullets, a policy known as **"dollar diplomacy."** American investments in Latin America helped those countries develop their industries and improve the lives of their peoples. If the Latin American countries did not follow the wishes of the United States, investments could be withdrawn.

Woodrow Wilson and his secretary of state, William Jennings Bryan, turned the policy into **"moral diplomacy."** They wanted to use negotiation in international affairs. Not wanting to pressure countries into decisions, Wilson wished to talk these countries into following the example of the United States. He believed that "the force of America is the force of moral principle." Wilson tried to promote democratic principles and secure American interests overseas while maintaining peace on all fronts. Wilson's policy proved overly idealistic, and before he left office the president had been forced to send troops into the Dominican Republic, Haiti, and Mexico.

In Asia

In the late 1800s China was becoming one of the most profitable trading spots in the world. Britain, France, Germany, Russia, and Japan had divided China into **"spheres of influence."** Each of these countries controlled all the trading operations within its "sphere,"

445

Sagamore Hill

Theodore Roosevelt's home, Sagamore Hill, has twenty-three rooms and is built in the Queen Anne style. His family eventually gave the estate to the government, and today the National Park Service preserves the homestead as the Sagamore Hill National Historic Site.

The furnishings of the home reflect Roosevelt's interests. His big-game hunting produced several trophies, samples of which are scattered throughout the house. His intellectual interests are apparent as well. His ability to read in three languages would have been put to good use with the approximately six thousand books in the house. Portraits of historical figures demonstrate the importance he placed on the study of history.

While Roosevelt was president, he sometimes used his home for official duties. Before government buildings were air conditioned, the president, Congress, and the Supreme Court left Washington between April and October. Government business could be transacted from any place, though, with the help of a telephone. Sagamore Hill served quite capably as a summer White House from 1902 to 1908. Most notably, Roosevelt was awarded a Nobel Peace Prize for Russo-Japanese peace negotiations that he conducted in the library at Sagamore Hill.

Progressive Foreign Policies

The foreign policies of the three progressive presidents marked a radical shift from the past (just as progressive *social* policies—discussed in the next chapter—caused a radical shift in policies that is still felt today). How were all three presidents' policies similar? *(They wanted to use the power of the federal government to promote "good" abroad.)* Ironically, the progressives could not agree on the best way to use America's power. Which policy do the students believe would create the most bitterness and long-term harm in America's relations with other countries? *(Answers will vary.)* Note the striking parallel to Jimmy Carter's emphasis on promoting human rights abroad. Foreign policy again became a hot topic after the Cold War ended, as President Clinton shifted back and forth between advancing economic interests and human rights.

American Activity in China

Americans had been somewhat active in China before the Open Door Policy went into effect. In 1844 the Treaty of Wanghai opened five major Chinese ports to American trade. Besides setting low tariffs on American goods, the treaty allowed missionaries to enter China. Over the remaining years of the nineteenth century, missionaries pointed thousands of Chinese to the gospel and started many churches. Because the United States had not been as involved in the exploitation of China as other powers had, U.S. missionaries had much success.

Open Door Policy

Those countries that had fought for spheres of influence in China resisted the Open Door Policy. But Americans believed in the necessity of open, unrestricted commerce. The policy reflected prevailing American sentiment that the United States must promote its principles around the world in order to keep vital trade lines open.

Boxer Rebellion

The Boxer Rebellion actually presented the opportunity for John Hay's Open Door Policy to be put into effect in China. Notice that America's kind treatment of the Chinese in the aftermath of the incident helped create a strong friendship between the two countries.

The Rise of Modern Japan

Emperor Mutsuhito, Japanese ruler from 1867 to 1912, contributed much to the creation of the modern state of Japan. He took the title Meiji, or enlightened rule. His Imperial Charter Oath, issued in April 1868, established the pattern for the Meiji period. According to the oath, the Japanese government would seek to modernize its nation, looking to the West for ideas.

As part of its modernization program, the Meiji government tackled the reform of education, the military, communication and transportation systems, banking,

or division of the country. The United States, however, had missed out in this arrangement and was now ready to seek some trading opportunities of its own.

China and the Open Door Policy—Some of the foreign powers in China wanted more than control of trade—they wanted land. Some European nations as well as Japan began to seize land, literally creating their own colonies. The United States objected to such European and Asian colonization in China. Americans wanted all of China to be open to everyone.

In 1899 Secretary of State John Hay sent a series of circular letters to those countries involved in China. These memos formally stated an **Open Door Policy.** No nation would have its own sphere any longer: all of China would be open to all nations on equal terms. No more Chinese land was to be seized. Germany and Japan were not at all eager to follow this policy, but to go against it, they would have to risk the wrath of two major powers, America and Britain. Consequently, Germany and Japan agreed. Since Chinese territories were not united and no army existed to protect them, China had no choice but to tolerate the invasion of foreign traders. Even so, some Chinese took action. They formed a secret group called the Society of Righteous and Harmonious Fists. Foreigners called them the Boxers because one of their rituals was shadowboxing.

The Boxers decided to force all foreigners to leave China. The uprising began in rural areas and then moved to Peking (now Beijing), the capital of China. The Boxers surrounded the sections of the city where foreigners lived and terrorized the foreigners. Some foreigners were murdered. Boxers also attacked and killed many Chinese Christians. The foreigners and Chinese Christians took refuge together and tried to hold out until help could arrive.

446

The United States acted to protect the lives of its citizens. The first relief expedition on June 10, 1900, was forced back. By August, John Hay had played European powers against each other enough to engineer an international force of twenty thousand men. These soldiers marched from Tientsin (TIN tsin) to Peking and freed the hostages.

Some of the eleven countries involved thought they should get land. But under the Boxer Protocol, signed September 7, 1901, none of them did. Ten high Chinese officials responsible for the **Boxer Rebellion** were executed and twenty-five Chinese forts destroyed. Giving up, China had to make damage payments totaling $333 million over the next forty years.

The United States government put most of its share into a fund for educating Chinese students in America. Schools and colleges in China were also built with this money. In addition, American churches and mission boards sent personnel and money to China. Because of such efforts, the Chinese response to the United States was friendlier than to other imperialist powers. The United States and China remained friends until the Communists took over that land in 1949.

The United States and Japan—After Commodore Matthew Perry and the United States Navy opened Japan to trade with the outside world in 1853, Japan quickly grew to be a powerful Asian country. In less than forty years Japan transformed itself into a modern industrial nation. Japan also gained the technical know-how that allowed it to become a modern military power. It became a militaristic nation by building up a strong army and navy.

Being a militaristic nation is a short step from being an imperialistic one. Japan had demanded a sphere of influence from China, and in 1894 and 95 the Japanese easily defeated the Chinese and took the land they

---

World Powers Then and Now

The text alludes to all of the world powers in 1900—Britain, France, Germany, Russia, Japan, China, and the United States. (Britain was more than a world power, however. It can be classified as a superpower.) Perhaps the most objective way to distinguish a world power from a minor power is the amount of money that a country spends on military technology. Based on that criterion, the only superpower today is the United States, and the list of world powers includes the same countries as those in 1900. Note how much the relationship

between these superpowers has changed. Now China is a Communist country, and Germany is a republic. Locate these countries on a map.

Reports on Relations with China and Japan

Ask the students to bring in an article on current foreign relations with China or Japan. Compare modern issues to the issues in 1900. Note the continuing prominence of trade.

A Strong Military—Guarantor of Peace?

Explain to the students the debate over the impact of building a powerful military. Liberals tend to argue that a strong military increases tension and excites a dangerous arms race, while conservatives typically argue that a strong military encourages peace. How would the students evaluate the effectiveness of the Great White Fleet?

wanted. The Japanese also joined the international force that defeated the Boxers, and in 1905 they defeated Russia in the Russo-Japanese War.

John Hay and President Roosevelt sought to use American power in Asia to maintain a **balance of power.** President Roosevelt could see that Japan would soon be one of the great powers and might be a threat to the rest of the world. He believed that the power of the United States could be used to offset Japan's power and that the United States should command the respect of the world. In 1905 President Roosevelt persuaded representatives from Russia and Japan to meet him at Portsmouth, New Hampshire. There he helped negotiate a treaty that maintained a balance of power in Asia while upholding Chinese independence. For his efforts he became the first American president to win a Nobel Prize for Peace.

In 1907 Roosevelt made a dramatic show of American military strength. He sent the entire U.S. battle fleet on a world cruise. While Congress protested the expense, the Great White Fleet, as the American ships were called, sailed on. The fleet visited the Japanese ports and so impressed the Japanese that their imperialistic designs were curbed for the time being.

SECTION REVIEW

1. Why did American naval officers want the United States to build the Panama Canal?

2. What were the terms of the Hay-Bunau-Varilla Treaty?

3. What famous quotation summarizes Theodore Roosevelt's foreign policy?

4. Who was John Hay? What policy did he propose for relations with China?

5. Who were the "Boxers"?

6. Why did Roosevelt send the U.S. battle fleet on a world cruise?

 Contrast the diplomatic philosophies of Theodore Roosevelt, William Howard Taft, and Woodrow Wilson.

SUMMARY

As imperialism became a common practice among the world's nations in the late 1800s, the United States began to break away from its traditional isolationist stance. After acquiring Alaska, Hawaii, and Midway Island peacefully, it entered the Spanish-American War in 1898. Although the United States intended only to aid Cuba, the war also resulted in adding new territories to the United States. The United States also began to boldly assert its strong position in world affairs after the turn of the century. American strength brought about the building of the Panama Canal, the opening of China to more foreign trade, and the establishment of the leadership of the United States in the Western Hemisphere.

447

and taxation. The development of industry also received much attention. Industrialists from America and Europe were called in to teach their methods. By the 1920s, *zaibatsu* (huge family-owned corporations) dominated the business landscape.

The government even reorganized itself. Japan established a constitutional government for the first time in 1889. The emperor became the head of state and supreme commander of the army and navy. He also had the privilege of appointing and overseeing government ministers. But he had to share some of the ruling power with the Diet, a two-house parliament.

Around the World with Nellie Bly

Late-nineteenth-century Americans found a heroine in reporter and traveler Nellie Bly. Bly, whose real name was Elizabeth Cochrane, began writing for the *Pittsburgh Dispatch* when she was just a teenager. She changed newspapers more than once during her journalistic career, but the focus of her writing remained the same: exposing corruption. Because of her subject matter, she was not always popular. Twice she was asked to leave a position. But her writing skill always won her another job.

What strongly captured Americans' interest, though, was Bly's trip around the world. Readers were familiar with the fictional travels of Phileas Fogg, a Jules Verne character who went around the world in eighty days. Bly became a real-life Phileas Fogg, but she completed the trip in seventy-two days, six hours, and eleven minutes, traveling on everything from a steamship to a rickshaw. She returned home to great acclaim. Those who would never have the means or inclination to make the trip themselves were able to experience Bly's travels through a commemorative board game.

Section Review Answers

1. so they could more easily defend both the Atlantic and Pacific coasts (p. 443)

2. The U.S. would control and fortify a ten-mile-wide strip of land on which a canal would be built. All nations could use the canal by paying a toll. (p. 444)

3. "Speak softly and carry a big stick, and you will go far!" (p. 444)

4. America's secretary of state; the Open Door Policy (All of China would be open to all nations on equal terms.) (p. 446)

5. a secret group of Chinese who were opposed to all foreign activity in China (p. 446)

6. He wanted to make a dramatic show of American military strength to discourage aggressive action. (p. 447)

 Theodore Roosevelt supported a "big stick" policy. He wanted to force proper behavior through military action. William Howard Taft adopted "dollar diplomacy." His idea was to control other countries through the promise of financial assistance or the threat of its withdrawal. Woodrow Wilson preferred "moral diplomacy," convincing countries to do the right thing through the persuasion of principle. (pp. 444-45)

Chapter Review Idea
Relations
Give your students the following list. Have them write two or three sentences explaining the relationships between the words.

- isolationism/imperialism/ humanitarianism
- humanitarianism/imperialism/ Dwight L. Moody
- Alaska/Midway/imperialism
- yellow journalism/William Randolph Hearst/Joseph Pulitzer
- Cuban dissatisfaction/yellow journalism/American investment
- de Lôme letter/U.S.S. *Maine*/Teller amendment
- Theodore Roosevelt/ Commodore Dewey/Battle of Manila Bay
- Theodore Roosevelt/Rough Riders/San Juan Hill
- Treaty of Paris/Guam/ Philippines/Puerto Rico
- Platt Amendment/Cuba/ Guantanamo Bay
- Finlay/Reed/Gorgas
- Panama Canal/de Lesseps/ Hay-Bunau-Varilla Treaty
- Roosevelt/"big stick"/ Roosevelt Corollary
- Roosevelt Corollary/"dollar diplomacy"/"moral diplomacy"
- Open Door Policy/China/Boxer Rebellion
- Great White Fleet/balance of power/Asia

Chapter Review

People, Places, and Things to Remember

isolationism	Teller amendment	Panama Canal
imperialism	Rough Riders	big stick policy
humanitarianism	Theodore Roosevelt	Roosevelt Corollary
Dwight L. Moody	battle of Manila Bay	William Howard Taft
Spanish-American War	Platt amendment	dollar diplomacy
yellow journalism	Guantanamo Bay	Woodrow Wilson
William Randolph Hearst	Walter Reed	moral diplomacy
Joseph Pulitzer	William Gorgas	spheres of influence
William McKinley	Emilio Aguinaldo	Open Door Policy
Dupuy de Lôme	Hay-Bunau-Varilla Treaty	Boxer Rebellion
U.S.S. *Maine*	John Hay	balance of power

Review Questions

Match these terms with their descriptions.

1. exploitation
2. humanitarianism
3. imperialism
4. isolationism
5. yellow journalism

a. meeting the physical needs of poor people
b. distorting the news to make it more exciting
c. taking advantage of a people's weakness
d. not getting involved in world affairs
e. taking control of foreign lands

Match each of the items below with the president with whom it is most closely associated.

6. moral diplomacy
7. de Lôme Letter
8. dollar diplomacy
9. "big stick" policy

a. William McKinley
b. Theodore Roosevelt
c. William Howard Taft
d. Woodrow Wilson

Fill in the blanks.

10. The sinking of the __ helped to trigger the Spanish-American War.
11. The __ assured Americans that action against Spain was intended to secure Cuban independence and not to build an American empire.
12. __ was a leader in the Philippines who wanted independence for his land.
13. Secretary of State __ negotiated a treaty with Panama and helped establish the Open Door Policy with China.
14. Several countries gained trading privileges in areas called __ in China.
15. The __ staged a rebellion in China because of their dislike for foreigners.

Questions for Discussion

16. Is humanitarianism good or bad? Explain your answer.
17. Does the news media still use yellow journalism today? Explain your answer.

448

Chapter Review Answers

1. c (p. 433)
2. a (p. 433)
3. e (p. 432)
4. d (p. 432)
5. b (p. 436)
6. d (p. 445)
7. a (p. 436)
8. c (p. 445)
9. b (p. 444)

10. *Maine* (p. 436)
11. Teller amendment (p. 438)
12. Emilio Aguinaldo (p. 442)
13. John Hay (pp. 444, 446)
14. spheres of influence (p. 445)
15. Boxers (p. 446)
16. Answers will vary. It is good to meet people's physical needs, but it is more important to meet their spiritual needs. So humanitarian work should never replace the preaching of the gospel.

17. Answers will vary. Although standards of reporting may be different today, the sensational still draws much attention.

History Skills

Sensationalism, Jingoism, and Impartiality

After the newspaper war of 1898, Pulitzer encouraged impartiality in his paper and tried to avoid sensationalism and jingoism. *Impartiality* means "not favoring one side of an issue." *Sensationalism* is "the use of exaggeration or shocking details to arouse curiosity." *Jingoism* is "loud support for aggressive action toward other countries." Decide whether each statement below shows *sensationalism, jingoism,* or *impartiality.*

1. The Cubans have rebelled because they believe their Spanish rulers have grossly mistreated them.
2. The Spanish devils have painted the town squares red with the blood of Cubans fighting for freedom.
3. American honor demands swift action against Spain because de Lôme dared to insult our president.
4. Clara Barton was one of the many nurses who rushed to the Havana harbor to care for the wounded American sailors.
5. The American army in Cuba has been almost wiped out by the dreaded yellow fever. Everywhere you look you can see dead bodies and feverish soldiers waiting to die.
6. Unless Congress ratifies the Treaty of Paris and takes its share of new territories, America is doomed to become a second-rate nation.
7. Dr. Walter Reed has proved that mosquitoes carry the deadly yellow fever.
8. If pip-squeak Colombia thinks it can blackmail America for $25 million, we'll show them who calls the shots around here!
9. The day before Panama declared its independence, American warships moved into position off the coast.
10. Before Gorgas went to work clearing the swamps, the rats were so thick that you couldn't take a step without touching one, and the mosquitoes were so thick they blocked the sun.

Extra! Extra! On another sheet of paper, rewrite the sentences that contain sensationalism or jingoism so that they are impartial.

History Skills

1. impartiality
2. sensationalism
3. jingoism
4. impartiality
5. sensationalism
6. jingoism
7. impartiality
8. jingoism
9. impartiality
10. sensationalism

Extra! Extra! (Answers will vary.)

Bring me your tired, your poor,
Your huddled masses yearning to breathe free,
The retched refuse of your teaming shore.
Send these, the homeless, tempest-tossed to me.
I lift my lamp beside the golden door.

(Engraved at the base of the Statue of Liberty)

For Americans the question "What nationality are you?" is sometimes hard to answer. Unlike people in many other countries, few Americans can trace their roots to the earliest inhabitants of this country. Many Americans have a long list of nationalities attached to their family history.

There have been several major waves of immigration. The first came in the early 1700s. At that time Pennsylvanian colonists began to worry about German and Scotch-Irish immigrants flooding into the colony. At least the Scotch-Irish spoke English, but the Germans? Colonists were sure that the Germans would change the whole colony, but they did not. The Pennsylvania Dutch (from the German word *Deutsch,* meaning "German") established a profitable farming region and became established members of early American society.

The next two waves of immigration occurred from the early nineteenth century to the early twentieth century. More than thirty million Europeans flooded into the United States. At first the immigrants came from Western Europe, but by the close of the century, most of the immigrants came from Eastern European countries. Many Jews facing persecution in Europe came to the United States in the early 1900s.

Another wave of immigration arrived in the 1980s and 1990s as Hispanic and Asian immigrants came into the nation. Refugees from Haiti and Cuba established large communities in New York City and Miami. Mexican immigrants crossed the border into America legally and illegally. Many went to Southern California to work on truck farms as migrant workers. (Truck farms are vegetable farms located within easy trucking distance to distribution centers.) Southeast Asians came into America fleeing poverty and government oppression.

Since the first colonist made landfall in North America, immigration has been a source of benefit and trouble. Each group that establishes dominance in a region feels threatened when newcomers enter that area. But newcomers often fill an important place in society. They bring new skills or are willing to work at important but low-paying jobs. By becoming productive citizens, they encourage growth in the economy. Why is it then that people are sometimes so resistant to new immigrants?

Three fears have dominated America's reaction to immigration. American's biggest fear has been that the new people will take jobs away from American citizens. In the early years when most Americans were farmers, there was plenty of land for all, and immigrants seemed less threatening to the economy. But as the country's economy focused on industry and people moved into the cities, citizens felt more threatened. In the late 1870s this fear was caused by the influx of Chinese immigrants, whose backbreaking labor made the Union Pacific Railroad possible. The Chinese immigrants were willing to do the hardest labor for long hours and low pay. Plus, they were willing to live without many of the special foods and other comforts that many Californians felt were essential. In reality, the Chinese did not take American jobs; Americans gave them up. When the railroad was finished, the Chinese created new jobs for themselves. However, when economic depression and crop failure hit California, politicians easily stirred opinions of worried Californians against immigrants. Emotions were so inflamed that in 1882 the Chinese Exclusion Act, which banned most Chinese from immigration, was passed. The ban remained in effect until World War II.

Another fear about immigration has been that American tax dollars will have to pay to take care of unemployed foreign-born citizens. However, statistics show that, except in isolated areas and in the case of illegal immigrants, the incomes of foreign-born citizens are the same as or higher than those of their American-born counterparts. Just like the Chinese in the 1800s, many new immigrants are quick to work long hours for less pay

Forces on American Society

Going Beyond

Have your students read the page and answer the following questions.

- What nationality dominated each of the four waves of immigration mentioned in the text? *(1st—German and Scots-Irish; 2nd—Western European; 3rd—Eastern European; 4th—Hispanic and Asian)*

- What are the three main fears about immigration? *(that immigrants will take jobs, that they will require American tax money for care, and that they will change America)*

- What challenge does immigration present for Christians? *(how to spread the gospel)*

Essay Idea

Have students write two or three paragraphs about the differences between immigration today and immigration in the 1700s.

and to do without things that American-born citizens think are essential. They also often combine family incomes to increase their standard of living.

As the trend in twentieth-century immigration has moved from Europe to South America, Asia, and underdeveloped countries, Americans are especially afraid that immigrants will change the nation. Immigrants do change America. From the beginning of our nation, every new group that has entered the Land of Opportunity has brought with it new ideas and new ways of doing things. These changes have brought challenges. Americans struggle with incorporating the newcomers into society, providing them with jobs, educating their children, and understanding their cultures.

In *Letters from an American Farmer,* written in 1782, J. Hector St. John Crévecoeur expressed his thoughts about this new nation filled with immigrants: "Here individuals of all nations are melted into a new race of men, whose labors and posterity will one day cause great changes in the world."

Melt they did, not by losing their original heritage and culture but by incorporating it with a shared American culture. Most people who have been here since their birth say, "I am an American," even if their parents are natives of a different country halfway around the world. And Americans did change the world. The United States' influence has mixed into the big cities around the world until travelers find the same language, hotels, fast-food restaurants, music, and entertainment available wherever they go.

For the Christian, the challenge is great. As the United States leaves its original standard of biblical morality, government is more accepting of other religions and cultures that do not honor God. But the challenge to Christians is not to fight against immigration and different cultures but to spread the gospel. God in His providence has brought all nations to America. In the United States, faithful Christians can present the gospel to all nations by simply walking across the street and telling their neighbors.

"Er . . . I can't spell that . . . From now on you will be known as Mr. Bobo Clown."

Progressivism

The last few years of the nineteenth century and the first few years of the twentieth century were exciting for America. These years contained good prospects for growth as a world power and as a prosperous nation. Cities and industries were expanding while technology was making more and more conveniences available to the American people. Yet while life in the United States had so much to offer, it also held many problems. Sins such as greed, dishonesty, and immorality afflicted the nation then as they afflict all nations. In recognition of the evils of society, many Americans began to try to right the wrongs and cure the ills in hopes of achieving social progress. Making life in America even better through reform was the goal of these "progressives," and their movement was called **progressivism.**

Changing American Life
Life was changing in the United States. New living and working conditions, new opportunities, new possessions, and new attitudes resulted from the changes and also brought more changes. Americans soon found that while some of these changes were pleasant, others were full of problems.

More People
The population of the United States at the turn of the century was seventy-five million,

452

CHAPTER 22	Lesson Plan Chart			
Section Title	**Main Activity**	**Pages**	**Time Frame**	
1. Changing American Life	Are the "Culture Wars" Any Different Today?	452-59	2-3 days	
2. The Progressive Era	The Danger of Popular Ideas	459-62	1-2 days	
3. Roosevelt Brings Progressivism to the White House	Labor Relations—An Open Question	463-65	½-1 day	
4. The Taft Administration	A Mock Interview	465-67	½-1 day	
5. Progressivism with a Democrat	Where Do You Stand?	467-69	½-1 day	
Total Suggested Days (including 1 day for review and testing)			5½-9 days	

and it was growing by over a million a year. Involved in this tremendous growth were a trend toward urbanization and the contribution of immigration.

By 1900 **urbanization** (UR bun ih ZAY shun), the movement of people to cities, had changed America. There were more cities, and the population in the cities was growing. Many young people reared in rural areas had moved to the cities seeking greater opportunities. Between 1860 and 1910 the percentage of Americans involved in agriculture decreased from sixty percent to thirty-one percent. By 1920 more than one-half of America's population lived in towns and cities. Urban areas, especially large cities such as New York, Philadelphia, Boston, and Chicago, became sprawling giants. Inner-city areas were often plagued by crowded tenements (apartments), poor sanitation, crime, and poverty.

America welcomed 5.2 million immigrants in the 1880s, 3.7 million in the 1890s, and in the peak decade between 1901 and 1910, 8.8 million. Almost all these immigrants faced problems in adjusting to their new home. In fact, not all of the original immigrants would become "Americanized." That plateau would be reached, however, by most of their children. Most of them learned English quickly, although the first few months of their early education was difficult. Few schools at this time offered bilingual education. Many foreign parents opposed it because they wanted their offspring to become a part of American life as quickly as possible.

The new immigrant groups contributed a great deal to the building of America. They extracted raw materials from the land and

A New York City policeman inspects the cluttered basement living room of a tenement house around 1900.

became the work force for many of America's diverse new industries. But immigrants brought more than labor. They brought the traditions and customs of their homelands as well, including their foods, music, and literature. All these things added more diversity to America's unique culture.

More Opportunity

America's millions were able to enjoy many opportunities to improve their lives and amuse themselves.

Education—Education was becoming more widespread. Throughout much of the 1800s, public education had been available at taxpayer's expense only on the elementary level. In 1860 there were only three hundred secondary schools in America, and only one hundred of them did not charge tuition. But by 1900, six thousand free secondary schools existed and by 1915, twelve thousand.

Opportunities for higher education reflected the same trend. Throughout the Civil War era, upper-class white males were about the only people who attended colleges or uni-

453

SECTION 1

Objectives

Students should be able to
1. Describe some general ways in which life was changing at the turn of the century.
2. Name two men involved in black education at Tuskegee Institute.
3. Explain the ways religion in America was changing near the turn of the century.

Urbanization and the Rest of the Nation

Most of the South, the Great Plains, and the western mountain areas did not participate in extensive urbanization. The South was still 80 percent rural in 1920.

Father of Progressive Education

The rise of modern science and evolution gave a new impetus to secular (nonreligious) education. A new breed of "social scientists" believed that science, not religion, could properly direct mankind's evolution. The leader of so-called progressive education, John Dewey, believed education should teach the child thinking skills to solve life's problems. Dewey was a leader in the philosophical movement known as secular humanism, which denies the existence of God

Student Activity A: Finding the Foremost Facts About Changing American Life

This challenging activity asks students to choose the best examples of changes in various aspects of American life at the end of the 1800s. Students need to develop their reading skills so that they can find the most important information in any historical narrative.

What Topic Have You Never Seen Before?

Have the students read silently a portion of the text in the first part of this chapter, and then have them point out subjects they have never seen before in their study of U.S. history. Your goal is to show them the dual themes of continuity and change: many subjects are repeated over and over but with a new twist.

Continuation of Chapter 14

In many ways, this chapter picks up where Chapter 14 left off, dis-

cussing social (as opposed to political) history. Throughout this chapter, show how the changes follow patterns similar to the changes in the earlier period (1800-1850). Also note any major changes. The title of Section 1 in Chapter 22 actually is the same as the title for Chapter 14. The theme is *change*.

Make a chart comparing modern life to life in 1900 (similar to the chart suggested on page 270 of the teacher's manual). Discuss transportation, communication, agriculture, industry, trade, and religion.

and replaces absolute standards of truth and morality with relative, pragmatic standards based on human experience (i.e., whatever works is right). Humanists affirm the basic goodness and perfectibility of man. In the eyes of humanists, the proper purpose of education is to unleash the good within the student and to free him to a self-realization of his perfection. Obviously, progressive education is directly contrary to Christian education, which sees mankind as corrupt through sin and in need of divine intervention.

Booker T. Washington

When Booker T. Washington was asked to run a school for blacks in Alabama, he was unaware of all the difficulties he would face. However, few men were as well prepared as Washington was for the task. Although born a slave in 1856, he went with his parents to West Virginia after emancipation. There he worked in poverty as a coal miner. One day he overheard two men talking about Hampton Institute, a school in Virginia for blacks. He determined to go there to get his education.

He got enough money to get to the school but still had to gain entrance. The head teacher hesitated to admit him as a student because of his poor appearance. As a test, she asked him to sweep out the reception room. Washington swept the room three times and then dusted it four times. Upon examining the room, the head teacher said, "I guess you will do to enter this institution."

To pay his room and board, Washington worked as a janitor for the school. After graduation he taught at a school in West Virginia, but eventually he returned to Hampton as a staff member. Samuel Armstrong, head of the Hampton Institute, received a letter from men in Alabama asking him to send someone to run a proposed school for blacks in the town of Tuskegee. They assumed he would send a white man, but instead Armstrong sent Washington.

versities. By 1900, however, increasing numbers of people, including blacks and women, enrolled, and those who did go to college had a wider choice of study. Many new curriculums designed to prepare students for more specific professions were introduced. For example, schools in agriculture and the mechanical arts multiplied, more elective courses became available, and more graduate schools offered advanced training.

Some of the colleges and universities were aided by millionaire businessmen who provided endowments (large sums of money) to finance specific programs or salaries. Some even founded schools. Tulane (1834), Cornell (1865), Drew (1866), Vanderbilt (1873), Johns

Self-educated Booker T. Washington founded Tuskegee Institute in 1881 as the first institution dedicated to the education of black Americans.

Hopkins (1876), and Stanford (1885) all bear the names of such educational **philanthropists** (fih LAN thruh pists; wealthy people who donate money to charitable causes). Philadelphia's Temple University (1884) was established by Russell Conway to educate young men who had talent and the desire to succeed but who lacked the money. The University of Chicago (1890) was founded with gifts made by John D. Rockefeller.

More educational opportunities also became available for women. In the Midwest and in the West women had an easier time getting university educations than elsewhere. They were admitted to most programs and attended classes with the men. But in the East women tended to be educated separately in women's colleges. It was unusual for women to attend state universities. Those who did needed to be strongly motivated in order to outlast the ridicule of male students.

Blacks were able to go to college too, but they almost always attended segregated schools founded just for them. The first black university, Lincoln University in Pennsylvania, opened its doors in 1854. Nashville's Fisk University and Howard University in Washington, D.C., were both founded in 1867.

The most famous black school was **Tuskegee** (tus KEE gee) **Institute** in Alabama, founded by **Booker T. Washington,** a self-educated former slave. The school's philosophy focused on hard work, self-worth, and self-reliance. An Iowa-educated botanist, Dr. **George Washington Carver,** aided the school's reputation and finances through his work. He found more than 300 new uses for the peanut and 118 uses for the sweet potato. He also explored ways to use pecans. His work was important because it helped the South become less dependent on its cotton crop.

A Rising Middle Class—Education and opportunities to work and advance in business

What's Wrong with Education in America?

As future voters and taxpayers, students need to develop clear convictions about public education. Discuss some of the latest debates about problems in public education—violence, evolutionary teaching, evil teachings about sex, poor scores on national tests, and so on. Also discuss some of the proposed solutions. Note that the teachers' union is fighting all efforts that favor parental choice, home schooling, and government support of private religious

schools. Students need to be able to defend private education.

Even before public schools were introduced, America was possibly the most literate society in the world. The colonial founders were convinced that the success of their venture depended on the biblical education of their citizens. Public schools did *not* arise to alleviate illiteracy. Instead, Unitarians, such as Horace Mann in Massachusetts, wanted to apply "scientific" methods to control education and to produce the kind of citizens the state government wanted. As it gathered strength in the

late 1800s, public education faced violent resistance from parents who wanted control over the education of their children. The fact that these parents lost their battle against state-run education does not mean that their arguments were wrong. In fact, if you look at the conditions in public schools today, it appears that the defenders of state-run "public" education were wrong.

Ask the students to imagine the types of arguments Americans might have used in the late 1800s to attack state-run education. Focus specifically on the arguments Christians would have used. *(Not only is the*

and industry helped many Americans improve their standard of living. A significant number of people who had been penniless immigrants, poor farmers, or poverty-stricken factory workers had found a way to improve their situation. Hard work and some business sense could bring financial gain. The fact that a person was born in poverty did not condemn him to stay there.

Only a few Americans became millionaires, and some never escaped poverty, but many Americans joined the ranks of the middle class. They had enough money to enjoy a comfortable home, adequate food, and some of the newly available consumer goods.

Leisure Time Activities

In the early 1800s, factories, mines, and other employers often demanded that their laborers work six days a week, often for a total of seventy hours or more. Complaints against such long hours (and the poor conditions and wages that often accompanied such labor) began to bring great changes during the era of progressivism. By 1910 the average workweek had dropped to 54.6 hours. Such a change gave many Americans some leisure time—time they could use to improve themselves or enjoy recreation and amusements.

Interest in both spectator sports and sports participation mushroomed. Baseball, basketball, and football were all relatively new sports that had developed in the United States. All three were popular, but baseball became the favorite. The first World Series took place in 1903. After baseball, boxing was America's most popular sport of the era. Watching heavyweights fight it out attracted many crowds. Rollerskating and bicycling were new crazes of the day, and many other sports, such as golf and tennis, were gaining attention.

Besides sports, amusement parks, concerts, theaters, and other attractions offered entertainment for Americans. There was a

Samuel L. Clemens is better known as Mark Twain.

surge of interest in opera and classical music, especially in areas where European immigrants had settled. Many symphony orchestra members and almost all the conductors had been born overseas. Of course immigrants packed the concert halls to listen to the music of European composers.

Although reading books was not new, literature did take on new importance in the era. Throughout the 1800s more people who became part of the middle class could read and had money for books. Reading then became more popular. Americans were especially fond of new American themes and regional settings. The most popular American writer of the day was **Samuel L. Clemens,** whose pen name was Mark Twain.

Magazines appealing to literary circles were common in the 1800s. But because they were expensive (thirty-five cents per issue), magazines like *Harper's* and the *Atlantic Monthly* never enjoyed wide circulation. The

When Washington arrived, he found that the only buildings available for the school were an old Methodist church and a shanty nearby. Both were in poor condition. Nevertheless, the school opened with thirty students enrolled. Washington was the only teacher. Washington recalled "that during the first months of school that I taught in this building it was in such poor condition that, whenever it rained, one of the older students would very kindly hold an umbrella over me while I heard the recitations of the others."

Eventually, Washington was able to move the entire school to an old plantation.

Today Tuskegee University offers sixty-eight different degrees. It includes about forty-five hundred acres of land and more than one hundred fifty buildings. Over one thousand people are now employed by the school.

Wage Hikes
In 1890 the average work week was 58 hours, and the average hourly wage was 21 cents. In 1910 the work week was 54.6 hours, and the wage was 28 cents. This was a 25 percent rise in total wages over that twenty-year period, with a decrease in working hours as well.

The First World Series
In October 1903 the first World Series was played between the Boston Puritans (Red Sox) and the Pittsburgh Pirates.

One interesting point about the series was the size of the ballparks. They were too small or rather the crowds were too big for them. Despite the efforts of the police, crowds drifted into the outfield. A few runs were the result of pop fly balls landing in the crowd and allowing for a ground rule of three bases.

455

government inefficient but it can also use its power to promote evil goals; God gave parents, not the government, the responsibility for education; people devalue anything that is free. Proponents of private education argued that government control would spread mediocrity, waste, and radicalism.) Stress that ideas have consequences, and the ideas of progressivism, expressed by John Dewey, have had results that we still suffer from today.

Is Leisure Time a Good Thing?

Discuss the rise of leisure time as a major issue in life. The Bible says that we are to work six days, and it generally associates leisure with laziness. But modern conveniences have made it possible for the average citizen to enjoy more leisure time than ever before. Discuss the value of leisure and how God wants us to use our spare time. Have the students look up the following verses and explain how they relate to the subject of leisure and spare time:

Mark 6:31; Ps. 90:12; I Cor. 7:29-31; Eph. 5:15-16.

Mary Baker Eddy

The founder of the Christian Science movement was born in Bow, New Hampshire, in 1821. She suffered from several mental and physical illnesses throughout her childhood.

In the 1860s Eddy became a follower of P. P. Quimby, a doctor of "mental healing." After his death, Eddy claimed much of his material as her own. Some portions of her book *Science and Health with a Key to the Scriptures* come directly from his writings. After an accident in 1866, she claimed to be healed and to have discovered "Christian Science."

After founding the Church of Christ, Scientist in 1879, Eddy continued spreading her beliefs through her writings. At the age of eighty-eight she founded the *Christian Science Monitor,* a newspaper that still exists today. Despite her death in 1910, the Christian Science movement continued to grow. Today there are churches in more than seventy countries.

Charles Taze Russell

In 1852 Charles Taze Russell was born in Pittsburgh. Despite being brought up in the Congregationalist Church, Russell soon rejected many doctrines of the Bible, including the reality of hell, the Trinity, the deity of Christ, and Christ's physical resurrection. By 1870, Taze had organized a Bible class that soon named him "pastor." In 1879 he founded a magazine that eventually became *The Watchtower Announcing Jehovah's Kingdom.* Today about eighteen million copies of the magazine are distributed worldwide.

Ellen G. White

Although she did not found the Seventh-day Adventist movement, Ellen G. White did help to popularize it with her claims of revelations from God. Born in 1827 at Gorham, Maine, White was raised in the Methodist Church. When she was nine years old, a girl at school got angry with her, threw a rock, and broke White's nose. The impact

invention of better printing presses and better methods of making paper eventually lowered prices. Publisher Hermann Cyrus Curtis introduced *Ladies' Home Journal* for ten cents a copy and *Saturday Evening Post* for only a nickel.

Different Values

America had received a godly heritage from its early Pilgrim and Puritan fathers. Even through the 1700s and early 1800s, most of the people who came to America were from a Protestant background. While many were not true Christians, most of these earlier Americans had a respect for the Bible as the Word of God and a belief in its moral standards. The immigration of the 1800s and the changes in American society, however, greatly altered the nation's religious attitudes.

Between 1860 and 1910 almost twenty-one million immigrants entered the United States. Some German immigrants were Lutheran, some Roman Catholic, and others rationalists (those who exalted man's reason above the revelation of God's Word). Most immigrants from Ireland were strong Roman Catholics. Later groups of Scandinavian immigrants were largely Lutheran, while Italian immigrants were usually Roman Catholics. Immigrants from eastern Europe were a mixed group including Mennonites, Russian Orthodox, Catholics, and Jews.

Almost all churches increased their memberships in these years, including the well-known "mainline" denominations such as the Methodists, Presbyterians, and Baptists. When some people began to feel that mainline denominations were not meeting their needs, they formed new denominations, such as the Holiness and Pentecostal groups. Several newly organized cults that denied some biblical truths also began during this period. For example, Mary Baker Eddy founded Christian Science, which teaches that "matter and death

are mental illusions," as are sin, pain, and disease. Seventh-Day Adventism grew under the leadership of Ellen G. Harmon White. Another cult, the Jehovah's Witnesses (Watchtower Society), was founded in 1872 by Charles Taze Russell. These cults offered attractive ideas to religious Americans who lacked knowledge of Bible doctrines. The cults won great followings, but they also blinded people to the truths of God's Word.

As German rationalists and some theologians cast doubts on the truth of Scripture, their ideas began to break down the standards of many religious groups in America. Some people began to accept the notion that the Bible was just a good book written by man. Men began to think that they had the right to examine Scripture and to say what parts were right and what parts were in error. This "liberalism" led ministers to emphasize a social

During the time of increased immigration, church membership across the nation grew.

Are the "Culture Wars" Any Different Today?

Ask the students to summarize the major subjects of debate in the modern "culture wars." *(education, social welfare, environment, religious freedom, equality, and so on)* How are they similar to the issues being debated during the progressive era? *(Many of them were the same.)* Note that the reformers, then as now, had a variety of motives, and many reformers were not Christians. Ask the students to find an article on the modern culture wars, or bring

in an article yourself. How might this article have been written in 1910?

Stress that progressivism marks a turning point in American culture that influences all aspects of American life. Its roots reach back to the Enlightenment ideas that invaded the colonies. The battle for the soul of America extended to the schools, the home, the church, and the government. Each of these topics is discussed in this chapter. Compare and contrast progressive ideas and their modern counterparts.

Enemies of the Gospel

As in Chapter 14, this section reminds students that Christians in America have never been free from attack. It was no easier to be a Christian in past eras than it is today. The purity of the church has always required constant vigilance. Modern Christians have no reason to grow discouraged by the attacks of the enemy. They need to learn to expect these attacks, and they should be encouraged by the example of past generations.

This temperance banner shows a table filled with the other vices associated with drinking.

gospel because doing good to mankind was obviously right. Many quit preaching the true gospel—repentance from sin and faith in Jesus Christ, who alone can give salvation—because they wished to think that man could solve his own problems. The focus of many American churches was quickly changing from God's provision for man's eternal need to man's abilities to solve temporal needs.

Some men, called **agnostics,** even scoffed at the existence of God, saying that man cannot know whether there is a God. The most famous agnostic, **Robert Ingersoll,** traveled the country giving lectures. People paid to hear him mock true faith, though many attended his lectures more out of curiosity than agreement.

In 1859 in England, one of the influential works of the nineteenth century was published. Written by **Charles Darwin,** *Origin of Species* proposed a theory of evolution. While most Americans did not readily accept evolution at that time, the theory began to influence both science and religious thought. In 1874 **Charles Hodge,** a leading conservative theologian, made what was probably the most successful attack on evolution. He attacked the evolutionary idea of natural selection, showing that it contradicted the existence of an all-powerful, all-knowing Creator.

While religious liberalism and other common philosophies prompted men to humanitarianism, they also hardened many Americans in their sin. But many Bible-believing pastors and evangelists were still preaching salvation through Christ. The existence of both liberal religion and true Christianity in American culture led to a mixture of religious goals in the progressive era. Some endeavors sincerely sought to reach souls for Christ. Others aimed at improving morals or living conditions, and some tried to do both.

Temperance Groups—The heavy use of alcohol had become a big problem in many areas of the country. Some immigrant groups were particularly heavy drinkers, and their actions were offensive to many others. Wherever alcoholism occurred, abuse of family members, increased poverty, and crime often followed.

Many religious Americans saw the need to correct the problem and formed **temperance societies** to fight against the evils of liquor. Most of them were associated with the Women's Christian Temperance Union (1874) or the Anti-Saloon League (1893). The efforts of these societies, combined with the efforts of evangelists who preached against the sin of drunkenness, led to the prohibition movement.

Interdenominational Organizations—Laymen founded interdenominational organizations that crossed church boundary lines.

was so severe that White was unconscious for three weeks. The incident left White disfigured and with traces of brain damage. When White was thirteen, her family came under the Adventist teachings of William Miller.

According to Miller, the Lord would return to earth between March 21, 1843, and March 21, 1844. After the first date passed, Miller modified his prediction to October 22, 1844. When that date passed, the Seventh-day Adventist movement went through what was called the "Great Disappointment of 1844." White helped to revive the Seventh-day Adventists the same year by claiming to have received a vision from God.

In the next few years, she claimed to have approximately two thousand "visions" and produced a number of writings about them. With her husband James White, she helped to spread the movement across America and even to Europe and Australia. While the Seventh-day Adventists gave credence to her claims, they refused to say they were divinely inspired. Since her death in 1915, Adventist scholars have become more critical of her works and have pointed out a number of contradictions.

Ask the students whether they have ever met a cult member. Allow volunteers to describe their experiences. Encourage students to recognize that these cults are not really meeting people's needs. The turnover rate in cults such as the Jehovah's Witnesses is drastic. True Christianity offers the only true hope of rest for the human soul.

"Humanist Manifesto I"

As mentioned in Chapter 14, "culture wars" have been fought throughout U.S. history. Modern movements are a natural outgrowth of progressivism and secular humanism. Read portions of the "Humanist Manifesto," published in 1933 and signed by many notables, including John Dewey. Have the students explain how the statements were in keeping with progressive ideas about man's ability to achieve perfection on earth.

Why Is Drinking Wrong?

If you have not discussed drinking in Bible class, now would be a good time to discuss the temperance movement. Even if students have already discussed drinking, now

would be a good time to review what they believe on the subject.

Billy Sunday

Although Billy Sunday grew up as an orphan in Iowa, he became a man twice successful in life—once by the world's standards and then by God's. In high school, Sunday amazed people by his speed. It was said that no one could outrun him. One day Cap Anson, owner of the Chicago White Stockings, saw Sunday and offered him a try-out for the team. Soon Sunday was playing in Chicago and helping them win three championships. He was only an average hitter, but he was a master at stealing bases (ninety-four in one season).

Sunday's baseball career did not last, though. In 1886, through the ministry of the Pacific Garden Mission, he accepted Christ as his Savior. Although he continued to play baseball for the next few years, he also began to work with the YMCA. Eventually, Sunday left baseball to join the ministry full-time. In 1896 he began preaching and holding revival meetings. In his early preaching days, he spoke mostly in small towns. Sunday referred to them as the "kerosene trail" because few of the towns had electricity. Soon invitations for Sunday started to come from larger cities. Between 1910 and 1920, he preached in almost every major city in the country.

In many of the cities, large tabernacles were built to house the crowds. The construction was carefully planned to ensure that Sunday's voice would be heard. To soften the noise of all the feet on the ground, they spread sawdust. When people came forward to receive Christ, they were said to "walk the sawdust trail."

Sunday's messages focused on the reality of Christ and salvation as well as the reality of Satan and hell. He also attacked the liquor industry, helping to bring about the passage of the Eighteenth Amendment.

In 1935 Sunday died of a heart attack. He had preached some three hundred revival campaigns across the United States. It is estimated that around one hundred million

"Rescue the Perishing"

As American cities grew in the 1800s, so did their problems. Sections of large cities such as New York became slum areas,—places where the poor, usually immigrants, lived close together in dirty, noisy tenements. The main "entertainment" in the slums was often found in saloons, where drinking, gambling, and other vices took much of the little money that the people had. Churches tended to move away from the slums, locating where more prosperous and "respectable" people could support them.

Some Christians did try to reach the people in the slums. They held services in rented halls, passed out tracts, and attempted to witness the people. One man, Jerry McAuley, wanted to do more. Born in Ireland in 1837, he came to New York City at the age of thirteen. McAuley soon became a thief; at the age of nineteen he was arrested for robbery and sent to prison.

In prison McAuley was converted through the testimony of a former convict. After getting out, McAuley thought that Christians were not doing enough to help the real "down-and-outs"—the drunks, prostitutes, and others who dwelt in the worst parts of the city. He decided to start a "rescue mission," a work located in the slums and designed to "rescue" people from sin. His Water Street Mission in New York City is usually considered the first rescue mission in the United States.

Probably the most famous rescue mission is the Pacific Garden Mission in Chicago. This mission was started in 1877 by Colonel George Clark and his wife, Sarah Dunn. D. L. Moody helped to name it. Thousands of people were reached for Christ through the Pacific Garden Mission. In 1886 a half-drunk baseball player named Billy Sunday heard a group of mission workers singing on a street corner. He followed them back to the Garden, where he was converted. Later, of course, he became a well-known evangelist.

Other people started rescue missions in other cities. Mel Trotter, for example, began a successful work in Grand Rapids, Michigan, and later helped found missions in other cities. Trotter loved the mission work because he had been saved in a mission. In 1897 he had stumbled into the Pacific Garden Mission. Although it was January, he was barefoot because he had sold his shoes to buy a drink. Converted, Trotter dedicated his life to reaching people like himself who had reached the bottom physically, mentally, and spiritually.

Rescue mission work varied in operation from city to city. Usually missions were open day and night to minister to anyone who came in. Services normally consisted of the singing of gospel songs, testimonies of converted sinners from the slums, and simple salvation sermons. The missions also tried to provide hot meals and a place to stay, at least for a night or two. Some more ambitious missions tried to provide work for their people. In these missions the people repaired clothing, made brooms, or did some other kind of work to help pay for their room and board.

Poor children such as these in Washington, D.C., were reached by gospel missions.

458

Relate Stories of Local Ministries

Discuss rescue missions and other local ministries that are supported by your church. Students could share their own experiences too. If possible, have a speaker come to share his experiences with those ministries. It would be interesting to find out about the history of the ministry—particularly the date it was founded, who founded it, and why.

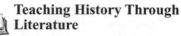

Teaching History Through Literature

There are several good biographies on the life and times of Billy Sunday, such as William T. Ellis's *Billy Sunday* (1959) and Fern Neal Stocker's *Billy Sunday: Baseball Preacher* (1985). BJU Press distributes Betty Steele Everett's *Sawdust Trail Preacher: The Story of Billy Sunday* (1987).

Defenders of the Faith

For an article about a defender of the faith against liberalism, see "Benjamin Breckinridge Warfield and the Defense of the Scriptures" by Mark Sidwell in *Scenes from American Church History.*

This book also includes "Sam Jones, Great Evangelist" by Bob Jones, "A.T. Pierson: Servant of God" by Christa Habegger, and " 'Plain Billy Sunday' " by Mark Sidwell.

Chapter 22 Progressivism

The Young Men's Christian Association (YMCA), which had originated in England, came to America. The "Y," as it was called, stressed four areas of growth: physical, educational, social, and religious. Another group of British origin was the Salvation Army. It provided relief for the poor and set up rescue missions to convert and rebuild the lives of those people who knew only defeat. Various other groups began rescue missions to work with such people. Probably the most famous rescue mission is Chicago's Pacific Garden Mission, founded in 1877. Other groups set up missions to work with specific immigrant groups.

Foreign Missions and Evangelistic Efforts—Americans were also concerned about taking the gospel to others. America sent out more missionary workers than any other country. The evangelistic and cultural impact of Christianity was so great at the end of the nineteenth century that some historians have called it the "Great Century of Christian Missions."

Important throughout the era was the work of evangelists and revival leaders. Camp meetings were held, but tents and brush arbors were abandoned for woodframe tabernacles. Some groups even held meetings at modern campgrounds with cabins for the visitors to stay in.

SECTION REVIEW

1. What is urbanization?
2. Who founded Tuskegee Institute?
3. List at least three ways in which the American laborer used his newly acquired leisure time.
4. What was one reason for the increased diversity of religious groups from 1860 to 1910?
5. List at least three cults that began during this time.

6. What does an agnostic believe?
7. What was the purpose of the temperance groups?

 How did German rationalism lead religion towards the social gospel?

The Progressive Era

Besides its growing spiritual needs, America's growing and changing society was beset with many other problems. Some of the problems were very big—too big for individuals to solve alone. The progressives began to look for help in solving America's problems. More and more they looked to government for the answers.

Progressive Aims

Progressives sought to abolish corruption and unfair practices in government, industry, labor, and even society. They were able to make permanent changes in the way the cities, the states, and the nation were governed, although social reforms were harder to accomplish.

A second progressive aim was to give people more say in governing. Some progressives believed that the evils of government could be cured by making government more democratic (giving individual citizens more power over laws and government officials). Some governmental practices thought commonplace today, such as primary elections and voting by secret ballot, were started by progressives.

Third, progressives believed that the quality of life in America could be improved by government. Many thought that government should improve society, that government was to be a minister of good. Some of the progressive ideals were definitely moral in tone. Combating crime in cities, establishing prohibition, and eliminating prostitution were among such moral aims.

people attended the meetings. More importantly, many came to know Christ and were saved from their sins.

SECTION 2

Objectives

Students should be able to
1. List the aims of progressives.
2. Explain the significance of the muckrakers.
3. Describe the major reforms made in government during this era.

459

Section Review Answers

1. the movement of people to cities (p. 453)
2. Booker T. Washington (p. 454)
3. watching or participating in sports; attending concerts, theater performances, amusement parks, and other attractions; reading books and magazines (p. 455)
4. immigration of non-Protestant peoples (p. 456)

5. Christian Science, Seventh-day Adventism, Jehovah's Witnesses (p. 456)
6. that we cannot know whether there is a God (p. 457)
7. to fight against the evils of liquor (p. 457)

 Rationalism caused men to question Scripture and to choose the parts they believed were correct. Many rejected salvation through Christ but

believed that doing good was right, so they promoted the social gospel. (pp. 456-57)

SECTION 2

Materials

• Activity B from Chapter 22 of the *Student Activities* manual

Progressivism 459

Boss Tweed

Boss Tweed was a leader of the New York City Democratic Party organization called Tammany Hall. Among the many corrupt dealings of Tammany Hall were schemes that charged city and county taxpayers exorbitant amounts of money for city expenses so that the excess could go into the pockets of Tweed and his friends. One of the biggest schemes involved a new county courthouse that should have cost about $500,000 but ended up with a price tag of over $8 million. The city's printing bill for two and one half years totaled a staggering $7 million. *Harper's Weekly,* with cartoons by artists such as Thomas Nast, helped bring attention to the corruption. (One of Nast's cartoons is shown on page 460; Tweed is the oversized character on the left.) Tweed was arrested in 1871, tried, and was sent to a debtor's prison, where he lived in modest comfort and was even allowed to visit his family when accompanied by his jailer. On one of these visits, Tweed escaped and fled the country. Nearly a year later, he was captured in Spain while working on a Spanish ship. The authorities there had identified him from a famous Nast cartoon. Tweed was returned to prison, where he died two years later.

Triangle Shirtwaist Company Fire

On March 25, 1911, one of New York City's worst disasters occurred. At the Triangle Shirtwaist Company building, a fire started on the eighth floor. The cause of the fire was never determined, although some believe it was a cigarette thrown carelessly on the floor. Whatever the case, the fire spread quickly, fed by the fabric used for shirts.

Although it was Saturday and nearly 5:00 P.M., many women were still working in the building. As news of the fire spread, the women headed toward the fire exits. Several escaped from the eighth and tenth floors. However, the ninth floor became the center

Uncovering Corruption

Progressives sought to correct widespread corruption through reform. Corruption existed on all levels of government: city, state, and national. In New York City, for example, William Marcy **"Boss" Tweed** milked the city of millions of dollars by using city funds to give himself and his friends large profits on city contracts. One example of corruption on the state level was the bribing of officials to give special favors to certain industries. In Pennsylvania, Standard Oil had been accused of doing everything to the state legislature except refine it. On the national level, the presidency of U. S. Grant had produced so many scandals that the term *grantism* became a synonym for illegal dealings in public office.

The spoils system used by Andrew Jackson and other presidents who followed him had allowed much corruption in the appointment of government employees. This was curbed in the late 1800s by the implementation of several civil service reforms that made merit, or ability, the standard by which jobs were awarded instead of loyalty to the political party in power. Even the reforms in the civil service system, however, were not enough to prevent some politicians from finding ways to abuse the policies.

Corruption was also rampant in industry. The public, especially western farmers, had been victimized by corrupt and unfair practices of the railroads. The railroads had been guilty of overcharging some customers while offering rebates to petroleum shippers. In states where timber was being harvested, some lumber companies stripped public lands for their own profit.

A cartoon from an 1871 issue of Harper's Weekly attacks the political corruption of Boss Tweed and his gang by asking, "Who stole the people's money?"

Some industrialists were not only dishonest in their business dealings but also unfair and even cruel to their workers. The workers often labored under terrible and unsafe conditions. Perhaps the worst disaster was the Triangle Shirtwaist Company fire in New York City in March 1911. Nearly 150 people, mostly girls and women, perished because doors had been locked to keep the workers on the job until the end of the shift. Because filtering systems in southern textile plants were rare, textile workers inhaled cotton lint dust. Some then contracted "brown lung" disease and later died from it. Long hours at low pay were normal. Since almost all jobs had the same hours and since employers exchanged lists of employees who caused trouble or went on strike, it did little good to try to change jobs. Women and children were also victimized by industry. Early efforts to protect women from some occupations and to forbid the employment of children under fourteen years of age failed.

460

Student Activity B: Progressivism

This prewriting activity gives students practice in summarizing the key points in a narrative.

Perpetual Discontentment

By 1900 Americans had experienced improvements in living conditions more than in any other period in history. Yet the cry was for "reform." Ask the students to explain what makes people perpetually discontented with their lot in life.

The Danger of Popular Ideas

Many Christians were swept up in the progressive movement, which appealed to their desire for morality and justice. Nevertheless, Christians became bedfellows with ungodly liberals who wanted to use government to perfect human society without God. A glaring lesson from this era is the danger of following the latest popular ideas. Christians need to understand their history so that they can know what is "new" and what is merely a rephrasing of an old philosophy. A knowledge of history enables students to expose the fallacies in the sup-

posedly new arguments. Discuss some popular political "fads" of the day, such as term limits, which are sometimes promoted on the promise that they will make government moral and spread righteousness. Then show the students that a biblical understanding of human nature should alert them to this "false advertising."

460   Chapter 22

Muckrakers: Journalists Who Exposed the Worst

If it had not been for muckraking journalists, it is possible that progressivism would have died; certainly it would have been less influential. **Muckrakers,** journalists who exposed society's ills, were given their name by Teddy Roosevelt. But the term was not original with him. It is the name of a character in John Bunyan's *Pilgrim's Progress* who was always looking down and could not look up even when offered a heavenly crown.

Muckraker journalists and authors named specific financiers, industrialists, and congressmen who undermined public interests. Muckraker **Lincoln Steffens** revealed city problems in articles for *McClure's*. Later they were put into a book, *The Shame of the Cities*. Steffens charged Philadelphia politicians with using the votes of "dead dogs, children, and nonexistent persons" to keep themselves in power.

Ida M. Tarbell was a Pennsylvania school teacher turned author. She had grown up near Titusville, Pennsylvania, at the height of Standard Oil's attempt to squeeze out its competitors. She later wrote a series of articles on the company's ruthless tactics. In 1903 the articles were printed in a two-volume work, *History of the Standard Oil Company*. Her book led to the court case requiring the company to break down its holdings.

John Spargo wrote of the ills of child labor and of the poverty that sent many children to school hungry each day. His work *The Bitter Cry of Children* (1906) aided the passage of child labor laws. Ray Stannard Baker attacked lynching, execution without trial, of blacks in southern states. **Upton Sinclair** used his novel *The Jungle* to show that Chicago meatpackers killed diseased cattle and used chemicals and dyes to cover up bad meat. His descriptions were effective enough to spark the final drive for the Pure Food and Drug Act.

The political and religious views of many of the muckraking writers were not sound, but their work did force some hidden problems to the attention of the American public and the government.

Revealing Society's Ills

Living conditions were worst in crowded cities. Rents were high and housing was limited, so the poor huddled together. Small, often one-room, apartments were common for entire families, who sometimes even kept boarders. More than 400,000 residents of New York City lived in windowless tenements. Twenty thousand more lived in damp cellar apartments where their rooms often flooded with water.

Epidemics were common. Diphtheria, smallpox, cholera, typhus, scarlet fever, and tuberculosis took many lives. Even "childhood" diseases such as measles, mumps, and chicken pox became dangerous under such conditions. Garbage created a terrible stench and became a breeding ground for insects, germs, and disease. Even where sanitation departments existed, they could not keep pace.

Insufficient water supply and inadequate plumbing were other urban problems. Many tenements did not have running water or indoor bathrooms. People got water from street wells. Because run-off water flowed into them, the water was impure. Fire hydrants were opened at certain times for bathing or other uses. Where indoor plumbing existed, it was usually shared by many people and was undependable.

While housing conditions for the poor were bad, those for people confined in prisons,

of the tragedy. There the exit doors were locked to keep women working until the end of their shift. Nineteen bodies were found next to the locked door.

Other women tried to escape by jumping out the windows. Most died from the fall. Even a safety net brought by firefighters did not help. Too many women jumped at the same time and broke through it. Although two elevators reached the floors on fire, the operators could take only a few women on each trip. In an act of bravery, three men from an adjacent building created a human chain across to a window on the eighth floor. Some women were able to cross on their backs to safety. Unfortunately, the men lost their grip and also fell to their deaths.

By the time the fire was put out, 146 people had died. In the aftermath, the New York legislature formed a commission to investigate factory work conditions. Several labor laws resulted.

The Jungle

Although Upton Sinclair's *The Jungle* exposed the evils of the meatpacking industry, the author had other reasons for writing. Sinclair meant for his book to focus on the plight of the workers. As a Socialist, Sinclair's goal was to alert people to the evils of big business. Unfortunately for him, people were more concerned about what was going into the meat they ate than the situation of the workers.

Shortly after *The Jungle* was published, the number of sales in domestic meat dropped by almost half. President Roosevelt sent two agents to see exactly what the heath conditions were. Their report was not encouraging. Meat was shoveled off dirty floors and stored in rotting boxcars. Food inspection laws were quickly passed. Sinclair said at the time, "I aimed for the public's heart, and by accident I hit it in the stomach."

Jacob Riis, Muckraker

In 1890 a book entitled *How the Other Half Lives* was published. In

---

Are Cities Bad?

Ask the students, "Are cities bad?"

Cities are a popular object of ridicule today, as though life would be better without cities. Liberals like to blame the environment for human sin. But students need to understand that city building and urbanization has been a characteristic of human history ever since Cain went out and built a city. The number and size of cities has increased steadily since the Tower of Babel, and it will probably continue until the vast majority of the world population lives in urban areas. Indeed, God's people will live in the massive new Jerusalem, which may measure two thousand miles on each side. God means for people to live in close fellowship.

Third World countries are currently going through the same trials that the United States faced a century ago when people flocked to the cities and slums rose up on the outskirts of town. Socialists like to blame capitalism and urbanization for these slums, and they suggest that the solution is more rigorous government control. But in reality, a free market appears to allow city-dwellers to make the best choices, and government bungling only worsens the problems. American slums proved to be temporary, and it was individual enterprise, not government inspectors, that got America out of the slums.

its pages author Jacob Riis exposed the condition of inner-city tenements in New York. However, the book's popularity was not so much from its text but from the line drawings that accompanied it. The drawings were based on photographs of the inner city taken by Riis.

Through his photographs Riis captured scenes of families inside their cramped tenements, homeless children sleeping on the streets, and alleys full of people with laundry hanging from above. Readers were shocked at what they saw. Theodore Roosevelt, then the New York police commissioner, wrote Riis, "I have read your book, and I have come to help." Eventually public reaction to the book brought about legislation to clean up New York slums.

Hull House

One of the most common misconceptions about Hull House was that the poor lived there. In reality, the residents were wealthy people who wanted to live among the poor and help them improve the neighborhood. Some of the more famous people who stayed at Hull House included the future president of General Electric, Gerard Swope; historian Charles Beard; and William Lyon MacKenzie King, the future prime minister of Canada.

mental hospitals, and other institutions were even worse. Filth and cruel treatment were commonplace.

Reforms

During this era many city officials had little ability, limited knowledge, and weak character. To overcome these problems, new methods of running city governments were tried. Rather than electing a mayor, some cities hired a trained expert called a city manager. Since his position did not depend on his popularity, the manager was under less pressure to bow to special interest groups. Other cities tried a commission form of government. Several commissioners were selected, and each was put in charge of a specific area of government. This system made it much easier to detect corruption.

Two states, Oregon and Wisconsin, were leaders in progressive reforms. Oregon reformed so many parts of its government that the package of ideas they tried was called the Oregon System. One new democratic practice was the **recall** of elected officials. If citizens became unhappy with the actions of an elected official, they could get a required number of signatures on a petition and force the official either to resign or to stand for special election, even if his term of office had not yet expired.

Two other government reforms enacted in many states were the initiative and referendum. An **initiative** allowed voters to propose their own legislation. First, a set number of voters' signatures had to be collected on a petition. Next, the proposed law would go on a ballot allowing voters to accept or reject it. **Referendums,** on the other hand, allowed voters to pass judgment on acts already passed by their state legislatures. A similar petition and voting system was used.

One other major government reform was the direct election of senators, brought about

in 1913 by Amendment Seventeen. Up to that time senators had been elected by state legislatures. The progressives believed that responsibility belonged to the people. They also believed that such an approach would put elections out of the reach of corrupt manipulators in state government. However, they failed to recognize that senators elected directly by the people would be more likely to follow the immediate desires of the public rather than stand for what was right for the nation in the long run. Thus a practical part of America's republican government was lost.

Many attempts were made to cure some of the problems of the cities. Individuals responded to the terrible conditions in tenements by founding settlement houses. The first settlement house, Toynbee Hall, was in Whitehall, a London slum. Americans modeled theirs after it. Besides providing food, clothing, and child care, the settlement houses offered recreation and classes to slum area women. America's first settlement house, called Neighborhood Guild, was founded in 1886 in New York City. Probably the most famous was Chicago's Hull House. **Jane Addams,** an avowed socialist, founded the work in 1889. She was assisted by Florence Kelly, who later channeled her energies into law. Her efforts led to the passage of child labor laws in several states.

Other citizens and social groups worked for improving prisons and mental institutions and for aiding people in other distressed conditions. While government stayed out of most of these social programs, it did begin to press regulations on industries' abuses of employees and consumers.

SECTION REVIEW

1. List three of the progressives' aims.

2. Who was "Boss Tweed"?

Discuss State and Local Reforms

Explain to your students the form of city government in your area and when it was instituted. Also find out whether your state constitution currently allows for recall, initiative, or referendum; find out when these amendments were passed. Also discuss any issues that recently came up for a vote or are coming up soon.

Section Review Answers

1. to abolish corruption and unfair practices in government, industry, labor, and society; to give people more say in governing; to use the government to improve the quality of life in America (p. 459)

2. New York City politician who mishandled city funds to make money for himself and his friends (p. 460)

3. recall, initiative, referendum (or the direct election of senators) (p. 462)

4. to provide better living conditions for the poor—food, clothing, child care, recreation, education, housing (p. 462)

 Because city managers were hired, not elected, they felt less pressure to give in to special interest groups. The commission form of government made it easier to detect corruption because there were several commissioners, each in charge of a specific area of government. (p. 462)

3. List three government reform ideas that gave more control to individual citizens.

4. What was the purpose of Toynbee Hall and Hull House?

 How did new methods of government help check corruption in cities?

Roosevelt Brings Progressivism to the White House

During the years when these issues of corruption, reform, and government regulation and aid were chief concerns for the country, Americans elected three presidents with progressive goals: Theodore Roosevelt, William Howard Taft, and Woodrow Wilson.

Theodore Roosevelt had been governor of New York when Tom Platt, the state political boss, discovered he could not control him. He then urged Republicans to nominate Roosevelt for the vice-presidency of the United States. Since the vice-presidency was thought to be a political graveyard, Platt hoped that it would shut Roosevelt up and keep him out of the public eye. However, when President McKinley was assassinated, Theodore Roosevelt became president. Although he believed it was "a dreadful thing" to gain the presidency that way, few people have enjoyed the office as much as Roosevelt did.

Roosevelt had some critics, but he gained a large popular following. He was wealthy and well educated, but his adventures as a cowboy and a soldier had given him an ability to identify with the people and endeared him to the public. A candy store owner even named a new toy, the Teddy bear, for him. A graduate of Harvard, Roosevelt spoke several languages and had written at least a dozen books before becoming president. Roosevelt was also a skilled politician with many progressive goals. Unlike many Republican leaders of the day, he wanted change and improvement for the nation's government.

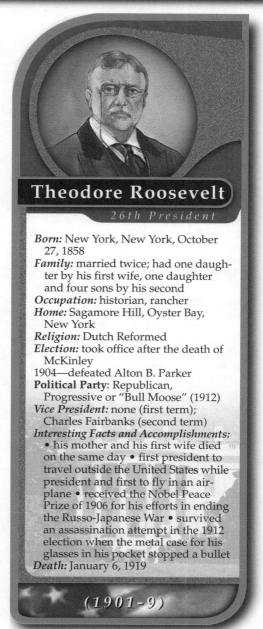

Theodore Roosevelt
26th President

Born: New York, New York, October 27, 1858
Family: married twice; had one daughter by his first wife, one daughter and four sons by his second
Occupation: historian, rancher
Home: Sagamore Hill, Oyster Bay, New York
Religion: Dutch Reformed
Election: took office after the death of McKinley
1904—defeated Alton B. Parker
Political Party: Republican, Progressive or "Bull Moose" (1912)
Vice President: none (first term); Charles Fairbanks (second term)
Interesting Facts and Accomplishments:
• his mother and his first wife died on the same day • first president to travel outside the United States while president and first to fly in an airplane • received the Nobel Peace Prize of 1906 for his efforts in ending the Russo-Japanese War • survived an assassination attempt in the 1912 election when the metal case for his glasses in his pocket stopped a bullet
Death: January 6, 1919

(1901–9)

463

Objectives
Students should be able to
1. Describe Theodore Roosevelt's rise to the presidency.
2. Describe some of the progressive actions of the government during

Assassination Attempt on Roosevelt

On October 14, 1912, Theodore Roosevelt was in Milwaukee preparing to address a crowd of his supporters. As he left his hotel, a man pushed through the crowd, aimed his gun at Roosevelt, and fired. Instantly, Roosevelt's stenographer, Albert Martin, rushed to restrain the gunman. He leaped onto the man's shoulder, grabbed him around the neck with one hand, and used the other to disarm him.

Meanwhile, Roosevelt fell backward. In a few moments, he got back up and told the people not to hurt the gunman, a fanatic named John Crank. Roosevelt had been hit but not fatally. The bullet had gone through his overcoat, spectacle case, and his folded speech manuscript in his pocket. Although slowed down, the bullet did manage to pierce Roosevelt in the chest. Despite his injury, he insisted on being taken to the auditorium to make his speech.

With his vest still stained with blood, Roosevelt mounted the platform and announced his injury. He instantly had a captive audience. The campaign speech went on for approximately an hour. Afterwards Roosevelt collapsed in weakness and was rushed to a hospital. But as he said in his speech, "it takes more than that to kill a Bull Moose." The Bull Moose survived, but his party did not. In the 1912 election, the Democratic candidate, Woodrow Wilson, won handily.

SECTION 3

Materials

• Activity C from Chapter 22 of the *Student Activities* manual

Student Activity C: The Progressive Presidents

This chart summarizes the main features of the three progressive presidencies. This type of activity gives the students practice in analyzing information so that they can make comparisons and contrasts. Students need to complete the chart as they

read through the last three sections of the chapter, or you can help them complete the chart during your lecture.

Roosevelt and Big Business

Roosevelt's first blow to big business was aimed at a holding company with a controlling interest in three major railroads. J. P. Morgan, James J. Hill, and Edward H. Harriman had united their genius to run these railroads for high profits. Roosevelt ordered prosecution of the group because they did not serve the "public good." The Supreme Court ruled against the railroads in the Northern Securities Case of 1904. It declared the holding company to be a trust that illegally restrained trade and forced the company to subdivide.

Teddy Bears

It is true that the teddy bear gets its name from Theodore Roosevelt, but how it happened is a subject of debate. One of the best-known stories involves a trip the president made to Mississippi in 1902. While he was there settling a border dispute, Roosevelt took some time to go hunting. An advance group of hunters found a bear cub, captured it, and tied it to a tree so that the president could shoot it. When Roosevelt arrived, he refused to shoot the captive animal, believing it was unsportsmanlike.

Clifford Barryman, a cartoonist for the *Washington Star*, heard about the story and used it in one of his cartoons. Soon almost everyone had heard about the bear. A store-owner named Morris Michtom decided to use the story to market a new toy in his Brooklyn store. He and his wife designed and made a toy bear and placed it in the store window with the cartoon and a sign that read "Teddy's Bear."

Theodore Roosevelt's Square Deal

Roosevelt believed that the government should control big business and promote competition. Government should also promote better working conditions and job safety. Roosevelt's views and his efforts to put big business under the government's thumb won over other progressives.

Like other progressives, Roosevelt believed that workers should receive just and fair treatment. Roosevelt's labor policy was shown in his handling of the United Mine Workers' strike in 1902. Workers demanded a shorter workday, raises, and recognition for their union. The strike dragged on for months as management refused to negotiate, and coal shortages caused public discomfort. Instead of siding with the owners and forcing the workers back to the mines, Roosevelt warned that he might use troops to run the coal mines. He also formed a special commission to help settle the dispute. This was the first time that the federal government had become a third party in settling a dispute between labor and management. Roosevelt claimed that he wanted to give both labor and management "a square deal." The question of whether such intervention is a proper use of federal powers remains. Nevertheless, a compromise reduced the working day for the miners to nine hours and raised pay by ten percent.

Protecting People and Resources

Upton Sinclair's *The Jungle* had exposed corruption in the meatpacking industry. In 1906 Congress passed the **Pure Food and Drug Act.** Federal inspectors gained the right to inspect all slaughterhouses and meat companies that shipped across state lines. Provisions forbade the use of harmful additives, even if they were designed to stop spoilage.

Many contemporary patent medicines, widely advertised and available over the counter or by mail, contained opium derivatives or a high percentage of alcohol. Although these medicines were often useful, they were also addictive. The Pure Food and Drug Act regulated the use of narcotics and required a list of contents on product labels. It also made it illegal to make unverifiable claims about medicines.

Another issue very dear to Roosevelt's heart was conservation. An outdoorsman, he readily responded to demands that the government protect lands for future generations to enjoy. America's first national park, Yellowstone, had become federal property in 1872. By 1901 there were three more national parks: Sequoia (sih KWOY uh; 1890), Yosemite (yoh SEM ih tee; 1890), and Mount Rainier (ray NEER; 1891). When Roosevelt left office in 1909, he had more than doubled the number of national parks, adding Wind Cave (1901), Crater Lake (1902), Mesa Verde (MAY-suh VURD; 1906), the Petrified Forest (1906), and Platt (1906).

To protect forest lands from loggers, Congress had started a forest reserve system in 1891. While Presidents Harrison, Cleveland, and McKinley had all added to the forest acreage, Theodore Roosevelt more than doubled the acreage in reserve. Theodore Roosevelt's close personal friend and a professionally trained forester, **Gifford Pinchot** (PIN show), was appointed chief forester. Pinchot not only helped to preserve America's forest resources but also set up a program to conserve its grasslands.

In 1902 Congress passed the New Lands Act, which permitted the sale of federal lands in arid areas. The money gained through such a sale was to pay for irrigation projects to make arid lands usable.

Roosevelt Steps Down

Although Theodore Roosevelt could have run again in 1908, he chose instead to hand-

464

Labor Relations—An Open Question

The text says of Roosevelt's first-time use of government power to settle a labor dispute: "The question of whether such intervention is a proper use of federal powers remains." Look back at the first two paragraphs on this page and have the students argue this question. Make the question personal. What if a student or his parent had a dispute with his employer? Would he want the federal government to help settle the dispute? Why or why not?

pick the next Republican presidential candidate. This was the first time since Andrew Jackson that a president in power had enough backing to do so. Theodore Roosevelt picked William Howard Taft, who had given him loyal service.

SECTION REVIEW

1. How did Roosevelt gain the presidency?
2. What was Theodore Roosevelt's attitude toward big business?
3. Whom did Roosevelt wish to be his successor?

 How did the power of the federal government increase during the progressive era?

The Taft Administration

William Howard Taft was a lawyer who had spent most of his career in the federal court system. Although Roosevelt had named him civil governor of the Philippines and later secretary of war, Taft preferred the courts. His lifelong dream was to be chief justice of the Supreme Court. However, he set aside that dream temporarily at the urging of Roosevelt. (In 1921, nine years after Taft left the presidency, he was appointed to the Supreme Court as chief justice by President Harding.)

Taft agreed with Roosevelt that government should control big business. However, when Taft won the 1908 election over Democrat William Jennings Bryan, the course he took as president was somewhat different from Roosevelt's. He followed the advice of Republican leaders more readily, and he did not publicly push progressive reforms. Although his methods and personality made him appear to be more easygoing than Roosevelt, Taft actually initiated eighty-nine antitrust suits, compared to Roosevelt's forty-three. But Taft was unable to dramatize his successes as Roosevelt had done. People saw only Taft's mistakes, and he left office a failure in the eyes of many Americans.

Taft's Term in Office

Nevertheless, Taft could claim many progressive actions. He helped to give the Interstate Commerce Commission more power to control the railroads, and he put telegraph and telephone companies under federal control. Taft backed reforms in the post office, created the Department of Labor to protect workers, and organized the Children's Bureau to end child labor. Also during Taft's administration the Sixteenth and Seventeenth Amendments to the Constitution were ratified. The income tax amendment (Sixteenth) gave government a source of revenues that would allow it to expand its activities greatly in later years. The Seventeenth Amendment required the direct election of senators.

The Republican Party Splits

Taft's political future was endangered by fighting within the Republican Party. Disputes over the passage of the Payne-Aldrich Tariff in 1909 made some Republicans think Taft had sold out Roosevelt's ideas. A bitter dispute between two of Taft's cabinet members over some western forest lands was the final straw. When Taft wanted Gifford Pinchot dismissed from his cabinet, Theodore Roosevelt came home from an African safari convinced that Taft had sold out progressive Republican principles.

The Election of 1912

Theodore Roosevelt had been home less than two months when he hit the campaign trail. He said that he was out to persuade voters to elect progressive Republicans to the House and Senate. But he was really widening the rift within the Republican Party and building his own support for the 1912 convention. By February 1912, Theodore Roosevelt "gave in" to the urging of progressive Republicans

465

Unfortunately, there was room for only 1,178 of the 2,224 passengers. Some of the lifeboats entered the water only half full, leaving around 1,500 people to drown or freeze to death in the twenty-eight-degree water.

Four hundred miles from the coast of Newfoundland, the *Titanic* began its last journey—12,500 feet to the ocean floor. It remained unseen by human eyes until 1985, when Robert Ballard's underwater research team discovered the ship's remains.

One of the last acts of Congress passed during Taft's administration was a law requiring two radio operators on passenger liners. Many more people might have been rescued from the *Titanic* had the law been made sooner. Another ship, the *Californian*, was less than twenty miles from the sinking *Titanic*. Its radio operator was off duty that night and did not receive the distress calls.

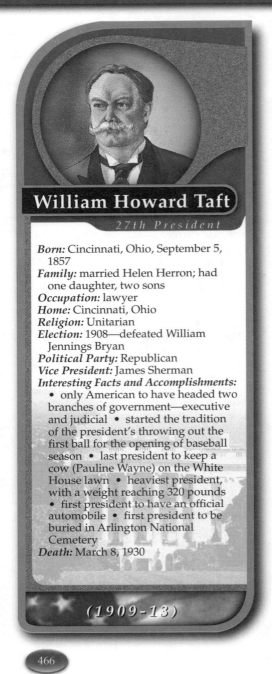

William Howard Taft

27th President

Born: Cincinnati, Ohio, September 5, 1857
Family: married Helen Herron; had one daughter, two sons
Occupation: lawyer
Home: Cincinnati, Ohio
Religion: Unitarian
Election: 1908—defeated William Jennings Bryan
Political Party: Republican
Vice President: James Sherman
Interesting Facts and Accomplishments:
• only American to have headed two branches of government—executive and judicial • started the tradition of the president's throwing out the first ball for the opening of baseball season • last president to keep a cow (Pauline Wayne) on the White House lawn • heaviest president, with a weight reaching 320 pounds • first president to have an official automobile • first president to be buried in Arlington National Cemetery
Death: March 8, 1930

(1909-13)

466

and announced, "My hat is in the ring. I will accept the nomination for president if it is tendered to me."

But Taft and his followers had the support of most of the Republican Party leaders. They helped him win the Republican nomination on the first ballot. Theodore Roosevelt declared that Taft Republican conservatives had stolen the nomination from him. Thus the new Progressive Party was launched, with Theodore Roosevelt as its candidate. When Roosevelt announced that he felt "as fit as a Bull Moose," his party became known as the **Bull Moose Party.** Theodore Roosevelt's political ideals were known as "The New Nationalism" and would have involved the federal government in still more areas had he won.

The Democratic candidate was New Jersey's progressive Democratic governor, Woodrow Wilson. His campaign catchwords spoke of the "New Freedom." He wanted strict government regulation to restore business competition. Although Roosevelt and Taft together got more votes than Wilson, Wilson won because of the split Republican vote.

Teddy Roosevelt flashes his famous grin.

shadow, Bush sometimes appeared weak and ineffective.

A Mock Interview

Assign groups of students to represent different people from around the country during the 1912 election—Democrats, pro-Taft Republicans, pro-Roosevelt Republicans, and Socialists. Pretend that you are Teddy Roosevelt and that you are going to hold a meeting with "the people." Give the groups a few minutes to prepare questions and to discuss the comments and charges they might make during such a discussion. Then open the floor for questions and follow-up comments from the crowd. Citizens must raise their hand and then "step up to the podium" to talk to the candidate.

Was Teddy a Demagogue?

Teddy Roosevelt's opponents called him a demagogue. Have a volunteer look up that word in the dictionary and read the definition to the class. *(a leader who obtains power by means of impassioned appeals to emotions and prejudices)* Do your students think that Roosevelt was a demagogue? If you did not discuss the characteristics of a great president in the last chapter, discuss them here. Was Roosevelt a poor loser when he lost the Republican nomination to Taft? Note the irony that Roosevelt had used the wheels of power four years earlier to get Taft elected, but he now accused Taft of using those same wheels to "steal" the nomination.

SECTION REVIEW

1. During his career, Taft headed what other branch of government besides the executive branch?
2. What were the provisions of the Sixteenth and Seventeenth Amendments?
3. The Republican split enabled what Democrat to win the 1912 election?

 Why was the Bull Moose party created?

Progressivism with a Democrat

Woodrow Wilson, son of a Presbyterian pastor, grew up in the South. His ideas reflected his background. He believed that there were two sides to every issue, "a right side and a wrong side," and he stubbornly hung on to principles, refusing to compromise. He had confidence in his judgment perhaps because he believed God had led him. He viewed men idealistically, sincerely believing that most people learned from experience and desired to do right. Politically, this view meant that he often underestimated his opposition, whether at home or abroad.

Wilson and Business

At first Wilson favored less government regulation of business than either Roosevelt or Taft. But rather than try to regulate large trusts, he believed that the government should break them up into smaller companies. He believed small companies would be less monopolistic and more likely to operate in the public interest. To deal with big business and get around the courts, which usually decided in favor of big business, Wilson took two steps. First, he set up the **Federal Trade Commission.** This independent regulatory agency had the power to get data from corporations and to issue orders to stop abuses. Second, Congress passed the **Clayton Anti-Trust Act** of 1914. This act closed some loop-

Woodrow Wilson and his wife, Edith, at his inauguration.

holes of the earlier Sherman Anti-Trust Act. It defined the unfair acts for which corporations could be fined or their executives jailed. The act also exempted both labor unions and farmers' cooperatives from antitrust laws so that these groups could lawfully protest unfair practices.

The Tariff and Income Tax

One of Wilson's major accomplishments concerned the tariff. Since the Democrats had gained majorities in both the House and Senate, Wilson had the support for the reforms he had proposed in his 1912 campaign. Wilson believed that a high protective tariff encouraged monopolies and led to higher charges for consumers. Lowering the tariff would force American businesses to compete with rivals and become more efficient. The **Underwood Tariff of 1913** gave the first major tariff decrease since the Civil War. The tariff rate on

467

SECTION 5

Objectives

Students should be able to
1. Explain Wilson's dealings with big business.
2. Describe the important changes regarding finances that came during the Wilson administration.
3. Name the two progressive amendments added during the Wilson administration and state their purpose.

Clayton Anti-Trust Act

Among other things, the Clayton Anti-Trust Act made it illegal for firms to charge one price to one customer and a second price to another when that action fostered monopoly. It said buyers did not have to sign contracts stating that they would never deal with the competition. It also made it illegal for the same people to be on the board of directors of several companies involved in the same types of business.

Oreo Chocolate Sandwich Cookies

In the same year that Wilson was elected to his first term, the National Biscuit Company introduced what they called a "tea biscuit." Since then the Oreo cookie has become a popular snack and desert treat. Its two chocolate wafers are made from Dutch cocoa and embossed with the famous Oreo name. Between the wafers a special icing called "slurry" is added.

Interestingly enough, nobody knows for sure where the name for the cookie came from. Wherever the name came from, it stuck, and so did the cookie as a favorite treat. Today over six billion Oreos are produced and consumed each year.

Section Review Answers

1. the judicial branch (as chief justice of the Supreme Court) (p. 465)
2. The Sixteenth created an income tax. The Seventeenth required the direct election of senators. (p. 465)
3. Woodrow Wilson (p. 466)

 because the Republican Party chose Taft again for its candidate and Theodore Roosevelt and his supporters felt that Taft had betrayed Progressive ideals (pp. 465-66)

Section 5

Materials

- The current Republican Party platform
- Activity D from Chapter 22 of the *Student Activities* manual

Why Study Presidents?

Many foreigners wonder why students of U.S. history pay so much attention to individual presidents. Ask students to answer this question. (*Presidential elections bring out the pressing issues that the average citizen cares about, and the president embod-* *ies or symbolizes the aspirations of all people in the nation. Even though the power of the president often seems limited, every president puts his distinct stamp on the course of events in the nation.*) Discuss the current president. How does his election and administration embody or symbolize the struggles of the average American?

Federal Reserve System

The Federal Reserve System was the final solution to the problem of keeping and regulating the nation's money. It followed the national bank, pet banks, and independent treasury systems discussed earlier in the book.

Crossword Puzzles

On December 21, 1913, Arthur Wynne delivered an early Christmas present to the world. The puzzle editor for the *New York World* designed a puzzle of connected blocks in the shape of a diamond. The first crossword puzzle was such a success that the puzzles became a regular feature in the Sunday edition.

As its popularity spread, crossword puzzles began to show up in other newspapers. In 1930 the first *Times* crossword puzzle was published. Today crosswords are found in newspapers around the world, and their loyal fans still take time out of busy schedules to solve them.

A Close One for Wilson

The 1916 election showed just how important each vote is in an election. If one more person had voted for Charles Evan Hughes in each California district, he would have become the next president of the United States.

Several other elections have been close calls. In the 1884 presidential election, Grover Cleveland defeated James G. Blaine by a majority of 1,047 votes within New York State. John F. Kennedy won the 1960 election by less than 1 percent of the vote in each election district.

In 1988 two Florida congressmen each won their seats by a single absentee vote. Another congressman from Alaska won his seat by eleven absentee votes. With election results like these, it is not surprising that politicians spend so much time and effort encouraging people to go to the polls and vote.

Woodrow Wilson
28th President

Born: Staunton, Virginia, December 28, 1856
Family: married Ellen Axson, and after her death, Edith Galt; had three daughters by his first wife
Occupation: lawyer, teacher, university president
Home: Washington, D.C.
Religion: Presbyterian
Elections: 1912—defeated William Howard Taft (Republican) and Theodore Roosevelt (Bull Moose) 1916—defeated Charles Evans Hughes
Political Party: Democrat
Vice President: Thomas Marshall
Interesting Facts and Accomplishments:
 • the first president with an earned Ph.D. • kept sheep on the White House lawn to crop the grass during World War I • played golf year-round to get over first wife's death; painted the balls black in the winter so that he could see them on the snow • had a stroke while in office, so his second wife managed much of his presidential affairs and is sometimes called "the nation's first lady president"
Death: February 3, 1924

(1913-21)

468

imports went down from forty pecent to less than thirty percent.

Since the Sixteenth Amendment had legalized the income tax, Congress used it to make up for the loss of tariff revenue. Incomes under $4,000 were not taxed. Annual incomes between $4,000 and $20,000 were taxed one percent. The income tax was a graduated tax: the more a person made, the higher percentage of his income he had to pay. The top bracket was six percent on incomes over $500,000. This beginning of income taxes paved the way for higher taxes and more government spending in the future.

Another financial reform accomplished during the Wilson presidency was the establishment of the **Federal Reserve System.** It set up twelve district banks under a national Federal Reserve Board. The Federal Reserve Banks served as bankers' banks. The district reserve banks could increase or decrease the amount of money in circulation. The Board could use its power to control many banking operations throughout the country and thus try to manage the nation's economy.

The Election of 1916

As the nation approached the 1916 election, Wilson was more and more preoccupied with events in war-torn Europe. Seeking to avoid American involvement in the conflict, his campaign slogan became: "He kept us out of war."

When Teddy Roosevelt refused to run as a progressive candidate, the Bull Moose Party dissolved. Progressive followers then had to decide whom to follow. Some backed Wilson because of his reforms, while others returned to the Republican fold.

The election of 1916 was a very close one. Wilson narrowly defeated Republican Charles Evans Hughes. Hughes was a former governor of New York and a Supreme Court justice. The key state in the election proved to be

Where Do You Stand?

With the students' help, write on the board all of the accomplishments during Wilson's administration. Then take a vote on each accomplishment to find out how many students would have supported the action and how many would have opposed it. Every student must be ready to defend his vote. Be prepared to give modern examples of similar issues and discuss how conservatives have typically voted.

The Republican Party Then and Now

Discuss the main tenets of the modern Republican Party (and even read from the party platform written during the last campaign, if you wish to download it from the Internet). Ask the students to make comparisons and contrasts with the party in 1916. Make similar comparisons between the old and new Democratic Parties. Note that parties can completely shift sides on such issues as the tariff, control of big business, and welfare.

Chapter 22   Progressivism

A New York City women's suffrage parade in 1913 calls for women to receive the right to vote.

entry of the United States into World War I. In addition to problems in Europe, Wilson faced problems in Latin America, where he tried to implement his moral diplomacy. With all this attention on actions in other lands, progressive politics began to fall by the wayside. Two major issues that were resolved, however, were the questions of prohibition and women's suffrage. To the delight of prohibitionists, the Eighteenth Amendment, banning the manufacture and sale of alcoholic beverages, passed in 1919. One year later, when the Nineteenth Amendment was passed, the suffragettes won their right to vote. However, the progressive era in American history was over.

California. Election returns from that state were late to arrive, and Hughes went to bed believing he was the next president. The next morning he found out that Wilson had been reelected.

Wilson's Second Term

During his second term Wilson was forced to focus on foreign affairs and the eventual

SECTION REVIEW

1. What system set up district banks to manage the nation's economy?

2. What gained most of the national government's attention during Wilson's second term?

3. What two major progressive issues were passed during Wilson's second term?

 How did the reduction of the tariff make the passage of the Sixteenth Amendment more important?

SUMMARY

Americans generally enjoyed great prosperity at the turn of the century, but they also realized that there were many problems in their nation. Greed, poverty, alcoholism, corruption in government, and other evils troubled many people in the United States, so Americans began to pressure government leaders to do something about these conditions. Progressive politicians campaigned for government reforms as well as regulations for industry. Although a few of the accomplishments of progressivism did prove helpful, their basic effect was to increase the government's activity and power in a search for solutions. Most people failed to realize that government could never solve the underlying problems of sin.

469

Section Review Answers

1. the Federal Reserve System (p. 468)

2. foreign affairs (World War I and Latin American problems) (p. 469)

3. prohibition and women's suffrage (p. 469)

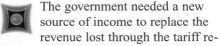 The government needed a new source of income to replace the revenue lost through the tariff reduction. It found that source in the income tax. (p. 468)

Chapter Review

People, Places, and Things to Remember

progressivism	Charles Darwin	referendums
urbanization	Charles Hodge	Jane Addams
philanthropists	temperance societies	Pure Food and Drug Act
Tuskegee Institute	"Boss" Tweed	Gifford Pinchot
Booker T. Washington	muckrakers	Bull Moose Party
George Washington Carver	Lincoln Steffens	Federal Trade Commission
Samuel L. Clemens	Ida M. Tarbell	Clayton Anti-Trust Act
agnostics	Upton Sinclair	Underwood Tariff of 1913
Robert Ingersoll	recall	Federal Reserve System
	initiative	

Review Questions

Match each of the following terms with its description.

1. agnostic
2. initiative
3. muckraker
4. recall
5. referendum
6. temperance society
7. urbanization

a. movement to the cities
b. says no one can know whether God exists
c. worked to prohibit alcohol use and abuse
d. one who reported poor conditions in society
e. voters' attempt to remove elected officials
f. voters propose legislation themselves
g. voters' reaction to a law already passed by their legislature

Answer the following questions.

8. What was the famous black school founded by Booker T. Washington?
9. What scientist helped to give that school a good reputation?
10. Name three religious cults that became popular around the turn of the century.
11. Who were the three progressive presidents?
12. What legislation helped to combat corruption in meatpacking companies and the abuse of patent medicines?
13. What was Roosevelt's party called in 1912?
14. What did the Sixteenth and Seventeenth Amendments do?
15. What is the term for the group of twelve banks and their board that regulate the nation's money system?

Questions for Discussion

16. In what ways was progressivism helpful to the country, and in what ways was it harmful?
17. How did America's government change during the progressive era?

470

Chapter Review Answers

1. b (p. 457)
2. f (p. 462)
3. d (p. 461)
4. e (p. 462)
5. g (p. 462)
6. c (p. 457)
7. a (p. 453)
8. Tuskegee Institute (p. 454)
9. George Washington Carver (p. 454)

10. Christian Science, Seventh-day Adventism, Jehovah's Witnesses (p. 456)
11. Theodore Roosevelt, William Howard Taft, Woodrow Wilson (p. 463)
12. Pure Food and Drug Act (p. 464)
13. Bull Moose Party (p. 466)
14. 16th—allowed a federal income tax; 17th—required the direct election of senators (p. 465)
15. Federal Reserve System (p. 468)

16. Answers will vary. Some abuses were corrected. Some freedom was lost.
17. Answers will vary. Agencies, regulations, and expenses grew.

History Skills

Types of Graphs

Graphs are a useful tool to display complex information in a simple format. The three basic types are line graphs, which show changes over time; bar graphs, which compare similar quantities to each other; and pie graphs, which compare individual quantities to the total.

Below are two graphs about changes in American life between 1860 and 1920. They are based on information supplied by the U.S. Census Bureau. Look at the graphs carefully and answer the questions that follow.

1. Which decade had the highest number of immigrants? How many came in that decade?

2. Approximately how many Americans lived in urban areas in 1860?

3. In what year did the number of urbanized Americans surpass the number of rural Americans?

Think About It—If you needed to create a chart showing the number of American cities whose population exceeded 100,000 from 1860 to 1920, which type of graph would you use: bar, line, or pie graph?

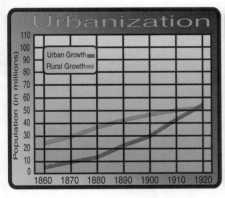

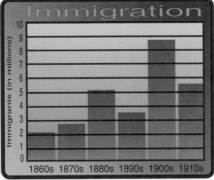

471

History Skills

1. 1900-1910; approximately 8.8 million

2. 6 million

3. 1920

 bar graph

Taking the Lead

Unit Six

This unit takes the students through both major wars of the century and the crash of the economy in the thirties. Your students will continue to see the decline in morality of Americans and a continued growth of government, especially during the Roosevelt administration.

Over There

A map of the world would be a helpful background for a bulletin board since your study covers two world wars. Use string and/or pushpins to show battle locations and fronts.

Another bulletin board could concentrate on events during the twenties and thirties. Photos of events and people scattered across the board with labels will make the era more real to your students. You may be able to download and print some photos from the Internet.

Materials

You will need the following special materials for your teaching of Unit Six.

- *Student Activities* manual for THE AMERICAN REPUBLIC for Christian Schools (Second Edition)
- WORLD STUDIES for Christian Schools, Second Edition (BJUP)
- Special speaker: a World War I model plane enthusiast
- *American History in Verse* by Burton Stevenson (BJUP)
- April 1994 issue of *National Geographic*
- *Scenes from American Church History* (BJUP)
- Special speaker: an antique collector or antique car enthusiast
- Video on Charles Lindbergh
- Special speaker: a person who experienced the Great Depression
- Video documentary on World War II
- December 1991 issue of *National Geographic*

CHAPTERS IN THIS UNIT:

23

WORLD WAR I

24

THE 1920S: DECADE OF CHANGE

25

CRASH AND DEPRESSION

26

WORLD WAR II

472

1914-17: The tank was a significant invention of World War I. Its ability to advance over rugged terrain was critical for trench warfare.

1920s: Home run hitter Babe Ruth was a great hero to the excitement-loving Americans of the Roaring Twenties.

Unit 6	Lesson Plan Chart		
Chapter Title	**Main Goal**	**Pages**	**Time Frame**
23. World War I	To recognize the total failure of imperialist and progressive ideas to solve international problems	475-93	4½-8 days
24. The 1920s: Decade of Change	To understand that moral decline is a recurring theme in civilization	494-511	5-7 days
Evolution	To identify ways in which evolutionary philosophy has affected society	512-13	½-1 day
25. Crash and Depression	To identify the fact that Americans faced with hard times will choose security over liberty	514-32	6-9 days
26. World War II	To discern God's providence in defeating the fascist powers and raising the United States to international power	533-55	6-10 days
Total Suggested Days			22-35 days

1930s: Economic troubles of the 1930s forced many men out of work. Soup kitchens provided warm meals for those in need.

1941: The crippling Japanese attack on the naval base at Pearl Harbor launched the United States into World War II.

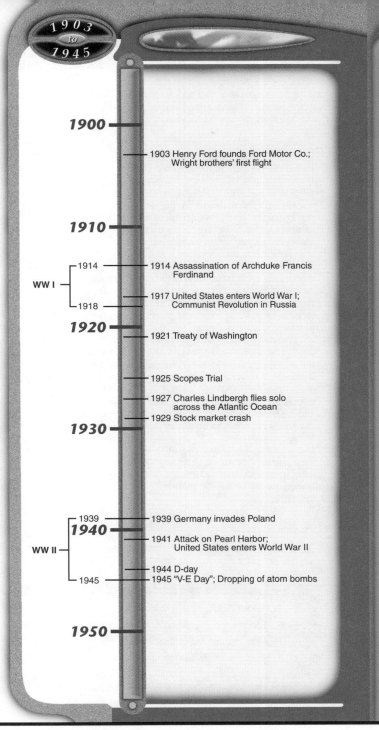

1903 to 1945

1900

1903 Henry Ford founds Ford Motor Co.; Wright brothers' first flight

1910

WW I
- 1914 — 1914 Assassination of Archduke Francis Ferdinand
- 1917 United States enters World War I; Communist Revolution in Russia
- 1918 —

1920 — 1921 Treaty of Washington

1925 Scopes Trial

1927 Charles Lindbergh flies solo across the Atlantic Ocean

1929 Stock market crash

1930

WW II
- 1939 — 1939 Germany invades Poland
- **1940** — 1941 Attack on Pearl Harbor; United States enters World War II
- 1944 D-day
- 1945 — 1945 "V-E Day"; Dropping of atom bombs

1950

• Photocopies of World War II songs and lyrics
• Special speaker: a veteran or someone with war memorabilia

Time Out

Ask the following questions about the time line. Have your students give the event and the date.

• What sparked World War I? *(1914 assassination of Archduke Francis Ferdinand)*

• In what year did World War I end? *(1918)*

• What event caused fear and poverty during the 1930s? *(the 1929 stock market crash)*

• When did the United States enter World War II? *(1941)*

• What event brought the United States into the war? *(the attack on Pearl Harbor)*

• What ended World War II? *(dropping of the atomic bombs)*

Roosevelt's "Nothing to Fear" Speech

Roosevelt's first inaugural speech set the tone for his forceful administration, which revolutionized American government. Read this excerpt. Then write the first five words of the sentence in the text that answers each question.

First of all, let me assert my firm belief that the only thing we have to fear is fear itself—nameless, unreasoning, unjustified terror which paralyzes needed efforts to convert retreat into advance. . . . Plenty is at our doorstep, but a generous use of it languishes in the very sight of the supply. Primarily this is because rulers of the exchange of mankind's goods have failed through their own stubbornness and their own incompetence. . . .

This nation asks for action, and action now.

Our greatest primary task is to put people to work. This is no unsolvable problem if we face it wisely and courageously. It can be accomplished in part by direct recruiting by the government itself, treating the task as we would treat the emergency of a war. . . .

We must frankly recognize the overbalance of population in our industrial centers and, by engaging on a national scale in a redistribution, endeavor to provide a better use of the land for those best fitted for the land. The task can be helped by definite efforts to raise the values of agricultural products and with this the power to purchase the output of our cities. . . . It can be helped by national planning for and supervision of all forms of transportation and of communications and other utilities which have a definitely public character. There are many ways in which it can be helped, but it can never be helped merely by talking about it. We must act and act quickly.

Finally, in our progress toward a resumption of work we require two safeguards against a return of the evils of the old order: there must be a strict supervision of all banking and credits and investments, so that there will be an end to speculation with other people's money; and there must be provision for an adequate but sound currency. . . .

If we are to go forward, we must move as a trained and loyal army willing to sacrifice for the good of a common discipline, because without such discipline no progress is made, no leadership becomes effective. We are, I know, ready and willing to submit our lives and property to such discipline. . . . I assume unhesitatingly the leadership of this great army of our people dedicated to a disciplined attack upon our common problems. . . .

It is hoped that the normal balance of executive and legislative authority may be wholly adequate to meet the unprecedented task before us. But . . . in the event that the national emergency is still critical, I shall not evade the clear course of duty that will then confront me. I shall ask the Congress for the one remaining instrument to meet the crisis—broad executive power to wage war against the emergency, as great as the power that would be given to me if we were in fact invaded by a foreign foe.

1. Whom did Roosevelt blame for America's hardships in the midst of plenty?
2. According to Roosevelt, how could the government help put people back to work?
3. What radical redistribution plan did Roosevelt propose (but never enact)?
4. How would Roosevelt respond to Hoover's emphasis on "rugged individualism"?

"Nothing to Fear"

1. the rulers of the exchange of mankind's goods —"the rulers of the exchange of mankind's goods have failed through their own stubbornness and their own incompetence"

2. by direct recruiting

3. planned to redistribute the population from the cities to the land

4. He would say that people must give up their individual desires for the good of all, to work toward a common goal—"we must move as a trained and loyal army willing to sacrifice for the good of a common discipline."

23

World War I

On June 29, 1914, Americans read in their newspapers of the assassination the previous day in Sarajevo (SAH RAH yeh voh), Bosnia, of Archduke Francis Ferdinand, heir to the Austro-Hungarian throne. Most Americans probably asked, "Where is Sarajevo, Bosnia?" Little did they realize how soon all their lives would be drastically affected by that political assassination in a little town on the Balkan Peninsula that few Americans had heard of. World War I would soon follow.

World War I shocked Americans. For three years—1914 through 1916—the United States looked on as "the Great War" ravaged Europe, destroying more property and life than any other war in history up to that time. Most

Americans believed that the war was Europe's affair. They agreed with President Wilson that Americans needed to be neutral in word and deed. They hoped that having the Atlantic Ocean between them and the conflict would keep America out of the war. In 1916 Americans had reelected Wilson because "he kept them out of war." But on April 6, 1917, hopes for staying at peace were dashed. The United States entered World War I.

The War As America Watched
The United States tried to mind its own business as the war began, but it could not help seeing the trouble that was brewing in Europe.

475

SECTION 1

Objectives

Students should be able to
1. List the four major reasons for World War I.
2. Describe the action or tactics of the war.

Imperialism in Africa

The continent of Africa was a tempting target for countries seeking to build empires. Though imperialistic activity was slow before 1880, by the time of World War I every country but Ethiopia and Liberia had been claimed by some European nation. France held the largest area, but most of its land was desert.

Powder Keg of Europe

Austria-Hungary, Russia, and Germany all had imperialistic ideas of extending their control into the Balkan area (the land between the Black and Adriatic Seas) because the Ottoman Empire was losing its grip on that region. Because of the political uncertainties there, the Balkans were called the "powder keg of Europe," and the assassination of the archduke was enough to set off an explosion.

Reasons for War

There were several reasons for Europe's turmoil, and one was extreme nationalism. A devotion to and a pride in one's own nation is a natural and proper feeling, but some countries had been building a distorted nationalism in their people in the years before the war. Some nations, like Germany, began to believe they had the right to build up and expand their country no matter what the effect might be on others.

Imperialism and militarism were two more reasons for the growing tensions in Europe. Several countries had or wanted large empires, and some were willing to fight each other to gain control of colonies or nearby territories. Several nations had built large armies to further imperial goals or protect possessions. Large and powerful military forces, however, were a threat to weaker neighbors and caused rivals to increase their forces as well.

Another major reason for the eruption of World War I was the alliances of European nations. In their effort to insure security against aggression, European nations had formed alliances, agreements to support one another militarily. The **Triple Alliance** included Germany, Austria-Hungary, and Italy, nations united by common imperialistic goals. The **Triple Entente** (on TONT; *entente* is a French word for "agreement") included Britain, France, and Russia, nations united by a common fear of Germany. Because these two opposing alliances involved all the major powers of Europe, once any of these powers entered a conflict, all the others were likely to be drawn in.

The Spark and Spread of War

The assassination of the Austrian archduke was the spark that ignited the conflict. Russia quickly came to the aid of Serbia, the little Balkan country that Austria-Hungary

Troops of both the Allies and the Central Powers spent much of the war locked in uncomfortable trench warfare.

Student Activity A: Experiences of War

This chart gives an excellent summary of the main information in the chapter. You will probably want to help the students complete the chart as part of your lecture.

Review Imperialism and Progressivism

As they have done in other chapters, the students need to see that ideas have consequences. Ask the students to summarize imperialism (Chapter 21) and to explain how it contributed to World War I. Also summarize the false, liberal views of man and of government that gave rise to progressivism. For a time, Americans blindly accepted the perfectibility of mankind and government. In God's providence, World War I struck classic liberalism a blow from which it never recovered.

The Scramble in Africa

You may want to review with the students what they learned in seventh-grade history by looking at *WORLD STUDIES for Christian Schools* (Second Edition) on pages 397- 402. This information combined with the side margin note on "Imperialism in Africa" will help them unite their studies.

Tanks such as this one became important weapons in World War I.

blamed for the deed. Thus Russia and Austria-Hungary were soon at war with each other, and the allies of both joined in the conflict.

On August 1, Germany declared war on Russia, and France joined with Russia against Germany and Austria-Hungary two days later. When German armies marched across the neutral country of Belgium to attack France, Britain quickly stepped into the war. A few other nations also took sides. Ahead was a long and bloody war between the **Central Powers**—Germany, Austria-Hungary, Bulgaria, and Turkey—and the **Allied Powers**—Britain, France, Russia, Italy, and later the United States. (Italy switched to the Allied side in 1915.)

Action in the War

Since the United States was not involved in the European alliances and rivalries, it had no reason in the beginning to enter the war with the other powers. It simply watched in

horror as soldiers slaughtered each other across Europe in their bitter fight.

Germany led the first major assault of the war by pressing its armies through Belgium to northern France. British troops came to France's aid before the Germans could take the country, however, and the two sides settled into trenches from the English Channel to the Rhine River. At the same time, the Russian armies began to attack Germany and Austria-Hungary from the east with little success.

The war dragged on with neither the Central Powers nor the Allies making large gains. However, both sides did introduce new weapons and equipment that made warfare more efficient and sometimes more brutal.

The British developed the tank, an armored vehicle that could fire shells while moving on caterpillar tracks. It was capable of almost continuous advance over rugged terrain. Soon the other powers developed their own tanks.

Austria-Hungary and the Balkans

Austria-Hungary had a strong interest in the Balkans. This volatile region on the empire's southeastern border could pose a danger, but it also presented an opportunity to acquire more territory. Austria annexed the province of Bosnia in 1908, against the wishes of other Balkan nations. Anti-Austrian groups sprang up to fight for Bosnia's independence. One of these groups, based in Serbia, sponsored the man who killed Francis Ferdinand. Austria-Hungary blamed Serbia for not stopping the group.

Slavic Peoples

The Slavs are the largest ethnic and linguistic group in Europe. They live mostly in Eastern Europe and share a common Indo-European language background, although Eastern Orthodox Slavs use a Cyrillic alphabet while Roman Catholics use the Roman alphabet. Russia has come to the aid of her fellow Slavs in Serbia more than once.

No Man's Land

Note that after the initial German thrust through Belgium, the fighting bogged down. The opposing armies dug trenches and spent most of the war in a stalemate, facing each other across a dangerous strip called "no man's land."

Development of the Tank

A tank is a vehicle that is both armed and armored. The idea for a moving vehicle of warfare originated with the chariot. Several variations of the idea were undertaken through the centuries. (One early tank pioneer was Leonardo da Vinci.) The tank finally achieved its modern look in World War I with the addition of caterpillar tracks. The heavy artillery fire and trench warfare of the Great War necessitated a heavily armored vehicle that could move capably over rugged terrain.

The word *tank*, which also refers to a container for storing liquid, came from India, where it described a pond. During World War I the British had to give their new armored vehicles a code name when they shipped them to France in case the enemy stole the crates. They chose "tank" because they thought the vehicles looked like tanks for holding benzene (a liquid developed from petroleum).

The Great War

World War I was called the Great War. It did not become World War I until the time of World War II.

Shell Shock

War had many ways of wounding a soldier. In addition to physical afflictions, there was psychological trauma. Many soldiers in World War I suffered from a condition commonly known as shell shock. Having been exposed repeatedly to the noise and horrors of the battlefield, their nervous systems collapsed. The behavior of shell shock victims ranged from apathy to extreme agitation. With proper rest and treatment, a soldier could recover from shell shock; however, disturbing memories might return periodically. Some afflicted with the condition became long-term residents of veterans' hospitals.

Slaughter on the Battlefield

The slaughter on World War I battlefields was staggering. On the first day of fighting at the Somme in July 1916, the British had 60,000 soldiers killed or wounded. Most were lost in the first half-hour of battle. In Belgium in April 1917, the British lost 150,000 soldiers in six days while their front line advanced only a few miles. The dead from this war numbered twice as many as the dead in all the major wars fought from 1790 to 1913.

On April 22, 1915, at the second battle of Ypres, the Germans unleashed a new deadly weapon: poison gas. Made from chlorine, the gas harmed the nose, throat, and lungs. Poison gases made whole armies temporarily helpless in the face of enemy attacks. Mustard gas, as it was called, soon became the most feared and common gas on the battlefield. About two percent of those who came into contact with it died. As a result, the gas mask was developed and became standard equipment in some war areas.

Fighting also took to the air. For a while the Germans used zeppelins, large aircraft similar to blimps, to bomb Britain. But because zeppelins were slow moving, they were soon replaced by the airplane. This new flying machine could be used for aerial reconnaissance, bombing, and "dogfighting." Dogfighting, shooting between enemy planes, became possible after machine guns were synchronized with the airplane's propellers. (Before that development in 1915, pilots could not fire their guns forward without shooting their own propellers.) Fighter pilots who shot down five or more planes became special heroes called "flying aces." Manfred von Richthofen, "the Red Baron," was Germany's top ace. Britain's flying hero was Mick Mannock, and when the United States entered the war, Eddie Rickenbacker became the most famous American ace.

Trucks and automobiles aided the transportation of military goods and personnel. Rifles, cannon, grenades, mines, and other weapons were improved or invented for effective fighting. And for battling on the sea, the Germans perfected the submarine. These "U-boats" (underwater boats) could remain unseen while launching a surprise torpedo attack against enemy ships.

The Wild Blue Yonder

America's air force had its beginnings in France during World War I. Actually, the first American air squadron was in the French armed forces. Since the United States did not have an air corps of its own at that time, many young Americans went to Europe to fly for France. At first these adventurers could join only the French Foreign Legion. They were forbidden by French law from enlisting in the regular French forces. Soon the law changed, though, and a group of young and wealthy Americans joined the French Air Corps. (The rich became pilots simply because before the war they were the only ones who had the money to buy planes and to learn to fly.)

Soon a group of these American pilots began petitioning the French government to form an all-American French squadron. Finally permission was granted, and in April 1916 the *Escadrille Américaine* (ES-kuh-DRIL uh-mehr-ih-CAN) was begun. When President Wilson complained that the name violated America's official neutral position, the squadron changed its name to the *Lafayette Escadrille*. The young men claimed that they were repaying France for the help that the Frenchman Lafayette had given the United States during the War for Independence.

The *Lafayette Escadrille* began with seven pilots and a lion cub for a mascot. During the war a total of thirty-eight men served as pilots for the group, and many of them died in their cockpits. When the United States entered World War I, the *Lafayette Escadrille* switched over to become the first American air squadron.

Display Model Airplanes

World War I is perhaps the most popular period among model airplane enthusiasts. Have the students bring in any models they may have and report anything they know about the planes and the pilots. If you know a model plane enthusiast, invite him or her to come and address the students.

Display Memorabilia from the War

If the families of any of the students have memorabilia from World War I, including medals and weapons, ask those students to share such items with the class, along with any stories of family veterans.

SECTION REVIEW

1. What event sparked the start of World War I?
2. List four of the causes of the war's outbreak.
3. What countries comprised the Allies? the Central Powers?
4. Which country made the first major assault?
5. What country developed the tank? poison gas?

 How did airplanes contribute to a nation's defenses?

Effects of the European War on America

Although the United States was not participating in the war, it was not totally isolated from the warring nations either. Transportation, trade, and diplomatic relationships with Europe were all affected by the war, and these matters concerned Americans.

Reasons for American Interest

Although President Wilson had stated that Americans should remain neutral, maintaining neutrality proved difficult for several reasons.

First, American sentiment favored the Allied cause. Although there were eleven million Americans who had some tie to Germany, there were substantially more who had British ties. America's background, its legal system, part of its form of government, and even its language were English. Americans also recalled that another ally, France, had come to America's aid during the War for Independence. Moreover, Americans had been upset by the German invasion of neutral Belgium.

A second factor was economic. Although American businessmen sold goods and lent money to both the Allied and Central Powers, more traded with Allied countries, especially Britain. Consequently, Americans were more sympathetic to Allied interests just to protect American investments.

Gradually the United States began aiding the Allies. Right after the outbreak of war, British and French agents had come to place orders with American firms. They contracted for shipments of grain, cotton, and other needed supplies. At first these countries had paid cash for their items and carried them home on their own ships. But when their cash ran low, they asked for and received loans. By early 1917 the United States had lent Britain over $1 billion and France over $300 million. The Germans protested that this violated neutrality because American-made shells and guns were killing Germans. Wilson, however, chose not to restrict these business deals. He believed that restricting them would help the Central Powers.

Another factor was Allied propaganda. Britain and France controlled the trans-Atlantic cables that brought the news to American newspapers. The Germans had to rely on the still imperfect radio to transmit messages to the United States. In addition, the Germans, with the few messages they did get through, did not project a good image to Americans. Because they emphasized hate and destruction, more anger than sympathy was aroused. The Allies easily won the Americans over just by reprinting German hate propaganda word for word. Germany's deeds were also harmful to its relationship with America. When it invaded Belgium, a violation of an earlier treaty, the German government explained away the betrayal by calling the treaty "a scrap of paper." About five thousand Belgian civilians who had resisted the Germans were executed. British propagandists were quick to let Americans know of this and other atrocities, including a few that never happened.

Violations of America's Neutral Rights

The biggest difficulty in maintaining neutrality revolved around Britain's and

---

Objectives
Students should be able to
1. Explain why American interest in the war grew.
2. Describe the British and German policies that violated American neutrality.
3. Describe the two incidents that prompted American entry into the war.

Who Was Right?
Germany and its leader, Kaiser Wilhelm, were guilty of some imperialistic, militaristic, and nationalistic errors, but so were most of the other European powers. For example, Germany violated Belgian neutrality, but the Allies later violated Greek neutrality in order to ensure that Greece did not join the Central Powers. Notice that Americans were divided in their support of the Allies and Central Powers in the early years because there was no clear-cut right side. This fact is significant in light of the outcome of the war and in contrast to the more obvious atrocities of Hitler's Nazi Germany and its allies in World War II.

Espionage and Sedition Acts
As is often the case in time of war, the U.S. government was worried about disloyalty during World War I. Congress passed two acts in 1917 and 1918 to prevent un-American activities. The Espionage Act made it illegal to discourage loyalty to the military or to send treasonous mail. The Sedition Act said that Americans could not obstruct the sale of war bonds or make harmful statements about the government, the Constitution, the flag, or the military uniform. Both laws were vaguely worded, leaving them open to interpretation.

Section Review Answers

1. the assassination of Archduke Francis Ferdinand, heir to the Austro-Hungarian throne (p. 475)
2. extreme nationalism, imperialism, militarism, and alliances of European nations (p. 476)
3. Allies—Britain, France, Russia, Italy, and the United States; Central Powers—Germany, Austria-Hungary, Bulgaria, and Turkey (p. 477)
4. Germany (p. 477)

5. tank—Britain; poison gas—Germany (pp. 477-78)

 They allowed soldiers to travel quickly into and out of enemy territory, checking conditions or dropping bombs. They also opened another arena for battle, the air. (p. 478)

SECTION 2

Materials

- *American History in Verse* by Burton Stevenson (BJUP)

- April 1994 issue of *National Geographic*

 Would We Be Neutral Today?

Intervention in foreign wars has become so common that Americans think of it as the norm. You need to help the students see the world as it was at the turn of the nineteenth century. They need to understand why it seemed so natural for Americans to stay neutral.

Have the students answer the following question in two different ways—from a modern perspective and then from the perspective of someone living in 1910. What

Victor Berger

A well-known case involving the Espionage Act was that of Victor Berger. Berger was originally from Austria-Hungary. He was elected to the House of Representatives from his adopted state of Wisconsin in 1910, becoming the first Socialist in that body. He lost two elections after that but was re-elected in 1918. Before his reelection, however, he was charged with violation of the Espionage Act because he had been publicly against American participation in the war. The other Congressmen, therefore, refused to let him take his seat. In a trial he was convicted of the charge and sentenced to twenty years in prison. He appealed the conviction; while he was out on bail, he ran in the election that was being held to fill the vacancy he had left in the House. He won the election, but Congress again did not allow him to take the seat. The Supreme Court reversed his conviction in 1921, and he was elected to the House yet again in 1922, remaining there until his death in 1929.

Submarines

It began in 1620 as a rowboat that was reinforced with iron and covered over with leather. It could remain submerged for hours at a depth of fifteen feet. When World War I began, it had developed to a vessel of 188 feet or longer, with a crew of twenty-six and the ability to travel underwater on battery and electric power at a speed of eight knots. It carried six torpedoes for military purposes. Today the submarine is a massive 560 feet long. Powered by nuclear reactors, it can travel at twenty-five knots while submerged. It carries ballistic missiles, which it can rapidly target on an enemy site, as well as torpedoes for defense. Sixteen officers and 156 enlisted men, working in two crews, operate it.

Christmas Truce of 1914

Christmas Day of 1914 was a memorable moment in the war. On that day, opposing soldiers got out of their trenches and met each

---

Germany's violations of America's neutral rights at sea. Since Britain was a small island nation, it was almost totally dependent on overseas trade for raw materials. Over the years Britain had developed the best and largest navy and merchant marine (trading) fleet. The United States had benefited greatly from trade with Britain, and it did not wish to lose that trade during the war. The United States wished to continue trade with Germany as well, but all sea trade with Europe was put in jeopardy by the naval strategies of Britain and Germany.

Early in the war Britain had put mines in the entrances to the North Sea. This was done to prevent nations from trading with Germany. However, instead of trading directly with Germany, some countries, including the United States, sent their goods to the Germans through neutral countries like the Netherlands, Denmark, or Sweden, who all resold them. Such actions angered the British, and they began to stop American shipping bound for neutral nations.

The British were ready to seize anything that could be useful to Germany. American ships were stopped at sea and ordered to British ports for searches. The time wasted pushed up the cost of goods. Sometimes foodstuffs spoiled before they could be delivered. The British claimed this action was necessary because of the danger of attack by German submarines. British firms also made "blacklists" of American firms that they suspected of trading with Germany through neutral nations. These actions angered Americans because they were a violation of the rights of a neutral country.

Britain did not receive all of America's anger, however. Realizing that Britain was dependent on foreign trade, too, Germany sought to cut British imports. Rather than using just a blockade, Germany chose to use

480

---

unrestricted submarine warfare. They fired on all ships in a designated war zone around Britain. Attacking neutral ships without giving them a warning and a chance to remove their passengers was a violation of international law. Therefore the United States protested Germany's policy as inhumane. Americans also said it violated the concept of freedom of the seas. Germans, however, argued that submarines were at a disadvantage. If they surfaced to give a warning, it was easy for even a merchant ship armed with guns to sink them.

Although the German Embassy put ads in newspapers warning Americans not to travel on British vessels, the warnings were ignored. In May 1915 a British liner, the *Lusitania,* was sunk without warning off the coast of Ireland. Among the 1,198 who perished were 128 Americans. President Wilson demanded that the Germans apologize and renounce this strategy. He later threatened to withdraw diplomatic recognition if another passenger ship was attacked. Germany cooperated for a while.

Growing American Fears

When the German offensives in France slowed, however, Germany decided that the only way to win the war was to cut Britain's supply lines and force her surrender. It could accomplish this by using its large fleet of U-boats. After the German announcement in February 1917 that it was going to resume its unrestricted submarine warfare, the United States broke off diplomatic relations with Germany.

Added to the submarine tension was the discovery of a German plot. Early in March the German foreign minister, Arthur Zimmermann, sent a telegram to the German minister in Mexico. In it he said that if war broke out between Germany and the United States, Mexico would be rewarded for entering the war against the Americans. Its reward

---

was the last big war? *(Persian Gulf War; Spanish-American War)* What other big wars have Americans fought in the past fifty years? *(Korean and Vietnam Wars; the Civil War)* What was the last big war on European soil and were Americans involved? *(World War II, yes; the Napoleonic Wars, no)* Who is the greatest world power? *(United States; Britain)*

Students need to ask themselves why the United States would take sides in foreign wars. Discuss any recent military actions, such as the Persian Gulf War, and summarize the reasons for U.S. involvement. Were

any of these issues at stake before World War I? Should America have remained neutral as long as they did during World War I? Should America stay neutral in most conflicts today?

Poetry Corner

You will find many poems about World War I in Burton Stevenson's *American History in Verse.*

"Abraham Lincoln Walks at Night" (Vachel Lindsay)

"The Road to France" (Daniel Henderson)

"Armistice Day" (Roselle Mercier Montgomery)

Nuggets from *National Geographic*

For an excellent review of the *Lusitania* findings, see "Riddle of the *Lusitania*" in the April 1994 issue of *National Geographic*. It explains the different theories of why the ship was sunk and how it went down so fast. The article also includes drawings and photographs of the findings.

When the S.S. Lusitania left harbor, no one expected that its first voyage would also be its last.

other on no man's land for a time of joint fellowship. The truce did not last long, but for a brief time the soldiers enjoyed peace.

Although the scene was unusual, it was not new to war. Soldiers of several conflicts have maintained friendly relations with the enemy when not in battle. British and French soldiers in the Peninsula War crossed to each other's lines, drew water together, and ate and played cards around the same campfires. Civil War soldiers traded coffee and newspapers, fished in the same ponds, and occasionally picked blackberries together. And men in the Boer War once went so far as to play a friendly game of football together.

Mexico and the United States

The Zimmermann telegram was especially upsetting to the United States because its relations with Mexico were not very good at the time. Mexico had experienced a revolution, and the new government was not friendly to America. America sent troops into Mexico twice, once in 1914 to defend its honor and once in 1916 to pursue the Mexican bandit Pancho Villa. Mexican president Venustiano Carranza insisted that the troops be withdrawn. They eventually were, but the situation was still tense at the time of the Zimmermann incident.

Jeannette Rankin

Jeannette Rankin was the first woman elected to the United States Congress. She represented her home state of Montana for two terms in the House of Representatives, elected in 1916 and 1940. A convinced pacifist, she opposed American participation in both World Wars. She was the only member of the House to vote against entry into World War II and the only member of Congress to vote against both wars. She never changed her views on war. When she was eighty-seven, she led a march in Washington, D.C., protesting the Vietnam War.

would be the return to Mexico of Texas, New Mexico, and Arizona.

British intelligence intercepted the telegram. The next day President Wilson asked Congress to arm American merchant ships, and he released the Zimmermann telegram to the public. The nation was outraged. When three more American merchant ships were sunk, the pressure increased. Finally, on April 2, 1917, a solemn president appeared before both houses of Congress asking for a declaration of war. Four days later, on April 6, 1917, the approval was given. The United States was joining the fight in Europe.

SECTION REVIEW

1. List at least three reasons for the difficulty of American neutrality.

2. How did some American ships attempt to get around Britain's blockade of German ports? What was Britain's response?

3. What German naval policy greatly angered Americans?

 What was the significance of the Zimmermann telegram?

481

The President's Difficult Choices

Ask the students to imagine that they are President Wilson or members of his cabinet. List each crisis described in this chapter. Call upon the students to summarize the issues that each crisis raised and the president's alternatives. Wilson vacillated between his role as a potential peacemaker and his need to protect the nation's interests. After each crisis, he could turn his cheek, mediate a peaceful settlement, increase supplies to the opposing side, increase the nation's military preparedness, or declare war. Each alternative had its pro-

ponents, and the president faced pressure from all sides. Every president faces a similar series of crises and difficult decisions. On few occasions do these decisions lead to war (which should be a last resort).

Section Review Answers

1. American sentiment favored the Allied cause; Americans wanted to protect investments with the Allies; Allied propaganda influenced Americans; Britain and Germany violated America's neutral rights (at least three). (pp. 479-80)

2. They sent goods to Germany through neutral countries. Britain began stopping and searching American shipping bound for neutral nations. (p. 480)

3. unrestricted submarine warfare (p. 480)

 Its plot to encourage Mexico to fight against the U.S. in exchange for America's southwestern lands enraged Americans and made them ready to fight Germany. (pp. 480-81)

SECTION 3

Objectives

Students should be able to
1. Explain the way the United States transported supplies to Europe.
2. Describe the way America increased production for the war effort.
3. Explain the way the United States financed the war effort.

Government Agencies and Powers

Notice the government agencies and powers that arose in response to the needs of the war. War has often given government the opportunity to expand its power with little opposition from the people.

American Legion

Established during World War I, the American Legion is the largest veterans' organization in the United States. Twenty officers of the American Expeditionary Force were asked how to improve troop morale. One man suggested a group for veterans, and the result of his suggestion was the American Legion.

The group today is open to any soldier who served honorably in a major American conflict (those conflicts that qualify are designated by the group). It focuses on aid for veterans, but it also promotes service and patriotism in communities. The GI Bill of Rights, which has provided many veterans with financial help for education and housing, was a proposal of the American Legion.

The United States at War

By the time the United States entered the war, the Allies were in a desperate condition. At one time, because of the success of Germany's unrestricted submarine warfare, the British people were down to a three-week supply of food.

The United States responded with huge shipments of supplies to Europe. To insure safe arrival, American ships traveled in groups

President Wilson stands before the Congress on April 2, 1917, asking the nation to join the fight in Europe.

called *convoys.* Naval destroyers with antisubmarine guns escorted them. With such protection, shipping losses were cut. The **convoy system** worked so well that not one of the two million American soldiers bound for Europe was lost at sea. Although American manpower gave a boost to Allied morale, the biggest contribution was in needed war materials. Food, clothing, munitions, ships, and vehicles poured into Europe. The Central

Powers were unable to match this production themselves and soon fell behind. To provide these needs for the Allied cause, America faced the challenge of gearing up for war. The peacetime economy and production needed to be channeled into a great effort for victory.

Military Preparedness

Since Americans feared having a strong standing army, its military force had purposely been kept small, consisting of only 200,000 men. Allied losses had already exceeded the size of the whole American army. The United States had only four hundred heavy guns and enough ammunition for a nine-hour bombardment. It had no tanks, and it lacked an air force. Now, suddenly, the United States had to train men, make equipment, and build ships to carry everything to Europe.

For the first time since the Civil War, the nation resorted to a draft. Under the Selective Service Act, local draft boards under civilian leadership supplied the men. The system worked well, and there was far less opposition to the draft than there had been during the Civil War. About four million men went into the service. The recruits were trained at thirty-two training camps across the nation.

Producing for the War

As America sent its soldiers off to battle, the entire nation had to adjust to the necessities of war. As a result the government had to begin many programs and agencies that could

SECTION 3

Materials

- Activity D from Chapter 23 of the *Student Activities* manual
- Construction paper and colored pencils or markers

The Difficulties of Raising an Army

Have the students imagine the problems that the United States faced in gearing up for war. They should list everything that needed to be accomplished and discuss

how each of these things could be accomplished.

1. Increase the size of the military from 200,000 to nearly 4,000,000 (use the draft or volunteers)

2. Train the military (open thirty-two camps; keep experienced troops together or use them as trainers)

3. Supply the military with food, clothes, and weapons (pay private industries or take over industry)

4. Ship the military to Europe (requisition private merchant ships or build more ships)

5. Send the troops into the battle lines (serve as replacements within existing armies or as a separate army)

6. Pay for salaries, equipment, and shipping (raise taxes or acquire loans)

All segments of the armed services joined together in the war effort.

American Junior Red Cross
President Woodrow Wilson announced the creation of the American Junior Red Cross on September 15, 1917. Eleven million young people joined the organization during World War I. They gave money to help children in other countries. They also worked on conservation at home. For example, they tended war gardens. Junior Red Crossers continued to serve in World War II—over nineteen million of them by 1945—but interest in the group dropped after the wars. Some young people felt that the Junior Red Crossers were not making really valuable contributions to the overall work of the Red Cross. The Junior Red Cross gradually ceased to be a separate group, being instead incorporated into its parent organization as Youth Services.

coordinate the war effort. Everything the American forces needed had to be obtained or manufactured and transported in a hurry.

The **War Industries Board** organized the industrial production needed. Factories were transformed to produce needed war materials—uniforms, guns, ammunition, vehicles, medical supplies. The board set criteria to standardize thousands of needed items and set economic priorities for the nation.

To insure that the railroads operated efficiently to carry the extra freight and passengers, the United States Railroad Administration took control of all railroads. It organized regional units, set rates and schedules, and set shipping priorities to insure that munitions (weapons, ammunition, and other war material) reached ports even if nonessential goods had to be held up.

The Fuel Administration had the job of conserving and directing the use of the nation's fuel. It asked the people to walk more and added "gasless days" to weekly calendars. Auto owners were asked to save

483

Student Activity D: Objectivity and Propaganda

Students need practice discerning the difference between objectivity and propaganda. World War I saw the first widespread use of modern propaganda.

Student Activity D: Finding Original Sources

This activity gives students practice in distinguishing primary and secondary sources of information about World War I. Discuss the merits and dangers of both kinds of sources in our quest for the truth.

 Recruitment Poster

Instruct the students to make World War I recruitment posters using construction paper, colored pencils or markers, and any other art supplies you have on hand.

Dixie Cups

A few years before the war broke out in Europe, an American named Hugh Moore stumbled across an idea for a new kind of cup. He was trying to sell water at a penny a cup. Customers were not especially interested in paying for water, but they did like the paper cups Moore used.

At that time health issues were receiving much national attention. Previously, the public had shared communal cups or dippers at public drinking places. But when a study revealed the abundance of germs on a public drinking vessel, Americans were shocked. Moore's Health Kups became extremely popular. In 1919 he renamed the product Dixie cups after the Dixie Doll Company near his house. In the years to come, his invention would be used to hold everything from soda to ice cream.

Influenza Epidemic

No one knows for sure where the influenza epidemic started. At the time, most people said it originated in Spain; in fact, the flu was called Spanish influenza. Many historians today think it began at Fort Riley, Kansas. After a dust storm in March 1917, over one thousand soldiers became sick with the flu, and forty-six died. When the regiment was sent to France, the epidemic hit there and spread across the battlefields.

At one point, the British navy was practically dry-docked because close to ten thousand sailors had the flu. The disease was deadly in the trenches as well. Some units had up to 80 percent casualty rates because of the flu, not the war. Approximately one-third of the American Expeditionary Force died from the disease. On ships bound for Europe, the death rate among troops was 20 percent. Things were so serious at one point that President Wilson considered not sending any more troops overseas. Doctors were stumped because they could find no way to combat the problem. No one knows which strain of flu the killer was. Most of the victims

gasoline so that trucks could run to carry war goods. The actions of these federal agencies designed to aid the war effort coordinated the activities of the nation in a remarkable way. They could do so because the national emergency had lessened the public's resistance to government power and restrictions. With Allied armies facing starvation, increasing America's food production received top priority. Herbert Hoover, who had already gained fame as organizer of a massive food relief program to Belgium, headed the Food Administration. Rather than force the public to conserve food, the administration set up a voluntary program. Americans were asked to make Mondays wheatless, Tuesdays meatless, and Thursdays porkless. Americans also raised their own vegetables in "Victory Gardens" so that more food would be available for the soldiers. With these efforts huge savings were made. Moreover, the people felt they were a part of the great war effort. Just before the war began the average annual amount of food shipped to Europe was 7 million tons. By 1919 it had reached 18.6 million tons.

The war also brought changes in the normal American work force. Since four million men were drafted, the normal work force was depleted. Because of the urgent need, many women now worked outside their homes for the first time. Some gratefully returned home when the war ended; others stayed on the job.

Volunteer groups were formed to support the "boys" in France. Memberships in the American Red Cross multiplied as women in local chapters met to roll bandages, knit sweaters or socks, and prepare packages to be sent abroad. Men who could not serve in the military also offered their time to support volunteer efforts.

Because the war caused a labor shortage, wages shot up and more jobs were available. Even with high taxes, loan drives, and

A Little Bird Named Enza

There was a little bird,
    Its name was Enza.

I opened the window,
    And in-flu-enza.

In 1918 this was the favorite poem of America's children. But the "little bird Enza" was no laughing matter. The deadly virus struck many American soldiers either while they were still in training or after they had arrived in Europe. In four months influenza killed twenty-one million people worldwide, more people than the war killed in four years. At the height of the epidemic, the last week in October 1917, twenty-seven hundred American soldiers died in Europe; twenty-one thousand American citizens died of the flu back home. But the flu was completely impartial: close to a quarter of a million Germans died as well.

The flu epidemic left as suddenly and mysteriously as it had come. By the middle of November 1918, it was over. Ironically, about the same time, so was the war. Some estimate that over forty million of the world's people died in the four years of World War I, and at least half of those were victims of the "little bird Enza."

A war bond rally in Atlanta encourages citizens to support the war effort.

increased prices for most goods, Americans were earning more than they ever had. Of course, prices went up for what the government bought too, raising the cost of fighting the war. To keep costs and wages under control, however, the government created the **War Labor Policies Board** to regulate laborers. While unions were allowed to organize and even showed significant gains in membership during the war years, the board stepped in to help settle disputes between labor and management. The board also set an eight-hour working day, stressed fair wages, and set standards for employing women and children.

The shortage of workers and the drop in immigration opened the doors of opportunity to black laborers. There was a movement of more than one-half million blacks to northern cities during the war. When the war ended, many blacks kept their jobs and remained in the North. This migration permanently changed the ethnic makeup of many northern cities.

Public Information

President Wilson did not want to leave anything to chance. He wanted Americans to know that their cause was just. To unite them behind the war effort, a Committee on Public Information was formed. Headed by journalist George Creel, 150,000 people became involved in a giant propaganda crusade to "advertise America." Talented artists designed war recruitment posters and ads. An army of lecturers appeared at local assemblies and even at silent movies. Called "four-minute men," they gave short talks on any number of patriotic topics and moved crowds to cheers or tears.

On the other hand the attitude toward the Central Powers or even things distantly related to them became negative. All things German were hated. Even though they had been in America for years and had proved their loyalty, some German Americans were sorely persecuted. Schools stopped teaching German, and school orchestras refused to play pieces by German composers such as

were young men and women who were otherwise strong and healthy.

Raggedy Ann
Children found new toys to play with in the decade of the Great War. One toy was actually a re-creation of an old favorite, the rag doll. In 1915 cartoonist John Gruelle and his daughter, Marcella, found an old rag doll. They fixed it up and called it Raggedy Ann after a character in a poem, "The Raggedy Man" by James Whitcomb Riley. Gruelle made up stories about the doll to amuse his daughter and eventually published them as *The Raggedy Ann Stories*. The book and accompanying doll were big hits. Ann got a brother, Andy, in 1920.

485

Dangers of "Total War"

War is always a threat to liberty. The challenges of World War I led to the most blatantly socialist system the American people had ever seen. In countries where democratic traditions are weak, autocratic governments arise in times of war and refuse to give up power even after the war is over. America has faced this danger as well.

Ask the students to list government actions or policies that led to a loss of liberties during World War I. *(the draft, standardized products, economic priorities instead of a free market, labor regulations, and propaganda)* The student text does not mention other limits created by the Espionage Act, the Trading-with-the-Enemy Act, and Sedition Act (see side margin note on p. 479). Uttering, writing, or printing "any disloyal, scurrilous, or abusive language" about the government or armed forces was a crime.

Lincoln Logs

War-era children also had the opportunity to build things with their toys. One popular building toy came courtesy of a well-known family in the architectural world. In 1876 Mrs. Anna Wright saw learning toys, including building blocks, used in a demonstration kindergarten. She ordered a set of toys for her son, Frank Lloyd Wright, and he became interested in building. Frank apparently passed on his appreciation for such toys to his son, John Lloyd Wright, also an architect. In 1917 John drew a design for toy-sized logs that kids could use for building. He called them Lincoln Logs.

Bach and Wagner. Sauerkraut became "Liberty Cabbage," hamburgers became "Liberty Burgers," and dachshunds were renamed "Liberty Pups." If you had caught the German measles, your mother would have been careful to tell the neighbors you had "patriotic spots" or "patriotic measles."

Paying for the War

The cost of the war was enormous. The United States spent about $24 billion, and the Allies borrowed $8 billion. About one-fourth of the money came from the new income and corporate taxes. The rest came from bank loans and loan drives.

Four times during the war the government went to the American people for money, raising more than $18 billion. "Liberty" and "Victory" loan drives were held in every community. Loan chairmen went door to door asking their neighbors to buy bonds. Workers also bought bonds at their places of employment. Buyers received "Liberty Buttons" for their lapels. Goals were set, and there were great celebrations when the drives went "over the top."

Even children became involved. They sold produce to earn money to finance the war, and they bought thrift stamps each week on "stamp day." A filled thrift card could be swapped for a $5 savings stamp; ten stamps on a card were proudly exchanged for a $50 bond.

SECTION REVIEW

1. What did the Selective Service Act do?

2. What was the purpose of the War Industries Board?

3. Name some of the changes made by the War Labor Policies Board.

4. How did America finance the war?

 How did the government attempt to unite Americans behind the war?

486

A young "doughboy"

Why Are Loans Necessary?

Students need to understand that governments cannot just "print money" to pay for a war. Traditionally, they have two options: raise taxes or borrow money. While the U.S. government did raise taxes significantly during World War I, the extra revenue still was not enough to pay for such a large-scale war. To borrow more money, however, the government could not just go to banks. Spare money is scarce in time of war. All Americans, from school children to retirees, had to sacrifice as much as they could. The need for every penny helps to explain the loan drives. The Germans were shocked by how much money America was able to raise and convert into war materiel.

Ask the students why they think the government no longer has loan drives. *(Answers will vary.)* The problem is that modern governments just go into debt and print more money. The result can be inflation, such as the inflation of the 1970s. Even worse is hyperinflation, which occurred in postwar Germany.

Although America got the money it needed through loans, this solution had long-term consequences too. The loans had to be paid back. Once the war was won, people were less willing to sacrifice, and they wanted their money back. The cycle of unpaid debts in the 1920s contributed to the worldwide depression of the 1930s. You can make a personal application, warning students about the dangers of depending on loans to pay for debt.

Section Review Answers

1. set up local draft boards under civilian leadership to supply men (p. 482)

Newly-arriving American "Doughboys" brought fresh enthusiasm to the tired Allied troops.

The American Forces "Over There"

The chief role of the navy was to get troops and supplies safely to Europe. Congress had voted for money to enlarge the navy before war broke out. During the war it tried to build or buy more ships to carry men and supplies to the troops fighting in Europe. It was on the battlefields, particularly those in northern France, that America's soldiers were needed.

The American Expeditionary Force

The American troops who joined the European fighting force were called the **American Expeditionary Force.** Although the United States declared war in April 1917, the first American troops did not arrive in Europe until the fall of 1917. The minimum training time was three months. Often the troops were called **"doughboys."** Most combat troops did not reach Europe until the spring of 1918 because of the period of training and other delays. The American Expeditionary Force (AEF) was commanded by General **John Pershing.** Pershing worked under Marshal **Ferdinand Foch** (FOSH), a Frenchman who served as Supreme Allied Commander. The British and French troops were weary and discouraged from three years of war, and the arrival of the "Yanks," as they called the Americans, was a welcome relief. The Allies wanted to place American doughboys in already existing armies and use them to replace British and French losses, but Pershing disagreed. Fearing that American

487

SECTION 4

Objectives
Students should be able to
1. Explain the way the United States financed the war effort.
2. Name the American and the Allied commanders.
3. Trace the American action in World War I.
4. Give the date of the armistice.

George M. Cohan
George M. Cohan wrote one of the most popular patriotic songs of the World War I era—"Over There." Born in 1878 in Providence, Rhode Island, Cohan started in show business young, starring in a vaudeville act with his parents and sister. Later, he did some writing and producing as well as acting, focusing often on patriotic themes. Besides "Over There," he also wrote the songs "I'm a Yankee Doodle Dandy" and "You're a Grand Old Flag."

The Language of War
The soldiers of World War I had their own way of speaking. For instance, certain names distinguished nationalities. A British soldier might be called Kitch; a Portuguese, Antonio; and a German, Alleyman or Fritz. Americans were called Sammy at the beginning of the war. Other terms that were a regular part of the soldier's vocabulary were *egg* (a hand grenade or bomb), *fleabag* (a sleeping bag or bedroll), *sausage* (an observation balloon), and *hopping the bags* (moving forward in an attempt to take ground).

---

2. to organize industrial production for the war effort (p. 483)

3. set an eight-hour workday, stressed fair wages, and set standards for employing women and children (p. 485)

4. through income and corporate taxes, bank loans, and loan drives (p. 486)

It established a Committee on Public Information that promoted the war through printed materials and lectures. (p. 485)

SECTION 4

Materials

- Activities C and E from Chapter 23 of the *Student Activities* manual

- *Scenes from American Church History* (BJUP)

The Making of a General

John Pershing had a talent for being in the right place at the right time. As a young officer he pushed hard for active service in the field, where chance for promotion was significant, and served with distinction in the posts he received. In Cuba he received a Silver Star for his part in the charge up San Juan Hill and was promoted from first lieutenant to captain. After the Spanish-American War, he received an assignment in the Philippines. There he ruled wisely, working hard to understand and build a rapport with the natives. He was promoted to brigadier general after a stint as an observer of the Russo-Japanese War. And his leadership in the tracking of Pancho Villa earned him the rank of major general. Though he never caught the outlaw, he was able to keep the United States out of war with Mexico.

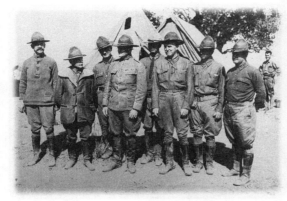

General John J. Pershing was called away from the conflict in Mexico to command the American forces.

morale would suffer, he requested that the American troops fight as a separate force. American units were then assigned their own segments of the front to defend.

Doughboys in Action

By the time the Americans arrived, the Germans had accomplished a major goal—getting Russia out of the fight. The Germans had aided the return of **Vladimir Lenin** to Russia in 1917 after the Russians had already overthrown their czar. Weary of war, the Russians followed Lenin in the Communist Revolution. Lenin had promised peace to the Russians, and he also had promised the Germans that he would pull Russia out of the war. When he gained power, he called Russian troops home and ended support for the Allied cause. Thus Germany had one less enemy to fight. The German armies that had been fighting the Russians could now be moved to the western front to fight France, Britain, and the United States.

The Central Powers launched an all-out offensive on the western front during the spring of 1918. The Germans hoped to reach the English Channel and also to take Paris. By June 3, 1918, they had reached the Marne River and were only about fifty miles from the French capital.

The combined American and French forces launched a counter-offensive and pushed the Germans back at a place on the Marne River called Château-Thierry (shah-TOH tyeh-REE). Next the Americans moved up to a hunting preserve called Belleau Wood (BEL oh) and stopped the Germans from making a run on Paris from that point. By the beginning of July, Paris was out of danger and the German advance was falling apart. Foch planned and carried off a massive assault at Amiens on August 8. The German general Ludendorff was to call it "the black day of the German army." Despite heavy German losses, Amiens was not the end of the war.

Shells stripped trees and leveled forests, leaving little protection for soldiers engaged in battle.

488

Student Activity C: War Diaries

This writing activity allows students to envision the Great War from the eyes of a soldier and his wife who are writing in their respective diaries.

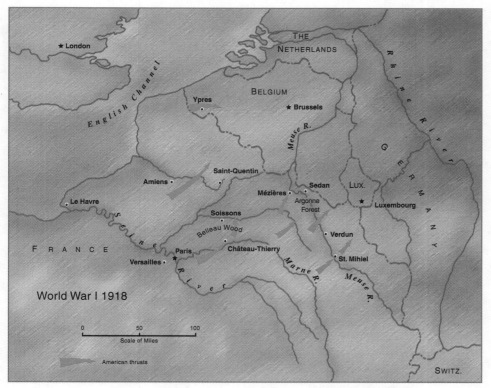

World War I 1918

0   50   100
Scale of Miles

American thrusts

General Pershing was determined to maintain an independent American force, but Allied leaders were putting strong pressure on him to integrate his troops into their already-existing armies. Finally, in exasperation at one meeting, having announced his refusal to budge from his position, Pershing walked out on the prime ministers of both Britain and France. Thereafter he was allowed to pursue his own strategy.

Demise of the Cavalry

The battle at St. Mihiel, significant as a major American victory, was also significant as the end of an era. General Pershing had sent three hundred cavalrymen into the battle. When machine guns started firing, however, the horses got scared, and most of them threw their riders. Using horses as weapons of war became a thing of the past.

With more than 250,000 American soldiers arriving monthly, Allied morale climbed. Pershing got permission to apply the separate strength of the U.S. Army as part of the larger counter-offensive. The place was St. Mihiel (SAHN mee-YEL), just south of Verdun. More than half a million doughboys came. An air corps of fifteen hundred planes was poised for takeoff, and thirty-two hundred French and American guns roared in protest against the German army. In forty-eight hours the battle was over.

Two weeks later the American forces launched an offensive into the Argonne (AHR gon) Forest. Foch had assigned the American troops the worst possible spot. American forces faced a maze of barbed wire, steel, and concrete. The hills and ridges offered almost perfect terrain for a German defensive. Historians have called this "the meat grinder offensive" because of the heavy losses.

By August 8 the British had broken through the German line. Having destroyed German resistance, the Allied troops moved swiftly across France, regaining lost lands for the Allies. The last major American activity took place in late October at Mézières, a link to the main German railway. By the end of September, however, the German commander, General Paul von Hindenburg, knew that all was lost.

489

Student Activity E: World War I

This map activity reviews the role of the American army in winning World War I.

Video on World War I Battles

Show a video on the U.S. battles of World War I. This visual reinforcement would help the names of these battles—Chateau-Thierry, Bellau Wood, St. Mihiel, and the Argonne Forest—to come alive for the students.

Sergeant York: Soldier of Christ

You may want to read "Sergeant York: Soldier of Christ" by Mark Sidwell in *Scenes from American Church History*.

An Armistice

Although it was nearly defeated, Germany did not surrender. It agreed to discuss terms of an armistice and an eventual end of the war. After the armistice, however, France and Russia disarmed Germany, and there was no further German discussion or involvement in the peace terms. (The Treaty of Versailles is discussed in the next lesson.) Germans became bitter over this treatment, and from that bitterness Hitler and the threat of World War II arose.

American Servicemen

Although World War I was a costly conflict, the number of Americans lost was relatively small. Of the more than twenty-four million American men who registered for the draft, not even three million were inducted into the military. Other men volunteered, but the total was still less than five million. Of that total army, approximately 115,000 died, and about half of those died not in battle but from disease.

SECTION 5

Objectives

Students should be able to

1. Name Wilson's plan for European peace and the provision he held to be the most important.
2. Name the "Big Four" at the peace conference and explain the viewpoint of each.
3. Describe the Treaty of Versailles and America's response to it.

Woodrow Wilson and the Senate

The U.S. Senate disliked the peace plan engineered by Wilson and his fellow leaders. A group led by Henry Cabot Lodge especially objected to the provision that the League of Nations would intervene if its members' territory or government was threatened. Senator Lodge had two key objections. First, there might be places where the United States would not want the League to intervene. Second,

---

At 11:00 A.M. on November 11, 1918, the slaughter stopped. Germany signed an armistice, or agreement to stop fighting. This day became an American national holiday called **Armistice Day.** (After World War II and the Korean War, the name was changed to Veterans' Day, honoring all veterans.)

The war had taken the lives of over eight million people and had left nearly twenty million wounded. The United States had lost 115,000 of its men in its year and a half of activity in the war. Over 200,000 Americans came home wounded. Although these casualties were light in comparison to those of the other major powers, Americans had known the heartache of war. Yet they hoped that this had been the "War to End All Wars" and the "War to Make the World Safe for Democracy." They believed they had fought for noble goals.

American soldiers and sailors in Paris.

SECTION REVIEW

1. What nickname was given to American troops?
2. Who was commander of the American Expeditionary Force?
3. Who was Marshal Foch?
4. When did the war officially end?

 Why did the Germans support Vladimir Lenin in his Communist Revolution?

Peace Comes to Europe

The end of the war brought many questions for the participants. How would Germany and the other defeated countries be treated? Would the victors claim conquered

490

---

territories and possessions? Could peace be maintained in Europe?

Wilson's Fourteen Points

Even before the war ended, Woodrow Wilson had proposed a set of guidelines to help rebuild European peace. His **Fourteen Points** had been announced in January 1918. Most of the points of his program centered on establishing a just peace and building a postwar world in which war would be less likely. The crucial point to Wilson was Point 14, providing for a **League of Nations.** He idealistically believed that an organization of cooperating nations could talk over problems and settle them peacefully, preventing future wars. Freedom of the seas, a ban against secret agreements, and general disarmament were some of the other key points.

President Wilson spoke of "peace without victory," urging generous terms that would preserve the German nation. He rejected territorial gains for the winners and **reparations,** or payment for damages by the losers. He said that weak nations should have the right of self-determination—that is, they could choose to be independent.

Section Review Answers

1. doughboys (p. 487)
2. General John Pershing (p. 487)
3. a Frenchman who served as Supreme Allied Commander (p. 487)
4. at 11:00 A.M. on November 11, 1918 (p. 490)

 He had promised to pull Russian troops out of the war; Germany could focus on the western front instead of having to divide her forces. (p. 488)

SECTION 5

Materials

- Activities B and F from Chapter 23 of the *Student Activities* manual
- Bibles

 Student Activity B: What God Says About War and Peace

This activity examines the Bible's lessons about just wars, especially in light of President Wilson's claim that America was fighting a just war to end all wars. It also emphasizes that earthly peace is temporary. Only in Christ can we find lasting peace (John 14:27).

American soldiers rest and recuperate in Paris, France.

The Paris Peace Conference

The Allied leaders met at the Palace of Versailles outside Paris on January 18, 1919, to shape the peace. President Wilson traveled to Europe to represent the United States at the conference himself. He believed that his presence would insure the victors' acceptance of a just and lasting peace. About two million people welcomed Wilson to Paris, regarding him almost as the savior of Europe. His reception strengthened his resolve to push for a treaty based on his Fourteen Points.

But the representatives from the other nations were equally determined. **Georges Clemenceau** (ZHORZH KLEM-un-SOH), the French premier, knew that his country had suffered at German hands in both the Franco-Prussian War and World War I. He wanted to ensure that Germany would never again be strong enough to hurt France. **David Lloyd George** represented Britain and **Vittorio Orlando,** Italy. These men plus Wilson were sometimes called

the Big Four. The nations that had lost and Russia were not included at the peace table. Thus the treaty has sometimes been called "a victors' peace." Leaving out the losers caused them to be resentful and to reject the treaty's provisions. Germany was forced to sign the **Treaty of Versailles** anyway on June 28, 1919. The other defeated countries signed other individual treaties. The 264-page Treaty of Versailles with Germany was very detailed. Against Wilson's wishes, it placed all the blame for the war on Germany and forced Germany to pay for its actions. Germany had to give up its overseas empire and some of its own land and resources. It had to allow foreign troops to remain on its land. Germany was also forced to pay huge reparations to Britain and France. While Wilson was disappointed about these and some of the other details of the treaty, he did convince the other leaders to provide for the formation of the League of Nations. Wilson believed that all the weaknesses of the

German and Allied leaders meet to sign the treaty to end the war in the Hall of Mirrors in the Palace of Versailles.

491

the United States did not want to be told by an outside party where it had to send troops. Though listening to a few suggestions, Wilson refused to make significant concessions to the senators.

Secret Treaties

Britain, France, and Italy had made secret treaties with one another early in the war. Clemenceau, Lloyd George, and Orlando felt bound by these treaties and forced the negotiations of the peace settlements to meet many of their demands. The demand for reparation payments would have an effect on the world economy in the 1920s, helping to trigger the Great Depression. The overall harsh treatment of Germany would influence that land to seek vengeance under Hitler's leadership in World War II.

Separate Treaties

Separate treaties were signed with the other Central Powers but were relatively minor in consequence compared to the Treaty of Versailles. The Treaty of Saint-Germain dealt with Austria, the Treaty of Trianon with Hungary, the Treaty of Neuilly with Bulgaria, and the Treaty of Sèvres with Turkey. Later Turkey secured a revision of its surrender terms in the Treaty of Lausanne (1923).

Debate Ideas

Have your students discuss and/or debate the following:

A lasting peace after World War I should have been based on Wilson's Fourteen Points.

The United States should have joined the League of Nations.

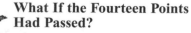

What If the Fourteen Points Had Passed?

After the Great War, Europe had a rare opportunity to lay the foundation for a

lasting "peace without victory." If the students are familiar with the basic events leading up to World War II, ask them to describe how world history might have changed if the European leaders had been kinder to Germany and if Wilson had been wiser in selling the League of Nations to the U.S. Senate. *(It is likely that the Nazis would not have risen to power and World War II would never have occurred.)* Then ask the students what purposes God may have had in hardening the hearts of the victors. *(God allowed the world to suffer one of its greatest tragedies. Events disproved*

man's false hope of achieving lasting peace.)

peace could be worked out through further negotiations in the league.

American Responses to the Treaty

When Wilson returned to the United States, he took the treaty directly to the Senate, whose approval is required for all treaties. Although most Americans probably supported the treaty, many senators were not pleased with it. Wilson had unwisely ignored the Republican leaders in the Senate while he helped formulate the treaty, and now those senators refused to ratify it without some changes. Wilson refused their changes, and the situation became deadlocked. Time passed, and the United States never did ratify the treaty. It simply declared the war to be over. Wilson was further disappointed that the United States did not join the League of Nations.

SECTION REVIEW

1. Who were the "Big Four" at the Paris Peace Conference, and what country did each represent?

2. What treaty stated the conditions for peace with Germany?

3. What key point did Wilson succeed in placing in the treaty?

4. How did the U.S. Senate respond to the treaty?

 What details of the peace process and treaty laid a foundation for German bitterness against the Allies?

SUMMARY

America had grown to be a powerful industrial nation by the beginning of the twentieth century. Although it attempted to remain aloof from the conflict that grew in Europe, its culture and interests made keeping a neutral position difficult. Eventually the nation abandoned neutrality and entered World War I in 1917. The United States made a gigantic effort to supply the faltering Allies with men and materials for the war effort. With this American aid the Allies defeated the Central Powers. President Wilson tried to persuade the delegates at the peace conference to follow his Fourteen Point program for establishing a lasting peace, but he found little support at the conference or in the United States.

492

Section Review Answers

1. Woodrow Wilson—United States, Georges Clemenceau—France, David Lloyd George—Britain, Vittorio Orlando—Italy (p. 491)

2. the Treaty of Versailles (p. 491)

3. the formation of a League of Nations (the last of his Fourteen Points) (p. 491)

4. It refused to ratify the treaty without some changes. (p. 492)

Germany was left out of the peace discussions. It was forced to accept all the blame for the war and to pay for its actions by giving up land, accepting occupation by foreign troops, and making large damage payments to Britain and France. (p. 491)

Chapter Review

People, Places, and Things to Remember

Triple Alliance
Triple Entente
Central Powers
Allied Powers
unrestricted submarine
  warfare
Lusitania
convoy system

War Industries Board
War Labor Policies Board
American Expeditionary
  Force
doughboys
John Pershing
Ferdinand Foch
Vladimir Lenin

Armistice Day
Fourteen Points
League of Nations
reparations
Georges Clemenceau
David Lloyd George
Vittorio Orlando
Treaty of Versailles

Review Questions

What significant event happened on each of the following dates?

1. June 28, 1914
2. April 6, 1917
3. November 11, 1918

Who was he?

4. Who was president of the United States during World War I?
5. Who commanded the American Expeditionary Force?
6. Who was commander of all the Allied forces?
7. Who were "the Big Four," and what country did each represent?

Write the appropriate term for each blank below.

When World War I broke out in 1914, Germany, Austria-Hungary, and the nations that sided with them were called the (8) , and Britain, France, and the nations that sided with them were called the (9) .

Germany's policy of (10) greatly angered Americans. It brought about the sinking of the *Lusitania* and eventually helped to prompt America to enter the war. The American soldiers who arrived in Europe were commonly called (11). They helped the Allies win the war. Fighting stopped on (12) Day.

Allied leaders met at Versailles to draw up a treaty. President Wilson's plan for peace consisted of (13), but most of his plan was rejected, except for the formation of a (14) to help settle international problems. Britain and France especially wanted Germany to pay reparations for the damages caused by the war. The resulting treaty with Germany, called the (15), was never signed by the United States.

Questions for Discussion

16. What were the advantages of the United States's remaining neutral during the early years of the war?
17. Should America have joined the League of Nations? Why or why not?

493

Chapter Review Answers

1. Archduke Francis Ferdinand was assassinated in Sarajevo. (p. 475)
2. America officially entered the war. (p. 481)
3. Germany signed an armistice to stop fighting. (p. 490)
4. Woodrow Wilson (p. 481)
5. John Pershing (p. 487)
6. Ferdinand Foch (p. 487)
7. Woodrow Wilson (United States), Georges Clemenceau (France), David Lloyd George (Britain), Vittorio Orlando (Italy) (p. 491)
8. Central Powers (p. 477)
9. Allies (p. 477)
10. unrestricted submarine warfare (p. 480)
11. doughboys (p. 487)
12. Armistice (p. 490)
13. Fourteen Points (p. 490)
14. League of Nations (p. 490)
15. Treaty of Versailles (p. 491)
16. Answers will vary. It could trade with both sides; it could avoid the casualties and expense of war; it could enter the conflict with a public that was more fully supportive.
17. Answers will vary. It probably would have made little difference since man's organizations can never ensure peace.

Goals

Students should be able to

1. Define and use the basic terms from the chapter.
2. Identify the three postwar problems discussed in the text.
3. Describe how economic prosperity helped bring moral decay.
4. **Understand that moral decline is a recurring theme in civilization.**

Clashing Cultures

In America the 1920s marked the transition from a predominantly rural society to a predominantly urban one. It took several years for the horse-drawn cart to be replaced by the automobile. That was a good thing for the early auto drivers, who frequently needed local farmers to come with a horse and pull their cars out of the mud.

Chapter Motivation

Review events from the previous chapter. Remind the students that even as America was reveling in its victory over evil in Europe, it began a moral decline from which it has never completely rebounded. Economic prosperity has drawn people even further from their dependence on the Lord. Progressivism has fostered a habit of looking to the government to take care of the nation's needs. Remind the students that moral decline is a recurring theme in civilization. Refer to other great countries and empires in which moral decline is seen.

Materials

SECTION 1

• Activity A from Chapter 24 of the *Student Activities* manual

SECTION 2

• Activity B from Chapter 24 of the *Student Activities* manual
• Magazines and old books containing pictures or images related to the 1920s

The 1920s: Decade of Change

With the end of World War I, most Americans looked forward to better times. Some thought that they could return to the ideals and ways of earlier days. Instead the 1920s, sometimes called the "Roaring Twenties," became a decade of startling changes.

In prewar years progressive Americans had united to check big industry and to gain reforms. Then they had united to wage a war that would make the world safe for democracy. In the twenties diversity replaced that unity. After sacrificing for a war, many Americans now wanted a good life for themselves. They wanted all the goods big industries could supply, and they were not as interested in righting society's wrongs. Since some of the restraints that they sought to throw off were biblical ones, the 1920s was an era when sin was practiced more openly than in earlier periods of American history.

While many Americans were prosperous enough to enjoy "a chicken in every pot and a car in every garage," as the Republicans promised in 1928, others struggled to put food on the table. Serious economic problems lurked below the surface prosperity of the era, and these problems led to calamity for many Americans as the decade closed.

494

CHAPTER 24	Lesson Plan Chart		
Section Title	Main Activity	Pages	Time Frame
1. Postwar Problems	How Was Communism a Unique Threat?	494-97	1 day
2. A Desire for Prosperity	Collage	497-501	1-2 days
3. Moral Decay	Why Was Prohibition a Failure?	502-7	1-2 days
4. Political Inaction	Charting Progressivism and Normalcy	507-10	1 day
Total Suggested Days (including 1 day for review and testing)			5-7 days

SECTION 1

Materials

• Activity A from Chapter 24 of the *Student Activities* manual

Postwar Problems

America emerged from the war with some attitudes and problems that would set the stage for the decade to come. First was a desire to stay out of any other foreign conflicts that might come along.

Isolationism and Peace

President Wilson had diligently sought American approval of the Treaty of Versailles with its provision for a new League of Nations. Because of his battle with the Senate, he decided to travel across the country and present his views to the people. While on his tour he had a stroke that left him unable to carry on his duties for a few weeks. In the remaining months of his presidency he never regained full strength; yet he continued to plead for the United States to ratify the treaty and join the league. The Senate and many Americans, however, feared that the obligations of the League of Nations would draw America into future wars. This fear and a general lack of concern for foreign affairs now that the war was over made most Americans ready to isolate themselves from problems outside the United States.

When the 1920 election came, the attitude of wanting to get back to business and forget about foreign problems resulted in a strong win for the Republican candidate, **Warren G. Harding.** His campaign, stressing a "return to normalcy," was victorious over that of James Cox, the Democrat. Ideas of signing the treaty and joining the league were soon forgotten.

Throughout the 1920s the United States remained true to its isolationist goals in that it stayed out of most foreign affairs. Wishing to cut expenses and to avoid temptation for future war, the government sought a way to trim down its navy. Harding's secretary of state, Charles Evans Hughes, and others believed that one cause of the war had been an arms race. Hence he suggested that the five major powers limit naval shipbuilding. This was done through the **Treaty of Washington** in 1921. Britain, the United States, Japan, France, and Italy scaled down their navies. For every five British or American ships built, Japan would be allowed three, and France and Italy one and three-quarters. The treaty, which allowed the United States to cut its budget, delighted Republicans, who were seeking bigger cuts in spending. Japan, however, considered the treaty unfair and turned its resentment against the United States in later years. In reality the treaty had little impact because the powers continued to increase their defenses by building smaller ships and submarines that were not limited under the agreement.

Another attempt to keep America free from the threat of future war was the **Kellogg-Briand Peace Pact.** Coolidge's secretary of state, Frank B. Kellogg, optimistically signed a treaty with sixty-two other nations in 1928. The countries agreed to outlaw war as a means of settling international disputes. As with most peace agreements, only some nations took it seriously. Men cannot establish peace on their own, and World War II would soon prove how futile their agreement was. It would also prove that the United States could not remain isolated from the world.

Depression

Following the war came a time of economic depression for the United States. The big demand for war products had kept industries and farms busy, but when the war was over, the demand dropped. Because many of the war products were no longer needed, factories had to change over to peace-time industry. It took time to build these new businesses. American farms had sent millions of tons of food to Europe during the war, but now Europe could start feeding itself again. There was no market for the great surplus of food.

495

SECTION 1

Objectives

Students should be able to
1. Describe America's isolationist attitude following the war.
2. Explain why there was a short economic depression following the war.
3. Describe the Red Scare that followed the war.

Mrs. Wilson

While Wilson was paralyzed and helpless from his stroke in 1919, only his wife and one advisor saw him. Some believe that Mrs. Wilson acted as president and made most of the decisions during that time, and thus she has been called the first woman president.

Kellogg-Briand Peace Pact

On August 27, 1928, fifteen key nations renounced war as an instrument of national policy. Forty-eight other nations later joined this pact for peace. Initially, French foreign minister Aristide Briand had proposed a pact between just the United States and France, hoping to enlist America as an ally in the event of another European war. Frank Kellogg knew what Briand was trying to do and instead proposed a treaty for all nations. Briand, of course, supported the popular measure.

Having no means of enforcement and being limited by various nations' self-approved exemptions, the treaty was virtually worthless. Ironically, the day the United

Student Activity A: Decade of Change

This chart summarizes the main content of the chapter, contrasting the progressivism of the 1900s and 1910s to the normalcy of the 1920s. Have the students begin the chart now for discussion during section four.

Commemorative Stamp

Design a stamp that commemorates a historical event or individual. Include a brief account explaining why the event or person deserves to be commemorated.

States Senate ratified the treaty, it also passed a bill to spend $274 million to build warships.

Veterans

In 1920 Congress had established the Veterans' Bureau to handle hospital bills and insurance claims for veterans. Congress passed two "Bonus Bills" to augment the low wages of those in the armed forces, but Harding vetoed both of them. In 1924 Coolidge vetoed a bill offering veterans a $1,000 life insurance policy after twenty years. Congress overrode that veto.

Farmers

When farm prices fell after the war, farmers banded together to seek aid through private and public channels. The American Farm Bureau began new chapters across the nation. Farm cooperatives were formed to store, market, and ship farm products more efficiently. A "farm bloc" of congressmen from all the major agricultural states banded together. They passed two bills to get the government to keep prices above parity (a set level) regardless of the market price. But Coolidge twice vetoed bills for such help. He believed the government should not be so actively involved in regulating the economy.

Ku Klux Klan

The Ku Klux Klan reemerged in 1915. Influenced by the patriotism of World War I, Klan organizers supported a native white population. Catholics and Jews were added to their blacklist. The group had between four and five million members in the mid-1920s but went down quickly afterwards. It did exercise enough influence in 1928, however, to prevent Catholic Alfred Smith from winning the presidency.

In reaction to World War I, Warren Harding kept America true to its isolationist goals.

Unemployment became a problem in the cities. Soldiers returning home from the war found few jobs available. War industries were closing down, and many jobs that were available had been taken by blacks and immigrants. For a while the blacks and immigrants were resented by white Americans who were without jobs. Unfortunately, violence eventually erupted from the frustration of the unemployed. Race riots occurred in both the North and the South. A new Ku Klux Klan arose in the South and Midwest to terrorize not only blacks but also Roman Catholics and Jews. New immigration laws were passed that set quotas (fixed numbers) of immigrants who could enter the United States. These laws were intended to stop the heavy flow of immigrants, especially those from the Roman Catholic countries of southern and eastern Europe.

Although the nation's economy picked up quickly and unemployment ceased to be a problem, veterans continued to pressure the government until they received a bonus of a $1,000 life insurance policy. The farmers' problems continued through the 1920s as high production and low prices continued. Although representatives of the farming states moved for government aid and regulation, President Harding and his successor, **Calvin Coolidge,** believed that the federal government should not interfere by regulating the farm economy.

Fear of Communism

Although Americans had read of events in Russia leading up to and including the Communist Revolution in 1917, few really were aware of the Communist presence until it involved them directly. Americans had heard reports of massacres in Communist Russia. A fear of communism began to grow, especially when Americans learned that the Communists intended to spread their rule. Leaders of the Soviet Union, as the Russian nation now

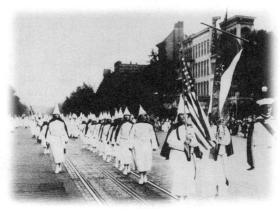

During the 1920s the Ku Klux Klan's focus included not only blacks but also Roman Catholics and Jews. Here Klan members parade in Washington, D.C. in 1928.

Lessons in Demobilization

The quick demobilization of the United States teaches valuable lessons for today. The presidents, both Democrat and Republican, believed that free enterprise could solve the problems of retooling industries and retraining soldiers. Note that modern presidents, such as Bill Clinton, proposed expensive federal training programs at the end of the Cold War. But history offers no proof that such expense is helpful.

How Was Communism a Unique Threat?

This is the first time that the students come face to face with the greatest enemy that the United States ever faced—Communism. Ask them to share what they know about Communism. Compare and contrast Communism with the other threats that the United States has faced. (Make special note of the rise of socialism and violent labor strikes.) Discuss how the attorney general dealt with terrorism then, and discuss measures the United States is taking today against terrorism. In what ways could terrorism undermine a democratic government?

called itself and the surrounding nations it controlled, had organized the Third International. This agency for world revolution would export communism anywhere, using any method. It was already making gains in Germany and Hungary.

The Communists had two political parties working in America by 1919. One of their aims was to create a struggle between common workers and the property-owning capitalists. During this time Americans began to think of any sign of worker discontent, and strikes in particular, as part of the Communist plot. In April 1919 there was also a wave of terrorist bombings. The post office intercepted letter bombs addressed to thirty-eight prominent businessmen or government officials, including John D. Rockefeller, Justice Oliver Wendell Holmes, and both the postmaster general and the U.S. attorney general. In June there were direct bombings. One bomb exploded in front of Attorney General A. Mitchell Palmer's home. In September a terrorist planted a bomb in front of the New York Stock Exchange, killing thirty-eight people.

Some have sarcastically called this period the "Red Scare," for some Americans did overreact to the Communist threat. However, we should remember that the threat itself was real. Believing that Communists were involved in the attacks, Attorney General Palmer crusaded for increased government investigation and arrests in these cases. Government agents raided offices of radical organizations and arrested 250 members of the Union of Russian Workers. In December the Labor Department sent 249 aliens, some of whom were Communists, back to Russia. Eventually the scare died down, but Americans maintained a fear of communism and its infiltration into the United States for most of the decade.

The fear of the Communists added to the resentment toward immigrants, many of whom were from southern and eastern Europe, where radical political ideas were spreading. Ill feeling toward both Communists and immigrants combined in a noted court case in 1921. Two Italian anarchists, Nicola Sacco and Bartolomeo Vanzetti, were arrested and tried for murdering two shoe company employees in a payroll robbery. They were found guilty and were sentenced to death. Protests led to the reopening of the case. Some charged that the two men had been sentenced to death because they were foreigners who held unpopular political views and not because they had committed a crime. The case dragged on for six years. Sacco and Vanzetti were convicted, and in 1927 the two were executed. Many, however, tried to make the case an example of injustice in American society.

SECTION REVIEW

1. What did Warren G. Harding stress in his presidential campaign?
2. What did the Treaty of Washington seek to limit?
3. What two groups tried to gain help from the government during the postwar depression?
4. What was the Red Scare?

 How was the Kellogg-Briand Peace Pact unrealistic?

A Desire for Prosperity

As Americans recovered from the war's effects, they developed a great desire for material prosperity. The humanitarian and reform goals of the earlier progressives were forgotten. They were replaced by desires for the possessions and the pleasures that the new decade was to offer.

Sacco and Vanzetti
Nicola Sacco and Bartolomeo Vanzetti were defendants in one of the most controversial trials of the twentieth century. Their accused crimes were robbery and murder. Both men had come to America from Italy in 1908, and neither had yet become an American citizen at the time of his arrest. In addition, both men were radical political anarchists. Their supporters claimed that their ethnic and political backgrounds prevented their receiving a fair trial.

Here are some of the arguments in the case. Witnesses identified Sacco as the shooter and Vanzetti as an occupant of the getaway car. In addition, both men were armed at the time of arrest and lied under official questioning. On the other side, the defense questioned whether prosecution witnesses could accurately identify the criminals after having had only a brief glimpse at the scene. Also, Sacco had an excuse for carrying a gun, and although the men did lie, it was only in response to questions about their radical political activities, which were highly unpopular in America at the time. The defense argued that the robbery was more likely the work of a professional criminal gang, and a convicted bank robber actually confessed to the crime.

Many were sympathetic to the men at the time of the trial. Opinion today is divided. Tests conducted in 1961 on Sacco's gun suggest that it was the murder weapon. Some have theorized that Sacco was guilty but Vanzetti was innocent. Whatever the truth of the crime, the trial put a spotlight on the American judicial system.

497

Red Flags

Two historical controversies are discussed on this page. Ask the students to find them. What words alert them to the controversy? *("Some have sarcastically called . . ." at the beginning of paragraph 2, and "Many, however, tried to make the case . . ." at the end of paragraph 3)* Can the students guess the viewpoint of this textbook's author? What should be their viewpoint? Can the students find any other controversial topics in this section, and do they know what position to take on them? *(the arms reduction Treaty of Washington, the Kellogg-Briand*

Peace Pact, new immigration quotas, and demands for farm aid)

Section Review Answers

1. a "return to normalcy" (p. 495)
2. naval shipbuilding (p. 495)
3. veterans and farmers (p. 496)
4. a strong fear of Communist infiltration in America (p. 497)

 It outlawed war as a means of settling international disputes, but it failed to realize that the treaty

would be worthless unless all nations abided by its terms. It also ignored man's natural sinful tendency toward conflict. (p. 495)

Objectives

Students should be able to
1. Explain the effects of the automobile, the airplane, and electric appliances on life in the 1920s.
2. Describe America's attitude toward business in the 1920s.

Charles and Frank Duryea

Brothers Charles E. and J. Frank Duryea developed one of the first gasoline-powered automobiles in America. They started a company in 1896 and built thirteen cars, all made exactly the same using interchangeable parts. Each car sold for $1,500. Although the company operated for only three years, it was the first to make a profit in the automobile business. The brothers went their separate ways, but both remained involved in the automobile industry.

First Motorcar Race

Frank Duryea won America's first motorcar race on Thanksgiving Day, November 28, 1895. The route took the racers from Chicago to Evanston, Illinois, and back. Six cars started the race, but only two finished. The weather was cold, and a fresh blanket of snow covered the ground. At a rate of less than ten miles per hour, Duryea took over nine hours to drive approximately fifty miles. The only remaining competitor pulled in almost two hours later.

Technology's Products

Inventions and improvements of industrial products greatly changed the American way of life in the 1920s. The automobile and the application of electricity to household appliances revolutionized daily life for many Americans.

The Automobile—The first successful American automobile had been built by Charles and Frank Duryea in 1893. Henry Ford had begun making cars in 1903, and many other automobile producers had also plunged into the business. Although cars had become common before the war, there were still many American families without a "horseless carriage." After the war, however, factories geared up to produce cars by the thousands. Families were eager to have their

The sleek, new Model A Ford began to roll off the assembly lines in the late 1920s.

own car, and the prices of all but the luxury models were affordable. Even if a family did not have enough money to pay for the car in full, they could buy it on the installment plan (paying for an item with weekly or monthly payments).

The great shift of transportation to the automobile had many direct effects on Americans. For example, the automobile allowed farmers to end some of the isolation of their lives in rural areas. When town was several hours away by horseback or horse and wagon, the farmer and his family ventured into town only a few times a year. With a car, however, the whole family could make the same trip in minutes, day or night. Now farm families could go to town often to shop or to attend social functions.

The automobile also changed the life of many city workers by making it possible for them to live away from the inner-city area where they worked. They could instead buy a house in the "suburbs" at the edge of the city and commute back and forth by car. With this practice came a by-product of the automobile—traffic jams.

Cars made travel easy for common Americans. As people began to drive everywhere, many other industries had to grow to meet the needs of these people and cars on the move. Service stations, motels, and drive-in restaurants, sprang up everywhere. Department stores, supermarkets, and other businesses were built 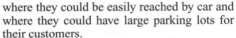 where they could be easily reached by car and where they could have large parking lots for their customers.

Other results of the popularity of the automobile were the spread of paved roads, the death of many people in automobile acci-

498

SECTION 2

Materials

- Activity B from Chapter 24 of the *Student Activities* manual
- Magazines and old books containing pictures or images related to the 1920s
- Special speaker: an antique collector or antique car enthusiast
- Video documentary on Charles Lindbergh

Student Activity B: Impact of Technology

This chart summarizes the impact of automobiles, airplanes, radio, and motion pictures on American life. Discuss the impact of these technologies on America today. What other revolutionary technologies should be added to the list (e.g., computers)? Based on what we know from the impact of the earlier technologies, what kinds of changes can we expect from new technologies?

Collage

Have your students design and make a collage for this decade. Put historical figures adjacent to symbols or items with which they are associated. Make a written guide to the collage to explain the people and symbols selected; tell why each is important. Bring in magazines, discarded books, or pictures downloaded from the Internet for students to use, or have them draw their own pictures.

dents, and even fast getaways for criminals as they fled from the scenes of their crimes. The automobile certainly made the average American's way of life more mobile.

The Airplane—Although the airplane was not a major form of transportation for most Americans in the 1920s, the airplane won admiration for its capabilities. In 1903 Orville and Wilbur Wright had made what is generally accepted as the first successful powered flight. World War I boosted aviation. Soon the government provided airmail service between major cities. Budding pilots pursued their interests by putting on air circuses at county fairs and by taking people up for short rides over towns.

The biggest air sensation came in 1927, when a twenty-five-year-old aviator from Little Falls, Minnesota, won a prize for being the first to fly non-stop across the Atlantic Ocean. **Charles A. Lindbergh** (LIND BURG) flew his specially designed plane, the *Spirit of St. Louis,* from New York to Paris in thirty-three and one-half hours. When Lindbergh touched down in Paris, he became an instant hero. Called "Lucky Lindy" or "the Lone Eagle," Lindbergh came home to a ticker-tape parade in New York and an invitation to the White House. Wherever he appeared over the next few years, he was mobbed by admiring fans.

Lindbergh's transatlantic flight and the record flights of other pilots did much to encourage air transportation. The first public international passenger carrier was the Pan-American "Clipper." Regularly scheduled commercial flights soon connected all of the major American cities. They also linked America to European and South American capitals.

Charles Lindbergh captured the attention of the nation with his transatlantic flight in the Spirit of St. Louis.

Electric Wonders—Second only to cars in changing American society was electricity. By 1929 generators were producing more electricity in the United States than in the rest of the world combined. Nearly all American cities and towns had electricity by the 1920s, and some rural areas had it as well. Americans were ready not just for electric lights but also for fancy new gadgets to plug in.

Inventors added electricity to many already existing household appliances like the ice box, stove, iron, and washing machine. Housewives boasted of all-electric kitchens, complete with fan, water heater, toaster, coffee percolator, and waffle iron.

499

Kidnapping of Lindbergh Baby

It has been called the crime of the century. On March 1, 1932, sometime between 8:00 and 10:00 P.M., twenty-month-old Charles A. Lindbergh Jr. was taken from the second-story nursery of his parents' house near Hopewell, New Jersey. The kidnapper left a ransom note demanding $50,000.

Many (including Al Capone) offered assistance, but the investigation kept running into dead ends. John F. Condon, a retired educator, volunteered to act as a mediator between the kidnappers and the Lindberghs. He met twice with a man who called himself John, the second time delivering a $50,000 ransom to him. Attempts for recovery ended May 12 when a baby's body was found in a wooded area four miles from the Lindbergh house.

The mystery of who had committed the crime remained. A lead finally came through the discovery of some of the gold certificates paid out in the ransom. They were traced to Bruno Richard Hauptmann, a German immigrant. A search of Hauptmann's residence revealed $14,000 more of the ransom money hidden in the garage, and a missing board in his attic matched one of the rungs of the homemade ladder used by the kidnapper. Hauptmann was convicted of the crime and executed on April 2, 1936. The verdict seemed conclusive, but doubts still linger. Theories ranging from the guilt of a family member to the possibility that Charles Lindbergh Jr. is still alive keep mystery lovers intrigued.

An interesting footnote to the case is that one of the key investigators, the head of the New Jersey state police, was H. Norman Schwarzkopf, father of the Desert Storm commander.

Bring in a Collector or Car Restorer

If you know an antique collector or antique car enthusiast, ask him to bring in some items to share with the class. Ask the guest to tell how he got involved in the hobby and some of his activities and unusual experiences.

Advertising over the Years

Study a corporation that has a history of seventy-five years or more. Consider industries or products from your own area. Design an advertisement for the product at various times (e.g., 1925, 1950, 1975, and today). Interesting products include automobiles, telephones, and radios.

 ## Video Clips of Lindbergh

Make the most of studying Charles Lindbergh as the icon of his day by including video clips from his life. Discuss the reasons behind his stardom and the impact of stardom on his life. Many consider him to be the first superstar of U.S. pop culture.

Radio Beginnings

Dr. Frank Conrad was an important radio pioneer. Conrad, assistant chief engineer for the Westinghouse Company and an avid ham radio operator, established an experimental radio station in his garage in 1916. The station was used for military purposes during World War I. After the war Conrad began giving talks and playing music for other ham operators. His music selections were so popular that he decided to announce ahead of time what he was going to play; he described these programs as "broadcasts." A local music store offered to keep Conrad supplied with records if he would acknowledge the store as his supplier.

Conrad's broadcasts stirred widespread interest. A department store in Pittsburgh installed a wireless receiving station so that patrons could listen to them. The vice president of Westinghouse then decided to build a bigger transmitting station and continue this programming in the hopes of selling home receivers.

Will Rogers

William Penn Adair Rogers was born November 4, 1879, in the area that is today Oklahoma. As a young boy on a ranch, Rogers learned to ride and rope; he used these accomplishments to win a spot in the entertainment world, starring in Wild West and vaudeville shows. He made his Hollywood debut in 1918 as a silent film actor and continued with the industry after the introduction of sound. He was voted the most popular male actor in 1934. In addition to his role as entertainer, Rogers became known for his humorous political commentary. Both in the newspaper and on the radio, he gained a large following. Rogers died in a plane crash near Point Barrow, Alaska, in August of 1935.

Model T

"You can paint it any color, so long as it's black." Whether Henry Ford actually said it, this famous quotation demonstrates the sturdy nature

Of course, electricity was also applied to industry, where it powered large machines. When applied to the communications network, electricity further improved the quality of American life. The greatest mass communication device of the 1920s was the radio.

The basis for the invention of the radio was a sound transmitter invented by an Italian, Guglielmo Marconi (mahr COH nee), in 1895. The "wireless" could transmit messages without using the usual telegraph or telephone wires. Soon inventors began using the wireless to transmit the human voice. The resulting radio provided Americans with hours of news and entertainment. The Westinghouse Company made special home receivers and sold them in quantity during the fall of 1920. Station KDKA in Pittsburgh received its broadcasting license six days before the 1920 presidential elections. The first commercial broadcast—November 2, 1920—announced Harding's election to the presidency.

The radio soon changed the way Americans lived. News, music, entertainment, and advertising reached more than twelve million American homes by 1930. Many Americans listened to comedian Jack Benny, singer Rudy Vallee, and Will Rogers's comic impersonations of Calvin Coolidge. Broadcasts of sports events also gained large popular followings. With Americans from different areas listening to the same programs, some regional differences soon began to fade. The radio drew Americans closer to events and people that affected their lives. They could hear the voice of the president and other leaders, and they could hear broadcasts of events as they happened.

The assembly line idea, developed by Henry Ford, boosted industrial production in the 1920s.

Business Boom

After the initial depression that followed the war, America soon took off on an amazing business boom. Some workers had saved money during the war while wages were high. Others were making money on new businesses. They were all ready to spend it on automobiles, electric appliances, clothes, entertainment, and the new pleasures of the 1920s. When Americans did not have the money, they borrowed it or bought items on credit.

The demand for new industrial goods caused industries to grow. Many manufacturers used the mass production techniques devised by Henry Ford. He placed workers along a moving conveyer belt, where each performed a certain task or added a certain part to the product. By 1927 this assembly line allowed him to turn out a new car every twenty-seven seconds. Similar assembly lines turned out refrigerators, phonographs, and vacuum cleaners. Clever advertising campaigns convinced customers that they had to buy more and more of the new products.

500

Tour an Assembly Line

Tour a local assembly line—particularly an assembly line for some of the products mentioned in this chapter.

Debate Idea

Have your students discuss and/or debate the following statement:

The business of America has always been business.

Parallels to the Modern Church Growth Movement

Discuss the modern church growth movement, which treats the church as a marketing enterprise that should poll the neighborhood and develop programs to satisfy a "target audience." A marketing consultant named George Barna was inspired by the movement to begin surveying religion in America to find out how to reach people with the gospel. He argued that church is a business and that the customers are the "unchurched." His influential books, such as *Marketing the Church: What*

They Never Taught You About Church Growth and *User Friendly Churches*, questioned the effectiveness of traditional worship services. He claimed, "If a church studies its market, devises intelligent plans, and implements those plans faithfully, it should see an increase in the number of visitors, new members, and people who accept Christ as their Savior."

Discuss the dangers of this movement. What is the scriptural purpose of church services? (See Acts 2:42.)

The Man Nobody Knows

President Coolidge's pointed remark that "the business of America is business" reflected the nation's widespread enthusiasm for business—an enthusiasm that affected even religion.

Bruce Barton, a preacher's son who had become a famous advertising executive, wrote a book, *The Man Nobody Knows,* which portrayed Jesus as a model business-man. Christ, according to Barton, was "the founder of modern business. . . . He picked up twelve men from the bottom ranks of business and forged them into an organization that conquered the world." Christ, Barton said, was a "sociable man" and "the most popular dinner guest in Jerusalem." Barton claimed that Jesus practiced "modern sales-manship," persuading by asking pointed questions, and even advertising by using parables. Barton's favorite quotation from the Bible was Christ's reply to His parents in Luke 2:49: "Wist ye not that I must be about my Father's business?"

The Man Nobody Knows enjoyed great success. In the mid-twenties it was on the bestseller list for two years. Despite its popularity, however, the book revealed the author's lack of knowledge of true Christianity. In a book entitled *The Christ We Know,* conservative Bible teacher A. C. Gaebelein argued that Barton's sketch of Christ struck at the heart of Christianity by denying Christ's incarnation as the Son of God: "Can the conception of Christ as a businessman, as a leader, or advertiser or sociable man, give our conscience rest and bring us nigh unto God? No! Nothing but the blood of Jesus." Furthermore, Barton's book ended with Christ's death, not His resurrection. Clearly *The Man Nobody Knows* misinterpreted Christ's work, but it does show how religion and business were mixed in the 1920s. What Barton wanted to do was bring Christ down to the level of business rather than elevate business to the standards of Christ's teachings.

Big businesses were providing new jobs. Some Americans with money left over after paying routine expenses invested in the stock market. As stockholders were paid larger dividends, more people purchased stocks, even using credit to do so. Other people invested in real estate. Property, especially in Florida, became a tempting deal, as the land was presented as a future resort paradise. Thousands bought property and resold it for higher prices, although little development took place. Many people went into debt on these get-rich-quick land speculations.

Both public attitudes and government favored big business. While attitudes toward big business had been negative from 1880 to 1920, Americans now respected or almost worshiped business and businessmen. "The man who builds a factory builds a temple, and the man who works there worships there," said President Coolidge. Business had become the god of the age. Government rarely interfered with any of the growing business empires of the 1920s. And since the prosperity of business was most important, labor unions gained little while they appeared to be fighting against American business.

SECTION REVIEW

1. How did the automobile change life for farmers? for city workers?

2. What American pilot was a hero of the 1920s? What did he accomplish in 1927?

3. What basic mass production technique did Henry Ford introduce?

 How did the radio help to unify American culture?

---

of the Model T. Ford wanted to build a car for the common man. By using an assembly line to create many identical products, Ford was able to make automobiles affordable. Between 1908 and 1927, Ford produced fifteen million Model Ts. Only the Volkswagen Beetle had a longer run.

Curb Exchanges

Many stock exchanges started in the streets. The American Stock Exchange, for example, began as the New York Curb Exchange in 1849. The gold rush started in California that year, and many companies hoped to make substantial profits through mining. Brokers not associated with established stock exchanges gathered on the streets of New York's financial district to buy and sell shares in these companies.

Curb trading continued through the rest of the nineteenth century and reached the height of its popularity in the first two decades of the twentieth century. Brokers stood on the streets or sidewalks while telephone order clerks conducted their transactions from the windows of office buildings above. Brokers used distinctive means of identification. A colorfully striped jacket and bright yellow hat, for example, would help a clerk identify a man as a broker. Because the streets were so loud, brokers communicated with a one-handed form of sign language, a practice that is still followed in major stock exchanges. The curb exchange moved indoors in 1921 so that its transactions could be better regulated and recorded.

What element of salvation is Barna leaving out? *(Salvation is not a result of good persuasion; it is a result of the Holy Spirit's leading.)*

Section Review Answers

1. Farmers were less isolated; they could go to town often to shop or to attend social functions. City workers could live away from their inner-city workplaces and drive in to work. (p. 498)

2. Charles A. Lindbergh; first to fly nonstop across the Atlantic Ocean (p. 499)

3. the assembly line (p. 500)

 People from all regions of the country became more alike as they heard the same programs and listened together to the broadcast of national events. (p. 500)

Objectives

Students should be able to

1. Explain how the 1920s became a time of moral decay.
2. Describe some of the popular fads and amusements of the 1920s.
3. Describe ways that criminals defied Prohibition.
4. Explain the significance of the Scopes Trial.

Rin-Tin-Tin

Rin-Tin-Tin, or Rinty, one of America's best-loved dogs, made his film debut in 1923 in *Where the North Begins*. He was an instant success. Over the next seven years he (together with his eighteen doubles) made eighteen more adventure films, bringing in a total of over $5 million for his owner, Leland Duncan. In addition to his salary, Rinty was supplied with live orchestral music, a diamond-studded collar, and steak dinners with all the trimmings.

Sound in Films

Motion picture studios successfully introduced sound in the 1920s. The Warner brothers took the lead. Their earliest attempts involved music, not speaking. They started with short musical highlights, but these did not make enough money to pay for themselves. Then they developed a program with several musical numbers strung together for its first half and a full-length feature film with musical background for its second half. Although the audience enjoyed this program, they were crazy about *The Jazz Singer* (released in 1927), the first film to include sections of dialogue. Dialogue was included throughout a film in July of 1928. A switch to a simpler sound system, championed by William Fox, helped sound become widespread.

Moral Decay

The new prosperity of the 1920s helped to foster not only excessive materialism but also a flagrant disregard for moral standards by many. The horrors of war had prompted some of the soldiers who returned to take a "live-for-today" attitude. They wanted to experience all the pleasure they could, regardless of the future. Other Americans were affected by the new sights and sounds of the age. The changes sometimes challenged their values, especially if those values were not firmly grounded in the truths of God's unchanging Word.

In this era changes in morals and culture were more readily expressed than they had been in earlier times. Poets and novelists freely expressed their dissatisfaction with the world, its values, its standards, and its morals. They were quick to draw attention to Christians who were hypocritical or legalistic. Such Christians indeed brought reproach on God's name. Unfortunately, those same writers and artists refused to acknowledge that there were sincere Christians. They preferred instead to reject Christianity. Nor did they offer anything to replace what they had cast aside. Men and women were left in a moral vacuum, where many did not recognize right and wrong. Thus this generation was called "the lost generation."

In Pursuit of Pleasure

The young people of "the lost generation" sought satisfaction in many pursuits. Some were new and unusual and lasted. Others were passing fancies, or "fads," that soon faded. Some were harmless; others were harmful; a few were fatal.

Alvin "Shipwreck" Kelly set a record by sitting atop a flagpole for 145 days. His food and drink were hoisted to him in a bucket. While atop the pole, Kelly met the girl who became his fiancée when she came up to interview him. Others set records in marathon

dancing. Raccoon coats, crossword puzzles, and a Chinese-inspired game called mahjong (MAH-ZHONG) became popular. Silent movies were the rage through most of the decade. Movie stars became American heroes, although their lifestyles were rarely worthy of emulation. Clara Bow, Greta Garbo, Mary Pickford, Rudolf "the Sheik" Valentino, and Douglas Fairbanks soon were recognized faces throughout the nation. Comic stars Buster Keaton and Charlie Chaplin made viewers laugh.

America's young people were soon copying the dress, hairstyle, and mannerisms of the stars. "Bobbed hair," much shortened from earlier years, became popular for girls. For some, such imitations were signs of rebellion. The undisciplined lifestyle gave rise to the term "flaming youth."

Many women abandoned dress and conduct codes of the past to become **"flappers."** These rebellious girls became the symbol of the Roaring Twenties. Always restless, the flappers delighted in shocking their elders with short skirts, slang, new dances, heavy makeup, and drinking or smoking in public. The young people of the lost generation did not seem to care that the pleasures of sin are but for a season.

Pleasure-hungry people sought entertainment in the theaters of America.

SECTION 3

Materials

- Activity C from Chapter 24 of the *Student Activities* manual
- *Scenes from American Church History* (BJUP)

Compare the Roaring Twenties and Today

The number of parallels between the Roaring Twenties and the modern culture wars is surprising. Write down some key facts about the twenties and ask the students to name some modern parallels. A short sample includes record-setting fads, board games, movies, hairstyles, flappers, sports idols, sensational crimes, speakeasies, bootlegging, gang wars, attacks on Scripture, and the Scopes Trial.

Interest in sports grew too whether by actual participation, attendance at events, or listening to the radio. Women made names for themselves in sports. In 1926 Gertrude Ederle became the first woman to swim the twenty-two miles across the English Channel. Helen Wills slammed her way to glory on the tennis court.

College football drew thousands of fans. Harold "Red" Grange, the "galloping ghost" of the University of Illinois, received the longest ovation in the history of college football when he ran for four touchdowns within twelve minutes. Knute Rockne (NOOT ROKnee), a Norwegian immigrant who became head football coach at Notre Dame, unleashed his players' talents to thrill radio audiences each Saturday afternoon. The "Four Horsemen of Notre Dame," his running backs, dazzled their way to gridiron glories.

Boxer Jack Dempsey, who was described as having "a neck like a bull, a granite jaw, and fists like iron," drew in the first million-dollar gate for a sporting event. Horse and auto racing drew crowds. Some people were attracted to such sports, not for their excitement, but for a wrong reason, gambling.

Other famous names in sports included a baseball star George Herman "Babe" Ruth, a home run hitter for the New York Yankees; Bobby Jones won fame on the links as a golfer. Besides entering major car races, Barney Oldfield raced at county fairs. And a horse named Man O'War won twenty of the twenty-one races he entered.

The Roaring Twenties are memorable partly because there was a greater emphasis on the sensational. Murders and other forms of crime filled American papers. Each crime seemed more sensational than the previous

Babe Ruth began his baseball career as a talented pitcher, but he became a home run hitting hero for the New York Yankees.

one reported. Americans seemed to thrive on all the excitement they could find.

Accidents and human misfortune captured the attention of the press. A hero dog named Balto and a spelunker (spih LUNG kur; one who explores caves) named Floyd Collins were two of the big stories in 1925. Balto carried diphtheria antitoxin 655 miles across Alaska to Nome. To save lives, this lead dog covered the distance in a blinding blizzard while the temperature plunged to fifty below zero. Floyd Collins gained fame for his explorations of Mammoth Cave in Kentucky. On another cave adventure, however, a seven-ton boulder pinned him in. A thin reporter managed to wriggle down the treacherous hole to interview him. The vivid descriptions riveted the attention of the nation on Sand Cave, Kentucky, where Collins was trapped. Floyd's voice became weaker by the day. On the eighteenth day of reporting, there was no reply from the trapped man; he was dead.

503

Gertrude Ederle

When Gertrude Ederle was a young girl, her mother taught her to swim by tying a rope around her and letting her down into the water; Gertrude could swim on her own within three days. She began swimming competitively while still a girl and had set eighteen world records by the time she was seventeen. She was chosen for the 1924 U.S. Olympic swimming team and won a gold and two bronze medals.

Because the water was often choppy and the weather uncertain, the English Channel was a serious challenge for a swimmer. Ederle tried to swim the Channel on August 18, 1925, but was disqualified when a fellow swimmer tried to help her, thinking she was too tired to continue. On August 6, 1926, a rough, stormy day, Ederle successfully swam the Channel in 14 hours and 31 minutes. She was the first woman to swim the Channel and the fastest person to that date. Ederle became deaf later in life but used her talents to teach deaf children to swim. She was inducted into the international Swimming Hall of Fame in 1965.

Bobby Jones

He was not a professional golfer; the law was his profession. But Bobby Jones was the only golfer ever to win both amateur and open titles in the United States and Britain in the same year—a grand slam. In addition to winning thirteen major championships, Jones is known for founding the Masters tournament.

Knute Rockne

Knute Rockne earned fame as a football player and coach at Notre Dame. He was an accomplished student, graduating magna cum laude. But when he was offered a graduate assistantship in chemistry, he accepted it on the condition that he be able to help the football coach, Jesse Harper. When Harper retired in 1917, Rockne became the head coach. With 105 wins, 12 losses, and 5 ties, Rockne had the greatest all-

Student Activity C: Sports Trivia

This activity gives the students practice in using the world almanac to find sports trivia. Discuss the type of trivia that young people keep up with today. What are the pros and cons of sports enthusiasm in America? (NOTE: The second part of this activity will be completed in the next section.)

time winning percentage. He died in a plane crash in 1931.

Rockne's story won Hollywood fame with the 1940 movie *Knute Rockne All American*. In it the character of Rockne uttered the famous line, "Win one for the Gipper," a tribute to former Notre Dame quarterback George Gipp (played by Ronald Reagan), who had died of a viral throat infection eight years previously.

St. Valentine's Day Massacre

Al Capone and Bugs Moran were rival gangster leaders in Chicago. In early 1929 Capone associate Jack McGurn told Capone about problems he was having with Moran, and the two planned an assassination. The plan was simple. On February 14, 1929, a bootlegger tricked the Moran gang into meeting him at a garage to buy alcohol at a good price. Capone's hired assassins dressed like police officers and staged a raid on the garage. Moran's gang members lined up against the wall as ordered by the "officers" and were promptly shot. The assassins left the building with some of their own men as "prisoners," climbed into a stolen police car, and drove away, leaving behind six dead and one dying man. Capone and McGurn had impenetrable alibis, and no one was ever charged with the crime. Bugs Moran, the chief target of the assassination, was not in the garage when the massacre occurred.

Detroit police discover an illegal brewery during prohibition.

The Failure of Prohibition

Prohibition was also an important issue. In 1919 the Eighteenth Amendment had been ratified. It had established prohibition by making illegal the manufacture, sale, transportation, import, and export of intoxicating liquors as a beverage. The outlawing of liquor was supported by many Americans. Thousands had rallied to the temperance societies of the 1800s, and the progressives of the early 1900s had made prohibition a major issue.

By 1915 fifteen states had voted out "demon rum." By 1918 thirty-three states were in the prohibition column. Since the United States was selling all its surplus grain to the Allies for food, it was considered unpatriotic to make liquor. The prohibition amendment passed Congress and went to the states for ratification. Its widespread support at the time is evidenced by its quick approval. All the states except Rhode Island and Connecticut ratified it in just over a year. In most states prohibition won by a large majority.

Prohibition, however, proved difficult to enforce. The Volstead Act of 1919 made any beverage with more than 0.5% alcohol illegal. It also set up a Prohibition Bureau to enforce the law. But the bureau had a small budget and only three thousand agents to enforce the law. Soon the problems of prohibition appeared.

Illegal taverns called **"speakeasies"** appeared across the nation. The border with Canada, where alcohol was legal, stretched nearly three thousand miles. Officers could

Why Was Prohibition a Failure?

Most students will understand from the text that Prohibition was a failure due to lack of government support, but what was the real cause of its failure? *(People need changed hearts to see the harm of alcohol. Without that change, the government will always have a difficult time enforcing right.)* What issues does the government have difficulty controlling in the United States today? *(drugs, assisted suicide, abortion)* What should a Christian do about issues like these? Discuss the Christian's political responsibility and how moral decay affects a nation.

not effectively patrol the long border, and liquor flowed freely across it. The Atlantic seaboard also had its share of rum runners. **Bootlegging,** selling illegal liquor, became a big business and made many rich. Since it was legal to have alcohol for medicinal reasons, some people got it by doctor's prescription. Others made their own home brew in stills.

Violence often accompanied the criminals who organized bootlegging rings. "Scarface" **Al Capone,** leader of a large crime ring in Chicago, made $60 million on liquor alone in 1927. He and other ruthless criminals organized liquor networks to supply those who wanted liquor and were willing to pay any price for it. They also extended their activity to crimes such as illegal gambling and prostitution. Criminal gangs controlled these activities in certain areas, and if a rival gang tried to operate in another's territory, the gangs sometimes went to "war" with one another. Innocent people were killed in raids, and such crimes shocked the public. Although periodic crackdowns came, it proved hard to put these gangsters behind bars. Not only would the criminals refuse to testify against each other, but the gangs also threatened the lives of honest citizens called as witnesses and bought off judges and officials.

By the late 1920s it seemed apparent that prohibition was not working. More and more Americans cried out for its repeal, which finally came in 1933. Prohibition has been called the "noble experiment" because the government tried to do away with an evil in society. Liquor is certainly the source of much pain and sin, but laws cannot change the moral character of men. Only salvation through Jesus Christ can change the hearts of individuals. As long as most of society remains without Christ, it will reject restrictions on its moral actions.

Nevertheless, prohibition did bring some benefits. Less alcohol was consumed, and some people gave up drinking. There was less gambling. Alcohol-related diseases and deaths decreased, and sober workers were more efficient. When prohibition was repealed, liquor freely began to afflict Americans with its sad effects again.

Ridicule of True Christianity

Because many Americans of the 1920s wanted fortune and pleasure without moral restrictions, they attacked the authority of Scripture. They did not want to be accountable to God and the standards set forth in His Word. Instead they followed the ideas of men that gave them excuses for rejecting the truth of the Bible. The theory of evolution, popularized by Darwin, told men that God had not created them. They reasoned that if God was not their Creator, then they did not need His salvation.

They also found other ideas that they thought freed them from responsibility. The psychologist Sigmund Freud taught that man behaves the way he does because of subconscious drives. Men interpreted his writings to mean that people cannot help what they do; therefore, they should do whatever they please and not feel guilty. Even Albert Einstein, famous mathematician and scientist, added to the sense of moral freedom. His theory of relativity stated that time, space, and mass were not fixed or absolute. Although Einstein himself did not apply his theory to moral matters, many people began to think that everything was relative. These men said that there are no absolute rights and wrongs and that everyone should do what is right in his own eyes.

Of course the Bible clearly states the standard God has set for man. Men who preached about the responsibility of man to a holy God and the truth of Scripture soon found themselves scorned by the society around them. The greatest example of this scorn in the

505

Capone's Day in Court
Despite Al Capone's well-known criminal activities, the government could not get a conviction on him. Lack of solid evidence, together with intimidation of witnesses and bribery of officials, kept Capone free. With encouragement from President Hoover, however, government officials renewed their efforts to put Capone behind bars. They sought evidence of either income tax evasion or violations of Prohibition. Lawman Eliot Ness and his "Untouchables" pursued the bootlegging portion of Capone's operation.

The government finally moved on Capone in 1931. Not sure how long its case, focusing on the income tax evasion, would hold together, it agreed to allow Capone to plea bargain for a light sentence. Judge James Wilkerson, however, declared that he was not bound by such a bargain. Capone withdrew his guilty plea and prepared for a trial. Having identified the potential jurors, Capone's men tried to bribe them. In response, Judge Wilkerson switched juries the day the trial started. Capone was sentenced to eleven years in prison. He served eight of those years and then returned to his mansion near Miami, Florida, where he lived until his death in 1947.

Richard Hart
James Vincenzo Capone, Al's oldest brother, left home as a young man and headed west. An excellent marksman, Capone made a name for himself as a soldier in World War I and later as a lawman on the frontier. Taking the name Richard Hart, Capone served as a Prohibition enforcement officer, general peacekeeper, and, after Prohibition was repealed, town marshal. For many years even his wife and children did not know that Richard Hart was a member of the Capone family, but he resumed contact with his mother and brothers in the 1940s.

Scenes from American Church History
You may want to read "H. C. Morrison and the Holiness Movement" in *Scenes from American Church History.* Another account of the religion of this era is "William Jennings Bryan: 'He Kept the Faith.' "

For more on J. Gresham Machen, read "J. Gresham Machen and the Fundamentalist Movement." "Ford Porter, Gentle Fundamentalist" is another account of the

courage of a man opposed to liberalism in the church.

American Civil Liberties Union

The American Civil Liberties Union (ACLU) was organized in 1920. Its founders included Clarence Darrow, Felix Frankfurter, Jane Addams, Helen Keller, Norman Thomas, and John Dewey. It was set up as a public interest law firm with the purpose of protecting civil liberties.

Today's ACLU has offices on national, state, and local levels. It pays more than sixty attorneys and, in addition, has available the services of two thousand volunteers. A membership of approximately 275,000 supports the organization.

The ACLU has taken leadership in the defense of such causes as freedom of speech, rights of minorities, abortion and homosexual rights, and separation of church and state (resulting in the removal of prayer, Bible reading, and the teaching of Creation from public schools).

1920s came with a trial concerning the teaching of evolution in schools.

In the 1920s Christians, angry because evolution was being taught in the public schools, pressured state legislatures to pass laws forbidding teachers to teach evolution. The Tennessee state legislature passed such a law. John Scopes, a high school biology teacher, broke the law and was brought to trial. He was convicted and fined $100.

Actually, the **Scopes Trial** had been a publicity stunt of two businessmen in Dayton, Tennessee. Eager to attract attention to their town, they asked Scopes to teach evolution with the assurance that the American Civil Liberties Union would provide legal support. The two businessmen hoped that a dramatic

William Jennings Bryan had been a prominent politician during the Progressive Era, but his participation in the Scopes Trial brought him ridicule.

J. Gresham Machen (1881–1937)

J. Gresham Machen (MAY chun) was perhaps the most scholarly spokesman for the faith during the 1920s. He studied at some of the best schools in the United States and Europe and was a professor at Princeton Seminary until its liberalism caused him to leave. During the 1920s he believed that the Presbyterian church was falling away from Scriptural truth and wrote several scholarly books defending truths such as the virgin birth, the inspiration of the Bible, the atonement, and the bodily resurrection of Christ. Machen argued that if someone held other views, he was not a Christian.

After leaving Princeton Seminary in 1929 Machen helped found Westminster Seminary in Philadelphia, where he taught until his death. He also set up a new independent mission board because of liberalism in the denominational one. Because of his stand for the truth, Machen was dismissed from the Presbyterian church, and by 1936 he and other conservatives formed the Orthodox Presbyterian Church. One of Machen's best books is *Christianity and Liberalism,* an attack on modernism.

trial would draw attention to Dayton and thus attract industry to the town.

In the summer of 1925, the trial turned into the hoped-for gigantic media event. Two hundred reporters converged on the small town of Dayton, and for the first time a trial was covered by radio. One of the prosecutors was William Jennings Bryan, three-time Democratic presidential nominee. Clarence Darrow, a famous trial lawyer and agnostic, defended Scopes. H. L. Mencken (MENG kun), a nationally known reporter who made fun of Christians, called the people of Dayton "gaping primates" and the event in Dayton the "Monkey Trial."

506

Bryan testified in the trial and was ridiculed by Darrow. While Bryan was a staunch defender of the faith, he did not always handle Darrow's questions well. Bryan was not a Bible scholar or a scientist. Even though Scopes was convicted for teaching evolution, the trial had made Bible-believing Christians appear ignorant and unscientific. The Scopes trial was a disappointment to true Christians, yet they knew that their faith rested in the sure Word of God. Even in such an era of open sin and ridicule of the Bible, some men still stood firm as they preached the truth of Scripture.

SECTION REVIEW

1. Why were the people of the 1920s sometimes called "the lost generation"?

2. Who were the heroes and heroines of this generation?

3. What is "bootlegging"?

4. What famous trial took place as a result of the teaching of evolution? Where did it take place?

 Why did Prohibition fail?

Political Inaction

The presidents of the 1920s reflected the attitudes and goals of the day. They promoted the unhindered growth of business and the general enjoyment of prosperity. The business and prosperity were indeed enjoyable, but some of the nation's serious problems were brushed aside at the time. Eventually the fruits of the materialism and selfishness of the era turned out to be a severe crisis for the country.

Harding's Weakness

Warren G. Harding was a likable newspaper editor from the small town of Marion,

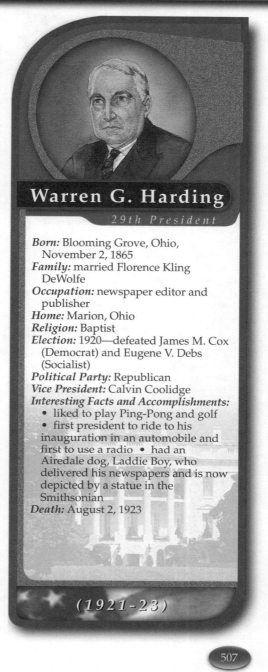

Warren G. Harding
29th President

Born: Blooming Grove, Ohio, November 2, 1865
Family: married Florence Kling DeWolfe
Occupation: newspaper editor and publisher
Home: Marion, Ohio
Religion: Baptist
Election: 1920—defeated James M. Cox (Democrat) and Eugene V. Debs (Socialist)
Political Party: Republican
Vice President: Calvin Coolidge
Interesting Facts and Accomplishments:
- liked to play Ping-Pong and golf
- first president to ride to his inauguration in an automobile and first to use a radio • had an Airedale dog, Laddie Boy, who delivered his newspapers and is now depicted by a statue in the Smithsonian
Death: August 2, 1923

(1921-23)

507

SECTION 4

Objectives
Students should be able to
1. Describe the Harding administration.
2. Explain why Coolidge was a popular president.
3. Name the man who followed Coolidge as president.

The Duchess
Daughter of a banker in the small town of Marion, Ohio, Florence Kling inherited the strong, independent spirit of her wealthy father. After she married Warren Harding in 1891, she took over the circulation department of his newspaper, the *Star*. She soon had the operation, as well as the newsboys, whipped into shape. When her husband became involved in politics, she took equal interest in his new activities. She worked hard to see him elected and, when he became president, reopened the White House to the public. (It had been closed due to President Wilson's poor health.) Harding called his wife "the Duchess."

Section Review Answers

1. because many of them threw off the moral restraints of the Bible and were left with no standards of right and wrong (p. 502)

2. movie stars (p. 502)

3. selling illegal liquor (p. 505)

4. Scopes Trial; Dayton, Tennessee (p. 506)

 because it lacked adequate means of enforcement and, more significantly, because it challenged man's sinful tendency to fight against moral restraint (pp. 504-5)

SECTION 4

Materials
- Activities C, D, and E from Chapter 24 of the *Student Activities* manual

Student Activity C: Presidents of the '20s

This activity reviews the terms associated with each of the three presidencies during the Roaring Twenties.

Alcohol in the White House

The Eighteenth Amendment prohibited the manufacture, sale, and transportation of alcohol within United States territory. Yet guests at poker parties at the Harding White House were served liquor.

Scandals of the Harding Administration

Other scandals of the Harding administration involved the attorney general, Harry Daugherty, and the head of the new Veterans' Bureau, Charles Forbes. Daugherty overlooked the corrupt schemes of his friends who were selling pardons, paroles, and liquor permits for cash. Forbes sold surplus medical goods for his own profit and pocketed money that was supposed to be used for the construction of veterans' hospitals.

Grace Anna Goodhue Coolidge

Grace Anna Goodhue grew up as an only child in the small town of Burlington, Vermont. She graduated from the University of Vermont and began teaching at Clarke School for the Deaf in Northampton, Massachusetts. She met Calvin Coolidge through the Congregational church they both attended.

Coolidge was a frugal man, and Grace managed their household well. With their two sons, they lived in a duplex in Northampton, even after Coolidge became the governor of Massachusetts. (Coolidge rented a room in Boston for a dollar and a half and came home each weekend.)

When she moved into the White House with her husband, Grace became one of the most popular hostesses in Washington, D.C. The combination of her fun-loving spirit and tactful kindness (together with her stylish beauty) endeared her to the capital and the nation. She took the role of First Lady very seriously and continued her responsibilities even when her sixteen-year-old son died unexpectedly.

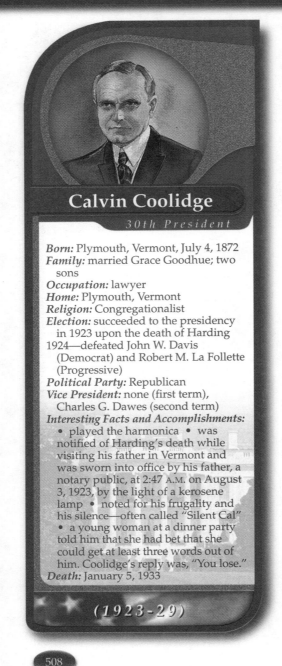

Calvin Coolidge
30th President

Born: Plymouth, Vermont, July 4, 1872
Family: married Grace Goodhue; two sons
Occupation: lawyer
Home: Plymouth, Vermont
Religion: Congregationalist
Election: succeeded to the presidency in 1923 upon the death of Harding 1924—defeated John W. Davis (Democrat) and Robert M. La Follette (Progressive)
Political Party: Republican
Vice President: none (first term), Charles G. Dawes (second term)
Interesting Facts and Accomplishments:
• played the harmonica • was notified of Harding's death while visiting his father in Vermont and was sworn into office by his father, a notary public, at 2:47 A.M. on August 3, 1923, by the light of a kerosene lamp • noted for his frugality and his silence—often called "Silent Cal" • a young woman at a dinner party told him that she had bet that she could get at least three words out of him. Coolidge's reply was, "You lose."
Death: January 5, 1933

(1923-29)

Ohio. He had come up the political ladder through Ohio politics, eventually becoming a U.S. senator. The political leaders in the state at that time were called the "Ohio Gang," and Harding did his share of favors for these friends to achieve his political success.

Harding had promised to get the country back to normal after the war, and since that was what the country wanted, he was easily elected to the presidency. It may also be noted that the 1920 election was the first time that women could vote for a president.

Once in office, Harding supported most of the popular programs of the day, especially big business. Unfortunately, he appointed many of his political friends to important offices in which they could use the government to promote their own gain. Although Harding was basically honest, his friends turned his administration into a great scandal. The most prominent criminal was Harding's secretary of the interior, **Albert B. Fall.** Fall persuaded Harding and the secretary of the navy to transfer control of government-owned oil reserves from the Navy Department to Fall's Interior Department. He then leased the reserves at Teapot Dome, Wyoming, and Elk Hills, California, to two oil men, who paid him back with several "loans" totaling $400,000. When Fall's crime was uncovered, he went to prison, the first cabinet member in history to be imprisoned for misdeeds in office.

Although not involved in public scandal for financial gain, Harding was weak and at fault personally for allowing the law to be disobeyed within White House walls. Harding was obviously a poor leader who failed to take his executive responsibility seriously. Instead of providing firm direction, Harding allowed national affairs to simply drift along without guidance. By the summer of 1923 Harding knew something was wrong. He told journalist William Allen White, "I have no trouble with my enemies. I can take care of them all right.

Progressivism Versus Normalcy

Ask the students to contrast the progressive presidents of the 1900s and 1910s to the presidents who led the "return to normalcy" during the 1920s. (See Activity A in the *Student Activities* manual.) Review the qualities of a great president. Note that all three progressive presidents—Roosevelt, Taft, and Wilson—are better known than the presidents of the twenties are. Nevertheless, conservative Republicans honor presidents who restrain government power, even if they get no personal glory.

Charting Progressivism and Normalcy

Discuss the chart from Student Activity A that your students should have completed by this time. Discuss which decade America most resembles today.

Compare Scandals

Compare the Teapot Dome Scandal with the scandals under Grant and modern examples of scandal (such as those under Bill Clinton). Can the students find any parallels between the weaknesses of the presidents and the scandals of their cabinets?

But my friends, White, they're the ones that keep me walking the floor nights."

Harding took a vacation to Alaska in 1923. On the way back the president became seriously ill July 28 in his hotel room in California. He died August 2. The officially listed cause of death was ptomaine poisoning. Since no one else in the party of sixty-five got food poisoning, however, it is more likely that he died of a heart attack. The **Teapot Dome Scandal** was uncovered after his death.

Coolidge's Administration

Calvin Coolidge, born in Vermont, had studied law in Massachusetts and entered politics there. He had gained a reputation as a "law and order" man when as governor of Massachusetts he had taken a stand during a Boston police strike in 1919. He declared, "There is no right to strike against the public safety by anybody, anywhere, any time," and forced the police back to work. To a nation that was in fear of disorder and crime, this stand won him admiration.

Succeeding to the presidency on Harding's death, Coolidge was in charge when most of the Harding scandals were revealed. By firmly prosecuting the corrupt officials, Coolidge won enough support to win the presidential election of 1924. Then he carried on the same basic policies that Harding had supported. While business appeared to be successful during the Coolidge administration, ominous conditions were developing. Because of the unwise speculation of investors, prices were going higher and higher on the stock market. Buying on credit was so popular that millions of Americans were in serious debt. Farmers were still overproducing and receiving low prices for their produce. These and other features of the American economy would soon lead the nation into calamity.

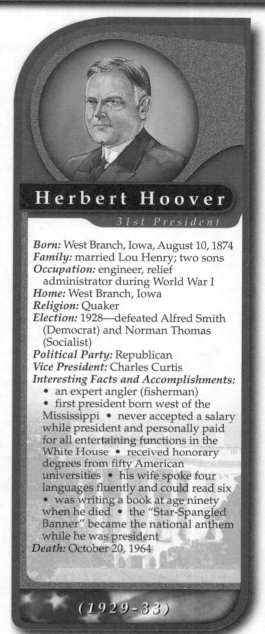

Herbert Hoover

31st President

Born: West Branch, Iowa, August 10, 1874
Family: married Lou Henry; two sons
Occupation: engineer, relief administrator during World War I
Home: West Branch, Iowa
Religion: Quaker
Election: 1928—defeated Alfred Smith (Democrat) and Norman Thomas (Socialist)
Political Party: Republican
Vice President: Charles Curtis
Interesting Facts and Accomplishments:
- an expert angler (fisherman)
- first president born west of the Mississippi • never accepted a salary while president and personally paid for all entertaining functions in the White House • received honorary degrees from fifty American universities • his wife spoke four languages fluently and could read six • was writing a book at age ninety when he died • the "Star-Spangled Banner" became the national anthem while he was president
Death: October 20, 1964

(1929-33)

509

A Life of Public Service

Before entering the White House, Herbert Hoover had already spent a good part of his life helping others. Traveling around the world as a mining engineer, Hoover was in China during the Boxer Rebellion. While his wife donated her time at hospitals, Hoover directed the building of barricades and at one point risked his life to rescue Chinese children.

At the onset of World War I, Hoover was in London. He helped the American embassy get American tourists home and then, as the result of his good work, received the assignment of feeding occupied Belgium. When America entered the war, he was named the head of the Food Administration, having to balance the food needs of soldiers at the front with those of civilians back home. After the war, the Allies asked him to organize food shipments for the hungry in Europe.

Travel Back in Time

Students know what was coming in the next two decades in U.S. history—the Great Depression and World War II. If they could travel back in time, what would they do with the information they know? Note that such information could be used for personal financial gain, or it could be used to warn the governments of the world. The challenge would be to make anyone believe you.

Star-Spangled Banner
Though written in 1814, "The Star-Spangled Banner" did not become the official anthem of the United States until the twentieth century. In 1916 President Woodrow Wilson ordered that the song be played at all naval and military occasions. And in 1931 Congress voted to make "The Star-Spangled Banner" the national anthem.

Hoover's Inheritance

The nation was still enjoying prosperity, however, when the election of 1928 came. The Republican candidate, **Herbert Hoover,** was swept into office by a nation satisfied with success. Hoover, a poor, orphaned farm boy, had proved his abilities by becoming a wealthy mining engineer and then devoting his talents to public service. His Democrat opponent, Al Smith, was a Roman Catholic and was against Prohibition. The nation was not yet ready to vote a Catholic into the presidency.

Hoover was talented, but he had inherited the impending fall from prosperity. The excesses of the twenties were about to result in disaster, and Hoover would be saddled with the responsibility for the Great Depression that was to come.

SUMMARY

The Roaring Twenties was a time of prosperity for the nation, following the sacrifices of World War I. Businesses boomed, and Americans enjoyed the new consumer goods and amusements. The United States generally isolated itself from foreign problems and distrusted foreigners within the country, while it concerned itself with issues and events at home such as Prohibition, Lindbergh's flight, and the fads of the "flaming youth." The 1920s was also a time of great decline in moral character. Americans pursued material possessions, often risking their future by buying too much on credit or speculating in stock and land. They ridiculed Christianity, rebelled against moral restraints, and turned to the pleasures of sin and selfishness. Although the decade was one of general prosperity, Americans would pay for some of their excesses with the hardships of the decade to come.

SECTION REVIEW

1. Name the three Republican presidents of the 1920s.

2. What act of corruption is associated with Albert B. Fall?

What conditions of the 1920s would help bring the nation's prosperity to an end?

Section Review Answers

1. Warren G. Harding, Calvin Coolidge, Herbert Hoover (pp. 507-9)

2. the Teapot Dome Scandal—using government property for his own profit (pp. 508-9)

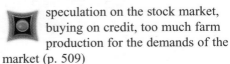
speculation on the stock market, buying on credit, too much farm production for the demands of the market (p. 509)

Chapter Review

People, Places, and Things to Remember

Warren G. Harding
Treaty of Washington
Kellogg-Briand Peace
  Pact
Calvin Coolidge

Charles A. Lindbergh
flappers
Prohibition
speakeasies
bootlegging

Al Capone
Scopes Trial
Albert B. Fall
Teapot Dome Scandal
Herbert Hoover

Review Questions

Match each of these men with the statement or description most closely related to him.

1. Al Capone
2. Calvin Coolidge
3. Albert B. Fall
4. Warren G. Harding
5. Herbert Hoover
6. Charles Lindbergh

a. America should "return to normalcy"
b. flew the *Spirit of St. Louis* to Paris
c. a Chicago gangster
d. organizer of Teapot Dome scheme
e. "the business of America is business"
f. inherited the fall from prosperity

Answer the following questions about the 1920s.

7. What two international agreements did the United States sign in the 1920s?
8. What was the "Red Scare"?
9. When was the first commercial radio broadcast, and what did it announce?
10. In what fad did "Shipwreck" Kelly participate?
11. What were the shockingly fashionable young women of the 1920s called?
12. When did Prohibition begin, and when did it end?
13. What is bootlegging?
14. In what famous trial was a teacher convicted of teaching evolution but biblical Christianity ridiculed?

Questions for Discussion

15. Why is the Roaring Twenties a good name for the 1920s?
16. Are fads ever bad? Explain your answer.

511

Chapter Review Ideas

Student Activity D: Lessons from History

The Roaring Twenties are rich with lessons for modern Americans who are struggling to understand moral decay and the human condition. This activity reinforces the deeper purposes for studying history. Ask the students to name more recent events that teach similar lessons.

Student Activity E: News Flash, 1920s Style

Students practice their creative writing skills by writing their own accounts of news stories from the 1920s, using the style of the day.

Chapter Review Answers

1. c (p. 505)
2. e (p. 501)
3. d (p. 508)
4. a (p. 495)
5. f (p. 510)
6. b (p. 499)
7. Treaty of Washington, Kellogg-Briand Peace Pact (p. 495)
8. a fear of Communist infiltration in America (p. 497)
9. November 2, 1920; Harding's election to the presidency (p. 500)
10. flagpole sitting (p. 502)
11. flappers (p. 502)
12. 1919; 1933 (pp. 504-5)
13. selling illegal liquor (p. 505)
14. the Scopes Trial (p. 506)
15. Answers will vary. The decade was roaring with activity—business, fads, amusements, faster transportation, sensational stories and crimes, and so on.
16. Answers will vary. Fads can be bad if they promote activity that is unbiblical.

Modern man expresses his beliefs every day. They are seen in politics, science, religion, education, and in many other areas. Some beliefs are expressed so frequently that they become accepted as truths—even by Christians. However, many widely accepted beliefs are far from the truths found in the Scriptures. Evolution is one of these beliefs.

Shortly after Darwin promoted the theory of evolution, philosophers began to apply it to every area of life. When William Jennings Bryan and Clarence Darrow debated evolution in 1925, they debated more than a theory of life's origin. They debated a way of thinking. According to the evolutionist, man is a well-developed animal; he was not created by God and therefore has no responsibility to Him. Any ideas of right and wrong were created by man, not by God.

Evolution's influence has been most obvious in the field of science. It is now common to hear scientists refer to the earth as "millions of years old" and life forms evolving slowly from simple to complex organisms. For instance, evolutionists look at the Grand Canyon and conclude that it formed over millions of years. A much simpler explanation might be that a catastrophic flood carved it out. Despite major gaps in evidence, scientists continue to accept evolution as a fact. They are like those mentioned in II Peter 3:5-6. ("For this they willingly are ignorant of, that by the word of God the heavens were of old, and the earth standing out of the water and in the water: Whereby the world that then was, being overflowed with water, perished.")

Once the field of science had accepted evolution, the theory moved into the field of education. Schools throughout the country receive funding each year from the National Science Foundation—an organization that also supports research on human evolution. The National Science Teacher's Association openly accepts the theory of evolution. Despite the ongoing debate between Creationism and evolution, NSTA states, "There is no longer a debate among scientists over whether evolution has taken place." When students hear that evolution is a fact and Creation is a myth, they begin to believe it.

512

It is not surprising that evolutionary thinking has spread to so many areas.

Evolution has also influenced economics. In the nineteenth century the German philosopher Herbert Spenser coined the evolutionary phrase "survival of the fittest," which means that life forms survive because they are strong and selfish. Ferdinand Lundberg sees a similar economic philosophy today. In his 1988 book *The Rich and the Super Rich* he states, "Standard doctrine holds that one should always pay the lowest possible wages and taxes, charge the highest possible prices and rents, and never give anything away unless the gift confers some hidden personal benefit." The doctrine might make sense if man were an animal. However, the Bible teaches that man is a unique being created in God's image. Romans 12:10 says, "Be kindly affectioned one to another with brotherly love; in honour preferring one another." Obviously the "standard doctrine" is not the doctrine of the Bible.

Evolution has had a growing influence on the American legal system as well. When laws are based on God's Word, they are unchanging, like the Bible itself. However, laws based on evolution are much different. If society is evolving, then the standards of what is right or wrong can change with it. For example, in 1993 the Hawaii Supreme Court ruled that the state could not deny same-sex couples marriage licenses without a "compelling reason." In Isaiah 5:20 and 24 God warns those who change the definition of right and wrong. "Woe unto them that call evil good, and good evil . . . their blossom shall go up as dust: because they have cast away the law of the Lord of hosts, and despised the word of the Holy One of Israel."

Effects from the theory of evolution are also very evident when it comes to social issues, such as abortion. Evolution is used to justify the killing of unborn babies because it is a natural practice among some animals. In *Science* magazine Barbara Burke writes, "Among some animal species, infant killing appears to be a natural practice. Could it be natural for humans too, a trait inherited from our ancestors?" While disabled and unwanted children may seem to serve little purpose

---

Materials

- Special speaker: an expert on Creationism
- Video on Creationism versus evolution

What Was It About?

After the students have finished reading, ask them the following questions?

- Where is the influence of evolution most easily seen? *(science)*

- What position has the National Science Teacher's Association taken on the truth of evolution? *(They say that scientists no longer debate whether evolution is true.)* Is this a true statement? *(No, much debate still occurs as scientists have difficulty making evolution work.)*

- How has evolution affected the standard of right and wrong? *(If evolution is true, then there is no standard except the current standard that has evolved from an evolving society.)*

 Special Speaker: Expert on Creationism

Invite someone to come to speak on the controversy between evolution and Creationism. Use the entire class period for the presentation and discussion.

Video on Creationism

If a special speaker is not available, show a video such as *Science and the Christian* (available from BJUP) or *God of Creation* (available from BJUP).

from an evolutionary world view, Christians know that God can use these lives greatly to His glory.

No doubt many Christians see the evil influences of evolution in these areas, but they may not notice it in others.

The Bible teaches that in the family the father should be the head of the household and that children should respect his authority. Evolutionists base the family structure on animal societies and "primitive" human society, where this authority is less important.

In the area of music, true standards of beauty come from God, not man. Melody, harmony, and rhythm all demonstrate the orderliness of God's universe. When they are skillfully blended, they create beautiful music. An evolutionist who disregards these standards can claim that any music is "good" no matter how it sounds.

The same principle applies to visual art. In New York City, for example, one museum advertised its exhibition as "a deliberate rejection of all the emblems of successful art: originality, integrity of materials, coherence of form." Any effort to push ahead the "evolution" of music and art into new forms is automatically labeled as good. Evolutionary thinking has allowed subjects focusing on sin to be called good.

With all the influence evolution has had, the world can seem a scary place for Christians. We are surrounded by those who oppose what the Scriptures teach. But God has a purpose for keeping His children in this sinful environment. The root of evolutionary thinking comes from a rejection of God. The only way people can change their thinking is through a change of heart. God has given Christians the privilege of presenting people with the only one who can do that—Christ.

Charles Darwin plots with Coco, King of the Monkeys, to take over the world with his "Theory of Evolution"

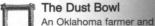

The Dust Bowl

An Oklahoma farmer and his sons battle the wind during a 1936 dust storm. The drought and the resulting dust bowl in the West were only more problems added to the nation during the depression.

Chapter Motivation

Ask students why they think Americans still remember the Great Depression. Why does it get so much attention? The Great Depression brought the biggest changes in America since the Civil War. Because no one wants a depression to return, we want to understand its causes. The Great Depression also matters because Americans voted for radical changes in their government. Modern Americans need to understand the motives behind these changes, and they need to decide whether the changes were worthwhile.

Materials

SECTION 1

• Activity A from Chapter 25 of the *Student Activities* manual
• Special speaker: a person who experienced the Great Depression

SECTION 2

• No materials

25

Crash and Depression

American businesses appeared to be flourishing as stock prices rose higher and higher in 1929. Although prices reached a new high in September, conservative investors were beginning to grow cautious. Those who sold stocks found fewer buyers, and prices began to slide down. By October, orders to brokers to sell surpassed orders to buy. On Thursday, October 24, a record-breaking thirteen million shares changed hands. Prices slid so low that investors lost $9 billion on that "Black Thursday." Many investors, who lost all of their money, could not pay the stock brokers the additional money that they owed. When the investors could not pay, brokers tried desperately to sell the stock, flooding the market still more.

A panic broke out the following Tuesday, October 29, when there were orders to sell sixteen million shares on the exchange. Fortunes made over a period of years vanished in minutes. Some people became so depressed they took their lives. This **stock market crash of 1929** signaled the beginning of the **Great Depression,** a time of hardship for many Americans.

The Fall of Prosperity

In 1928 during his election campaign Herbert Hoover had declared, "We in America today are nearer to the final triumph over

514

CHAPTER 25	Lesson Plan Chart		
Section Title	**Main Activity**	**Pages**	**Time Frame**
1. The Fall of Prosperity	Guest Speaker from the Depression	514-22	2-3 days
2. FDR and the New Deal	Relief, Recovery, Reform	522-27	2-3 days
3. Opposition to the New Deal	Bad Precedents of the New Deal	528-31	1-2 days
Total Suggested Days (including 1 day for review and testing)			6-9 days

poverty than ever before in the history of any land," but soon millions of Americans would join the ranks of the unemployed, the homeless, and the hungry. The Roaring Twenties ended with a national financial collapse that would afflict Americans for the next decade.

Causes of the Crash

The great desires for wealth and pleasure in the 1920s had much to do with the crash that followed, but there were several specific causes for the financial crisis.

Industrial Problems—Despite the overall air of prosperity in the 1920s, many common workers had already faced economic woes. Farmers were suffering from low prices. Textile workers and coal miners were hurt by layoffs as demand for their products declined. These workers could no longer buy the industrial goods that were filling the market. Eventually, many other Americans were running out of credit to buy more. With a decreased demand for goods, industrial output slowed. Laborers worked fewer hours or were laid off, cutting incomes and causing hardships. Since industries were often interdependent, when one cut back, others were forced to do the same. As consumer spending continued to drop, industrial expansion came almost to a standstill long before the crash actually took place.

Overuse of Credit—The use of credit, especially of installment buying, had grown steadily. While credit covered some of the early symptoms of economic illness, its unwise and often unrestrained use made things worse. Before long, people were having to make such high payments on the things they had bought on credit that they could not afford to buy anything new. Auto sales and construction lagged, and workers were laid off; these people were then unable to meet their payments at all. Merchants, who had extended the credit loans, lost money, and their businesses began to falter.

Speculation—In the late twenties newspapers carried accounts of people who had profited from get-rich-quick schemes. These speculators, often motivated by greed, bought properties at a low price, hoping to sell them quickly for a much higher price. Most had speculated in land or stock.

Land prices went up in the 1920s, especially in urban areas or near recreational settings as people moved outward to the suburbs. The biggest land boom was in Florida, where the semitropical climate attracted hordes of speculators. Miami alone boasted two thousand real estate offices in 1925. Those who had speculated early and bought good land did make big profits. But others who bought land on credit found they could not make their payments. Some people were swindled into buying undesirable lands and even swamps. In 1926 hurricanes struck, helping to put an end to the desire to invest in the area. Homes were left vacant, and few sales were made thereafter. Bank failures in Florida climbed when loans were not repaid.

While risky land investments did not tempt many Americans, stock speculation did. Prices of corporate stock had risen steadily beginning in 1927. By September 1929 stock prices were 400 percent higher than they had been in 1925. People of modest means were attracted to stock purchases. The ticker-tape machine allowed purchasers across America to follow price changes almost as they happened. The number of those "playing the market" grew to about 1.5 million in 1929. But most were not buying stocks to collect quarterly dividends. Rather, they wanted to sell stocks for quick profits when the prices rose. Many investors paid scant attention to the earnings of the companies they had invested in, an indication of the actual value of the stock. They assumed stock prices would keep going up no matter what the industries did.

SECTION 3
- Activities B, C, and D from Chapter 25 of the *Student Activities* manual

SECTION 1

Objectives
Students should be able to
1. List and explain four major causes of the economic crash.
2. Explain why there were runs on banks.
3. Describe the conditions faced by farmers and the unemployed.
4. Explain ways that Hoover tried to deal with the depression and explain the results.

The Crash and Suicide
When the stock market crashed in 1929, fortunes disappeared as well as many American hopes. Some feared that they would not be able to support their families, while others dreaded the loss of the lavish lifestyles they had enjoyed. Whatever the reasons, some thought suicide was the answer to their problems.

In a note, a vice president of Earl Radio Corporation revealed his ruined financial status after losing thousands of dollars. The note was found after he had jumped from the window of his eleventh floor hotel room in Manhattan. Jim Riordan, president of the County Trust Company, shot himself in the head. There were rumors that he had lost hundreds of thousands of dollars in the crash.

The materialism of the Roaring Twenties had caught up with many Americans. People had become so used to having things that they could not imagine a world without them. When the crash came, their god was destroyed. Thankfully, there is one God who cannot be destroyed and who is always there to help His children.

Student Activity A: Hoover vs. FDR

This chart summarizes the key differences between Presidents Hoover and Roosevelt. You will probably want to help the students complete the chart in class when you begin to discuss the Roosevelt administration. Discuss the continuing conflict between the two worldviews that the men represent.

Other Causes of the Depression

Explaining events such as the Great Depression is not always as easy as it seems. People behave in predictable ways, so it does not seem fair to blame that particular generation for being greedy, selfish, and shortsighted. Another explanation for the depression is the government's radical changes in money policy. Just as the depression of 1837 followed the Specie Circular (as mentioned on pages 245-47), the depression of 1929 followed the Federal Reserve's decision to withdraw money from circulation. A free market puts checks and balances on selfish decisions, but government intervention causes havoc on the economy.

Ask the students to think of other possible causes of the Great Depression. An obvious answer—but one that they may miss—is the Lord's intervention. The fact that economists have never been able to explain the depression satisfactorily should point our minds to God. Ask the students to consider His possible reasons for sending the depression. *(God may have wanted to put this prosperous, worldly generation through a severe test.)*

Early Depression in Florida

Before 1926, Miami had a booming tourism industry. New housing developments were springing up to accommodate a population that had reached thirty thousand. But in that year, two hurricanes hit Florida, bringing the depression to the region early.

More than 243 people died because of the two storms, and 1926 was recorded as the fourth deadliest and fifth costliest hurricane year in Florida history. The second hurricane is ranked as the twelfth deadliest U.S. hurricane in the twentieth century.

Miami was devastated. Whole subdivisions were wiped out, and streets were flooded in six to seven feet of water.

Ironically, even though the hurricanes put southern Florida in a depression, they actually helped other areas. In northwest Florida the hurricanes uprooted over four thousand old power poles. Gulf Power Company was forced to replace the poles, which helped modernize the area.

Ticker Tape Machine

The bad news of November 29 was not broken to investors gently. In fact, it rushed toward them, printed on thin sheets of paper from the ticker tape machine.

This little machine was invented in 1867 as a variation of Samuel Morse's telegraph machine. Like the telegraph, it received information by cable, but it also printed the information on strips of paper three-fourths of an inch wide. This feature was valuable for stockbrokers, who needed to keep updated on stock transactions throughout the day. As the little rolls of paper were fed through the machine, they were printed with the symbol for a stock, the number of shares, and the price of each transaction. Each brokerage firm would have a machine to keep them connected to the stock exchange.

The problem was made even more complex because brokers allowed investors to **buy on the margin.** The investors or buyers paid only part of the purchase price in cash, usually ten percent, and borrowed the rest from the broker, using the stock as collateral. The broker borrowed money from banks and corporations to cover loans made to his investors. If the value of the stock went up, there was no

The stock market seemed to be going strong just before the crash

problem. The buyer could repay his loan with interest and gain a profit. If the stock's value went below the value of the loan, however, the buyer's margin was "called in." The speculator then had to get more cash or risk loss of the shares along with his cash investment. If the buyer could not repay his loan, the broker could take the stock.

The system satisfied many and seemed to stimulate the economy. Stock prices climbed, and in March 1928 both the volume of shares traded and their value soared. The boom lasted through the summer of 1929, although econo-

mists were baffled because both prices and business profits were falling at the same time.

International Economic Problems—In addition to economic problems such as the lack of industrial expansion, the overuse of credit, and wild speculation on land and stock, several other problems helped to bring the downfall of prosperity. Many of these involved not only the financial operations of the United States, but also those of other countries, particularly European countries.

America had lent the Allies money during World War I, and the debts and their interest amounted to over $11 billion. War-torn Europe had little cash to repay this debt. In addition, the United States had passed a high tariff on foreign goods that kept European nations from trading with America. Without profitable trade, Europe could not repay the debt. The only source of money for repayment to American creditors was the money they received from German reparations payments. Yet the Germans were also too poor to make these large payments for the war as the Treaty of Versailles had demanded. To this complex situation of international debt was added the fact that Americans began to lend Germany millions of dollars to rebuild the country, but Germany used the money to make the reparations payments. When the crash came, most of the money from these international loans was lost, and the end of American credit and prosperity threw Europe into a severe depression too.

Conditions of the Depression

Once the crash came, most Americans lost all their optimism. They saw prosperity disappear, and most had little hope that it would

516

Dangers of Credit

Explain life in America before the invention of the credit card. People discouraged debt, and loans were frowned upon. Most debts were "secured," or backed, by an item of value that the borrower would surrender in case the debt was not paid. Discuss how life has changed since then and the dangers of unsecured loans. Also discuss unwise business practices today. Banks and automobile manufacturers appeal to customers to buy on credit. Solomon warns that "the borrower is servant to the lender" (Prov. 22:7).

The War Debts Cycle

Illustrate the foreign economic crisis by drawing three arrows that form a circle. The first arrow should say *German Reparations,* pointing to *Allied War Debt,* pointing to *U.S. Loans.* The loans to Germany complete the cycle. When the depression stopped the flow of loans, all the nations in the cycle were hurt.

return very soon. Investments, money, jobs, and even homes were no longer safe.

The Run on Banks—People became increasingly afraid that the money they had deposited in banks would be lost. Some drew money out of banks to pay their brokers. Others panicked and withdrew all their money. Banks could not keep pace with the demand. In the last two weeks before Hoover left office, depositors pulled out $1 billion. Banks ran out of cash and were forced to close their doors, some permanently. Others reopened to offer depositors only a percentage of their total deposit.

Banks had unwittingly contributed to the collapse through unwise extension of credit. In September 1927 there was $1.3 billion out in loans. The same month in 1929 the total had risen to $8.5 billion. When many of these loans could not be repaid, the banks ran out of money. By 1931 about five thousand banks had closed their doors. Not all were large, but some were; the failure of the Bank of the United States in New York City affected 400,000 people.

Unemployment—Millions of Americans were thrown out of work by the depression. By 1931, thirteen million Americans, one of every four workers, were unemployed. While some workers kept their jobs, they labored only a few days a week or a few hours a day. Others who kept their jobs took wage cuts.

The loss of a man's job usually meant no steady income for his family. Even so, the family needed food. The mortgage or rent payments had to be made. Any person or business that had given credit was now beating on the

The depression caused great despair and suffering among America's poor, but conditions for families in the Dust Bowl became especially difficult.

door to receive payment. The situation seemed desperate to millions of Americans.

Wives and mothers helped out the best they could. They took in laundry and took cleaning jobs. If families had an empty room or children could double up, they took in renters. They planted gardens and canned vegetables to save on grocery bills. Clothing was patched; socks were darned. Children wore hand-me-downs. Sometimes unemployed husbands or older sons left home to search for work in another town.

Many families could not continue paying the installments on their loans. Because of

"Migrant Mother"

During the depression the state of California hired Dorothea Lange to photograph and document the conditions of migrant workers there. While working in Nipomo, California, in 1936, she saw a young migrant woman with her children. From this incident comes Lange's famous photo called "Migrant Mother," shown on this page.

Years later in the 1960 issue of *Popular Photography,* Lange recounted the incident. "I saw and approached the hungry and desperate mother, as if drawn by a magnet. I do not remember how I explained my presence or my camera to her, but I do remember she asked me no questions. I made five exposures, working closer and closer from the same direction. I did not ask her name or her history. She told me her age, that she was thirty-two. She said that they had been living on frozen vegetables from the surrounding fields, and birds that the children killed. She had just sold the tires from her car to buy food. There she sat in that lean-to tent with her children huddled around her, and seemed to know that my pictures might help her, and so she helped me. There was a sort of equality about it."

517

Guest Speaker from the Depression

Invite an elderly person to class to relate childhood experiences of the depression, or have students interview a relative or family friend (on tape or in writing).

Hoovervilles

As the depression deepened, Hoovervilles sprang up across the United States. These poverty dwellings were usually located on the outskirts of major cities, where employment opportunities and services were greater. The homes in these towns were built from anything the people could get their hands on. Tents, tar paper, box wood, cardboard, car parts, spare lumber, and scrap metal were all used as building material.

Other "Hoover" Expressions

Much of the blame for the Great Depression was placed on President Herbert Hoover. In addition to "Hoovervilles," a number of depression expressions bore his name. A "hoover wagon" was a car pulled by mules. A "hoover flag" was an empty pocket turned inside out. A "hoover blanket" was a newspaper, and a "hoover hog" was a jackrabbit or armadillo ready for eating.

Hoover-ball

One "Hoover" expression that developed was not related to the depression. White House physician Admiral Joel T. Boone developed a game called "Hoover-ball" as part of the president's fitness plan. Boone designed the game to be played in a short amount of time to fit the president's schedule and still give a good workout.

The game was played on a court and scored similar to tennis. However, the rules were more similar to those used in volleyball. Teams of 2-4 players used a six-pound medicine ball to score points. A server would throw the ball over the net, and the opponent would have to catch it and throw it back as quickly as possible. Each team would attempt to throw the ball in an area on the court where the opposite team could not catch it.

Today Hoover-ball is still played in certain areas. In Hoover's home state of Iowa, the Hoover-ball National Championship is held at the annual Hooverfest.

Soup kitchens provided many people their only meal of the day.

mortgage foreclosures, some eventually lost their homes. Some moved to abandoned boxcars or hastily built shacks on the edges of towns. Since these poverty dwellings were blamed on the president and his policies, they were called "Hoovervilles." Many who needed help were aided by others. Family members helped their relatives. Friends and churches also offered help. People helped each other, trading their skills and materials.

The depression forced most Americans to lower their living standards. For many the depression destroyed their sense of independence and accomplishment. It was difficult, especially for a family's primary breadwinner, to be unemployed, unable to support his own family. Some men searched for work in vain and then waited for handouts at soup kitchens or stood in bread lines. Sometimes they gleaned fields, scavenged city dumps, or searched for food in garbage cans. It was not uncommon to see once-prosperous men selling apples on the street corner. A few men tried to escape from their troubles by jumping on freight trains to ride the rails as hobos.

The depression forced some Americans to reexamine their values. They found they could live on less. For Christians the depression offered many opportunities to trust the Lord in new ways. They continually saw God's provision for His people as He supplied their needs. They saw anew the truth of Psalm 37:25: "I have been young, and now am old; yet have I not seen the righteous forsaken, nor his seed begging bread." Yet during this economic depression, there was no significant major religious revival. Many Americans, when hard

How Would Your Life Change?

Have the students discuss ways their life would change if another depression struck. Why are they not willing to implement these money-saving changes now?

If someone's family already saves money in interesting ways, ask him or her to share examples.

"I Remember the Drought"

The droughts of the 1930s created desperate conditions for farmers. One victim of the droughts recalled his family's situation:

"I know from experience what it means to have no rain. For three years in the thirties we had very, very little rain. There was no pasture for the cows on our dairy farm. My dad chopped down trees so the cows could eat leaves all summer. They would bellow when they heard Dad chopping. We had to make leaf haystacks, which the cows ate in the winter. The grass was so thin Mother used a hand rake and a gunnysack to pick up the hay. The winds blew every day, day after day. The grasshoppers were the only ones who were happy and multiplied easily. They skinned the thistles to live. We poisoned them at every turn. . . . To this day, I still conserve [water] and feel that it's almost a sin to use too much of it because you just don't know when it might be scarce again."

pressed, turned not to God but to the government.

Further Farm Problems—Few farmers had been prosperous, even in the booming 1920s. They produced so much grain, livestock, and other farm products that prices had stayed low. Many farmers could not make payments on farmland they had bought or on the cars, equipment, and other items that they had bought on credit. Without higher prices for their products, many were in danger of losing their farms.

Conditions for farmers became even worse, especially on the western edge of the Central Plains and on the Great Plains, where the **"Dust Bowl"** brought extreme poverty. This area, already semiarid, had first been overgrazed by cattle. Then with the increased demand for food during World War I, it had been plowed into farms. Since there had been enough rainfall then, farmers were able to make money. But in the 1930s droughts came,

Dust clouds blocked out the sun for miles

519

Rail Hoboes

During the depression thousands of people traveled across the United States hidden in or on top of railcars. Most were young men, but young women and even whole families used the rails too.

Each hobo had his own reason for riding the rails. The majority of them were out of work and just trying to survive. Sometimes families who were unable to support all of their children would send the older ones out on their own. For those turned out, the rails were the best way to travel and search for work. Others simply traveled for the taste of adventure. Now known as "yuppie hoboes," these young people may have even come from wealthy families.

At the end of the depression, some hoboes went home; others continued life on the rails. Some went on to be famous. Louis L'Amour (author), H. L. Hunt (oil billionaire), William O. Douglas (Supreme Court justice), and Art Linkletter (television personality) were all hoboes for a time.

Dust Storms

The dust storms that swept through the American plains during the depression were both natural and manmade disasters. Soil erosion occurs naturally from the winds, but the farmers sped up the process. The wheat they grew replaced the grass of the plains, which anchored the soil. When droughts came, the soil hardened, crumbled, and blew away in the wind.

The walls of dust sometimes reached heights of two miles and widths of one hundred miles. Wind carried the dust at speeds of up to fifty miles per hour. When the dust clouds swept over, the sun was blotted out and houses and cars were covered. The temperature would drop as much as forty degrees, and the air would be thick with static electricity. People would get shocked if they touched anything metal.

Some storms carried dust so far that it reached cities on the East

Coast. Even ships as far as three hundred miles from the coast sometimes got dusted.

Bonus Army

When the "Bonus Army" first arrived in Washington, the police were in charge of the situation. Police Superintendent Pelham D. Glassford actually helped provide aid for the 20,000-plus demonstrating and allowed some of them to stay in vacant government buildings around the capitol. However, as the protest wore on, the army played a more important role. The general directing their operations would eventually play major roles in World War II and the Korean War—Douglas MacArthur.

The Bonus Army incident turned out to be a rough spot in MacArthur's outstanding career. One story claims that the veterans were evicted by MacArthur's troops as the general rode down Pennsylvania Avenue in his best uniform and on a white horse. While the horse story has since been disproved, MacArthur's actions are still questioned.

One major question was whether MacArthur disobeyed an order from President Hoover. Hoover sent a message telling MacArthur to keep his troops from entering the main veteran camp until the women and children had been removed. However, the debate is whether the general actually received the note. His executive assistant, Brigadier General Moseley, claimed that he did, but three other witnesses denied it.

Whatever the case, MacArthur did not apologize for his actions. He believed they were necessary to prevent a possible overthrow of government led by Communists in the country. While Communism had grown in popularity in the depression, few in the Bonus Army were connected with it. In fact, the other veterans harassed two hundred Communists who posed as veterans.

adding to the farmers' economic woes. First the crops dried up. Next the land turned to dust. Then winds whipped the rich topsoil off the dry exposed ground. By late fall of 1933, "black blizzards" blew from west to east across the country. The clouds of dust darkened skies as far away as Albany, New York. By 1934 the lands from Texas to Canada were ravaged by the dust storms. The soil drifted into banks like snow. Cars had to use their headlights in the daytime. Families put wet towels in window sills and under doors to keep out the choking dust. Livestock died of thirst. Thousands of farm families fled from their homes. Some went to areas, especially in

During the depression Herbert Hoover tried to be optimistic about the prospects for the American economy and people.

California, where farm workers were needed to tend vegetable fields and orchards.

Hoover's Plight

President Herbert Hoover tried to deal with the onset of the depression by being optimistic. The more people panicked, the more damage was done to the economy, and so he tried to encourage Americans to believe that these trials would soon pass and business would boom again. Few people seemed to listen. Stock prices continued to fall as investors tried to sell. Runs on banks continued, and industry remained inactive. Although Hoover was not responsible for the problems that beset America, he was the president, and thus he received most of the blame for everything that was going wrong.

The Veterans Demand Aid—The veterans of World War I had been promised a life insurance bonus to be paid in 1945. Although the veterans were no worse off than most other Americans in the depression, many began to ask for the government to pay them part of the face value of their insurance policies at an earlier date. In the spring of 1932, Walter Waters, an unemployed veteran from Oregon, journeyed east to the capital to pressure Congress to pay the "bonus." Soon men from all parts of the country joined him. About 20,000 veterans became a part of this "Bonus Army" and camped on a low-lying muddy area near the Potomac River. The men were there most of the summer. When the Senate defeated the Bonus Bill, many veterans left, but a few thousand remained. Hoover refused to meet with them, but he did ask Congress to advance them money from their insurance policies so they could get home. They were told that any who were left after July 28 would be evicted. At this point radicals in the group tried to start a riot. After two policemen were beaten to the ground, two Bonus marchers were killed. Hoover then opted to use troops, and the soldiers routed the veterans and set fire to their shacks. Although stern action was needed, Hoover received much criticism for treating the veterans harshly.

Hoover's Theory—The President was not insensitive to how the depression was affecting Americans. He believed first in "local responsibility. The best hearts and brains of every community could best serve their neighbors." He believed that creating government agencies to handle the problems would give the sufferers more red tape than relief. His position was that federal funds should be used only after all voluntary and local resources were exhausted.

When federal monies were used, Hoover believed they needed to be carefully regulated. They should not be given directly to people as a **dole,** or handout, such as welfare is today. Instead, they should be used for projects so that the effects of the funds would benefit more people. If cities and states, for example, were given loans to pay for public works projects, they could hire local people who would benefit from the employment.

Hoover did not believe in government regulation of big business. He saw federal control of activities as an invitation to dictatorship, corruption, waste, and inefficiency. He defended personal freedoms against government encroachment. He greatly feared socialism. He also wanted to keep the federal budget balanced, so he was reluctant to spend large amounts of money for aid programs.

Hoover's ideas were basically good, but he soon met opposition. Sound though his policies might have been, they required both time and the cooperation of the people to bring the desired results. Many Americans saw only their immediate hardships and wanted relief right away. When the president's ideas brought no quick remedy, many Americans began to complain.

Franklin Delano Roosevelt won votes with his enthusiasm and "New Deal"

Hoover did try to establish programs to help the people. He set up some government work projects to employ thousands of men and supply useful work. Public buildings were constructed, and in 1931 construction was started on what became Hoover Dam on the Colorado River. The federal government also subsidized the building of thousands of miles of roads.

In January of 1932, Congress passed Hoover's bill creating the **Reconstruction Finance Corporation.** It could lend up to $2 billion to businesses, industries, and banks to undertake projects that would employ more men. Therefore, there would be less need for

Hoover Dam "High Scalers"

One of the most dangerous jobs in building Hoover Dam was clearing the canyon walls of loose rocks. From ropes secured on top of the canyon, men called high scalers risked their lives to do this job. The men working below were in danger of being killed by falling rocks unless the debris was removed. Even pebbles could become deadly when falling from hundreds of feet up.

Ropes were secured on the top of the canyon and extended down the side. At the end of one rope, a chair like that on a swing was attached for a man to sit in. The high scaler was attached to another rope that he could rappel down when his work was done. Once he was in position on his chair, a jackhammer was lowered to the high scaler.

High scalers had to be agile climbers and unafraid of working at high altitudes. Many were former sailors or circus performers. Although their pay was 40 percent higher than that of most workers, their job was more risky. High scalers had to maneuver around a network of ropes, air hoses, and electrical lines hanging around them. Often they worked above each other, so they needed head protection to protect from rocks and dropped tools. Those who had hard hats wore them. Others improvised by dipping their soft hats in tar and letting it harden.

On occasion, high scalers would swing on their ropes, performing aerial acrobatics for the other workers. In one instance, however, acrobatic skills were a matter of necessity. An engineer who had been inspecting the work on the canyon wall slipped and began to fall. Oliver Cowan, a high scaler working below him, heard the man's cry, swung out on his rope, and caught the engineer's leg. Another high scaler soon arrived to help raise the stunned man back to safety.

It's Hard Being a Conservative

Ask the students to answer the question "Why is it easier for progressives/liberals to win the support of voters than it is for conservatives?" Men such as Roosevelt promised to use government money to solve people's problems, but Hoover and other conservatives argued that the job of the American republic is to give individuals the liberty to solve their own problems.

Students need to recognize the tension between security and liberty. The government can provide one or the other but not both. In times of crisis, human nature seeks security at the expense of liberty. The Founding Fathers placed restraints on human nature's tendency to overreact in a crisis. Students need to be prepared for this danger when new crises arise in the nation.

Discuss how liberal and conservative politicians present their arguments in modern debates. What "crises" are liberals using to appeal for more government programs at the expense of liberty? Why are their arguments so appealing? *(fairness, equality, safety, compassion)* What are some of the most powerful appeals conservatives make? *(liberty, individualism, pride, tradition)*

Objectives

Students should be able to
1. Describe the circumstances of FDR's election to the presidency.
2. Explain ways Roosevelt obtained support for his New Deal programs.
3. List several of the New Deal programs and their purposes.

Assassination Attempt

Roosevelt was the first and last president to be elected to a fourth term in office. However, if it were not for an alert spectator, he might have been remembered for not even beginning his first one. Shortly before his inauguration, the president-elect traveled to Miami, Florida. After a cruise on Vincent Astor's yacht on February 15, Roosevelt was driven through Bay Front Park as part of a parade.

At one point, the car stopped, and Roosevelt sat up on the back seat to give a speech. At that moment a man named Giuseppe Zangara fired a 32. caliber pistol from the crowd. The target was Roosevelt, but none of the five shots hit him. Zangara, who was only five feet tall, had fired while standing on a box. A woman nearby pushed him when she realized what was happening.

The bullets hit four bystanders and the mayor of Chicago, Anton Cermak, who was riding with Roosevelt. Cermak was hit in the abdomen and fell from the car. He was quickly helped back in and rushed to the hospital. Nearly three weeks later, Cermak died of his wound.

Zangara, who had been arrested, was convicted of the murder and sentenced to death. On March 21 he went to the electric chair and was executed. He took to the grave the real reason for the assassination attempt. No strong motive was ever determined.

direct relief. Congress also approved the president's request for twelve Federal District Home Loans Banks. These banks could lend money to loan associations, banks, and insurance companies, who in turn could aid homeowners who were having trouble making mortgage payments.

Despite these actions, Hoover continued to receive criticism. The steps he took were not dramatic enough to satisfy the many Americans who were still waiting for help.

SECTION REVIEW

1. What were four specific causes of the financial crisis?
2. What does it mean to "buy on the margin"?
3. What were "Hoovervilles"?
4. What natural disaster hit farmers on the plains?
5. Why did the "Bonus Army" travel to Washington, D.C.?

 How did Herbert Hoover want to handle the nation's financial problems?

FDR and the New Deal

While Hoover was reluctant to take dramatic action, discontent grew. Because many Americans continued to blame Hoover and the Republicans for the problems of the depression, the Democrats gained followers.

The Election of 1932

The election of 1932 was one of the most decisive in American history. The Republicans renominated Herbert Hoover. The Democrats chose New York's governor, **Franklin Delano Roosevelt,** and John Nance Garner of Texas as his running mate. Some Americans believed that the regular parties were not solving America's problems, so they turned to radical leaders. The Socialist party nominated Norman Thomas, and the Communists ran William Foster.

The President's Polio

Even though President Roosevelt had a disability, he did not let it interfere with his political aspirations. Stricken with polio in 1921 at the age of thirty-nine, Roosevelt was permanently paralyzed from the hips down. To most people that would have signaled the end of any political career. To Franklin Delano Roosevelt it was just another obstacle to push aside on his way to the highest office in the land.

It was not always easy. Roosevelt had to use metal braces just to stand. In order to minimize the effect of his disability on the public, Roosevelt refused to be seen in his wheelchair. He had to be helped to "walk" up to the podiums to give his speeches. One time the podium had not been fastened down, and it and the president went tumbling off the platform into the orchestra pit. Returning to the reset stand, Roosevelt simply picked up his speech right where he had left off. For traveling, he had a railroad car with a special elevator and a special wheelchair.

Roosevelt's condition also gave him a special burden for the similarly disabled. He was constantly visiting the hospitals and working with disabled children or soldiers. He had a car designed with hand controls, and often he would take a particularly discouraged child for a ride and talk. Always the child returned with a positive attitude and a desire to go on. Roosevelt also invested heavily in a treatment center at Warm Springs, Georgia. The springs there had a therapeutic effect on those who used them.

Whatever one's view of Roosevelt's political philosophy, his courage and perseverance in confronting his physical limitations must be admired and applauded.

Roosevelt campaigned with buoyant enthusiasm and confidence. He favored programs that were very costly, while promising to cut government spending by twenty-five percent. He promised the voters a **"New Deal,"** and many were drawn to him because

---

Section Review Answers

1. industrial problems, overuse of credit, speculation, and international economic problems (pp. 515-16)
2. to purchase stock by paying part of the price in cash and borrowing the rest from the stock broker, using the stock as collateral (p. 516)
3. areas of shacks that became the dwellings of the poor and homeless (p. 518)
4. the "Dust Bowl" (p. 519)

5. to seek early payment of a life insurance bonus that had been promised to them (p. 520)

 He preferred that local and volunteer organizations provide relief. Where he did intervene, it was to give money to businesses or state and local governments that could, in turn, create jobs and loans for the public. (p. 521)

SECTION 2

Materials

• No materials

 Pages from U.S. History

Discuss excerpts from Roosevelt's famous First Inaugural Address, included on page 474.

The First Modern Politician

Ask the students to reread the descriptions of President Roosevelt and list ways that he set the precedent for a "modern politician," who wins public favor by any means possible. *(hid his infirmity so that he would look good in front of cameras, publicly helped needy children, promised to cut spending but also favored costly programs, promised*

he gave hope for strong actions that might bring change.

Hoover praised "rugged individualism" and encouraged voluntary efforts by industry and labor to deal with their problems. Although Hoover also pledged more government action than before, by the fall of 1932 millions of voters were convinced that Hoover's way would not work. Roosevelt carried forty-two of the forty-eight states to become the new president.

Putting the New Deal into Action

Franklin D. Roosevelt brought optimism to a depressed nation when he took office March 4, 1933. With confident voice he asserted, "This great nation will endure as it has endured, will revive and will prosper. . . . The only thing we have to fear is fear itself. . . . We do not distrust the future of essential democracy. The people of the United States have not failed. In their need they have registered a mandate that they want direct, vigorous action."

Roosevelt and his advisors, a **"Brain Trust"** of college professors (most of whom were from Columbia University), were ready to take that "vigorous action." The president began by proclaiming a **bank holiday,** closing banks temporarily, to stabilize banking. Next he called Congress into special session to deal with the crisis and to put his policies into effect. Then he went on the radio for the first of his many "fireside chats" to the nation. A good public speaker with an understanding of people, Roosevelt radiated warmth, even on the radio. He made extensive use of press conferences, seeking to make the press his allies. As allies they could sway lagging public opinion to rally support for his ideas. Soon there appeared a long line of legislation and programs that would be FDR's New Deal.

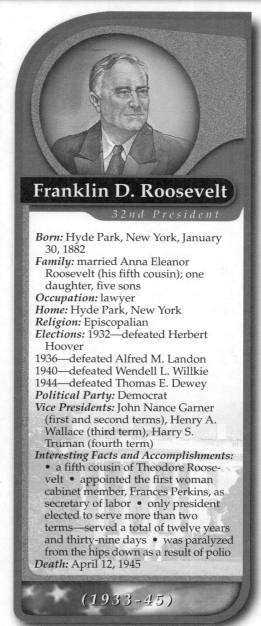

Franklin D. Roosevelt
32nd President

Born: Hyde Park, New York, January 30, 1882
Family: married Anna Eleanor Roosevelt (his fifth cousin); one daughter, five sons
Occupation: lawyer
Home: Hyde Park, New York
Religion: Episcopalian
Elections: 1932—defeated Herbert Hoover
1936—defeated Alfred M. Landon
1940—defeated Wendell L. Willkie
1944—defeated Thomas E. Dewey
Political Party: Democrat
Vice Presidents: John Nance Garner (first and second terms), Henry A. Wallace (third term), Harry S. Truman (fourth term)
Interesting Facts and Accomplishments:
• a fifth cousin of Theodore Roosevelt • appointed the first woman cabinet member, Frances Perkins, as secretary of labor • only president elected to serve more than two terms—served a total of twelve years and thirty-nine days • was paralyzed from the hips down as a result of polio
Death: April 12, 1945

(1933-45)

523

Fireside Chats

Shortly after taking office in March of 1933, President Franklin D. Roosevelt addressed the nation in his first radio "fireside chat." Roosevelt was already familiar with using the radio. As governor of New York, he made radio speeches two or three times a month, but now he had a much larger audience.

Roosevelt made his speeches very candid. He believed that if he was going to be reaching people in their living rooms and kitchen, he should speak to them as a neighbor. He chose simple words and phrases that the majority of American people would understand, and he made sure the talks were not too long.

Each fireside chat was carefully crafted. Roosevelt would meet with a team of professional speechwriters and dictate a rough draft of what he wanted. From there the team would set to work refining the speech and presenting it back to the president. Some chats went through as many as twelve revisions before they were given. Even then Roosevelt rarely read them word for word. He would ad lib phrases that came to him in the moment of delivery.

The term *fireside chat* was coined by CBS reporter Hally Butcher just before Roosevelt's second radio address. Other reporters soon began to use the term, and eventually so did Roosevelt. His first thirteen chats dealt mostly with the depression crisis. Roosevelt used his speeches to explain and justify the New Deal to Americans. Soon, however, the chats turned to international issues. Roosevelt explained World War II and the part America would play in it.

By the time of his last address on January 6, 1945, Americans were familiar with the sound of Roosevelt's voice and his opening words: "My friends."

---

vigorous action, developed a memorable theme—a New Deal, used his abilities as a good public speaker in fireside chats, sought to make the press his ally)

Make comparisons with a modern politician, such as Bill Clinton. Explain to the students that politicians are big imitators. They carefully study the lives and works of winners to find the "secrets" to their success. Discuss any recent trends in politics that are considered secrets to success, such as town hall meetings, focus groups, and websites.

Make a Time Line of FDR

Make a vertical time line of the life of FDR with the dates going up the middle. On one side place events from the president's personal life and on the other place national events.

Dangers of National Debt

Discuss the founders' opposition to national debt. Is it ever fair for one generation to borrow from the next generation for its own benefit? In other words, is it right that teenagers today should pay interest on debts that previous generations have accu-

mulated in the spending spree from the 1960s through the 1990s?

In 1938 Congress replaced the AAA with the Soil Conservation and Domestic Allotment Act. With this legislation, farmers were to be paid government money not for withdrawing lands from production but for practicing soil conservation. A second AAA retained the soil conservation features while allowing the secretary of agriculture to regulate by quotas the amount of crops producers could sell. Those exceeding their quotas were fined.

Early New Deal Legislation—Congress, realizing that the American people wanted the action that Roosevelt promised, became a "rubber stamp," approving almost anything the president proposed. In the first one hundred days, legislation for New Deal programs moved quickly.

As soon as Congress convened after Roosevelt's inauguration, it passed the Emergency Banking Act. This act suspended all banking activity, creating a bank holiday until banks could restabilize. The Treasury Department had the power to decide which banks were sound enough to reopen. Half of the banks, holding ninety percent of all banking resources, were back in operation by March 15. Only about one bank in twenty never reopened. When the banks reopened three weeks later, confidence returned and more than $1 billion was redeposited.

In May 1933 Congress also approved Roosevelt's creation of the Federal Emergency Relief Administration (FERA). This temporary agency (later replaced by the WPA, or Works Progress Administration) had $500 million in federal money to disburse. The agency provided funds for the states to use for relief needs. The money was to be channeled into work relief where possible so that the recipients would work for their pay. However, because the immediate need seemed so great, more of it went out as direct relief (doles) than as work relief.

Congress founded the Home Owners' Loan Corporation in June of 1933. This agency bought mortgages from holders and rewrote them on easier payment schedules. By 1936 one-fifth of all mortgaged nonfarm homes had mortgages under this agency. It was one of the most popular of the New Deal relief acts.

While the general public got relief through FERA and the Home Owners' Loan

Corporation, special efforts were made to help farmers. The Farm Credit Administration (FCA) refinanced mortgages for farmers who would have lost their lands. The government also hoped to restore the farmers' purchasing power through the **Agriculture Adjustment Act** (AAA). To raise farm prices, farmers were asked to cut production. Rather than sell their products at a loss, the farmers were told to destroy crops. In 1933 they were asked to plow under between one-quarter and one-half of their crop. Milk was poured into ditches; grain was burned; cattle, sheep, and hogs were killed. Cotton and wool were stored in warehouses and held off the market until greater need would raise the prices.

Ironically, while this was being done, many Americans were hungry or in need of clothing. Yet the action seemed to offer hope to the farmers because they were being paid to cooperate with the plan. The act allowed the government to pay farmers for not producing crops. The government also bought surplus crops that it planned to store and sell when prices were higher. Farm income did go up about fifty percent over the next two years.

Despite the AAA's immediate benefits for the farmers, it was soon attacked. When the policies forced farm prices up, consumers had to pay more for their goods. Moreover, the subsidies for not producing were given to landowners. In the South, where sharecropping was used, the landowners were not the ones who actually farmed the land. The sharecropper who had labored on the land did not receive any benefits. In fact, he often lost money because he had to cut his production. Meanwhile the landlord received all the monetary gain.

In 1936 the Supreme Court nullified the AAA, but a dangerous precedent had already been set. Many farmers became dependent upon government subsidies. Farmers would

Rule by the Wise Few

Ask the students to discuss how some of the Founding Fathers might have responded to Roosevelt's administration if they had been alive at the time. Note Jefferson's charges against George III and ask whether the same charges could have been made against Roosevelt: "He has erected a multitude of new offices, and sent hither swarms of officers to harass our people and eat out their substance." How might Roosevelt and his "Brain Trust" have defended themselves? *(Times have changed; the emergency calls for emergency measures. Note that this at-*

titude is consistent with progressivism's acceptance of the "evolution" of society and government. We still hear these arguments today.)

Ask the students whether the American people of our day would accept rule by a "Brain Trust," proposing dozens of new laws to regulate life in America. *(The answer is surely no, and students need to recognize how shocking Roosevelt's power was.)* Discuss how the modern government bureaucracy, consisting of nearly three million Americans, makes rules to govern the lives of citizens. This unelected bureau-

cracy is even more powerful than Roosevelt's Brain Trust, and it did not exist before the New Deal.

Ask students whether Americans could ever return to the small government of the 1920s. Even if Americans could return, should they? *(If Americans want to return to the principles on which the nation was founded, they must make what appear to be "radical" changes in order to undo the radical changes introduced in the 1930s.)*

This political cartoon shows Uncle Sam's approval of the cooperation between labor and management under the NRA.

soon regain those subsidies and agricultural regulation, and they would protect them. Such policies require tremendous government expense while they artificially control the industry. Other New Deal programs would similarly hamper other industries from adjusting to the market demands.

The **National Recovery Administration** (NRA) was designed to help businesses recover from the effects of the depression. The logic behind the act was to eliminate "wasteful competition" among firms. Codes were written and given to businesses. Each company was assigned a share of the national market and given annual production quotas. The codes also set maximum hours to be worked and minimum wages. An additional provision required a company to recognize a union if the majority of the employees wished to form one. Each firm or business that complied with the NRA codes was allowed to display the NRA's Blue Eagle seal. Rather than clutching arrows in its talons as on the Great Seal, this eagle clutched lightning bolts and a gearwheel. The NRA was soon criticized as a violation of the free enterprise system. Big businesses seemed to be favored over smaller ones, and the consumer was caught in the middle when prices

Relief, Recovery, and Reform

Carefully explain the three phases of Roosevelt's program: relief, recovery, and reform. Draw a chart and ask the students to put each program under the appropriate heading. Note that the programs often had overlapping purposes. Discuss which programs met their immediate objectives (+), which were declared unconstitutional (!), and which still exist (*). Mark each with the appropriate symbol on the chart.

The names of all the programs are not important, but the precedents they set are very

Relief	Recovery	Reform
Civilian Conservation Corps (CCC)	bank holiday	TVA+*
Federal Emergency Relief Act (FERA)!	Emergency Banking Act	Banking Reform Act that created the FDIC*
Agriculture Adjustment Act (AAA)+!	end of the gold standard	Securities and Exchange Commission*
Home Owners' Loan Corporation*	National Recovery Administration (NRA)!	National Labor Relations Act
Works Progress Administration		Social Security*
		(Wagner) National Labor Relations Act
		Fair Labor Standards Act

important. Students need to be able to use these old programs as illustrations when they face debates about new programs, such as Head Start and AmeriCorps. So many government activities that students take for granted—federal aid to farmers, summer jobs for young people, government-assisted home loans, government-run utilities, the FDIC, child labor laws, and minimum wages—were once controversial.

Crash and Depression   525

went up. The Supreme Court declared the NRA unconstitutional in 1935.

Another law established the **Civilian Conservation Corps.** This act gave unemployed young men jobs and at the same time conserved natural resources. In the seven years of its existence, the CCC employed two and a half million young men.

In May 1933 Congress also established permanent New Deal agencies with long-range as well as immediate goals. The **Tennessee Valley Authority** (TVA) involved seven southeastern states. The agency provided public power projects on the Tennessee River. The thirty multipurpose dams produced and sold electric power, controlled floods, eased erosion, manufactured fertilizer, and created recreation areas. Because it involved the federal government in areas where it had never been involved before and put the government in the position of competing with private companies, the act was controversial.

Further Action—Americans were generally pleased that the new president was taking firm actions to deal with the depression. When one measure did not work, Roosevelt quickly tried another one. The actions, however, were not bringing a real economic recovery to the nation, and millions were still in need. Roosevelt continued to experiment with new programs that he hoped would solve some of the problems. In 1935 he launched the Works Progress Administration (WPA). This agency put more people to work on construction projects. WPA workers built hospitals, schools, parks, playgrounds, and airports.

Eventually the WPA was extended to other areas, including the arts. Actors, actresses, and directors were employed to put on programs. Authors were hired under the Federal Writers' Project to write historical and geographical guides for the forty-eight states. Artists were hired under a Federal Art Project.

The Cees Get Passing Grades

They planted over two billion trees and spent 6.5 million man-hours fighting forest fires. They built over 420,000 dams, fixed up old parks and built new ones, and built or improved miles of trails and access roads. They made thirty dollars a week, twenty-five of which was sent home to help support their families. "They" were the *Cees,* the young men who worked for the Civilian Conservation Corps.

There were over two and one-half million jobless youths hired by the Civilian Conservation Corps. The CCC was the most popular New Deal program; even the Republicans praised it. It was the first relief agency to go into action. Some have called the Cees "The Tree Army," and others, "The Soil Soldiers." The program lasted from 1933 until World War II, when most of the young men were called into the armed forces.

The camps for the Cees were directed by army officers. Extracurricular activities were usually oriented toward sports, particularly boxing. Rising time was 5:45 A.M. and taps was at 10:00 P.M. The food had the flavor of Army meals with lots of potatoes and bologna. For most of the men, the times spent in the Cees were rewarding, and for some it was character building. Hard outdoor work kept them busy. The conservation emphasis gave meaning to their efforts. The money sent home to help their families gave them a purpose. It is easy to see why the Civilian Conservation Corps received the most praise of any of Roosevelt's programs.

Students need to ask themselves whether these programs were wise and should be continued.

Red Flag: TVA

The student text says TVA was "controversial," but most Americans take it for granted today. Ask the students why it was controversial. *(It was a socialistic program on a grand scale.)* Discuss the alternatives to government-run utilities. Note that several conservatives have called for the privatization of TVA.

Discuss the fundamental question of whether the federal government should use tax money to provide services for those who live in inaccessible places where electricity and other benefits are expensive to implement.

A recent example of this debate occurred during the 1990s when Al Gore argued that the federal government had an obligation to build a cable network to every community in the nation. He claimed that every American had a right to access the "information superhighway." But this so-called right would have cost as much as $200 billion, and it raised the question of whether rural people had a "right" to the tax money of others so that they could enjoy the same benefits as city-dwellers. Private companies eventually built the new Internet links, without the waste and inefficiency the government program would have entailed.

Unions and Freedom of Assembly

The Constitution guarantees freedom of assembly to groups such as labor unions. So why was the National Recovery Administration (NRA) declared unconstitutional, and why did conservatives oppose the

They painted murals in public buildings such as post offices. The National Youth Administration (NYA) helped young people. High school and college students were hired for part-time jobs that enabled them to stay in school. Together the WPA and NYA provided jobs for almost five million Americans.

Even though Roosevelt took many daring actions, some New Deal critics believed that the president was not doing enough to relieve the poverty of many Americans. Some suggested radical plans to distribute wealth and won many supporters. One such critic was Dr. Elmer Townsend, a retired California medical doctor who designed a plan to help the elderly. His plan required the government to pay each person over sixty a $200-a-month pension. The money for the pensions would come from a national sales tax. To receive pensions, retirees would have to agree to spend every cent each month. He thought such spending would pump up the economy.

Another radical plan was proposed by Huey Long, a masterful politician from Louisiana. He suggested taxing large incomes heavily to provide a minimum income for the poor. Another popular speaker with a plan was Father Charles Coughlin, a Detroit priest who had a nationwide radio broadcast. He suggested government-stimulated inflation, government takeover of certain industries, and a guaranteed living wage for laborers. He also wanted to overhaul the currency system and abolish the Federal Reserve System for regulating the nation's banks. Most of the ideas of these critics were even more socialistic than Roosevelt's programs, and they would have led the government deeper into debt. They also would have discouraged people from working for their money.

Roosevelt countered these ideas with a government-sponsored insurance plan. It offered smaller monthly pensions by giving federal aid to the states for the elderly as well as funds for unemployment insurance, aid to dependent children, and public health programs. The old age insurance, commonly called **Social Security** today, was only a part of the program. The program was to be financed by a federal tax on wages (one percent in 1935) paid by both employer and employee.

Roosevelt supported the National Labor Relations Act of 1935, also called the Wagner Act. With it he tried to salvage some of the benefits labor had been offered under the now-outlawed NRA. This act encouraged the growth of labor unions. The largest labor union, the American Federation of Labor, now faced competition from another union, the Congress of Industrial Organizations. Formed in 1935, this union boasted a membership of 3.7 million within two years. Other regulations intended to help workers came with the Fair Labor Standards Act in 1938. It established the nation's first legal minimum wage and maximum hours for workers producing goods that crossed state lines. The wage was twenty-five cents per hour, and the workweek was to be forty-four hours. The act also forbade children under sixteen from working in most industries.

SECTION REVIEW

1. Who were the presidential candidates in 1932?

2. What New Deal provisions were made for the nation's farmers?

3. How did the Works Progress Administration and the National Youth Administration provide relief for Americans?

4. What did the old age insurance come to be called?

 How did Franklin Roosevelt seek to gain America's confidence?

Minimum Wage

Ever since the Fair Labor Standards Act established the minimum wage in 1938, the level has increased throughout the years. The following chart represents this gradual change.

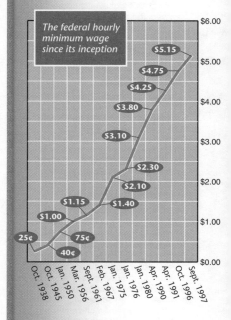

The federal hourly minimum wage since its inception

(Wagner) Labor Relations Act? The Constitution allows people to join organizations, but it does not allow the federal government to grant special privileges to select organizations. Such favoritism limits the freedom of individuals and the freedom of opposing organizations. If a businessman or laborer dislikes a labor union, he should be free to speak out against it and to cut off all relations with it. Roosevelt's labor laws violated the freedom of businessmen to run their businesses as they chose. Many conservatives have argued that labor unions should be free to form, but they must earn political clout by attracting voluntary supporters.

Section Review Answers

1. Herbert Hoover, Franklin Delano Roosevelt, Norman Thomas, and William Foster (p. 522)

2. The Farm Credit Administration refinanced their mortgages to help them keep their farms, and the Agriculture Adjustment Act tried to control farm production to raise prices. (p. 524)

3. by providing them with jobs (pp. 526-27)

4. Social Security (p. 527)

 He met Americans' demand for action with the introduction of many recovery measures. He sought to win the press over to his side through press conferences, and he also went directly to the American people with his radio "fireside chats." (p. 523)

Eleanor Roosevelt

Only two Roosevelts have held the office of president, but a third one has also played an important role in the public arena. Eleanor Roosevelt made a major contribution to her husband's longevity in the White House. She traveled across the United States promoting the New Deal. In 1933 alone, she covered forty thousand miles.

Jesse Owens: 1936 Olympics

In May of 1931, the International Olympic Committee awarded the 1936 summer Olympics to Germany. The United States and several other nations considered boycotting the games because of Nazi Germany's racial practices and belief in the superiority of the Aryan race. German citizens who were Jewish or members of other minorities were unable to participate in the games. In the years leading up to the games, the German sports program focused on demonstrating the superiority of the Aryan race.

While several American Jews did boycott the games, the United States sent an official team. Among the members was a black athlete named Jesse Owens. Owens and several other athletes delivered a strong blow to the Nazi beliefs. Owens captured four gold medals, a feat that would not be matched until 1984 by Carl Lewis. Besides winning the 100-meter, 200-meter, and 4x100 relay, Owens set an Olympic record in his long jump victory.

A story has persisted that Hitler refused to congratulate Owens on

Opposition to the New Deal

Although Roosevelt had gained office with a large popular vote, there were many who opposed him. Liberals and leftists opposed him because they did not think that his New Deal policies had gone far enough. They believed that the New Deal needed to be more socialistic, providing for government ownership of certain industries or providing people with income at government's expense.

Conservatives also voiced their opposition. Under Roosevelt's New Deal, the government had gained control in areas previously left to private interests. Conservatives distrusted such governmental control and feared the extension of the government's power into more areas. The New Deal was giving the federal government wide powers over industry and commerce, areas that were not government's rightful sphere. Roosevelt's agencies were replacing the free enterprises of capitalism with the government regulations of socialism. Federal powers gained during the crisis of the depression would never be curbed in the decades to come. The Supreme Court decisions in 1935 and 1936 outlawing several New Deal measures and agencies fueled the conservative opposition and reflected its thinking.

The Election of 1936

The New Deal president faced a political test in the 1936 election. A group called the American Liberty League unsuccessfully sought to block the president's renomination. The Democrats, however, chose Roosevelt on the first ballot. The party platform praised the New Deal and promised similar additional reforms.

During his first term Roosevelt had been working to change the Democratic Party's image. Until 1935 he had urged business, agriculture, bankers, and workers to settle conflicts among themselves. But in 1935 he began using the government's power to alter the bal-

ance between employees and employers, and between the rich and the middle class or poor. He tried to identify the Democratic Party with the underprivileged. Blacks, urban immigrants, and workers tended to join the Democratic Party from this time on.

Although Roosevelt had refused to support both civil rights regulations and an anti-lynching law in 1936, blacks still voted for him. The depression hit the poor especially hard. Poor blacks and whites were particularly grateful for the New Deal's financial relief. Many blacks believed that the Roosevelt's programs had saved them from starvation. The public works projects offered blacks employment at equal wages with whites (although they were not allowed to work with whites). Such policies landed FDR seventy-five percent of the black vote in 1936.

The Republicans had lost heavily in the congressional elections in 1932 and 1934. Because they lacked a leader and a program to attract voters, a 1936 win looked impossible as well. The Republicans ran Alfred M.

FDR's policies that helped blacks brought him seventy-five percent of the black vote in 1936.

SECTION 3

Materials

• Activities B, C, and D from Chapter 25 of the *Student Activities* manual

Student Activity B: Evaluating the New Deal

This prewriting activity covers one of the most controversial, momentous periods in U.S. history. It is similar to the History Skills activity on Reconstruction in the student text, page 381.

 Viewpoints on the New Deal

Divide the class into groups representing various perspectives on the New Deal—poor farmers, poor labor, middle class workers, and business owners. Choose one student to represent each of the main nominees for president in 1936. Have each candidate come up with a theme for his campaign and list three main reasons he should be elected (or his opponent rejected). If the candidates are wise, they will seek reasons that appeal to a majority of voters. Then read each reason and have the different groups vote on whether they

would support it. Students should see the difficulty that the Republican nominee faced.

President Roosevelt and his wife, Eleanor.

Declining Popularity of the New Deal

Roosevelt's strong win and congressional support encouraged him to challenge the make-up of the Supreme Court. Because it had struck down several New Deal measures, FDR became more and more critical of the court's conservative nature.

In February 1937 he presented a plan to "pack" the Supreme Court with new justices. He hoped that adding to the number of justices would protect his New Deal measures. Roosevelt requested that the number of justices be increased from nine to as many as fifteen. Each time a justice reached seventy and did not retire, FDR wanted to appoint a new justice. This court-packing plan would have allowed him to add justices who would support his programs.

For the first time, Congress defeated a Roosevelt request. They saw his action as a serious threat to the balance of power among the branches of government. Increasing the court's size in this way would have limited the independence of the judicial branch by giving the president more power to control it.

The New Deal had reached high tide in 1936. In 1937 it ebbed. Suddenly there was a **recession,** a slump in business that was supposed to be less serious than a full depression. The decline between September 1937 and June 1938 was one of the worst in American economic history. The stock market dipped and industrial production declined. In early

Landon, who had been a progressive governor in Kansas. Using the phrase "America Is in Peril," the Republicans criticized the New Deal for its overthrow of traditional ways and for betraying its promises to the people.

Although Landon campaigned hard, he carried only two states, Maine and Vermont. Roosevelt beat him by more than eleven million votes. The Congress elected in 1936 was also heavily Democratic.

his victories and left the stadium. However, historians have concluded that the insult was probably unintentional.

Although Owens may not have had a close friend in the führer, he did become friends with the German long jumper Ludwig ("Luz") Long. During the long jump competition, Owens came close to fouling out of the qualifying round. Before Owens's last attempt, Long approached him and suggested that he make a mark in the ground just before the takeoff board to help position himself. Owens took the advice, qualified, and eventually took the gold medal while Long took the silver. Long was the first to congratulate him.

Hindenburg

With a length of 803.8 feet and a diameter of 135.1 feet, the *Hindenburg* was one of the largest aircraft ever built. Inside her metal frame were sixteen gas cells able to hold over seven million cubic feet of hydrogen. At a top speed of eighty-four miles per hour, the *Hindenburg* could make the trip from Friedrichshefan to Lakehurst in a few days.

Passengers onboard the ship could travel in relative comfort. Although the cabins were small and sparse, the passengers spent most of their time in the ship's other rooms. The ship had a fifty-person dining room, a reading and writing room, a smoking room, a lounge with a baby grand piano, and a promenade from which passengers could view the earth below.

The *Hindenburg* made ten trips to Lakehurst in 1936. However, during its flight on May 6, 1937, something went terribly wrong. The ship was two hundred feet from the ground and beginning its landing when flames appeared near the tail. Within seconds the flames spread over the whole ship, and the *Hindenburg* crashed tail first to the ground. Of the ninety-seven people onboard, thirteen passengers and twenty-two crewmen died. One ground crew member was also killed.

Checks and Balances at Work

Ask the students to explain how the founders' system of checks and balances worked during the economic crisis of the 1930s. While the nations in Europe were wracked by political turmoil and rising fascism, Roosevelt failed in his effort to assume dictatorial powers. Congress, even though it was controlled by his own party, refused to go along with his court-packing plan. The courts limited the worst examples of the New Deal. But in response to Roosevelt's threat, the Supreme Court softened its conservativism. (Also, soon after

the court-packing plan, several justices retired, which allowed Roosevelt to put a majority of progressives on the bench.)

The cause of the disaster has never been fully explained. Theories have included sabotage by an anti-Nazi group, a lightning strike from an electrical storm, and insurance fraud. Recently, a researcher named Addison Bain has attempted to disprove that the ship's hydrogen ignited and destroyed the ship. Instead, he concludes that the skin of the ship contained a flammable substance. When the fire started, the skin burned like dry leaves. Whatever the cause, the tragedy was enough to end interest in commercial air travel in airships.

"War of the Worlds"

During the golden age of radio, stations tried to get the listeners' attention just as the media does today. On October 30, 1938, the Columbia Broadcasting System succeeded in a bigger way than they expected. That Sunday evening the station broadcasted a radio drama called "War of the Worlds," based on a science fiction novel written by H. G. Wells. Orson Welles (no relation to the author) and his band of actors performed a dramatization of an alien invasion of earth. The program was set up as a fictional musical variety show. It was interrupted at intervals by faked newscasts bringing news of the aliens landing around New Jersey and attacking people.

At the beginning and throughout the show, announcements were made to clarify that the show was a radio drama. However, many people did not hear the disclaimers and spread the news. People across America began to panic. Some hid in basements while others gathered up possessions and fled to subways. A few even wrapped their heads in wet towels to survive poisonous gas attacks by the aliens.

The "War of the Worlds" showed the power the media could have in convincing people that something was true.

1937 federal spending had dropped off. This spending cut reduced personal incomes and in turn cut the purchasing power that had been artificially sustaining industry's production.

Roosevelt had accepted the use of government spending to get the economy started up, even if it meant going into debt. But when the government reduced its spending after four years, the pumped-up economy did not stand on its own. It was becoming evident that the New Deal measures had only helped to cover the problems; they had not brought the United States recovery.

Consequences of the New Deal

The New Deal had improved conditions from their 1932 depressed state in some respects. Business profits and farm prices were up; unemployment was down. Annual per capita income had gone up from $678 in 1933 to $925 in 1939. Electricity had been extended to many rural areas, and other public works had improved buildings and parks and encouraged conservation. These benefits, however, had come at a tremendous price for the country—the growth of federal power and federal spending.

Perhaps the one positive thing that the New Deal had accomplished was the restoration of people's faith and confidence in America. Roosevelt, despite the dangers and failures of many of his programs, had offered hope and action for people who were in a panic. People trusted him to do something about their problems.

In 1939, however, after six years of Roosevelt programs, the United States had not really recovered from the depression. Prices for farm products were still low. Overall manufacturing production and corporate profits lagged far behind 1929 levels. Nine million Americans were still unemployed.

Roosevelt's money policies and excessive spending had a great effect in the following years. He had taken the United States off the gold standard in 1933. Paper money and coins were no longer convertible into gold coins. Although this action did little to aid the economy at the time, it gave the government much power over national currency for the future. And because of its high spending, the New Deal had left the country with a record debt. The national debt in 1933 was $2.6 billion. In 1939 it was $6.5 billion. Unfortunately, in future years the precedents of high government spending and unbalanced budgets continued. The public just did not want the government to cut back on what they were used to having.

Families, such as this one on their way to Oregon, traveled across the nation to wherever jobs might offer relief from the depression.

530

Bad Precedents of the New Deal

Ask the students to reread the discussion of the "Consequences of the New Deal" (pp. 530-31). List all of the bad precedents of the 1930s: government power over national currency (the end of the gold standard),

growth of federal spending, record debt, increased executive power, increased size and scope of the federal government, government intervention in private enterprise, help to farmers and industrial workers, and belief that the public is entitled to government aid during a crisis. Students should recognize that all of these precedents continue to affect us today.

New government programs usually have long-term consequences, so citizens need to be wary of every suggestion for new laws. Discuss current debates over proposed laws. What bad precedents would they set?

Ask the students to summarize the fundamental lesson of this chapter: "Even when government programs fail to solve the nation's problems, the programs continue and grow."

In the long run the New Deal brought other changes. The government, especially the executive branch, had greatly increased its power. Under Roosevelt both the size and scope of the federal government had been greatly increased. Unfortunately, once the government assumes the responsibility for something, it rarely gives up control. And when the people give up their personal rights and responsibilities to government, they rarely get them back.

The government had also intervened in the economy and perhaps even managed it. The economy was no longer based solely on private enterprise. Although private businesses remained the mainstay of economic activity, government had assumed a major role. The government had taken responsibility for individual and national economic welfare. It had provided special help to farmers and industrial workers. It left Americans with the idea that when there was a crisis in future years, the government would help them then, too. Some people now believed that they were entitled to public help if they became victims of any circumstances over which they had no real control.

The depression was a time of great trials for many Americans and for the nation as a whole. Those who lived through it learned many lessons about the uncertainty of money and positions in this world. Too few, however, learned to trust in God fully in the midst of their hardships. It was easier to ask the government for aid. We who are Christians must realize that men and governments may fail. The only one worthy of our trust in any crisis is our Savior, Jesus Christ. He who feeds the birds of the air and clothes the lilies of the field is certainly able to take care of His own children. "But seek ye first the kingdom of God, and his righteousness; and all these things shall be added unto you" (Matt. 6:33).

SECTION REVIEW

1. What groups of voters did the Democratic party begin to attract in 1935?

2. What Republican candidate ran against Franklin Roosevelt in the 1936 election?

3. Why did Roosevelt want to increase the number of Supreme Court justices?

4. What positive things did the New Deal accomplish?

 Why was it difficult for the government to cut back its role in society after the New Deal era?

SUMMARY

The stock market crash in 1929 signaled the end of a generally prosperous and carefree time for the nation. It also signaled the beginning of a severe economic depression that would last throughout the 1930s. Bank failures and business closings plagued the country after the crash, and millions of Americans began to experience the hardships of unemployment, the loss of their homes or farms, and even hunger. In their distress, many looked to the government to give them aid. When President Hoover's reactions did not bring them quick relief, they turned to Franklin Roosevelt for swift action. He offered one New Deal program after another in an attempt to bring recovery. The programs increased government power and federal debt, but they ultimately failed to solve the underlying problems of the depression. The American people survived the trying times of the 1930s, but in the process they learned to depend on government aid and regulation to protect them from crisis.

 531

Section Review Answers

1. the underprivileged, reforming liberals, blacks, urban immigrants, and workers (p. 528)

2. Alfred M. Landon (pp. 528-29)

3. so that he could add justices who would support his programs (p. 529)

4. the restoration of people's faith and confidence in America (p. 530)

 The American public got used to having the things the government was giving them. And in times of crisis in the future, Americans expected the government to take care of them. (pp. 530-31)

Student Activity D: Modified True/False
This activity reviews the main concepts in the chapter.

Student Activity D: The New Deal's "Alphabet Soup"
This activity reviews the major New Deal programs.

Chapter Review

People, Places, and Things to Remember

stock market crash of
  1929
Great Depression
buy on the margin
"Dust Bowl"
dole
Reconstruction Finance
  Corporation

Franklin Delano
  Roosevelt
"New Deal"
"Brain Trust"
bank holiday
Agriculture Adjustment
  Act

National Recovery
  Administration
Civilian Conservation
  Corps
Tennessee Valley
  Authority
Social Security
recession

Review Questions

Define each of the following terms.

1. Dust Bowl

2. buying stock on the margin

3. dole

4. bank holiday

5. recession

Match each of the following terms with its description.

6. Great Depression
7. Social Security
8. New Deal
9. Brain Trust
10. Reconstruction Finance
    Corporation

a. Roosevelt's group of advisors
b. Hoover's aid program
c. "old age insurance"
d. the 1930s
e. Roosevelt's attempt to bring the nation relief
   and recovery

The New Deal contained many programs and pieces of legislation that were commonly known by their initials. For that reason they were sometimes called an "alphabet soup." What were the full names of the programs listed below, and what did each one do?

11. AAA
12. NRA
13. CCC
14. TVA

Questions for Discussion

15. Is the Social Security program, established during the New Deal, a benefit to the nation? Explain your answer.

16. How did the depression change Americans?

Chapter Review Answers

1. the drought-stricken area of the Plains where many farmers were ruined during the depression years (p. 519)

2. paying part of the price with cash and borrowing the rest from a stock broker with the stock as collateral (p. 516)

3. a handout (p. 521)

4. closing banks temporarily to stabilize banking (p. 523)

5. a slump in business considered less severe than a full depression (p. 529)

6. d (p. 514)

7. c (p. 527)

8. e (p. 522)

9. a (p. 523)

10. b (p. 521)

11. Agriculture Adjustment Act—asked farmers to cut production to raise prices (p. 524)

12. National Recovery Administration—tried to eliminate "wasteful competi-

tion" by regulating businesses (p. 525)

13. Civilian Conservation Corps—employed young men for public projects (p. 526)

14. Tennessee Valley Authority—provided for public power projects on the Tennessee River (p. 526)

15. Answers will vary.

16. Answers will vary. It destroyed their optimism. It made them more dependent on the government.

26

World War II

O n Sunday morning, the seventh of December in 1941, the Japanese bombed Pearl Harbor in Hawaii. The attack on the American naval base resulted in the sinking or disabling of nineteen American ships, the destruction of nearly two hundred planes, the deaths of over two thousand men, and the wounding of more than one thousand more. The treacherous surprise attack prompted President Franklin D. Roosevelt to address Congress the next day with these words:

Yesterday, December 7, 1941—a date which will live in infamy—the United States of America was suddenly and deliberately attacked by naval and air forces of the Empire of Japan.

Roosevelt then asked the Congress to declare war, and immediately America was thrown into a conflict not only with Japan but also with Germany and Italy. The United States had joined the worldwide conflict known as World War II.

Trouble Brewing

Although Americans fighting in World War I had idealistically believed that they were "fighting a war to end all wars," in less than twenty-five years Americans were back on the battlefields. The conditions leading to the conflict were many; the troubles had begun almost before the guns of World War I had cooled.

533

CHAPTER 26	Lesson Plan Chart			
Section Title	Main Activity	Pages	Time Frame	
1. Trouble Brewing	World War II Videos	533-36	1 day	
2. World War II Begins	Student Activity A: Steps to War	536-41	1-2 days	
3. America Enters the War	Student Activity C: War in Two Theaters	541-43	½-1 day	
4. American Efforts in Europe	Costly Mistakes	544-47	1-2 days	
5. The War in the Pacific	Student Activity E: The Balloon Pops in the Pacific	547-51	1-2 days	
6. The End of the War	Red Flags—The Decision to Drop the Bomb	551-53	½-1 day	
Total Suggested Days (including 1 day for review and testing)			6-10 days	

- Photocopies of World War II songs and lyrics
- A recording of "God Bless America"

SECTION 4
- Activity D from Chapter 26 of the *Student Activities* manual
- Special speaker: a veteran or someone with war memorabilia

SECTION 5
- Activity E from Chapter 26 of the *Student Activities* manual
- (Home school) War games

SECTION 6
- Activity F from Chapter 26 of the *Student Activities* manual

SECTION 1

> **Objectives**
> Students should be able to
> 1. Describe the rise of dangerous leaders in Germany, Italy, and Japan.
> 2. Name the Latin American foreign policy of the United States in the 1930s.

Hitler's Ruse

Hitler cleverly avoided the restrictions of the Treaty of Versailles as he trained Germans for eventual service in his armies. He organized youth groups and sports groups with the underlying purpose of military training. The *Hitler Jugend* (Hitler Youth) gave young men from age fourteen to eighteen the opportunity to go on military excursions with real army units. Younger boys eagerly wore the uniforms of the *Jungvolk* (Young Folk). "Hiking clubs" became popular and taught the Young Folk to march in formation and obey orders like military men. The 1936 Olympic games were held in Munich, and they gave the Germans the opportunity to train for pistol and rifle teams. The League of Air Sports trained pilots and supervised glider clubs under the leadership of Herman Göring, the eventual head of the *Luftwaffe* (German Air Force). One of Hitler's generals also bargained with the Soviet Union for permission to train armies and develop equip-

Leaders of War

Not everyone was pleased with the outcome of World War I. The peace settlements had satisfied only a few of the participants. Most countries had not gotten all they wanted from victory or had lost much more than they wanted to lose from defeat. Some of this dissatisfaction aided the rise of three strong imperialist countries in the 1930s.

Hitler Builds His Third Reich—The German nation was most upset by the Treaty of Versailles. That settlement had placed all the blame for the war on Germany and had stripped the country of some of its land, its colonial possessions, its strong army, and its self-respect. The treaty had also forced a large debt upon Germany to be paid to the Allies as reparations. Humiliated by these terms of defeat, Germany struggled through the 1920s. In the midst of the downcast German people, however, there arose a man who gave Germany a hope for future greatness.

Adolf Hitler gained Germany's attention in 1924 with the publication of his book *Mein Kampf* ("My Struggle"). In it he preached the injustice of the Treaty of Versailles, blamed the Jews for Germany's problems, and declared the superiority of the German race. Hitler also organized the National Socialist German Workers Party, or **Nazi Party,** around his leadership. He denounced communism (which the Germans greatly feared at that time), and he proposed a strong, organized Germany that would become a powerful leader of the world.

Although many Germans did not accept Hitler at first, they found Nazism to be full of excitement and pageantry, and almost no one wanted to be left out. Calling Hitler the *Führer* (leader), many joined in his support, believing that they were building a Third Reich (German empire) that would last for a thousand years. They believed that Hitler would restore Germany to its rightful place in the

world. They believed the promises Hitler made in his speeches with more enthusiasm than many Christians today carry the gospel to the lost. A few people continued to mistrust him, but their influence was not strong enough to reverse his power.

As depression increased German despair in the early 1930s, Hitler and his Nazi Party swept into power. He became the German chancellor in 1933 and was given the powers of a dictator. He soon began to violate the Treaty of Versailles by sending troops into the Rhineland area near France and by organizing German men and boys into groups for military training. Hitler also set German scientists to work developing new weapons and materials that could be used in war. His power and ambition would soon threaten world peace.

Mussolini Moves to Conquer—Italy was also disappointed after World War I. It had switched to the Allied side during the war but had not received the extra territories it wanted when the war ended. Suffering from economic and political problems after the war, Italy allowed **Benito Mussolini** to seize power in 1922. Mussolini, called *Il Duce* (DOO chay; the leader), was the leader of a party that favored nationalism and opposed communism. Like Hitler, he had organized military groups across Italy. As dictator, Mussolini built efficient railroads and major highways, provided houses and lands for sixty thousand peasants, and made other improvements in Italy. Although he denied freedom to the people, he promised to give Italy back the pride of a bygone era by establishing a "Second Roman Empire." Such promises initially caused his followers to rank him with Julius Caesar.

Mussolini's first attempt to expand his empire began in 1935, when Italian soldiers crossed the Mediterranean to attack the African land of Ethiopia. Ethiopian tribesmen faced Italy's machine guns and bombers with

534

Student Activity B: Alternative Outlining

This prewriting activity helps students to overview the outline of the chapter and then to consider alternative ways to outline the information in the chapter.

Popularity of World War II

Ask the students to share what they know about World War II and the sources of their information—books, movies, family history. Ask them to describe any books at their home or any books they have ever checked out from the library that deal with

World War II. Tell them that more books have been written about this period of history than perhaps any other period. Ask them to give some reasons for this. *(It was the biggest war in world history in terms of numbers and territory, and it changed the course of the world. The scale of the war and its recent occurrence enable us to find innumerable stories of heroism and villainy.)*

Let Students Teach

It is possible to let the students do much of the teaching in this chapter, while you sim-

ply fill in the details. Many students will already be well versed in the war. Ask them to give their favorite part of the war, and then have them share what they know when you get to that part.

Never Again—Studying the Causes of War

Ask the students to explain the value of understanding the causes of World War II. As with all war, we study the causes so that we can prevent another war like it. Ask the students whether a new world war would be

spears and rifles. Although Europe and the United States looked on in horror, no one went to Ethiopia's aid.

Mussolini found an ally in Hitler. Both men had formed **fascist** (FASH ist) **governments,** strong dictatorships that stressed nationalism and power. They formed an alliance called the Rome-Berlin Axis. Later, Japan joined this alliance, becoming the third of the **Axis powers.**

Changes in Japan—Japan's industrial and military power had been growing since the turn of the century. A group of military leaders had gained control of Japan, and they intended to increase Japanese power in China and in other areas of Eastern Asia and the Pacific. These leaders were convinced that Japan had deserved greater recognition as a world power after World War I. They convinced the Japanese people that the United States was a threat to further growth of the Japanese Empire and that Japan should establish control of the trade and resources of Eastern Asia.

After World War I, the League of Nations had assigned Japan the responsibility of governing some Pacific islands formerly held by Germany. Fortifying these islands enabled Japan to invade China and take over the northern region called Manchuria in 1931. The United States believed that Japan's conquest of Manchuria was wrong, but the United States's request to the League of Nations to take action against Japan was ineffective, and Japan stayed in Manchuria. Since no American possessions in the Pacific were yet threatened, the United States did nothing except to slightly strengthen their defenses in the Philippines.

Roosevelt and Foreign Policy

The United States was aware that the growing powers of Hitler, Mussolini, and the Japanese military leaders were threatening the delicate balance of world peace. Even so, the isolationist attitude that had ruled in the 1920s also prevailed in the 1930s. Most Americans were more concerned that the nation take care of the problems of its own economic depression than that it get involved in foreign affairs. They hoped that the limits set for navies and the peace pacts signed by major nations in the 1920s would be enough to discourage future war. Americans did want the League of Nations to take appropriate actions against the threatening powers. Yet the League was very weak and never able to act as an effective restraint against villainous nations.

President Roosevelt was among those who wanted the United States to take a major role in foreign affairs. But without popular support little was done about the trouble that was brewing in Europe and Eastern Asia. A significant step, however, was accomplished in the United States's relationships to the countries of Latin America. President Hoover had initiated a **"Good Neighbor Policy"** in dealings with these lands, and Roosevelt continued the policy. Instead of marching into Latin American countries with a "big stick" when troubles arose, as had been done since the presidency of Theodore Roosevelt, the United States began

Benito Mussolini promised the Italians a second Roman Empire.

535

ment on Soviet soil in return for aiding a Soviet military buildup.

Fascism

Both Hitler and Mussolini introduced fascist governments to their countries. However, the ideas behind fascism were not new. Earlier societies and philosophers had promoted the state over the individual. In ancient Sparta, men were taken at an early age and placed in schools to train them to serve in the military. Individuals had a greater loyalty to the city-state than to their family. In the nineteenth century the German philosopher Georg Friedrich Hegel argued that a person was important only as part of the state, not as an individual. Another nineteenth-century philosopher named Friedrich Nietzsche promoted fascism through his belief that man could become perfect by forcibly exerting his will. The fascist movements, which adopted these ideas, succeeded in Germany and Italy for a number of reasons. In both countries charismatic leaders were able to inspire the people and to use propaganda to promote fascism. The depressed economic conditions in both countries made the people more willing to accept change. And in the case of Germany, the harsh conditions set by the Treaty of Versailles after World War I gave the people reason to blame others for their problems.

Japan's Leadership

Hideki Tojo was the leading Japanese military officer active in Japan's expansion of power.

---

likely today. If so, where might it be fought, and who would fight on each side?

Discuss Rogue Nations

Under their fascist leaders, Germany, Italy, and Japan became "rogue nations." A rogue nation ignores fundamental principles of international relations. They willingly use any means necessary to increase their power. The two most common types of rogue nations are Communist countries, such as China, and radical Muslim nations, such as Iran. Ask the students to consider U.S. relations with these countries and its relations with the fascists during the 1930s. Are these countries or their leaders any less dangerous?

 World War II Videos

Several excellent World War II documentaries are available. Use the video over several days. Use appropriate portions for each section of the chapter. This will help to make the war seem more real to your students.

Objectives

Students should be able to

1. Describe German expansion and the policy of appeasement.
2. Trace Hitler's successful advances in Europe as the war began.
3. Describe the battle of Britain.
4. Explain the failure of Hitler's invasion of the Soviet Union.
5. Describe American opinions and policies as the United States watched the war.

to let these countries handle their own affairs. The Good Neighbor Policy did much to improve relations with these countries, which had grown tired and suspicious of U.S. intervention in their lands.

SECTION REVIEW

1. What event brought the United States into World War II?
2. What two European leaders built strong military dictatorships after World War I?
3. What part of China had Japan conquered?
4. What was the general attitude of Americans toward foreign affairs in the 1930s?
5. What new policy was the United States following in its dealings with Latin America?

 How did the end of World War I prepare Germany for the start of World War II?

World War II Begins

In the late 1930s the world watched as Hitler began his conquest of European territory. His actions soon made France and Britain realize that something had to be done about this fascist leader.

German Expansion

Because other nations had not really protested Hitler's disregard of the Treaty of Versailles, Hitler chanced violating it again by uniting Austria (a German-speaking land) with Germany in 1938. In four weeks Austria came under Hitler's control. Foreign powers still did not protest too strongly against him, so he next demanded the Sudetenland, an area in Czechoslovakia. He claimed that the 3.5 million Germans who lived there "deserved to be a part of the Fatherland." However, he had secretly instructed his military to invade Czechoslovakia if he did not gain it peacefully by October 1, 1938. Hitler promised that this would be "the last territorial claim I have to make in Europe."

German soldiers stand shoulder to shoulder at a 1935 Nazi rally.

Great Britain's prime minister, Neville Chamberlain, and Hitler reached an agreement during a meeting in Munich, Germany. Chamberlain thought that if Europe would "appease" Hitler by giving in to his demand, peace would be saved. Many Europeans were relieved that war had been avoided, but they soon found that giving in to evil often causes it to resurface in an uglier form. Chamberlain returned to Britain and announced that there would be "peace in our time." **Winston Churchill,** who would soon take Chamberlain's place as prime minister, violently disagreed, saying, "You chose dishonor, and you will have war!"

Although Hitler took the Sudetenland peacefully, the **appeasement** did not work. About six months later, Hitler forcefully took over all of Czechoslovakia. Europe began to realize that Hitler intended to keep increasing

---

Section Review Answers

1. the bombing of Pearl Harbor by the Japanese (p. 533)
2. Adolf Hitler and Benito Mussolini (p. 534)
3. Manchuria (p. 535)
4. isolationist—they were more worried about problems at home than abroad (p. 535)
5. "Good Neighbor Policy" (p. 524)

 Feeling that everything had been taken away from them and staggering under the weight of a huge debt, Germans were ready for a leader like Hitler who expressed their grievances and seemed to offer the return of self-respect. (p. 534)

SECTION 2

Materials

- Activity A from Chapter 26 of the *Student Activities* manual

Student Activity A: Steps to War

This activity simplifies the sequence of causes and effects that led the United States into war. You can use this activity or a simplified version—the History Skills activity on page 555.

Discuss Appeasement

The main lesson of this section is the danger of appeasement. It is clearly wrong for a nation or an individual to back down on its obligations, no matter what the threat. Death is better than dishonor. The Allies were bound by the Versailles treaty to

his power and his empire. No European nation was safe.

By the spring of 1939, Hitler wanted Poland. This time both Britain and France warned that such action would lead to war. Hitler ignored them, saying, "Our enemies are little worms. I saw them at Munich." But Hitler was worried that the Soviet Union would also protest his actions. He realized it

Neville Chamberlain thought that his agreement with Hitler had saved Europe from war.

would be unwise to fight too much of Europe at one time. Therefore, in August he signed a nonaggression pact with **Joseph Stalin,** the dictator of the Soviet Union. They agreed not to attack each other as they both expanded their territory. Although Hitler had said that he hated the Communist Soviet Union, he would wait until later to attack that enemy. The stage was now set for the beginning of World War II.

War Envelops Europe

On September 1, 1939, Hitler unleashed his mechanized war machine on Poland. Hundreds of bombers soared over Poland while armored tanks, called *panzers,* and thousands of soldiers moved in to take control. The Soviet Union also attacked Poland from

the east. Within hours Poland had lost almost all hope for avoiding conquest. A few Poles continued to resist for several weeks, but the fall of Poland was complete before the month ended. The world had seen a new type of warfare—"lightning war," or **blitzkrieg.** Nine more European countries soon would fall under Nazi control as the Germans advanced.

Britain and France, the **Allies,** knowing that Hitler had to be stopped, declared war on Germany on September 3, 1939. They rushed to prepare their armies, but little fighting took place for eight months. Then on April 9, Hitler's forces took control of Denmark and Norway. A few weeks later, on May 10, 1940, Hitler staged another blitzkrieg, sending his forces into Belgium, the Netherlands, and Luxembourg. The Belgians and the Dutch, unable to fight against his strong armies, soon became conquered states. Next, by-passing France's heavy fortifications, the Germans moved into France through the Ardennes Forest. Britain sent soldiers and equipment to help France, but the Allied army of 338,000 men was forced to retreat to northern France near the port of Dunkirk. The Germans rushed to cut off an escape across the English Channel. Having trapped the Allied army at Dunkirk, the Germans waited for their air force to finish the task. Bad weather, however, prevented German planes from bombing the fleeing forces. Meanwhile, the British and French brought every available boat to Dunkirk. Fishing boats, steamers, yachts, and even lifeboats were used to evacuate the Allied army. Fishermen, dockworkers, merchants, and farmers all helped ferry the army across

Blitzkrieg
Hitler's "lightning war" was first demonstrated in Poland on September 1, 1939. Fifty years earlier, the blitzkrieg would not have been possible. The development of the internal combustion engine changed everything. No longer did troop movement depend on how fast men could march or where rail lines ran. Trucks could move men and artillery across diverse terrain. Planes could drop men behind enemy lines. Tanks offered protection and firepower as German troops swept over enemy territory.

Today it is hard for us to imagine armies without mechanized forces, but at that time tanks, trucks, and airplanes were new in the war arena. Hitler used these elements to the fullest to take over large portions of Europe.

Dunkirk
The evacuation of the Allied troops from Dunkirk was made possible by the bad weather. This protection for the Allied troops from almost certain annihilation is often cited as an instance of providential control over history.

 537

respect the boundaries of Czechoslovakia. Students need to understand that in their own lives they should never appease the flesh or the Devil. The events leading to World War II are an amazing parallel to the lives of individuals who appease evil.

Students also need to consider the flip side of appeasement. When should the United States ignore evildoers in the world? Supporters of U.S. intervention around the world constantly raise the specter of "appeasement" as an argument against isolationists. But clearly it is not the United

States's job to suppress every dictator that raises his head.

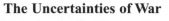 The Uncertainties of War

Statesmen throughout the ages have argued that war should be the last resort of diplomacy because it is too unpredictable to be assured of success. Emphasize to the students that no one foresaw the possibilities of a blitzkrieg. Even Churchill himself was unaware of the potential danger to ships and troops. The lack of preparedness of the Allies led to the col-

lapse of France and the near annihilation of the British army.

Ask the students to discuss the surprising course that other wars have taken in U.S. history. In particular, recall that in the Civil War the North thought that they could beat the South in a matter of weeks. Students need to look for other examples of unwise optimism as they read about later wars, such as Korea, Vietnam, and the Persian Gulf. Stress to the students that any time the U.S. government clamors for war, they should be wary. The fighting will rarely be as easy as is first promised.

The "Great Wall" of France

After World War I, many Frenchmen were still worried about Germany. The Germans had invaded France not only in that war but also in the Franco-Prussian War (1870-71). Few people believed that Germany would remain weak for long.

To protect themselves the French considered several solutions. Charles de Gaulle and others thought France should build up its tanks and planes. Joffre argued for a line of fortresses on France's eastern border. Pétain argued along similar lines, but he wanted the fortresses to be stronger. André Maginot, a lifelong civil servant, worked out a compromise between Joffre and Pétain that would eventually become the Maginot Line. Although Maginot did not design the fortifications, he was the one who tirelessly promoted them and convinced the French people of their necessity.

In history the Maginot Line is remembered as a failure. Hitler's troops succeeded in invading France and controlling most of the country. However, the only real flaw of the system was that it did not extend far enough to the north. After World War I, Belgium was France's ally, which prevented fortifications from being built on that border. When Belgium declared itself neutral in 1920, France built some minor fortifications there but nothing compared to the Maginot Line. During the war Germany penetrated France through this northern gap. Some German forces did assault parts of the Maginot Line, but most were repelled. When the fortresses surrendered, it was not because they were captured but because higher French officials ordered it.

Other Heroes

Although the pilots of the RAF are given the most credit for winning the battle of Britain, many other people helped in the victory. Radar operators kept track of incoming German planes and quickly alerted the RAF. This information was vital considering the low number of

the Channel to safety. The evacuation of an army, however, was hardly enough to save France. On June 14, 1940, German troops entered Paris. France had fallen to the Nazis.

While Hitler was conquering the French, Mussolini announced that Italy was joining Germany in the fight against the Allies. Mussolini had already taken control of Albania before the war began, and he intended to gain more land from an Axis conquest of Europe.

Britain Stands Alone

With the fall of France, Britain stood alone to face Hitler and Mussolini. Most believed that the Germans would cross the English Channel to invade and conquer the

Many believed the evacuation of Dunkirk was a miracle.

British Isles, but Hitler chose another way to try to defeat Great Britain. He ordered devastating bombing raids on English cities, including the capital, London. These bombing attacks became known as "the battle of Britain." They began in July 1940 and lasted for one year.

The Germans hoped to drive Britain's Royal Air Force (RAF) from the skies and to force a surrender by inflicting heavy damage on civilians. The RAF courageously tried to

Smoke rises around St. Paul's Cathedral in the aftermath of the battle of Britain.

protect Britain from the bombings. Because of a shortage of pilots, RAF pilots made as many as five flights a day to defend their homeland. Their efforts prevented the fall of Britain. The new prime minister, Winston Churchill, said of the RAF, "Never in the field of human conflict was so much owed by so many to so few." Had the attacks continued, the outcome might have been different. But the British determination to stop Hitler persuaded him to seek another approach to victory.

Hitler Turns Against the Soviet Union

Although mired in a stalemate in Great Britain, Hitler was winning elsewhere. German armies had control of Hungary and Rumania by the spring of 1941. Turkey had signed a treaty of neutrality. In early summer Hitler swept into southeastern Europe. Bulgaria, Yugoslavia, and Greece were soon Axis victims.

Hitler then made a decision that would have tremendous consequences—a decision to attack the Soviet Union. Hitler believed that the British were holding out in the hope that the Soviets would change sides and come to the aid of the Allies, so he wanted to crush the

Soviet Union before it could turn on him. He also wanted Soviet resources for German use. While the Germans were still fighting the Allies in Western Europe, Hitler's generals tried to warn him that opening up another front, or battleground, in the East would be unwise. Expanding the war into the Soviet Union late in the summer could be dangerous, but Hitler did not listen. On June 22, 1941, the blitzkrieg against the Soviet Union began. Hitler thought he could take control of the land in just eight weeks.

At first the Russian people accepted Hitler's armies as a relief from the terrors of Stalin's Communist rule. However, they soon learned that the Nazis were not friendly. Germans ravaged Soviet towns and tortured the Russians they met. The Russians began to use a "scorched earth" policy. Instead of leaving crops and livestock for Hitler to use to feed his men, the Russians, as they retreated, burned their crops and killed their animals. Thus the supplies the German army had hoped to capture were gone. With every mile conquered, the supply lines back to Germany became longer.

In mid-October German troops were only forty miles from Moscow, and they had killed over two million Russians. Even though the autumn days grew shorter and temperatures grew colder, Hitler refused to stop and wait until spring for further action. He did not want to give Stalin more time to ready his defenses. So the Germans marched on with only their summer uniforms and lightweight oil for their vehicles. Ironically, a century before, Napoleon had been in the same situation and found that the Russian winter was far more dangerous than Russian troops. But Hitler had not learned from history. On December 6, as the freezing Soviet winter closed in, the Soviet troops attacked Hitler's cold and weary forces, and they actually broke through the German lines. The Soviet army and the Russian winter

Axis-Controlled Area 1941

had kept Hitler from defeating the Soviet Union.

American Sympathies and Fears

Americans looked at European affairs with increased alarm. The European dictators had made it clear that they were opposed to any form of republican government. Some Americans feared that if Britain fell, Germany might try to wage war on the United States. Most Americans generally opposed Hitler and wanted the Allies to win. Yet since Congress had passed a series of neutrality acts in the 1930s, Americans were limited in what they could do to help the Allies.

In 1939 Congress had allowed the Allied powers to buy war materials from American companies if the Allies paid cash and carried the supplies on their own ships. Congress also passed a Selective Service Act in 1940. Once again young men aged twenty-one to thirty-

British pilots. It kept the pilots in the right place at the right time.

All along the coast, a series of long-range radar towers created an invisible net. Any plane above five thousand feet could be detected as far as one hundred miles away. Lower-flying aircraft occasionally went through the net undetected, but short-range radar towers usually spotted them. Once a radar operator detected an aircraft, the information was relayed to a Fighter Command's Headquarters. Trained civilians also kept track of the plane visually, using binoculars and height-measuring equipment. At Fighter Command the information was plotted on a huge map of the coast. All around the map, workers used long magnetic sticks to move markers representing planes. A balcony above the map allowed the British leaders to see exactly what was happening across the coast and to make decisions based on the situation.

Where? How Far?

In anticipation of a German invasion, the British government ordered the removal of signs which indicated the direction of and distance to towns and cities. This tactic was intended to confuse the Germans if they ever invaded. It succeeded in confusing many travelers.

This 1930s political cartoon warns that America's policy of isolationism in the face of Hitler's Nazi threat was placing the United States in great danger.

five were required to register for possible military service. Some 375,000 men were drafted and started training to be ready for attack. But since the armistice in 1918, America had not been concerned with building a strong armed force; so the new soldiers had to train on old or substitute equipment until new pieces were available.

Many Americans still feared war and wanted to avoid it at all costs. The America First Committee, with such prominent members as Charles Lindbergh, and other organizations pleaded for American neutrality. Roosevelt ran for a third term as president in 1940, and he won. Because of the fear of war, however, Roosevelt had to promise that he would keep American boys out of a foreign war, a war that did not directly involve the United States.

As the battle of Britain was threatening to crush the Allies in the summer of 1941, President Roosevelt decided that Britain des-

perately needed more help. He sought a way for the Allies to obtain vital war equipment from the United States more easily. Congress complied by approving the **Lend-Lease Act.** This act permitted the president to send equipment to any nation in which the receipt of such equipment might be vital to American defense. Rather than paying with money, the countries could pay with property, services, or equipment for American use. In this way the United States received land for

Adolph Hitler salutes Nazi soldiers in a parade in Munich.

seven air bases in exchange for war supplies sent to Britain.

Americans also began to realize that the European Axis powers (Germany and Italy) might not be their only enemies. Japan had joined the Axis powers, and it was pursuing interests in Asia. Japanese forces had already entered Southeast Asia; Australia, New Zealand, or the Philippines might be Japan's

America First

The existence of the America First Committee, led by such prominent men as Charles Lindbergh, is surprising to modern Americans. The group appears shortsighted and profascist. But in reality, many of their leaders were attempting to continue America's tradition of isolationism. Even in recent years, leaders such as Patrick Buchanan promoted an official position of America First. If you think it is appropriate, divide the class and have them argue the two sides of the debate that raged in 1940. Lindbergh was willing for Britain to fall to

the Nazis. Why? *(It was widely believed that Soviet Communism was at least as dangerous as Nazism, and isolationists hoped the two evil systems would destroy each other.)* Students need to understand the dangers of making assumptions about the philosophical basis for various political views.

Promises, Promises

Like Wilson, Roosevelt made campaign promises to keep the United States out of war. But it is clear that he believed the United States should enter the war. In fact,

historians argue that Roosevelt acted as a masterful politician, doing everything he could to change public opinion and bring the country into war. Congresswoman Clare Boothe Luce charged that FDR "lied us into war because he did not have the political courage to lead us into it." Do the students see any evidence of his politicking? *(He worked with Congress and patiently waited until the right time to introduce the Selective Service and later the Lend-Lease Act. He broke off trade with Japan, knowing that it might lead to war. His secret meeting with Churchill in August*

next target. Most Americans did not know that Japan also intended to take control of a vast area in the Pacific. The Japanese were strengthening their position in Asia in preparation for their attack on American possessions in the area.

President Roosevelt decided to forbid almost all trade with Japan. The strain between the two nations increased as Japan continued to expand its power in defiance of American interests. In November 1941, Japanese diplomats arrived in Washington for talks. At the same time, however, Japanese aircraft carriers were sailing across the Pacific to take up positions within bombing distance of Hawaii.

The bombing of Pearl Harbor devastated the American Navy and brought America into World War II.

SECTION REVIEW

1. With what major power did Hitler make a nonaggression treaty that he later broke?

2. Hitler's invasion of what country actually triggered World War II?

3. Which countries did Hitler capture between September of 1939 and June of 1940?

4. What was the German strategy in the battle of Britain?

5. What was the Lend-Lease Act?

 Why was Hitler's decision to invade the Soviet Union unwise? Why did he do it anyway?

America Enters the War

The attack on the naval base at **Pearl Harbor** on December 7, 1941, put an end to American neutrality. When the United States declared war on Japan after the attack, Japan's allies, Germany and Italy, also declared war on the United States. The war now directly involved America in a fight against all the Axis powers.

The attack on Pearl Harbor was a great blow to the United States Navy. The damage was severe, but heavier losses were avoided

because the American carrier fleet was at sea that Sunday morning. Nonetheless, the United States had much to do to prepare itself for the long fight ahead.

Manpower for War

Following Pearl Harbor, patriotic volunteers deluged army and navy recruiting centers. Eventually about sixteen million Americans, one in eleven, wore military uniforms. Those Americans who sincerely believed that war was wrong registered as

541

SECTION 3

Objectives
Students should be able to
1. Name the event that brought the United States into the war.
2. Describe ways in which Americans went to work for the war effort.
3. Describe ways in which Americans produced or conserved materials for the war effort.
4. Explain the "Hitler first" policy.

America Goes To War
For months before the Pearl Harbor attack, President Roosevelt had actually been hoping for an event that would bring the United States into the war. The American public was reluctant to enter the war without some kind of clear attack on the United States. Roosevelt had even sent American naval patrols nearer and nearer to Europe hoping to provoke a German attack, but Hitler had been careful not to give the United States an excuse to enter the war while he was busy with other Allied enemies. After Pearl Harbor, however, Hitler had no choice but to fight the Americans too.

Carrier Warfare Begins
Even as new technology made Hitler's blitzkrieg possible, it also played a crucial roll in the Japanese attack on Pearl Harbor. In 1910 an American stunt pilot named Eugene Ely landed a plane on a ship. By 1941, the airplanes launched against the Americans were coming from Japanese carriers, ships designed for aircraft. Without these huge ships, the small fighters would have run out of fuel before reaching Hawaii.

The Japanese attack required secrecy to be successful. Lieutenant Commander Minoru Genda had to plan the massive attack and yet preserve radio silence. Ironically, the solution came to him while watching an American newsreel showing four American carriers

---

1941, mentioned on page 543 of the student text, shows he was planning for war.)

Section Review Answers

1. the Soviet Union (p. 537)

2. Poland (p. 527)

3. Denmark, Norway, Belgium, the Netherlands, and Luxembourg (p. 537)

4. to drive Britain's Royal Air Force from the skies and to force a surrender by inflicting heavy damage on civilians (p. 538)

5. an agreement that the U.S. would provide needed supplies for the Allies in return for property, services, equipment, or other items useful to the U.S. (p. 540)

 In opening another front, the Germans had to divide their forces; it is always more difficult to make progress with a divided focus. In addition, the timing of the attack put Germany in the middle of the Soviet Union as the dangerous Russian winter closed in. Hitler hoped to capture valuable

resources and to end British hopes that the Soviets would come to their aid. (p. 539)

SECTION 3

Materials

- Activity C from Chapter 26 of the *Student Activities* manual

- December 1991 issue of *National Geographic*

- Materials for making a recruitment poster

traveling together in formation. In contrast, the Japanese usually kept their carriers spaced apart by up to one hundred miles. Genda realized that if he kept his carriers together the attack could be coordinated visually rather than by radio.

The strategy was put into action; and on December 7, 1941, the Japanese launched their attack. The carriers enabled the Japanese fighters to wreak havoc at the American naval base. However, the same strategy that helped bring Japanese success also brought failure. The Japanese had hoped to find four American aircraft carriers at Pearl Harbor. Instead, they found none. The *Lexington* and the *Enterprise* were delivering marines to Wake and Midway Islands. The *Hornet* and the *Yorktown* were not even in the Pacific. With their carriers intact, the Americans could still use their air power to fight back against the Japanese.

conscientious objectors and served in the medical corps or in nonmilitary roles.

Women also became involved in the war effort in military or civilian jobs. Some served in the Women's Army Corps (WACS); others joined the Women's Naval Reserve or the WAVES (Women Accepted for Voluntary Emergency Service). The WASP (Women Airforce Service Pilots) helped to fly aircraft from the factories to air force bases. Although women were not assigned to combat roles, they did serve overseas, especially in tasks that freed men to fight.

More women also became a part of the job force, taking the places of men who were drafted. Posters picturing "Rosie the Riveter" were used to recruit women to join workforces everywhere. Some joined the Red Cross, and others worked with the USO (United Service Organizations), entertaining troops and providing other services.

As some jobs previously closed to them opened up, black Americans joined the workforce in larger numbers than ever before. Blacks also enlisted in all-black units in the armed forces.

Beginning February 1, 1943, Japanese-Americans could enlist, too. They trained as an all-Nisei (American-born Japanese) force. Because of their Japanese association, however, most were sent to fight in Europe. Some Japanese-Americans did do intelligence work in the Pacific, cracking the secret Japanese telegraph codes.

Materials for War

The United States entered the war without materials and preparation for the conflict, but Americans rose to meet the challenge. Factories were soon retooled to produce war goods, such as jeeps and tanks, rather than cars. Through teamwork and sacrifice, production doubled in less than four years. By 1945 more than 300,000 planes, 100,000

tanks and self-propelled guns, 2.5 million military trucks, 1.1 million rifles and carbines, 400,000 artillery weapons, and 50 billion rounds of ammunition had become a part of the American arsenal.

Shipbuilders set to work to increase the United States's naval fleet. Ships dubbed "Liberty Ships" were christened as quickly as every three and a half working days. Liberty Ships were employed to carry war materials to far-flung fronts. Aircraft carriers, destroyers, submarines, and other vessels also were built with amazing speed.

To meet the ever-increasing need for war goods, Americans at home had to sacrifice during the war. After 1942, automobiles were no longer made for private sale. Gasoline and

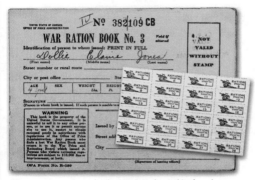

The government used ration stamps, issued to Americans in ration books, to limit purchases of goods that were in short supply during the war.

oil as well as meat, butter, sugar, coffee, most canned or frozen goods, and shoes were rationed (restricted in use) because of shortages. Americans received books of ration stamps. They could buy a rationed item only if they had an unused stamp for it. When scarce products were available in stores, there were often long lines to buy them. Little was thrown away. Drives to collect tin cans, waste

542

• Photocopies of World War II songs and lyrics

• A recording of "God Bless America"

Student Activity C: War in Two Theaters

This chart summarizes events in the European and Pacific Theaters. You will probably want to help the students complete the chart during your lectures.

Nuggets from *National Geographic*

"Pearl Harbor: A Return to the Day of Infamy" in the December 1991 issue of *National Geographic* covers the story of the immediate cause of America's entrance into World War II. Good pictures and memoirs are included.

Recruitment Poster

Make recruitment posters for World War II. Appeals for WAACs included "Back the Attack, Be a WAAC! For America Is Calling," "Speed Them Back, Join the

WAAC," and "I'd Rather Be with Them—than Waiting for Them."

Songs and Song Composition

Sing a song from World War II. Perhaps have the class write their own lyrics for the tune. Songs include "Goodbye Momma, I'm Off to Yokohama" and "To Be Specific, It's Our Pacific."

National Hymn: "God Bless America"

Although "God Bless America" was not composed during the thirties, that

The "Big Three"
The third meeting of the Big Three at Yalta is discussed on page 546.

paper, aluminum, and scrap iron became common.

As they had in World War I, most Americans patriotically added to their food supply with "victory gardens." These vegetable gardens popped up everywhere: in backyards, along edges of parking lots, in zoos and parks, and in window boxes. By 1943 they supplied Americans with a third of all their vegetables. These efforts ensured that there would be more food available for the boys fighting in the war. Americans also bought war bonds to help pay for the war effort.

The supply lines used to carry goods to the armed forces stretched around the globe. In addition to supplying its own men, the United States supplied much of the Allied forces. President Roosevelt called the United States "the arsenal of democracy."

Mapping the War

As commander-in-chief of all American armed forces, the president mapped the war strategy with the help of the leading military officers and advisors. Roosevelt also met with Britain's prime minister Winston Churchill. Their first meeting was held secretly aboard an American destroyer off the coast of Newfoundland in August 1941, before the United States had joined in the war on the Allied side. Later the Arcadia talks, held near Washington, D.C., made public the Allied leaders' "Hitler first" policy. This policy made Nazi Germany the first target. The United States agreed that the Germans were the biggest threat to the Allies. Once Hitler was defeated, Japan could not stand long.

Other meetings among Allied leaders allowed them to discuss their military strategy and to plan for dealing with the problems that would be faced after the war was over. At Casablanca (CAS uh BLANG kuh) in Morocco in January 1943, the Allies decided to invade

Europe through Sicily and Italy. After Hitler had turned against the Soviet Union, that country had joined the Allies. Therefore, at the next meeting in Teheran (TEH uh RAN) in Iran, Soviet dictator Joseph Stalin joined the meet-

Stalin, Roosevelt, and Churchill, the "Big Three," met at Teheran to discuss war strategy.

ings. Stalin pressed for the Allies to invade northern Europe to take pressure off his troops. With the fall of France and the end of the battle of Britain, most of the fighting was taking place in the east between the Germans and the Soviets. Stalin was promised a second European front to take the pressure off the eastern front in return for his promise that the Soviet Union would help defeat Japan once Hitler was defeated.

SECTION REVIEW

1. About how many Americans served in the armed forces during World War II?

2. Name three military organizations in which women served. How did women help the cause at home?

3. What had to be done with America's factory production?

 How were civilians able to aid the war effort?

543

---

is when it became famous. Irving Berlin wrote the song in 1918 and laid it aside, but in 1938 as war in Europe was approaching, Berlin decided to write a song of peace. He brought "God Bless America" out again, improved it, and then gave Kate Smith exclusive rights to sing it. Bring in a recording of the song (by Kate Smith if possible) and play it for the class. Afterwards discuss the lyrics and why some people believe this should be the United States's national anthem rather than "The Star-Spangled Banner."

Section Review Answers

1. sixteen million (p. 541)

2. WACS, WAVES, and WAFS; they became part of the job force, joined the Red Cross, and worked with the United Service Organizations (p. 542)

3. It had to be retooled for the production of war goods. (p. 542)

 They limited their consumption of certain products; recycled tin cans, paper, aluminum, and iron; and

grew gardens to make sure that the soldiers had adequate food and supplies. (pp. 542-43)

Objectives
Students should be able to
1. Trace the Allied operations in North Africa, Italy, and France.
2. Explain the significance of the Normandy invasion.
3. Describe the defeat of Germany.

American Efforts in Europe

Although the United States did not totally neglect events in the Pacific, it sent its major forces into the European portion of the conflict first.

Attacking North Africa

Prior to Germany's invasion of Russia, Italy had launched a major campaign in the deserts of North Africa. The British, however, defeated the Italians and threatened to drive them out of Africa altogether. In order to prop up his faltering ally, Hitler sent German troops, called the "Afrika Korps," to Africa under the brilliant command of the "Desert Fox," General Erwin Rommel (ROM ul). By clever maneuvering and swift movement, Rommel succeeded in driving back the British. He even threatened to drive into Egypt and capture the Suez Canal. The battle lines in North Africa shifted back and forth for hundreds of miles in 1941 and 1942, as first Rommel and then the British were victorious.

By the middle of the year 1942, however, American troops began to arrive. Under the skilled command of General **Dwight D. Eisenhower,** the Americans landed in western North Africa and began to push east toward Libya. The British in the meantime began to drive west from Egypt. With this "Operation Torch," as the African campaign was called, the Allies crushed the Axis forces between them. Rommel and some of his men escaped to Europe, but 240,000 Axis troops surrendered to the Allies in Tunisia in May of 1943.

The Allies Attack Italy

Although Hitler had lost in North Africa, he now fought to keep "Fortress Europe," or the lands that the Reich held in Europe. The Allies under American General George Patton launched "Operation Husky" to free Italy by invading Sicily, the island off the tip of Italy. American troops under General Mark Clark and British troops under General Bernard Montgomery then crossed to Italy. Working their way up the Italian coast, the Americans captured Naples in October 1943. But the push to take Rome was slowed by Germans who were entrenched in the mountains. It took four months for the Allies to travel through Italy's snow-clad mountains.

As they had done in World War I, the Italians decided to switch sides. They overthrew Mussolini, surrendered to the Allies, and declared war on Germany. Although the American forces freed Rome on June 4, 1944, fighting continued with German forces in Italy for another year. The Allies decided to focus their assault elsewhere in Europe. Leaving behind the fewest possible troops to hold the German force where it was in Italy, General Eisenhower worked in Britain to prepare for a bigger invasion. American generals Omar Bradley and George Patton and British general Bernard

Tanks were ideally suited for the desert terrain in the North African campaigns.

SECTION 4

Materials

- Activity D from Chapter 26 of the *Student Activities* manual
- Special speaker: a veteran or someone with war memorabilia

 Student Activity D: The Rubber Band Snaps in Europe

This map acquaints students with all of the European places discussed in the text.

How Many Battles Can You Name?

Discussions of the American Revolution and the Civil War are filled with famous battle names. But World War II is a series of "operations" and objectives. Students probably cannot name many battles. Why? With the introduction of tanks and paratroopers, battles were fought on a large scale with rapidly shifting lines. No longer did war consist of distinct pitched battles between two opposing armies.

 ### Display War Memorabilia

Families of students or church members are likely to have interesting memorabilia from World War II, including medals and weapons. Ask for a volunteer to share them with the class, along with any stories of family veterans. You might also display model airplanes.

European Theater, 1943-44

Scale of Miles
0   100   300   500

Allied thrusts
Axis controlled

Montgomery assisted Eisenhower in the planning.

The Allies began preparations for a great invasion of Germany through France, "Operation Overlord." They assembled men and equipment in southern England while they sent planes on bombing attacks in Germany. The RAF planes conducted night raids over German cities, systematically destroying two and a half cities per month. The American air force bombed by day, focusing on industrial and military sites.

Invasion at Normandy

At dawn on June 6, 1944, the largest invasion force in history moved into position in the English Channel. Twenty miles away, across the Channel, lay the German-held northwest region of France, called Normandy. Allied leaders had considered tide schedules and

545

"Nuts!"

Hitler's last effort to win the war came in 1944 at the battle of the Bulge. It was more than a single battle. It was a campaign in southern Belgium and the Ardennes Forest in Luxembourg. The Germans focused their attack at one point in the Allied line held by inexperienced divisions. The Allies were forced to retreat, and the German advance created a bulge in the frontline.

Within the bulge, a pocket of resistance remained. The American 101st Airborne Division still controlled the city of Bastogne. Facing cold weather, low supplies, and a German siege, the Americans stubbornly refused to surrender. On December 22, the Germans sent a message to the Americans demanding their surrender. On reading the note Brigadier General Anthony McAuliffe replied, "Aw, nuts!" The other officers decided that "Nuts!" was the perfect response to send back to the Germans. When the Germans asked the American messenger to explain the word, he harshly told them that it meant the Americans were not going to give up and if the siege continued, the Germans would be killed.

Needless to say, the Germans were not happy with the reply and continued their attack even through Christmas Day. Allied aircraft dropped provisions and weapons to the Americans inside Bastogne. Finally on December 26, the Fourth Armored Division of Patton's Third Army moved against the bulge. The force moved forward until they reached Bastogne and relieved the 101st Airborne. Early in 1945 the German bulge was finally pushed back, and the Allies moved forward. By May of that year, Germany had surrendered.

weather reports when they picked June 6 as **"D-day,"** the day for the operation to begin. General Eisenhower led the Allied forces in the Normandy invasion. He announced by radio, "The tide has turned. The free men of the world are marching together to victory." The D-Day invasion was the turning point of the European war.

While the Allied air forces sought to provide air protection, American soldiers landed on Normandy beaches code-named Utah and Omaha, and the British landed on other nearby beaches. German defenses were strong, and the Allied landing was challenged. Losses were heavy, but a beachhead was secured. The Allies then pushed inland yard by yard and mile by mile across some of the same ground fought over in World War I.

On August 25, after a grueling, three-month battle, the Allies liberated Paris. German resistance collapsed rapidly after Paris fell, and by October, just two months later, the Allies had advanced all the way to the Rhine River. But in mid-December the German retreat stopped. Hitler launched an immense counterattack into Belgium in an attempt to recapture the strategic port of Antwerp and divide the Allied forces. Although the Germans did not succeed in taking the port, they did succeed in pushing the Allied lines sixty miles westward at one point. This "bulge" in the lines allowed the Germans to surround an American division in the Belgian town of Bastogne. Other Allied forces rushed to the trapped forces in the resulting **battle of the Bulge.** After a month of battle, the German attack began to slow. The Allies moved in to free those in Bastogne and started pushing the Germans

back toward Germany again. Hitler's forces were faltering.

German Defeat

As the Americans and other Allies fought northward from Italy and east from the Rhine, the Soviets were fighting their way west toward Berlin. Although the American forces probably could have won the race and arrived at Berlin first, they elected not to, concentrating instead on capturing Nazi forces and liberating concentration camps.

The Soviet Union broke the promises it made at Yalta, setting the stage for the Cold War to come.

An additional factor that kept them from Berlin was the **Yalta Meeting** of FDR, Churchill, and Stalin in February 1945. There Soviet "special interests" in Eastern Europe were recognized in return for Stalin's promises of entry into the Pacific war and of holding postwar elections in any countries the Soviets liberated. The Soviet promises proved worthless, but nonetheless, Roosevelt thought these agreements necessary, and Churchill was forced to go along. Yalta would prove to be the

Costly Mistakes

No war is fought without mistakes, some of them costly. Do the students recognize any serious mistakes in Allied strategy? What consequences did they suffer? *(Many historians criticize the decision to focus on mountainous Italy rather than the "soft underbelly" in the Balkans).*

By agreeing to stay out of Yugoslavia and Eastern Europe, Roosevelt allowed the Communists to take over.

Another mistake was allowing the Soviets to reach Berlin first, thus dividing Germany

in two. Eastern Europe still remembers with bitterness the "ghost of Yalta." The American people need to know about mistakes from the past so that they will be less likely to make similar mistakes in the future.

Another potentially costly mistake occurred during the Casablanca Conference between Roosevelt and Churchill. Roosevelt told the press that he would demand "unconditional surrender." As a result of this controversial announcement, it is certain that the antiwar movement was silenced in Germany and the German government faced utter ruin.

The collapse of all German leadership helped the Communists to set up a puppet government there.

Debate Idea

Have your students discuss and/or debate the following:

The Yalta agreement violated American national security interests in World War II.

Berlin suffered great destruction from intense bombing near the close of the war.

last meeting of these two leaders with Stalin. Within a few months Roosevelt was dead, and Britain elected a new prime minister to replace Churchill.

Berlin fell on May 2, 1945, two days after Hitler committed suicide. On May 7, 1945, the Germans surrendered at a schoolhouse near Rheims (REEMZ). An elated America paused briefly to celebrate **"V-E Day"** ("Victory in Europe") on May 8. All efforts could be centered on forcing the Japanese to surrender in the Pacific.

SECTION REVIEW

1. Where was the first major battleground for American soldiers against the Germans in World War II?

2. What country was liberated from Axis rule under "Operation Husky"?

3. What actions did the RAF and the U.S. Air Force take against Germany so that the Allies could invade it?

4. Where and when did the largest invasion in history take place? What was this day called?

5. When did Germany finally surrender?

 How did the conference at Yalta increase the power of the Soviet Union?

The War in the Pacific

While the war in Europe was being won, events in the Pacific did not come to a standstill. America put men, ships, and planes into the Japanese conflict as it was able, but the early results were discouraging.

The Japanese Advance

The same day that Japan attacked Pearl Harbor, it also struck at other major targets in the Pacific, including the Philippines. At that time the Philippines still belonged to the United States, and the islands served as an important American base in the Pacific. On Christmas Eve, 1941, the Japanese made their second large-scale landing on the Philippines. By January they held Manila. The American-Filipino troops, under General **Douglas MacArthur,** held only the Philippine peninsula of Bataan (buh TAN) and the small, nearby island of Corregidor (kuh REHG ih DOR). But when it was realized that it would be impossible for American forces to keep the Philippines, MacArthur was ordered to leave. The United States did not want to risk the capture of a valuable general; so MacArthur escaped to safety in Australia. As he left, he promised the Filipinos, "I shall return."

With supply lines cut off, the American troops remaining in the Philippines ran low on supplies. They suffered from disease and starvation. Even in their weakened condition, they battled to defend Bataan, but it was not enough. On April 9, 1942, most troops on the Bataan peninsula had to surrender to the Japanese. The captured Allied troops were forced to march in tropical heat, without food or water, for sixty-five miles to a prison camp. Thirteen thousand of the American forces in the Philippines had escaped to Corregidor. By early May the Japanese were shelling the island constantly. Finally the remaining men

547

SECTION 5

Objectives
Students should be able to
1. Trace the extent of the Japanese advance.
2. Describe the battles of the Coral Sea and Midway.
3. Explain the American strategy for defeating the Japanese in the Pacific.
4. Explain the success of the kamikaze attacks.

Section Review Answers

1. North Africa (p. 544)

2. Italy (p. 544)

3. The RAF bombed German cities. The U.S. Air Force bombed industrial and military sites. (p. 545)

4. Normandy; June 6, 1944; D-day (pp. 545-46)

5. May 7, 1945 (p. 547)

 There, with Allied consent, it gained a foothold in Eastern

Europe that would lead later to domination. (p. 546)

SECTION 5

Materials

- Activity E from Chapter 26 of the *Student Activities* manual

- (Home school) War games

 Student Activity E: The Balloon Pops in the Pacific

This map acquaints students with all of the places in the Pacific discussed in the text.

The Thach Weave

Compared to the Japanese Zero fighter plane, the American F4F Wildcat lacked maneuverability. The Zero could turn sharper and climb faster, giving it a definite advantage in a dogfight.

Lieutenant Commander J. S. Thach came up with a solution to this problem. He designed a looser four-plane formation that would allow the Wildcats to cover each other. In essence, the planes would act as a team in battle. If a Wildcat was being chased by a Zero, it would begin a spiraling dive. Another Wildcat would start a similar dive that would intertwine with the first giving it opportunity to shoot the pursuing Zero. The navy soon made the "Thach Weave" a standard tactic for their pilots.

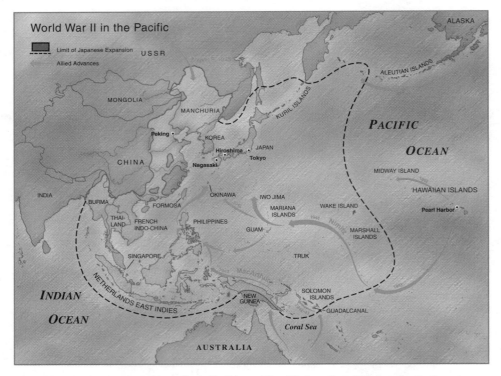

World War II in the Pacific

Limit of Japanese Expansion

Allied Advances

ALASKA · USSR · MONGOLIA · MANCHURIA · Peking · KOREA · Hiroshima · JAPAN · Tokyo · Nagasaki · CHINA · INDIA · BURMA · FORMOSA · OKINAWA · IWO JIMA · MARIANA ISLANDS · THAI-LAND · FRENCH INDO-CHINA · PHILIPPINES · GUAM · SINGAPORE · NETHERLANDS EAST INDIES · INDIAN OCEAN · NEW GUINEA · Coral Sea · AUSTRALIA · KURIL ISLANDS · PACIFIC OCEAN · ALEUTIAN ISLANDS · MIDWAY ISLAND · HAWAIIAN ISLANDS · Pearl Harbor · WAKE ISLAND · MARSHALL ISLANDS · TRUK · SOLOMON ISLANDS · GUADALCANAL

surrendered. The Japanese controlled all of the Philippines.

Meanwhile, the Japanese had also captured most of Southeast Asia and many of the islands in the Pacific. In June the Japanese turned northward and even snatched two of the Aleutian Islands just off the tip of southern Alaska. To America's dismay, the Japanese seemed to control the entire region of eastern Asia and the western Pacific.

American shipyards and munitions factories were gradually making progress. They were soon able to launch and equip new aircraft carriers within fifteen months from the time their construction began. Soon, battleships, aircraft carriers, and escort vessels sailed westward to help push back the Japanese.

The Rising Sun Begins to Set

In the spring and summer of 1942, Americans saw a ray of hope in the Pacific war. On April 8, 1942, the aircraft carrier *Hornet* secretly sailed within seven hundred miles of the Japanese mainland. Sixteen B-25 bombers under the command of Jimmy Doolittle shocked the Japanese by dropping bombs on Tokyo and other Japanese cities. This successful operation was a tremendous boost to the morale of the Americans.

After the bombings, Japan changed its war strategy. The Japanese split their force of aircraft carriers. Two were sent to harass Allied naval supply lines near Australia. The other four giant carriers moved into the middle of the Pacific, acting as magnets to draw the United States into battle there. Because the

548

Which War Presented Greater Challenges?

Ask the students which of the two world wars presented the greatest challenge, as far as converting the nation to war production. *(The answer must be World War II because the United States faced a greater threat to its transports [because of submarines], the United States had to fight on two fronts [Europe and the Pacific], and the United States had to provide supplies for more allies [the Soviet Union, in particular].)* The nation's effectiveness is amazing, and it disproved the tyrants' fantasy that Americans had "gone soft" under democracy and capitalism. Ask the students whether they would be willing to make similar sacrifices today.

Preparedness is an old question. Many experts argue that the United States will not have time to "prepare" for the next war because it will be over too quickly. That is one argument given to support a large standing army. Is it a valid argument?

Japanese lacked the productive power to fight a long war, they gambled everything on a quick victory.

The Japanese aircraft carriers heading for Australia used the Coral Sea as an approach lane. In May of 1942 they met an American naval force led by two aircraft carriers, the *Yorktown* and the *Lexington*. The resulting three-day **battle of the Coral Sea** was unusual because it was the first sea battle in which all of the fighting was done by airplanes. The Japanese force turned back, and one of its carriers was sunk. The *Lexington* suffered such extensive damage that it had to be destroyed, but the battle successfully stopped Japanese advances toward Australia.

The other Japanese aircraft carriers had headed toward Midway Island, an American island west of Hawaii. The Japanese hoped to attack the island base and then lure American carriers into a battle. But by this time American naval intelligence had cracked the Japanese radio code and had advance warning. Planes from American carriers bombed the Japanese ships in advance, preventing the attack on Midway. The Americans sank three Japanese carriers in a few minutes, and the fourth went down the next day. The cost to America was also high. The Americans lost one aircraft carrier, and most of the planes and their pilots had been shot down. However, the huge Japanese sea offensive was stopped, and the Japanese navy had suffered a defeat.

The Americans then planned a strategy to capture the Japanese-held islands in the Pacific. Starting with the southern islands, American naval forces would work their way

The cost of the battle of Midway was high, including the loss of the U.S.S. Yorktown, but "Avenger" torpedo bombers helped win the day.

northward until they reached islands that were within bombing distance of Japan. General MacArthur would head one operation that would push northward from New Guinea to the Philippines. Admiral **Chester Nimitz** (NIM itz) would "island-hop" across the mid-Pacific, taking certain key islands in three chains: the Gilberts, the Marshalls, and the Marianas. Then both forces would converge on the Japanese mainland.

MacArthur Moves Northward

The Japanese, meanwhile, had almost finished an airfield on **Guadalcanal** (GWOD ul kuh NAL) in the Solomon Islands near New Guinea. From there they could bomb Allied convoys at will. Consequently, MacArthur began his offensive there in 1942, but it took six months to drive the Japanese out. The Japanese fought tenaciously, and American casualties were heavy. Finally, the marines dynamited the island's caves to force out the last Japanese defenders.

The American attack on New Guinea became bogged down and was saved only

549

Midway Code Breaking

Admiral Yamamoto had a good plan for capturing Midway Island. He planned to send some forces to attack the Aleutian Islands off the coast of Alaska. The American Pacific Fleet, according to his estimation, would sail north from Midway to rescue the Aleutians. Once they sailed away from Midway, his main invasion force would seize the island. By the time the American fleet turned around, the island would be in Japanese control and Yamamoto could focus on attacking the fleet.

That was the plan, but it is not how things turned out. American code breakers discovered Yamamoto's plan to use the Aleutians as a diversion. However, they were not sure the main target was Midway. Coded Japanese messages referred to the target only as AF. To verify the target, Admiral Nimitz had the Midway garrison broadcast that they were out of fresh water. He made sure the message was sent in a code that the Japanese had already deciphered. Two days later the American code breakers intercepted a Japanese message saying that AF was out of water. Midway was definitely the target. When the attack on the Aleutians came, the Pacific Fleet remained near Midway, anticipating the Japanese invasion force.

War Games

More war games have been developed for World War II than any other war. Of special value are the grand strategy games that allow students to weigh the same choices that Roosevelt and his generals considered when making their war plans. Two popular board games are Axis & Allies and Third Reich. These games require several hours to learn and play (especially Third Reich). If your students are already familiar with the games, you might want to ask them to share some of the insights they have gained about alternative strategies.

General MacArthur honors his promise to return to the Philippines.

The Americans learned lessons for future attacks. The Japanese did not surrender easily. Two months of bombing before landing troops became normal. Thousands of tons of explosives would be hurled shoreward by battleships at Japanese targets from this point on.

After launching such attacks in the Marshall Islands, the Nimitz forces recaptured Guam in the Marianas. Next, they retook the sea east of the Philippines from the Japanese. The fleet then angled northward toward **Iwo Jima** (EE-woh JEE-muh). This small island, only seven hundred miles from Tokyo, had been a station from which the Japanese could intercept American bombers headed for Japan. If the United States could capture it, Iwo Jima could serve as an emergency landing and refueling stop for American bombers. It could also provide a takeoff point for shorter-range fighter planes. But Iwo Jima proved to be the costliest chunk of rock and black sand taken by the U.S. Marine Corps in their 168-year history. Over five thousand marines died during its capture in early 1945.

when General MacArthur airlifted fifteen thousand troops there. By October 1944 MacArthur's forces were ready to retake the Philippines, landing first at Leyte (LAY tee). Many liberty-loving Filipino fighters who had hidden in the mountains and jungles now undertook guerrilla warfare to help the Americans free the Philippines. MacArthur said, "I have returned. By the grace of Almighty God, our forces stand again on Philippine soil, soil consecrated by the blood of our two peoples." By March 1945 the forces had moved northward and had freed the Philippine capital of Manila on the island of Luzon.

Nimitz Moves West

The first target of Admiral Nimitz's Pacific operation was Tarawa, the largest atoll (a ring-like island of coral) in the Gilbert Islands. After bombing the island for a whole week and pounding it for hours with heavy gunfire, the Americans did not expect much resistance. They soon discovered how well the Japanese held out. While American losses soared, the Japanese resisted until only seventeen of more than forty-five hundred defenders remained alive.

As war with the Japanese intensified, the Allied seamen began to fear a new type of Japanese attack: the **kamikazes** (KAH mih KAH zeez). Kamikazes were suicide attack planes. Their pilots deliberately hurled these

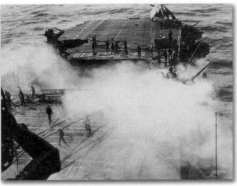
Sailors attempt to control the blaze after a kamikaze plane crashes into the U.S.S. Enterprise.

The Image of Iwo Jima

Point the students to page 533—the famous image of soldiers raising the flag during the battle for Iwo Jima. How is this a fitting image of America's effort during the war?

planes at an enemy target. Such attacks were a product of the Japanese belief that the highest gift one could give the emperor was one's life. Furthermore, Japan had lost both its first-rate pilots and its best planes. In kamikaze warfare out-of-date planes could be loaded with explosives and flown by inexperienced pilots who had only to dive into a ship. The results were devastating. Kamikazes sank 30 ships, damaged 368 more, and killed 11,000 sailors. In spite of the kamikaze attacks, the American forces pushed on toward Japan.

Taking **Okinawa** (OH kih NOW wah) was the last obstacle to reaching the Japanese mainland. The assault on Okinawa began in April 1945 and was completed in June. The Japanese fought hard; over 110,000 died, leaving 11,000 to surrender. But now Americans were just 325 miles from mainland Japan and were able to attack both Japan's industrial and population centers. In one ten-day bombing blitz American planes turned thirty-two square miles of factories into wasteland. Fire bombing of residential areas was especially destructive because the Japanese homes were built close together and were constructed of highly flammable materials.

SECTION REVIEW

1. What American general was forced to evacuate while attempting to hold the Philippines?

2. What two American military leaders took command of much of the action against Japan?

3. An airfield on which of the Solomon Islands took the Americans six months to capture?

4. What small island base had the Japanese used to keep American bombers from Japan? How many marines died in its capture?

5. What was the last American conquest before attacking the Japanese mainland?

 Why did the Japanese use kamikazes despite the tragic waste of human life?

The End of the War

American forces were closing in on all sides, and Japan was suffering heavily from bombing raids. The American military had learned, however, how hard the Japanese would fight. Many feared that it would take hundreds of thousands of American lives to invade and conquer Japan.

The Beginning of the Atomic Era

In 1933, as Hitler gained power and took action against the German Jews, physics professor Albert Einstein took refuge in the United States. Aware of the Nazis' efforts to develop a uranium bomb, Einstein wrote the president in July 1939 to advise him of the possibilities and dangers of such a weapon. Leaders in the United States decided to set up a secret program to make such a bomb before the Germans could.

A group of brilliant scientists joined this **"Manhattan Project."** In Los Alamos, New Mexico, the Manhattan Project engineers assembled the materials for the bomb. At dawn on July 16, 1945, the first device was successfully tested in New Mexico.

On April 12, 1945, Franklin Roosevelt, by then in his fourth term as president, died from the effects of a stroke. The day after **Harry S. Truman** stepped into the presidency, he was told of the Manhattan Project. He decided that it would be better to end the war quickly with the new weapon than to spend countless thousands of lives in an invasion of Japan. Although in later years people debated Truman's approval of dropping the bomb, Truman wrote in his *Memoirs,* "Let there be no mistake about it. I regarded the bomb as a military weapon and never had any doubt that it should be used."

551

---

with Japan. The Japanese could have also tried to surrender to the Soviets. This possibility drew an increasingly negative response in the United States as relations with the Soviets turned sour.

Many modern historians have focused on Soviet-American relations in regards to the decision to drop the bomb. Some argue that the main motivation for the decision was not to force Japan to surrender but to intimidate the Soviet Union. While attending the Potsdam Conference with Churchill and Stalin, Truman learned that the atomic bomb had been successfully tested. He was described as a "changed man" when next he met with Stalin. He had more confidence and determination to resist Stalin's ambitions.

Another possibility is that the decision was made to keep the Soviets from participating in an invasion of Japan. This motivation does not seem so odd considering the Soviet Union's postwar actions. Almost every area in Europe liberated by the Soviets came under Communist control. A joint operation in Japan might have resulted in a situation similar to that in Germany, where the Western Allies and the Soviets rushed to defeat the Nazis. The seeds of another Cold War conflict might have been sown.

Germany and the Bomb

Germany had nearly perfected the atomic bomb before its defeat, and thus the development was vital to the United States. Imagine what Hitler could have done had he gained the atomic bomb first.

It is interesting to note that the scientists of the Manhattan Project had built only three bombs. One was used in the test in New Mexico, and the other two were dropped on Japan.

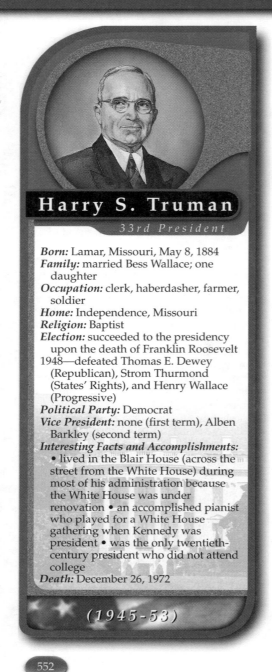

Harry S. Truman
33rd President

Born: Lamar, Missouri, May 8, 1884
Family: married Bess Wallace; one daughter
Occupation: clerk, haberdasher, farmer, soldier
Home: Independence, Missouri
Religion: Baptist
Election: succeeded to the presidency upon the death of Franklin Roosevelt 1948—defeated Thomas E. Dewey (Republican), Strom Thurmond (States' Rights), and Henry Wallace (Progressive)
Political Party: Democrat
Vice President: none (first term), Alben Barkley (second term)
Interesting Facts and Accomplishments:
• lived in the Blair House (across the street from the White House) during most of his administration because the White House was under renovation • an accomplished pianist who played for a White House gathering when Kennedy was president • was the only twentieth-century president who did not attend college
Death: December 26, 1972

(1945-53)

552

A "mushroom" cloud rises above Nagasaki, Japan, following the atomic explosion in 1945.

On July 26, when President Truman met at Potsdam in Germany for a conference with the major powers, he issued the **Potsdam Declaration.** It demanded that Japan surrender unconditionally or face total destruction.

Although the original military leaders in Japan's war effort were no longer in power, the new premier refused to surrender. Eleven days later, on August 6, 1945, at 8:15 A.M., an American bomber dropped a single uranium bomb on **Hiroshima** (HIR uh SHE muh). Although it was only a little more than two feet in diameter and ten feet long, the bomb's explosive power was equal to twenty thousand tons of dynamite. The blast killed eighty thousand Japanese civilians, and an equal number suffered radiation burns.

After another warning to surrender was ignored, the United States dropped a single plutonium bomb, called "Fat Boy," on **Nagasaki** (NAH guh SAH kee) on August 9. This bomb flattened the city and killed about forty thousand people.

Peace

The next day Japan sued for peace. On August 15, 1945, the Japanese people heard the voice of their emperor Hirohito. In a taped radio broadcast, the emperor told his subjects

Red Flags—The Decision to Drop the Bomb

The last paragraph on page 551 analyzes the controversial decision to drop the atomic bomb. Divide the class into opposing sides on the issue, and ask them to research the arguments given on both sides.

that the war was over. Americans at home ran into the streets, temporarily leaving their jobs, and hugged one another from sheer joy.

Although a few Japanese groups in distant spots continued to fight, the war was really over. On August 21 General MacArthur was in Tokyo. As he watched the same flag that had flown over the U.S. Capitol on December 7, 1941, go up over the reestablished American embassy, he said, "Let it wave in full glory as a symbol of hope for the oppressed and as a harbinger of victory."

On September 2, 1945, MacArthur accepted two of the emperor's representatives on board the battleship *Missouri* anchored in Tokyo Bay. There they signed the formal treaty of surrender.

World War II was the costliest war in history. It is estimated that over fifteen million soldiers and twenty million civilians died in the war. The United States lost nearly three hundred thousand of its military personnel,

and many more were wounded. On top of its human effort and loss, the nation spent about $300 billion on the war.

Americans returned to peacetime with great relief that the price had been paid and the war had been won. It then remained for them to take their place in the postwar world.

SECTION REVIEW

1. What was the Manhattan Project?

2. Who became president before the war ended?

3. On what two cities were the atomic bombs dropped?

4. Where, when, and by whom was the Japanese surrender accepted?

5. How many American servicemen died in the war?

 Why has there been debate over Truman's decision to drop the atomic bomb?

SUMMARY

The fascist governments that arose in Germany and Italy began to threaten Europe in the late 1930s, while Japan's militaristic government wanted more control in Asia and the Pacific. The desires of these nations led them to band together as the Axis powers and brought Britain and France into war against them in 1939. Hitler's German armies soon took control of most of Europe, including France. For over a year, Britain stood alone against the Axis powers. The United States aided the Allied cause by supplying materials but was unwilling to join the war until Japan bombed the American naval base at Pearl Harbor in December 1941.

With that attack, the United States entered the war and began to build its military strength to defeat its enemies. With Britain, the United States concentrated first on defeating Hitler and Mussolini in Europe. Campaigns were launched in North Africa, Italy, and France, and the Allied advances finally brought victory in Europe on May 8, 1945.

In the east the Japanese had taken control of much of Southeast Asia and the Pacific Islands. They had even taken control of America's Philippine Islands. But American forces began to battle back, winning control of island after island until they reached islands within bombing distance of Japan. Rather than risk a large-scale invasion, the U.S. dropped two atomic bombs on Japan. This action forced the Japanese to surrender and ended World War II in August 1945. The United States emerged from the war as leader of the free world and as a nation with many postwar problems.

553

Look Ahead

Students are about to begin the final unit of the book. Ask them to put themselves in the place of the common citizen at the end of World War II. What had they suffered? What costs would they bear? What prospects did the future hold? Ask some students to give an optimistic view and some a pessimistic view. Note that even Truman hoped that the good relations with the Soviet Union would carry over into the postwar era.

Students must recognize that the people had only a glimmer of the coming Cold War. The disappointments of the coming years are an essential part of any evaluation of the success of World War II. Like so many other wars, victory seemed empty. Christians know that no war can solve mankind's basic problems, and they also know that wars must be fought until Christ's return.

Section Review Answers

1. American research project to develop the atomic bomb (p. 551)

2. Harry S. Truman (p. 551)

3. Hiroshima and Nagasaki (p. 552)

4. on the battleship *Missouri;* September 2, 1945; Douglas MacArthur (p. 553)

5. nearly 300,000 (p. 553)

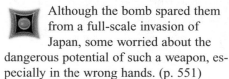 Although the bomb spared them from a full-scale invasion of Japan, some worried about the dangerous potential of such a weapon, especially in the wrong hands. (p. 551)

Chapter Review

People, Places, and Things to Remember

Adolf Hitler	Lend-Lease Act	Guadalcanal
Nazi Party	Pearl Harbor	Iwo Jima
Benito Mussolini	conscientious objectors	kamikazes
fascist governments	Dwight D. Eisenhower	Okinawa
Axis powers	D-Day	Manhattan Project
Good Neighbor Policy	battle of the Bulge	Harry S. Truman
Winston Churchill	Yalta Meeting	Potsdam Declaration
appeasement	V-E Day	Hiroshima
Joseph Stalin	Douglas MacArthur	Nagasaki
blitzkrieg	battle of the Coral Sea	
Allies	Chester Nimitz	

Review Questions

What word(s) is (are) best described by each of the following phrases?

1. strong dictatorships that stressed nationalism and power

2. giving in to demands in an attempt to settle a disagreement peacefully

3. a swift attack of bombers, tanks, and troops—a "lightning war"

4. young men who were sincerely opposed to war and were thus allowed to serve in noncombat roles instead of regular military service

5. Japanese planes flown on suicide missions to destroy American ships

Match each of the following men with his country.

6. Franklin Roosevelt   a. Britain

7. Benito Mussolini   b. Germany

8. Joseph Stalin   c. Italy

9. Adolf Hitler   d. Soviet Union

10. Winston Churchill   e. United States

Match the appropriate letter on the time line with the event that occurred on that date. Also describe the significance of each event.

1939	1940	1941	1942	1943	1944	1945
A		B			C	D E

11. V-E Day   14. bomb dropped on Hiroshima

12. attack on Pearl Harbor   15. D-Day

13. Hitler invades Poland

Questions for Discussion

16. Should the United States have been better prepared for World War II? Should it be constantly prepared for war? Explain your answers.

17. How does a man like Hitler gain such popularity and power? Could such a man rise to power in the United States? Explain your answer.

History Skills

Steps to War

Although America's change from total isolationism to all-out war seemed sudden, it was provoked by a long series of events. To trace these events, use the reactions listed below to complete the chart on your own paper.

Foreign Action	American Reaction
1. Treaty of Versailles (1919)	
2. Treaty of Washington (1921)	
3. Kellogg-Briand Peace Pact (1928)	
4. Japan's conquest of Manchuria (1931)	
5. Allies' failure to pay war debts (early 1930s)	*bitterness at the Allies' ingratitude*
6. Italy's conquest of Ethiopia (1935)	
7. Germany's capture of the Rhineland (1936)	
8. Britain's appeasement (1938)	
9. Allied declaration of war (1939)	
10. fall of France (1940)	
11. Japan's entry into Southeast Asia (1941)	
12. Germany's invasion of Russia (1941)	*secret agreement with Churchill to defeat "Hitler first"*
13. Germany's sinking of U.S. convoys (1941)	
14. Japan's attack on Pearl Harbor (1941)	

American Reactions:

"lend-lease" policy
"cash-and-carry" policy
ban on most trade with Japan
disillusionment with foreign wars
declaration of war against the Axis powers
hope that naval competition would cease
horror at fascist aggression, but no action
worldwide realization of the Nazi threat to
   peace

hope that nations would avoid future
   wars to settle disputes
decision to shoot submarines on sight
no protests at the violation of the
   Versailles Treaty
disappointment after appealing to the
   League of Nations

History Skills

1. disillusionment with foreign wars

2. hope that naval competition would cease

3. hope that nations would avoid future wars to settle disputes

4. disappointment after appealing to the League of Nations

5. (given)

6. horror at fascist aggression, but no action

7. no protests at the violation of the Versailles treaty

8. worldwide realization of the Nazi threat to peace

9. "cash-and-carry" policy

10. "lend-lease" policy

11. ban on most trade with Japan

12. (given)

13. decision to shoot submarines on sight

14. declaration of war against the Axis powers

Preparing for the Future

Unit Seven

This final unit gives your students an opportunity to apply to the current era what they have learned from successes and failures in history. As you teach this unit, you should review many of the themes that have surfaced in previous chapters—not only the consequences of moral decay, government intervention, and citizen apathy, but also the amazing flexibility of the Constitution and God's providential care for His people.

Facing the Future

Put on the bulletin board a time line from the founding of the United States to the present. Have your students illustrate different decades with events that fit. At the end of the time line, post either Jeremiah 29:11 or II Chronicles 7:14 as an encouragement to your students that God is still in control.

Materials

You will need the following special materials for your teaching of Unit Seven.

- *Student Activities* manual for THE AMERICAN REPUBLIC for Christian Schools (Second Edition)
- Special speaker: someone to talk about life in the fifties
- Video about the threat of nuclear holocaust during the Cold War
- Special speaker: someone to talk about life under the threat of nuclear holocaust
- A copy of JFK's inaugural address
- A copy of the February 1993 issue of *National Geographic*
- A copy of "Letter from a Birmingham Jail" by Martin Luther King Jr.
- Video documentary on the civil rights movement
- A copy of Reagan's first inaugural speech
- Special speaker: an expert in computer technology

CHAPTERS IN THIS UNIT:

RECOVERY, COLD WAR, AND COEXISTENCE

THE SIXTIES— NATION IN CRISIS

RISE OF THE RIGHT

BRIDGE TO THE 21ST CENTURY

556

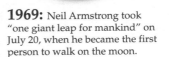

1963: Led by Martin Luther King Jr., 250,000 people marched on Washington, D.C. to show their support for civil rights legislation.

1969: Neil Armstrong took "one giant leap for mankind" on July 20, when he became the first person to walk on the moon.

1950s: Hula-Hoops were popular with the children of the postwar baby boom.

Unit 7	Lesson Plan Chart		
Chapter Title	Main Goal	Pages	Time Frame
27. Recovery, Cold War, and Coexistence	To understand that the world will never be safe for democracy	559-77	5-7 days
28. The Sixties—Nation in Crisis	To identify the internal battles for democracy being waged in this era	578-603	5½-9 days
29. Rise of the Right	To determine characteristics of a good president and how to choose a president	604-22	4½-6 days
30. Bridge to the 21st Century	To identify modern problems as the same problems returning from the past	623-45	5-6 days
Total Suggested Days			20-28 days

1974: President Richard Nixon left office in the wake of a scandal surrounding a burglary at the Democratic Party's National Campaign Headquarters and the subsequent cover-up by the White House.

1991: After five weeks of intensive bombing in the Persian Gulf War, it took ground troops just one hundred hours to force the surrender of Iraqi troops in Kuwait.

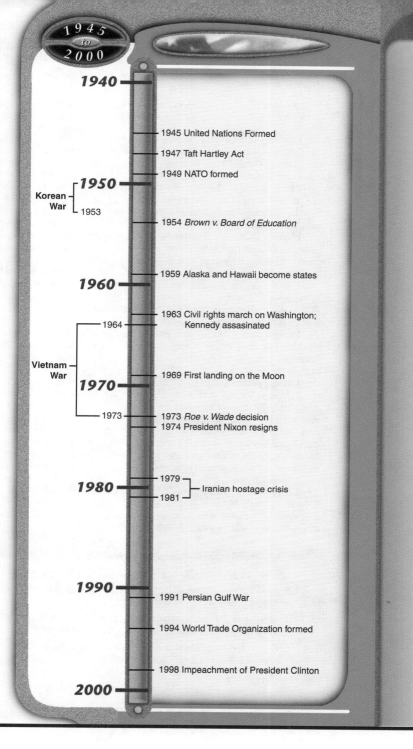

1945 to 2000

1940

1945 United Nations Formed

1947 Taft Hartley Act

1949 NATO formed

1950

Korean War — 1953

1954 *Brown v. Board of Education*

1959 Alaska and Hawaii become states

1960

1963 Civil rights march on Washington; Kennedy assasinated

Vietnam War — 1964

1969 First landing on the Moon

1970

1973 *Roe v. Wade* decision

1974 President Nixon resigns

1980

1979 — Iranian hostage crisis
1981 —

1990

1991 Persian Gulf War

1994 World Trade Organization formed

1998 Impeachment of President Clinton

2000

Time Out

Ask the following questions about the time line. Have your students give the event and the date.

- What are the names and dates for the three wars in this era? *(Korean War, 1950-53; Vietnam War, 1964-73; Persian Gulf War, 1991)*

- What year was John F. Kennedy assassinated? *(1963)*

- What event changed the boundaries of the United States? *(statehood of Alaska and Hawaii in 1959)*

Unit VII: Preparing for the Future

King's "I Have a Dream" Speech

Rev. Martin Luther King used his gifts as a speaker to rally support for civil rights legislation. Read this conclusion to his powerful speech. Then answer the questions.

I say to you today, my friends, that in spite of the difficulties and frustrations of the moment, I still have a dream. It is a dream rooted in the American dream.

I have a dream that one day this nation will rise up and live out the true meaning of its creed: "We hold these truths to be self-evident, that all men are created equal."

I have a dream that one day on the red hills of Georgia the sons of former slaves and the sons of former slaveowners will be able to sit down together at the table of brotherhood.

I have a dream that one day even the state of Mississippi, a desert state sweltering with the heat of injustice and oppression, will be transformed into an oasis of freedom and justice.

I have a dream that my four little children will one day live in a nation where they will not be judged by the color of their skin but by the content of their character.

I have a dream today.

I have a dream that one day the state of Alabama, whose governor's lips are presently dripping with the words of interposition and nullification, will be transformed into a situation where little black boys and black girls will be able to join hands with little white boys and white girls and walk together as sisters and brothers.

I have a dream today.

I have a dream that one day every valley shall be exalted, every hill and mountain shall be made low, the rough places will be made plain, and the crooked places will be made straight, and the glory of the Lord shall be revealed, and all flesh shall see it together.

This is our hope. This is the faith with which I return to the South. With this faith we will be able to transform the jangling discords of our nation into a beautiful symphony of brotherhood. With this faith we will be able to work together, to pray together, to struggle together, to go to jail together, to stand up for freedom together, knowing that we will be free one day.

This will be the day when all of God's children will be able to sing with new meaning: "My country, 'tis of thee, sweet land of liberty, of thee I sing. Land where my fathers died, land of the pilgrim's pride, from every mountainside, let freedom ring."

And if America is to be a great nation, this must become true. So let freedom ring from the prodigious hilltops of New Hampshire. Let freedom ring from the mountains of New York. Let freedom ring from the heightening Alleghenies of Pennsylvania!

Let freedom ring from every hill and molehill of Mississippi! From every mountainside, let freedom ring!

When we let freedom ring, when we let it ring from every village and every hamlet, from every state and every city, we will be able to speed up that day when all of God's children, black men and white men, Jews and Gentiles, Protestants and Catholics, will be able to join hands and sing in the words of the old Negro spiritual, "Free at last! Free at last! Thank God Almighty, we are free at last!"

1. Does King appeal to any values that you support? What are some of them?

2. King appeals to equality, expressed in the Declaration of Independence. What does King believe is "the true meaning" of this creed?

3. King appeals to universal justice, prophesied by Isaiah (40:3-5) and explained in Luke 3:2-6. How does King apply this passage?

4. King appeals to freedom, promised in John 8:34-36 and expressed in the Negro spiritual "Free at last!" What does King mean when he says, "We will be free one day"?

"I Have a Dream"

1. (Most students will answer yes.) the American dream, equality, brotherhood, freedom, justice, character, the glory of the Lord, hope, faith, working together, prayer, country, unity

2. He believed that minorities have a right to expect equal treatment without prejudice. In other words, the federal government has a duty to secure equal treatment, regardless of the desires of the states or the people.

3. He speaks of a time when people, working together, would transform America and bring "a beautiful symphony of brotherhood."

4. He believed that social action will one day free all people, not just from slavery but from the prejudice of others. He rejoiced in his hope that mankind can bring happiness on earth.

27

Recovery, Cold War, and Coexistence

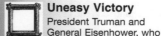 **Uneasy Victory**

President Truman and General Eisenhower, who helped to shape postwar America in the years following World War II, shake hands to celebrate victory in Europe. However, shading the celebration is the realization of another foe that threatens—Communism.

Chapter Motivation

Even though America had helped other nations win a war for democracy, the next thirty years continued the fight against Communism. Remind your students that there are always men and governments that desire to control others and remove their freedoms. Democracy is hard to maintain and is constantly threatened. Ask the students to look for God's control in the events of the fifties and sixties.

Materials

SECTION 1
- Activities A and C from Chapter 27 of the *Student Activities* manual
- Special speaker: someone to talk about life in the fifties
- Paper for a wall time line

SECTION 2
- No materials

SECTION 3
- Activity B from Chapter 27 of the *Student Activities* manual

---

t 7:00 P.M. (EST) on August 14, 1945, President Harry Truman announced to the nation that Japan had finally accepted the terms of surrender. Church bells rang. Whistles blew. Troop ships halfway across the Pacific turned around and headed home. World War II was over! Four years of conflict on the battlefields, on the seas, and in the air had come to a halt. The United States was at peace.

The war was over, but the United States faced new challenges that would prove to be almost as trying as the war had been. The world after the war was not the same as the one that had existed before. New problems, new threats, and new fears emerged in the postwar era. But the country would also have new opportunities and new technology that would bring a new prosperity.

Home from the War

The end of the war brought nine million men in uniform home to civilian life. It brought the retooling of industries to produce peacetime goods instead of guns and tanks. It opened the way for new inventions, new styles, and new fads to change America's way of life.

CHAPTER 27	Lesson Plan Chart		
Section Title	Main Activity	Pages	Time Frame
1. Home from the War	Guest Speaker Who Lived During the Fifties	559-63	1-2 days
2. Postwar Problems	Learning from Past Victories	564-67	1 day
3. Cold War Crises	Student Activity B: Hot Spots During the Cold War	567-72	1-2 days
4. The Eisenhower Era	Why Do Foreign Affairs Matter?	572-75	1 day
Total Suggested Days (including 1 day for review and testing)			5-7 days

SECTION 1

Materials

- Activities A and C from Chapter 27 of the *Student Activities* manual
- Special speaker: someone to talk about life in the fifties
- Paper for a wall time line

SECTION 4
• Activity D from Chapter 27 of the *Student Activities* manual
• Video about the threat of nuclear holocaust during the fifties
• Special speaker: someone to talk about life under the threat of the nuclear holocaust

SECTION 1

Objectives
Students should be able to
1. Describe the economic conditions that followed the war.
2. Explain how the places and ways people lived changed in the years after the war.
3. Describe Truman's Fair Deal.

Record Industry
Not only did television bring changes for postwar America, but so did new technology in the phonograph industry. The 78 rpm records of the thirties and forties were replaced with 33⅓ rpm long-playing records in stereophonic sound for serious music lovers and with 45 rpm records that became a hit with teenagers. A new type of music, rock-and-roll, gained popularity in the late 1950s and began a trend of encouraging teenage rebellion and recklessness.

Levittowns
After World War II, many Americans were eager to move from their cramped city apartments. Government measures such as the GI Bill had given the means to move, but builders like William and Alfred Levitt gave them a destination.

During World War II the Levitt brothers had obtained a contract with the federal government to build homes for defense workers. It was in these years that they learned how to build houses cheaply and quickly. They put their skills to good use in 1947 by building a suburban housing development on New York's Long Island.

Changing Times

Many Americans feared that a depression would follow World War II as it had World War I or that the nation would return to the hardships of the Great Depression. Instead of another depression, however, Americans found plenty of jobs, and they kept businesses booming with their desire for more and more material goods. They wanted new comforts and labor-saving devices such as dishwashers, automatic washers, electric dryers, power lawn mowers, and boats. The easy availability of credit encouraged such purchasing.

Since some consumer goods had been either rationed or totally unavailable during the war, people were now ready to buy what they could not buy before. In 1944 factories had produced 100,000 planes and only 70,000 passenger cars. In 1949 only 6,000 planes were produced, but 3.7 million passenger cars rolled off assembly lines. The major problem was that so many goods were in demand, and factories could not produce enough to satisfy the public. Prices on many goods skyrocketed until the demand was met. But as more factories got in gear to produce needed items, inflation settled down, and the economy became stable.

Another aid to Americans after the war was the **GI Bill.** Fearful that soldiers returning from war would be unemployed, as many were after World War I, Congress passed a bill that helped the veterans move right into civilian life. Veterans were granted benefits in many areas, including help in finding jobs and money for education and for home purchases.

While the young men were away at war, many young couples had postponed marriage. With the war over, many newlyweds began to start families, and the resulting **"baby boom"** created tremendous new demands, which changed over the years as the children grew. A demand for housing was followed by a demand for baby goods such as baby food,

Better communication through radio and television spread fads across the nation at lightning speed. This girl enjoys the Hula-Hoop.

diapers, and strollers. When these children started school, there were acute shortages of classrooms and teachers.

With housing shortages in the early postwar years and the high cost of land in the cities, more Americans became willing to move to the suburbs. Contractors built homes cheaply and quickly, using the techniques of mass production. Bulldozers graded the lots, and work crews came to lay water, gas, sewer,

560

Student Activity A: The Postwar Administrations

This chart summarizes the key events under Presidents Truman and Eisenhower. You may want to help the students complete the chart in class as you lecture.

Guest Speaker Who Lived During the Fifties

If at all possible, bring in a guest speaker to talk about life in the fifties and to answer students' questions. In particular, ask the speaker to talk about changes in

cars, the interstate highways, fads, the statehood of Alaska and Hawaii, the St. Lawrence Seaway, and even the Cold War. Have the students prepare questions ahead of time (and give these to the guest speaker ahead of time).

The Downside of the GI Bill

By this point, the students should be questioning the wisdom of each new government program they read about. They should recognize that most programs have a downside. Can the students find the downside to the GI Bill? Anytime the federal govern-

ment intervenes in private enterprise and education, there are unintended consequences. Just as state-run elementary and secondary education helps to explain the education woes in America today, federally funded college education has been blamed for problems in colleges and universities. Pouring money into schools of higher learning led to waste and experimentation on expensive new programs. With the easing of financial restraints, the cost of college education skyrocketed while quality fell. An even worse result of federal money is the strings attached. The federal govern-

Beginning in the 1950s, the interstate highway system changed the landscape of America by allowing people in the outlying country to drive quickly to city jobs. Urban sprawl became common around major cities.

and electrical lines. They were followed by carpenters, who built row after row of identical houses. Roofers, plumbers, electricians, and painters applied their skills as well. Rolling fields turned into suburbs in a few weeks or months.

Most (about ninety-five percent) of those who moved to homes in the suburbs were younger whites. Cities were left to be occupied by the poor (mostly the elderly and racial minorities). Since cities could not collect heavy taxes from the poor, they had to function with less money. Thus cities started to decay and sought government aid for urban renewal projects.

To live in the suburbs, Americans needed more cars. Two-car families became common because the breadwinner needed a car to drive to work and the family wanted to use another.

With more cars came more automotive-related industries like service stations and car washes. Shopping centers were started in order to cut the travel distance to stores. Cities spread out so much that some described the situation as "urban sprawl."

Naturally, the traffic increased, and commuter traffic jams became more common. These problems and the desire to be able to move troops and equipment in case of war prompted the government to promote more and better highways. In 1956 a **Federal Aid Highway Act** was passed. This allowed construction of 41,000 miles of interstate highways at a cost of $28 million over thirteen years. Increased use of auto, truck, and air transportation cut back the use of railroads.

With cars, highways, and the availability of new jobs, Americans were willing to move

On 1,200 acres of potato farmland, the Levitts and their workers laid out street after street and built home after home. The Levitts reduced home building to twenty-seven steps. Different materials were dropped off at sites throughout the day, and each worker specialized in one particular task. Trees were laid out exactly twenty-eight feet apart, and houses were built on two models, the Cape Cod and the Ranch house.

Several cost-cutting measures were used in construction. Instead of building basements, the Levitts installed radiant heat coils in the concrete slabs. Sheetrock walls replaced plaster ones. Metal pre-assembled cabinets were installed instead of wooden ones. One of the most distinguishable features was a large wall of windows in the back of the house. Not only did this practice save the Levitts from building another wall, but it also made the house seem bigger by giving a broad view of the back yard.

In the first week of sales, over three hundred homes were sold. Prices started at $6,990, but Levitt soon raised them by $1,000 dollars. Still, it was a good deal, and many people were willing to pay the price. Buyers agreed to follow rules, such as mowing the lawn once a week, not hanging laundry on weekends, and not building fences.

The Levitts' success in New York inspired them to build other Levittowns in New Jersey, Pennsylvania, and Florida. Many other suburban developers followed the Levitts' pattern as well. However, some people began to criticize Levittowns as symbolizing a growing conformity in American culture. According to them, all the houses looked the same, and everyone conformed to prescribed social roles. While these criticisms seemed justified at first, once people got settled they began to individualize their homes. Many built on additions for extra living space or added carports and garages. In fact, Levitt homes have changed

561

ment places demands on schools before they can receive federal money.

Federal grants and loans might seem like a good thing, especially to young people who face a steep bill for college. So this is an ideal time to test students' willingness to live by principle rather than pragmatism, to oppose government handouts even when they are enticing.

A Time Line of the 1950s

Hang a time line on the wall and write the foreign and domestic events in their proper places as you discuss them in class. Or have

students prepare their own time lines with categories for social, political, literary, and economic events for the 1950s.

Discuss Urban Sprawl

Discuss recent debates about urban sprawl, particularly in your area. Based on what the students have learned, do they think government regulation is the solution?

Old Debates About Internal Improvements

Throughout this unit, help the students to see how modern problems are parallel to

problems Americans have faced in the past. When they read about the Federal Aid Highway Act, what similar issues do they remember from the past? *(turnpikes, canals, and railroads)* Do they remember the issues on both sides of the debate? *(Opponents say federal involvement leads to graft and inefficiency, and it appears to be a misappropriation to take money from one region in order to benefit people of another region. Proponents say it ultimately benefits the whole nation.)* Have your students form their own opinions. Can

so much that they are presenting a difficulty for the Smithsonian. The institution has been searching for an unmodified original Levitt home for its collection. Only a few exist, and their owners are not yet willing to give up their homes.

Wham-O

The Wham-O Manufacturing Company of California launched some of America's greatest postwar fads. Richard Knerr and Arthur "Spud" Melin, two recent college grads, started the company in 1948 by marketing slingshots and boomerangs. However, their first fad-starting product came ten years later after an Australian friend visited them. He told the two about bamboo hoops used in Australian gym classes. This ancient torso-trimming instrument, called the Hula-Hoop, was used as far back as the fourteenth century in England and even in ancient Greece. Its name came from seventeenth-century missionaries to Hawaii who thought users looked like they were performing the Hawaiian hula. Knerr and Melin made a few changes to satisfy a modern market. Instead of vine, wood, or metal, they made their Hula-Hoop out of another fairly new product—plastic. Sold in a number of bright colors, Hula-Hoops started a craze of unprecedented size across America. In the first year alone, between 60,000 and 100,000 hoops sold. Not all were under the name "hula," though. Wham-o was unable to get a patent, and soon "spin-a-hoops" and "hoop-d-dos" also appeared on the market.

Just as the Hula-Hoop fad was dying out, Wham-O introduced another fad into American culture. Knerr and Melin hired a carpenter and inventor named Fred Morrison to join their company. He had developed a plastic flying disc he called the "Pluto Platter." Wham-O marketed the disk in 1957, but the product's real popularity came after a few changes in 1958. While visiting some Ivy League schools, Knerr saw students throwing pie tins to each other and yelling,

from their hometowns and to relocate. They moved to sections of the country that offered new jobs. The West, especially California, offered the biggest attraction. The South and the Southwest also grew in population. This was the beginning of the **"sunbelt migrations,"** movements toward the areas of the country with warmer climates.

The war had produced changes in technology. Scientists had worked hard during the war to find new materials and inventions that would improve the war effort and supply substitutes for materials that were in low supply. Now that the war was over, some war inventions and materials had peacetime applications. New medicines and vaccines had been developed for diseases. Synthetic fibers, plastics, and other new materials became useful for industries. New hybrid crops, insecticides, machinery, fertilizer, and better irrigation techniques allowed American farmers to grow more crops than ever before. These changes in American agriculture have sometimes been called the **"green revolution."**

Changes in technology also affected the use of leisure time. Although the television had been made workable as early as 1927, it

President Truman holds the Chicago Tribune, which incorrectly predicted the outcome of the 1948 presidential race.

was not perfected until after World War II. In 1946 there were seven thousand television sets. By 1950 there were four million and by 1960 there were 74 million. Television had many effects on Americans. One was the lessening of regional differences as people from the North, South, East, and West all watched the same programs.

Crazes were also common in the postwar decade. More than thirty million Americans purchased Hula-Hoops, large plastic rings that could be twirled for exercise. A Walt Disney television series based on the life of a frontier hero, Davy Crockett, led to a whole series of products. Children carried Davy Crockett lunch boxes and wore coonskin caps and buckskin jackets while singing about the "King of the Wild Frontier."

The Fair Deal

Although the depression of the 1930s had ended, many people still wanted the government aid that Franklin Roosevelt's New Deal had given them. Americans wondered if the new president, Harry Truman, would continue support of similar programs. Their answer came in September 1945. The president called Congress into special session to present a twenty-one-point domestic program that he called a **"Fair Deal."** The policies were similar to those of the New Deal but established the GI Bill, provided better treatment of black Americans, increased aid to science and public education, and subsidized medical insurance. Not all of Truman's ideas were accepted by Congress, but they helped give the American people some assurance that the government would continue to come to their aid.

One of the issues that did not go Truman's way was the control of labor unions. During the days of high inflation after the war, laborers wanted higher wages without price increases. Some of the unions resorted to major strikes to get their way. Auto, steel,

---

they give historical examples to defend their position?

The Fair Deal and the "Do Nothing" Congress

Students may read that Truman called the Republican-controlled Congress of 1947 the "do nothing" Congress. Help the students to recognize the danger of accepting his evaluation. Would they have supported Truman's "Fair Deal," which was an even more socialistic extension of the New Deal? By fighting the president's efforts to extend government power and programs,

were the Republicans "do nothing" congressmen? What is implied by this phrase? *(Good leaders introduce more government programs.)* You might want to make comparisons to the Republicans who withstood President Clinton's later efforts to extend government power over health care. The fact that their fight to restrain government spending did not produce any legislation does not mean that they were not doing their job.

coal, and railroad workers went on strike for higher wages. With the growing number of strikes, some Americans thought that unions had gained too much power. Truman had difficulty controlling the labor unrest himself, but he did not like the way the Republican Congress dealt with it either.

Congress passed the **Taft-Hartley Act** of 1947 over the veto of Truman. The act limited the powers of unions by giving employees more freedom to work against unions. The bill outlawed the closed shop, a practice that forced businesses to hire only union members. It permitted states to pass laws prohibiting union shops that required workers to join the union within a certain date of their hiring. In addition, unions had to give a sixty-day notice before changing or ending work contracts. During that time they could not strike. Moreover, if a proposed strike threatened the nation's health or safety, an eighty-day **injunction,** a court order forbidding the strike, could be issued. During that time the strikers and the management were required to settle the dispute through negotiations.

In the years following the war, **civil rights** (rights guaranteed by the Constitution to every American citizen) for America's blacks became an increasingly important issue. Although Congress rejected Truman's civil rights legislation, the president did try to lessen discrimination against blacks through the influence of his position.

Both the North and the South practiced segregation. Although not required by law in the North, segregation existed in fact. Blacks generally lived in their own neighborhoods and went to black neighborhood schools and businesses. In the South **Jim Crow laws** segregated blacks from whites in schools, theaters, restaurants, and on buses.

Changes came slowly. In 1946 President Truman appointed the President's Committee on Civil Rights. In 1948, by executive order, the president banned segregation in the armed forces. In World War II President Roosevelt had issued an executive order saying that the federal government would not contract its business to any firms that discriminated against minorities. President Truman continued the policy and also formed a committee to investigate instances of alleged discrimination.

These actions during the Truman administration advanced the civil rights movement. Other changes were made to help integrate blacks in other areas. In 1947 Jackie Robinson became the first black to play major league baseball when he joined the Brooklyn Dodgers. Higher education also began to open to blacks as the University of Oklahoma began to admit blacks to graduate school in 1948.

Truman's idea of giving a Fair Deal to the American people helped him win the presidential election of 1948. He had not been especially popular in his first few years as president. Political pollsters said his Republican opponent, Thomas E. Dewey, was a sure winner, and newspapers printed on election night declared the same. But when the ballots were counted, both the pollsters and the papers were wrong. Truman had waged an exhausting campaign, traveling across America making speeches from the end of a railroad car. The public apparently admired his fighting spirit. "I met the people face to face," he explained, "and . . . they voted for me."

SECTION REVIEW

1. How did the GI Bill help veterans?

2. What parts of the country did many Americans move to in the postwar years?

3. What was Truman's domestic plan called?

4. What act limited the powers of labor unions?

 How did the "baby boom" and suburban life affect the American economy?

563

"Frisbie." The name came from William Russell Frisbie, a baker who printed his name on the pie plates that came with his pies. Knerr liked the name and changed Wham-O's flying disk to the "Frisbee." Although the Frisbee did not generate the same craze that the Hula-Hoop had, it has been a more permanent part of American culture.

Other Legislation of the Era

Other legislation in 1947 included the establishment of the presidential line of succession. The Speaker of the House and president pro tempore of the Senate are in line after the vice president. Next are the members of the cabinet in order of the creation of their departments. The Twenty-second Amendment, passed in 1951, also addresses the presidency. It limits a president to two terms of office or, in the case of a vice president elevated to the presidency, a maximum of ten years in office. This amendment was in reaction to the extended presidency of Franklin Roosevelt and represents a recognition of the dangers of allowing one man to lead the government for a prolonged time.

Jackie Robinson

Jackie Robinson broke the color barrier in baseball in April 1947. In that year he signed a contract to play with the Brooklyn Dodgers for $5,000 with a $3,500 bonus. In his first game against the Boston Braves, Robinson went hitless, but he scored the winning run. On a sacrifice bunt, the Braves' first baseman fielded the ball but hit Robinson in the back with it. A double by Pete Reiser drove him home and allowed the Dodgers to win 5-3.

 Viewpoints on the Taft-Hartley Act

Divide the class into representatives of big business, labor unions, small businessmen, and workers outside the labor unions. Have each group present its opinions on the Taft-Hartley Act. Note that pro-business Republicans passed the law to curb the special privileges that Roosevelt had granted labor unions.

Student Activity C: Presidential Election of 1948

This activity allows students to create their own election map and pie charts on the unusual election of 1948.

Section Review Answers

1. It gave them benefits in finding jobs, getting an education, and purchasing homes. (p. 560)

2. the West, the South, and the Southwest (p. 562)

3. "Fair Deal" (p. 562)

4. Taft-Hartley Act (p. 563)

The "baby boom" and suburban life created greater demands for baby goods, housing, and transportation. Related industries also grew. (p. 560)

Objectives

Students should be able to
1. Describe how the Allies dealt with Germany after the war.
2. Describe how the United States dealt with Japan after the war.
3. Explain the Marshall Plan.
4. Name the three parts of the United Nations and evaluate the activities of that organization.

Adolf Eichmann

As the Nuremberg Trials continued, the name of Adolf Eichmann continued to surface. This man headed a Jewish affairs department within the Gestapo. He and his men hunted down Jews as the Nazis moved into Russia. He was responsible for sending millions of Jews to Nazi death camps. And he was missing. At least that was what authorities believed.

Actually, Eichmann had been captured, but he was using the alias Otto Eckmann. Knowing he would eventually be found out, Eichmann escaped from the American prison near Nuremberg and hid in the mountains of central Germany. There he became a chicken farmer and changed his name to Otto Henninger. As the search for him continued, Eichmann moved to Italy and, with the help of the underground Nazi movement, escaped to Argentina.

Under the name Ricardo Klement, he started a new life as a rabbit farmer and a foreman at a Mercedes-Benz plant. His true identity was concealed until 1959, when the Israelis received a tip regarding his location and his alias. Agents secretly kept him under surveillance, gathering important information to confirm his identity. Undercover agents even asked him for directions while secretly taking pictures of him with a camera hidden in a briefcase.

Finally, the Israelis grabbed Eichmann as he got off a bus.

Postwar Problems

The United States emerged from World War II as the most powerful nation in the world, but it now had one strong rival—the Soviet Union. These two nations had fought as allies in the war, but the differences of these two postwar world powers would create great tensions. As Europe and Eastern Asia lay in ruin after the havoc of war, they needed help for rebuilding from the superpowers. The problem was that American ideas on how they should be rebuilt often conflicted with the demands of the Soviet Union.

Postwar Germany

Because Germany's government under Hitler had been defeated, the Germans were left without a government at the war's end. To fill this power vacuum, the Allies divided Germany into four sectors, or sections. American, British, and French troops occupied the three western sectors. The Soviets occupied the fourth sector—the eastern part of Germany closest to the Russian border. The Soviet Union quickly showed that it would have its way in that sector by making sure that its economy and politics were communist-controlled. Tensions developed in Germany. These tensions later resulted in major problems between the United States and the Soviet Union.

The Allies were also concerned about dealing with Germany's former Nazi leaders. As Allied troops liberated the German-occupied areas of Europe, they discovered concentration camps. Terrible atrocities had taken place in these camps. As many as six million Jews and millions of other Europeans had been exterminated in the Nazi-driven Holocaust. The Allies decided to try the Nazi leaders publicly as war criminals. The trials began in 1945 in Nuremberg, Germany, and further unraveled the grim story of Hitler's Germany. In October 1946 the international court at the **Nuremberg trials** condemned twelve Nazi leaders to death for "crimes against peace" and "crimes against humanity." The trials of lesser Nazi officials continued over many more months, though more quietly.

Dealing with Japan

Japan had been destroyed by the war. Her cities and harbors lay in ruin. Her merchant fleet had been sunk. The United States avoided trouble with the Soviet Union over the rebuilding of Japan by taking sole responsibility for helping that country. Truman appointed General Douglas MacArthur to head a military government in postwar Japan that could supervise its recovery.

Japanese officials meet Americans on the U.S.S. Missouri *to sign documents of surrender.*

564

SECTION 2

Materials

• No materials

Debate Ideas

Have your students discuss and/or debate the following:

The United States received significant benefits from joining the United Nations.

General Douglas MacArthur should have been permitted to bomb China

and cross the Yalu River in pursuit of North Korean forces.

The Nuremberg Trials were an illegitimate means of assessing and punishing Germany for its World War II crimes.

The United States should withdraw its support from the United Nations.

Learning from Past Victories

Ask the students to put themselves in the position of the victors at the end of World War II. Write on the board the international

problems that have to be solved, and then discuss alternative solutions. Americans were deeply concerned about the possibility of another world depression, the rise of radicalism among the dispossessed poor, and the potential for a new war.

After having won the biggest and costliest war in history, Americans had many options in their treatment of their vanquished foes. The United States wanted to demilitarize and democratize Germany and Japan; it feared that the industries of those countries might be used for war again. Once the students consider the options that the

The United States helped the Japanese write a new constitution. The Japanese elected a legislative body and gave rights to all citizens. Women got the right to vote. As in Germany, war criminals went to trial. In an effort to help rebuild the lives of the Japanese and to instill spiritual values, General MacArthur encouraged missionaries to come to Japan. Thus the door to Japan again opened to the gospel.

The UNRRA (United Nations Relief and Recovery Administration) sent aid to the Japanese from 1945 to 1948. The United States was the chief donor to this organization, which provided food, clothing, and medicine to meet immediate needs. Japan quickly rebuilt, soon becoming a thriving industrial nation. In 1951 the United States ended its military occupation of Japan. The United States had helped Japan to rebuild, gaining her as a powerful ally for the free world.

The United States Aids Europe

Europeans, who had seen World War II fought on their own lands, had suffered more than Americans. Millions of their soldiers and civilians had been killed. Millions of the survivors were homeless, wandering from place to place seeking shelter and food. To many of these "displaced persons" life seemed hopeless. There was no one to hire them. The wartime governments of the defeated countries no longer existed, and the winners were so deeply in debt from their own war efforts that they could do little to help. Bombing and fighting had destroyed most industries. Railroads and roads were in ruin. Because they had been bombed or burned, farmlands did not produce, and near-famine conditions existed in Europe.

The United States went to work aiding Europe. First it furnished aid through the UNRRA. Immediate needs were met through shipments of tons of food, clothing, and medicine. Because communists could and did make easy inroads among the discontented and downtrodden, the United States demonstrated a special concern for such people in an effort to keep them from ignorantly accepting communist influence.

On June 5, 1947, Secretary of State **George Marshall** proposed a vast new aid program for Europe. He asked Congress for huge sums of money to rebuild the European countries ravaged by war. The **Marshall Plan** offered aid even to Eastern European countries already subjected to Soviet control. But the Soviet Union rejected the offer. It would not allow its satellites (Soviet-dominated countries) to take advantage of the offer.

Although the Marshall Plan cost a great deal (more than $12 billion), it did aid European recovery. The Western European countries that received American help rebuilt quickly and soon surpassed their prewar production.

The Formation of the United Nations

Throughout World War II the Allies had held eleven conferences to plot strategy and deal with problems. The idea of a postwar peace-keeping organization to replace the League of Nations was voiced at the meeting in Teheran late in 1943. Because of increased tensions among the Allies, especially between free countries and the Soviet Union, the topic was raised again at Yalta in February 1945. The Big Three—the United States, Britain, and the Soviet Union—called for a meeting of nations at San Francisco to write a charter for another world peace-keeping organization.

On April 25, 1945, just thirteen days after the death of President Roosevelt, President Truman welcomed delegates from fifty nations to San Francisco. During the two months of discussion, the delegates had many arguments. Some threatened to leave the meetings because the Soviet demands were too selfish. Finally, enough concessions were

After signing a statement of willingness to stand trial, he was smuggled out of the country to Israel. Although the Argentinean government was angry about the Israelis' tactics, they did not ask for Eichmann's return. Eichmann was kept in a high security prison and charged on fifteen counts of war crimes. He was found guilty of all of them. Eichmann was hanged, and then his ashes were spread over the Mediterranean to ensure he would not rest on Israeli soil.

The United Nations

The United Nations's organizational meeting at San Francisco was preceded by a planning meeting at Dumbarton Oaks in Washington on August 21, 1944. Roosevelt had promised the Soviet Union advantages in the United Nations when the topic was discussed at Yalta. The difficulty of dealing with the Soviet Union on the formation of the UN became increasingly evident through the Dumbarton Oaks and the San Francisco meetings.

An additional problem for the United States concerning the UN is its finances. The United States has been the major contributor for its projects and programs from the beginning. Few other nations have paid their fair share. Russia and its former satellites have often withheld funds.

565

United States had, they will better appreciate the generous choices it made. Perhaps never before has a victor been so good to its enemies and converted them into lasting allies. Ironically, the Soviet ally became America's great enemy, and its former enemies became its allies.

Comparison with the League of Nations

Have the students research and compare the League of Nations and the United Nations. Make a chart to show the similarities and the differences.

The UN in the News

Ask the students to find an article on some issue related to the UN today, or bring in an article and discuss it with the class. How have the issues changed, and how are they similar?

Secretary of State George Marshall meets with Nationalist China's President Chiang Kai-shek and his wife.

made to forge a charter for the new **United Nations** organization.

A permanent world headquarters for the United Nations was established in 1947 when John D. Rockefeller Jr. provided $8.5 million to construct a building. The city of New York gave land; the United States provided a generous loan of $65 million. The new headquarters opened in 1952.

The Organizational Structure of the United Nations—The three most important parts of the U.N. are the **General Assembly,** the **Security Council,** and the **Secretariat.** The General Assembly was to be somewhat like a legislature. Every member nation was to send a representative. By 1999 it consisted of the delegates of 185 countries. The General Assembly really has little power, however, since the nations are not forced to abide by its decisions.

The Security Council had five permanent member nations and six (now ten) nonpermanent members. The latter are elected by the General Assembly for two-year terms and are usually drawn from the smaller countries. The Security Council is the strongest part of the U.N. because it has the power to enforce U.N. policy with military action. But because any one of the five permanent members (Britain, the United States, France, China, and the Russian Federation) can exercise veto power to stop a decision, the council's power is frequently curtailed. It has acted successfully only in minor disputes or when the Big Five decided to use force. During the Cold War, the Soviet Union vetoed more than a hundred decisions of the council—more than all the other members combined. Moreover, when the seat of Free China was given to Communist China, the chance of a veto by a Communist power doubled.

The final major body of the U.N. is the Secretariat. The Secretariat is a type of executive branch, composed of U.N. agencies and administrators that handle the daily affairs of the organization. It is headed by a secretary-general elected by the General Assembly.

Weighing the Successes of the United Nations—From a Christian viewpoint it is admirable to settle disputes peacefully, as the United Nations intends. Knowing the possible consequences of today's weapons, few people want war. Yet no matter how strong and exemplary the desires for peace may be, the sinful nature of man works against them.

Although some people and nations believe that it is important to do right and keep one's

566

word, others are mainly concerned with what will benefit them most. Sinful man will often do what he can to get ahead, even if he must disregard the rights of others to do so. Because they are led by sinful men, countries are often guilty of unjust actions. Communist countries in particular tend to honor an agreement only when it benefits them. Appealing to a higher level, that of honoring God, is fruitless because God means nothing to them. Thus, agreements made in the United Nations have little chance for success.

Moreover, the record of the U.N. shows its ineffectiveness. It has neither brought peace nor ended war. Since its founding, at least seventy-five wars have erupted in the world, and more than one-third of the world's population has come under communist domination. The member nations of the United Nations fall into three major categories—free world nations, communist nations, and the **third world.** (The third world includes the many poor nations of Africa, Asia, and Latin America.) Because the third-world nations are generally poor and politically unstable, communist influences have often swayed these countries to accept communist ideas and side with the Soviet Union in disputes at the United Nations. This communist influence creates problems for the United States in its dealings with these third-world countries. In addition, the existence of the U.N. in New York has allowed many foreign countries to spy in the United States legally, a practice contrary to the best interests of Americans.

Although the words of Isaiah 2:4—"They shall beat their swords into plowshares, and their spears into pruning hooks: nation shall not lift up sword against nation, neither shall they learn war any more"—appear in the U.N. headquarters, in God's Word the verses refer to Christ's coming kingdom. Only after Christ's return to earth will there be true peace. The United Nations cannot stop that turmoil; only God can. Yet Christians are not to be troubled over these things. The Christian's refuge is not in the organizations of man, but in the arms of the almighty God.

SECTION REVIEW

1. Which section of Germany came under communist control?
2. What changes occurred in Japan under U.S. supervision?
3. What plan was developed for giving aid to Europe after the war?
4. What are the three bodies of the United Nations? Which body is the strongest?

 Why has the United Nations been unable to achieve its goal of international peace and security?

Cold War Crises

Because the threat of Hitler and Nazism was great, the United States and the Soviet Union became allies in World War II. When the war was over, however, the United States soon learned that the Soviets were out to gain all they could in the postwar disarray. In the years after the war there developed what was called the **Cold War.** The United States and the Soviet Union did not go into a direct military conflict with each other, but they found themselves in many disputes that sprang from the tensions between them. Fear of a third world war erupting between the two countries was often present.

At Yalta Stalin had pledged to hold free elections in Poland and in other areas where the Soviets took control. But he had no intention of allowing any nation that the Soviets occupied to choose its own form of government. By organizing communist parties in the countries of Eastern Europe even before World War II, the Soviets had laid the groundwork for communist takeover. As Soviet troops moved in to occupy Eastern Europe at

567

SECTION 3

Objectives
Students should be able to
1. Define Cold War and containment.
2. Describe the circumstances that led to the Berlin airlift.
3. Describe the relationship of the United States to China since World War II.
4. Explain the circumstances and results of the Korean War.

Problems with the Soviet Union

In connection with the end of the war and America's postwar problems with the Soviet Union, remember that the Soviet Union had begun World War II as Hitler's friend under the nonaggression pact. The Soviets had rushed into Poland to collect the spoils alongside the Nazis. Only when Hitler turned against the Soviet Union did that country join the Allied cause. Also, Stalin had agreed at Teheran and Yalta to help defeat Japan once Hitler was defeated. That help did not come until three months after V-E Day, however. The Soviets waited until August 9, the day the second atomic bomb was dropped on Japan, to declare war on Japan. By then Japan was, for all practical purposes, defeated. So the Soviet declaration only allowed the Communists to rush into Japanese-held areas on the Pacific coast and gain control for themselves. In addition, the Soviets did not allow free elections in the lands they had "freed" in Eastern Europe. All of these deplorable actions appalled the United States, but no one wanted further war.

Origins of the Cold War

The Cold War technically began in 1945 with a state of hostility between the United States and the Soviet Union. Understanding the animosities between the two superpowers, however, requires looking back over the preceding hundred years. The United States

---

Section Review Answers

1. East Germany (p. 564)
2. Japan wrote a new constitution, elected a legislative body, gave the vote to all citizens, tried its war criminals, opened its doors to missionaries, and through aid became a strong industrial nation. (p. 565)
3. Marshall Plan (p. 565)
4. General Assembly, Security Council, and the Secretariat; the Security Council is the most powerful (p. 566)

 The United Nations has failed in its mission because of man's sinful nature. Not until Christ returns to this earth will there be lasting peace. (p. 567)

SECTION 3

Materials

• Activity B from Chapter 27 of the *Student Activities* manual

Student Activity B: Hot Spots During the Cold War

This chart summarizes Communist and American activities in the various regions of the world during the Cold War. You will probably want to discuss the answers in class. The text discusses seven countries/regions, but the chart asks the students to choose four.

was suspicious of czarist Russia in the nineteenth century for several reasons: their government was totalitarian; the country was isolated and backward, having ended serfdom officially as late as 1861 and not having experienced the Industrial Revolution, as well as the great cultural movements of the West. In the nineteenth century, Russia was a potential threat in the Pacific Northwest, a challenge lessened by the U.S. purchase of Alaska. In the early twentieth century, losses in the Russo-Japanese War and World War I revealed Russia's backwardness.

The Bolshevik Revolution of 1917 further alienated Russia from the West. Communism was not only totalitarian but also antireligion and aggressive, threatening revolutionary movements in the rest of the world. By withdrawing from World War I in 1918, Lenin had made victory against the Central Powers more difficult. Mistrust was so strong between America and the Soviet Union that the United States did not give diplomatic recognition to that nation until 1933. American political rhetoric between the wars was strongly anti-Communist.

Just as in World War I, the Soviet Union was an ally in World War II, and U.S. relations with Stalin became more complicated. President Roosevelt, along with British prime minister Churchill, believed an alliance with the Soviet Union against Hitler was the best way, though not a perfect way, to defeat Nazi Germany. This "marriage of convenience" forced Hitler to fight a two-front war, thus placing him in a serious strategic disadvantage. Curiously, American propaganda during the war revamped the images of Stalin and the Soviet Union, making both "good guys." The American news media participated in this "makeover." During this wartime alliance, the Soviet Union received lend-lease assistance from the United States.

But even during the wartime cooperation, there were serious divi-

the war's end, they placed communists in government positions. In this way they took over the governments of Bulgaria, Yugoslavia, Albania, Rumania, Poland, Hungary, and later Czechoslovakia. To ensure that these countries remained in the communist camp, Red Army units remained in each nation, keeping pro-Soviet leaders in control despite opposition from the people.

On March 5, 1946, Britain's World War II leader, Winston Churchill, came to Fulton, Missouri, to speak at Westminster College. Churchill graphically described the problem in Eastern Europe: "From Stettin in the Baltic to Trieste in the Adriatic, an **iron curtain** has descended across the Continent." From then on countries under communist control were said to be "behind the Iron Curtain." This political and military barrier soon came to represent the differences in beliefs between the two sides. Churchill believed that the West would have to take firm action to halt future communist expansion.

The Truman Doctrine: Containing Communism

The Soviets soon proved Churchill's point by showing that they were not content to control only Eastern Europe. Their next goal was to claim the oil-rich Middle East.

Allied troops had occupied Iran during World War II to keep open its vital oil supply. When the war ended, American and British troops withdrew, but Soviet troops remained. Soviet-inspired rioting took place, and Iranian troops who sought to restore order were kept from doing so. When Iran, with American backing, complained to the U.N., the Soviet troops left.

Meanwhile, communist-led guerrillas in Greece were gaining ground in their efforts to take control. Turkey also seemed to be on the brink of tumbling into the Soviet camp. President Truman finally saw that it was

essential for the United States to "contain" communism, that is, to stop the Soviets from overtaking more governments. To carry out the **containment** policy, the president asked Congress to approve $400 million for military aid to support the pro-Western governments in Greece and Turkey. The idea of using military aid to support pro-Western, anti-communist governments soon got the name **Truman Doctrine.**

Confrontation in Germany

When Germany was divided among the Allies after the war, the country's old capital of Berlin was in the middle of Soviet-controlled East Germany. Because Berlin was such an important city, the Allies agreed to divide its control among themselves. It had four zones, one each for France, Britain, the United States, and the Soviet Union. Supplies were shipped to the French, British, and American zones of Berlin from the West by truck or train across Soviet-held lands.

When the United States, Britain, and France decided to combine their sectors of Germany, the Soviet Union responded by denying all road, rail, and river access across East Germany to Berlin, beginning June 24, 1948. This violation of the Yalta agreement left two million residents of West Berlin without food and other supplies. The Soviet Union thought that its blockade would force the Allies out of Berlin. Stalin also believed that his action would undermine the confidence of the European Allies in the United States.

President Truman responded quickly to the Soviet threat. He announced that the United States would use a massive airlift to West Berlin. For the next 321 days, more than 250,000 flights carried supplies into West Berlin. More than 2.5 million tons of supplies were airlifted to the blockaded city. The Soviets did not attack the planes, as some had predicted. When the Soviets realized that the

United States was prepared to keep the **Berlin airlift** going indefinitely, it lifted its blockade in May 1949.

Since the Soviet Union had taken such a strong grip on East Germany, attempts for unification of Germany seemed futile. In September 1949, the United States, Britain, and France allowed the sectors of Germany they held to become an independent nation. The new Federal Republic of Germany (West Germany) was formed, with Bonn as its capital.

Alliances and Aid

Because of the Soviet threat to the parts of Europe that remained free, President Truman believed that these nations needed more than financial aid. He asked Congress for military support and the formation of a joint alliance, with the United States as a member. The alliance, called the **North Atlantic Treaty Organization** (NATO), united the Western European nations of Britain, France, Italy, Portugal, the Netherlands, Denmark, Norway, Belgium, and Luxembourg, as well as the North Atlantic countries of Canada, Iceland, and the United States. In 1952 Greece and Turkey joined, and in 1959, West Germany. These nations agreed to provide money, troops, and military equipment for mutual protection. General Dwight D. Eisenhower became the first supreme commander of NATO forces. America's membership in NATO meant a change in its long-standing policy of isolationism. It was the first peacetime alliance that the United States had ever joined for the possible defense of other nations.

The Soviets, responding to the Berlin airlift and the formation of NATO, gathered representatives of their Eastern European satellites in Warsaw, Poland. The Soviets then organized their own military alliance, called the **Warsaw Pact.** The Warsaw Pact nations included Poland, Albania, East Germany,

Bulgaria, Rumania, Czechoslovakia, Hungary, and the Soviet Union.

The China Question

Just as postwar Europe was undergoing change, so was the Far East. China became a special problem. China was the most populous nation in the world. The communists, led by **Mao Zedong,** were poised to gain control of the country after World War II.

China had suffered from fighting warlords and domineering foreign countries in the decades before the war. Generalissimo **Chiang Kai-shek** had emerged as leader of the strong "Nationalist" group in China. The United States had made trade agreements with

With promises of land for the poor, Mao Zedong gained control of China for the Communist Party. Chiang Kai-shek and the Nationalists fled to Taiwan.

sions between the Soviet Union and the other Allies over the timing and location of the second front, the one from the west, against Hitler. Stalin wanted it soon and in Western Europe. The Allies were slow to begin the second front, finally starting it in June 1944, three years after Germany had invaded Russia. Churchill wanted the attack in southeastern Europe, closer to the Soviet Union, thereby giving the Communists less of a free hand in Eastern Europe after liberating it from the Nazis. Roosevelt convinced Churchill that the invasion should take place in France.

In the spring of 1945 when the common enemy that bound them together was defeated, the United States and the Soviet Union reverted to a familiar pattern of hostility. Soon the Cold War was underway.

Truman and NATO

President Truman proposed the organization NATO in his 1949 inaugural speech, along with what was called his "Point Four Program." That program involved offering more aid to underdeveloped nations for the improvement of their economic and living conditions so that they would be less likely targets for Communism.

China and the Cold War

With the Soviet Union as the main adversary during the Cold War, the role of China in that era is often overlooked. China is important, if for no other reason, as the most populous nation in the world. That nation played a role in intensifying the Cold War and also in helping to end it.

China has had an uneven relationship with the West. By the end of the nineteenth century, the American Open Door policy brought China, against her will, into commercial contact with the West. In the early twentieth century, China's imperial era ended when Sun Yatsen founded a republic. It foundered due to two threats. One was Japanese aggression in the 1930s and 1940s. The other was the opposition of the Communist leader

Unprecedented NATO

Stress that NATO—the first peacetime defensive alliance in U.S. history—had no precedent in the country's history. Can the students find any period in America's past similar to the one that led to NATO? Did the circumstances warrant this change in policy? Since the Cold War has ended, some have wondered whether any circumstances would justify an end to NATO and a return to isolationism. Has the United States entered such a period?

China Policy

Review U.S. policies toward China over the years. China is potentially one of the great powers of the world. When have the two countries been friends, and when have they been foes? Note the immigration restrictions, the Open Door policy, the Boxer Rebellion, U.S. support of Chiang Kai-shek, the World War II alliance, and the modern split between Taiwan and the mainland. Emphasize that finding the right policy toward China has never been easy.

After the loss of China to the Communists, political parties in the United States did a

lot of finger pointing, asking, "Who lost China?" But in reality, the level of U.S. responsibility for the outcome of internal conflicts in other countries is debatable. The United States felt compelled to withdraw its military support from China's corrupt nationalist government. The same question can be asked in relation to many other countries: "Should the United States support a corrupt democracy that does not enjoy the support of its people?" This question has arisen in Korea, Vietnam, Latin America, and Africa. Bring up recent examples in the news.

Mao Zedong. In 1919 the United States made an agreement with Japan that gave it special rights in China. That led to massive protests in China, and Mao rose to power with that movement. His Communism was mixed with Chinese nationalism, whether anti-Western or anti-Japanese, and that unfortunately made him popular with the masses.

Until 1927 Chiang Kai-shek, Sun Yat-sen's successor, had worked with Mao, but at that point Chiang kicked the Communists out of his "nationalist" party. A civil war between Chiang and Mao continued for the next twenty years. During the World War II era, they united against the Japanese threat, but in 1945, with that threat removed, they resumed their civil war. Chiang, as a non-Communist, had the support of the United States, but by 1949 Mao had defeated his opponent and claimed the Chinese mainland for Communism. With China's fall to Communism and the Soviet Union's production of its first atomic bomb, 1949 was one of the worst years during the Cold War. Communism presented an impressive geographical, military, and ideological front.

China played pivotal roles in two of the Cold War's worst episodes—the Korean and Vietnam Wars. In 1950 North Korea invaded South Korea, and Mao supported the action. Douglas MacArthur sought to attack China because of her support for the Communist North Koreans, but President Truman, unwilling to get bogged down in a land war in Asia against China, fired the general. Under Eisenhower, an armistice ended the fighting but did not resolve any of the underlying problems in Korea.

China also played a key role in ending the Cold War. As it had supported North Korea, China also aided North Vietnamese Communists in their effort to conquer South Vietnam. President Nixon, in a bold strategic move to help end the Vietnam War, opened relations with China in a 1972 presidential visit to that country. China had not

Chiang and had aided the Chinese against Japan in World War II. Chiang's efforts to defeat the Japanese in China and to control China, however, were being sabotaged from within his own party by corruption and internal conflicts. Some American troops were sent to aid Chiang, but they were pulled out in 1947.

Almost immediately China was again engulfed in war. This conflict was between the communists, led by Mao, and the Nationalists, led by Chiang. Mao's forces were highly motivated. The communists had promised to give land to the poor. By 1949 the communists had gained control of the mainland. They forced Chiang to flee with his army to the coastal island of Taiwan, where he set up Nationalist China (also called the Republic of China or Free China). Mainland China became the communist "People's Republic of China."

The presence of communism in China posed a new threat. China and the Soviet Union signed the Sino-Soviet Pact in February 1950, confirming American suspicions that the communists might try to work together against the free world. President Truman, and several presidents who followed him, steadfastly supported Chiang and his government on Taiwan, at least in theory. Some Americans preferred, however, to recognize the communist People's Republic, which controlled the mainland, as the one legitimate government of China. Americans knew that the Chinese communists were persecuting Christians, squelching free ideas, and killing or imprisoning those who opposed Chairman Mao. Even so, in 1979 the United States reversed its policy and recognized Communist China instead of Free China.

Korea and the Korean Conflict

China was not the only communist target in Eastern Asia. The Soviet Union had begun

to take a grip on part of Korea before World War II ended. As the United States was defeating Japan, the Soviet Union was pouring troops into Korea. The Yalta agreement allowed the Soviets to occupy Korea north of the 38th parallel. The Soviets again promised that at the proper time, free elections would be held. Of course, the communists established

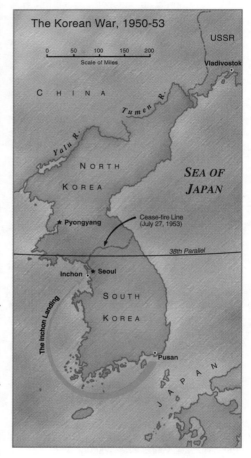

The Korean War, 1950-53

Contrast Korea with Previous Wars

The Korean War was unlike anything the United States had ever fought before. Ask the students to find those differences and draw conclusions about the wisdom of wars for the current generation. *(The Korean War was never officially declared; the United States military sought authorization from an international organization; and the president was content with a stalemate rather than victory. The national interests that we fought to achieve were "murkier" than those of any previous war. As a result of this new type of war, the basic issues* *were never settled, and the United States was forced to maintain a military force in South Korea for the next fifty years.)*

their style of government in North Korea in the meantime. South Korea held its own elections, and the Republic of Korea was formed with Seoul as capital. Korea, like Germany, was thus divided—part communist, part free.

Talks were held in hopes of unifying Korea, but they broke down. Then North Korea invaded South Korea on June 25, 1950. The U.N. Security Council quickly called an emergency session to deal with the crisis. It demanded North Korea's immediate withdrawal. When the troops were still there two days later, the Council suggested that the U.N. aid South Korea. (The Security Council was able to approve this because the Soviet Union was boycotting sessions at that time.)

That same day President Truman committed American planes and ships to support the South Koreans. On June 30 American troops were ordered to Korea. Within a week the U.N. voted to send a peacekeeping force to Korea to seek an end to the conflict. Since four-fifths of its men were American, President Truman was allowed to pick its commander. He chose General Douglas MacArthur, the most experienced American Pacific officer.

Truman hoped the troops could drive communist troops out of South Korea. But a shortage of needed equipment and American unreadiness produced a shabby start for the **Korean War.** North Korean troops, well equipped by the Soviets, continued to push their way south. By the end of August, U.N. forces held only the southeastern corner of Korea near Pusan. MacArthur then surprised the North Koreans by going behind their lines and attacking from Inchon. All the ground lost was regained in two weeks.

When the troops reached the 38th parallel, a decision was needed. Truman and the U.N. approved MacArthur's order to cross into North Korea. The U.N. hoped that MacArthur's northward push would lead to reunifying Korea. On October 26, 1950,

General MacArthur's public denunciation of President Truman for limiting the war in Korea ended his military career.

MacArthur's advance guard reached the Yalu River, the dividing line between North Korea and China. China reacted by sending more than two hundred thousand "volunteers" across the Yalu River into North Korea to stop the U.N. forces.

Fierce fighting broke out, and U.N. troops were pushed back past the 38th parallel down into South Korea. MacArthur now believed that winning a land war in Korea required the bombing of Chinese bases and supply lines in China. MacArthur declared, "There is no substitute for victory."

President Truman and his advisors, however, thought differently. They were now content simply to restore the boundary to the 38th parallel. Although MacArthur pushed for all-

been given diplomatic recognition by the United States since 1949. Instead, America had recognized Taiwan, where Chiang and his defeated nationalist forces had fled in 1949, as the real China. Taiwan also held China's seat in the UN. Nixon sought to play China against the Soviet Union, hoping that Soviet fears of a U.S.-China relationship would cause the Soviet Union to be more cooperative in seeking peace in Vietnam and nuclear arms reductions.

By the late 1970s, China had gained recognition by the United States and was placed on the UN Security Council. With the collapse of the Soviet Union, Communist China looked less threatening, and most Americans saw it merely as a huge market for American goods.

SECTION 4

Objectives
Students should be able to
1. Describe the circumstances in Vietnam during the 1950s.
2. Name the new Soviet leader and the new policy that developed between the Soviet Union and the United States.
3. Explain how Fidel Castro turned Cuba to Communism.
4. Name the two states that joined the Union in 1959.

Communist Expansion

The United States met problems with Soviet-inspired Communist expansion attempts in other places besides those mentioned in the text. For example, a pro-Soviet government in Guatemala was unseated through the influence of Eisenhower's secretary of state, John Foster Dulles.

Eisenhower's Foreign Policy

In the campaign of 1952, Republicans preached change in Cold War foreign policy. Truman's limited war, containment, and coexistence with Communist principles, they argued, had failed. Eisenhower proclaimed, "I will go to Korea," and implied a plan for victory. Eisenhower's rhetoric and that of his secretary of state, John Foster Dulles, was strongly anti-Communist, but their actual record, according to historians, is otherwise. Some look at the 1950s and see problems that are unresolved and passed on to the 1960s, while others admire Eisenhower for his unwillingness to use force to deal with military crises.

Several incidents indicate that Eisenhower did not solve diplomatic and military problems but just postponed them and passed them on to John F. Kennedy. In Korea he negotiated an armistice that ended the fighting but did not resolve the problem of a divided Korea. The military tension in that country remains to this day. A

out war and total victory, Truman decided on a limited war with very specific aims. He did not want to risk the use of nuclear weapons in Korea. He was also afraid that the Soviet Union might fight back somewhere in Europe or Asia if the United States pushed for control of North Korea. When MacArthur publicly denounced the president's policy of limited war, Truman removed him from his command.

In July 1951 talks for a cease-fire started, but both the talks and the fighting dragged on. Following his election in 1952, President Dwight D. Eisenhower traveled to Korea to revive the stalled talks. A cease-fire was signed on July 27, 1953, restoring the 38th parallel as the boundary. There was to be a demilitarized (nonfortified) zone between communist North Korea and free South Korea.

SECTION REVIEW

1. What was the name for the barrier between communist-controlled countries and the West?
2. What idea promoted the use of military aid to carry out the United States's containment policy?
3. How did the United States keep West Berlin from falling into communist hands?
4. What military alliance was formed to halt the threat of Soviet aggression in Europe?
5. Who was the leader of Free China? Who led the communist takeover of China?
6. Whom did Truman choose to lead the U.N. forces in Korea?

 How was the Cold War a different type of war from World War I and II? Why?

The Eisenhower Era

Both the Republicans and Democrats would have been happy to have World War II hero Dwight D. Eisenhower as their candidate in 1952. He ran on the Republican ticket against Adlai E. Stevenson, governor of Illinois. The public decided that they "liked Ike" (as he was called), because his grandfatherly image made many Americans feel comfortable. Eisenhower won handily.

Southeast Asia

Problems with communist expansion continued during the Eisenhower era. The Southeast Asian area of Indochina (Vietnam, Cambodia, and Laos) became a target for communist control. The area had been a French colony, but after World War II French control in the land was deteriorating. **Ho Chi Minh,** a communist leader, tried to gain independence for Vietnam. His forces defeated the French at Dien Bien Phu in May 1954. The United States did not intervene with troops at this time because it did not want to risk another land war in Asia.

The conflict was referred to an international conference in Geneva, Switzerland, for settlement. As in Germany and Korea, it was decided that there would be two Vietnams. North Vietnam under Ho Chi Minh would be communist. South Vietnam would be noncommunist and would receive American support. But North Vietnam was not content. Using guerrilla tactics it attacked, seeking to gain control of South Vietnam. Before long the United States discovered that the North Vietnamese were receiving Chinese and Soviet military aid.

Activities in Korea and Indochina not only had made the United States tense but also had alarmed other free countries in Southeast Asia and the southern Pacific. Therefore, in 1954 eight countries formed an alliance to contain the spread of communism there. The **Southeast Asia Treaty Organization** (SEATO) united the United States, Britain, France, Australia, New Zealand, Thailand, Pakistan, and the Philippines. The United

 572

Section Review Answers

1. Iron Curtain (p. 568)
2. Truman Doctrine (p. 568)
3. They airlifted supplies to the blockaded city. (p. 568)
4. North Atlantic Treaty Organization (p. 569)
5. Chiang Kai-Shek; Mao Zedong (p. 569)
6. General Douglas MacArthur (p. 571)

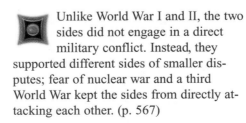 Unlike World War I and II, the two sides did not engage in a direct military conflict. Instead, they supported different sides of smaller disputes; fear of nuclear war and a third World War kept the sides from directly attacking each other. (p. 567)

SECTION 4

Materials
- Activity D from Chapter 27 of the *Student Activities* manual
- Video about the threat of nuclear holocaust during the fifties
- Special speaker: someone to talk about life under the threat of the nuclear holocaust

Why Do Foreign Affairs Matter?

This is a U.S. history book. But the book is filled with events in other countries. Ask the students why the United States cared about politics in Eastern Europe, Greece, Turkey, Germany, Japan, China, Korea, Southeast Asia, the Soviet Union, and Cuba.

States agreed to aid any of these nations threatened by an aggressor. By the end of 1955, America was sending military advisors to South Vietnam to train Vietnamese forces. The United States also pledged to aid Taiwan if it was attacked by mainland China.

Soviet-American Relations

The United States had become the leading nation of the free world. America could no longer remain isolated from international affairs as it had in earlier times. Because the interests of the United States were affected by conditions abroad, it had to get involved in international problems. America's greatest international problems lay in the Cold War tensions with the Soviets. The affairs between the United States and the Soviet Union were always gaining world attention.

In July 1955 Britain, France, the Soviet Union, and the United States met in Geneva, Switzerland, to attempt to put to rest some of the Cold War tensions. About the only thing that was agreed on was that they would not resort to war to resolve differences. President Eisenhower suggested that the United States and the Soviet Union submit to air inspections of each other's military installations to see whether there were missiles present. The Soviets, however, rejected the idea.

The Soviet Union was struggling to project a new image. Stalin had died in 1953, and **Nikita Khrushchev** (KROOSH chef), his successor, claimed to be critical of the former leader's terror tactics. One time he declared that the Soviets wanted to be friends and promote peace with the United States; yet Soviet intentions had not really changed. At another time Khrushchev threatened, "We will bury you."

The United States and the Soviet Union settled into a policy of **"peaceful coexistence."** The two countries agreed to try to settle the many tension-filled situations between

them without hostility. They also tried to arrange events that would promote goodwill between the two countries. Khrushchev even visited America in 1959, the first Soviet leader to do so. Unfortunately, the attitude of peaceful coexistence committed the United States to settling each issue with the Soviets peacefully even if Soviet wrongs were not stopped or punished.

European Developments

Further examples of Soviet communist oppression came in Eastern Europe. People in the Soviet satellite countries were unhappy under communist rule. In October 1956, freedom fighters in Hungary bravely led a revolt. They pleaded for help from the West on short-wave radio broadcasts, but help never came. For four days the people of Hungary had hope. Their revolt forced Soviet troops to leave their capital of Budapest. But then the Soviet army rolled back down the streets in tanks and crushed the freedom fighters. The freedom fighters were brave, but with only homemade grenades and their bare hands, they could not stop the tanks.

The Soviet invasion of Hungary was brought before the U.N. That body voted to condemn the Soviets. When the Soviets ignored the U.N. decision, the U.N. took no real action. Because the nations feared that aid to Hungary might start a third world war, the Soviets ruthlessly crushed the freedom movement with no hindrance from the free world.

Cuba

Latin America soon became another source of Cold War tensions. Communism was winning support in the region because so many of the people were poor and uneducated. Many believed the communist promises. The growth of communist activity in Latin America alarmed Americans since it brought the Soviet threat closer to home.

573

policy of nonrecognition toward mainland China remained the same as it did under Truman. When protests against Communist rule broke out in Hungary in 1956, Eisenhower offered only rhetorical support. Policy toward Communist Eastern Europe continued as it had under Truman. When Castro, a Communist, took over Cuba in 1959, Eisenhower took no military action to reverse it.

Liberal historians tend to look more positively at Eisenhower's foreign policy record. He was a peace president, a strong leader who avoided war whenever possible. His military background, perhaps, made him more cautious about military intervention. Instead of expanding the Korean War, as some conservatives wanted, he stopped the fighting through negotiations. He did not sanction an invasion of mainland China in order to satisfy Taiwan or anti-Communists in America.

Even Eisenhower's harshest conservative critics would concede that he was wise in staying out of the Vietnam War, which escalated in 1954 when the defeated French left and the Geneva Accords divided the country into a Communist north and a non-Communist south. Ho Chi Minh continued his fight for a united Communist Vietnam, but Eisenhower gave only aid, not large numbers of American troops, as did Kennedy and Johnson later. His intervention with Khrushchev in the 1956 Suez crisis and his failure to intervene in Hungary that year or in Cuba in 1959 solidified, for some, his credentials as a peacemaker. Khrushchev's visit to the United States in 1959 and the resulting good will enhanced a pacifist image.

Help the students to recognize how much the world scene had changed after World War II. For the first time in history, democracy was engaged in a worldwide struggle against a foe whose primary purpose was to wipe out democracy and free enterprise. The whole free world looked to America for help and guidance, while the rest of the world plotted and schemed against her.

What lessons does the Cold War hold for us today? Although the United States no longer faces such a determined enemy, the whole world still looks to the United States as a friend or a foe. Every decision our representatives make has a direct impact around the world. The nation cannot shirk or ignore its God-given duties. The next generation must clarify the country's role. Christian teachers must challenge their students to be responsible U.S. citizens and future leaders. Future generations cannot adequately do their job without an understanding of events following World War II.

Anti-Communism at Home

A major theme of domestic politics in America during the early Cold War years was anti-Communism. Americans were concerned not just with foreign aspects of Communism—Eastern Europe, Korea, and Vietnam—but also with aspects affecting the United States. Communism was gaining ground around the world, and one popular explanation, real or imagined, was that traitors and spies inside the U.S. government were helping the enemy.

The most famous episode of anti-Communist suspicion was the Hiss case. In 1948 Congressman Richard Nixon of the House Un-American Activities Committee was investigating subversives in government. He discovered through the testimony of a former Communist, Whittaker Chambers, that Alger Hiss, a former New Dealer and State Department official, had been a Communist in the 1930s and had arranged for secret documents to be transferred to the Soviets. The charge was a bombshell. Hiss denied the charges under oath. In 1950 in a second trial, he was convicted of perjury after an earlier trial had deadlocked. The statute of limitations had expired for spying. Hiss was sentenced to five years in prison, but more importantly he became a symbol for right wing and left wing feelings about the Cold War. Conservatives looked at Hiss as a symbol of big government and weak policies toward Communism, the reason for Communist advances in Eastern Europe and in Asia. The episode also catapulted Nixon into national politics. Truman and liberal Democrats continued to defend Hiss.

The Alger Hiss case also gave credibility to later charges by Senator Joseph McCarthy that Communists inside the U.S. government were helping the enemy. Other factors reinforced the suspicion: the uncovering in 1950 of the Rosenburgs, spies who had given atomic secrets to the Soviets, and the Communist invasion of South

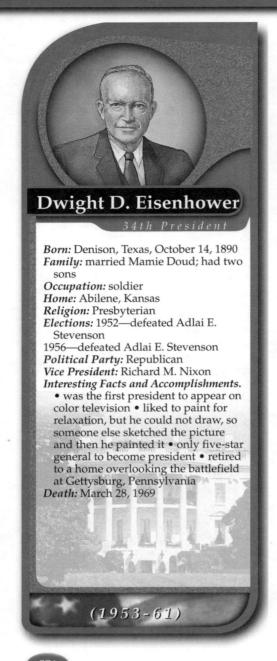

Dwight D. Eisenhower

34th President

Born: Denison, Texas, October 14, 1890
Family: married Mamie Doud; had two sons
Occupation: soldier
Home: Abilene, Kansas
Religion: Presbyterian
Elections: 1952—defeated Adlai E. Stevenson
1956—defeated Adlai E. Stevenson
Political Party: Republican
Vice President: Richard M. Nixon
Interesting Facts and Accomplishments.
  • was the first president to appear on color television • liked to paint for relaxation, but he could not draw, so someone else sketched the picture and then he painted it • only five-star general to become president • retired to a home overlooking the battlefield at Gettysburg, Pennsylvania
Death: March 28, 1969

(1953-61)

574

The most disturbing communist gain for the Americans was that of Cuba. In 1959 Americans heard that Fulgencio Batista, a long-time dictator of Cuba, had been overthrown by a revolutionary leader, **Fidel Castro.** Although the State Department was aware of Castro's communist leanings from the outset, the American people were not. Thus Americans idealistically believed that conditions might get better in Cuba if Castro took control.

Instead, conditions got worse. Castro, a cruel dictator, jailed thousands of his political enemies. He seized the property of Americans and American business investments in Cuba and declared himself a communist. Cuban refugees attempted to escape Castro's regime by fleeing to Florida any way they could. Some flew; more floated on rickety boats. Soon Soviet aid was on its way to Cuba. The Caribbean was no longer an American lake. Ninety miles off Florida lay a communist threat to American freedom.

Activities at Home

The United States was involved in some important activities at home during the Eisenhower era. Two of the most pleasant accomplishments were the completion of the **St. Lawrence Seaway** and the addition of two new states. In 1954 the United States and Canada had undertaken a joint project called the St. Lawrence Seaway. The two countries cooperated to deepen the St. Lawrence River and build canals and locks where necessary. The completed seaway allowed ocean-going vessels to sail from the Atlantic Ocean through the seaway to the Great Lakes. The project helped the economies of both nations and turned cities along the Great Lakes into major inland seaports. The moving water through the seaway was also used to provide electrical power.

The Threat of "the Bomb"

Describe to the students what life was like under the constant threat of nuclear attack. Students would enjoy hearing human-interest stories from someone who lived during that time. Or you could show clips from training films produced by the government. Interestingly, fear of world destruction even influenced films, as horror movies spawned new creatures like Godzilla.

Ask the students whether this fear of world destruction led to a revival. Why or why not? *(It did not. Again, man trusted in his own ability to save himself.)* What current dangers could again bring the world into such a state of fear? *(terrorism, biological disaster, climatic change)* These dangers have the advantage of keeping people focused on issues beyond self-gratification. Ask the students whether they are ever afraid of anything. Has peace been good for the world?

Soviet Views on the Cold War

Ask the students to consider what the Soviet people during the Cold War must have thought about U.S. activities and dangers of future war. Note that the Russian people had suffered greatly from foreign invasion twice during the century, and they had a natural suspicion of military forces near their border. Also, it was easy for them to find flaws in American society.

Interestingly, some liberal historians actually blame the United States for starting the Cold War. Why might they make this

In 1959 Congress admitted two territories to the Union. Alaska and Hawaii became the forty-ninth and fiftieth states. Alaska and Hawaii differ from the other states because they are noncontiguous, or unattached, territories away from the other forty-eight states. The states are also unique because of their populations. About one-fifth of Alaskan citizens are Indian (Eskimo, Aleut, or other tribes). One-half of Hawaii's citizens descend from Japanese, Chinese, Filipino, or Korean immigrants. The additions of Alaska and Hawaii gave the United States an even wider cultural heritage.

SECTION REVIEW

1. Who was elected president in 1952? What party did he represent?

2. What alliance was started to contain communism in Southeast Asia?

3. What Latin American country turned communist in 1959? Who became its leader?

4. How did the St. Lawrence Seaway benefit the United States and Canada?

 Was it dangerous for the United States to agree to a policy of "peaceful coexistence" with the Soviet Union?

SUMMARY

The United States emerged from World War II as the prosperous leader of the free world. Americans eagerly returned to peacetime activities, but international problems continued to concern the nation. Because of communist actions after the war, great tensions arose between the United States and the Soviet Union. The two nations avoided a direct shooting conflict, but a "Cold War" continued between the two throughout the 1950s. The ideals and demands of the United States and the communists clashed in Germany, Korea, and many other areas of the world. The new United Nations organization did little to stop regional conflicts and did not control the spread of communism. All the while, the United States continually provided protection for the free world and increased its aid to faltering free nations. The United States found its new role as world leader to be both expensive and entangling.

Korea that same year. Senator McCarthy exploited the issue with speeches and congressional hearings. Democrats and liberals were on the defensive; they did not want to appear sympathetic to the Communists. In 1950 Congress passed the McCarran Act, which required Communists to register. McCarthy and Republicans used the anti-Communist issue effectively in the 1952 elections, and the results were Eisenhower's election as president and a Republican-dominated Congress. With Republicans in charge of the government, the dynamic shifted for McCarthy. His attacks on the State Department and the U.S. Army were less successful. In the long run, Richard Nixon was more effective than McCarthy as an anti-Communist crusader. McCarthy, despite lack of evidence, used his anti-Communism crusade as a political weapon, and in 1954 his Senate colleagues censured him. Three years later he died.

575

---

conclusion, and why is it so outrageous? *(They argue that America's strong military and nuclear power made the Soviet Union feel insecure. But the Communists never hid their hatred of capitalism and their desire to take over the world.)*

Section Review Answers

1. Dwight D. Eisenhower; Republican (p. 572)

2. Southeast Asia Treaty Organization (p. 572)

3. Cuba; Fidel Castro (p. 574)

4. It opened the Great Lakes to ocean-going vessels and allowed the water to be used for electrical power. (p. 574)

 It sometimes committed the United States to peaceful solutions that did not punish Soviet wrong-doings. Without fear of United States retaliation the Soviets could continue to spread Communism. (p. 573)

Chapter Review Idea
Student Activity D: Geography of the Postwar World
This activity reviews the connection between events and countries mentioned in the chapter.

Chapter Review

Terms

GI Bill
baby boom
Federal Aid Highway Act
sunbelt migrations
green revolution
Fair Deal
Taft-Hartley Act
injunction
civil rights
Jim Crow laws
Nuremberg trials
George Marshall
Marshall Plan

United Nations
General Assembly
Security Council
Secretariat
third world
Cold War
iron curtain
containment
Truman Doctrine
Berlin airlift
North Atlantic Treaty
  Organization
Warsaw Pact

Mao Zedong
Chiang Kai-shek
Korean War
Ho Chi Minh
Southeast Asia Treaty
  Organization
Nikita Khrushchev
peaceful coexistence
Fidel Castro
St. Lawrence Seaway

Review Questions

Answer each of the following questions.

1. What legislation initiated the interstate highway system?
2. What did President Truman call his domestic program?
3. Who devised a plan for helping the war-torn countries of Europe?
4. What are the three important divisions of the United Nations?
5. What two states entered the Union in 1959?

Explain the meaning of each of the following terms.

6. baby boom
7. green revolution
8. Nuremberg trials
9. Cold War
10. peaceful coexistence

Match each of the following men with his country.

11. Fidel Castro   a. Communist China
12. Chiang Kai-shek   b. Free China
13. Ho Chi Minh   c. Cuba
14. Nikita Khrushchev   d. Soviet Union
15. Mao Zedong   e. Vietnam

Questions for Discussion

16. Why is the United Nations unable to maintain world peace?
17. What would have happened if the United States had taken an isolationist position after World War II?

Chapter Review Answers

1. Federal Aid Highway Act (p. 561)
2. Fair Deal (p. 562)
3. Secretary of State George Marshall (p. 565)
4. General Assembly, Security Council, Secretariat (p. 566)
5. Alaska and Hawaii (p. 575)
6. the large number of babies born in the years following World War II (p. 560)
7. new developments in seeds, machinery, chemicals, and production techniques that helped farmers increase their production dramatically (p. 562)
8. the trial of Nazi leaders in an international court, beginning in 1945, on charges of war crimes (p. 564)
9. a time of high tension between the Soviet Union and the United States but without direct military conflict between the two nations (p. 567)
10. the U.S./Soviet agreement to settle disputes peacefully and to promote good will between themselves rather than to increase hostilities (p. 573)
11. c (p. 574)
12. b (p. 569)
13. e (p. 572)
14. d (p. 573)
15. a (p. 569)
16. Sinful men cannot ensure peace on earth.

History Skills

Using the Library: Report on the United Nations

The library is an essential resource in writing special projects for history class. Your text gives some information but not everything you need. Find a copy of a world almanac, encyclopedia, or other library resource to answer the following questions about the current status of the UN.

1. Where are UN headquarters?
2. Approximately how large is the UN staff?
3. How many nations are members of the UN?
4. What years did each of these nations become members of the UN: Australia, Germany, Japan, Egypt, Italy, Vietnam?
5. Where can you send for a copy of the UN charter?
6. How many votes does each nation get in the General Assembly?
7. What are the five permanent members of the Security Council?
8. What are the current ten nonpermanent two-year members of the Security Council?
9. How many votes are necessary to pass a measure in the Security Council?
10. Who is the current secretary general of the Secretariat?
11. How much was last year's UN budget?
12. What is the "executive branch" of the UN?
13. What is the "judicial branch" of the UN?
14. How long is each UN judge's term of office?
15. Where does the UN court meet?

577

---

17. Communism would probably have expanded over far more lands than it did.

History Skills

1. New York City
2. **see almanac**
3. **see almanac**
4. 1945; 1973; 1956; 1945; 1955; 1977
5. Office of Public Information, United Nations, New York, NY 10017
6. one
7. China, France, Russia, United Kingdom, United States
8. **see almanac**
9. nine
10. **see almanac**
11. **see almanac**
12. Secretariat
13. World Court
14. nine years
15. The Hague, Netherlands

Goals

Students should be able to
1. Review the presidencies of Kennedy, Johnson, and Nixon.
2. Identify the important civil rights changes in the decades reviewed.
3. Define and use the basic terms of the chapter.
4. **Identify the internal battles for democracy being waged in this era.**

The People Speak Out

Protests, such as this anti-war demonstration, were a common sight in the sixties. Standing for a cause became a popular part of the youth culture in the sixties and seventies.

Chapter Motivation

In this chapter, the students will learn about the continued problems of big government and threats to democracy. Challenge the students to see the internal threats to democracy in this chapter. Remind them that the more the government takes public money in an effort to heal national wounds, the less accountable the public will feel to bind the wounds themselves.

Materials

SECTION 1
- Activities A and B from Chapter 28 of the *Student Activities* manual
- A copy of JFK's inaugural address
- Picture books and magazines as resources for a collage, mural, or display
- February 1993 issue of *National Geographic*

SECTION 2
- A copy of "Letter from a Birmingham Jail" by Martin Luther King Jr.
- Documentary video on the civil rights movement

28

The Sixties— Nation in Crisis

The 1960s marked the beginning of a turbulent era in American history, filled with riots, assassinations, and images of war. The nation experienced a crisis on every front, from the breakdown of morals at home to military defeats abroad. Traditional beliefs came under attack in the schools, churches, courts, homes, and legislatures. In spite of great advances in science and medicine, American civilization appeared to be in decline. The dark days continued into the 1970s when the president was forced to resign in disgrace in 1973. After over a decade of effort, the government had also failed to end poverty and racial prejudice. Meanwhile, communism continued to menace the world.

Kennedy's New Frontier

The sixties began with the bright hopes of a young senator who challenged America with a dream of conquering a "New Frontier."

The Close Election of 1960

The Republicans chose Eisenhower's vice president, Richard Nixon, as their candidate in 1960. The Democrats chose Massachusetts Senator **John F. Kennedy.** Kennedy's running mate was Texan Lyndon B. Johnson, the well-known Senate majority leader. With this ticket the party hoped to win the votes of both northern and southern Democrats. Kennedy was young, only 43, and he was a Roman Catholic. In a major change from earlier campaigns,

CHAPTER 28	Lesson Plan Chart			
Section Title	Main Activity	Pages	Time Frame	
1. Kennedy's New Frontier	JFK's Inaugural Address	578-84	1-2 days	
2. The Quest for Civil Rights	Viewpoints on Civil Rights	584-88	1-2 days	
3. The Undeclared War in Vietnam	Student Activity C: Summary of the Vietnam War	588-94	1-2 days	
4. The Fall of Richard Nixon	Discuss Modern Environmentalism and Other Issues	595-600	1 day	
5. The Watergate Scandal	Discuss the Meaning of the Watergate Scandal	600-602	½-1 day	
Total Suggested Days (including 1 day for review and testing)			5½-9 days	

SECTION 1

Materials

- Activities A and B from Chapter 28 of the *Student Activities* manual
- A copy of JFK's inaugural address
- Picture books and magazines as resources for a collage, mural, or display
- February 1993 issue of *National Geographic*

SECTION 1

Objectives
Students should be able to
1. Name the candidates in the 1960 election.
2. Identify the Peace Corps and the Alliance for Progress as two of Kennedy's foreign programs.
3. Explain the significance of the construction of the Berlin Wall.
4. Explain America's reaction to Kennedy's death.
5. Describe Johnson's "Great Society" program.

John F. Kennedy makes his inaugural speech with President Eisenhower and Mrs. Kennedy looking on.

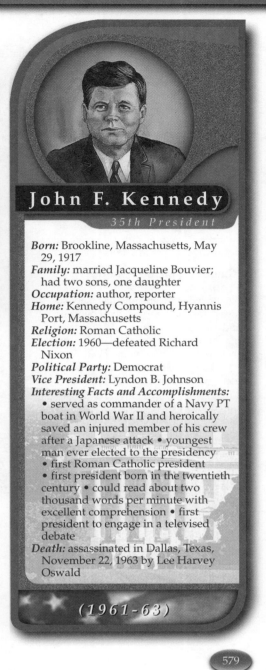

John F. Kennedy
35th President

Born: Brookline, Massachusetts, May 29, 1917
Family: married Jacqueline Bouvier; had two sons, one daughter
Occupation: author, reporter
Home: Kennedy Compound, Hyannis Port, Massachusetts
Religion: Roman Catholic
Election: 1960—defeated Richard Nixon
Political Party: Democrat
Vice President: Lyndon B. Johnson
Interesting Facts and Accomplishments:
• served as commander of a Navy PT boat in World War II and heroically saved an injured member of his crew after a Japanese attack • youngest man ever elected to the presidency • first Roman Catholic president • first president born in the twentieth century • could read about two thousand words per minute with excellent comprehension • first president to engage in a televised debate
Death: assassinated in Dallas, Texas, November 22, 1963 by Lee Harvey Oswald

(1961-63)

U-2 Spy Plane
Before the election in 1960, the United States faced another Cold War crisis. The Soviets shot down an American U-2 spy plane over the Soviet Union. The Soviets captured the pilot, Frances Gary Powers, who had parachuted to safety. The Soviets accused the United States of spying and used the incident as an excuse to cancel a scheduled summit with Eisenhower in Paris.

Nixon and Kennedy engaged in a series of four television debates. Kennedy entered the debates as an underdog, but he used his youthful appearance and charm to good effect. In contrast, Nixon seemed to lack energy and appeal. The election was a close one. Out of 68.3 million votes cast, Kennedy won by only 120,000. This was less than one vote per precinct (local voting place). The election highlighted the importance of individual votes even in a large country.

Kennedy's Mixed Domestic Program
Kennedy's campaign had promised a new program, the **"New Frontier."** Kennedy pressed for measures similar to those of the New Deal—economic aid to poor areas, medical insurance for the aged (called Medicare), aid for college students, and an ambitious space program. In his inaugural speech, Kennedy challenged Americans to "ask not

579

Student Activity A: Time Line of the Sixties

This time line divides the key events of the 1960s by year and topic. You may want to help students complete the time line during your lectures.

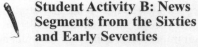

Student Activity B: News Segments from the Sixties and Early Seventies

This activity requires students to look at events from the perspective of a television producer. In addition to challenging the students' creativity, the goal is for them to rec-

ognize the limits of the television medium and to see the potential for slanting the news.

Anything New Under the Sun?

As the students read through each section, ask them to look for issues and situations they have seen before. Very few of the themes in this chapter are new. JFK and LBJ merely sought to extend the New Deal in new ways. Even moral decay is an old theme, reaching back before the Roaring Twenties and the Gilded Age. Foreign affairs took a new turn, but the biggest

changes were the reasons for war and the conduct of war. Students need to be making comparisons and contrasts so that they can discern the wisdom and folly of leaders. As they develop their discernment in the laboratory of recent history, they will be better prepared to evaluate current and future leaders in Washington.

JFK's Inaugural Address

Read from JFK's inaugural address or play a recorded clip so that the students can see the sense of optimism he conveyed. The two key statements are his

Peace Corps

Some of the many Peace Corps projects involved the digging of wells or the building of water systems that would provide clean drinking water. Of course such work is good and needful, but it can be appropriately contrasted with the work of spreading the gospel by Christ's words in John 4:13-14. "Whosoever drinketh of this water shall thirst again: but whosoever drinketh of the water that I shall give him shall never thirst; but the water that I shall give him shall be in him a well of water springing up into everlasting life."

Berlin Wall

The Soviet Union wanted the West out of Berlin. Nikita Khrushchev demanded that all Western troops withdraw and allow Berlin to become a "free" city. Khrushchev threatened that if his demand was not met, he would make a new treaty with the East Germans that would sever Western access to Berlin. President Kennedy and other Western leaders would not back down from their determination to hold on to West Berlin, but East Germans were fearful of the consequences of a Western withdrawal. Many migrated to the West, causing great consternation among Soviet and East German leaders. A wall was erected in August 1961 to stop this flood of frightened refugees.

The main portion of the barricade ran approximately twenty-six miles through the center of the city. The primary barrier was a wall constructed of huge slabs of concrete and varying in height from twelve to fifteen feet. The top of the wall was covered with concrete tubes, barbed wire, or other impediments. Beyond the wall (in East Berlin), an area of no man's land was secured by such things as barbed wire, armed guards with dogs, mines, trenches, and watchtowers. A second wall enclosed that neutral area. All citizens of East Berlin who lived within one hundred meters of the Wall were required to register with the government, and some

what your country can do for you; ask what you can do for your country." Furthermore, he asked America's enemies to join the United States in a quest for lasting peace.

Since Kennedy's victory was a narrow one, and since southern Democrats often voted with House and Senate Republicans, Kennedy's "New Frontier" met opposition in Congress. Congress agreed to a few of Kennedy's goals—such as raising the minimum wage to $1.25 per hour, passing the Trade Expansion Act, and making improvements in the Social Security system. But it rejected Medicare, aid to college education, and a bill to create a department of urban affairs.

Kennedy's Mixed Foreign Program

President Kennedy had several ideas for helping needy countries and spreading peace. As he was implementing these plans, however, they were cut short by the Cold War.

Peace Corps—One popular idea, which Kennedy introduced in 1961, was a volunteer program called the Peace Corps. The "best and brightest" Americans—teachers, engineers, technicians, and businessmen—agreed to dedicate two years of their lives to help improve conditions in poverty-stricken countries. More than sixty countries received help in improving their schools, medical care, and conservation.

Many of the goals of the Peace Corps were good, but it met only a few temporal needs. It provided no permanent solutions for the world's needs. Christians should realize that although helping the poor and needy is good, people have a spiritual need that only the Lord Jesus can satisfy.

Progress in Latin America—Realizing that Cuba was training soldiers to spread communism throughout the region, Kennedy announced an **Alliance for Progress.** Under this plan almost $12 billion went to Latin American nations to provide housing, schools, and health clinics or hospitals in the 1960s. It was hoped that relieving poverty would ease some of the unrest that allowed communism to spread. Unfortunately, money cannot improve people's minds and hearts. The large expenses of the program served mainly to encourage corruption instead of benefiting the poor.

President Kennedy looks over the Berlin Wall into communist-controlled East Berlin.

The Berlin Wall—Kennedy had several dangerous confrontations with the Soviets. Thousands of East Germans—mostly professional people—were escaping into the free city of West Berlin. As a result, in 1961 the Soviet dictator, Khrushchev, ordered the construction of a concrete wall around West

---

request for service of country and his claim that America would make any sacrifice during the Cold War in the defense of liberty. Evaluate the rhetoric of the speech. Does it reflect sound principles, or is it just sweet platitudes?

Collage of the Sixties

Bring in picture books and magazines from which your students can choose materials to make a collage, mural, or display that reflects life in this time period. (You could make photocopies of the book and magazine photos.) Include works

of art, musical titles (patriotic, religious, classical, and popular), painters, books (authors), entertainers, and sports figures of this decade. Students should write a synopsis of their findings and should include a description or explanation of their collage, mural, or display.

Media Reports in the Sixties

Have your class research how reporters, photographers, and war correspondents treated and influenced a war, an important issue, or a famous event during the sixties.

Lessons from Latin American Policy

Ask the students to compare the Alliance for Progress with past policies toward the nations in Latin America. Note the similarity to Taft's dollar diplomacy and the difference from Teddy Roosevelt's "big stick" policy. Neither money nor force has solved the region's problems. What can students conclude from this experience? Give enough information to prepare the students for Reagan's new approach in the 1980s. Also, look for reports on Latin American policy today.

Berlin. Armed guards stood waiting to shoot any who tried to cross the **Berlin Wall.**

President Kennedy responded by sending more troops to West Berlin. In 1963 he made a dramatic nighttime visit to the Berlin Wall, while thousands of Berliners lit candles to show their support of freedom. Kennedy expressed his support with these memorable words, spoken in German, "Ich bin ein Berliner." ("I am a Berliner.") Nevertheless, the wall was a blow to the free world.

On the Brink of War with Cuba—Under Communist dictator Fidel Castro, Cuba's problems were growing worse. Castro had seized all American property in Cuba and refused to pay for any of it. President Eisenhower, in reaction, had cut Cuban sugar imports and later had broken off relations completely. Castro's economic policies caused great hardships for the people. As life under Castro's regime worsened, many Cubans fled to the United States. With so many pro-democracy Cubans in Florida, the Central Intelligence Agency (CIA) devised a plan to train fifteen hundred of them to overthrow Castro. Soon after taking office, Kennedy allowed the plan to proceed. The CIA believed that when the Cubans heard about the invasion, they would rally to their cause.

Unfortunately, nothing went as planned. On April 17, 1961, the force landed at the **Bay of Pigs,** but Castro's forces easily repelled the invasion because Kennedy withheld promised air support. More than four hundred exiles died, and the rest were captured. Castro was able to use the unsuccessful invasion to embarrass the United States.

Problems with Cuba grew worse. On October 14, 1962, American U-2 spy planes flying over Cuba confirmed suspicions that the Soviet Union was shipping missiles to Cuba, missiles that could carry nuclear bombs and destroy American cities. The nation was horrified when President Kennedy announced the presence of the missiles and his decision to blockade Cuba. United States warships surrounded the island, ready to stop and search any Soviet vessels that violated the blockade. Kennedy also demanded that the Soviets remove the missiles, and he put the nation's armed forces on full alert.

Khrushchev was enraged. He blamed Kennedy for pushing mankind into nuclear war. But after a week of the tense standoff, he sent Kennedy a message on October 28 offering to remove the missiles if the United States promised never to invade Cuba. As suddenly as it had begun, the **Cuban Missile Crisis** was over. Kennedy's secretary of state, Dean Rusk, boasted, "We're eyeball to eyeball, and I think the other fellow just blinked." But he said nothing about the U.S. side of the bargain, which would have serious consequences for decades to come.

A Slight Thaw in the Cold War—In the wake of the Cuban Missile Crisis, the United States and the Soviet Union wanted to ease tensions. A "hot line," a direct telephone line between the White House and the Kremlin in

People hoped in vain that the Nuclear Test Ban Treaty was a sign that the Cold War was thawing.

581

had to leave their homes. (Upper-story windows or rooftops had too much potential for escape routes over the wall.) The rest of West Berlin (that which was not bordered by East Berlin) was also surrounded by a wall or some other type of barrier. In all, approximately 110 miles of barricades surrounded the city.

A Jelly Doughnut

The phrase *ein Berliner* in Kennedy's statement to the people of West Berlin had a meaning Kennedy never intended. Because he added the article *ein* in front of *Berliner*, he changed himself from a citizen of the city of Berlin to a jelly doughnut.

Operation Mongoose

Although the attempted invasion at the Bay of Pigs was a miserable failure, President Kennedy was not resigned to letting Castro go his way. He wanted to continue to place pressure on the dictator. In November 1961 the Kennedy administration made plans for a new program code named Operation Mongoose.

Mongoose had an operating force of approximately four hundred Americans and two thousand Cubans, a fleet of speedboats, and an annual $50 million budget. Its purpose was to undermine the government of Fidel Castro. Its activities were generally covert and ranged from sabotage of shipping (e.g., contaminating an outgoing shipment of sugar) to intelligence gathering.

Mongoose's activities continued through the resolution of the Cuban Missile Crisis. The operation was officially terminated October 30, 1962, but three sabotage teams that were commissioned by Mongoose had already left for Cuba, and one carried out its mission on November 8.

Recent Events in Cuba

Discuss recent issues involving Cuba. In 1999 Fidel Castro was the only remaining Cold War warrior still in power. Failures such as the Cuban Missile Crisis had long-term consequences for millions of people. The trade embargo lasted more than twenty-five years.

Moscow, the Soviet capital, was installed in 1963. The same year at Geneva, Switzerland, the United States, Britain, and the Soviet Union signed a Limited Test Ban Treaty. They agreed that there would be no above-ground testing of nuclear weapons. Each nation was to tell the others of any underground tests and was to police itself. But France and China, who also had nuclear weapons, refused to sign the treaty.

The End of Camelot

When Kennedy came to office, the musical *Camelot* was popular on Broadway. The play retold the story of King Arthur's Round Table and his dream of creating a new England where truth, justice, and equality would reign. Seeing a parallel between King Arthur's dream and that of Kennedy, some began to refer to Kennedy's administration as "Camelot." The dreams of Camelot came to an abrupt end on November 22, 1963. While traveling down a street in Dallas, Texas, the president was shot by Lee Harvey Oswald. Kennedy was only forty-six. The reasons for the assassination remain a mystery.

After his death Kennedy became a hero. Even people who disagreed with Kennedy's politics remembered the things they liked about him—his youth, his idealism, and his vitality. Kennedy seemed to represent optimism for America's future. Congress quickly passed many of Kennedy's New Frontier programs, which had been stalled in Congress, as memorials to the late president.

LBJ's Great Society

Lyndon B. Johnson took his oath of office on the presidential airplane, Air Force One, after Kennedy's death. Since Johnson had

been on Capitol Hill for thirty-two years, serving in both the House and the Senate, he knew the political system and how to work it. A powerful and persuasive man, he was able to get bills passed. Johnson called his legislative program **"The Great Society."** His program was supposed to help America bring "an end to poverty and racial injustice . . . in our time."

LBJ's Election to Four More Years—But before Johnson could achieve all his goals, he first had to win the election of 1964. His challenger was a conservative senator from Arizona named **Barry Goldwater.** He represented a small but growing branch of the Republican Party that openly denounced big government programs, wanting government "out of our pocketbooks and out of our bedrooms." Goldwater voted against the Civil Rights Act, not because he supported racial discrimination, but because he wanted citizens to be free to run their own lives. The liberal wing of the Republican Party was embar-

Shock and grief shows on the face of Jacqueline Kennedy as Lyndon Johnson is sworn into the office of President on Air Force One shortly after the assassination of President Kennedy.

The Aftermath of Assassination

Compare and contrast the aftermaths of Lincoln's assassination and JFK's assassination. Both men became heroes, and their failures were easily forgotten. But in Kennedy's case, his program succeeded better after his death than it had before, whereas Lincoln's program for Reconstruction died on the vine. Ask the students to explain why. *(Factors include the skills of the vice presidents, the political views of the leaders in Congress, and the bitter disputes over the Civil War.)*

Was It a Mistake to Choose Goldwater?

Goldwater lost by a landslide. Should the Republicans have concluded that they made a mistake to choose him as their nominee? Students need to recognize that presidential elections have a value that goes far beyond the current winner or loser. Candidates are positioning themselves for future elections, and different wings of the party are struggling to present their ideas to the American people, hoping that their ideas will eventually take root. As we look back, Goldwater's election is considered a water-

shed in the rise of the Republican Right, which swept Reagan into office in 1980. In fact, Reagan won national recognition because of his spellbinding speech during Goldwater's nomination. Make parallels to the most recent presidential election so that students can see the long-term goals of the participants. Someday the students, as voting citizens, should push their party to make decisions based on principle rather than pragmatism.

rassed by Goldwater, and the press published his blunt statements about eliminating Social Security and using nuclear weapons to win the war in Vietnam, if necessary. Democratic ads frightened voters with the threat of nuclear destruction. LBJ won the contest by a landslide, receiving 61 percent of the vote.

War on Poverty—Forty million Americans did not share in the nation's rising wealth during the 1950s. This hidden minority was stuck in a "culture of poverty," according to a blockbuster book called *The Other America* (1962) by Michael Harrington. Johnson took up the cause of the poor in his Great Society, declaring a "War on Poverty." He created a Job Corps, similar to the Peace Corps but focusing on the needs at home. Other Great Society programs included aid to distressed areas of the eleven states in Appalachia, a food stamp program for poor families, and a Head Start Program for underprivileged children who needed a "head start" in education before they started regular school. Johnson also asked Congress to pass new legislation for labeling and packaging food, drugs, cosmetics, and household supplies.

In 1965 Johnson pushed through several more programs of the Great Society. Medicare and Medicaid gave qualifying Americans two months of low-cost hospital care and allowances for other medical costs. The government added two new cabinet positions—Housing and Urban Development, and Transportation.

All of these programs were expensive, costing more than the government brought in. Overspending put the nation in debt, a problem that would plague America for the next twenty years. The Great Society also made Americans more dependent on government programs and gave the federal government more power over people's lives.

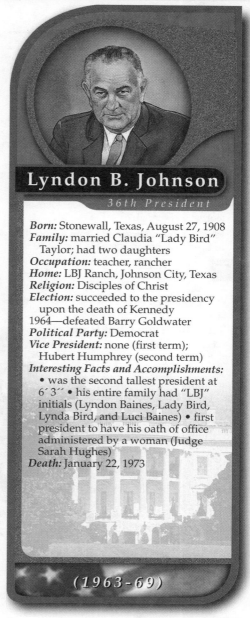

Lyndon B. Johnson
36th President

Born: Stonewall, Texas, August 27, 1908
Family: married Claudia "Lady Bird" Taylor; had two daughters
Occupation: teacher, rancher
Home: LBJ Ranch, Johnson City, Texas
Religion: Disciples of Christ
Election: succeeded to the presidency upon the death of Kennedy
1964—defeated Barry Goldwater
Political Party: Democrat
Vice President: none (first term); Hubert Humphrey (second term)
Interesting Facts and Accomplishments:
• was the second tallest president at 6´3´´ • his entire family had "LBJ" initials (Lyndon Baines, Lady Bird, Lynda Bird, and Luci Baines) • first president to have his oath of office administered by a woman (Judge Sarah Hughes)
Death: January 22, 1973

(1963–69)

583

topple Castro angered elements of organized crime. They apparently felt double-crossed.

How does the Mafia relate to the assassination? Again, according to this scenario, Oswald did kill the president, but his links to Communists gave the mob cover. To keep Oswald from talking, he was killed. Investigators discovered much later that Jack Ruby, Oswald's killer, had links to the Chicago Mafia, where he had worked before moving to Dallas.

Again, there is only circumstantial evidence to support this conspiracy theory, but given the sordid private life of Kennedy and the public's ongoing fascination with him and his family, conspiracy theorists will continue to have grist for their mills for years to come.

Radical Shift in Immigration Policy
The Democratic Congress of 1965 made a watershed decision that had a profound impact on the nation, though its fruits were not fully evident for another thirty years. They opened the door to non-European immigrants. Concerning the decision, Republicans said that the Democrats wanted to increase their voting base, which traditionally comes from the working class and the poor. The Democrats, however, argued that they were removing a prejudicial policy and allowing families to be reunited.

Nuggets from *National Geographic*
Poverty grips the part of the nation known as Appalachia. "In the Hearts of Appalachia" in the February 1993 issue of *National Geographic* describes the lifestyles and culture of Appalachia.

Why Do Americans Like Government?
Ask the students to explain why Americans were so supportive of the massive government programs that LBJ pushed through Congress. What had caused such a dramatic change in America's fundamental dislike of a strong central government and high taxes? After all, the country was founded because of this issue. It can be argued that the schools no longer instilled traditional values. But another explanation is the reform tradition and the philanthropy tradition in America. If the government truly could help the poor, Americans were willing to sacrifice for them. But, as students will see in their study of the 1990s, Americans were disillusioned by their bad investment. It is never easy to explain the motives behind voters' choices.

Objectives
Students should be able to
1. Explain the significance of the *Brown v. Board of Education* case.
2. List and describe the major civil rights legislation and amendments of the 1960s.
3. Name the most prominent black civil rights leader of the 1960s.

Separate but Equal
The 1896 case that had established the "separate but equal" principle was *Plessy v. Ferguson*.

Changing Strategies of Civil Rights Activists
The American civil rights movement, bringing revolutionary change not only to America but also to the world, has been central to politics since the 1950s. Over time the techniques used by its advocates have varied, and their adaptability has made the struggle one of the most successful and imitated in the world. They shifted from legal assaults and peaceful protests to violence.

The founding of the NAACP in 1910 began a legal strategy to end racial segregation. Lawyers for the organization challenged segregation in the courts, winning small victories over the decades until the big victory came in 1954 with the *Brown* decision. Although it took two more decades to implement school desegregation, the *Brown* decision marked a high point in the legal battle for black civil rights.

The following year, 1955, Martin Luther King Jr. launched a bus boycott to end discrimination in that city's bus system. The action broadened the civil rights struggle to include mass action—huge public protests by blacks and sympathetic whites. King's success led to more protests. In 1960 the Student Nonviolent Coordinating Committee organized sit-ins at dime-store lunch counters to

SECTION REVIEW

1. What was the name Kennedy gave to the program for his administration?
2. What was the purpose of the Peace Corps?
3. In what city did the Soviets build a wall to stop escapes from the communist-controlled area?
4. What two situations in Cuba created problems for the United States?
5. Why did Kennedy become a hero after his death?
6. What name was given to Lyndon Johnson's legislative program?
7. What conservative senator from Arizona lost to Lyndon Johnson in the election of 1964?

 Considering the election of 1960 as well as more recent ones, do you think television has had a positive impact on the political process? Explain your answer.

The Quest for Civil Rights
Despite LBJ's skills in passing legislation, he soon came face to face with two insurmountable problems that would fill the headlines during his years in office. One was the Vietnam War. The other was civil rights.

Civil rights has stirred controversy since the Constitutional Convention. The term originally referred to the right of every citizen to receive equal treatment before the law. Despite the guarantees of the Constitution and the brave service of black soldiers in World War II, black Americans were still being denied many of their civil rights in postwar America. Their long struggle to gain equality came to be called the *civil rights movement*.

The Courts Intervene in Civil Rights
An 1896 Supreme Court case had allowed blacks to be separated from whites as long as facilities were theoretically equal. For many years the National Association for the Advancement of Colored People (NAACP) worked quietly to get judges to end inequalities. After a series of cases, black graduate students were allowed to seek an education in white universities because at the time there were no black schools on the graduate level that offered equal training.

But eventually lawyers challenged the idea of "separate but equal" facilities. In 1954 in ***Brown v. Board of Education,*** the Supreme Court ruled that segregation of children in public schools based solely on race violated the equal treatment that all citizens were guaranteed under the Fourteenth Amendment (see p. 159). The *Brown* case applied to schools in seventeen states. Schools were told to inte-

Influential black leader Martin Luther King Jr. leads the 1963 March on Washington where blacks and whites rallied in support of civil rights legislation.

Section Review Answers
1. "New Frontier" (p. 579)
2. to help improve conditions in poverty-stricken countries (p. 580)
3. Berlin (pp. 580-81)
4. the failed invasion at the Bay of Pigs and the Cuban Missile Crisis (p. 581)
5. because he became a symbol in Americans' minds of optimism for the future (p. 582)
6. "The Great Society" (p. 582)

7. Barry Goldwater (p. 582)

 Answers will vary. Appearance or charisma may become more important than the substance of a candidate's positions. On the other hand, greater exposure of candidates may allow the average citizen to be more informed politically.

SECTION 2

Materials
• A copy of "Letter from a Birmingham Jail" by Martin Luther King Jr.

• Documentary video on the civil rights movement

grate "with all deliberate speed." However, some school districts did not start to integrate until 1969 or later.

President Eisenhower did not put particular pressure on the states to integrate. He hoped the states would follow the court's instructions on their own. When challenged by the government of Arkansas, however, Eisenhower put the state National Guard under his control to insure the safe enrollment of black students at Little Rock's Central High School in 1957.

President Kennedy took a stronger stand to enforce existing laws and to act on the *Brown* case. In less than three years, the Justice Department took action to integrate 183 schools. In September 1962 and June 1963, Kennedy sent federal marshals to the Universities of Mississippi and Alabama to ensure that black students could enroll.

The **Twenty-third Amendment** passed during the Kennedy administration. It gave the residents of the District of Columbia the right to vote in national elections. Since the district's population was heavily black, this was regarded as a step forward in civil rights.

Early Civil Rights Protests

Black activists did not rely on the courts alone. In 1955 Rosa Parks, a seamstress in Montgomery, Alabama, rode a city bus home after a hard day at work. Tradition and the law divided the bus into two sections, with blacks sitting in the back. But Mrs. Parks sat at the rear of the white section, in one of the few empty seats on the bus. When a white person asked her to give it up, she refused and was arrested. To show support for her action, other blacks started a bus boycott. They refused to ride city buses for over a year, depriving the buses of desperately needed money. Finally the city ended the bus law.

A small group pickets in front of an apartment complex to protest the failure of the complex to rent to minorities.

Blacks tried other forms of protest—sit-ins at white lunch counters, kneel-ins at churches, and wade-ins at schools. "Freedom riders" rode from place to place in the South, seeking to integrate the buses and to encourage blacks to register to vote. Everywhere they went, civil rights demonstrators faced angry white mobs; they were ridiculed and beaten, and some were murdered. Police employed tear gas, cattle prods, and attack dogs to stop protesters in Birmingham, Alabama, in early 1963. A bomb destroyed a black church in Birmingham, killing four girls.

The biggest single demonstration took place at the U.S. capital in August 1963. Organized by Martin Luther King Jr., its purpose was to rally support for proposed civil rights legislation. About 250,000 blacks and whites participated in the **march on Washington,** where King delivered a memorable address, repeating the phrase "I have a dream." King spoke of an ideal America where liberty and equality would be a reality for all—both black and white.

protest their segregation practices. The following year the Congress of Racial Equality sponsored freedom rides into the Deep South to dramatize racial discrimination in public facilities. The crusade gained much sympathetic coverage from the media and much white middle class support for big marches, the most notable being in Washington in 1963 when King delivered his memorable "I Have a Dream" speech. Civil rights as a mass movement reached a climax with a flurry of legislation in Congress. The 1964 Civil Rights bill ended racial segregation in public accommodations; the 1965 Voting Rights bill empowered federal officials, not white southerners, to register blacks for voting; and the 1968 Open Housing bill ended legal segregation in housing.

With the successes came problems. In 1965 in the Watts section of Los Angeles, one of the worst race riots in American history occurred, and for the next few summers blacks continued to riot, loot, and burn their neighborhoods in major cities. King's death in 1968 encouraged black radicals, such as the Black Panthers, to turn toward violence in their struggle. Calls for "black power" replaced the cries for integration. Many blacks rejected white liberals who had been their allies during the 1950s and 1960s. Black militancy ultimately alienated whites in politics and the media, bringing an end to the civil rights movement and helping to usher in a conservative backlash in the 1970s.

Twenty-third Amendment
The Twenty-third Amendment was very difficult to pass. Conservatives opposed the idea of allowing a city of government workers to vote. They argued that the founders of the Constitution did not want elected officials to abuse their powers to win votes.

585

Read "Letter from a Birmingham Jail"

Read portions of Martin Luther King Jr.'s influential "Letter from a Birmingham Jail," which defends the need for civil disobedience. A copy of this may be found on the Internet or in books of famous speeches.

Pages from U.S. History

Have the students read King's "I Have a Dream Speech" on page 558 and answer the questions. Be sure to discuss the original meaning of the statements that King quotes. In addition to the questions on page 558, ask the students what King means by brotherhood among "all of God's children." As a liberal ecumenicist, King looked forward to an event on earth among people of many faiths. But the Bible defines God's children as those who place faith in Christ (Gal. 3:26-28), and it says that they look forward to unity in heaven (Rev. 7:9). Ask the students whether King's speech appeals to reason or to emotions. They should recognize that King uses emotional symbols to influence people's attitudes and actions, but he fails

to make clear that his dream of equality, justice, freedom, and brotherhood is radically different from what the country's Founding Fathers and orthodox churches have advocated.

*Thousands and thousands of protesters cover the green from the
Washington Monument to the Capitol during the March on Washington.*

Congress Passes Civil Rights Legislation

Following the march on Washington and
Kennedy's assassination, Congress rallied to
pass new civil rights legislation. The **Civil
Rights Act of 1964** forbade racial segregation
and discrimination in schools and public
places, such as motels. The federal government would no longer make contracts with
private companies that discriminated, and it
would no longer give money to institutions
that discriminated in their hiring practices.

The **Twenty-fourth Amendment** (p.
165), ratified in 1964, forbade states from
levying poll taxes. This tax required voters to
pay a fee before they could vote. Poll taxes
were popular in the South because they kept
both poor blacks and poor whites from voting.

The **Voting Rights Act of 1965** ended
long-standing injustices in voting in federal
elections. Although the Fifteenth Amendment
(1870) kept the states from denying any one
race the right to vote, southern states had gotten around the law in a variety of ways. Many
required literacy tests. Often these not only
tested reading knowledge but also required
understanding of obscure, difficult portions of
state constitutions. Blacks who sought to register had also been harassed. The new act gave
the national government the power to register
blacks in states where the registered black vote
was significantly lower than census population. Federal officials also had the power to
check any complaints of discrimination.

Divisions Among Civil Rights Leaders

The civil rights movement heard many
conflicting voices. A Baptist minister, **Martin**

President Johnson signs the Voting Rights Act of 1965 ensuring black voters' rights as black leaders look on.

North. But he had many enemies, especially after a visit to Mecca in 1964 that caused him to embrace racial harmony and to denounce the "black racism" of the Nation of Islam. Gunmen killed Malcolm X at a rally in New York City the following year.

Radical young blacks were also attracted to Stokely Carmichael, who advocated "black power." No one was sure what the term meant, but its slogan—"violence is as American as cherry pie"—frightened many whites and angered conservative blacks, who feared its effects on the progress of the civil rights movement.

While the nation's attention was drawn to the segregation laws of the South, it overlooked the social prejudice that had segregated black communities in the North and on the west coast. **Urban riots** broke out in several cities. Just days after the passage of the Voting Rights Act in 1965, rioters burned a black community in Los Angeles known as Watts. Thirty-four people died, and property damage exceeded $35 million. The next year rioters burned parts of Detroit and Newark, and dozens more were killed. The looting and destruction shocked Americans. Another blow to the civil rights movement came in April 1968. A white assassin killed Martin Luther King Jr. while he was standing on a hotel balcony in Memphis, Tennessee. King's murder set off a wave of violence in black neighborhoods across America. In spite of government efforts to improve civil rights, the dream of racial harmony seemed far away.

Luther King Jr., was the first black leader to win national prominence. King founded the Southern Christian Leadership Conference. But instead of preaching the gospel, the conference spoke of liberating the poor and underprivileged through social action. King helped to organize the bus boycott in Montgomery, and he was jailed during the demonstrations at Birmingham. While in the Birmingham jail, he wrote an influential "letter" advocating nonviolent, passive resistance—also called civil disobedience—to raise public awareness of unjust laws.

Some black leaders rejected King's "soft" views, however. Among them was **Malcolm X,** a convert to the Nation of Islam (the Black Muslims), who preached black supremacy and the need to create a separate black nation to keep the black race pure. Malcolm X's preaching won a large audience, especially in the

Nation of Islam

In 1930 a silk salesman in Detroit named W. D. Fard founded the Nation of Islam, whose followers were commonly known as Black Muslims. He believed that Islam was the true religion of the black man since it started with the "blacks" of Asia and Africa. He combined Muslim teachings with a quest for black autonomy; one of his goals was to have a separate nation within the United States for blacks.

Fard disappeared in 1934, but he had a faithful disciple who continued his work. Elijah Poole was born in Georgia in 1897 but moved to Detroit to work in an automobile factory in 1923. He met Fard in 1930 and became devoted to the Black Muslim cause, receiving from Fard the last name of Muhammad as testimony of his devotion. Shortly after Fard's disappearance, Muhammad reestablished the group in Chicago. He set Fard up as a deity—Allah—and declared himself to be Allah's messenger. He continued Fard's emphasis on black separation; whites were "devils."

Upon Elijah Muhammad's death in 1975, his son Warith Deen Muhammad took over the leadership of the Nation of Islam. Significant changes followed. The group moved toward Sunni Islam. Membership was no longer exclusively black, and followers became known as Muslims rather than Black Muslims. Even the organization's name changed from Nation of Islam to the World Community of Al-Islam in the West to American Muslim Mission.

There is a Nation of Islam today, but it is separate from the American Muslim Mission. Louis Farrakhan led a group of people away from the main movement in 1978. His group holds to the black separatist teachings of Elijah Muhammad, and members call themselves Black Muslims.

587

Video on Civil Rights Movement

Watch a documentary video on the civil rights movement. Make sure that your students view the video with scriptural principles in mind and not just blind emotionalism. Preview the video carefully for sections that may be too violent.

Viewpoints on Civil Rights

Since the Civil War, Americans have not agreed on the best way to give blacks equality in society. Note the fundamental difference between Booker T. Washington and the NAACP. Washington argued that blacks should earn an equal place by their own hard work, while the NAACP believed that there were too many political hindrances for blacks ever to have a chance. At first the NAACP worked through the courts, but the 1960s saw the rise of civil disobedience and more radical approaches designed to force the issue.

Divide the class into different factions and have them research some of the arguments that each faction gave. Ask the students to explain how a Christian should decide on the best alternative. Obviously, they want everyone to enjoy full liberty and opportunity, but none of the methods have succeeded in achieving these goals. Christians make choices based on principles, not whatever "works." Ironically, unhampered freedom in the United States has created more equality of wealth and position than any other government system in world history.

Objectives

Students should be able to

1. Name the resolution that gave the president authority to send troops into conflict in Vietnam.
2. Describe the difficulties of fighting the war in Vietnam.
3. Describe American opinions toward the war in Vietnam.
4. Explain the circumstances and results of the election of 1968.
5. Define Vietnamization.

Gulf of Tonkin Resolution— Background

The Gulf of Tonkin Resolution played a significant role in the Vietnam War. It was the statement upon which both President Johnson and President Nixon claimed congressional support of their actions. The resolution received overwhelming support. It passed the House by a vote of 416 to 0 and the Senate by a vote of 88 to 2. However, in intervening years the incident that provoked the resolution has been called into question, and the question is whether it ever actually occurred.

The South Vietnamese were attempting to subvert the government of the Communists in North Vietnam in any way possible (as were the North Vietnamese to the government of South Vietnam). America assisted the South Vietnamese in their subversive efforts. As part of that assistance, the U.S.S. *Maddox* was conducting electronic espionage in the region of the Gulf of Tonkin in August 1964. On August 2, three North Vietnamese patrol boats attacked the *Maddox*. In the fighting that followed, one of the patrol boats was sunk and the others retreated. Although this attack caused concern over future North Vietnamese intentions, the *Maddox* was not violating international law by its presence in the region and so was ordered to continue its

---

SECTION REVIEW

1. What major court case affected civil rights? What practice did it declare to be unconstitutional?

2. What black seamstress sparked a bus boycott by her refusal to give up her seat for a white person?

3. Who was the most prominent black civil rights leader? What famous phrase did he use during the march on Washington?

4. What three pieces of civil rights legislation were passed after President Kennedy's assassination? What did each accomplish?

 What would you identify as the greatest threat to the civil rights movement? Why?

The Undeclared War in Vietnam

The biggest single issue in foreign affairs in the 1960s was the **Vietnam War.** Lyndon Johnson inherited the conflict that had been brewing in Southeast Asia for nearly a decade (pp. 572-73). During Johnson's administration, Vietnam became a raging issue as American involvement increased.

Increasing American Involvement

Although Eisenhower had pledged that he would not allow South Vietnam to fall to Communists and had supplied financial aid, Kennedy was the first president to send large numbers of Americans. By November 1963, the United States had 16,000 troops in Vietnam. Most served as "advisors," training the Vietnamese to fight their own war.

President Johnson campaigned promising not to send American boys "to do what Asian boys ought to be doing for themselves." Nevertheless, he became increasingly concerned that

Southeast Asia would be conquered by the Communists as China had been in 1949.

In August 1964 Johnson found an opportunity to justify an increase in American involvement in the war. He announced on television that North Vietnamese patrol boats had attacked two American destroyers in international waters off the coast of Vietnam in the Gulf of Tonkin. The president reported this incident to Congress and requested power to act. The resulting **Gulf of Tonkin Resolution** said that the United States was now ready "to take all necessary steps, including the use of armed forces" against the North Vietnamese. The resolution was not a declaration of war, but it gave the president broad powers to increase American activity in Vietnam.

American activity in Vietnam was hotly debated in the United States. Leaders who favored increased American presence in Vietnam, or an "escalation" of the war, were called **hawks.** Those who wanted the United States to pull out completely were called **doves.** Under Johnson, the number of troops in Vietnam escalated rapidly. In May 1965

American soldiers stand back and watch as a Viet Cong base camp goes up in flames.

Section Review Answers

1. *Brown v. Board of Education;* segregation of children in public schools based solely on race (p. 584)

2. Rosa Parks (p. 585)

3. Martin Luther King Jr.; "I have a dream" (pp. 585-87)

4. The Civil Rights Act of 1964 forbade racial segregation and discrimination in schools and public places; the Twenty-fourth Amendment forbade states from levying poll taxes;

the Voting Rights Act of 1965 ended injustices in federal election voting. (p. 586)

 Answers will vary. Possibilities include man's sinful nature and unwillingness to change or the violence of radicals on the fringes of the movement.

SECTION 3

Materials

• Activity C from Chapter 28 of the *Student Activities* manual

Student Activity C: Summary of the Vietnam War

This simple question-and-answer activity summarizes the key events in the Vietnam War. The first part of the activity refers to the previous chapter.

more than half a million Americans were on Vietnamese soil.

A Sticky Situation

The United States was committed to protecting the free government of South Vietnam. The United States effort might have had a better chance of success had Vietnamese politics been free of corruption and had the South Vietnamese people consistently backed their own government, but this was not so. During the war the United States had to fight not only the Communists from the North but also Communist supporters in the South. The **Vietcong,** Vietnamese Communists who had stayed in South Vietnam after the division of the country, carried out guerrilla warfare against Americans and the South Vietnamese troops.

The Vietnam War

0   100   200   300
Scale of Miles

America's Disadvantages in the Rice Paddies of Vietnam—The United States entered the conflict with other disadvantages. Since Congress had never officially declared war, technically the country was engaged in only a police action. The United States feared that if it declared war, many more countries would join the fight, leading even to world war. Yet thousands of Americans were dying in Vietnam for a cause that politicians were still debating. As the war dragged on, it seemed that the United States was not fighting to win anything. There seemed to be no glorious cause to rally public support.

Furthermore, although the United States had the most modern and sophisticated weapons, it could not use this advantage easily in Vietnam. In World War II the United States had defeated Germany by bombing its industrial cities. North Vietnam had no large industrial plants but rather thousands of little shops scattered across the land. The trees and terrain also made bombing difficult. American bombers found it difficult to identify targets on the **Ho Chi Minh Trail,** the route that the Vietcong forces used to move their men and goods. Even when they identified specific targets, success was not guaranteed. For example, one log bridge was destroyed at least twenty times, but the North Vietnamese kept rebuilding it in only a few days. Moreover, the North Vietnamese received a steady stream of military supplies from both China and the Soviet Union.

In addition, United States servicemen could not identify the enemy. To the servicemen, the North Vietnamese and Vietcong looked just like the loyal South Vietnamese. While those in the cities usually supported the Americans, in rural areas no one knew whom to trust. The Vietcong even employed children to lob hand grenades at American soldiers. Children killed many soldiers; yet when

operations. Two days later the *Maddox* was sailing with another destroyer, the *Turner Joy,* when sonar readings appeared to indicate the presence of enemy torpedoes. Both ships opened fire, and one of them reported having sunk two enemy vessels. Yet no personnel on either boat had actually seen any ships or heard any gunfire. Later, a commander on the *Maddox* acknowledged the possibility that they were mistaken in their belief of an attack. Nevertheless, President Johnson, without getting a firm confirmation of the facts, used the incident to promote the escalation of war with North Vietnam.

Gulf of Tonkin Resolution—Ramifications

The powers granted by the Gulf of Tonkin Resolution became the source of great debate. Such powers allowed a president to entangle American military personnel in conflicts or potential conflicts as he wished, and Congress could not force the president to pull troops out of such a situation. Thus, an undeclared war could go on indefinitely. Congress later passed legislation to avoid this problem in the future. The War Powers Act, passed in 1973, required a termination of hostilities within ninety days after the president had sent troops into conflict unless Congress authorized a continuation or unless war was officially declared.

Contrast Korea and Vietnam

After they read the section on Vietnam, the students should be able to explain why the Vietnam War turned out so differently from the Korean War. Make comparisons and contrasts as you look for the answer. *(Both were police actions; both propped up corrupt regimes; both were fought to contain Communism; and both enemies were supported by powerful Communist countries. Unlike the Vietnam War, the Korean War was short; America had allies in Korea; the Korean War followed on the heels of victory during World War II; and the Koreans* *started the war with a direct assault by a conventional army.)*

Understanding the Student Protests of the Sixties

Among the most important movements to shape American society in the late twentieth century were the student protests and hippie movement of the sixties. Their opposition to the Vietnam War helped end that war and thereby change the nation's foreign policy. Furthermore, they revolutionized American colleges and universities by insisting on easier academic and moral standards; and their counterculture, with its rock music, drugs, immorality, and shabby dress and hair, forever changed American culture.

A major question for historians is why young people at that particular time became so rebellious. The causes are complex. One was demographic. The postwar baby boom created a huge demographic bulge in the population, which increased about 30 percent between 1945 and 1960. Those babies became college students by the midsixties, and universities became unbelievably overcrowded. In addition, with more students the competition became fiercer. Also, before the midsixties, colleges were strict, with high academic and moral standards. Colleges were seen as part of the establishment, which, according to the students, was responsible for problems such as the Vietnam War. By the late sixties, therefore, colleges became tense places, and many students resorted to protests and violence against the administration.

Other factors also contributed to the student revolt. An underlying cause was the baby-boom generation's rejection of their parents' materialism. The "affluent society" of the American postwar era placed a premium on hard work and the accumulation of wealth. Young people in the sixties were correct in discovering that middle-class materialism did not satisfy; however, they were wrong in their remedy. Instead of searching for spiritual fulfillment, they sought refuge in rock music, drugs,

U.S. Marshals bodily remove one of the protesters during a violent anti-Vietnam demonstration at the Pentagon Building.

children were killed in the war, the American public was appalled.

Radical Youth on the Home Front—A greater threat than the enemy in Vietnam was the lack of unity at home. As war continued, political activists who strongly opposed the war gained increasing public attention. A **"New Left"** movement, led by Communist sympathizers, grew among disenchanted Americans and civil rights workers looking for a new cause. Many college students, who were subject to the draft, joined the protests. A few defiant ones burned their draft cards and the American flag. Some young men fled to Sweden or Canada. In October 1965 more than ninety cities had antiwar demonstrations. A left-wing organization, the Students for Democratic Society, was in the forefront. In April 1967 antiwar marches in New York and San Francisco attracted up to 300,000 people.

The antiwar movement was the most visible outpouring of a radical change in thinking and morals among American young people.

For years, schools and liberal churches had been teaching that mankind is evolving and that there are no absolute standards of right and wrong. Young people took this teaching to heart. Hippies and other radical youths rejected their parents' vain search for happiness through hard work and acquiring wealth. The so-called **counterculture** toppled all symbols of morality and authority. They adopted standards completely different from their parents' "old-fashioned" culture, choosing long hair, brightly painted clothes, and "hip" vocabulary. They believed the world could solve its problems if everyone just started loving each other as innocent children. "All we need is love," claimed one popular rock song.

The counterculture was a logical outgrowth of Romantic philosophy taught in the schools. Romanticism argues that nature is good and that civilization is corrupt. Youths wanted to return to their natural state. Many of them indulged in drugs and sexual immorality in an effort to achieve complete freedom and happiness. They were wrong, of course. In the seventies and eighties the country reaped the bitter fruit of this foolish rebellion, as American society sank to new lows.

North Vietnam's Surprise—The Tet Offensive

By clever use of guerrilla warfare and supplies from the Soviet Union and China, the North Vietnamese, led by Ho Chi Minh, made headway against the South. If they could just prolong the war, they believed they would win because Americans would give up and pull out.

To slow the stream of supplies flowing into North Vietnam, the United States began bombing the northern port of Haiphong and the capital city, Hanoi. The bombings were extremely effective. Each time the bombings were stepped up, however, the wily Ho Chi Minh hinted that he might go to the peace table if the bombings halted. Liberal politicians convinced LBJ to slow the bombings, only to allow the Communists time to move in more troops and supplies.

In spite of the setbacks, the president and his leading general, William Westmoreland, expressed optimism in public in 1967. They expanded the air war and sent additional American soldiers into battle. Some believed the fight would be over in two to three years.

Over the Christmas holidays of 1967, the United States called another ceasefire. As usual, the Communists used the lull to their advantage. This time, however, they moved huge quantities of supplies and troops into South Vietnam. Large numbers of strangers walked or rode into South Vietnam's cities. Many more funerals were held than usual, bearing coffins stuffed with weapons, not corpses.

Helicopters swoop in to airlift members of the 2nd battalion.

With their troops in position, the North Vietnamese and the Vietcong unleashed a surprise attack on January 30, 1968, the Chinese New Year (the Tet). They waited until shortly after midnight, when all the partiers were asleep. From one end of the country to the other, they fired on police stations, military bases, government buildings, radio and power stations, and foreign embassies. They captured the old imperial city of Hue (HWAY) and assaulted Saigon, the capital city.

But American forces counterattacked and regained what was captured within a few weeks. Nevertheless, the Tet Offensive was a serious blow to support for the war effort at home. Televisions, radios, magazines, and newspapers falsely reported the incident as a miserable defeat for America. Such reports, along with the growing casualty list, increased sympathy for the doves.

The Violent 1968 Election

The 1968 election arrived in the midst of the turmoil over Vietnam. Most Americans expected Lyndon Johnson to win reelection easily. But the disastrous Tet Offensive encouraged some of his opponents in the Democratic Party. The campaign of Eugene McCarthy, an antiwar senator from Minnesota, gained momentum. With the support of college students, he did extremely well in the New Hampshire primary in March 1968.

McCarthy's success led another senator from New York, **Robert Kennedy** (the brother of the late president), to try his chances in the race. Five days after the New Hampshire primary, Kennedy threw his hat into the ring. He counted on the popularity of his name, as well as

immorality, and rebellion. The dress of the typical young person of the late sixties—long hair, ragged jeans, T-shirts, and sandals—illustrates the rebellion against middle-class values.

Assassination of Robert Kennedy

It was in the early hours of the morning on June 5, 1968. Robert Kennedy had spoken to an enthusiastic crowd of supporters in a ballroom in Los Angeles's Ambassador Hotel after winning the California Democratic presidential primary. He left the ballroom shortly after midnight to give a press conference in another room. His escorts took him on a shortcut through the hotel kitchen. There a twenty-five-year-old Palestinian immigrant, Sirhan Sirhan, fired a .22-caliber revolver at the candidate. Kennedy was hit three times. Five others were also wounded, but only Kennedy's wounds were fatal. He died the next day. Sirhan was tried for and convicted of first-degree murder. He was sentenced to death, but his sentence was reduced to life in prison in 1972 when California's death penalty was declared unconstitutional. Sirhan's supposed motive was anger over Kennedy's support for selling fighter jets to Israel. As was true after JFK's assassination, some questioned whether the man caught was the true and only assassin.

591

George Wallace for President

George Wallace entered the race for president four times, three times as a member of the Democratic Party (1964, 1972, and 1976) and once as a member of the independent American Party (1968). Although his views were radical, he gathered a fair amount of support. When running independently in 1968, he got his name on the ballot in all fifty states and received ten million popular votes. While running for the Democratic nomination in 1972, Wallace was shot at an outdoor rally in Laurel, Maryland. In a wheelchair after that, he was unable to regain his campaigning momentum. He ran again for the Democratic nomination in 1976, but Jimmy Carter defeated him handily. In 1983 Wallace took his last political office, the governorship of Alabama (a position he and his first wife had each held previously). Interestingly, this formerly ardent opponent of integration appointed more blacks to political office than any other figure in Alabama history.

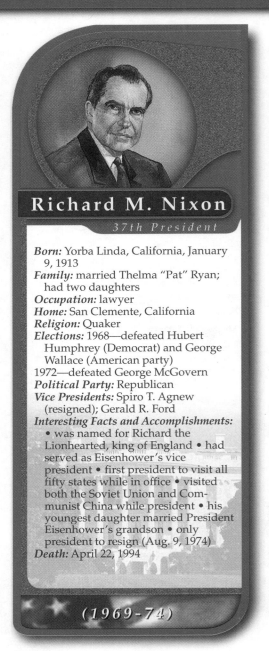

Richard M. Nixon
37th President

Born: Yorba Linda, California, January 9, 1913
Family: married Thelma "Pat" Ryan; had two daughters
Occupation: lawyer
Home: San Clemente, California
Religion: Quaker
Elections: 1968—defeated Hubert Humphrey (Democrat) and George Wallace (American party)
1972—defeated George McGovern
Political Party: Republican
Vice Presidents: Spiro T. Agnew (resigned); Gerald R. Ford
Interesting Facts and Accomplishments:
• was named for Richard the Lionhearted, king of England • had served as Eisenhower's vice president • first president to visit all fifty states while in office • visited both the Soviet Union and Communist China while president • his youngest daughter married President Eisenhower's grandson • only president to resign (Aug. 9, 1974)
Death: April 22, 1994

(1969-74)

592

his support among minorities and labor unions.

Johnson's nomination was no longer a certainty. A political poll revealed that only thirty-six percent of the country supported him. On March 31 Johnson stunned the country with an announcement that he would bow out of the election. Immediately his vice president, **Hubert Humphrey,** declared his candidacy to replace Johnson.

Robert Kennedy beat the pack to become the front-runner among the Democrats. But on the night of his greatest victory in the California primaries, an Arab radical assassinated Kennedy in a Los Angeles hotel. This was a blow from which the Democrats could not recover. They held their party convention in Chicago and chose Humphrey as their candidate. But the convention was marred by a wave of antiwar riots and demonstrations.

The Republicans revived the hopes of Richard Nixon and put him on their ticket with Spiro T. Agnew of Maryland. A third party, the American Party, ran George C. Wallace, an Alabama governor noted for his opposition to integration. He shopped for votes from those who were tired of high taxes, liberal court decisions, and federal interference in the lives of citizens. The election was close between Nixon and Humphrey, but Nixon won.

Pulling Out of the War

Nixon inherited an unfinished war in Vietnam and a "no-win" war policy, as well as a huge national debt and an economy that was nearly out of control. Ignoring the advice of his Council of Economic Advisors, President Johnson hoped to fight a war, keep the Great Society programs, and still limit inflation without a tax increase. Since he was already unpopular, Johnson had no desire to raise taxes. But he did not want to cut programs, either. To escape the consequences of the difficult choices, he lied. When congressmen talked to him about a tax increase and discussed the cost of the war, Johnson gave false figures. The war was costing $100 million a day. The White House, however, reported a much lower cost.

Not wanting to repeat the failures that had ended Johnson's career, Nixon made it his priority to end American involvement in Vietnam "with dignity." Nixon intended to pull large numbers of ground troops out of Vietnam while continuing intensive bombing raids. Yet he did not want the United States to appear defeated.

Vietnamization—In the fall of 1969, Nixon announced his proposal for the **Vietnamization** of the war. This meant that the responsibility for the fighting would gradually be returned to the South Vietnamese. The United States would continue to support the South Vietnamese with supplies, air attacks, and other assistance. As Vietnamization was carried out, more American troops came home. When Nixon took office, 543,400 Americans were in Vietnam. An accelerated American pullout left 157,000 by December 1971, and only 24,000 by the end of 1972.

The success of Vietnamization depended on continued American support for the South Vietnamese and America's determination to force North Vietnam to honor its agreements. But while Americans pulled out of Vietnam, the Communist leaders built up their force of North Vietnamese soldiers and Vietcong, and they continued to stockpile supplies from Communist China and the Soviet Union.

In April of 1970 President Nixon announced a temporary expansion of the war across Vietnam's border into Cambodia, where Communist soldiers were lurking in safe hideouts. The Communists would withdraw to supply bases in Cambodia between attacks on

> **The Twenty-sixth Amendment**
>
> Because eighteen-year-olds were eligible to be drafted for military duty but were not able to vote, many Americans argued that the voting age should be lowered. The **Twenty-sixth Amendment** was passed in 1971 to lower the voting age from twenty-one to eighteen. Supporters said that an American who is old enough to die for his country is old enough to vote.

Americans in South Vietnam. Without bothering to seek Congress's approval, Nixon ordered the Cambodian bases bombed. In 1971 the United States also attacked Vietnamese forces in Laos.

American response to these actions, especially the move into Cambodia, was predictable. Demonstrations erupted on college campuses. At **Kent State University** in Ohio, students disobeyed the instructions of the Ohio National Guard to disperse. When the soldiers felt threatened, they panicked and fired into the crowd, killing four students. A similar riot at Jackson State University in Mississippi led to two more deaths. In a regular war, such dissent and riots would have been punishable, perhaps even defined as treason. In an undeclared war, Americans tolerated such acts, and some even cheered them on.

Paris Peace Talks—Meanwhile Nixon sought to get the North Vietnamese to the peace table. It took six weeks to get the two sides into the same room in Paris because the Communists argued about the shape of the table and the seating order. The talks broke up when the secretary of the Communist Party left in anger. Nixon responded with air strikes and heavy bombing of Hanoi and Haiphong, North Vietnamese cities. In addition, the U.S. Navy mined Haiphong's harbor. "The Christmas blitz" was heavy enough that North Vietnam came back to the peace talks and signed a ceasefire on January 24, 1973.

593

Jane Fonda

Jane Fonda was one of the most famous and most visible of the antiwar protesters. The culmination of her antiwar activities was a trip to North Vietnam in August 1972. After two weeks of touring the country, Fonda gave a radio address to American servicemen fighting in the region. In her speech she praised the North Vietnamese and criticized America (President Nixon in particular) for its pursuit of the war. Many Vietnam veterans resented Fonda after this trip, although in a 1988 television interview she apologized for causing them pain.

Evaluate Vietnamization

Given the difficulties in Vietnam, what would the students have done if they were president in 1969? The results of Vietnamization were disappointing and predictable, but did the United States have a better option? Ever since America's loss in Vietnam, the Pentagon and the State Department have tried to learn the lessons so that the nation would never lose another war. The United States applied these lessons when it entered the Persian Gulf War. One of the keys to success was a clear set of achievable objectives. Discuss any recent debates about new military conflicts. Show the students any evidence of the president's fear of the "ghost of Vietnam."

American Exit from Vietnam

The saga of the Vietnam War ended dramatically for several hundred Americans. As South Vietnam teetered on the edge of collapse, American embassy personnel, together with the Vietnamese who had worked for them, were evacuated by helicopter from the roof of the U.S. embassy in Saigon. The South Vietnamese government then collapsed on April 29, 1975.

The steel staircase on the roof of the embassy, by which fleeing embassy workers scrambled to the safety of the rescue helicopters, was preserved when the former embassy was demolished in the summer of 1998. It is on display at the Gerald R. Ford Museum in Grand Rapids, Michigan, and stands as a symbol not only of the burning drive for freedom but also of the ignoble end to America's involvement in Vietnam.

End of South Vietnam

When the Communists took control of South Vietnam, they renamed Saigon "Ho Chi Minh City" after their leader, who had died in 1969. Many South Vietnamese tried to leave the country immediately, and others tried after they began to see the terrors of life under Communism. Many left by boats of all kinds, hoping to make their way by sea to a nearby free country. These fleeing Vietnamese were called "boat people."

In the early 1980s the Wall was built to honor veterans of Vietnam who, despite the outcome of the war, served their country faithfully.

North Vietnam used the lull to rebuild its forces. When the Communists attacked Saigon in 1975, Nixon's successor, Gerald Ford, asked Congress to increase aid to South Vietnam, but Congress refused. The cause of South Vietnam was lost. The last American troops left Saigon in the spring of 1975. Within two weeks of the American departure, Saigon fell to the North Vietnamese. In the years following, reports of Communist massacres and inhumanity regularly found their way out of Southeast Asia.

The Cost of Vietnam—The cost of the Vietnam War was high: more than 58,000 Americans killed; 300,000 wounded; and about $140 billion spent. But the war cost far more. War veterans came back to a disillusioned country. Few were welcomed as heroes; most were ignored. Memories of past victories made it hard to understand the purpose of wasting lives in Vietnam. It was not until 1982 that a national memorial for the Vietnam dead was dedicated.

The war left several questions unanswered. To what extent should the press be allowed to report the actions of the military? How much power should the president have to wage war? Should Americans entangle themselves in foreign conflicts that might end without victory? The fate of missing soldiers troubled the nation as well. Nearly six hundred prisoners of war in Vietnam were released in 1973, but over two thousand soldiers that were listed as missing in action (MIA) are still unaccounted for.

Congress reacted to the cost of this undeclared war by limiting the president's power to fight such wars in the future. The **War Powers Act** (1973), vetoed by Nixon but overridden by Congress, defined the circumstances necessary before the president could go to war, and it required that all action be ended in thirty days unless Congress authorized action beyond that.

SECTION REVIEW

1. What action of Congress gave President Johnson the authority to increase American involvement in Vietnam?

2. What were the South Vietnamese Communists called?

3. Name three disadvantages the United States military faced in Vietnam.

4. How did American young people respond to the Vietnam War?

5. What was "Vietnamization"?

6. When did the last American troops leave Vietnam? What was the result of their departure?

 How was Vietnam different from American wars before that time? How did these differences affect public reaction?

 594

Section Review Answers

1. Gulf of Tonkin Resolution (p. 588)

2. Vietcong (p. 589)

3. With no official declaration of war, the conflict seemed to lack purpose. America's technology was not a great advantage in the jungles of Vietnam. And U.S. servicemen had trouble identifying the enemy. (p. 589)

4. Many took part in antiwar demonstrations; some young men refused to be drafted. (p. 590)

5. gradually returning the responsibility for fighting the war to the South Vietnamese (p. 593)

6. the spring of 1975; Saigon fell to the North Vietnamese within two weeks (p. 594)

 The Vietnam conflict was not even a war officially. It lacked clear direction and seemed to make no progress toward a satisfying conclusion. As a result, Americans at home did not rally to support the action or the soldiers as they had in previous wars. In addition, Vietnam was the first military action to be covered extensively by television. Constant images of death and destruction aroused strong animosity toward the conflict.

The Fall of Richard Nixon

Richard Nixon took office at the end of the turbulent sixties. He appealed to people he called "the silent majority"—decent, law-abiding, tax-paying Americans. Although anti-war protests continued for a while, unrest seemed to be disappearing. Americans approached the next decade with hopes for an end to the turmoil. President Nixon's leadership gave the country a new confidence. But in the end, he resigned in disgrace, and his administration left the country in shambles.

Détente in Foreign Affairs

Unlike President Johnson, whose interest had been in domestic affairs, Nixon's emphasis was on foreign affairs. He dealt with the problem of Vietnam, and he gained friendlier relations with Communist China and the Soviet Union. Though Nixon had earned a reputation in the Senate as a "cold warrior" against communism, he brought in a new era of **détente,** an easing of tensions, with the Soviet Union. Nixon relied heavily on Dr. **Henry Kissinger,** a Harvard professor born in Germany who became his special advisor. In 1973 Kissinger became Nixon's secretary of state.

Treaty with the Soviets—In May 1972 President Nixon made a trip to the Soviet Union to discuss a Strategic Arms Limitations Treaty (**SALT**). Both nations agreed to restrict the types and number of nuclear warheads and missiles. They also made trade agreements and an agreement to cooperate on scientific and space projects. Conservative opponents of these agreements said they were worth little more than the paper on which they were written because of the Soviet Union's history of ignoring treaties. However, the agreements did have considerable political value at home.

Friendship with Communist China—China closed its doors to the West when the

Ping-Pong Diplomacy

"It doesn't matter whether you win or lose, but how you play the game." So the saying goes, but in April 1971 the question on everyone's mind was who was playing and where. In that year the American Ping-Pong team made a daring trip into Communist China, becoming the first American delegation to visit in twenty-two years. Henry Kissinger was already involved in secret negotiations to ease tensions with China, but the two nations needed something more to break the ice. Ping-Pong was the answer.

Under an invitation from Chinese Prime Minister Zhou Enlai, the team traveled to Beijing for a tournament. The fifteen Americans took sightseeing trips to the Great Wall and Shanghai, and they met with the prime minister himself. When it came time to play, eighteen thousand eager fans crowded into Beijing's Indoor Stadium. The Americans were not sure what to expect. Thankfully the match was "friendly." Though the Chinese were world-class champions, the Americans were able to keep the games close. The Chinese narrowly won the men's games, 5-3, and the women's, 5-4. The Chinese players had been easy on them, the visitors admitted. While the Americans lost in Ping-Pong, they won in diplomacy. The stage was set for formal talks. Three months later, Kissinger made a formal visit of his own. President Nixon's historic visit followed the next year.

The success in Beijing opened the door for "sports diplomacy" around the world. Team competition showed the common people just how much they shared with people of other lands. For example, after years of bitterness over the Iranian hostage crisis, a wrestling team helped to thaw U.S. relations with Iran in 1998. The Iranians treated the American players like kings, prompting several more wrestling teams to crisscross the ocean to compete. More recently, an American baseball team played in Cuba, where baseball is the national passion. Perhaps America's future ambassadors should wear sneakers instead of dress shoes.

595

Efforts at détente eased Chinese and American relations enough for President Nixon to make a visit to the Great Wall of China in 1972.

Shuttle Diplomacy in the Middle East—The Middle East was a constant source of worry. In October 1973 Egypt and Syria, armed with modern weapons from the Soviet Union, launched a surprise attack against Israel, America's ally. The first week of the Yom Kippur War devastated Israel's army, but in the second week Israel took the offensive. A brilliant thrust across the Suez Canal threatened the rear of Egypt's army. The Soviet Union prepared to send troops to assist the Arab states, but it held back after Nixon put America's nuclear forces on alert. Nixon also flew nearly two billion dollars in military hardware to strengthen Israel.

Secretary of State Henry Kissinger became the go-between to help restore peace. Over several months planes shuttled him back and forth from the United States to Damascus, Syria; to Cairo, Egypt; on to Tel Aviv, Israel; and back home again. The **shuttle diplomacy** brought an end to the bloodshed but no permanent peace agreement.

Communists took over in 1949. Americans feared that some day China might join forces with the Soviet Union, even though the two countries were bitter rivals. In 1971 Kissinger seized an opportunity to open relations, making a secret trip to China. There he made arrangements for a presidential visit in February 1972. Accompanied by American reporters and camera crews, Nixon toured the Great Wall, attended banquets, and met with Chinese leader Chairman Mao Zedong.

This opening of diplomatic relations with the People's Republic of China, however, hurt America's support of "Free China," its former allies during World War II who had fled to the island of Taiwan. When the United States recognized Red China, the U.N. admitted it into that organization and expelled Taiwan. The United States ended its diplomatic relationship with Taiwan on January 1, 1979, even though it is one of America's largest trade partners.

Failure to Fix the Struggling Economy

When he came to office, Richard Nixon inherited both a war debt and runaway inflation. Under the Johnson administration, the American public never sacrificed at home the way they had in other wars. Americans continued to buy all the material goods they wanted while the government spent money not only for the war but also for growing domestic programs, such as caring for the poor. The increases in government aid discouraged pri-

596

The Space Race

The Soviets dropped a "bomb" on the United States on October 4, 1957. The bomb was the news that **Sputnik I** had successfully entered orbit. After the news flashed across the country, shocked faces appeared on every street corner. How could they do it? How could the Communists be the first to develop the technology to launch a satellite into space? The United States would never be the same.

Rather than raise their hands in surrender, Americans took up the challenge and entered the space race. Americans had a long way to go. A month after the launch of Sputnik, another Soviet rocket carried a dog into space. In April 1961 yet another bomb dropped. The Soviets announced that the cosmonaut Yuri Gagarin had orbited the earth. In response, President Kennedy committed the nation to the most ambitious science project in its history: land a man on the moon by the end of the decade.

Congress established the National Aeronautics and Space Administration (**NASA**) to run the new space program, and it put aside money to promote science and math education in the classroom. Many tense years passed, but it soon became apparent the United States had pulled ahead in the race. NASA overcame the complex problems one by one. The Mercury spacecraft were the first to enter orbit, and the Gemini missions tested the technology to dock two craft in outer space. Finally, the Apollo spacecraft blasted 385,000 miles to the moon.

On July 20, 1969, word came back to NASA that "the Eagle has landed." Neil Armstrong, the commander of Apollo 11, clambered out of the Eagle lunar module and was the first to set foot on the moon. The world listened in awe as he declared, "That's one small step for man, one giant leap for mankind." President Nixon called the astronauts to congratulate them.

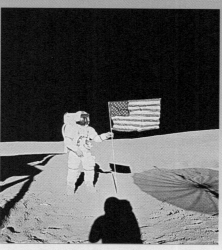

Apollo 14 astronaut Alan Shepard poses for a picture on the moon.

Progress in the Space Race
After the successful completion of the *Apollo* moon landing, NASA began to founder. The Soviets launched the first manned space station, *Salyut I,* in 1971. The United States followed two years later with *Skylab,* launched on May 14, 1973.

A Monetarist View of the Causes of Stagflation
Many explanations have been given for the stagflation in the 1970s. (Stagflation refers to a stagnant economy in recession with high inflation.) Monetarists, who like to blame inflation and depression on government interference with the money supply, blame Nixon's decision during his first term to devalue the dollar. To gain the short-term benefits of higher economic growth rates and lower unemployment, Nixon separated the U.S. dollar from the gold standard, and the U.S. Federal Reserve cranked up the printing presses. Too much money in circulation always leads to higher prices. The short-term benefits gave way to a long-term economic crisis that endured through the rest of the decade. Not until the Fed reined in the money supply under Reagan did the government kill the beast of stagflation. But before that, three presidents embarrassed themselves in frantic efforts to curb inflation through price controls or volunteer efforts.

vate efforts to end poverty; the government would end it for them.

Wage and Price Controls—Nixon tried to curb inflation by slowing government spending and by increasing taxes. With less money in circulation, people would not be able to buy as much. But such action often results in an economic **recession**. (A recession is a slowdown in the economy, a time when businesses produce fewer products and must get rid of some of their workers.) This was the result of Nixon's action. To make the recession less painful to the average American—and to help his own chances of reelection—Nixon raised

government spending to create new jobs, but this action only increased the national debt.

Nixon decided to use the power of the federal government to curb inflation, despite the outcries of conservatives. In August 1971 he ordered wage and price controls. All wages, prices, and fees were frozen at August levels for ninety days. When the ninety days were up, the Cost of Living Council was organized. Under its guidelines some increases were allowed. Nixon's wage and price controls, however, did not deal with the causes of inflation—excessive government spending and national debt. They only temporarily con-

Discuss the Modern Space Program

Find articles on the current space program, including a new space station and a manned flight to Mars. Why does the space program generate so little excitement today compared to the Space Race of the 1960s? Discuss the legitimate reasons for space exploration, then and now. Is it appropriate for the federal government in a free republic to fund science?

Debate Idea

Have your students discuss and/or debate the following:

The space program is profitable.

The Arab oil embargo was a reaction against America's support for Israel in the Yom Kippur War (1973-74). See page 596 for a discussion of this war.

Roe v. Wade

The "Roe" of *Roe v. Wade* was Norma McGorvey of Texas. Because she was denied her desire to have an abortion, she sued the state of Texas. The Supreme Court decided in a 7-2 ruling that a woman had an unrestricted right to an abortion within the first three months of pregnancy. This unrestricted right was applied essentially to the time when the baby would be unable to survive outside the mother's womb. A woman's right to privacy justified this ruling. The First, Ninth, and Fourteenth Amendments were used to "support" this right to privacy. Justices William Rehnquist and Byron White were the dissenters in the case.

trolled some of its symptoms. The controls artificially slowed inflation to about three percent annually. But with the end of these controls in 1973, inflation doubled. In 1974 it almost doubled again to 12.2 percent.

Arab Oil Embargo—An unexpected hardship arose when Arab nations, angry over American support of Israel, ordered an embargo (complete ban) on American oil shipments in October 1973. Since the United States imported one-quarter of its oil from Middle Eastern countries, the **oil embargo** hurt Americans. To compound the problem, the federal government's price controls prevented businesses from selling gasoline at higher prices in order to discourage buyers. Instead, gas stations were forced to close down, or they limited how much each customer could buy. Motorists had to wait in long lines at gasoline stations. When price controls were lifted, prices of gasoline, fuel oil, and petroleum-based products, such as plastics, rose dramatically. Complex government rules and regulations limited the freedom of businesses to find creative ways to adapt to the changes.

President Nixon offered no convincing solution to the problem. He asked Americans to conserve energy. Smaller cars that got more miles per gallon became popular. Car pools or "ride-sharing" became common practices in big cities. Many Americans spent vacations close to home. Congress lowered the speed limit to 55 mph, and it approved a pipeline across Alaska to mine oil reserves above the Arctic Circle. The oil embargo also encouraged Congress to spend money on new programs to develop alternate sources of energy.

The **energy crisis** eased somewhat when the Arab nations lifted their embargo in March 1974. Although OPEC (the Organization of Petroleum Exporting Countries) halted its embargo, it steadily raised crude oil prices. Some extremist Muslim countries, such as Libya and Iran, hoped to destroy America with

exorbitant prices. More moderate OPEC members, such as Saudi Arabia, argued that ruining the economies of Western industrialized countries would ultimately hinder their ability to buy oil. Unable to agree on prices and production limits, OPEC countries split, and oil again flowed freely.

Failure to Restrain the Liberal Courts

Nixon's Court Appointments—President Nixon had the opportunity to appoint four justices to the Supreme Court, including a new chief justice. The Warren Court, the liberal court of the 1950s and 1960s, had grown unpopular with many Americans who believed it protected criminals and tied the hands of the police. In state after state, criminals had been freed on legal technicalities. When Chief Justice Earl Warren retired in 1969, Nixon replaced him with **Warren Burger.** He filled later vacancies by nominating Harry Blackmun, Lewis F. Powell, and William H. Rehnquist. Burger was a grave disappointment to conservatives. Although the Burger Court limited the scope of some landmark decisions of the Warren Court, it did not reverse them.

Roe v. Wade—Unfortunately, there were not enough conservatives on the court to prevent a liberal decision on abortion. In *Roe v. Wade* (1973), the court decided that a woman had the right to abort her unborn child within the first three months of pregnancy. The ruling overturned the abortion laws of all fifty states. Since then nearly 1.5 million abortions have been performed each year. This legalized murder destroys nearly one-third of all American babies each year.

Growth of Federal Powers

A growing list of issues in the 1960s, such as the environment and women's rights, led to a rapid growth of federal powers in new areas of private life.

The Search for Clean Air and Water—
The modern **environmentalist movement,** a concern about man's relationship to his environment, was launched by the publication of Rachel Carson's book *Silent Spring.* Published in 1962, the book alarmed Americans about the harmful impact of pesticides, such as DDT. Under LBJ, the government spent billions of dollars to clean up lakes and rivers. The first lady, Lady Bird Johnson, led a crusade for "the beautification of America." But cities and states took primary responsibility for regulating their own industries and pollution.

A nationwide protest called Earth Day on April 22, 1970, encouraged the federal government to step in. That year Congress established the Environmental Protection Agency (EPA) to oversee environmental regulations. The Clean Air Act of 1970 (amended in 1977

Phyllis Schlafly gained national attention as the outspoken opponent of the Equal Rights Amendment. Her warnings against the negative effects of the amendment helped to stop its passage.

and 1990) regulated air pollution. The Water Pollution Control Act (1972) and later the Clean Water Act (1977) regulated water pollution. Nixon also signed the Endangered Species Act in 1973, granting bureaucrats the power to decide which species are threatened and how to protect them. Environmentalists complained that the law was too weak, and conservatives complained that it was too arbitrary. Bureaucrats had a free hand to limit industry and construction, such as logging and dams, without even analyzing the costs and benefits.

New Rights Movements—In the wake of the civil rights movement among blacks, many other groups began pressuring the government to give them what they believed were their rights as citizens. Among the civil rights movements was a protest among low-paid Hispanic grape pickers in California, led by César Chavez. Another protest, called the American Indian Movement (AIM), gained strength among militant Indians and won notoriety when members seized a government trading post at Wounded Knee, South Dakota, in 1973. The most prominent of the new civil rights movements was the **women's rights movement,** sparked by the publication of Betty Friedan's book *The Feminine Mystique* in 1963. Friedan mocked the lives of moms who stayed at home and raised kids in "a comfortable concentration camp."

While some joined the women's rights movement to earn equal pay, others sought far more. The radical National Organization for Women (NOW), cofounded by Friedan, pushed for legal abortions and easy divorce laws. NOW also supported the **Equal Rights Amendment (ERA).** The harmless-sounding amendment to the Constitution stated, "Equality of rights under the law shall not be denied or abridged by the United States or by any state on account of sex." Conservative women, led by Phyllis Schlafly, denounced

Indian Rights
Indians were among the many groups of Americans who became more vocal about their rights during the 1960s. Indian leaders demanded repayment for the many treaties that the federal government had broken or ignored. Some protests became violent. A group of Indians seized a government trading post at Wounded Knee, South Dakota, in 1973 (see page 382). A member of the radical American Indian Movement, Leonard Peltier, killed two FBI agents at the Pine Ridge reservation in 1975. Though the violence was regrettable, it drew attention to legitimate complaints about mismanagement of the Bureau of Indian Affairs. In a sense, this program was the United States's first experiment in socialism, and it had proved to be a disastrous failure.

Homosexual Rights and the Stonewall Riots
Homosexuals at a bar in New York City rioted during a police raid, barricading the police in the building and attempting to burn it down. Homosexual rights activists cite the so-called Stonewall Riots as the start of the homosexual rights movement. President Clinton honored this event by declaring the Stonewall Inn on the National Register of Historic Places.

599

Discuss Modern Environmentalism and Other Issues

Students are now reading about issues that remain in the news today. Discuss recent legislation dealing with environmentalism and have the students summarize both sides of the issue. Conservatives do not want to see America's resources trampled, but they argue that a free society will do a better job of developing resources than government bureaucrats. Liberals, on the other hand, do not believe that free men can be trusted to act in the "public interest."

Discuss other issues in this section to guide your students in thinking scripturally rather than emotionally about these issues.

Objectives
Students should be able to
1. Describe the circumstances that led to Nixon's resignation.
2. Explain Congress's reaction to the Watergate scandal.

the ERA because it would give the federal government virtually unlimited power to impose rules on daily life. She claimed that feminists would use the amendment to abolish time-honored traditions that respect the obvious differences between the sexes—everything from separate bathrooms for women to the ban on women in combat. Congress passed the ERA in 1972, but its supporters could not get enough states to ratify (confirm) the amendment, even after liberals in Congress granted extra time.

SECTION REVIEW

1. What two Communist countries did Nixon visit?

2. Who conducted shuttle diplomacy to help stop the bloodshed in the Middle East?

3. Who launched the first satellite into space? What was Neil Armstrong's historical accomplishment?

4. How did Arab countries react to American support for Israel?

5. Whom did Nixon appoint as chief justice? What landmark decision was passed under his court?

6. What group of Americans made a special push for civil rights at this time? What piece of legislation did they unsuccessfully champion?

 What happens to private citizens when government begins getting more involved in their lives?

The Watergate Scandal

Nixon won reelection in 1972 by a landslide, defeating a liberal Democrat, Senator George McGovern of South Dakota. Pleased with détente, a stable economy, and favorable developments in Vietnam, the people felt confident under Nixon's leadership. But soon cracks began to appear in the image of the Nixon administration.

Resignation of the Vice President—Nixon's running mate, Vice President **Spiro T. Agnew,** was charged with accepting bribes from construction companies while he had been governor of Maryland. He was also charged with income tax evasion, to which he pleaded no contest (similar to pleading guilty). Facing a possible prison sentence, Agnew resigned the vice-presidency on October 10, 1973. He was the first vice president to resign since 1833 and the first vice president ever to resign because of a criminal charge.

For the first time since its ratification in 1967, the Twenty-fifth Amendment was used to pick a new vice president. Following the guidelines in the amendment, Nixon selected Gerald R. Ford, a Michigan congressman. He took the oath of office on December 6, 1973.

The Watergate Cover-up—The president himself got into trouble after five men were arrested for breaking into the Democratic Party's National Campaign Headquarters and planting electronic listening devices during the election of 1972. The break-in took place in an office building in Washington, D.C., named **Watergate.** The press learned that the arrested men were members of President Nixon's committee for the reelection of the president (mockingly called CREEP). No evidence turned up that Nixon knew about the break-in, but suspicions grew that he had tried to cover up the crime after he learned about it.

The trial of the Watergate burglars and two other Nixon officials began in January 1973. One of the burglars claimed that the witnesses had committed perjury (lied in court). He also said that the men had been told to plead guilty by someone higher in the administration.

In May of 1973 the U.S. Senate began its own independent investigation of the Watergate scandal. The investigation soon discovered that the White House had secretly

---

Section Review Answers

1. the Soviet Union and China (p. 595)

2. Secretary of State Henry Kissinger (p. 596)

3. the Soviet Union; the first person to set foot on the moon (p. 597)

4. They ordered an embargo on American oil shipments in October 1973. (p. 598)

5. Warren Burger; *Roe v. Wade* (p. 598)

6. women; the Equal Rights Amendment (p. 599)

 They begin to lose some of their freedom. They may also become less efficient if their activities are limited by government regulations. And their sense of personal responsibility and initiative may be damaged.

SECTION 5

Materials

• Activity D from Chapter 28 of the *Student Activities* manual

made tape recordings of all the president's office conversations. By listening to the tapes, the committee would be able to determine the president's role in the cover-up, if any. But when the courts ordered Nixon to turn over the tapes, the president refused. He argued that he had executive privilege and that turning them over would endanger national security.

Nixon's Resignation—The American people were outraged. They wrote angry letters to Congress asking for Nixon's impeachment. The House Judiciary Committee then began hearings on fifteen charges. The president responded by turning over the tapes to a new special prosecutor. However, some of the tapes were missing, and an eighteen-and-a-half minute section had been erased on one tape. Nixon claimed it was a secretary's error. When a court order asked for more tapes, the president refused to comply. However, he did supply a tape transcript. The transcript showed that the president had known about the efforts to cover up Watergate, although he was not necessarily the instigator.

Watergate dragged on. Believing that no man can act above the law, Republicans turned against the president. By the end of July, the House Judiciary Committee voted to impeach the president for obstructing justice, misusing his presidential powers, and refusing to comply with their requests for evidence. When the committee showed its determination to examine additional charges, the president's lawyers persuaded him to release more transcripts. These showed that the president not only had known of the burglary but also had acted to stop an FBI investigation of it. The president's position was now hopeless. Rather than face a trial before the Senate that would

lead to his removal, President Nixon resigned on August 9, 1974, the only president ever to do so.

The Watergate conspiracy troubled the public, not only because of the political corruption but also because of the president's virtually unlimited power. Actually the power of the president had been increasing steadily since the time of Franklin Roosevelt. In response, Congress acted to prevent another Watergate. It forbade the president from refus-

Seemingly unaware of his disgrace, Nixon gives his famous victory sign as he prepares to leave the White House.

601

Meaning of the Watergate Scandal

The Nixon scandals of the early 1970s are significant at several levels. In sheer magnitude, Watergate dwarfs other presidential scandals in American history—Grant's, Harding's, and even Clinton's. It involved more than just an illegal break-in at the Democratic Party headquarters in the Watergate complex. It included illegal campaign contributions, political sabotage or "dirty tricks," and the break-in at Daniel Ellsberg's psychiatrist's office. Two attorney generals, several presidential aides, the IRS, the FBI, and the CIA were all tainted by the scandal. And most dramatically, a president resigned, an unprecedented event in American history.

The question that still haunts students of the scandal is why someone as smart as Nixon would do something so dumb. We will never know fully what went on in his mind, but we can give a general answer to that question. Nixon's overwhelming desire was to win reelection in 1972. Nixon feared an Edmund Muskie candidacy for 1972 because a moderate Democrat would be more difficult to beat. Thus, Nixon and his aides were desperate to know Democratic strategy for the fall campaign and, therefore, to avoid any surprises. Nixon also wanted to know if the Democrats had any "dirt" that they could use against him.

Another issue that motivated Nixon and his aides was a sincere belief that a Democratic victory in 1972 would jeopardize a successful end to the Vietnam War. Daniel Ellsberg had earlier released the Pentagon Papers, secret documents about earlier presidents' handling of the war. During Ellsberg's trial, Nixon wanted him discredited, so Nixon's aides broke into Ellsberg's psychiatrist's office looking for embarrassing material. The discovery of this break-in led to a mistrial. To thwart future "leaks," Nixon and his aides created the "Plumbers Unit," a

Discuss the Meaning of the Watergate Scandal

Ask the students to contrast the Watergate scandal with the other presidential scandals in U.S. history. Why was it worse than any other? (See margin note above.) Ask the students to share examples of political cynicism that they have heard. Discuss the basis for this cynicism and the proper Christian response.

clandestine White House committee that used extralegal tactics to win the '72 election and to protect Nixon. In the end, Nixon's personal lust for power brought him down.

Watergate proved to be a threat to democracy. It is clear now that Nixon did not trust the democratic electoral process. If he had, he would not have resorted to illegal campaign contributions or sabotage of political enemies. Perhaps the most dangerous aspect to the scandal was Nixon's use of "spies" to accomplish his ends. He was attempting to do on the domestic level what the CIA had been doing in foreign lands—subvert the natural processes of government.

The scandal did incalculable damage. The presidents who followed Nixon found it difficult to take decisive action in domestic or foreign affairs. Nixon's "imperial" presidency led to a weaker presidency. The year following his resignation, the Vietnam War ended in a disgraceful loss for South Vietnam. President Ford was unable to get congressional support for more aid to that government. To this day, Americans mistrust governmental institutions, from the White House on down. Also, the nature of the press changed. Investigative reporting, or finding the next scandal, drives the media and only intensifies Americans' cynicism about public officials.

ing to release budget funds set aside by Congress in order to stop a congressional program or action. It strengthened the Freedom of Information Act, allowing the public more access to government documents. A Federal Campaign Reform Act in 1974 placed a limit on the amount of money private individuals could give to candidates, hoping to limit the use of contributions to "bribe" candidates.

The American political system successfully exposed and dealt with the Watergate conspiracy rather than pushing it under a rug. It showed that the president was not above the law. The Constitution's system of checks and balances worked. Yet Nixon's corruption seriously damaged the prestige of his office, and he undermined the faith of the American people in their political leaders. Beginning in 1974, the percentage of Americans using their hard-won right to vote declined dramatically. Many wondered whether America would ever recover.

SUMMARY

The decade of the 1960s was a trying time for the United States. Divided opinions on major issues, such as civil rights and the Vietnam War, created crises that hurt all Americans. Media reports of violence stirred fears and unrest. While the Great Society attempted to regulate and improve American life, the only obvious result was a rapid increase in the national debt. The assassinations and resignations made historians wonder whether America had become a morally corrupt civilization, like the ancient Roman empire, in steady decline.

SECTION REVIEW

1. Who was Nixon's first vice president? Why did he leave office?

2. What was the crime that Nixon was accused of trying to cover up?

3. What important sources of evidence did investigators try to get from the White House?

4. What was President Nixon's response to the impeachment process?

 Was it necessary to include an impeachment clause in the Constitution? Defend your answer.

Section Review Answers

1. Spiro T. Agnew; because of criminal charges of accepting bribes and income tax evasion (p. 600)

2. a break-in at the Democratic Party's National Campaign Headquarters and the planting of electronic listening devices during the 1972 election campaign (p. 600)

3. tapes of the president's office conversations (p. 601)

4. He resigned on August 9, 1974. (p. 601)

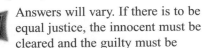 Answers will vary. If there is to be equal justice, the innocent must be cleared and the guilty must be punished. If one person is placed above the law, the judicial system is threatened.

Chapter Review

Chapter Review Idea
Student Activity D: Evaluating What You Read
Now that students are near the end of the school year, they should recognize alternative perspectives, especially the Christian perspective, on controversial events. You will probably want to complete this activity in a class discussion.

People, Places, and Things to Remember

John F. Kennedy	Malcolm X	détente
New Frontier	urban riots	Henry Kissinger
Alliance for Progress	Vietnam War	SALT
Berlin Wall	Gulf of Tonkin Resolution	shuttle diplomacy
Bay of Pigs	hawks	Sputnik I
Cuban Missile Crisis	doves	NASA
Lyndon B. Johnson	Vietcong	recession
the Great Society	Ho Chi Minh Trail	oil embargo
Barry Goldwater	New Left	energy crisis
Brown v. Board of	counterculture	Warren Burger
Education	Robert Kennedy	*Roe v. Wade*
Twenty-third Amendment	Hubert Humphrey	environmentalist movement
march on Washington	Vietnamization	women's rights movement
Civil Rights Act of 1964	Kent State University	Equal Rights Amendment
Twenty-fourth Amendment	Twenty-sixth Amendment	(ERA)
Voting Rights Act of 1965	War Powers Act	Spiro T. Agnew
Martin Luther King Jr.	Richard Nixon	Watergate

Review Questions

Indicate whether each of the following items is most closely associated with (A) President Kennedy, (B) President Johnson, or (C) President Nixon.

1. Watergate
2. the Great Society
3. Vietnamization of the war
4. Gulf of Tonkin Resolution
5. the New Frontier
6. Cuban Missile Crisis

Match each of the following items with its description.

7. Berlin Wall
8. *Brown v. Board of Education*
9. Peace Corps
10. *Roe v. Wade*
11. Tet Offensive

a. Communist attack on South Vietnam
b. barrier between East and West Germany
c. legalized abortion
d. overturned "separate but equal" policy
e. sent American volunteers to needy places

Answer these questions about the 1960s.

12. Whose shuttle diplomacy temporarily ended Middle Eastern bloodshed?
13. Who was the first man to walk on the moon?
14. What black preacher led much of the civil rights activity of the 1960s?
15. What three Democrats ran for the presidential nomination in 1968?

Questions for Discussion

16. Was the civil rights movement of the 1960s necessary? Why or why not?
17. Why do you think the assassination of leaders often enhances their reputations?

Chapter Review Answers

1. C (p. 600)
2. B (p. 582)
3. C (p. 593)
4. B (p. 588)
5. A (p. 579)
6. A (p. 581)
7. b (p. 580)
8. d (p. 584)
9. e (p. 580)
10. c (p. 598)
11. a (p. 591)
12. Henry Kissinger's (p. 596)
13. Neil Armstrong (p. 597)
14. Martin Luther King Jr. (p. 587)
15. Eugene McCarthy, Robert Kennedy, Hubert Humphrey (pp. 591-92)
16. Answers will vary.
17. Answers will vary. It is difficult to criticize someone who has been murdered.

29

Rise of the Right

n many ways, the crisis of the 1960s still haunts the United States. Radical youths from the "hippie" generation eventually entered positions of leadership as writers, teachers, and politicians. From their lofty perches, these leaders proclaimed their radical ideas. Yet in the years following Watergate, Americans slowly came to see the bad consequences of big government and unrestrained morals.

Signs of a reawakening of conservative ideas appeared on every hand. On July 4, 1976, Americans of all types celebrated the **Bicentennial,** the two-hundredth anniversary of the Declaration of Independence. The event rekindled memories of the values that had made America great. A renewed drive to restore traditional values climaxed in the election of Ronald Reagan, a conservative on the "right" who promised to restore America's greatness. In just ten short years after the Bicentennial, the country was again enjoying a booming economy and new pride. That year the nation celebrated the one-hundredth birthday of the Statue of Liberty, and the next year it marked an even greater event—the bicentennial of the Constitution.

Ford, the Unelected President

The nation suffered through two weak presidents after Nixon resigned. Vice President Gerald R. Ford took the oath of office the day Nixon left. Ford's position was difficult: the public had not elected him as

---

CHAPTER 29	Lesson Plan Chart		
Section Title	**Main Activity**	**Pages**	**Time Frame**
1. Ford, the Unelected President	Checklist of Presidents' Strengths	604-7	½-1 day
2. Carter, the Peanut Farmer	Human Rights in Foreign Policy?	607-10	1 day
3. The Reagan Revolution	Reagan's First Inaugural Speech	611-15	1 day
4. Bush's Problem with "the Vision Thing"	Why Did Bush Do It?	615-21	1-2 days
Total Suggested Days (including 1 day for review and testing)			4½-6 days

either vice president or president. He saw the need to restore the public's confidence in the presidential office. He promised "openness and candor" and said he was only an ordinary man who would try to do his best. Ford also promised regular news conferences so that the public would be informed of his actions. He chose as his vice president a former New York governor from the liberal wing of the Republican Party, Nelson Rockefeller. He kept Henry Kissinger, Nixon's secretary of state, and said that he would pursue a foreign policy like Nixon's.

Ford's Pardon of Nixon

One month into office Ford ignited a controversy that he never lived down. He pardoned Richard Nixon. By pardoning Nixon for any crimes he might have committed while in office, Ford angered many of his main supporters. He said that trying the former president would subject the country to added agony. Some Democrats, however, accused him of making a "buddy deal" with the president in exchange for his nomination as vice president. Many Americans were dismayed that the former president could go free while the men serving under him remained in jail for their crimes.

Ford's Failed Effort to Whip Inflation

When Gerald Ford took office, Nixon's wage and price controls had failed to check inflation. In 1974 inflation reached a record 12.2 percent.

Ford could do little directly to solve the main cause of the problem. An independent government agency that was created in 1913, called the Federal Reserve, controlled the supply of money in the country. (Too much paper money in distribution makes prices go up.) At first, Ford pushed for a voluntary anti-inflation crusade. Called WIN (Whip Inflation Now), the plan urged consumers to stop

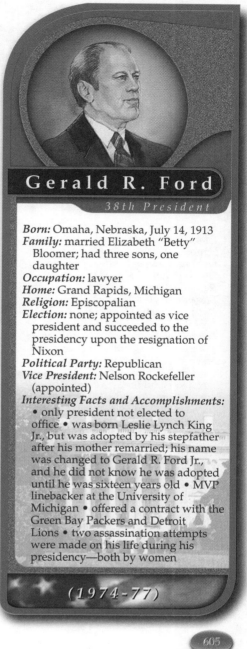

Gerald R. Ford

38th President

Born: Omaha, Nebraska, July 14, 1913
Family: married Elizabeth "Betty" Bloomer; had three sons, one daughter
Occupation: lawyer
Home: Grand Rapids, Michigan
Religion: Episcopalian
Election: none; appointed as vice president and succeeded to the presidency upon the resignation of Nixon
Political Party: Republican
Vice President: Nelson Rockefeller (appointed)
Interesting Facts and Accomplishments:
• only president not elected to office • was born Leslie Lynch King Jr., but was adopted by his stepfather after his mother remarried; his name was changed to Gerald R. Ford Jr., and he did not know he was adopted until he was sixteen years old • MVP linebacker at the University of Michigan • offered a contract with the Green Bay Packers and Detroit Lions • two assassination attempts were made on his life during his presidency—both by women

(1974–77)

605

Objectives

Students should be able to
1. Define what "strike" Ford had against him from the beginning of his administration.
2. Name the controversy that Ford ignited in his first month in office.
3. Explain how Ford failed to "whip" inflation.

Ripening Apple

The quest to build a personal computer began in earnest in the 1970s with the development of the microprocessor. A couple of unlikely candidates took up the task in 1976. Stephen Wozniak spent his childhood making voltmeters, ham radios, calculators, and some games, but he was never comfortable in the classroom. After high school he attended the University of Colorado but flunked out. Along with other computer hobbyists, he started the Homebrew Computer Club. Among those who attended was another college dropout named Steven Jobs.

Jobs worked with Atari as a game designer, but his real interest was in personal computers. He convinced Wozniak to work with him on a marketable prototype. Working in Jobs's garage, the two created the Apple I computer. To cover the cost of their project, Wozniak sold his programmable calculator and Jobs sold his Volkswagen Bug. Although it included only a circuit board, they were able to sell the Apple I to a local electronics supplier and launch the Apple Company.

In 1977 the company introduced the Apple II, which came in a plastic case and included color graphics. While the Apple I was designed initially for computer hobbyists, the Apple II was intended more for the general user. It was an instant success, but in the field of computers, success is fleeting. IBM soon introduced a personal computer of its own, forcing Apple to make improvements

presidents numerically based on presidential qualities. Make a profile sheet for each president. Keep track of why each president scored the way he did in each category. After you finish reading the chapter, tally class scores to find out who the winner is.

on theirs. They introduced the Apple III and the Apple Lisa, but neither was very successful. Jobs realized that neither he nor Wozniak had the business skills to keep Apple competitive, so he convinced John Sculley, then president of Pepsi-Cola, to become CEO for Apple.

With Sculley in charge, the company introduced the Macintosh computer in 1984. It was successful but not enough. Sculley began to make major changes within the company. By the end of 1985, both Wozniak and Jobs had resigned. After a decade of economic ups and downs, Apple looked as if it would fail completely. However, in 1996 Apple took control of a company known as NeXT. NeXT's president was none other than Steven Jobs.

Under Jobs, Apple hit the market with a series of successful computers. The PowerMac G3, iMac, and the PowerMac G4 all helped to put Apple back in the profit column. By the end of the decade, Apple had reestablished itself as a competitive force in the field of personal computers.

Carter as a Candidate in 1976

As ineffective as Jimmy Carter may have been as president, he was an ideal candidate in a post-Watergate era. America was at a low point. The economy plummeted to a postwar nadir. Losing the Vietnam War placed the United States in one of its weakest positions of the Cold War. The Watergate scandal had thoroughly discredited Republicans. All of these factors gave Democrats great hope for the 1976 election.

Carter presented himself as an outsider, someone uncorrupted by the failures in Washington. Not a lawyer or a politician from Washington, this one-term governor of Georgia described himself as a peanut farmer, and he cast off the three-piece suit for flannel shirts and blue jeans. In reaction to the dour Nixon, Carter made his broad grin a trademark.

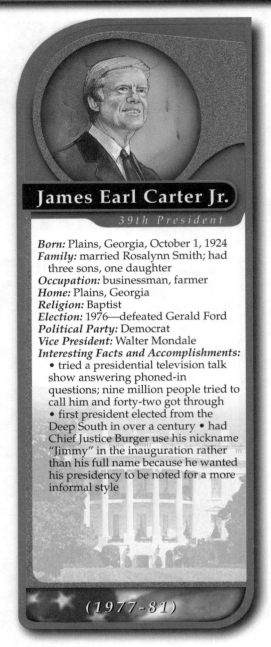

James Earl Carter Jr.
39th President

Born: Plains, Georgia, October 1, 1924
Family: married Rosalynn Smith; had three sons, one daughter
Occupation: businessman, farmer
Home: Plains, Georgia
Religion: Baptist
Election: 1976—defeated Gerald Ford
Political Party: Democrat
Vice President: Walter Mondale
Interesting Facts and Accomplishments:
• tried a presidential television talk show answering phoned-in questions; nine million people tried to call him and forty-two got through
• first president elected from the Deep South in over a century • had Chief Justice Burger use his nickname "Jimmy" in the inauguration rather than his full name because he wanted his presidency to be noted for a more informal style

(1977-81)

606

buying high-priced goods, and it asked workers not to seek wage increases. But since workers and businesses believed they were the victims, rather than the causes, of inflation, they ignored WIN. The economic recession grew even worse as the Federal Reserve raised interest rates (one of the tools it uses to limit the amount of money in circulation). Sales of new products fell; the number of workers out of work climbed above nine percent.

President Ford then requested a tax cut and less government spending. Liberal Democrats who controlled Congress approved the tax cut, but they spent more and more money on new programs. Ford vetoed sixty-one bills in an effort to hold down the growth of government, but inflation continued to spiral upward.

Ford's Failed Election Campaign

Ford decided to run for president in 1976. Because he had not been in office long, he had not made many of his own policies. Moreover, the Republican Party was still recovering from the shame of Watergate. Ford's inability to solve the nation's problems gave Democratic leaders assurance that "we could run an aardvark this year and win."

Out of the many candidates running for president, the Democratic Party picked little-known **Jimmy Carter,** a former one-term governor of Georgia. Carter stressed his honesty and his lack of ties to politics in Washington. Because he had taken a strong stand on civil rights in Georgia, he won black voters. He also enjoyed a following among labor unions. In spite of his natural advantages, Carter ran a lackluster campaign and defeated Ford by only a narrow margin, 51 to 48 percent.

From Vice Presidency to Presidency

How many vice presidents during the twentieth century became presidents? *(six—Theodore Roosevelt, Harry S. Truman, Lyndon B. Johnson, Richard M. Nixon, Gerald Ford, and George Bush)* How many of them served two terms? *(only Nixon, but he lost his first election at the end of his vice presidency)* Why is it so difficult for vice presidents to win and keep the presidency? *(They are held responsible for their predecessor's legacy.)*

SECTION REVIEW

1. Whom did Ford choose for his vice president?

2. What controversial step did Ford take shortly after becoming president?

3. What was Ford's plan to lower inflation? Why did it fail?

4. What was Jimmy Carter's political background?

 Do you agree with Ford's decision to pardon Nixon? Why or why not?

Carter, the Peanut Farmer

President Jimmy Carter entered office with high hopes. Democrats controlled both houses of Congress by large margins, and Americans were looking for someone to solve the pressing problems of the day. He wanted to bring new faces to Washington and to use the same simple, down-home style he had used to run his father's peanut warehouse in Georgia.

But the inexperience and idealism that helped Carter win the election greatly hindered his effectiveness in office. He failed to make the necessary effort to win support for his programs. He also got bogged down in the details of governing and failed to spell out the principles that guided his administration. Few people, even in his own party, really knew the president's long-term goals. To make matters worse, Carter did not have a solid grasp of foreign affairs.

Carter's Domestic Failures

Amnesty for Draft Dodgers—One of President Carter's first acts was to offer **amnesty,** or a group pardon, to those who had illegally dodged the draft during the Vietnam conflict. The president wanted to heal the rifts left by the war. But to Americans who had complied with the law and lost family members, the action was an insult. The number of people who took advantage of the amnesty

was smaller than expected. Some draft dodgers snubbed the offer because they believed accepting it was an admission that their actions had been wrong.

Double-Digit Inflation—Economic troubles mushroomed under Carter. To escape inflation, consumers were borrowing money to get what they wanted before prices went up. With more money in circulation, inflation only increased faster. The annual inflation rates were "double-digit"—over ten percent. Workers, unable to afford the higher prices, demanded higher wages. At the same time, interest rates on loans reached some of the highest levels in years. People could not afford home mortgages, so builders found themselves out of work. Related businesses suffered, and unemployment rose.

Like Ford, Carter proposed to curb inflation by slowing the growth of federal spending and by revising the tax system. He asked people to accept voluntary wage and price controls but had little success. His tax bill was supposed to cut taxes for the poor by closing

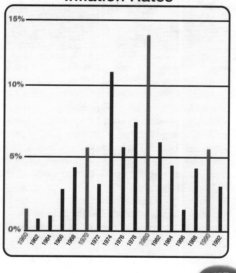

Inflation Rates

607

SECTION 2

Objectives

Students should be able to

1. Identify Carter's domestic and foreign policy failures.

2. List the leaders involved in the Camp David Accords and the countries they represented.

3. Identify the Muslim ruler who encouraged the taking of hostages at the American embassy in Iran.

Section Review Answers

1. Nelson Rockefeller (p. 605)

2. He pardoned Nixon for any crimes he might have committed while in office. (p. 605)

3. WIN, a voluntary crusade in which consumers would stop buying high-priced items and workers would not seek raises; these groups saw themselves as victims, not problems, and refused to sacrifice to seek a solution (pp. 605-6)

4. He had been the governor of Georgia for one term. (p. 606)

 Answers will vary. The country had been through much turmoil, and it did need to begin a restoration of faith in its government. But if President Nixon was guilty of a crime, he should have been punished to uphold the integrity of the judicial system.

Section 2

Materials

• No materials

Carter's Three Mile Scare

In an attempt to calm the nation, President Jimmy Carter decided to visit Three Mile Island shortly after the accident occurred. Even as the president made his way to the site, workers were still trying to determine whether the reactor was going to blow up. One theory, later disproved, suggested that a hydrogen bubble was building and that it was only a matter of time before a huge explosion occurred.

On arriving in Harrisburg, Pennsylvania, Carter was informed about the hydrogen bubble theory. Despite the danger, Carter could not turn back without creating greater fear among the public. He continued on to the Three Mile Island nuclear power plant. The tour group made their way through the plant, wearing special boots to protect them from radioactive water on the floor.

Once outside the accident area, Carter and the others checked their dosimeters—tools that measure radiation. Carter's read seventy-eight millirems. It should have been at zero. For a few minutes there was a panic because it appeared that the president had been exposed to radiation. Finally, the workers realized that some of the dosimeters had not been recharged and set at zero. Carter was fine.

loopholes open to the rich. But by the time Congress finished with the bill, it had reduced some taxes for the wealthy, while it raised Social Security taxes on everyone.

Dependence on Foreign Energy—From 1973 to 1977, the cost of imported oil for the nation skyrocketed from $8 billion to $40 billion a year. President Carter devised a program that he believed would end dependence on foreign oil. First, he wanted nationwide conservation. Second, he created a cabinet-level Energy Department to oversee programs to help American companies to search for new oil fields and to develop alternative energy sources. Next, he proposed **deregulation,** an end to price controls, on gas and oil. He hoped

President Carter drives away from visiting Three Mile Island days after safety systems narrowly avoided a nuclear disaster.

that higher prices would encourage conservation and the search for oil at home. Carter also wanted to tax profits on oil and use this money to fund his government programs. His plans were set back when Muslim radicals took power in Iran and cut oil production in 1979, creating an energy crisis reminiscent of the 1973 oil embargo.

President Carter believed that increasing the use of nuclear power might help solve the energy crisis. But he faced opposition on all sides. Conservatives complained that nuclear power required a massive monopoly run by the central government rather than free enterprise. Liberals complained about the hazards of nuclear waste and nuclear accidents. Their fears became reality on March 28, 1979, at the **Three Mile Island** nuclear power plant near Harrisburg, Pennsylvania. The nuclear reactor's cooling system failed. Before the reactor could be shut down, radioactive steam was released, contaminating the water in a backup stream. Although the backup system worked and the immediate crisis passed, the accident prompted antinuclear protests and hampered the building of more nuclear power plants.

Carter's Humiliation in Foreign Affairs

In his inaugural address Carter declared that human rights would be central in his foreign policy. "Because we are free, we can never be indifferent to the fact of freedom elsewhere," he said. "Thus people everywhere should have freedom to make political choices, exercise their ideas free of intimidation or persecution, and to own property." Although such ideas sound wonderful, they are hard to impose on countries where the United States has little influence.

Controversy over the Panama Canal "Surrender"— The United States had signed a ninety-nine-year lease on the Panama Canal, beginning in 1903. Panamanian nationalists were now demanding that it be put under their control immediately. Carter entered negotiations and in 1977 signed the **Panama Canal Treaty.** The United States agreed to transfer control of the canal by the year 1999. The United States, however, retained the right to intervene with military force if the canal's neutrality were ever threatened.

The Senate approved the treaty after hot debate. Those who supported the treaty believed that the United States had no right to the Canal Zone. Many Americans, however, attacked the "surrender" of a canal that

---

Compare the Weaknesses of Ford and Carter

Both Ford and Carter are considered weak presidents. Compare and contrast their circumstances and legacy to understand the different ways they were weak. The Republican Ford stood up against a liberal Democratic Congress, but he was hampered by the aftermath of Watergate. Carter enjoyed the advantage of a Democrat-controlled Congress, but he lacked the political skill to pass legislation. Both presidents were helpless in the face of inflation and the congressional spending spree.

Ask the students what makes a president great. Note that circumstances are almost as important as the person. Even good people can accomplish little unless circumstances are in their favor.

Human Rights in Foreign Policy?

Discuss the pros and cons of Carter's desire to base foreign policy on the promotion of human rights. Note that his idealism resembles that of Woodrow Wilson. Contrast this approach with the pragmatism of Henry Kissinger, who was willing to overlook the evils of dictatorships if it furthered the United States's interests in the Cold War.

The place of human rights in U.S. foreign policy remains an unsettled question. Leaders of other nations have acknowledged that they are careful not to offend the United States because of the potential ramifications. If a president shows no concern about human rights abuses, then he emboldens Communists and other totalitarian states to repress dissidents. On the other

Americans had worked and died to build. They also feared that under Panamanian rule, the canal might fall into communist hands.

Camp David Accords Between Israel and Egypt—One of the few successes that Carter claimed in foreign affairs was the successful conclusion of talks begun under the previous two Republican administrations. Kissinger's shuttle diplomacy helped to persuade Egypt and Israel to end their fighting. Egypt's leader Anwar Sadat took the next step, accepting an invitation to visit Israel's prime minister Menachem Begin (BAY gin) in Tel Aviv. Carter took this opportunity to invite Sadat and Begin to Camp David, a presidential

Carter, Begin, and Sadat seem pleased at the success of the Camp David meetings.

retreat in Maryland. They reached a historic accord, or agreement, with Carter acting as mediator. In September 1978 Sadat and Begin signed the **Camp David Accords.** Israel agreed to return the Sinai Peninsula; Egypt agreed to become the first Arab nation to recognize Israel's right to exist.

Senate Rejection of SALT II—Carter continued negotiations with the Soviets for another Strategic Arms Limitations Treaty.

However, he offered the Soviets a new set of proposals. One of his aims was to guarantee equality in bombers and nuclear missiles. This slowed the talks, and the treaty called SALT II was not signed until March 1979. When Carter submitted the treaty for Senate approval, however, both the Senate and the press reacted negatively. Opposition grew when the Soviet Union invaded Afghanistan in

Jimmy Carter and Leonid Breshnev signed the SALT II Agreement, but the Senate later withheld approval.

1979, and the disappointed president withdrew the treaty.

Soviet Invasion of Afghanistan—The Soviet invasion of Afghanistan deeply angered Americans. Claiming they had been invited into Afghanistan, the Soviets executed the Afghan president soon after their paratroopers landed. Their plans to set up a puppet regime were hindered by Afghan guerillas who took to the hills. Although Carter had earlier stated his opposition to secret military operations, he let the Central Intelligence Agency (CIA) channel aid to Afghan freedom forces. Carter's punishment for the Soviets was weak, however: he stated that the United States would

hand, Carter showed that an overemphasis on human rights could be embarrassingly ineffective in promoting American interests abroad. For example, consider Panama. During Clinton's administration, Communist China stepped in to run some of the key facilities in the Panama Canal after the United States pulled out. This action violated the treaty between the United States and Panama, but the United States had relinquished its authority to enforce the treaty.

Training Students to Be Naysayers

The study of the Carter administration gives you a good opportunity to check whether students have developed their skills of analysis over the course of the year. Since Carter was a moderate liberal, it is likely that most students would have opposed his election. If this is the case, they should be suspicious about every policy he pursued. Pick out any of his foreign or domestic policies at random and see whether the students can explain the reasons that conservative Republicans would have op-

posed him. (The most difficult example will be the Camp David Accords, but even in this "triumph," Israel's position remained tenuous, and Egypt's pretense of accepting Israel has proved empty.)

not take part in the 1980 Olympic Games, to be held in Moscow.

The Iranian Hostage Crisis—On November 4, 1979, America faced a new crisis. In the Middle Eastern country of Iran, a group of radical students stormed the U.S. embassy compound and took sixty-six Americans hostage. The students soon revealed their connections to Iran's new Muslim ruler, the **Ayatollah Khomeini.**

The **Iranian hostage crisis** caught most Americans by surprise, but it shouldn't have. The United States had aided the former ruler of Iran, the shah. The Iranian people were fed up with his self-serving rule and revolted. The shah was forced to flee the country, and Khomeini emerged as ruler. In a nation suffering from deep economic problems and widespread unemployment, Khomeini easily stirred up hatred toward the shah and his supporter, the United States. In October 1979

The Ayatollah Khomeini easily stirred his nation's resentment of the United States's support of the shah of Iran into hatred against all Americans.

President Carter allowed the shah, ill with cancer, to enter the United States for medical treatment. Carter made his decision on humanitarian grounds, ignoring his advisors' warnings that the Iranians would retaliate.

Carter gave only a feeble response. He froze Iran's assets (investment money) in America. Then he cut off the importation of Iranian oil. Carter made one attempt to rescue the hostages by military force, but it was a fiasco. A helicopter collided with a transport plane, killing eight soldiers, and the commandos had to abort their mission hundreds of miles from their objective. This failure only added to America's feelings of frustration and humiliation. The American people were incensed that Khomeini and his country had paralyzed the United States in such a way.

The situation changed when Iran's neighbor, Iraq, invaded in September 1980. The ancient foes locked horns in a deadly war that would last eight years and send over three hundred thousand Muslims to their graves. Khomeini offered to release the American hostages on three conditions: free Iranian assets, promise never to interfere in Iranian affairs, and return the shah's wealth. Since the United States had no legal access to the shah's money, it refused. The crisis did not end until Reagan's inauguration. On January 21, 1981, after 444 days in captivity, the American hostages were set free.

SECTION REVIEW

1. What did Carter do for those who had illegally escaped service in Vietnam?

2. How high did inflation go during Carter's term of office?

3. What alternative source of energy did Carter push? What event seriously damaged support for his program?

Section Review Answers

1. He offered amnesty, or a group pardon, to them. (p. 607)

2. double-digit—over ten percent (p. 607)

3. nuclear power; the accident at Three Mile Island nuclear power plant (p. 608)

4. 1999 (p. 608)

5. Israel and Egypt (p. 609)

Answers will vary. The cause of Iranian hatred stemmed further back than President Carter's term of office. However, weak leadership certainly did nothing to deter the incident and likely prolonged it.

4. By what year was Panama to receive control of the Panama Canal according to the Panama Canal Treaty?

5. The Camp David Accords brought peace between what two Middle Eastern nations?

 Was Carter's weak leadership responsible for the Iranian hostage crisis? Explain your answer.

The Reagan Revolution

Carter faced a formidable opponent in the election of 1980, California's former governor **Ronald Reagan.** Reagan's speeches were direct, sincere, and stirring. He had run for president twice before, nearly unseating Ford in the 1976 election. Tired of the failures under Carter, Americans were ready to listen to Reagan's conservative proposals. Reagan promised to strengthen the national defense, to cut the size of the federal bureaucracy, and to get big government "off the backs of the people." He offered to restore American strength and pride, and the people were ready for a change.

On election night, Reagan carried all but six states. Riding "on the coattails" of the president, Republicans won enough seats to take control of the Senate by a small margin. Although Democrats still held a majority in the House, a group of moderate Democrats sometimes voted with the Republicans. This meant that, in his early years as president, Reagan was able to get his programs passed by Congress, especially laws dealing with the economy and with military spending.

Reagan's New Direction in Domestic Policies

Reagan's first priority was to solve the problems at home. He offered a new approach to the economy, and he promised to restrain the liberal courts.

Supply-side Economics—The causes of inflation are complicated. An easy way to

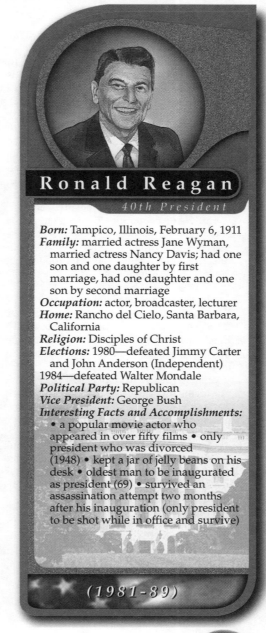

Ronald Reagan
40th President

Born: Tampico, Illinois, February 6, 1911
Family: married actress Jane Wyman, married actress Nancy Davis; had one son and one daughter by first marriage, had one daughter and one son by second marriage
Occupation: actor, broadcaster, lecturer
Home: Rancho del Cielo, Santa Barbara, California
Religion: Disciples of Christ
Elections: 1980—defeated Jimmy Carter and John Anderson (Independent) 1984—defeated Walter Mondale
Political Party: Republican
Vice President: George Bush
Interesting Facts and Accomplishments:
• a popular movie actor who appeared in over fifty films • only president who was divorced (1948) • kept a jar of jelly beans on his desk • oldest man to be inaugurated as president (69) • survived an assassination attempt two months after his inauguration (only president to be shot while in office and survive)

(1981–89)

611

SECTION 3

Objectives
Students should be able to
1. Define *supply-side economics.*
2. Describe the changes in the Supreme Court during the Nixon and Reagan administrations.
3. Describe Reagan's policy toward the Soviet Union.
4. Name the two groups involved in the revolution in Nicaragua.
5. Identify the event that hampered Reagan's effectiveness at the end of his second term of office.

Ronald Reagan's Background
The second half of the twentieth century's most successful president and a conservative icon, Ronald Reagan brought a very diverse background to the White House. Ironically, many factors about his past are at odds with the conservative views he espoused later in life.

Before the 1950s, Reagan was a Democrat, even a liberal one. He had supported Franklin Roosevelt and his New Deal and its continuation under Harry Truman. Later as president, Reagan often would quote Roosevelt favorably, so to some degree he retained a fondness for him. As president of the Screen Actors Guild, Reagan was popular among Hollywood liberals and leftists. In 1950, when Richard Nixon ran against the very liberal Helen Douglas for the U.S. Senate in California, Ronald Reagan endorsed Douglas, but she did not want the endorsement publicized for fear it would reinforce her leftist image.

In the 1950s Reagan slowly shifted to the right. In 1952 he supported Eisenhower over Stevenson, as he did again in 1956. In 1962 he switched his party registration to Republican. Why did Reagan change so dramatically? He cited his years as leader of the Screen Actors Guild, during which he saw the destructive influence of the left

---

SECTION 3

Materials

• A copy of Reagan's first inaugural speech

• Illustration of a Laffer curve

Reagan's First Inaugural Speech

Select portions of Reagan's first inaugural speech and ask the students to cite the main goals of his administration. Discuss how well he reached his goals.

and of Communism in Hollywood. Also his success in television, first for GE Theater and later "Death Valley Days," made him wealthier; and like many who become wealthier, he became more conservative. Some also credit the influence of his wife Nancy, whom he married in 1952.

There are certain other ironies, given the support of Reagan by the religious right in the 1970s and 1980s. He was divorced, although that factor was neutralized by the fact that his first wife, Jane Wyman, sought it and that Reagan had been happily remarried since 1952. Also, Reagan's show business background made him an unlikely hero of the right since over the years Hollywood has done little to strengthen the morals of America.

Laffer Curve

As part of his "supply-side economics" approach, Reagan adopted the Laffer curve theory. This theory was proposed by Dr. Arthur Laffer of Reagan's Economic Policy Advisory Board. It was based on two assumptions. First, it said that if there was a zero percent income tax, then obviously there would be zero income tax revenue generated. Second, it said that a one hundred percent income tax would also generate zero revenue. In other words, the government would not get any money by taxing nothing, but it also would not get any money by one hundred percent taxes because people would find it pointless to generate income if it was simply all taxed away. With this in mind, the theory suggested that there must be a point between a zero and a one hundred percent income tax at which the most revenue could be generated. The trick was to find it.

Some critics claim that the Laffer curve theory was a failure because Reagan failed to balance the budget. However, the claim is unfair considering the evidence. Reagan and his economic advisors estimated that income taxes were too high. According to the

explain it is that the supply of money is greater than the supply of products that people can buy. (Too much money is chasing too few goods.) Under these circumstances, businesses must raise prices. The government can stop businesses from raising prices in several ways. One option is to take money away from buyers through taxes and high interest rates. Reagan suggested another way. He focused on the other side of the equation: make more products available by reducing taxes and regulations on businesses and investors. Industries would then have more money to make products. Reagan called this positive approach **"supply-side economics."** He argued that tax cuts would increase the amount of tax money that the government would collect. Critics referred to his magic plan as "voodoo economics" or "Reaganomics." Both sides waited to see what would happen.

In 1981 Congress passed the first part of Reagan's plan by cutting inheritance and gift taxes, corporate taxes, and income taxes. The Economic Recovery Tax Act of 1981 included the largest income tax cut in American history—a 25 percent reduction for each taxpayer. To help balance the budget, the president also hoped to cut the size of the government bureaucracy and to slow down increases in federal spending in almost every area except the military. But the House of Representatives, which is responsible for budget bills, showed little interest in reducing federal spending. Democratic leaders in Congress accused Reagan of being hard-hearted and wanting to hurt the poor.

Before the tax reforms were passed, the country fell back into a deep recession. The president agreed to some tax increases, such as taxes on cigarettes and airline tickets, to ease worries that the government was not earning enough money, but otherwise he called on Americans to "stay the course" he had proposed. The recession lifted, and in

1983 the United States entered its longest period of continuous economic growth in history. Inflation disappeared, and jobs were abundant. As the decade wore on, Democrats watched government income from taxes almost double, just as Reagan had hoped. But Congress continued to spend money even faster than it came in. Government debts mounted to record levels, threatening America's long-term prosperity.

Reagan's Stab at a More Conservative Court—Another goal of the Reagan administration was to restore law and order. This required replacing liberal judges with more conservative ones. President Reagan's first appointment to the Supreme Court was the first woman on the Court, **Sandra Day O'Connor.** Afterward the president named Justice **William H. Rehnquist,** a conservative justice already on the court, to replace Chief Justice Warren Burger when he stepped down. Another conservative appointment, Antonin Scalia, helped to tilt the high court away from its liberal predecessor. However, O'Connor—and a later appointment Anthony Kennedy—disappointed conservatives. While they ruled in favor of strong criminal laws and police powers, these appointments refused to overturn abortion.

Chief Justice Warren Burger administers the oath to Sandra Day O'Connor, the first woman to serve on the Supreme Court.

Was This a Revolution?

Begin the discussion of the Reagan administration by considering the expression "the Reagan Revolution." First, ask the students to explain what a revolution is. Then discuss the sense in which the nation might go through a revolution. Historians question whether the changes were mistakenly labeled as a "revolution." Give both sides of this debate. No one can deny that Reagan failed to accomplish everything he wanted, primarily because Republicans did not control the House. The Republican takeover of the House in 1994 was also called a revolu-

tion. In the sense that they had been barred from the seats of power for nearly sixty years, that election was a revolution. But they found themselves just as hamstrung as Reagan because the president at the time was a Democrat, and he vetoed almost everything they tried to pass.

The most valuable lesson from this discussion is that the founders intentionally set up checks and balances to prevent a revolution. The lingering effects of the progressive liberalism in the early 1900s would take at least two decades (the 1980s and 1990s) to change. Any candidate who

promises to revolutionize America during his administration is either deceived or lying. Changes come much more slowly, as students will see during the next few years of their lives.

Illustrate the Laffer Curve

Make a simple illustration of taxes and revenue to show the logic of the Laffer curve (above). Is this common sense or "voodoo economics"?

Reelection by a Landslide—The Democratic Party nominated former Vice President Walter Mondale to face Reagan in the 1984 elections. But he surprised many by promising to raise taxes and by choosing a woman as his running mate—Geraldine Ferraro, a liberal congresswoman from New York. The Democrats attacked the high debt, the military build-up, and the limits on spending for social programs. However, Americans trusted the president, and he led in the polls the entire campaign. On election night he carried every state but Mondale's home state of Minnesota. It was one of the biggest landslides in American history.

Reagan's Foreign Triumphs

Reagan was just as successful abroad as he was at home, but it took longer for Americans to see the fruit of his labors.

Bare Knuckles Toward the "Evil Empire"—President Reagan was a vocal opponent of communism. Carter's friendly relationship with the Soviets had turned to frost—if not ice— before Reagan even took office. The Soviets had invaded Afghanistan, and Soviet-equipped Cuban troops were fighting America's ally in Angola, Africa. Moreover, the Soviets were installing long-range missiles in Eastern Europe. Tensions increased in 1983 when the Soviets shot down a Korean airliner with 61 Americans on board, including a U.S. congressman. (The Soviets claimed the plane had crossed its border and was spying.) The Soviets also backed Poland's crackdown on workers demanding greater freedom. Reagan made no attempt to melt the frost. Indeed, he boldly condemned the Soviet Union as an "evil empire."

President Reagan wanted to negotiate limits on nuclear arms, but he took a different tack from Carter. Liberal Democrats argued that the best way to make peace with the Soviets was to voluntarily reduce the U.S. military, allaying Soviet fears of American aggression. Reagan, on the other hand, believed the best way to achieve peace was a strong military. He set aside money to develop a modern bomber, called the B-1, and he asked for further research on nuclear and chemical weapons. By removing Soviet hopes

President Reagan addresses Congress.

of ever defeating the United States, he believed the Soviets would have no choice but to negotiate a better peace agreement. When the Soviets stalled during talks in 1982, Reagan daringly placed more nuclear missiles in Western Europe.

Reagan's tough stand made American allies nervous, but he stuck to his policies. A sore spot among Soviet leaders was Reagan's ambitious proposal, the Strategic Defense Initiative (SDI). SDI's aim was to develop a defense system that could knock down nuclear missiles aimed at American cities. The liberal

Laffer curve, lowering taxes would result in higher revenue. Reagan tested the theory in 1981 with the Economic Recovery Act, which included a large cut in the income tax. The result was a doubling of government income. The Laffer curve worked. Unfortunately, government spending counteracted any gains the tax cut created. Thomas Jefferson once said, "If we prevent the government from wasting the labors of the people under the pretense of caring for them, they will be happy."

613

Star Wars II

When Reagan first proposed his Strategic Defense Initiative (SDI), it faced severe criticism from within and without the country. Many said it would upset the delicate balance of power that existed between the United States and the Soviet Union. Once Reagan left office, the program (dubbed "Star Wars") had its budget cut drastically, and some programs were even canceled. The need for the program seemed outdated when the Soviet Union collapsed in 1991. But Star Wars was not dead.

By the end of the nineties, both Republicans and Democrats were calling for missile defense for the nation. The Soviet Union may have been gone, but many of the nuclear warheads were still around. Now they were in the hands of smaller nations, many with unstable governments. Nuclear technology was not a well-kept secret either. Unsettling evidence showed that Chinese spies working in the United States had been stealing nuclear information. Up to thirty nations also had ballistic missile technology that would allow them to fire warheads over long distances. When North Korea test fired a three-stage missile over northern Japan, the call for security intensified.

In 1999 the House and the Senate both passed bills to construct a national missile defense system. It was Reagan's SDI all over again but with the new name "Ballistic Missile Defense Organization." Clinton reversed Democratic policy and set aside $10.5 billion dollars over five years to build the system. The new Star Wars plan has less to do with space though. While Reagan's SDI included x-ray lasers fired from space satellites, the sequel focuses on land- and sea-based defense rockets.

Forty years of Soviet domination end with the tearing down of the Berlin Wall.

press mockingly called SDI the **"Star Wars"** program. But the Soviet Union suffered a crisis of leadership, as the Soviets realized they could not keep up with America's dynamic economy and sophisticated technology. Three of the Soviet Union's old-guard leaders died within a three-year span. Finally, **Mikhail Gorbachev,** a young leader brimming with new ideas, came to power in 1985. That same year he became the first Soviet leader to meet with Reagan. A second meeting on arms limitations two years later in Reykjavik, Iceland, collapsed because Reagan refused to give up SDI. Meanwhile, discontent was growing within the Soviet Union. A desperate Gorbachev finally gave in to Reagan's demands. On December 9, 1987, the two leaders signed the historic Intermediate Nuclear Forces (INF) Treaty, which eliminated most of Europe's medium-range nuclear missiles, a first step toward further reductions.

Battling Middle-Eastern Terrorism— Early in Reagan's first term, civil war and foreign intervention in Lebanon led the U.N. to send in peace-keeping troops. American marines were stationed in Lebanon as a part of this force. But on October 23, 1983, a truck loaded with heavy explosives ran through a series of barricades and slammed into the marine headquarters on the outskirts of Beirut. The suicide attack killed over two hundred marines, and Reagan pulled the remaining force out of the country.

Elsewhere in the Middle East, Muslim terrorists led a series of attacks on Westerners. When intelligence officials in the United States learned that Libya's leader, **Muammar Qaddafi,** was behind some of the terrorism, and after Qaddafi added new threats against the United States, Reagan responded with a surprise bombing raid. The attack on March 31, 1986, was brief, but it quieted the terrorist rampage.

Reagan Doctrine in Latin America— After Castro's rise to power in Cuba, the United States made every effort to limit the spread of communism. Struggling with poverty, unequal wealth, and evil dictators, Latin America was a breeding ground for revolution. A small island in the Caribbean—Grenada—became a focus of concern after Reagan took office. An anti-American government, which had ruled Grenada since the 1970s, allowed Cuba to build a major runway which could be used to fly supplies to communist rebels throughout the region. The threat increased after rebels overthrew and executed Grenada's president in 1983.

The resulting civil war in Grenada threatened the lives of about seven hundred American students enrolled in medical school there. Fearing for their own safety, several Caribbean nations asked the United States to intervene. In a surprise attack, American paratroopers, joined by forces from five Caribbean nations, restored peace to Grenada. The United States finished the airstrip and oversaw a free election in 1984, while American troops remained in Grenada only a matter of weeks.

Another dangerous revolution had taken place before Reagan took office. With the help of Cuban advisors, the **Sandinistas** had set up

614

a Communist government in Nicaragua. In response, the CIA had begun channeling aid to the freedom-fighting rebels, called **Contras** (short for the Spanish word for counter-revolutionary). President Reagan feared that revolution would spread to Nicaragua's neighbors. Reagan was particularly concerned about El Salvador, the most crowded nation in Central America. At first Congress went along with Reagan's plans to give aid to the Contras and to El Salvador. Eventually, however, the unstable conditions raised fears that America might be pulled into another conflict like Vietnam. Investigators also found that some Contras were guilty of violating human rights.

The Iran-Contra Affair—An incident came to light in 1987 that hampered Reagan's effectiveness in the final years of his presidency. The administration had arranged the sale of weapons to Iran in exchange for Iran's help in freeing some Americans who had been captured and were being held hostage in Lebanon. The president apparently approved this deal, contrary to his official stand against bargaining with terrorists. The situation grew worse when it was learned that some of the profits from the sale of the weapons were being sent by third parties to aid the Contras in Nicaragua.

Congress had cut all government aid to the Contras at the time of the transactions, so Reagan's enemies charged that he had violated the law. Reagan claimed he knew nothing of this diversion of funds. Many Americans believed him, but opponents made much of his apparent lack of control. Congress hired an independent counsel (lawyer) to investigate, but after he spent almost seven years and $37 million, no one was ever convicted. The counsel's report concluded, "President Reagan's conduct fell well short of criminality which could be successfully prosecuted."

SECTION REVIEW

1. How did "supply-side economics" propose to lower inflation?

2. Who was the first woman appointed to the Supreme Court?

3. Which Soviet leader agreed to come to the bargaining table with Reagan?

4. What were the Communist rulers in Nicaragua called? Who were the freedom fighters that were trying to overthrow them?

5. One of the complaints in the Iran-Contra affair was that weapons were sold to Iran. What was the other complaint?

 Do you agree with Reagan's view that the best way to achieve peace is to build a powerful military? Defend your answer.

Bush's Problem with "the Vision Thing"

The Reagan Administration marked a turning point in the history of the nation and of the world. The year Reagan left office, 1989, communism collapsed in Eastern Europe. Two years later, the Communist leader of the Soviet Union stepped down, and fifteen new countries rose out of the ashes of the former empire. The American system of government and free enterprise had proved victorious. The Cold War that had dominated the last half of the twentieth century was finally over. All eyes now turned to the president of the United States to guide the free world into the next century. Americans were ready for sweeping changes at home, now that the specter of communism had stopped haunting Europe. Who was the right man to lead the nation?

Reagan proposed that his vice president, **George Bush,** would be the best man to carry on his vision. Unlike Reagan, however, Bush was a pragmatist (a person who believes that

---

SECTION 4

Objectives
Students should be able to
1. Explain the difference between Reagan's and Bush's leadership philosophies.
2. Identify the high point in Bush's administration.
3. List the government scandals during Bush's administration.
4. Describe Bush's domestic failures.

615

Section Review Answers

1. by reducing taxes and regulations on businesses and investors in order to make more products available (p. 612)

2. Sandra Day O'Connor (p. 612)

3. Mikhail Gorbachev (p. 614)

4. the Sandinistas; the Contras (pp. 614-15)

5. that some of the profits had been used to aid the Contras in Nicaragua (p. 615)

 Answers will vary. There are no guarantees of peace. However, considering man's sinful nature, it is always a good idea to be prepared.

SECTION 4

Materials
• Activities A, B, and C from Chapter 29 of the *Student Activities* manual

The SALT and START agreements (discussed on the facing page) both dealt with the modern arms race but in different ways. SALT I and II set the upper limits on the number of select nuclear weapons that both countries could possess. However, these agreements said little about new nuclear technology, and they lacked any real power without surveillance to ensure enforcement.

Under the Reagan administration, the START agreements were launched. They focused on an actual reduction of nuclear arms by both sides. In total, START I called for a 30 percent reduction of U.S. and Soviet nuclear arsenals. Under START II the arsenals are not to exceed 3,000-3,500 warheads by 2003. The agreements also included on-site inspections, satellite surveys, and an exchange of data that would ensure measures were being enforced.

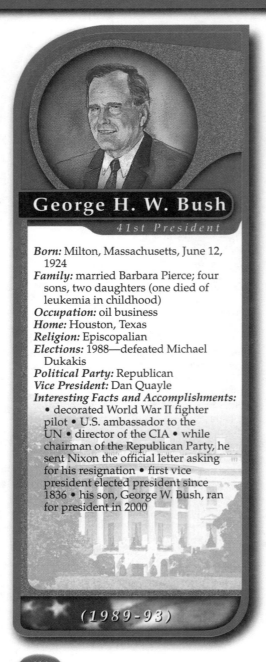

George H. W. Bush

41st President

Born: Milton, Massachusetts, June 12, 1924
Family: married Barbara Pierce; four sons, two daughters (one died of leukemia in childhood)
Occupation: oil business
Home: Houston, Texas
Religion: Episcopalian
Elections: 1988—defeated Michael Dukakis
Political Party: Republican
Vice President: Dan Quayle
Interesting Facts and Accomplishments:
• decorated World War II fighter pilot • U.S. ambassador to the UN • director of the CIA • while chairman of the Republican Party, he sent Nixon the official letter asking for his resignation • first vice president elected president since 1836 • his son, George W. Bush, ran for president in 2000

(1989-93)

616

whatever works best is right). This Eastern "gentleman" accepted many of the traditional values with which he was reared, yet he rarely spoke of right and wrong. Instead, he spoke of the views of "my generation" and "your generation." He voiced support for many of Reagan's policies, not based on principle but on practical concerns. He was an uninspiring speaker who once admitted that he lacked "the vision thing."

In Reagan's Shadow, Election of 1988

The election of 1988 pitted George Bush against a liberal governor from Massachusetts, Michael Dukakis. During his eight years in Reagan's shadow, Bush had remained a mystery to the American people. When Reagan picked him as a running mate in 1979, Bush was a "moderate" Republican with a lifetime of experience in public service and foreign affairs. Bush now struggled to establish a separate identity. He wanted to soften Reagan's strictly conservative message. "I want a kinder, gentler nation," Bush said in his acceptance speech at the Republican convention. He spoke of solving the nation's social ills by kindling the vast resources of the American people as "a thousand points of light."

After a shaky start, Bush rallied support largely by returning to Reagan's popular positions: American strength at home and abroad. He also vowed, "Read my lips—no new taxes." The result for Bush and his running mate, Dan Quayle, was a solid win on election day. Bush's election was in many ways a vote of approval for Ronald Reagan. Bush became the first vice president since 1836 to replace the president under whom he served. Unfortunately, like that earlier president, Martin Van Buren, Bush inherited serious troubles that demanded immediate attention.

Foreign Affairs

In foreign affairs President Bush brought the same resolve as his predecessor. His experience and skill led to major triumphs in Panama and the Persian Gulf, but he was slow to see the significance of sweeping changes in China and the Soviet Union.

Invasion of Panama—Bush faced several international crises with amazing success. His first major triumph involved Panama's drug-dealing leader, Manuel Noriega, whose criminal activities had become an embarrassment to the U.S. government. Reagan had attempted to remove Noriega peacefully, but in vain. In December 1989 Noriega went too far. His troops killed a U.S. marine and attacked an American couple, and then the general declared war on the United States. In the early morning hours of December 20, Bush launched Operation Just Cause. Within days American troops had crushed Noriega's forces and captured the general, at a cost of only twenty-three American lives. Noriega became the first foreign head of state to be captured and tried in a U.S. court. He was convicted in 1992 of drug trafficking and sentenced to forty years in prison.

Protests Break Out in China and the Soviet Union—Meanwhile rumblings were heard on the other side of the globe. The Cold War was coming to an end, but Bush was slow to see the significance of events. Chinese students led a massive protest at Beijing's Tiananmen Square in 1989, hoping to spread democracy to their Communist land. When tanks crushed the protest, killing over two thousand people, Bush refused to take any action. Indeed, when it came time to renew China's "most-favored-nation" trade status, Bush did so.

A similar series of events was taking place in the Soviet Union. As that "evil empire" began to tear apart, Bush continued to support its Communist leader, Gorbachev. Bush spoke with Gorbachev about creating a "new world order," and they negotiated a nuclear arms reduction treaty (START). Bush was slow to

support the reformer Boris Yeltsin, even when it became obvious that he was the people's choice to lead Russia out of communism.

The Persian Gulf War—Bush reached a high point in his career when he negotiated an international alliance to stop Iraq's invasion of Kuwait in 1990. The dictator **Saddam Hussein** had invaded this tiny, oil-rich neighbor, hoping to win glory for himself and easy wealth for his nation. But Bush vowed, "This will not stand." A UN directive (order) told Hussein to withdraw by January 15, 1991, and it authorized the allies to use "all necessary means" to liberate Kuwait if Hussein did not comply. The U.S. Congress also approved war, if necessary. It was America's first official declaration of war since World War II.

President and Mrs. Bush meet with troops stationed in Saudi Arabia before the conflict known as the Gulf War.

The brief **Persian Gulf War** (January 16 to February 27, 1991) began with five weeks of massive, around-the-clock bombing. It was followed by a surprise ground attack in the desert. General Norman Schwarzkopf secretly ordered soldiers and tanks to move into the desert west of Kuwait. This force circled around the Iraqi army and trapped it in

Stealth Technology

In Operation Just Cause and Desert Storm, a new form of technology was used. Since the seventies, American engineers had been secretly designing a jet that could go undetected by radar defenses. The strategy was to design the jet's body to reflect as little energy as possible. To achieve this, engineers limited the angles of the jet to give it a flat design. In a prototype design, the back tail fins were pointed inward, but this caused another problem. Heat from the exhaust reflected off the fins. The final design had the fins pointing outward.

To keep the jet invisible on radar, every precaution was taken. Mesh covers over the engine intakes protected against internal reflections. The skin of the plane was made of radar-absorbent material. The canopy was coated with a substance to make it impenetrable to radar. Even screw heads were redesigned to ensure they would not cause reflections. As a way of reducing the jet's noise, exhausts were soundproofed, and the turbine was made to give off a high-pitched whine instead of a loud scream.

At the time of the Panama invasion, the stealth jet, called the F-117 Nighthawk, was ready for service. Six jets were sent on missions, but two returned unneeded and another two had their mission canceled. The final two completed their bombing mission undetected by enemy radar.

During the Persian Gulf War, the F-117 saw more action. In the first twenty-four hours of the war, the jets accounted for 31 percent of the targets attacked. One target was particularly memorable for CNN viewers. A bomb from an F-117 destroyed the Al-Kark Communications Tower. CNN's television signal was transmitted from there. When the bomb hit, the station suddenly went blank. Reporters Peter Arnett and Bernard Shaw had to continue the broadcast without the aid of video.

Compare Reasons for Past Wars

Mention some of the United States's previous wars—Tripolitan War, Mexican War, Spanish-American War, World War I, World War II, Korean War, Vietnam War—and ask students to recall the reasons for each war. How was the Persian Gulf War different? Was the war justified even though the United States had no alliances with the countries involved and no immediate threat to its property? A war's being successful does not mean it is right, and even if a war is justified, the manner in which it is fought (e.g., under UN directives) is not

necessarily right. Did the Persian Gulf War set a precedent that the United States should follow in other places?

Stealth technology has continued with the development of the Stealth B-2 Bomber. These and other high-tech weapons reveal what war may be like in the twenty-first century.

Bank Scandal

The BCCI (Bank of Credit and Commerce International) scandal—the worst in banking history—shocked the international community. On July 5, 1991, the United States and other major banking countries seized BCCI assets, worth an estimated $20 billion. The United States indicted the president and founder of BCCI for fraud and racketeering. One million depositors in seventy countries lost money. Investigators later discovered that the bank had been involved in secret arms deals and bribes around the world. Clark Clifford, a powerful leader in the Democratic Party and BCCI attorney, was indicted the following year for taking bribes. The head of Saudi Arabia's intelligence pleaded guilty to a BCCI conspiracy to take control of First American Bank, chaired by Clifford.

Perspectives on Corruption

Human nature always encourages graft and corruption in government as well as industry. America's founders wanted a small government that stayed out of business, except to defend the law. Lawmakers were supposed to be regular citizens—not professional politicians—who met for a few weeks each year to pass laws and then went back to their normal lives. They believed that big government would promote abuse of taxpayer money, whether by greedy politicians or crooked businessmen.

The massive assault called Operation Desert Storm began five weeks of the most intensive American military effort since World War II.

Kuwait. The Iraqi army surrendered en masse. The ground war was over within one hundred hours, and Americans rejoiced that the ghosts of the Vietnam War had vanished. Yet the cream of Hussein's army, the Republican Guard, remained safe at home in Iraq. Schwarzkopf, his hands tied by UN directives, could not move north to capture Hussein.

In the wake of victory, Bush's popularity ratings soared to an unprecedented 89 percent. No leading Democrat wanted to run against him in the next election. Yet Bush's decision to place United States troops under UN directives would come back to haunt him. Hussein remained in power and continued to take actions that embarrassed the United States.

Government Scandals and Demands for Reform

The U.S. government was rocked by a series of financial scandals beginning in 1989. Many liberals said that these scandals were a sign of the greed and decadence caused by Reagan's deregulation of banking, business, insurance, and health care. Yet blame quickly spread to the Democrat-controlled Congress.

Savings and Loan Bankruptcies—The first scandals involved savings and loan (S & L) banks, which began to go bankrupt because of unsound investments and a drop in oil prices. The federal government had to spend over $300 billion to keep Franklin D. Roosevelt's promises to safeguard individuals' bank accounts. This cost the average taxpayer roughly $3,000. Efforts to sell the bankrupt S & Ls proved to be a nightmare of waste and fraud.

Other Business Scandals—Health care overcharges, insurance fraud, empty retirement funds, and similar instances of dishonesty hit the headlines during the same period. Most of the scandals had a similar theme: the government guaranteed benefits but provided insufficient regulation. Liberals argued that the government needed more regulation. Conservatives argued that the government needed to stay out of private business.

Congressional Scandals—Congress was embarrassed by its own scandals. In 1989 Congress passed the so-called "Ethics Reform Act." In exchange for giving up money for speeches (honoraria), Congress gave itself a massive pay raise and established automatic annual cost-of-living adjustments (COLAs). In 1993 alone, the COLAs gave congressmen a pay raise of $4,100, which they never had to vote for. Taxpayers were furious. States responded by ratifying the Twenty-seventh Amendment on May 7, 1992. The amendment reads, "No law, varying the compensation for the services of the Senators and Representatives, shall take effect, until an election of Representatives shall have intervened."

In 1992 news leaked that a majority of congressmen had serious House Bank overdrafts. It became clear that they were abusing the perks of office. They were allowed to overdraw on their checking accounts without penalties, while taxpayers paid the interest. The House Ethics Committee released names of 247 congressmen who had overdrafts.

A more serious scandal, involving the House Post Office, came to light. Investigators found that congressmen were abusing their privileges to pay office expenses and to buy stamps. The most infamous case involved the powerful chairman of the Ways and Means Committee, Dan Rostenkowski. He was eventually sent to jail for pocketing over ten thousand dollars worth in money for stamps, hiring employees who were paid for work they never did, and using his congressional staff for private work (at a total cost of half a million dollars to taxpayers).

Many Americans decided that wealthy incumbents (officeholders) had lost touch with the people who elected them. Support grew for **term limits**—restrictions on the number of years that a congressman can stay in office. During the 1992 elections, fourteen states passed laws to limit senators to twelve years and House members to anywhere from six to twelve years. The number of states with term limits increased to twenty-two after the 1994 elections.

Domestic Failures

Bush's domestic policies sent mixed signals to the nation. Conservatives were concerned about his liberal compromises, while liberals were disappointed with his conservative stands. He said he opposed abortion, but he appointed a Supreme Court justice who upheld *Roe v. Wade.* He said he opposed big government intrusion into business, but he increased the minimum wage from $3.35 to $4.25. He said he supported business, but the 1991 Clean Air Act cost businesses around $30 billion per year. He said he wanted to simplify government, but the number of pages devoted to regulations rose from 47,418 under Reagan to 67,715 under Bush. He said he supported traditional values, but he became the first president to invite homosexuals to visit the White House when he signed the Hate Crimes Statistics Act.

The "Education President"—Ronald Reagan had campaigned against Washington's control of education, but his promise to disband the cabinet position went unfulfilled. In contrast, George Bush promised to become the "education president." The federal government's involvement in education grew rapidly under his administration. His favorite program was Head Start, begun by Lyndon B. Johnson in the 1960s. Even though studies indicate that the advantages of early education fade away by second or third grade, spending for this federal program grew dramatically under Bush: from $600 million to $2.8 billion.

An Education Summit in 1989 agreed on six national goals that American schools should meet by the year 2000. Bush proposed America 2000, a plan to bring American schools up to these goals. Bill Clinton, the governor of Arkansas who was a leader at the summit, later converted this program into Goals 2000. It set "voluntary" standards for textbooks and testing that states must meet in order to receive federal funds. Yet poor performance on standardized tests continued to embarrass the nation.

Disabilities Act—President Bush signed the **Americans with Disabilities Act,** which went into effect in 1992. The landmark law prohibited job discrimination based on disabilities. It also required local governments and businesses to provide better conditions for

Supporters look on as President Bush signs the Americans with Disabilities Act of 1990.

Foley's Folly

Speaker of the House Tom Foley (D-Wash.) was so angered by a popular vote to institute term limits (and keep him from running for re-election) that he went to court to overturn the vote as unconstitutional. Disgusted voters kicked Foley out during the 1994 elections. Foley became the poster boy for those who advocate term limits as a way to oust elitist leaders.

Clarence Thomas Confirmation Hearings

Except for the Senate hearings for Robert Bork in 1987, the confirmation hearings for Clarence Thomas in 1991 were the most controversial in modern history. Bush appointed a conservative, anti-abortion black to replace the outgoing liberal Supreme Court justice Thurgood Marshall. At the last minute, Anita Hill, who had worked for Thomas ten years earlier at the Equal Opportunity Employment Office, came forward and accused Thomas of making lewd advances toward her. The senators at first praised her for her bravery, but their search for the truth became confused when Thomas categorically denied all of the accusations. He accused the liberal senators of a "high-tech lynching." Someone was lying, but the senators described both of them as exemplary Americans. The media portrayed Hill as an innocent, mainstream lawyer. They ignored reports of her close connections with leading feminists. Only after the trial did the public become aware of Hill's potential motives for lying. Thomas was confirmed after a close vote. During his first year, he proved to be one of the Court's most conservative justices. Meanwhile, the national conscience was alerted to the problems of sexual harassment, and liberals began pressing for stricter laws against it.

Note the following ways in which truth was handled loosely in these highly political hearings. Bush said he selected Thomas because he was "the most qualified" man on

---

Discuss Term Limits

Discuss the pros and cons of term limits. The arguments are strong on both sides of the issue. Supporters point to the tendency of power to corrupt and the tendency of those in power to abuse their power to stay in office. But opponents believe that the people should be free to vote as they choose. They also are wary of any fundamental changes in the basic structure of the republic because such changes usually have unintended consequences. For example, they fear that term limits would weaken the power of elected officials and actually strengthen the power of unelected experts from each party who run the offices and do the real work of the representatives.

Students need to learn to have the same wariness about constitutional changes that purport to stem the effects of man's sinful nature. Sin finds a means to worm its way out of any legislative restrictions. It is interesting to note that the Republicans took control of Congress without the passage of a term limits amendment, and the push for term limits died soon afterward.

his list, not because he was conservative and black. Thomas refused to discuss his views on abortion and other issues, claiming that he had no fixed views. And the senators gave Anita Hill a hearing even though her accusations would never have been permitted in a court of law. She waited ten years to make her complaints, and she had no corroborating witnesses.

Americans with Disabilities Act

In addition to dealing with the employment of disabled persons, the Americans with Disabilities Act pushed for greater accessibility for the disabled in the workplace and in public facilities. Some routine changes that were often made in response to the act were the installation of grab bars and access ramps and the lowering of public telephones. Restaurants and stores had to consider the width of their aisles (for wheelchair accessibility) and to have employees available to provide any assistance necessary (e.g., reading a menu or a price tag for a blind customer).

Rodney King—First Trial

The controversial trial of the officers accused of using excessive force against Rodney King was moved outside Los Angeles to lessen racial tensions. Four black jurors were barred when it was found that the NAACP had attempted to influence them; consequently, there were no blacks on the jury. The media aroused national emotions by continually replaying brief snippets of the beating while ignoring the case for the defense. Later, black columnist Walter Williams said, "Having seen the complete amateur video and trial evidence, I agree with the jury in its acquittal verdict."

The Riots

In the aftermath of the acquittal verdict, angry mobs pulled motorists from their vehicles and killed them. In addition to 53 deaths, there were 2,400 injuries, 5,500 fires, and 3,000 arrests for looting. Korean businesses were

---

the disabled. Companies with fifteen or more employees were required to hire and promote people with disabilities. The greatest opposition to the act came from small businessmen, who feared that the new costs would put them out of business. Many Americans also feared the unclear definition of disability, which allowed people with AIDS and mental conditions to claim they had a "disability." The law brought a flood of expensive lawsuits.

This law aroused the ire of conservatives who opposed federal interference in business and local government. The concept of "rights" for the disabled departed from historic civil liberties and rights. The Disabilities Act encouraged a widespread movement against **unfunded federal mandates** (federal requirements that the federal government does not pay for). The law cost in excess of $60 billion in its first few years.

Los Angeles Riots—The most significant domestic crisis during the Bush administration was the **Los Angeles riots** (April 29–May 3, 1992)—the deadliest riots in modern American history. Fifty-three people died and over $1 billion in damage occurred in America's second largest city. The rioting had many similarities to the race riots of the early 1960s. (During the 1965 Watts riots in Los Angeles, thirty-four people died.)

The rioting began when a state court found four white police officers not guilty of charges that they used excessive force against a black motorist named Rodney King. King, who had been driving drunk, was chased for eight miles at 115 miles per hour. His passen-

The Los Angeles riots in response to the beating of Rodney King were the deadliest riots in modern American history.

gers surrendered, but the 6' 4", 240-pound King knocked down two officers and continued resisting arrest. A bystander videotaped much of the scene, including an estimated fifty-six blows against King by officers wielding billy clubs and flashlights. The media aroused the anger of viewers by continually replaying segments of the beating.

The Los Angeles city police were unprepared for the havoc that followed the acquittals. Looting and murder spread through the inner city of Los Angeles, where gang and ethnic rivalries had been simmering for years. Motorists were pulled from their vehicles and killed by angry mobs. Bush promised to bring the officers to trial in federal court on charges of violating King's civil rights. (Two were convicted). The president and Congress also agreed to send more than $500 million in emergency aid. A jury later ordered the city of Los Angeles to pay King $3.8 million.

The 1990 Budget Deal and Economic Recession—The greatest concern among economists during the Reagan-Bush years was

---

What Was the Worst Thing Bush Did?

Ask students to imagine themselves as voters during the 1992 election. Looking back on the four years under Bush, what would they have considered the worst thing he did? Write down all of the answers and keep a tally. The text mentions several things that conservatives disliked. It is interesting to consider which of them led to his defeat.

Student Activity A: The Cost of Federal Bureaucracy

This is an interesting interdisciplinary activity that helps students to visualize the significant changes in national debt, federal spending, trade imbalances, and inflation between 1970 and 1990.

Economics 101

Review the difference between national debt, deficit, recession, and depression.

Why Did Bush Do It?

Conservatives around the country drew in their breath when Bush announced on television his decision to raise taxes. They could not believe he would "surrender" so glibly to the liberal Democrats in Congress. The conservatives' prophecies of an election disaster proved true two years later when Bill Clinton upset Bush. Ask the students to imagine the reasons Bush gave to justify his action. Why did he not recognize the consequences of his actions? *(Bush wanted to prove his willingness to go to any lengths to balance the*

---

mounting national deficits. (A deficit is a shortage in the amount of tax money that the government makes each year in order to pay its expenses. The government creates a deficit when it spends more money than it makes in one year.) The inability of Congress and the White House to harness big spending led Bush to make the most disastrous decision of his career. Democratic leaders in Congress promised to cut spending if he would accept a large tax increase. So Bush abandoned his campaign pledge of "no new taxes." **The 1990 budget deal** did not tame the deficit, but it did ruin Bush's credibility.

Continued government spending, new taxes, and the high cost of regulations helped bring an end to the "Reagan Revolution." Even though the country enjoyed low interest rates, low inflation, and low gas prices, a recession gripped America (and the rest of the world). While Bush focused on foreign diplomacy after the breakup of the Soviet Union, Americans wanted action to help the slow economy at home. Not until his State of the Union Address in January of the election year did Bush outline his domestic policy. Although he borrowed many proposals from conservatives, his past practices did not match

his new talk. His re-election campaign blamed Congress for the country's troubles and asked Americans to kick the Democrats out so that the Republicans could have a chance. He defended "family values" and attacked the character and "tax-and-spend" policies of his Democratic opponent, Bill Clinton. But voters did not listen to him.

SECTION REVIEW

1. What historical record was set with Bush's election?
2. Where did Chinese students hold a major protest? What was Bush's response to the demonstration?
3. What action caused the United States to declare war on Iraq?
4. Congressional scandals led to public support for laws that would do what?
5. The Los Angeles riots were in response to a trial surrounding the beating of what black motorist?

 Some conservatives argued that Bush did more harm than good to the cause of conservatives. Why would they say this?

SUMMARY

The United States entered its third century carrying a heavy load. The Watergate scandal had left the presidency weak. Growing national debt and inflation threatened the economy. The communists made advances in Southeast Asia and Latin America, and terrorists stalked the Middle East. But the election of Ronald Reagan marked the beginning of a new era of hope for America. While struggles continued between liberals and conservatives, it appeared that traditional values might take new root in America soil.

perhaps hardest hit by the looting. The government slowly escalated its response: a city police tactical alert, a complete mobilization of six thousand police officers, a call of the National Guard, and finally an entry of federal troops.

Rodney King—Second Trial
The nation watched with concern the outcome of the new trial promised by President Bush. The American Civil Liberties Union opposed the retrial because it seemed to be an unconstitutional double jeopardy. This time the local, state, and federal governments made extensive plans to quell possible new riots. On April 18, 1993, the verdict returned with two officers innocent and two guilty (Sgt. Stacey Koon and Officer Laurence Powell). No one seemed satisfied, but no further rioting occurred.

Skewed Justice?
An ironic twist in the Rodney King case occurred a few months later in the trial of two black men who had severely beaten a white truck driver during the Los Angeles riots. Although a news camera videotaped the gruesome scene, the jury said the men were not guilty of attempted murder or aggravated mayhem. Instead, they were convicted on minor charges.

Iran-Contra Conclusion
One of Bush's last acts in office was to pardon several government officials involved in the Iran-Contra affair. The charge against most of them was that they had withheld information or otherwise obstructed the congressional investigation. Former secretary of defense Caspar Weinberger was one of the highest profiled to receive a pardon. His pardon was controversial to some, even though he had not been proved guilty of any crime.

621

budget, and he hoped that Americans would understand that the nature of the economic emergency justified his broken pledge. It appears he even thought he was being courageous and self-sacrificing in the interests of the public good. But his lack of devotion to principle and his lack of understanding about human nature and government blinded him to the unwillingness of liberals to restrain spending. His pragmatism allowed him to sacrifice his word for immediate ends.)

The Bush administration taught a hard lesson about the dangers of electing an

unprincipled pragmatist as president. Ask the students whether they think it would have been better for Republicans to nominate a conservative, even if he had lost the 1988 election. Even today Christians debate the merits of electing an "electable" candidate as opposed to a principled candidate.

Section Review Answers
1. first vice president since 1836 to be elected to replace the president under whom he served (p. 616)
2. Beijing's Tiananmen Square; he refused to take any action and even re-

newed China's "most-favored-nation" trade status (p. 617)
3. Iraq's invasion of Kuwait (p. 617)
4. limit congressional terms (p. 619)
5. Rodney King (p. 620)

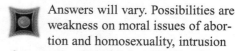 Answers will vary. Possibilities are weakness on moral issues of abortion and homosexuality, intrusion of government into business and education, and failure to keep his promise of no new taxes.

Chapter Review Ideas

Student Activity B: Lessons from Bad News

This is a good opportunity for students to evaluate the "bad news" of the 1970s and the "good news" of the 1980s. Americans proved that they can learn from their mistakes. You will probably need to make this a class activity.

Student Activity C: Presidents After Nixon

This activity reminds students of the key events during the four administrations after Nixon's resignation.

Chapter Review

People, Places, and Things to Remember

Bicentennial	supply-side economics	Persian Gulf War
Jimmy Carter	Sandra Day O'Connor	term limits
amnesty	William H. Rehnquist	Americans with
deregulation	Star Wars	Disabilities Act
Three Mile Island	Mikhail Gorbachev	unfunded federal mandates
Panama Canal Treaty	Muammar Qaddafi	dates
Camp David Accords	Sandinistas	Los Angeles riots
Ayatollah Khomeini	Contras	1990 budget deal
Iranian hostage crisis	George Bush	
Ronald Reagan	Saddam Hussein	

Review Questions

Answer these questions.

1. What two bicentennial celebrations did America have during the 1970s and 1980s?

2. What was President Carter's greatest foreign relations triumph?

3. What two groups were fighting against each other in Nicaragua in the 1980s?

4. Who was the first woman appointed to the Supreme Court?

5. What was the most significant domestic crisis during the Bush administration?

Match these men with their descriptions.

6. Mikhail Gorbachev   a. Iranian Muslim ruler

7. Saddam Hussein   b. Libyan leader

8. Ayatollah Khomeini   c. Soviet leader

9. Muammar Qaddafi   d. Iraqi leader

10. William Rehnquist   e. chief justice appointed by Reagan

Indicate whether each of the following items is most closely associated with (A) President Ford, (B) President Carter, (C) President Reagan, or (D) President Bush.

11. pardon of Richard Nixon

12. Persian Gulf War

13. supply-side economics

14. Grenada invasion

15. Iranian hostage crisis

Questions for Discussion

16. Compare and contrast Reagan and Bush.

17. Should the United States have become involved in the Persian Gulf War? Would it have been better to remove Saddam Hussein from power?

Chapter Review Answers

1. Declaration of Independence, Constitution (p. 604)

2. Camp David Accords (p. 609)

3. Sandinistas and Contras (pp. 614-15)

4. Sandra Day O'Connor (p. 612)

5. the Los Angeles riots (p. 620)

6. c (p. 614)

7. d (p. 617)

8. a (p. 610)

9. b (p. 614)

10. e (p. 612)

11. A (p. 605)

12. D (p. 617)

13. C (p. 612)

14. C (p. 614)

15. B (p. 610)

16. Answers will vary. Both could claim foreign policy triumphs, though Bush gave too much control to the UN in the Gulf War. In domestic affairs, Reagan wanted less government involvement while Bush's policies tended to promote more.

17. Answers will vary.

Additional Thought Questions

1. How do you think history books will describe the Bush administration fifty years from now?

2. Is it fair to lump Reagan and Bush together in a period called the "Reagan-Bush years"?

30

Bridge to the 21st Century

Stealth Fighter
F-117 Nighthawks, popularly known as stealth fighters, first saw action in the Persian Gulf War in 1991. Their advanced antiradar technology heralded a new era in warfare.

Chapter Motivation
In this chapter your students should see that several themes from history are resurfacing. Ask the students to look for problems in the republic that have arisen as politicians have tampered with the Constitution.

Materials

SECTION 1
- Activities A and B from Chapter 30 of the *Student Activities* manual

SECTION 2
- No materials

SECTION 3
- Activities C and D from Chapter 30 of the *Student Activities* manual
- Bibles

SECTION 4
- No materials

SECTION 5
- Special speaker: an expert on computer technology

Americans were expecting a rosy future after the death of communism in Europe. Yet the next few years severely tested the nation's ability to adjust to the new world. As events unfolded, Americans worried that moral corruption was eating away at the heart of the republic, posing a greater threat to the country than Soviet tanks ever had.

A New Face in Washington

The year 1992 came during a period of great transition in America. The Cold War had just ended. Around the world, socialists were in full retreat. Americans finally saw the failure of Franklin D. Roosevelt's New Deal and Lyndon B. Johnson's War on Poverty. These ideas now looked dated and unsuited for the challenges of the twenty-first century.

The 1992 Election

The Democratic Party began searching for a way to break the party's liberal image after Ronald Reagan's landslide victories. Governor Bill Clinton of Arkansas and other young Democrats met to discuss new ideas in a forum called the **Democratic Leadership Council.** They got an opportunity to test their ideas in the election of 1992 when it became

623

CHAPTER 30	Lesson Plan Chart		
Section Title	Main Activity	Pages	Time Frame
1. A New Face in Washington	Does Character Matter?	623-28	1 day
2. The Republican Revolution of 1994	Can Congress Lead a Revolution?	628-30	½ day
3. Culture Wars	Student Activity C: What God Says About Modern Issues	630-33	½ day
4. Confronting Society's Problems	Could You Do Any Better?	634-35	½ day
5. Clinton's Trials	Failure of the Constitution?	635-39	½-1 day
6. Foreign Policy in the 21st Century	Debate Isolationism and Interventionism	639-44	1-1½ days
Total Suggested Days (including 1 day for review and testing)		5-6 days	

SECTION 1

Materials

- Activities A and B from Chapter 30 of the *Student Activities* manual

Student Activity A: Current Events

This activity asks the students to find articles on eleven topics discussed in this chapter and to write a summary of the articles. You can assign any number that you wish the students to find. You might

SECTION 6
• World map
• List of arguments for isolation-
ism and interventionism

SECTION 1

Objectives

Students should be able to
1. Identify the Democrats'
strategy for the election of
1992.
2. Explain how Clinton used
his mandate to change
social policy.
3. Name the major contro-
versies of Clinton's first
term in office.

Promises, Promises

As part of his "New Covenant,"
President Clinton wanted to reform
government ethics, reduce the
deficit, increase government "investments" in job programs, reform the health care system,
improve welfare, and make abortions free and rare.

Clinton's Nominees

The first lesbian ever confirmed by
the Senate was Clinton appointee
Roberta Achtenberg, an outspoken homosexual activist. She once
tried to force Boy Scouts in San
Francisco to approve homosexual
scoutmasters. Her job as assistant
secretary in the Department of
Housing and Urban Development
was to ensure fair housing and
equal opportunity.

Other Clinton nominees had legal
problems. Zoë Baird, a female appointee for attorney general, had
hired illegal aliens and not paid
Social Security taxes for them.
Kimba Wood, Clinton's second
choice for the position, turned out
to have similar problems. Ron
Brown, his black appointee for
commerce secretary, eventually
got the position but only after he
faced accusations of receiving
bribes from the government of
Vietnam. Controversies over other
nominations plagued Clinton over
the next four years.

obvious that the "Reagan Revolution" had fallen apart under George Bush.

Bill Clinton won the Democratic Party's nomination in spite of incredible obstacles, including accusations of adultery, marijuana use, and draft dodging. Clinton hammered away at Bush's domestic policies, hoping to

Ross Perot (on the right) charmed audiences with his folksy humor during the three-way debates of the 1992 election.

draw attention away from his foreign suc-
cesses. Daily the media reported the latest bad economic news. Clinton's campaign headquarters boldly stated his message: "It's the economy, stupid." He successfully portrayed

himself as a moderate "New Democrat" who wanted to change America.

Conservatives, led by columnist Pat Buchanan, also attacked Bush's mixed record. Bush apologized for breaking his "no new taxes" pledge in 1990, promising to fight taxes in the future. But he never convinced voters of his sincerity. Suspicious of both major candidates' promises to cut spending, a billionaire named **Ross Perot** entered the race as an independent candidate. He promised drastic measures to wipe out the deficit. Many voters turned to this outsider, who even took the lead temporarily in opinion polls.

On election day, Clinton won by a large margin in the electoral college (370 to 168), but he lacked deep support. Ross Perot gained the largest number of third-candidate votes since Teddy Roosevelt in 1912. Democrats won no seats in the Senate, and they lost nine in the House. Also, Clinton failed to attract a majority of the popular vote (43% Clinton, 37% Bush, 19% Perot). Democrats credited their win to Clinton's campaign skills and the country's anger against the "failed trickle-down policies of the 1980s"; Republicans blamed a weak economy, bad press, and Bush.

Controversial Nominations

Like his idol, John F. Kennedy, President Bill Clinton began his administration with grand (and sometimes contradictory) dreams, which he called a "New Covenant" with the American people. But like JFK, Clinton found himself mired in controversy and unable to push his programs through Congress.

Once elected, Bill Clinton had to choose between old liberal ideas or the new ideas of the Democratic Leadership Council. Clinton quickly made his decision. He decided to work with the old liberal establishment, and he began by nominating controversial liberals to government posts. Clinton said he wanted to

624

have them share their articles as you study those topics in the chapter.

Compare Intraparty Conflicts During Recent Elections

Point out some of the issues during the most recent election and show how they are a continuation of issues raised by the Democratic Leadership Council during the 1992 election. Note how both major parties are divided on the best way to define themselves. The debate concerns the level of government intervention in social issues

(such as abortion) and economic issues (such as welfare).

Does Character Matter?

Ask the question that was raised during the 1992 election: "Does character matter?" Why would anyone say no? This is a fool-
ish question, and the students need to be able to explain why. The Bible teaches that all our actions are a product of our inner character (Prov. 4:23). A man who violates his sacred marriage vows is likely to violate his vows as president. Share with your class

recent examples of presidents who claim that their private life is their own business.

Use the profile list that the students devel-
oped while studying the previous chapter to check whether President Clinton has the character qualities that make a good president.

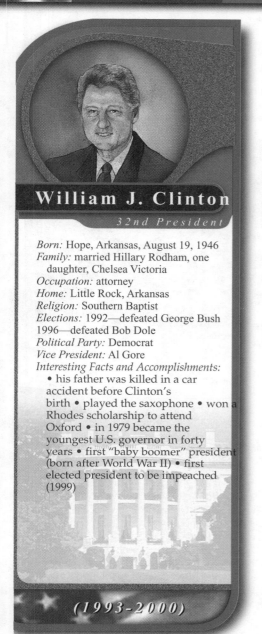

William J. Clinton

32nd President

Born: Hope, Arkansas, August 19, 1946
Family: married Hillary Rodham, one
   daughter, Chelsea Victoria
Occupation: attorney
Home: Little Rock, Arkansas
Religion: Southern Baptist
Elections: 1992—defeated George Bush
   1996—defeated Bob Dole
Political Party: Democrat
Vice President: Al Gore
Interesting Facts and Accomplishments:
   • his father was killed in a car
   accident before Clinton's
   birth • played the saxophone • won a
   Rhodes scholarship to attend
   Oxford • in 1979 became the
   youngest U.S. governor in forty
   years • first "baby boomer" president
   (born after World War II) • first
   elected president to be impeached
   (1999)

(1993–2000)

create a diverse cabinet of women and minorities that reflected the mix in American society. But his liberal appointments contradicted this description. The only moderate in the cabinet was his treasury secretary.

Along with his efforts to include minorities and women in government, Clinton promised "to make a real effort to include in my administration members of the gay and lesbian community." In the first year he appointed almost thirty open homosexuals to key posts. Controversy over these and other nominations plagued Clinton throughout his first term in office.

Controversial New Social Policies

Clinton claimed that the 1992 election gave him a mandate (a command by the people) for change. However, his first acts as president were to promote social change, not economic change, and these acts caused an uproar that would not die down. Two days after assuming office he removed several limits that Reagan had placed on how government money was used to pay for abortions. Days later he kept a campaign promise to end a ban on homosexuals in the military. Such actions angered conservatives and distracted attention from his efforts to help the economy.

All of Clinton's cabinet members supported liberal social policies. His health secretary Donna Shalala was a prime example. One of her first actions was to push "children's rights." These so-called rights are laid out in the **UN Convention on the Rights of the Child,** a treaty passed in 1989 but never signed by the United States. It grants every child freedom of religion, freedom of association, the right to family planning (including abortion), the right to use his own language, and the right to have "rest and leisure." The administration made an intense effort to get the Senate to sign, but conservative Senators defeated this threat to the authority of parents.

625

UN Convention on the Rights of the Child

The UN Convention on the Rights of the Child is easily accessible on the Internet. Read some of the provisions and discuss them with your class so that they understand the dangers of children's rights. Of particular interest are the freedom of speech (Article 12), the right to receive information of all kinds through any media of the child's choice (13), freedom of conscience and religion (14), freedom of association (15), the right to privacy (16), the right to family planning (24), the right to use his own language (30), and the right to have "rest and leisure" (31). Note that Article 19 could be used to take children away from Christian parents if spankings are considered "physical violence" and preaching about sin and hell is considered "mental violence." God has given parents, not the government, the duty of raising children to fear God (Eph. 6:4).

Ruby Ridge Debacle

The attack on the Waco compound was the culmination of a growing problem—the creation of new "federal crimes" that were once the concern of the states. "Federalizing" crimes began with Prohibition. By 1990, over fifty federal agencies and commissions had been granted the right to carry weapons and make arrests. Among the biggest were the Drug Enforcement Agency, the Environmental Protection Agency, and the ATF. By harassing and sometimes entrapping innocent citizens, these agencies aroused suspicions that they were part of a liberal "conspiracy" to undermine the Bill of Rights, especially the Second Amendment, which says that gun ownership is "necessary to the security of a *free* state."

Before the Waco disaster, a very disturbing incident occurred at a cabin on Ruby Ridge in northern Idaho. The ATF entrapped and besieged alleged white supremacist Randy Weaver in 1992. U.S. marshals first shot his fourteen-year-old son in the back and killed him; then they shot his unarmed wife in the head while she was standing at the door of their cabin holding her ten-month-old baby. A jury later found Weaver not guilty for killing a federal marshal during the siege.

Propornography Justice Department

The Clinton administration sought to change the way that federal prosecutors could deal with obscenity and child pornography cases. First, it sought a ruling from the Supreme Court that prosecutors must prove that the defendant knew the minority status of video performers (*United States v. XCitement Video*). In addition, it wanted prosecutors to have to prove not only that the photographer had pornographic intent, but also that the children themselves were "lasciviously engaged in sexual conduct" (*United States v. Knox*). Clyde DeWitt, a defense attorney for pornographers, wrote in *Adult Video News,* "The voice of

The leading cheerleader for the president's social policies was his surgeon general, Dr. Joycelyn Elders. She was well known for her support of homosexuals and her attack on what she called the pro-life "love affair with the fetus." Elders used her office to promote controversial views, such as sex education beginning in kindergarten. In 1993 she even suggested that the government consider legalizing drugs to reduce violent crime. The president later fired Elders when her public statements became too embarrassing.

Clinton made two other appointments in his first year that showed his liberal priorities. The first was a feminist on the Supreme Court named Ruth Ginsburg, who opposed all limits on abortion. The second appointment was his attorney general, **Janet Reno,** the first woman ever to head the Justice Department. She believed crime could be solved if the government would help children to grow up in a good environment. In her view, the "war on crime" should emphasize social programs that prevent people from becoming criminals.

After taking office, Reno showed her liberal colors. Her first priority was to clamp down on pro-life sit-ins at abortion clinics. With her backing, Democrats in Congress passed the **Freedom of Access to Clinic Entrances** (FACE) law, making most abortion protests a federal crime.

A new controversy erupted soon after Reno's appointment. On February 28, 1993, the Bureau of Alcohol, Tobacco, and Firearms (ATF) raided a seventy-seven-acre compound in Waco, Texas, because it believed cult leader **David Koresh** was stockpiling illegal arms. The poorly organized raid failed, leaving four

agents dead. After a fifty-one-day standoff, Reno ordered tanks to break into the compound and spread tear gas. The compound went up in flames, killing Koresh and seventy-two of his followers. Conservatives ridiculed the handling of the initial raid and Reno's

The compound of cult leader David Koresh went up in flames when federal officials tried to force their way in.

decision to force a violent end to the standoff. Bitter over the ATF's actions, a radical named Timothy McVeigh marked the second anniversary of Koresh's death by bombing a federal office building in Oklahoma City. The huge blast killed 168 people.

Controversial New Programs

With Democrats controlling the White House and both houses of Congress, Clinton declared "an end to the deadlock and drift and a new season of American renewal." During the election, Clinton had set three priorities for the first one hundred days of his administration. First, he wanted a new budget that slashed spending and raised taxes only on the rich. Second, he wanted to reform welfare so

Discuss the Wisdom of Federal Crimes

Discuss the wisdom of making so many crimes a federal issue rather than a state issue. The Founders feared a powerful "police state" run by the central government because of the potential for abuse. The temptation for politicians to act "tough on crime" is another instance of Americans' willingness to surrender liberty in return for greater security.

that people went back to work after two years. Third, he wanted to reform the health care system to stop spiraling prices and to guarantee insurance for everyone. Clinton also made many side promises.

Higher Taxes—By the time of his inauguration, Clinton had already begun to backpedal on his pledges. When he finally presented his first budget, it called for new government programs, higher taxes for everyone, and few spending cuts (except in the military). Clinton proposed a record-breaking $496 billion increase in taxes. The budget barely passed Congress without a single Republican vote. This "deficit-reduction" plan did not reduce anything except the rate of growth of the national deficit. Government spending, along with taxes, grew significantly. Nevertheless, the president claimed a victory and moved on.

Bigger Government—During the election, Clinton preached against waste and inefficiency in government. But regulations grew rapidly under his leadership. Immediately after taking office, Clinton signed a backlog of big-government legislation that past Republican presidents had vetoed. The Family and Medical Leave Act forced businesses to give employees twelve weeks of unpaid leave to care for newborn babies or seriously ill family members. Another intrusive law was the Brady Bill. States had to complete background checks before customers could buy guns.

Clinton also took up the banner of the environmentalists. His secretary of the interior imposed stiff restrictions on the use of government lands in the West. To protect the threatened spotted owl in the Pacific Northwest, Clinton held a Forest Conference "to build a consensus on a balanced policy to preserve jobs and to protect the environ-ment." His compromise literally shut down logging in federal forests, and thirty thousand loggers lost their jobs.

Clinton kept one of his most popular campaign pledges, designed to promote community service. Similar to Kennedy's Peace Corps, **AmeriCorps** offered federal money to stu-

Over one hundred thousand young people have served their communities through AmeriCorps.

dents who wished to work off their school bills through community service. In return for two years of full-time work, volunteers received $14,800 in living expenses, a $9,500 credit toward higher education, and free health care and child care benefits. Their hourly wage, excluding benefits, was $7.27. AmeriCorps "brought the taxpayer the $30,000 'volunteer,'" complained one senator.

Health-Care Disaster—The issue that proved to be the supreme test of President Clinton's ability to pass a liberal agenda was health-care reform. He set his wife, **Hillary Rodham Clinton,** over a task force to develop a plan. In November 1993 he introduced her massive 1,342-page plan to Congress.

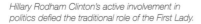

Hillary Rodham Clinton's active involvement in politics defied the traditional role of the First Lady.

reason has found its way into government."

During Clinton's time in office, fewer pornographers were convicted of crimes. Only six criminal cases in 1996 involved obscenity violations, as opposed to seventy-eight in 1989 under George Bush.

Dark Side of the Health Care Plan

Under the Clinton health care plan, one-seventh of American businesses would come under government supervision. In addition, all Americans would be required to pay insurance premiums that would cover abortions.

Republican Alternatives

Conservatives offered alternative "free-market" plans, such as tax breaks for employees or tax-free savings accounts to cover medical expenses.

Drug Policy

President Clinton showed little concern for the war on drugs in his first two years in office. The director of the Office of the National Drug Control Policy (the drug czar) had his staff reduced from 146 to 25, and over a thousand members of military units devoted to antidrug activities lost their jobs. Ranking Democratic representative Charles Rangel of New York observed that he had "never, never, never seen a president who cares less about this issue."

Reaching Out to Atheists

The Clinton administration hosted perhaps the first formal White House meeting with an organized atheist group. The atheists expressed concerns about civil rights "violations" against nonbelievers. For instance, some places restrict atheists from becoming notary publics or from taking public office, and the Boy Scouts require a statement of faith in God. Ron Barrier of American Atheists said, "Hopefully this will open up lines of communication between the atheist community and this administration and any subsequent administration."

Student Activity B: How Clinton Lost the Health Care Debate

This activity tests the students' ability to find logical fallacies. It also gives them a concrete example of the dishonesty that led to Clinton's downfall.

SECTION 2

Objectives
Students should be able to
1. Identify Newt Gingrich and describe the Contract with America.
2. Identify the budget battle that shut down the government.
3. Analyze the effectiveness of the "Republican Revolution."

Election Overturn
As a result of the 1994 elections, Republican governors headed eight of the nine largest states. (Florida was the only exception.) One of the most closely watched shifts in American politics was the breakdown of the Democrats' "Solid South." For the first time since Reconstruction, Southerners elected a majority of Republicans to the U.S. Congress.

Gingrich's Third Wave
After the 1994 election earthquake, the media and the public scrambled to find out who Gingrich, the little-known Speaker of the House, was and what he was after. He explained to reporters that he planned to run a "third-wave, world-market-and-opportunity-oriented" House. In opening ceremonies of the new Congress, the former history professor gave his colleagues a list of books to read that explained his views.

The book that revealed the most about Gingrich was *Creating a New Civilization: The Politics of the Third Wave* by Alvin and Heidi Toffler. It claims that human history has gone through three revolutions—the flourishing of agriculture, the Industrial Revolution, and the modern information revolution. As futurists, the Tofflers assert that the old order is decaying and that we must revolutionize world government to succeed in the "new

At first Americans were attracted by the promises of making insurance available to everyone at low costs. By January 1994, however, the national mood had shifted. The economy was booming, and the annual rise in medical costs had fallen. Support waned as taxpayers began to see how Clinton's plan would create a huge program, eventually costing more than Social Security.

In spite of growing opposition, the president refused to compromise. In the end no measures came to the floor for a vote.

SECTION REVIEW

1. What independent candidate won wide support during the 1992 election?

2. What did Clinton indicate would be his priority if elected?

3. List four women whom Clinton nominated for high office and their positions.

4. Who led President Clinton's task force on health care reform?

 What are the advantages and disadvantages of having health care paid for by the government?

The Republican Revolution of 1994

Clinton faced many problems in his first two years, but voters were most upset by his failure to meet his goals. Smoking and drug use were on the rise. Crime became so bad that it moved ahead of the economy as Americans' greatest concern. The country wanted action.

Contract with America
An outspoken Republican in the House named **Newt Gingrich** came up with a plan that he hoped would help his party win big in the 1994 midterm elections. Republicans in the House joined together to sign a **Contract with America,** promising to bring up ten pop-

Newt Gingrich, the first Republican Speaker of the House in forty years, actively sought support for his revolutionary ideas.

ular bills for a vote—if elected—in the first 100 days of the next Congress.

As the numbers came in on election night, analysts were astounded by the clear rebuff of the president. For the first time in forty years, voters handed control of the House over to the Republicans, by a comfortable margin of 230-204 (with one independent). The GOP also won control of the Senate (52-48) and most governorships.

First Hundred Days of the 104th Congress
The newly elected Republicans knew that voters wanted results. Gingrich, who was elected Speaker of the House, moved quickly to put his supporters in positions of power. By overlooking senior congressmen, he proved his dedication to renew Congress and to push through his conservative program.

Bob Dole, who became the majority leader in the Senate, was less dedicated to change. Like his colleagues in the Senate, Dole had not signed the Contract with

628

America, and he did not feel obligated to support it.

Realizing that his first actions would set the tone of the next two years, Gingrich began fulfilling the Contract on the very first day. In addition to the ten bills that it promised to bring up for a vote in the first hundred days, the Contract promised eight reforms in the way the House ran. After working fourteen hours on the first day, congressmen passed all eight of them. For example, one reform required Congress to obey the regulations that it had imposed on the rest of the nation.

The remainder of the first hundred days was no less hectic. Every one of the promised bills was brought to the floor for a vote. The three most important bills would have radically changed the balance of power established by the Constitution. Two were amendments to the Constitution. The **balanced budget amendment** would make Congress balance the budget by the year 2002, and the term limits amendment would limit congressmen to twelve years of office in each house of Congress. The third major bill instituted the **line-item veto.** It gave the president the right to cut individual items in the federal budget without approval from Congress.

The energy with which the House pushed the Contract was impressive. The line-item veto passed the House and Senate with ease. Term limits got a majority of votes, but not the two-thirds it needed. The balanced budget amendment passed in the House but failed in the Senate by only one vote. All of the other bills in the Contract passed the House in some form.

Budget Battles

The initial success of the House was mostly symbolic. The legislation still had to go to the Senate and receive the president's signature. The only bill that had become law was a restriction on future unfunded mandates. The greatest test of the Republican Congress was

its effort to prepare a serious plan to balance the budget. Gingrich acknowledged that every other issue was secondary to his primary goal—to balance the budget by the year 2002.

The Uncompromising Freshman Class—The Republicans had no illusions about the battles that lay ahead. In the face of hostile media attacks, they would have to convince Americans to accept large cuts in government benefits and services. Yet the seventy-three members of the House freshman class felt up to the challenge.

In February 1995 the president unveiled a $1.6 trillion budget that—even Democratic leaders conceded—failed to make the tough choices needed to stop the rising deficit. To the world's amazement, the House drafted an alternative plan that would really balance the budget. As anticipated, Democrats condemned the Republicans as "extremists" who wanted to balance the budget on the backs of the aged and poor.

Two Train Wrecks—As the Republican spending bills (thirteen in all) began moving through Congress, Clinton started vetoing them. As the summer wore on without a budget agreement, the nation prepared for a "train wreck," or a **government shutdown.** Under the Constitution, the federal government can spend money only when Congress has approved it by law. If the government failed to pay its debts, it would wreak havoc on world finances. Both the president and Congress hoped that the other side would accept a compromise before the shutdown.

Despite the pressure, House freshmen would not give in. Either the president would accept a real balanced budget, or he would get no budget at all. As the train wreck loomed in November 1995, the Senate leaders flinched. They passed a "continuing resolution" that would keep the government running under the old budget. But the House demanded some cuts first, and the president vetoed the resolution. As a result, all "nonessential" government

629

age." They claim that even the American Constitution is outdated: "The system of government you fashioned, including the very principles on which you based it, is increasingly obsolete. . . . It must be radically changed and a new system of government invented—a democracy for the twenty-first century." The Tofflers also advocate a new moral order, including polygamy and group marriage.

The Speaker's futurism helps to explain why so many people considered him bombastic and arrogant. Throughout his tenure, Gingrich had the lowest popularity ratings on record. Traditional conservatives feared that their leader might become an albatross around their necks.

House Reforms
These are the eight reforms that the 104th Congress passed on its first day:

1. Require Congress to obey the laws and regulations that it has imposed on the rest of the nation.
2. Hire an independent auditor to uncover waste, fraud, or abuse in Congress.
3. Cut committee staffs by one-third and eliminate three full committees and twenty-five subcommittees.
4. Limit the terms of committee chairmen to six years; limit the term of the Speaker to eight years.
5. Ban proxy votes by absent committee members.
6. Open committee meetings to the public.
7. Require a three-fifths majority to increase taxes.
8. Use honest budget figures that do not adjust for inflation (zero base-line budgeting).

Conservatives and Neo-Conservatives

Ask students to define a conservative. *(One possibility: "A person who opposes change and who wants to conserve the best elements of the past.")* Find evidence that Gingrich was a "neo-conservative," not a conservative in the traditional sense of the word. (See margin note on pages 628-29.) He called for three drastic changes in the Constitution. Discuss the potential dangers of each one of these changes for the separation of powers.

Another sign of a "neo-conservative" is his desire to keep government programs but to use them for conservative ends. For example, a neo-conservative continues to give money to states for welfare and education, but he wants to give the states more freedom in the use of the money.

 Can Congress Lead a Revolution?

Throughout this chapter, ask the students to recall parallels from U.S. history to help them to understand the dynamics of recent events. Can they think of other

times that Congress and the president were at odds over the future direction of the country? Was Congress ever able to overcome presidential opposition and take control of the direction of the nation? *(Consider the Radical Republicans of the late 1860s, who eventually won a two-thirds majority in Congress because of Johnson's obstinacy. In Clinton's case, however, Republicans had a bare majority, and Clinton made every effort to avoid appearing obstinate.)*

SECTION 3

Objectives

Students should be able to

1. Compare the moral decay of the twenties to that of the nineties.
2. List liberal, conservative, and religious solutions to moral decay.
3. Evaluate the culture wars based on God's Word.

Pro-euthanasia Justice Department?

In 1998 Attorney General Janet Reno removed the last federal obstacle to physician-assisted suicide in Oregon, where a state referendum in 1994 had legalized the practice. The Justice Department decided not to prosecute doctors who prescribe or provide lethal doses of drugs. In doing so, Reno overruled the Drug Enforcement Agency, which had determined that doctors who help suicides could be prosecuted under the federal Controlled Substances Act.

The Bible on Euthanasia

The Bible is clear that active euthanasia is wrong. Even its supporters see the potential for abuse. Dr. Jack Kevorkian's fifteenth "patient" pleaded with him to remove the mask supplying carbon monoxide. As a pathologist, Kevorkian is not qualified to deal with psychological problems and depression. Legalized euthanasia puts pressure on patients who may not want to be financial burdens. Easy death diminishes respect for the dignity of human life. Guidelines for legal euthanasia also fail to acknowledge that patients sometimes recover from "terminal" conditions.

Consider the following biblical principles regarding euthanasia. God expects people to choose life, not death (Deut. 30:19). God made man in His image; therefore, to take the life of an innocent person is a capital offense (Gen. 9:6). God intentionally uses trials to teach patience (Rom. 5:3; James 1:3). The desire to eliminate a

services, such as parks, shut down. For six days the treasury department juggled money to keep the government paying its bills, but it could not keep up for long.

The House finally agreed to a compromise, but not until the president signed a pledge to seek a serious balanced budget in seven years. But the president's next budget proved to be another sham. When the House rejected Clinton's budget, the government shut down again just before Christmas. Again the Senate, led by Republican Bob Dole, caved in. Outmaneuvered by moderates in their own party, Republicans in the House gave up. The Republican "revolution" never recovered from this blow. Republicans needed a Republican president to sign their revolution into law.

The Resignation of Newt Gingrich—Republican leaders took many hits from Democrats. House Speaker Newt Gingrich came under fire when he signed a $4.5-million book deal with a company that stood to benefit from a bill under debate in the House. Democrats also accused Gingrich of improperly using tax-deductible money to fund a college course he taught. The attacks weakened Gingrich's power as speaker. After the Republicans did poorly in the 1998 midterm elections, Gingrich stepped down, and no charismatic leaders rose up to take his place.

SECTION REVIEW

1. What did the Contract with America promise?

2. What were the three most important bills of the Contract? Name one that passed both the House and the Senate.

3. What was the result of the standoff between the House and Clinton over the budget?

 Why does the federal debt tend to grow, and why is reducing it so difficult?

630

Culture Wars

While politicians were arguing over balanced budgets and taxes, another set of issues was moving to the forefront of national concerns. For the first time since the Roaring Twenties, the economy was booming and the country faced no major foreign threats. Polls showed that the nation's concerns had shifted from the economy and foreign affairs to social issues, such as welfare reform, education standards, and juvenile crime.

Recognition of Moral Decline

Lifestyles changed rapidly in America during the Nineties. People had more time and money for play and recreation. Modern technology provided novel ways to fill time. Computers, compact discs, and cellular phones were commonplace by the end of the decade. Yet evidence was mounting that something was missing.

The decline in America's "traditional values" became a topic of national debate after Vice President Dan Quayle gave his famous "Murphy Brown speech" during the 1992 election campaign. In that speech, he blamed America's woes on its moral decline, symbolized by the television sitcom Murphy Brown, which glorified unwed mothers. At the time, the liberal media scoffed at him. But Americans started to reconsider their views.

Most Americans are pragmatists who care whether a system works, not about the philosophy behind it. Taxpayers could tolerate spending of their money on noble programs; however, they became angry when the programs did not work. Democrats had spent $3.5 trillion of taxpayers' money in their war on poverty, while the poor had grown poorer. Americans, who had spent 2 percent of their income on federal taxes in 1960, now spent 24 percent. "We're getting a very bad buy for our money," Gingrich concluded, and Americans seemed to agree.

Section Review Answers

1. to bring up ten popular bills for a vote in the first one hundred days of the next Congress (p. 628)

2. balanced budget amendment, term limits amendment, line-item veto; line-item veto (p. 629)

3. The Republicans gave up on their stringent demands. (p. 630)

 Once a program starts providing benefits, people demand more and more. Few people willingly give

up benefits they get for "free" from the government. (pp. 629-30)

SECTION 3

Materials

- Activities C and D from Chapter 30 of the *Student Activities* manual

- Bibles

 Student Activity C: What God Says About Modern Issues

This activity shows the students that the Bible is relevant to modern issues. In particular, it shows that mankind cannot solve its own problems without God and that the modern understanding of human rights does not match God's description of human rights and responsibilities.

Even the liberals acknowledged that thirty years of government spending had not produced the kind of country they had hoped for. Crime and poverty were up. Rap and rock music were increasingly violent. Television lost all sense of modesty. In 1993 two influential articles in the Atlantic Monthly and the Wall Street Journal blamed illegitimate births for ruining America. The percentage of illegitimate births had risen from 5 percent in 1960 to over 26 percent in 1990, and the numbers

The nation was shocked by the random violence on April 20, 1999, when two teens gunned down twelve fellow students and a teacher at Columbine High School in Littleton, Colorado.

kept getting worse. The articles argued that the breakup of the family led to most other social ills, such as poverty, crime, drugs, and even homelessness.

Proposed Solutions to Moral Decay

Now that everyone agreed about the existence of a problem, the debate shifted to understanding its cause and finding a solution.

Liberal Solutions—Many liberals, including Bill Clinton, sounded almost conservative in their proposals. They talked about the importance of "family," "community," and "traditional values." First lady Hillary Rodham Clinton even published a book on child rearing entitled *It Takes a Village*. The title was taken from an old African proverb, "It takes a village to raise a child." But her views were, in fact, anything but conservative. **Communitarians** hold the old socialist idea that the whole community shares responsibility for the lives of its members. "How dare you believe you have the right to raise your children by yourself," said a leader in the Children's Defense Fund, a children's rights organization once headed by the first lady.

Communitarians believe that the answer to the culture wars is for governments and communities to promote love and acceptance of all minority groups—whether based on religion, ethnic background, lifestyle, or "sexual orientation." In their view, society will improve when people are free to discuss their beliefs openly and to make choices without fear of disapproval.

New Right Solutions—After abortion was legalized in 1973, a faction called the **New Right** began swelling the ranks of the Republican Party. Religious people from all denominations were worried that the government was defending and promoting wickedness. The New Right was credited with helping Ronald Reagan win the 1980 election. Members of the New Right believed that families, not the government or the "community," must solve America's moral decline. Indeed, this group attacked big government as a major cause of America's problems.

A leader of the New Right was **Rush Limbaugh.** Although the liberal media branded him as an extremist, his radio show attracted twenty million listeners each week. His first book, *The Way Things Ought to Be* (1992), was the most popular nonfiction book in over ten years, selling 4.5 million copies in its first year. Rush—as his listeners called him—attracted a large audience of "pocketbook conservatives" who were tired of the government taking their money and giving nothing in return. Although he supported

financial burden is against God's plan, for life is more valuable than money (Mark 8:36-37). God often brings back a soul from the brink of death (Job 33:29-30). There is an appointed time for every person to die (Eccl. 3:1-2). And finally, it is God who holds the power of life and death (Ps. 104:29-30).

631

Biblical Perspective on Euthanasia

Discuss what the Bible says about euthanasia. Have the students look up the verses noted in the margin above. Note that states began to pass laws specifically banning physician-assisted suicide, but two federal courts overturned them in 1996. (One court struck down Washington's law using the "right to privacy" arguments that legalized abortion. Another court struck down New York's law because it is not "rationally related to any legitimate state interest.") Students must understand that God gave all governments an obligation to promote good and resist evil (Rom. 13:1-4). God does not recognize a "right" to privacy.

Discuss Parallels with the Twenties

Discuss parallels between the nineties and the Roaring Twenties. Note that evil is not a new thing, and in some ways things were worse then than they are now. *(Give several specific examples. For instance, gangs armed with machine guns are not patrolling the streets.)*

Time Travel

Have the students imagine that politicians during the 1960s could go forward in time to the 1990s to see the results of their programs. What might have happened to the War on Poverty and other programs if Congress and the president had enjoyed this opportunity?

Politicians need to make an effort to forecast the long-term results of their policies. How does knowledge of history help them to make wise forecasts? Should the politicians in the 1960s have been able to forecast the failure of their programs?

Gambling Hits the Jackpot

A key target of the religious right was gambling. Outlawed since the early 1900s, gambling made a comeback in the 1960s. Many states began to legalize—and even to run—new gambling operations. The first state lottery appeared in 1963 in New Hampshire; lotteries were established in thirty-six states by 1997. At the same time, the number of states with gambling houses (or casinos) grew from two to twenty-five. By the end of the 1990s, casinos were attracting more than double the number of people attending major-league baseball games.

Fortunately, communities began fighting back. Activists warned their friends and neighbors about the destructiveness of gambling, and they sought signatures on initiatives to limit its spread. The Christian Coalition joined the National Council of Churches in 1996 to form the National Coalition against Legalized Gambling. That same year the president signed a law establishing a commission to study the social and economic impact of gambling in America. The final report, released in 1999, suggested numerous limitations on the gambling industry and denounced many of the trends in state-sponsored gambling.

Cooperation for Reform

Since the 1940s, a large number of conservative believers have emphasized the need for Christians to become active in social reform. In the introduction to Carl Henry's *The Uneasy Conscience of Modern Fundamentalism* (1947), a leading pastor named Harold Ockenga argued, "The church needs a progressive Fundamentalism with a social message." Ockenga coined the term *New Evangelical* to describe these "progressive" believers who wished to reform America by cooperating with liberals in the church. Since then, New Evangelicals (or simply Evangelicals) have been trying to break down the walls between Roman Catholics, Protestants, and Charismatics in

some good positions, his pride, profanity, and sarcasm dismayed many Christians. He was concerned not so much with moral standards as with freedom to get rich without interference.

Solutions from the Religious Right—The conservative group that caused the most controversy was the **religious right,** comprised of various Christian leaders and organizations. This branch of the New Right believed that the country needed to return to traditional, "Judeo-Christian" values. The best-known organization in the 1970s was the Moral Majority, headed by the Rev. Jerry Falwell. The religious right receded into the background after the election of Reagan in 1980, but it gained new strength when the party began looking for Reagan's successor. Pat Robertson, the Charismatic host of television's 700 Club, campaigned for president in 1988. Although he lost, he started a grassroots movement called the **Christian Coalition.** Members became heavily involved in politics, seeking to elect conservatives to local offices and school boards. They wanted to revitalize America from the ground up.

Evaluation of the Culture Wars—Most Bible-believing Christians agree on the cause of America's problems: Americans have rejected God's truth and cannot find a substitute. But Christians do not agree on the solution to the moral crisis.

Promoting a no-nonsense conservative message, Rush Limbaugh became the most popular talk-show host in America.

Conservative Christians known as New Evangelicals believe that they need to join Roman Catholics and other Protestant groups to combat a common enemy—immorality and secular humanism. A rival group of Christians, known as Fundamentalists, offers an old-fashioned solution to society's problems. Like many of the nation's forefathers, they believe the nation's only hope is the salvation of souls by God's grace through faith in the Son of God, who shed His blood for man's sins. Fundamentalists are not seeking to restore "culture" or "tradition," which has changed throughout American history. They believe God's people should be salt and light in a sin-cursed world by proclaiming the truth of Scripture and by separating from sin (II Cor. 6:14-15).

Although most Fundamentalists believe voting is a civic duty, they oppose the view that it is their duty to join with false denominations against evil. Religious compromise harms the one institution that has the answers for America—the church. The effort of Evangelicals to influence politics has confused Americans about the true meaning of "Christian." The religious right advocates civic virtue and moral laws, whereas the Bible teaches that the letter of the law kills (II Cor. 3:6-17). Only the gospel brings life and true "liberty," as people are changed from the inside out.

Religion and Politics

Explain the impact of the new wave of immigration—newcomers from Asia and Latin America—on religious diversity in America. It is interesting to note that religious differences usually carry over into differences in political views. Help the students to identify the major religious groups in your region (and across the country), and explain the diversity of political views.

Student Activity D: Modern Conveniences in Your Home

This home survey will help the students recognize just how much their lives are dominated by modern technology.

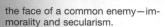

Generation X

A generation is a group of people born and living around the same time. Because they share similar experiences, members of a generation are alike in many ways. You have already read about the youth of the Roaring Twenties. You also read about the Baby Boomers, the first generation born after World War II. But what of the generation after that? The Baby Boomers received so much attention that those who came after were nearly forgotten. As Boomers aged, however, people began wondering about the next generation. What were they like? How did they live? Suddenly, everyone was talking about this unknown group. Advertisers, not knowing how to describe them, borrowed the generic term "Generation X".

Generation X is made up of Americans who were born in the 1960s and the 1970s. The members of Generation X often were home alone. Mothers worked in increasing numbers, and divorce was on the rise. These children took part-time jobs in record numbers when they reached their teen years. They also had more schooling as a group than any previous generation. But when they entered the job force, they had trouble finding really good jobs. Faced with an uncertain job market and the prospect of supporting the large, aging Baby Boomer population, many Xers grew pessimistic about the future.

Generation X looked at society differently from the way their parents had. Their lonely childhood caused a craving for relationships. Wanting to make a difference for others, many volunteered for community service. They turned away from the

pursuit of money; money was a means and not an end. At the same time, they liked the luxuries that money could buy. They lived at home longer and married later. Finally, they were the first generation to grow up with advanced technology, experiencing its blessings as well as its problems.

Most significantly, Generation X rejected absolute truth. No one could say he had the truth because truth was different for each person and situation. America became a land of diversity, not just of races and cultures but also of philosophies. Public schools taught that each new idea was acceptable. Tolerance was the theme of the day. People forgot that God's standards of right and wrong apply to everyone (Rom. 3:10-12), and the only way anyone will reach heaven is to trust in Jesus Christ alone (Acts 4:12).

Generation X enjoyed a series of activities that came to be known as extreme sports. Involving everything from skateboarding to skydiving, this new brand of sport tested the limits of human ability. Its fans saw extreme sports as a way to put adventure back into American life. But it also makes sense that people with few guidelines for their behavior and pessimism about the future would have little fear of risking their lives.

Even though you are technically not part of Generation X, maybe you can see some of its characteristics in your own generation. How would you describe your generation, and what do you think its members will be like in the future? Think about how you can reach your generation for Christ.

the face of a common enemy—immorality and secularism.

In 1994 twenty Roman Catholics and twenty Evangelical leaders signed a document asking members of the two religious groups to accept each other as Christians. "We dare not by needless and loveless conflict between ourselves give aid and comfort to the enemies of the cause of Christ," stated the twenty-five-page "Evangelicals and Catholics Together: The Christian Mission in the Third Millennium." Some of the areas where the two communities should "contend together" were the "right ordering of civil society," "religious freedom," "legal protection for the unborn," "parental choice in education," "opposition to pornography," and "anti-religious bigotry in entertainment media." Leaders included Pat Robertson, Cardinal John O'Connor of New York, and Chuck Colson, a famous Southern Baptist who heads Prison Ministries.

Section Review

1. According to communitarians, who makes sure that children are brought up right?

2. What event in 1973 gave rise to the New Right?

3. Name a leading figure of the New Right.

4. What do Fundamentalists see as the only solution to society's problems?

 Should Fundamentalists join the Christian Coalition? Explain your answer.

633

Discuss the Modern Generation

Ask the students to summarize the features of "modern culture" that differ from any period in America's past. Challenge them to explain events and trends that gave rise to these features of modern culture. *(Possible answers include the corrupting power of "pop culture" [such as MTV], the commercialization of professional sports, and the rising power of the media.)*

Your students may not realize that the modern television ratings were a direct result of the culture wars in the 1990s. Conservatives complained about sex and violence on television, and Clinton responded by supporting government oversight of the industry. In fear of losing their freedom, television executives decided to regulate themselves. Ironically, many conservatives scoffed at the value of these ratings, arguing that they would actually worsen the situation. Their warning proved true. The television producers believed that as long as they labeled the offensive elements in their programs they had no more restraints.

Section Review Answers

1. the community (p. 631)

2. legalization of abortion (p. 631)

3. Rush Limbaugh, Jerry Falwell, or Pat Robertson (pp. 631-32)

4. the gospel (p. 632)

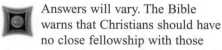 Answers will vary. The Bible warns that Christians should have no close fellowship with those who oppose the true gospel (II Cor. 6:14).

Welfare Reform Act

The Welfare Reform Act changed the welfare system in six ways.

Aid to Families with Dependent Children would no longer be an entitlement. Instead, states would have the freedom to set their own eligibility standards and the level of assistance.

Welfare recipients would have a five-year lifetime limit on assistance (with exceptions for reasons of "severe hardship").

Over a seven-year period, states were to require at least half of their single-parent recipients to work at least thirty hours a week.

States would be awarded additional funds for reducing illegitimacy. Underage mothers could receive benefits only if they lived in an adult-supervised household and attended high school.

The definition of "disabled" children whose parents would qualify for additional cash payments was tightened.

Immigrants would not receive welfare assistance until they had been five years in residence. In addition, states would have the option of reforming the way in which Medicaid benefits were given to noncitizens.

Goals 2000

Under Goals 2000, nineteen secular educators, appointed by the president, would run the powerful new National Educational Standards and Improvement Council (NESIC). Like a national school board, NESIC began developing national standards for curriculum and testing. After the NESIC

Welfare lines were cut in half soon after the passage of the Welfare Reform Act.

Confronting Society's Problems

After the budget battles of 1995, the Senate went to work on other bills, beginning with the House's Contract with America. The Senate approved the line-item veto, and the president signed the bill (although the Supreme Court later declared this law unconstitutional).

Congress passed some significant new legislation, too. The Telecommunications Bill deregulated the cable, telephone, and television industries. Republicans hoped the bill would spur new competition, cheaper rates, and the construction of a private "information superhighway." Another major overhaul of government regulations was the "Freedom to Farm Act." It phased out several New Deal programs that had paid farmers not to plant crops. Moderate Republicans joined Democrats to pass a bill raising the minimum wage from $4.25 to $5.15.

Welfare Reform

The Republican Congress also wanted to overhaul the federal government's welfare system. The president had already vetoed two bills. But to the surprise of conservatives and the dismay of liberals, he signed the **Welfare Reform Act** in 1995. For the first time since FDR's New Deal, the government rolled back

its guarantee of financial aid for the poor. The law required welfare recipients to go back to work within two years, and it put a lifetime cap of five years for assistance. Rather than continuing to run the welfare system from Washington, the law gave states freedom to spend the money as they chose.

National Education Standards

After Clinton failed to take over the health care industry in 1993, he sought another cause to champion. He picked education. Costs kept going up, while student performance was going down. In his 1997 State of the Union Address he claimed, "My number one priority as president for the next four years is to insure that Americans have the best education in the

Home schools became increasingly popular during the 1990s.

world." He pushed for a long list of government programs to improve education.

Clinton's interest in education went back to his days as governor of Arkansas, when he helped produce Bush's Education 2000 proposal (see p. 619). After becoming president, Clinton signed a bill that he hoped would become a watershed in American history. The **Goals 2000**: Educate America Act established a new bureaucratic system that set "voluntary" standards that states must meet to receive federal funds.

SECTION 4

Materials

- No materials

Could You Do Any Better?

No matter what politicians have offered to reform farming, welfare, and education, they have received criticism from American citizens. Ask the students why it is so difficult to make reforms in such areas. *(Government has already obligated itself to providing benefits. It is much easier for the government to stay out of an issue than it is*

for the government to extricate itself once it has gotten involved. Once a program begins, the government has new obligations that it must weigh before making changes.)

Ask the students whether they could come up with a fairer, more reasonable solution to problems in welfare and education. *(Discuss the problems created by simply cutting off all federal funds that states have been using to pay for welfare and education. The states must make major changes in their bureaucracy and tax structure to keep paying the bills.)*

Conservative Republicans believed that states and local communities should handle education and most other social issues, as they had been doing for hundreds of years. They argued that lack of money was not the problem, and more money was not the solution. The Republican Congress took out some parts of Goals 2000, but they feared to repeal it outright. In fact, yearly spending on Goals 2000 increased to over half a billion dollars.

Meanwhile, support grew for alternative solutions. One of the most popular ideas was **educational vouchers.** Instead of the government's deciding where students would attend school, the government would give parents vouchers (or scholarships) that they could "spend" at any school of their choice. But the leaders in public education fought the voucher system, calling it a threat to public schooling in America.

Efforts to Stop Social Evils

Republicans passed a series of bills on serious social issues. Perhaps the most significant was a ban on **partial birth abortions.** Even some feminists agreed that this cruel procedure went too far. (The doctor draws the baby's body out feet first, inserts an instrument into the base of its head, and suctions out the brain.) Sadly, President Clinton vetoed the bill in the name of "the right to choose."

Republicans passed a major bill on another issue of concern—homosexuality. Courts in Hawaii were attempting to legalize homosexual marriages in their state. If such marriages became legal, the Constitution would require all other states to recognize homosexual marriages. In response, Congress passed a bill limiting benefits, such as health insurance, to traditional marriages between men and women. The president publicly ridiculed the bill as "gay-baiting." But when it reached his desk, he quietly signed it late at night.

SECTION REVIEW

1. Name two acts of Congress that rolled back New Deal programs.

2. What law created "voluntary" standards for schools across America?

3. Name two social issues that revealed President Clinton's true liberal character.

 Are educational vouchers a good idea? Defend your answer.

Clinton's Trials

After the Democrats lost in the 1994 election, President Clinton began an all-out effort to raise money to win the next election. His party blanketed the nation with expensive television advertisements. During the campaign, Clinton spent more money on advertising than any other candidate in history had. But his reelection did not bring an end to his hardships.

The Never-Ending 1996 Campaign

Clinton ran a brilliant campaign. He stayed focused on a few important ideas, and he avoided any controversies. He presented himself as a New Democrat, again declaring, "The era of big government is over." Rather than presenting his own programs, he let others attack him on both sides—the liberals on the left and the "radical" Republicans on the right. He wanted Americans to see him as someone they could trust in the middle. Clinton took advantage of the president's "bully pulpit" to push small, popular reforms, such as recommending school uniforms and limits on teen smoking.

The Republicans' choice for president was Senate Majority Leader Bob Dole of Kansas—another pragmatist like George Bush. During his many years in the Senate, he had made friends around the country. His political connections made it easy for him to

635

---

released the first series of curriculum standards, critics noted that the U.S. history standards contained nineteen negative references to the anti-Communist Joseph McCarthy but did not mention such figures as Paul Revere and Thomas Edison. "They make it sound as if everything in America is wrong and grim," complained Lynne Cheney. The Senate voted 99-1 to condemn the standards. The new Republican Congress dismantled NESIC and other controversial elements of Goals 2000.

Affirmative Action in Question
During the 1990s, opposition mounted against affirmative action. Although the Civil Rights Act of 1964 outlawed discrimination, it did not specify how to implement itself. By the early 1990s, at least 160 federal laws and guidelines gave preferences to minorities and women.

In 1995 the U.S. Supreme Court declared that government agencies could no longer give preferences to minorities and women unless they had experienced actual discrimination. President Clinton ordered a review of affirmative action programs, but he kept each one alive.

In 1996 Californians passed Proposition 209, ending affirmative action in state colleges and universities as well as in government employment and contracting. President Clinton's attorney general tried to overturn the law in court but was unsuccessful.

SECTION 5

Objectives
Students should be able to
1. Evaluate the budget deal of 1997.
2. List the scandals of the Clinton administration.
3. Analyze the results of the impeachment proceedings.
4. Compare Johnson's impeachment with Clinton's.

Section Review Answers

1. Freedom to Farm Act and the Welfare Reform Act (p. 634)

2. Goals 2000: Educate America Act (p. 634)

3. partial birth abortions and homosexuality (p. 635)

 Answers will vary. If parents pay taxes for schools, they should have a right to choose how that money is spent. However, the danger of government financing of education is that the

government always regulates how the money is spent. If the government dislikes a Christian policy, such as preaching against homosexuality and abortion, the government can demand a change or take away the money. (pp. 634-35)

SECTION 5

Materials

- Special speaker: an expert on computer technology

Communications Technology

Communication became an obsession in the last part of the twentieth century. More people were exchanging more information at faster rates than ever before. Drivers took their phones with them in their cars. Important documents crossed the country instantly through fax machines. Cable and satellite subscribers had hundreds of television channels to watch. And people carried pagers for both business and personal use.

Possibly the greatest change in communications was the introduction of the Internet, a system that allows computers to share information over phone lines or cables. Government researchers developed the Internet in 1969 to connect computer scientists and engineers working on military projects. Large universities and research companies soon joined up. For several years, government and education kept the Internet to themselves, and the system was difficult to use. But two developments changed the Internet into an information highway for the entire nation.

The first development was the creation of tools for finding information. Regardless of how much data it held, the Internet would not be valuable without a practical way to look up a topic. Two tools helped organize the Internet. Browsers allowed users to view documents easily, and hypertext joined together documents on related topics through underlined words or phrases. (The researcher could use his mouse to click on one of the underlined portions and be taken to a document on that subject.)

The second development was a change of control. Though the government had developed the concept of the Internet, it gradually stepped back and let private companies take leadership. The Internet developed from a center for professional research and communication into a marketplace and a high-tech post office. Advertisements popped up along with information; consumers made on-line purchases with their credit cards (yearly sales were estimated to grow from $272 million in 1993 to $108 billion ten years later); and people from all over sent personal notes via e-mail or joined strangers in "chat room" discussions.

The Internet has become a growing part of American life, so Christians, like others, are trying to determine how to deal with it. They do not want to miss the opportunity to influence large numbers of people easily. At the same time the Internet can be dangerous. Large amounts of ungodly material confront the user (though tools to block objectionable sites are available), and Internet browsing can waste a great deal of time. So how should a Christian handle the Internet? Whether on the Internet or off, the key is to follow Ephesians 5:15-16: "See then that ye walk circumspectly, not as fools, but as wise, Redeeming the time, because the days are evil."

raise money and to win the Republican nomination. But he had several handicaps. He had a sharp tongue, he was old (over seventy), and he was unable to express a clear vision for America's future. Furthermore, Dole had offended conservatives in his own party by compromising during the budget battles.

For months, the media had predicted that Clinton would win by a landslide. But when the votes were finally tallied, he failed to win even a majority (receiving only 49 percent of the votes). Dole took 41 percent. Ross Perot, who again ran as an independent, got 8 percent. The races for Congress were close, but the Republicans held on to their majority.

Debate Ideas

Have your students discuss and/or debate the following:

The Social Security system should be abolished.

The welfare state undermines the work ethic.

Education vouchers would improve education in America.

Special Speaker on Computer Technology

Have a special speaker talk about advances in computer technology. He or she could also discuss ways that computers will be used in the future and how these advances will change our lives.

The Information Age

Many sociologists have begun comparing the impact of the computer age (or "Information Age") to the impact of the Industrial Revolution. Review the changes to American culture that followed the rise of industry and cities. Is it likely that computers could have a similar impact on daily life? Discuss how computers could one day change everyday patterns at home and work. Computers are even changing politics; politicians are able to make direct contact with their constituents and supporters.

Balanced Budget at Last?

Despite all of the accomplishments of the Republican Congress, their most basic need remained unchanged: balancing the budget.

After weeks of talks, the president and Congress hammered out a compromise. Unlike the revolutionary 104th Congress, the new congress did not propose to eliminate any major government programs or departments. In fact, spending for the Education Department jumped 34% in the first year of the new budget plan.

The booming economy made the budget deal possible. At the last moment, the Congressional Budget Office found $225 billion in unexpected money. The so-called budget deal spent more than if Congress had kept the old budget and never reached a deal!

In spite of the budget's shortcomings, it created a surplus in 1998, the first surplus in thirty years. This surplus was possible only because the government included income from Social Security taxes, although this money was supposed to be set aside to pay future retirement costs. The "surplus" completely changed the debates in Washington. No longer did representatives argue about spending cuts; the question became how to spend the extra money.

No End to Scandals

While President Clinton was busy trying to assure his place in history, a steady stream of scandals undermined his ability to lead the nation. Questions about his character had plagued him since before he became president. In 1992 he promised to appoint "the most ethical administration in the history of the Republic." But ethical questions hurt his party in the 1994 midterm elections and later in the 1996 campaign.

Scandals in the Cabinet—Three members of Clinton's cabinet came under criminal investigation during the first four years of Clinton's administration. Judges appointed an **independent counsel** in each case. (A "counsel" is a lawyer who gives legal advice or conducts a court case.) Democrats had created the first independent counsel during Nixon's Watergate scandal so that someone outside the administration could investigate wrongdoing within the administration.

Scandals in the White House—Clinton's past came back to haunt him in office. One scandal involved his past investment in a resort in northeastern Arkansas, called Whitewater Development Corporation. The **Whitewater scandal** was a complicated web of questionable relationships between politicians, law firms, and businessmen while Clinton was governor of Arkansas. As the investigation wore on, over a dozen people pleaded guilty to various crimes. The most

Instead of "Building a bridge to the twenty-first century," President Clinton left a legacy of scandal.

Most Investigated President in History

At least eleven committees in Congress planned to investigate some aspect of President Clinton's scandals during the first year of his second term. He earned the dubious distinction of being "the most investigated president in history."

Travelgate

Soon after Clinton moved into the White House, a miniscandal called "Travelgate" began. His administration fired the staff of the White House Travel Office and gave the profitable jobs to Clinton's friends from Arkansas.

Background to Whitewater

The Whitewater scandal broke early in the 1992 election campaign. But after Clinton claimed he had lost money in the 1978 land deal, the press ignored it. How could there be any wrongdoing if he lost $69,000?

The first questions arose while federal investigators were studying the 1989 failure of a savings and loan (S&L) called Madison Guaranty. They wished to find out why it had been allowed to stay open—costing taxpayers millions of dollars when it finally closed. To their surprise, the owner of the S&L, James McDougal, turned out to be a friend and business partner of the Clintons. The group had invested in a 230-acre real-estate development at Whitewater in 1978. In addition, the state regulator who let the S&L stay open was a friend and appointee of Governor Clinton. Even worse, the lawyer who represented the S&L before the state regulator was the governor's own wife, Hillary Rodham Clinton, an employee of the Rose Law Firm.

The conflicts of interest were obvious. The question for federal investigators was this: Did McDougal illegally divert S&L money to help Clinton pay off debts from his 1984 governor's race and from the failing Whitewater project?

637

Budget Battles Today

Update the students on the latest budget battles in Congress. (Or ask them to bring in articles.) Ask them to look back into America's past to find the periods when the budget was a focus of politics. Although economic issues may loom large in our day, we know that other issues are likely to take their place in the future, just as they have in the past. What issues do the students foresee replacing the economy and the budget? *(Morals and cultural decline are leading contenders for political debate.)*

Compare Clinton's Scandals to the Past

Compare and contrast the social conditions in America during past scandals and the social conditions surrounding Clinton's scandals. Note that the Grant scandals occurred during the evil Gilded Age, and the Harding scandals occurred during the corrupt Roaring Twenties. Is it true that the president is often a reflection of his age? Look at other presidents, beginning with Washington, and evaluate how they reflected the strengths and weaknesses of their generations.

Independent Counsel Investigation

When the Whitewater story resurfaced in December 1993, James McDougal claimed that the Clintons had all of his files. But the Clintons said their files were incomplete. Republicans began pressing for an independent counsel. Democrats joined the demand when news leaked that the Rose Law Firm was shredding its files related to the S&L. On January 20, 1994, Attorney General Janet Reno appointed lawyer Robert Fiske to head the investigation. Fiske sent investigators to the Rose Law Firm and subpoenaed many top Clinton officials to testify. But Fiske came under fire for whitewashing some troubling issues, such as White House deputy counsel Vincent Foster's suicide. Republicans pressured Congress to renew the Independent Counsel Law, which requires a panel of federal judges to appoint the counsel. The law was renewed, and a panel of judges subsequently chose former solicitor general Kenneth Starr to replace Robert Fiske.

By January 1996, nine people had pleaded guilty in the Whitewater investigation. Another four men in the treasury department had resigned because of their efforts to keep the White House informed about the investigation.

More on Impeachment

The honorable thing for the president to do during the impeachment trial was to resign, as Nixon had done. Over a third of the newspapers in the country called for his resignation, realizing that it was dangerous for the nation to be led by a dishonest man that neither allies nor enemies of the nation could respect. But President Clinton vowed to remain in office to the last day of his term, without any thought of how his actions might hurt the nation.

Clinton's own friends in the Senate prepared a censure statement that described his relationship with Lewinsky as "shameful, reckless, and indefensible." The Democratic

embarrassing confession came from Webster Hubbell, a former law partner with Hillary Clinton. The president had appointed Hubbell to a high position in the Justice Department. Unable to put the scandal behind him, Clinton asked the Justice Department to hire an independent counsel in 1994.

Another scandal hit the papers in the 1996 election season. The press learned that the White House had obtained confidential files from the FBI on hundreds of Republicans. The president called the incident an innocent mistake, but Filegate embarrassed the administration.

Campaign Finance Scandals—A whole new scandal began to pour out after the 1996 election. It involved the way Democrats—and the president in particular—had raised funds for the campaign.

The president had been consumed with raising money. Clinton knew that raising campaign money on government property was illegal. (This law was intended to keep people from bribing politicians.) Nevertheless, the Clintons and the Gores invited wealthy contributors to over a hundred "coffees" at the White House, and they opened the Lincoln Room for overnight stays.

The public was deeply troubled by reports that some of the campaign money had come illegally from foreigners in Asia who were trying to influence votes. The Democratic Party promised to send back over $1.5 million from questionable sources, but the party did not even know where to send some of the money. One of the money raisers, John Huang, later told investigators that Communist China had contributed to the president's campaign indirectly through Asian companies. The Clinton administration was further embarrassed by reports that China had acquired American computer and missile technology which it was using to develop long-range nuclear missiles.

Impeachment of the President

The scandal that led to the impeachment of President Clinton came from an unexpected source. A former beauty queen from Arkansas, Paula Jones, sued him in 1994 for sexual harassment—and she had witnesses. The president raised over a million dollars for a "legal defense fund," and he used the money to delay the case until after his 1996 reelection. He appealed to the Supreme Court, claiming that his duties as president gave him special privileges to avoid such trials while in office. But he lost his appeal in 1997.

The trial attracted much publicity. Defense attorneys called many witnesses to testify about the president's character. The case took an unexpected turn when a young woman named Monica Lewinsky appeared. At first she claimed under oath that she had committed no immoral acts with the president. Secret audio tape recordings by a friend of Lewinsky later showed that she had lied and was covering up. President Clinton himself appeared on national television waving his finger at the camera and declaring his innocence.

A judge eventually dismissed the Jones case, but not before the damage had been done. **Kenneth Starr,** the independent counsel investigating the Whitewater scandal, received court approval to investigate the president's part in lying to the grand jury and the attempted cover-up. The president refused to admit any wrongdoing, and he made every legal effort to block Starr's investigation. For nine months he kept up the lies, deceiving his cabinet and his friends, as well as the American people. The president's denials forced Starr to dig deeper into embarrassing, personal details. Finally, after great expense and time, Starr uncovered undeniable evidence that contradicted the president's version of the story. Starr sent his evidence to the House, listing thirteen impeachable offenses.

Contrast America's Two Impeachments

Unlike Clinton, Andrew Johnson was not elected—he succeeded Lincoln after his assassination. Johnson faced impeachment in a political power struggle, not over criminal conduct.

Failure of the Constitution?

A popular question during the impeachment and trial was "Is the Constitution Working?" Supporters of the president argued that the Constitution was never meant to be used as a political weapon to bring down an opponent. Others said that the process was successful because the embarrassment will force future presidents to avoid conduct similar to that of President Clinton, whether or not such conduct leads to removal.

It is interesting to note that the founders' original design for impeachment was ruined by the direct election of senators. The founders intended that the trial be held by men who were not influenced by the whims of public opinion.

Four articles of impeachment came to the floor of the House for a vote on December 19, 1998, and two passed. The two articles claimed that the president had committed perjury (lied before a court) and had obstructed justice (hidden evidence from a court). President Clinton became only the second president ever impeached.

The Senate then heard the case for the removal of the president from office. When it came time to cast votes, not one Democrat voted in favor of the articles of impeachment. Robert Byrd, a respected senator from West Virginia, admitted on television that the evidence was clear, but he voted against conviction anyway. The Democrats argued that removal from office was too extreme a punishment. Several "moderate" Republican senators voted with the Democrats, too. But the vast majority of Republicans voted for conviction, even though most Americans were against them and the vote might hurt their party. The number of senators voting in favor of conviction fell below even a simple majority of 50. (The Constitution requires a two-thirds majority—67 of 100—to remove the president from office.)

Polls showed that 70 percent of Americans approved of the president's performance, a higher rating than President Reagan ever received. Polls also showed that respect for his character had fallen lower than respect for Nixon's had at any time during the Watergate scandal. Americans apparently did not care that the president broke the law, violated his sacred marriage vows, took advantage of a twenty-one-year-old employee, and lied repeatedly, as long as the economy was performing well. Conservatives in the New Right lamented the "collapse of

Secretary of State Madeleine Albright

American civilization." President Clinton had promised a "bridge to the twenty-first century," but his actions raised questions as to whether he was instead leading the American republic to its destruction.

SECTION REVIEW

1. What strategy did President Clinton use to win the 1996 election?

2. What scandal involved Bill Clinton's business investment in northeastern Arkansas?

3. What independent counsel presented evidence for Clinton's impeachment?

4. On what two counts was President Clinton impeached?

 Why do you think so many people supported Clinton during his scandals?

Foreign Policy in the 21st Century

"Character doesn't matter," boasted Clinton's defenders. But in foreign affairs, America soon saw how much character really does matter. Bad judgment can threaten peace around the world, bringing a quick end to the nation's prosperity and balanced budgets. Clinton's lack of character ended up aiding America's potential enemies, offending America's allies, and destabilizing the world. In the view of many analysts, President Clinton failed to follow a clear set of principles to guide his foreign policy. He made quick decisions as emergencies arose, rather than taking preventative measures.

The president was fortunate to avoid several potential disasters in his first term. He hoped to shine during his second term. He selected a whole new team of foreign advisors after several cabinet members quit. **Madeleine Albright,** the first

Senators further warned that his conduct "creates disrespect for laws of the land; . . . brought shame and dishonor to himself and to the office of the president; [and] violated the trust of the American people."

"High Crimes and Misdemeanors"
Representatives in Congress never resolved the most fundamental question related to the trial of President Clinton: Did his conduct fall under the definition of impeachable offenses given in the Constitution? Conservative constitutional scholars gave explanation of the terms based on the context of the day in which they were written. In British legal tradition (from which the United States got the concept of impeachment), "high crimes" refers to crimes in high office, not to "big" crimes as opposed to "little" crimes. The word *misdemeanors* refers to "bad behavior," not to the modern concept of lesser crimes.

Republicans Vindicated
The Republicans were vindicated in their actions in the impeachment when the judge in the Paula Jones case held the president in contempt of court for lying and obstructing justice, fining him a large sum of money. The judge's decision was the first of its kind against a president.

SECTION 6

Objectives
Students should be able to
1. Identify the first female secretary of state.
2. Discuss Clinton's dealings with Communist countries.
3. Define multilateralism.
4. Explain changes to free trade under Clinton's administration.

639

Section Review Answers

1. Clinton let others attack him from both sides so that he could appear as someone in the middle whom Americans could trust. (p. 635)

2. Whitewater (p. 637)

3. Kenneth Starr (p. 638)

4. perjury and obstruction of justice (p. 639)

 Answers will vary. It appears that most Americans had accepted the philosophy of moral relativism.

Perhaps they also felt it would be hypocritical to expect more of their leaders than they did of themselves. (p. 639)

Section 6

Materials

• World map

• List of arguments for isolationism and interventionism

The Ripple Effect of Dishonesty

Explain to the students that all the nations of the world keep up with events in the

United States. Foreign leaders are constantly assessing the president of the United States to comprehend his personality, principles, and goals. Whenever a president makes a threat and keeps his word, as President Reagan did when he fired the air traffic controllers, it has a direct impact on foreign relations because foreigners know the president will keep his word and carry out his threats.

As the students read about President Clinton's administration, however, they need to be alert to instances of blustering and threats that were never carried out. Ask

woman to serve as secretary of state, made an aggressive effort to solve the world's problems with the help of the U.S. military.

Battling the Military

Having avoided the draft and joined demonstrations against the Vietnam War in his youth, Clinton faced a difficult task earning the respect of the military. Yet his first act as commander in chief—to end the ban on homosexuals—angered generals and privates alike. His second act was to speed up the reduction in the size of the military. He hoped that improved efficiency would enable a smaller army to continue its preparedness for two wars at once. His layoffs, wage freezes, base closures, and homosexual policy caused a mass exodus of good soldiers. Poor planning in foreign actions—along with the unnecessary deaths of servicemen—discouraged new recruits.

Dealing Softly with Communists

When Clinton assumed office, communism appeared to be in its death throes. Only four countries remained under its shadow. But by failing to adopt a clear policy toward

Bill Clinton often met with Boris Yeltsin of Russia to discuss the future of democracy in Russia.

regions once dominated by communism, the president allowed a host of new dangers to take root.

Resurgence of Communist China—After the fall of the Soviet Union, Mainland China became the dominant communist power in the world. During the 1992 election campaign,

Shanghai became a prosperous port city after China's communist leaders opened the door to free enterprise.

Clinton attacked Bush for keeping the Most Favored Nation (MFN) trade status with China despite its human rights abuses at Tiananmen Square. Though China openly increased its abuses against Christians and dissenters, Clinton renewed MFN status anyway. He said he feared that American businesses might lose a chance to get rich in one of the world's fastest growing markets.

In the meantime, China continued a massive buildup of arms and began to make threatening gestures toward America's friends in the Far East. One of the touchiest issues was the status of Taiwan, which China considered a rebel province. Clinton responded with a policy of "strategic ambiguity," unlike in the past, when the United States had made plain its intention to protect its trading partner with force, if necessary.

them to consider how this influenced foreigners in their relations with the United States. Character does matter. Discuss the current situation in America, as well, to find examples of leaders who keep their word or of those who cannot be trusted.

Hot Spots

Point to a world map and ask the students to name the countries that are most often in the news and tell why. An alternative activity is to have students bring in newspaper pictures portraying American involvement in other countries. Post these pictures on

the map beside the appropriate countries. Perhaps you can do some research and put a star over all of the countries in which at least one thousand American troops are now stationed.

Ask the students to explain why Christian citizens of this country need to know about world geography and world history. *(They need to know about the hot spots, in particular, where the United States may become involved in the future.)* This activity helps to prepare the students for their study of geography in ninth grade.

The NATO Alliance

Current Members
(also includes the U.S., Canada, and Iceland)

New Members in 1998

Possible Future Members

Nuclear Threat in North Korea—Communist North Korea was another embarrassment. In 1993 it threatened to withdraw from the **Non-Proliferation of Nuclear Weapons Treaty (NPT).** Under this treaty, the five nations with nuclear weapons agreed to prevent any new countries from developing or buying nuclear weapons. The other nations of the world agreed to this treaty only so long as they felt relatively safe. But the development of a nuclear bomb in North Korea could touch off a nuclear arms race in Southeast Asia with deadly results. American allies begged for a tough stance, but Clinton was more casual. He eventually agreed to help North Korea build two nuclear power plants if it promised to stop trying to make nuclear weapons. Unfortunately, the delay gave the communists extra time to collect material to build nuclear weapons without any guarantee that the weapons program had stopped.

The NPT, first signed in 1968, came up for renewal in 1995. Fearing a new arms race, President Clinton convinced many countries to make the treaty permanent. In return, the five declared nuclear powers—Russia, the United States, China, Britain, and France—promised to work harder to reduce their stockpiles. But some of the most dangerous countries in the world, such as Iran and Pakistan, refused to sign.

Expanding NATO into Eastern Europe—Clinton also failed to develop a consistent approach toward the formerly communist countries of Eastern Europe and the former Soviet Union. He almost blindly put his support behind the Russian reformer Boris Yeltsin. When Yeltsin used Russian troops to force his will on the former republics, Clinton remained silent.

The countries of Eastern Europe, who feared new Russian aggression, looked to the West for help. The expansion of NATO remained a touchy issue. Russian nationalists hated the thought of NATO troops at their doorstep. After years of talks, Russia signed a historic agreement in 1997 that gave it a voice in NATO in return for allowing Eastern European nations to join. In 1999 three new members joined NATO—Poland, the Czech Republic, and Hungary.

The radical changes in the NATO alliance took place without public debate at home. The shift in policy raised grave concerns. Would NATO be able to respond to local wars? What

641

Compromise to Extend NATO
As part of its agreement with Russia, NATO promised that it had no "intention" of moving troops or nuclear weapons into Eastern Europe.

Trade with Vietnam
To "open markets" for American business, Clinton lifted a ban on trade. Veterans were outraged because the Communists had not made a serious effort to locate 1,609 American soldiers missing in action since the Vietnam War. The man who helped make the deal, Commerce Secretary Ron Brown, had once been offered money from Vietnam to help it gain access to American trade.

Confused Policy Toward Cuba
The president sent conflicting signals to Fidel Castro, the Communist leader of Cuba. Clinton wanted to open trade despite Republican opposition. But in the summer of 1994, when Castro opened the door for boat people to flee to the States, Clinton's solution was to reverse America's thirty-six-year-old open-door policy and to confine the refugees to tents at the American base at Guantanamo Bay. As talks wore on, the squalor of the twenty-three thousand refugees became an embarrassment to the administration. Clinton agreed to increase the number of legal immigrants if Castro promised to stop future illegal immigration. Clinton also agreed to accept the Guantanamo refugees, and he promised to use the U.S. Coast Guard to turn back illegal refugees. Cuban-Americans and conservatives were furious at this policy. "What if such a policy had been adopted at the Berlin Wall?" they asked.

As the number of Cuban boat people declined, a group of Cuban-American pilots, known as "Brothers to the Rescue," switched their activity from rescuing rafts to dropping leaflets calling for revolt. On February 24, 1996, Cuban fighter jets shot down two of their unarmed planes, killing all four men onboard. In

---

Debate Isolationism and Interventionism

Christians realize that the well-being of America depends on the blessing of the Lord and not the devices of men (Isa. 31:1, 3). Honoring the Lord is the best foreign policy. Nevertheless, the students need to choose sides on the issue of America's role in world affairs. Some debates about government are not necessarily issues of "right or wrong" but "strong or weak." Put the following list of arguments on the overhead. Then debate and decide which is the strongest argument.

Arguments for isolationism:

1. "Entangling alliances" go against tradition.

2. Each country needs to defend itself.

3. America does not have the power to right every wrong.

4. Many of the countries America supports are corrupt and undemocratic.

5. America's involvement with NATO and the UN has not prevented wars.

6. Americans cannot impose their will on the rest of the world.

Arguments for interventionism:

1. America has close cultural ties to Europe.

2. The United States has an obligation to honor commitments made during the Cold War.

3. As the most powerful country, the United States is obligated to help the weak.

4. America's businesses depend on open markets and free commerce.

response, President Clinton gave up his efforts to normalize relations with Cuba. He agreed to sign a Republican bill to tighten economic sanctions.

Rise in Worldwide Terrorism
One positive development following the end of the Cold War was the release of the last Muslim-held hostages. Muslim extremists could no longer play superpower against superpower. Yet Islamic extremism remained a threat to international peace and security. Following the example of Iran, radical Muslims in every country hoped to win popular support and to take over their governments.

The United States and its friends became the focus of this terrorism. The worst Islamic attack on American soil came on February 26, 1993, at the World Trade Center in New York City. Muslim radicals planted fifteen hundred pounds of explosives in a van parked in the complex's underground parking garage. The blast killed six, wounded one thousand others, and destroyed millions of dollars of property. The FBI moved swiftly to arrest the four men directly involved and indicted in absentia the ringleader, Ramzi Ahmed Yousef. Investigators uncovered another plot to bomb several buildings and landmarks around New York City and to assassinate several political leaders. The men involved in both bombing conspiracies were followers of a religious leader named Sheik Omar Abdel Rahman. Years earlier this radical cleric had been tried and acquitted in Egypt as a supporter of Anwar Sadat's assassination. Abdel Rahman surrendered to authorities in 1993 and was convicted in U.S. federal court in 1996.

Terrorists have attacked American forces in the Middle East also. On November 13, 1995, terrorists blew up a U.S. military building in Riyadh, Saudi Arabia, killing five Americans and two others. In May 1996 the Saudis beheaded the four men who confessed to the crime without letting the FBI question them. One month later, a

if dictators rose to power within the alliance itself? One of the new NATO members—Hungary—did not even share a border with the rest of the NATO alliance.

Working with the United Nations

When he took office, Clinton wanted the United Nations (UN) to become the policeman of the world. He adopted a policy of **multilateralism**—listening to many nations before making decisions that every side can agree on. Conservative Republicans accused him of shirking his responsibilities. They preferred a policy of unilateralism—making decisions alone in America's clear national interest. With so many conflicting voices, the UN proved that it could not take timely action. Events showed the world just how ineffective the UN-U.S. alliance was.

Somalia—The first failure occurred in the famine-stricken African country of Somalia. Without public approval, President Bush had sent American troops to Somalia in December 1992 to help the UN protect aid shipments and to restore order. When the UN decided to disarm the warring factions, the most powerful "warlord," General Aidid, fought back. As the killing of UN troops mounted, the UN and the United States began a fruitless effort to capture Aidid. Chief of Staff Colin Powell requested tanks and heavy armament to protect his troops, but Secretary of Defense Les Aspin turned him down, fearing that this move would be too provocative. Clinton eventually sent army specialists called Rangers to track Aidid down. But Americans watched in horror as Somalians shot down a helicopter, captured the pilot, and dragged a soldier's body through the streets. The failed raid cost eighteen lives. As a result, Clinton ordered the withdrawal of American forces from the country.

Haiti—Watching the catastrophe in Somalia were other rogue leaders of the world.

Among them was a military regime in the poverty-stricken Caribbean island of Haiti. Haiti's military leaders decided to back out of negotiations to reinstate President **Jean-Bertrand Aristide,** whom they had overthrown in a 1991 coup. For a year Clinton blustered about armed intervention if the military rulers refused to return to negotiations.

In the fall of 1994 Clinton ordered an invasion. He appeared on television to defend his decision, condemning the murderous "thugs" who had established the "most violent regime in our hemisphere." Even as the warplanes were in the air, however, Clinton allowed a three-man team to negotiate with the head of these murderers, Lt. Gen. Raoul Cedras. The negotiators—which included former president Jimmy Carter—convinced Cedras to accept generous terms of resignation. The U.S. even paid the general $10,000 per month in return for the use of his home and other buildings in Haiti. Later when American troops handed the mission over to the UN, Clinton declared the mission a "remarkable success." After an operation that cost more than $1 billion however, Haiti remained a bloody, poverty-stricken land.

Civil War in Former Yugoslavia—After the end of the Cold War, the most explosive region in the world was the Balkan Peninsula in Eastern Europe. The former Communist country of Yugoslavia, which consisted of a complex variety of competing ethnic groups, broke up into five countries. A bitter civil war erupted in 1992 in Bosnia, one of the former republics of Yugoslavia. Three ethnic groups—Muslims, Serbs, and Croats—savagely fought each other in a three-way war. The UN sent in 23,000 "peacekeeping" troops, but they were powerless to stop the bloodshed. George Bush, who was president at the time, refused to involve American troops. During the 1992 election campaign,

5. Isolationism failed to prevent the United States from entering two world wars.

6. The spread of peace and free trade will help everyone.

 Updates on Countries

Ask the students to report on conditions in one of the countries mentioned in this chapter. In particular, ask for reports on countries in which the U.S. military intervened, such as Somalia or Haiti.

Calendar Capers
Have the students design and make an illustrated calendar of events pertaining to our country's history or to events that center on a single theme. Divide the class into twelve groups. Post a list of events and the dates they occurred. Have each group illustrate one month with pictures of their own design or with prepared pictures. (Examples: individual presidents, authors, artists, composers, inventors, wars, etc.) Sources include historical almanacs and encyclopedias.

The American Ideal
Ask your students, "If you could make an ideal America, what would it be like?" Then have them write a paper describing their ideas. Consider the political, economic, religious, and social features of America. Lead them in their thinking by asking the following questions. What would be your ideals for each of the areas mentioned? How do your ideals differ from what exists today? How could you rally the public behind your goals? What would you do about those who do not share your

Clinton ridiculed him for not taking action to stop the "ethnic cleansing," or systematic murder of ethnic minorities. But Clinton softened his stance after he became president. For the next three years Clinton shifted back and forth between threatening to bomb and silence.

Meanwhile, American advisors secretly trained Croatian troops. These troops launched a surprise attack in 1995 that drove

Bombed-out homes were a common sight after the violent breakup of Yugoslavia.

out the Serbs living in the eastern part of Croatia and threatened the Serbs living in Bosnia. Clinton finally decided to send U.S. jets to bomb the Serbs. Now the Serbs were ready to come to the peace table. In November 1995 President Clinton invited the warring factions to meet at a military base in Dayton, Ohio. To encourage the peace negotiations, he promised to send 20,000 American troops to Bosnia to keep the peace.

The warring leaders signed the **Dayton Accords,** and an uneasy peace settled over the Balkan Peninsula. But the accords had many embarrassing flaws. The new "unified" government in Bosnia would have two separate armies, two legislatures, and two courts. To avoid criticism, President Clinton promised that the troops would stay only "about one year." Four years later they were still there.

Air War in Kosovo—In fact, Clinton increased U.S. commitments in the Balkan region. When rebels took up arms in Yugoslavia's southern province of Kosovo, the president demanded that Yugoslavia make peace with them or suffer the wrath of NATO bombs. When the Yugoslav government refused to back down, the president sent warplanes and cruise missiles to bomb the country. It was the first time NATO had ever attacked a sovereign nation. After over fifty days of bombing, the Yugoslav leader caved in. But by then, Serb attacks had forced approximately one million Kosovars from their homes. The U.S. military had yet another costly "peace" to enforce.

Increasing World Trade

Clinton claimed two major successes in foreign trade. One was the passage of an agreement with Mexico and Canada, called the North American Free Trade Agreement (**NAFTA**). During the election, Clinton ridiculed the free trade agreement signed by Bush and the other heads of state. But after taking office, he decided to support NAFTA if it included labor and environmental guarantees. With strong Republican support, Congress passed NAFTA late in 1993.

The president's other success in world trade was the passage of the eighth round of GATT (General Agreement on Tariffs and Trade). After World War II, the nations of the world held seven "rounds" of negotiations to make trade easier. By 1990, tariffs (taxes on trade) had fallen from 40 to 5 percent, and the volume of world trade had exploded. An eighth round of talks in Uruguay, begun in 1987, sought to reduce tariffs by another third. It also addressed unfair trade practices. But the nations could not come to an agreement. Clinton changed the basic purpose of the agreement, as he had done with NAFTA, to include new environmental standards and a

three-thousand-pound bomb in a truck killed nineteen American servicemen at their housing complex, Khobar Towers, near Dharan. The Saudis also failed to cooperate in the investigation of the Khobar bombing. Some observers thought that the Saudi government might be trying to hide its failure to protect the Americans from Syrian military officials it had allowed into the country. President Clinton suspected Iran in the Khobar blast.

Still further attacks occurred in Africa. On August 7, 1998, terrorists bombed U.S. embassies in Nairobi, Kenya, and Dar es Salaam, Tanzania, killing 258 and wounding more than 5,000. These bombings appeared to be linked to wealthy Islamic radical Osama bin Laden. He reportedly sponsored an international network of terrorists that targeted the United States. The United States responded to the attacks with quick, decisive military action. On August 20, cruise missiles were launched both at a terrorism training center in Afghanistan and a pharmaceutical manufacturing facility in Khartoum, Sudan. The pharmaceutical facility was believed to be a manufacturing site for nerve gas. The United States chose a military response because of the lack of cooperation on terrorism it had been receiving and because of the need to deter further aggressive actions against American diplomatic facilities.

643

ideals? What hindrances would keep America from reaching your ideal?

A Double Standard Toward Kosovo

Discuss Clinton's double standard in his treatment of Taiwan and Kosovo. Ask the students to find the many amazing parallels in the countries' circumstances but the opposite reactions by the U.S. State Department. When Taiwan merely hinted that it was considering changing its policy to one of being an independent country rather than the rightful possession of mainland China, the Clinton administration delayed various

exchanges and threatened to cut off military assistance to show its displeasure. Taiwan had been separate for fifty years, but Clinton reaffirmed America's "one-China" policy. He said this even though China's civil-rights abuses have been far more atrocious than those of the Serbs. When China threatened to bomb Taiwan with neutron bombs if it continued its pursuit of independence, Clinton backed off on U.S. commitments to help Taiwan as laid out in the Taiwan Relations Act (1979). Clinton explained, "I didn't think this was the best time to do something which might

excite either side or imply that a military solution is an acceptable alternative."

Meanwhile in Kosovo, a site of importance to the Serbs' national identity since they fought there for freedom from the Turks in 1389, the Kosovar minority declared independence from Yugoslavia in 1991. The liberation army had resorted to terrorism to achieve its aims, and the Serbs responded with force. Kosovar leaders dealt in drug traffic to raise money for their cause. With little to fear from the Serb military, Clinton went to war to help the Kosovars, sparking a violent purge of Kosovo by the Serbs.

World trade reached record levels in the 1990s.

large bureaucracy. The member nations finally approved a permanent **World Trade Organization** (WTO) in 1994 to enforce GATT. Ironically, Clinton had changed free trade into "managed free trade" under international bureaucrats.

SUMMARY

The end of the Cold War brought a sigh of relief to all nations. The people of the United States hoped the country would enter a new century of peace and unprecedented prosperity. But their election of President Clinton proved that prosperity requires much more than the right laws. The people need to honor righteousness, and their leaders need to be men of good character. The future success of America remained in question as the twenty-first century dawned.

SECTION REVIEW

1. Who was the first woman to serve as secretary of state?

2. Name two Communist countries in Asia with which President Clinton failed to deal firmly. What threat did each of them pose to the United States?

3. What three new members joined NATO in 1999? What danger did this expansion of NATO pose to the United States?

4. What three ethnic groups fought each other in Bosnia? What peace agreement tried to calm the conflict?

5. What two successes did Clinton claim in foreign trade?

 In Clinton's view, what role should the UN and NATO play in promoting peace in the post–Cold War era? Do you agree with him?

Which country has a better claim to independence? Why would the United States support drug-dealing terrorists but balk at helping a stable democracy that fought by its side in World War II and has become its sixth largest trade partner?

Section Review Answers

1. Madeleine Albright (pp. 636-40)

2. China and North Korea; China—arms buildup and aggression against American friends; North Korea—development of nuclear weapons (pp. 640-41)

3. Poland, the Czech Republic, and Hungary; the U.S. might be called on to intervene in situations which contradict its principles or best interests (pp. 641-42)

4. Muslims, Serbs, and Croats; Dayton Accords (pp. 642-43)

5. NAFTA and GATT (p. 643)

 policeman of the world; answers will vary, but God Himself opposed a one-world government when He told the descendants of Noah to spread throughout the world (p. 642)

Chapter Review Answers

1. Kenneth Starr (p. 638)

2. Madeleine Albright (pp. 639-40)

3. Newt Gingrich (p. 628)

4. Ross Perot (p. 624)

5. Rush Limbaugh (p. 631)

6. c (p. 642)

7. b (p. 629)

8. a (p. 637)

Chapter Review

People, Places, and Things to Remember

Democratic Leadership Council
Bill Clinton
Ross Perot
UN Convention on the Rights of the Child
Janet Reno
Freedom of Access to Clinic Entrances
David Koresh
AmeriCorps
Hillary Rodham Clinton
Newt Gingrich

Contract with America
balanced budget amendment
line-item veto
government shutdown
communitarians
New Right
Rush Limbaugh
religious right
Christian Coalition
Welfare Reform Act
Goals 2000
educational vouchers

partial birth abortions
independent counsel
Whitewater scandal
Kenneth Starr
Madeleine Albright
Non-Proliferation of Nuclear Weapons Treaty (NPT)
multilateralism
Jean-Bertrand Aristide
Dayton Accords
NAFTA
World Trade Organization

Review Questions

Identify each of the following people.

1. This independent counsel presented evidence for impeaching Bill Clinton.

2. This was the first woman to serve as secretary of state.

3. This man became speaker of the House after Republicans took control in the 1994 elections.

4. This independent presidential candidate promised serious measures to fix the economy.

5. This conservative broadcaster gained a large following through his radio show and books.

Match these terms to their definitions.

6. consulting many nations about decisions

7. power to cut individual budget items

8. lawyer who investigates government corruption

a. independent counsel

b. line-item veto

c. multilateralism

Answer these questions.

9. What was the 1994 Republican campaign promise to take prompt action on popular legislation?

10. What peace agreement was signed by parties fighting over Bosnia?

11. What was President Clinton's solution to America's education problems?

12. What was the grassroots political movement of the religious right?

13. What organization was created to enforce fair trade practices?

Questions for Discussion

14. Is America a Christian nation? Explain your answer.

15. Should governments attempt to "legislate morality"? Why or why not?

645

Chapter Review Idea

Student Activity E: Comparing Clinton to a Past Democratic President

This activity summarizes the key elements of the Clinton administration and helps students to contrast them with his predecessors. President Clinton was deeply concerned about his legacy—he wanted to be remembered as a strong president, not another Jimmy Carter. Which president was he most like? To answer this question, different students need to be prepared to discuss Franklin D. Roosevelt, Harry S. Truman, John F. Kennedy, and Jimmy Carter.

Year Review Idea

Supplemental Activities

Please consider setting aside a week at the end of the year to complete and discuss the supplemental activities at the end of the *Student Activities* manual. Students need to look back at everything they have learned and see how it all fits together. You may even want to have a year-end test on the presidents and the eras of U.S. history. Some of the most important lessons you can teach cannot be taught until after the students have finished the book.

---

9. Contract with America (p. 628)

10. Dayton Accords (p. 643)

11. Goals 2000 (p. 634)

12. Christian Coalition (p. 632)

13. World Trade Organization (p. 644)

14. Answers will vary. Though America's founders were influenced by biblical principles, the nation has moved away from its moral foundation. And those who truly know Christ as Savior are in the minority.

15. Answers will vary. Government regulations will never change hearts, but they can check the excesses of sinful men.

More Thinking Questions

1. Was Bush's defeat in 1992 a repudiation of Republican policies as Clinton claimed?

2. Compare and contrast the Bush administration and the Clinton administration.

3. Twenty years from now, what do you think historians will consider the greatest accomplishment and the greatest failure of President Clinton's administration?

4. Why do polls show widespread support for "family values," while statistics indicate that morals are worse than ever?

5. Should Christians denounce the immorality of their leaders? (See Luke 3:19-20.)

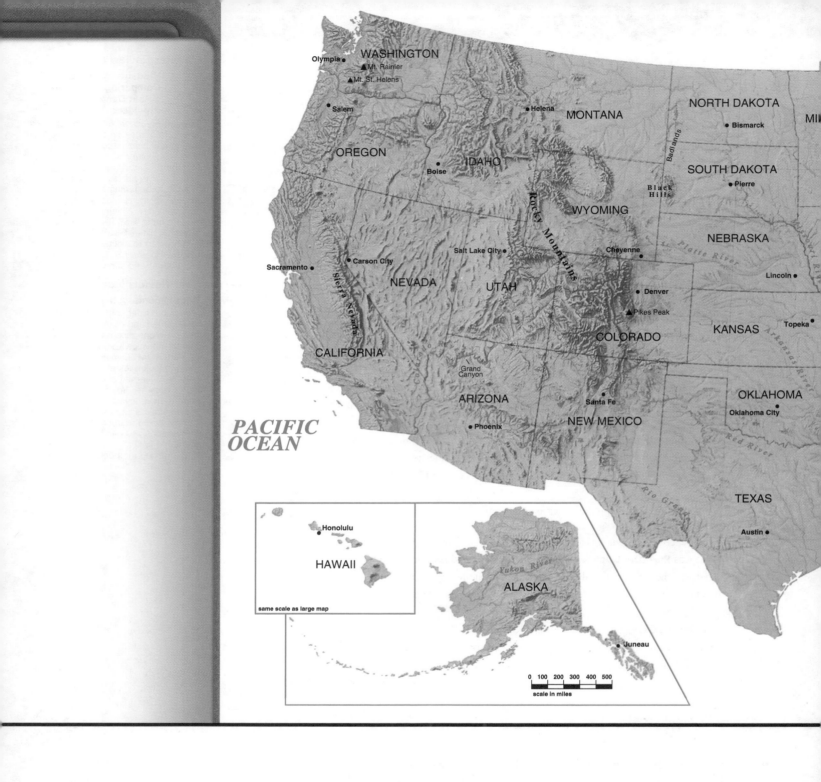

WASHINGTON
Olympia •
▲ Mt. Rainier
▲ Mt. St. Helens
• Salem

OREGON

IDAHO
• Boise

MONTANA
• Helena

NORTH DAKOTA
• Bismarck

SOUTH DAKOTA
• Pierre

Badlands

Black Hills

WYOMING
Rocky Mountains

NEBRASKA
Platte River

• Cheyenne
Salt Lake City •
NEVADA
Carson City •

UTAH

Lincoln •

Sacramento •

Sierra Nevada

• Denver
▲ Pikes Peak

COLORADO

KANSAS
Topeka •

CALIFORNIA

Colorado

Grand Canyon

Arkansas River

OKLAHOMA

ARIZONA

Santa Fe •

Oklahoma City •

PACIFIC
OCEAN

• Phoenix

NEW MEXICO

Red River

Rio Grande

TEXAS

Austin •

• Honolulu

HAWAII

same scale as large map

Yukon River

ALASKA

• Juneau

0   100   200   300   400   500

scale in miles

646

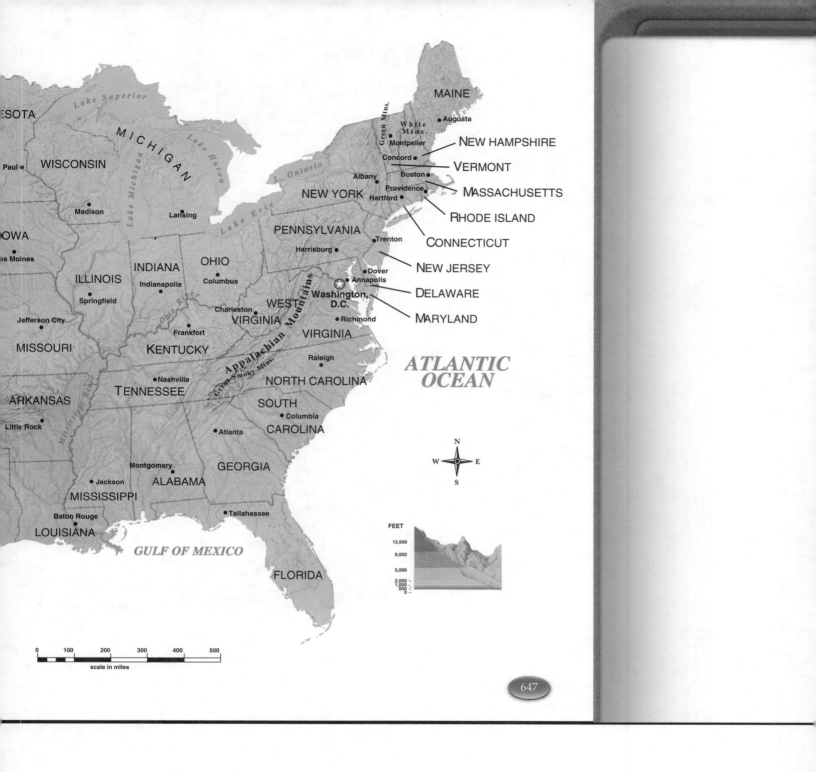

MAINE

Green Mtns.

White Mtns.

• Augusta

Montpelier •

NEW HAMPSHIRE

Concord •

VERMONT

Albany •

Boston •

MASSACHUSETTS

Providence •

Hartford •

RHODE ISLAND

NEW YORK

CONNECTICUT

PENNSYLVANIA

• Trenton

Harrisburg •

NEW JERSEY

• Dover

Annapolis •

DELAWARE

Washington, D.C.

MARYLAND

• Richmond

VIRGINIA

MINNESOTA

Lake Superior

MICHIGAN

Lake Huron

St. Paul •

WISCONSIN

Lake Michigan

L. Ontario

Madison •

Lansing •

Lake Erie

IOWA

Des Moines

OHIO

INDIANA

Columbus •

ILLINOIS

Indianapolis •

Ohio River

Springfield •

Charleston •

WEST VIRGINIA

Jefferson City •

Frankfort •

MISSOURI

KENTUCKY

Appalachian Mountains

VIRGINIA

Raleigh •

Great Smoky Mtns.

NORTH CAROLINA

ATLANTIC OCEAN

• Nashville

ARKANSAS

Mississippi River

TENNESSEE

SOUTH CAROLINA

Little Rock •

Columbia •

Atlanta •

CAROLINA

N

Montgomery •

GEORGIA

W E

• Jackson

ALABAMA

S

MISSISSIPPI

Baton Rouge •

Tallahassee •

LOUISIANA

GULF OF MEXICO

FLORIDA

FEET

12,000

9,000

5,000

2,000
1,000
500
0

0   100   200   300   400   500

scale in miles

647

Index

653

657

Photo Credits

The following agencies and individuals have furnished materials to meet the photographic needs of this textbook. We wish to express our gratitude to them for their important contribution.

ADN-Zentralbild
Suzanne R. Altizer
American Red Cross
Architect of the Capitol
Agence France Presse (AFP)
Associated Press
Chessie System
Kindra Clineff
George R. Collins
Colonial Williamsburg Foundation
Corbis-Bettmann
Corel Corporation
Cumberland Gap National Historical Park
Department of State, U.S.A.
Digital Stock
Dover Publications, Inc.
Thomas DuRant
Eastman Chemicals Division
Michael Evans
Gene Fisher
Ford Motor Company
Franklin D. Roosevelt Library
Richard Frear
Kenneth Frederick
George Bush Presidential Library
George Bush Presidential Materials Project
GeoSystems Global Corporation
The Gingrich Group
Harpers Ferry Center
Harry S. Truman Library
Historical Documents Company
Imperial War Museum
Jimmy Carter Library

John F. Kennedy Library
Brian D. Johnson
Tim Keesee
W.S. Keller
Reed Kelley
Jack Kightlinger
Bob Krist
Library of Congress
Lyndon Baines Johnson Library
Mr. & Mrs. Albert Maghan
Fred Mang, Jr.
Robert Matthews
Metropolitan Museum of Art, New York
Montana Department of Commerce
Mt. Vernon Ladies Association
Museum of the City of New York
National Aeronautics & Space Administration (NASA)
National Archives
National Cotton Council of America
National Park Service (NPS)
New York Convention and Visitors Bureau (NYCVB)
New York Public Library
New York State Department of Commerce
North Carolina Division of Tourism, Film & Sports Development
Oregon Economic Development Department
Argyle Paddock
Pana-View Slides
Pennsylvania Division of Travel Marketing

Pennsylvania Historical Museum and Commission
Philadelphia Convention & Visitors Bureau
Photo Disc, Inc.
Premiere Radio Networks
Princeton University
Puerto Rico Tourism
Wade Ramsey
Ed Richards
Abbie Rowe
Phyllis Schlafly
South Carolina Department of Parks, Recreation & Tourism
Pete Souza
Tennessee Tourist Development
Texas Tourist Development Agency
Brad Trent
Peter Turnley
Unicorn Stock Photo
Union Pacific Railroad
United Press International (UPI)
United States Air Force
United States Capitol Art Collection
United States Marine Corps
Unusual Films
Virginia Tourism Corporation
The White House
Woolaroc Museum, Bartlesville, Oklahoma
www.arttoday.com
Young Americans Foundation
Zion National Park, Utah

Chapter 19

Architectural Iron Works, 13th-14th Streets and Avenue "C", Lith.: Sarony, Major & Knapp, Museum of the City of New York, 36.18.3, Gift of Mrs. J. Insley Blair 387; Montana Department of Commerce 388; NYCVB 390; Digital Stock 391, 393(backgrounds); Union Pacific Railroad 394(both); Library of Congress 397, 398, 400, 404(left); Pennsylvania Historical Museum and Commission 403; NPS, photo by Richard Frear 404(right)

Chapter 20

Brian D. Johnson 408; Kenneth Frederick 409; Library of Congress 412, 413; Photo Disc, Inc. 414, 423; Dover Publications, Inc. 416; Digital Stock 418, 421(backgrounds); National Archives 420, 424, 425(both), 426; NPS, photo by Fred Mang, Jr. 422, photo by W.S. Keller 427

The West

Photo Disc, Inc. 431(left, right); Digital Stock 431(middle); ©1998 GeoSystems Global Corporation 431(map)

Chapter 21

NPS, photo by Richard Frear 432, 445; Library of Congress 434, 439(both); www.arttoday.com 436; Digital Stock 438(background); Puerto Rico Tourism, photo by Bob Krist 442(top); Unusual Films, courtesy of Tim Keesee 442(bottom); Photo Disc, Inc. 444

Chapter 22

National Archives 452, 453; Library of Congress 454, 455, 457, 458, 460, 466, 467, 469; Suzanne R. Altizer 456; Digital Stock 463, 466, 468(backgrounds)

Unit 6 Opener

National Archives 472(top), 472-73, 473(top); Library of Congress 472(bottom)

Chapter 23

Ed Richards 475; Imperial War Museum 476; National Archives 477, 478, 481, 483(both), 487, 488(both), 491(bottom); Library of Congress 482; Unusual Films, courtesy of Tim Keesee 485, 490; courtesy of Mr. & Mrs. Albert Maghan 486; American Red Cross 491(top)

Chapter 24

Library of Congress 494, 496(top), 499, 500, 503, 506; National Archives 496(bottom), 502, 504; Ford Motor Company 498; Digital Stock 507, 508, 509(backgrounds)

Chapter 25

Library of Congress 514, 516, 517, 519, 520, 521, 525, 528, 530; National Archives 518(both), 529; Digital Stock 523(background); courtesy of the North Carolina Division of Tourism, Film & Sports Development 526

Chapter 26

National Archives 533, 535, 536, 540(right), 541(both), 549, 550(both); www.arttoday.com 537; Imperial War Museum 538(left), 544; Library of Congress 538(right), 540(left), 543, 549(inset); Unusual Films, courtesy of Tim Keesee 542(both); Franklin D. Roosevelt Library 546; ADN-Zentralbild 547; Digital Stock 552(background); United States Air Force 552

Unit 7 Opener

National Archives 556(top), 557(top); NASA 556(middle); UPI/Corbis-Bettmann 556(bottom); United States Marine Corps 557(bottom)

Chapter 27

NPS, photo by Abbie Rowe, courtesy of Harry S. Truman Library 559; UPI/Corbis-Bettmann 560; Photo Disc, Inc. 561; National Archives 562, 564, 569, 571; www.arttoday.com 566; Digital Stock 574(background)

Chapter 28

George R. Collins 578, 594; National Archives 579, 584, 585, 586, 588, 590, 591, 596, 601; Digital Stock 579, 583, 592(backgrounds); John F. Kennedy Library 580, 581; Lyndon Baines Johnson Library 582, 587; NASA 597; courtesy of Phyllis Schlafly 599

Chapter 29

The White House, photo by Pete Souza 604, photo by Michael Evans 612, photo by Jack Kightlinger 613; Digital Stock 605, 606, 610, 616(backgrounds); National Archives 608; Jimmy Carter Library 609(both); CORBIS/AFP 610; Young Americans Foundation 614; George Bush Presidential Materials Project 617; United States Marine Corps 618; George Bush Presidential Library 619; CORBIS\Peter Turnley 620

Chapter 30

Corel Corporation 623, 644; George Bush Presidential Library 624; Digital Stock 625(background); Associated Press 626, 631; Unicorn Stock Photo 627(top), 634(top); The White House 627(bottom), 637, 640(bottom); The Gingrich Group 628; ©1998 Brad Trent/Premiere Radio Networks 632; Photo Disc, Inc. 633, 634(bottom), 636, 640(top); Department of State, U.S.A. 639; Tim Keesee 643

The States of the Union

Order of Admission into Union	State	Year of Admission	Postal Abbrev.	Capital City	Nickname	Area in Sq. Miles
1	Delaware	1787	DE	Dover	Diamond State, First State	2,044
2	Pennsylvania	1787	PA	Harrisburg	Keystone State	45,308
3	New Jersey	1787	NJ	Trenton	Garden State	7,787
4	Georgia	1788	GA	Atlanta	Empire State of the South	58,910
5	Connecticut	1788	CT	Hartford	Constitution State	5,018
6	Massachusetts	1788	MA	Boston	Bay State, Old Colony	8,284
7	Maryland	1788	MD	Annapolis	Old Line State, Free State	10,460
8	South Carolina	1788	SC	Columbia	Palmetto State	31,113
9	New Hampshire	1788	NH	Concord	Granite State	9,279
10	Virginia	1788	VA	Richmond	Old Dominion State	40,767
11	New York	1788	NY	Albany	Empire State	49,108
12	North Carolina	1789	NC	Raleigh	Tar Heel State	52,669
13	Rhode Island	1790	RI	Providence	Little Rhody	1,212
14	Vermont	1791	VT	Montpelier	Green Mountain State	9,614
15	Kentucky	1792	KY	Frankfort	Bluegrass State	40,409
16	Tennessee	1796	TN	Nashville	Volunteer State	42,144
17	Ohio	1803	OH	Columbus	Buckeye State	41,330
18	Louisiana	1812	LA	Baton Rouge	Pelican State	47,752
19	Indiana	1816	IN	Indianapolis	Hoosier State	36,185
20	Mississippi	1817	MS	Jackson	Magnolia State	47,689
21	Illinois	1818	IL	Springfield	Land of Lincoln, Prairie State	56,345
22	Alabama	1819	AL	Montgomery	Heart of Dixie, Cotton State	51,705
23	Maine	1820	ME	Augusta	Pine Tree State	33,265
24	Missouri	1821	MO	Jefferson City	"Show Me" State	69,697
25	Arkansas	1836	AR	Little Rock	Land of Opportunity	53,187
26	Michigan	1837	MI	Lansing	Wolverine State	58,527
27	Florida	1845	FL	Tallahassee	Sunshine State	58,664
28	Texas	1845	TX	Austin	Lone Star State	266,807
29	Iowa	1846	IA	Des Moines	Hawkeye State	56,275
30	Wisconsin	1848	WI	Madison	Badger State	56,153
31	California	1850	CA	Sacramento	Golden State	158,706
32	Minnesota	1858	MN	St. Paul	North Star State, Gopher State	84,402
33	Oregon	1859	OR	Salem	Beaver State	97,073
34	Kansas	1861	KS	Topeka	Sunflower State	82,277
35	West Virginia	1863	WV	Charleston	Mountain State	24,231
36	Nevada	1864	NV	Carson City	Sagebrush State, Silver State	110,561
37	Nebraska	1867	NE	Lincoln	Beef State, Cornhusker State	77,355
38	Colorado	1876	CO	Denver	Centennial State	104,091
39	North Dakota	1889	ND	Bismarck	Sioux State, Flickertail State	70,702
40	South Dakota	1889	SD	Pierre	Coyote State, Sunshine State	77,116
41	Montana	1889	MT	Helena	Treasure State	147,046
42	Washington	1889	WA	Olympia	Evergreen State	68,139
43	Idaho	1890	ID	Boise	Gem State	83,564
44	Wyoming	1890	WY	Cheyenne	Equality State	97,809
45	Utah	1896	UT	Salt Lake City	Beehive State	84,899
46	Oklahoma	1907	OK	Oklahoma City	Sooner State	69,956
47	New Mexico	1912	NM	Santa Fe	Land of Enchantment	121,593
48	Arizona	1912	AZ	Phoenix	Grand Canyon State	114,000
49	Alaska	1959	AK	Juneau	The Last Frontier	591,004
50	Hawaii	1959	HI	Honolulu	Aloha State	6,471
	District of Columbia	1791	DC	Washington		70

The Presidents of the United States

Presidents	Term	Political Party	Home State	Vice-President
George Washington	1789-1797	None	Virginia	John Adams
John Adams	1797-1801	Federalist	Massachusetts	Thomas Jefferson
Thomas Jefferson	1801-1809	Republican	Virginia	Aaron Burr
				George Clinton
James Madison	1809-1817	Republican	Virginia	George Clinton
				Elbridge Gerry
James Monroe	1817-1825	Republican	Virginia	Daniel D. Tompkins
John Quincy Adams	1825-1829	Republican	Massachusetts	John C. Calhoun
Andrew Jackson	1829-1837	Democrat	Tennessee	John C. Calhoun
				Martin Van Buren
Martin Van Buren	1837-1841	Democrat	New York	Richard M. Johnson
William H. Harrison	1841	Whig	Ohio	John Tyler
John Tyler	1841-1845	Whig	Virginia	
James K. Polk	1845-1849	Democrat	Tennessee	George M. Dallas
Zachary Taylor	1849-1850	Whig	Louisiana	Millard Fillmore
Millard Fillmore	1850-1853	Whig	New York	
Franklin Pierce	1853-1857	Democrat	New Hampshire	William R. King
James Buchanan	1857-1861	Democrat	Pennsylvania	John C. Breckinridge
Abraham Lincoln	1861-1865	Republican	Illinois	Hannibal Hamlin
				Andrew Johnson
Andrew Johnson	1865-1869	Republican	Tennessee	
Ulysses S. Grant	1869-1877	Republican	Illinois	Schuyler Colfax
				Henry Wilson
Rutherford B. Hayes	1877-1881	Republican	Ohio	William A. Wheeler
James A. Garfield	1881	Republican	Ohio	Chester A. Arthur
Chester A. Arthur	1881-1885	Republican	New York	
Grover Cleveland	1885-1889	Democrat	New York	Thomas A. Hendricks
Benjamin Harrison	1889-1893	Republican	Indiana	Levi P. Morton
Grover Cleveland	1893-1897	Democrat	New York	Adlai E. Stevenson
William McKinley	1897-1901	Republican	Ohio	Garret A. Hobart
				Theodore Roosevelt
Theodore Roosevelt	1901-1909	Republican	New York	Charles W. Fairbanks
William H. Taft	1909-1913	Republican	Ohio	James S. Sherman
Woodrow Wilson	1913-1921	Democrat	New Jersey	Thomas R. Marshall
Warren G. Harding	1921-1923	Republican	Ohio	Calvin Coolidge
Calvin Coolidge	1923-1929	Republican	Massachusetts	Charles G. Dawes
Herbert Hoover	1929-1933	Republican	California	Charles Curtis
Franklin D. Roosevelt	1933-1945	Democrat	New York	John Garner
				John Garner
				Henry A. Wallace
				Harry S. Truman
Harry S. Truman	1945-1953	Democrat	Missouri	Alben W. Barkley
Dwight D. Eisenhower	1953-1961	Republican	Pennsylvania	Richard M. Nixon
John F. Kennedy	1961-1963	Democrat	Massachusetts	Lyndon B. Johnson
Lyndon B. Johnson	1963-1969	Democrat	Texas	Hubert H. Humphrey
Richard M. Nixon	1969-1974	Republican	California	Spiro T. Agnew
				Gerald R. Ford
Gerald R. Ford	1974-1977	Republican	Michigan	Nelson A. Rockefeller
Jimmy Carter	1977-1981	Democrat	Georgia	Walter F. Mondale
Ronald Reagan	1981-1989	Republican	California	George Bush
George Bush	1989-1993	Republican	Texas	Dan Quayle
Bill Clinton	1993-2001	Democrat	Arkansas	Al Gore